Research Methods and Statistics in **Psychology**

SAGE Foundations of Psychology

Series editors:
Craig McGarty, Murdoch University
Alex Haslam, University of Queensland

SAGE Foundations of Psychology is a series of texts intended to provide an introduction to key areas of psychology. Books in the series are scholarly but written in a lively and readable style, assuming little or no background knowledge. They are suitable for all university students beginning psychology courses, for those studying psychology as a supplement to other courses, and for readers who require a general and up-to-date overview of the major concerns and issues in contemporary psychology.

Published titles:

Statistics with Confidence
Michael J. Smithson

An Introduction to Child Development (2nd edition)
Thomas Keenan and Subhadra Evans

An Introduction to Personality and Intelligence
Nick Haslam

Second Edition

Research Methods and Statistics in
Psychology

S. Alexander Haslam and **Craig McGarty**

Los Angeles | London | New Delhi
Singapore | Washington DC

Los Angeles | London | New Delhi
Singapore | Washington DC

SAGE Publications Ltd
1 Oliver's Yard
55 City Road
London EC1Y 1SP

SAGE Publications Inc.
2455 Teller Road
Thousand Oaks, California 91320

SAGE Publications India Pvt Ltd
B 1/I 1 Mohan Cooperative Industrial Area
Mathura Road
New Delhi 110 044

SAGE Publications Asia-Pacific Pte Ltd
3 Church Street
#10-04 Samsung Hub
Singapore 049483

Editor: Michael Carmichael
Editorial assistant: Keri Dickens
Production editor: Imogen Roome
Copyeditor: Neville Hankins
Proofreader: Leigh Timmins
Indexer: Christine McCoy
Marketing manager: Alison Borg
Cover design: Wendy Scott
Typeset by: C&M Digitals (P) Ltd, Chennai, India
Printed and bound in Great Britain by Ashford
Colour Press Ltd

MIX
Paper from
responsible sources
FSC® C011748

First published 2014

Library of Congress Control Number: 2013941889

British Library Cataloguing in Publication data

A catalogue record for this book is available from
the British Library

ISBN 978-1-4462-5597-1
ISBN 978-1-4462-5596-4 (pbk)

To our teachers, who, when we knew nothing of these things, gave us direction and purpose

Contents

Contents

Contents

Preface

Although we always had great ambitions for this book, when we set about writing it we had no idea how successful it would go on to be. Indeed, since completing *Doing Psychology* (the first instantiation of this text), between us we have written or edited 14 other books and although many of these have been very well received, none has had anything like the same popular appeal. Accordingly, when our colleagues at Sage asked us to put our heads together to produce another updated edition we felt that we owed it to the tens of thousands of readers of earlier versions to see if we could. Happily, this not only proved to be possible, but also served to remind us why we had been so enthusiastic about the original venture and, in the process, to rekindle much of our passion for the issues that this book explores.

Indeed, our own careers in the intervening years owe much to the content of this book and the thinking that went into it. This is because, while at one level this can be seen as a 'how to' text that explains the procedures involved in designing, conducting and reporting research, at another level it is also a 'why to' text that attempts to explain why doing certain things is important and why particular debates matter – encouraging readers to engage not just with the details of the research process but also with the bigger picture. In this sense the book is not so much a manual as a manifesto. Moreover, this is a manifesto that we have endeavoured to live out in our own careers as research scientists and in our collaborations with colleagues around the world.

Through all this, there are two key points on which the original idea for this book hinged, to which we have tried to remain faithful. The first is that *research in psychology matters*. It makes a difference to people's lives. We therefore have a responsibility to do it as well as we possibly can, and we have no choice other than to learn about the range of issues that this book addresses. The second is that *research in psychology is exciting* – or at least should be. For this reason, as you learn about research methods we want to you to engage with the points that we discuss not because you have to, but because you want to. Indeed, we are confident that if we can help you to engage in this way, you will experience this excitement yourself and become a far more effective researcher in the process.

With a view to bringing these features of·the text to the fore, there are a number of substantial changes that we have made for this edition. Most obviously, we have updated the book through the inclusion of images and Research Bites. These are intended to provide a space to step back from the text and reflect on the ways in which it relates both to issues in the world at large and to contemporary debates in psychology. In order to reflect the instruction you are likely to receive in any classes you take, we have also replaced sections of the text in which statistical tests were performed by hand with instructions (and accompanying images) that explain how to perform these using a statistical program. As well as updating the coverage of experimental design, survey research and ethics, this edition also includes a much more expansive coverage of qualitative methods.

All of these various changes represent responses to the very large amount of feedback that we received on the previous edition. As well as being extremely detailed, this was also extremely encouraging. Indeed, above all else, it is the generosity of our colleagues in helping us to rise to the challenges of putting together a new edition that we most appreciate. But as well as acknowledging this, we also want to recognize the large number of people who helped in the production of previous editions.

When first writing *Doing Psychology* (which was published in 1998), Mike Calford, Wolfgang Grichting, Judith Harackiewicz, Kate Reynolds and Jennifer Sanderson provided comments on selected chapters for which we were extremely grateful. Others, including Mike Innes, Michael Platow and John Turner, provided very instructive input in specific content areas. Mariette Berndsen, Chris Cooper, Richard Jennings, Jason Mazanov, Penny Oakes, Rina Onorato and Russell Spears provided additional observations and suggestions that were helpful too. Ziyad Marar at Sage also deserves to be singled out for his constant encouragement and his commitment to the Foundations of Psychology series as a whole and for entrusting ongoing oversight of our work to the ever-attentive Michael Carmichael. The editorial work of Lucy Robinson, Jane Evans and Richard Leigh was also superb. However, at the time we reserved our highest category of thanks to Michael Cook, Catherine Haslam, Duncan McIntyre and Mike Smithson who all worked very long and very hard to provide detailed and extremely insightful comments on entire drafts of the text.

When we put together the first edition of *Research Methods and Statistics in Psychology* (published in 2004) we again received very helpful input from a large number of colleagues including Steve Brown, Carole Burgoyne, Sue Burney, Kerry Chalmers, Barbara David, Nellie Georgiou-Karistianis, David Goble, Kristina Macrae, Elinor McKone, Annie Mitchell, Don Mitchell, Jonathan Potter, Judy Slee, Janet Tweedie and Andy Wills. We were grateful to Zoe Elliott at Sage and Bob Wilson at Footprint for their continued commitment to the book and their unwavering confidence in our efforts. Richard Leigh and Lauren McAllister provided extremely helpful input at proof stage, as did Lucy O'Sullivan who also compiled the indexes. Finally, we also wanted to thank the many students who had provided us with positive feedback on *Doing Psychology* and assured us that our continued endeavours were worthwhile.

Students also need to be thanked for motivating and helping us to improve this second edition. We are grateful too to our colleagues Andrew Livingstone, Blake McKimmie, Thomas Morton, Anna Rabinovich, Joe Sweetman, Anne Marthe van der Bles and Renate Ysseldyk for their thoughtful input. At the same time we would like to extend special thanks to Christine McCoy who carefully reread the entire manuscript and to Robin Lupton and her many great colleagues at Sage for their sterling work in guiding us through this process.

Finally, unlike previous editions, this one includes a formal dedication. This is to those teachers who initially fired up our passion for psychological research and who showed us how to do it better and how to have fun while we were at it. Thank you.

Alex Haslam and Craig McGarty (2013)

The Authors

Alex Haslam is Professor of Psychology and Australian Laureate Fellow at the University of Queensland. Together with colleagues, he has written and edited 11 books and over 200 research articles and chapters. His most recent books are *The New Psychology of Leadership: Identity, Influence and Power* (with Steve Reicher and Michael Platow, 2011), *The Social Cure: Identity, Health and Well-Being* (edited with Jolanda Jetten and Catherine Haslam, 2012) and *Social Psychology: Revisiting the Classic Studies* (edited with Joanne Smith, 2012). He is former Chief Editor of the *European Journal of Social Psychology*, former President of the Psychology Section of the British Science Association, and currently on the editorial board of eight journals (including *Scientific American Mind*). He is a Fellow of the Canadian Institute for Advanced Research and of the Association for Psychological Science. He is also a recipient of the European Association of Social Psychology's Kurt Lewin Medal for research excellence, the British Psychology Society's Award for Excellence in Teaching, and a National Teaching Fellowship from the Higher Education Academy.

Craig McGarty is Professor of Social and Political Psychology at Murdoch University. He received his undergraduate training in psychology at the University of Adelaide and his PhD from Macquarie University in 1991 (where he was a tutor from 1985 until 1989). He

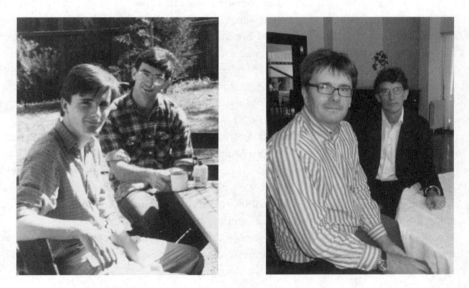

Photos P.1 and P.2 A study in developmental psychology: The authors in 1988 and 2013 (Alex on the left, Craig on the right).

spent 1990 as a lecturer in social psychology/social interaction at the University of Western Sydney and moved in 1991 to the Australian National University as a research associate. He was Reader and Head of the School of Psychology before moving to Murdoch University in Western Australia as the Director of the Centre for Social and Community Research and then Director of the Social Research Institute. He has worked on a wide range of topics in experimental social psychology and his current research includes a social audit of the aspirations and solutions of a remote Indigenous community and studies of the reconciliation process in post-genocide Rwanda. His books include *Stereotypes as Explanations* (with Vincent Yzerbyt and Russell Spears, 2002) and *Categorization and Social Psychology* (1999).

Key Features of this Book

Engaging text – designed to encourage understanding of, and interest in, the process of conducting research in psychology.

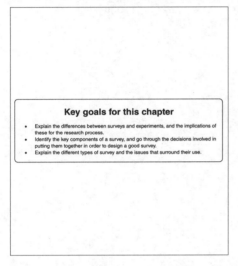

Key goals for each chapter – designed to structure your approach to the material it addresses.

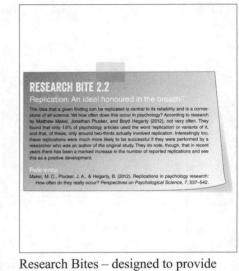

Research Bites – designed to provide you with practical insights that arise from contemporary discussions of research practice.

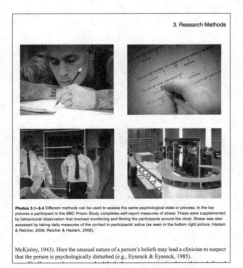

Photographs – designed to reinforce key points and encourage critical reflection.

Test Yourself questions – designed to test your understanding as you progress through each chapter.

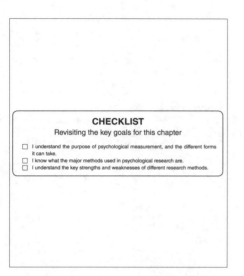

CHECKLIST

Revisiting the key goals for this chapter

- [ ] I understand the purpose of psychological measurement, and the different forms it can take.
- [ ] I know what the major methods used in psychological research are.
- [ ] I understand the key strengths and weaknesses of different research methods.

End of chapter checklist – designed to confirm that you have achieved each chapter's key goals.

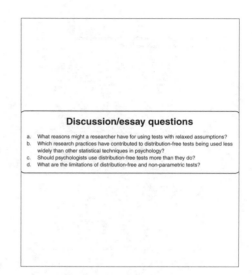

Discussion/essay questions

a. What reasons might a researcher have for using tests with relaxed assumptions?
b. Which research practices have contributed to distribution-free tests being used less widely than other statistical techniques in psychology?
c. Should psychologists use distribution-free tests more than they do?
d. What are the limitations of distribution-free and non-parametric tests?

Discussion questions – designed to stimulate reflection on the key issues addressed in each chapter.

Exercises – designed to test your knowledge in an active and practical way.

behavioural measures Measures designed to gain insight into particular psychological states or processes that involve recording performance on particular activities or tasks.

behavioural trace measures Measures designed to gain insight into behaviour that examines phenomena associated with that behaviour. For example, footprints in the sand could provide a behavioural trace of where people have walked, and this could be used to measure people's preference for particular parts of a beach.

behaviourism An approach to psychology that asserts that human behaviour can be understood in terms of directly observable relationships (in particular, between a stimulus and a response) without having to refer to underlying mental states. Behaviourism was the dominant approach to psychology for most of the first half of the 20th century.

dimension Any property of people or things on which they can differ (e.g., intelligence or height). Different people and things can therefore be situated or placed at different points along any dimension and it is possible to differentiate between them in terms of the positions they occupy (e.g., for measurement or assessment purposes).

dynamic mental processes Aspects of psychology that are seen to be common to people in general, but which are changeable over time (e.g., mood and judgement).

extraneous variable Any variable that is not of immediate interest to a researcher but which may pose a threat to validity because it compromises the interpretation of research findings. This is usually because it obscures the measurement of processes of interest.

generalization The process of making statements about the general population on the basis of relevant research (e.g., experiments or surveys).

instrument Any procedure or device used to assess or measure psychological or behavioural phenomena (e.g., intelligence, attitudes, eye movements).

physiological measures Measures of physiological states or processes (e.g., skin conductance and blood flow) used in psychological research to gain insight into particular psychological states or processes.

population The complete set of events, people or things that a researcher is interested in and from which any sample is taken.

Glossary – designed to clarify the definition of key terms as they are introduced in each chapter.

Research methods: A checklist for research evaluation and improvement

Table 3.1

Potential problem	Question to ask	Potential improvement
Poor or limited choice of measure	Have researchers used an appropriate measure to investigate the psychological process or state in which they are interested?	Consider the different types of measures that could be used to investigate the issue at hand (e.g., behavioural, self-report, physiological). Consider the advantages and disadvantages (as well as the practicalities) of using different types of measure or different measures of the same type. If appropriate, design and conduct research that involves these alternative measures.
Extraneous variables	Are research findings contaminated by factors that are not of immediate concern to the researchers?	Think broadly about factors that are not addressed in the research but which may be affecting the findings (and their interpretation). Take steps to eliminate these (for more detail, see Chapters 4 and 5) or to compensate for them by using multiple methods.
Unrepresentative sampling	Is the experimental sample representative of the sub-population from which it is drawn and is the sub-population representative of the general population of interest?	Consider the implications of any unrepresentative sampling that has occurred. If necessary, take steps to improve the sampling procedure (e.g., by using random sampling; for more detail see Chapter 5) and then attempt to replicate the research findings.
Confounding	Is assignment to experimental conditions associated with an additional variable that is not of immediate interest to researchers (and which they had not intended to manipulate) but that could be having an impact on the findings?	Take steps to eliminate the impact of confounding variables by controlling for them. This is typically done by manipulating the independent variable of interest under conditions where the level of the confound is held constant.
Lack of experimental control (in quasi-experiments and surveys)	Is the interpretation of a relationship between an IV and a DV compromised by a failure to manipulate the IV experimentally?	Consider ways in which it might be possible to manipulate an IV experimentally. If none is feasible, and an IV has not been manipulated experimentally, try to generate alternative explanations of the relationship and be careful to avoid the correlational fallacy of implying that the IV caused the DV (for more detail, see Chapter 10).
Poor or limited choice of method	Have the researchers used an appropriate method to investigate the psychological process or state in which they are interested?	Consider the different types of method that could be used to investigate the issue at hand (experimental, quasi-experimental, survey, case study). Consider the advantages and disadvantages (as well as the practicalities) of using alternative methods to supplement and extend the research. If appropriate, design and conduct research that involves these alternative methods.

Research evaluation and improvement checklist – designed to provide you with an easy-to-access summary of best practice that you can refer to in the future.

Further reading

Over the past few years correlation and regression techniques have become much more popular as a means of analysing psychological data. Cohen's (1988) book provides a very good introduction to this area, which underlines the importance of looking beyond statistical significance. Miles and Shevlin's (2001) text provides a good user-friendly introduction to the possibilities of such analysis and to the various ways in which it can be conducted.

Cohen, J. (1988). *Statistical power analysis for the behavioral sciences* (2nd ed.). Hillsdale, NJ: Erlbaum.
Miles, J., & Shevlin, M. (2001). *Applying regression and correlation: A guide for researchers and students*. London: SAGE.

Further reading – designed to point you in the right direction when you want to know more about a given topic.

Companion Website – providing supplementary material for instructors and students, including an annotated research report, details of hand calculations of statistical tests, statistical tables and data files. www.sagepub.co.uk/haslamandmcgarty2e

Introduction

Key goals for this chapter

- Explain the purpose of this book.
- Explain the book's structure and how to use it.
- Motivate readers to engage with the book's goals and to read on.

'Why do I have to do this?'

Students are typically drawn to study psychology out of a sense of curiosity. They are interested in questions like 'What makes people love or hate each other?', 'How does our mind solve difficult problems?' and 'How do children develop a sense of morality?'. Such questions are potentially among the most interesting that can be explored in any academic setting. Not surprisingly, most students quickly find out that these and many other psychological topics can be fascinating to learn about and investigate.

The same can rarely be said for a student's first course on research methodology or statistics. When embarking on these courses most students often just ask themselves 'Why do I have to do this?'. The question is asked partly out of genuine confusion, but also with a sense of foreboding – the study of methodology and statistics has the reputation for being dull, difficult and distressing. Few things have the same reputation for making people both bored and fearful at the same time.

Despite these concerns, the people responsible for laying down the guidelines for teaching in psychology continue to demand that students endure the trials and tribulations of a training in research methodology and statistics. Why spoil the fun? Why expose students to material that they may dislike and may turn them off studying psychology altogether?

It may be comforting to conclude that academic psychologists are sadists. Some probably are. But academics have little to gain from making students' lives miserable just for the sake of it. Nowadays almost all academic departments are keen to attract and retain as many students as possible. Accordingly, a number of very good reasons need to be put forward to encourage perseverance with material that many find difficult. So what are they? As we see it, the case for asking (indeed, demanding) psychology students to come to grips with issues of methodology and statistics rests on the following points.

First, it needs to be emphasized that one of the key transformations that students of psychology undergo in the course of their study is from being *consumers* of psychological knowledge to being *producers* of it. Before coming to university, most budding psychologists (like most other members of the general community) have been exposed to a range of relevant research. Psychology is the stuff of everyone's lives and for this reason it provides excellent material for television, radio, newspapers and everyday conversation. In the formal media, journalists and commentators give us neatly packaged versions of the psychology of prejudice, fear, stress, physical attraction, memory, and so on. Yet a key part of a person's academic training as a psychologist is to be able to participate *actively* in the research process. This role involves more than just supporting or challenging different versions of psychological truth with opinions and beliefs (something that any intelligent person should be able to do). It means being able to do so on the basis of carefully gathered and critically tested scientific evidence. Clearly we cannot do this unless we understand how to gather and how to test that evidence.

A second reason for studying methodology and statistics is related to the first. In order to understand and evaluate research conducted and reported by others, we need to have some

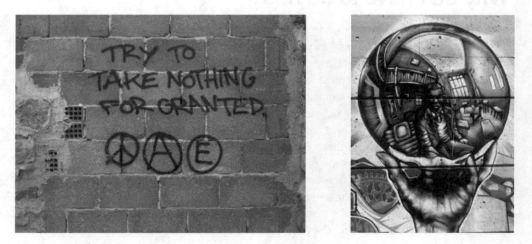

Photos 1.1 and 1.2 In our daily lives, we are exposed to people's theories of psychology all the time – as we strive to understand and explain our own behaviour and that of other people. Training in psychological research methods should allow you to interrogate the quality of these theories and to reflect critically on their utility and value.

insight into the procedures and assumptions by which their work has been guided. We may be suspicious of a person who uses a survey to make claims that eating a particular food will improve eyesight, or who concludes on the basis of an experiment that wearing a particular brand of jeans will make us more attractive to members of the opposite sex. By fully understanding the strengths and limitations of the research methods used we can find out whether our suspicions are well founded. Indeed, we can be fairly sure that it is precisely because so many people do *not* have this type of understanding that a great deal of important research continues to be misunderstood. It is also because so few people really understand these issues that certain research strategies continue to have appeal for those who want to use research to *conceal* truth rather than *reveal* it.

If the above reasons seem too idealistic and abstract, then a third reason is purely pragmatic. If you are reading this book you are likely to have one of two futures in mind. Either you are going to become a psychologist (in which case you will actually be doing research in the near future) or you are going to get a job where your psychological training will be very useful. In both cases, the ability to conduct, analyse and interpret psychological research is likely to serve you well. Indeed, of all the skills that a degree in psychology should impart, these are probably the most useful – and therefore the most marketable.

Of course psychology is not the only discipline that trains students to use research methods and statistics. However, because psychology students approach these issues in an attempt

RESEARCH BITE 1.1
The importance of a hungry mind

An analysis by Sophie von Stumm, Benedikt Hell, and Tomas Chamorro-Premuzic (2011) sought to identify the best predictors of academic performance. Unsurprisingly perhaps, a person's intelligence was the best predictor. However, they also found that this was matched by the combined predictive power of effort and intellectual curiosity. They conclude that succeeding in academic fields (such as psychology) is not just a question of being smart and trying hard, it is also about having a hungry mind. In support of their case, they quote Samuel Johnson's observation that 'curiosity is, in great and generous minds, the first passion and the last'.

Reference
Von Stumm, S., Hell, B., & Chamorro-Premuzic, T. (2011). The hungry mind: Intellectual curiosity is the third pillar of academic performance. *Perspectives on Psychological Science*, 6, 574–588.

to understand human behaviour, their expertise has a general and much sought-after relevance. This expertise is particularly relevant in fields such as advertising, marketing, teaching, politics, policy making and in almost all managerial and executive roles.

This is not to say that studying research methodology and statistics will get you a well-paid job, or that you would necessarily want a job in which this knowledge played a central role. However, taking the above three points together, we believe that this knowledge should enhance your ability to make reasonable inferences about human behaviour and to evaluate critically the inferences drawn by others. These are probably the most directly applicable skills that can be imparted and developed through the study of psychology as a whole.

Finally, though, we would like to think that acquiring and mastering these skills could actually be intellectually rewarding and stimulating *in itself*. In light of the gloomy expectations with which you may have started reading this book, this may seem to be a tall order. A major objective of this book is to make the idea seem a little less outrageous than it might otherwise have been.

The structure of this book and an overview of the chapters

In writing this book our broad objective has been to make studying research methodology and statistics a positive experience. So in order to get our points across we have tried to use words and figures rather than numbers and equations wherever possible. Note, though, that it is not easy to do good psychological research. For that reason you may find some of the material that we have to deal with quite challenging.

Some people might suggest that one way to make the book more readable would be to take out *all* the numbers, *all* the equations, *all* the technical procedures and *all* the jargon. You may think this is a very attractive proposition. However, it will not be much help when you need to apply your knowledge, or when you progress to more advanced courses in which familiarity with this material is essential. Although the technical jargon we deal with can be hard to understand at first, mastery of it will ultimately make it much easier for you to communicate with other psychological researchers.

In this book we aim to provide a comprehensive examination of the research *process*. We have structured the chapters so that they present an ever-sharpening focus on the various aspects of research. We begin by asking very general questions about research motives and objectives. We then work through the main strategies that can be employed to reach those objectives. Finally, we consider the key statistical techniques typically associated with each strategy.

In this way, we address in sequence the key questions that are raised at different stages in the research enterprise: from the general ('What am I trying to do here?') to the specific ('How confident can I be that two groups of people really are different?'). We have outlined the structure of the next eight chapters in Figure 1.1.

In Chapter 2 we consider why people are motivated to conduct psychological research in the first place and the broad goals they set themselves when they do. We also identify

Figure 1.1 Structure of Chapters 2–9

properties that are generally considered the hallmark of good research and that are therefore most prized by members of the research community. Not surprisingly, because these properties can be viewed as prescriptions for research practice (effectively telling researchers what they should and should not aim for), there is controversy about their appropriateness and utility. For example, although we strongly endorse the view that psychology is a science, this scientific status is neither unproblematic (what does it mean?) nor uncontested (is it really?). In this chapter we outline these and other controversies, and some of the major camps into which researchers fall.

In Chapter 3 we discuss the main strategies that researchers employ to address different types of research question. We start by looking at precisely what psychologists measure and observe in their research, and at the basis and consequences of measurement decisions. We then look at the aims of measurement in *experimental*, *quasi-experimental*, *survey* and *case-study* research. We outline the key features of each of these four methods and the kinds of conclusion each allows researchers to draw. We consider the factors that determine when each method is used and discuss the relative strengths and weaknesses of each.

In Chapter 4 we examine the experimental method in detail and explore how experiments are designed and conducted in psychology. In particular, we focus on the *choices* that using the experimental method involves, their consequences, and the factors to be considered when making them. These choices include decisions about who should participate in a study, what things should be controlled and what should be measured. Similar considerations are also central to Chapter 5 where we look at survey methodology and design. In both chapters we emphasize the types of *inference* that the various methods allow the researcher to make and consider how features of research design impact on our ability to make particular types of inference.

Chapters 6 to 9 introduce statistical concepts that are essential to almost all psychological research. These will form the backbone of the statistical knowledge that you will need to take from this book into more advanced courses or into a research setting. However, because our aim is to help you become a researcher rather than a mathematician, we generally downplay the algebraic and computational aspects of the statistics we introduce. It is our belief that the main obstacles to becoming a good researcher are conceptual not mathematical, so it is on overcoming these conceptual problems that we have chosen to expend most of our (and your) energy. For 99% of readers the mathematical (mainly algebraic) skills required to take you through this book will be ones that you acquired at high school (though your memory may need a bit of refreshing). We want to make it clear that statistics are not weapons of torture heralded from some alien world in order to confuse and deceive. Instead they are natural and sensible tools that are used in research (and other) contexts to make certain features of reality easier to grasp.

All the research methods discussed in Chapters 3 to 5 have one feature in common – they ultimately require the collection of research *data*. The first stage in handling almost all research data involves simply summarizing their most important features. In Chapter 6 we discuss the procedures most commonly used for describing data: those involved in representing typical data and the spread of data. This chapter thus includes our first attempt to make numerical statements about the properties of a given set of data. In other words, it introduces us to *descriptive statistics*.

Chapter 7 deals with a second class of statistics, those used to determine whether our *inferences* are sensible – that is, to make statements about what is going on in our research and about how our research findings relate to underlying reality. These inferences allow us to determine how likely it is that a given event has occurred by chance, and hence how 'special' it is. *Inferential statistics* allow us to establish, for example, how unlikely it is that if you asked a class of students to take a multiple-choice exam their average score would be above 65% if they were responding randomly. If this event is extremely unlikely and if you find that the average class score is above 65%, then this tells you that their performance is, in some sense, remarkable.

In fact, though, researchers do not (or should not) just ask endless questions and get people to do different things on the off chance that something remarkable will crop up. Instead, these types of activity are usually carried out in the context of a specific research question or *hypothesis* (a statement of what the effect of one thing should be on another). For example, a researcher may have a hypothesis that a particular class will perform well on an exam – perhaps because they are very bright, or have studied very hard, or have been well taught.

Inferential statistics are normally used as part of a *hypothesis-testing* exercise, as they allow the researcher to make qualified judgements about the degree of support for a particular hypothesis. Chapter 8 discusses these procedures as they are applied by researchers who are interested in comparing two sets of data that have been obtained in different situations (e.g., comparing the test performance of two different classes of students, or the same class at different times). Chapter 9 then discusses these procedures as they are applied to examine the *relationship* between *variables* (where a variable is simply a *dimension* on which people may differ, such as age, mood or intelligence). Chapter 10 examines situations in which more than two data sets are compared. Finally, Chapter 11 looks at a range of inferential statistics that are used to deal with categorical, proportional and ranked data (e.g., where researchers are not comparing two classes' test scores, but the proportion of people in the two classes who passed).

While the previous chapters focused on the way in which researchers collect and analyse numerical data, the next two chapters provide an alternative perspective on the research process by looking at a class of techniques in which research findings are non-numerical. Here the emphasis is not on quantitative examination of the psychological process (e.g., in terms of scores, speed or accuracy), but rather on *qualitative* approaches that attempt to discover and communicate the rich texture of particular forms of behaviour (e.g., language, movement and interaction). Approaches such as these are particularly useful when the essence of a phenomenon or process is at risk of being lost or changed through quantification. For this reason they are often used by researchers who are critical of quantitative approaches or who want to check that a quantitative approach does justice to the topic in which they are interested. Chapter 12 focuses on what we refer to as *classical qualitative methods* – methods that focus on the process or organizing data in particular ways and abstracting relevant features from those data. Chapter 13 focuses on what we refer to as *contextual qualitative methods* – methods that emphasize the context in which data are found and that seek to preserve this context within the analytic process.

Chapter 14 steps back from the mechanics of conducting and analysing different forms of research to explore research *ethics*. As with the issues dealt with in Chapter 2, these are some of the most thorny in the research process. Leaving our consideration of these until the end of the book may appear to be inconsistent with the book's overall structure and the sharpening focus of the chapters. However, this chapter appears here not because it was an afterthought, but because we believe that it is necessary to have a full understanding of what the research process entails before one can reflect on its ethical implications and appropriateness.

Our concern in Chapter 14, as in all the others, is not so much to argue for one position over another (though we do express our opinions). Instead we set out the various considerations and positions with which researchers need to be familiar, and on which they need ultimately to take a stance themselves. This discussion also serves to take the book full circle, ending up by locating the research process within the world of people's values, perceptions and behaviour – the world that research sets out to understand and interpret. Sciences do not exist outside society but are a part of it, and scientific ethics express and reinforce the bond between science and society. This is especially apparent in psychology because the topics that it deals with are often quite sensitive and can sometimes be extremely controversial.

Chapter 15 concludes our coverage of research methods and statistics by attempting to bring together all the material discussed in the book within an integrated analysis of the research process as a whole. This analysis centres around the observation that when they conduct psychological research, all researchers have to confront different forms of *uncertainty*. The chapter discusses what these forms are, and how each can best be dealt with.

A key point here is that it is generally impossible (and also undesirable) to eliminate all uncertainty from the research process. Nonetheless, one hallmark of a good researcher is the ability to *manage uncertainty appropriately*. Accordingly, a major objective of this book is to help you acquire this ability.

How to use this book

This is a book that we want you to *read*. That may sound rather obvious, but in many respects it is quite radical. This is because other methodology and statistics books often serve primarily as instruction manuals to which people turn only in times of crisis (either because they have forgotten how to do something or because they need to revise for an exam). There is nothing wrong with having books for this purpose and most seasoned researchers need to have a good one. However, for someone coming fresh to the topic, this sort of text is not especially inviting. One would hardly seek to inspire literature students by giving them a reference book, so why would you do it for psychologists?

Indeed, it was the idea of writing a book that students could *read* that motivated us in the first place. So, as with most other books, we would recommend that the best way to use this one is to *start reading it at the beginning and work through to the end*. Having said that, it is quite likely that the instructor on any course you are taking will advise you that there are certain sections you should focus on and others that you can skim through. This will often be appropriate (depending on the course you are taking), but we think that as your career as a psychology student and researcher develops you will find it useful to return to the book to fill in any gaps in your knowledge. In this sense the book is designed to serve as a resource for researchers of all levels of sophistication.

It is clear, however, that, unlike most detective novels (and despite our best intentions), your reading is unlikely to be sustained simply by a desire to get to the end. We have deliberately avoided major twists of plot and we try to provide solutions to most of the mysteries on the spot. Partly to overcome any lack of intrigue, we have punctuated the text at regular intervals with relevant Test Yourself exercises. These are designed to ensure that you process the material we present as actively as possible and that, as you progress, you understand the most important issues and concepts. All questions are asked in multiple-choice format and range in difficulty from those that are relatively easy (*) to those that are quite (and sometimes very) difficult (***).

We opted for the strategy of asking questions of different degrees of difficulty for three reasons. First, we hoped that this strategy would serve to vary the pace of the text and make it more engaging. Second, we thought that giving this form of graded feedback was more realistic as it will give you insight into how well you are progressing relative to the kinds of benchmark that your instructors are likely to apply in the exams and tests *they* set you. It is quite likely that these exam questions will not be of uniform difficulty, but will be designed to differentiate between students on the basis of how much they have learned. Finally, some of the concepts and issues we discuss *are* difficult, so we felt it would be misleading to make questions about these artificially easy, just to make you feel good. Indeed, we suspect you may actually feel better if you are able to answer some of the more difficult questions.

These Test Yourself exercises are presented in boxes set aside from the main text. In the shaded portion of each box we talk through the answer to the question, outlining both what makes one answer correct and what makes the others incorrect. In each case we recommend that if you get a question wrong (and we would be surprised if this never happens), you go back over the preceding text to identify the source of any confusion or misunderstanding. Test Yourself 1.1 is an example of a fairly easy question.

To consolidate this process of continual active learning and revision, at the beginning of each chapter we try to make it clear what the three core goals of each chapter are. At the end of the chapter we then revisit these questions in the form of a checklist so that you can reflect on what you have read and the understanding you have acquired as a result. Along the way we have also included images and accompanying text to try to make some key points salient, as well as Research Bites (such as the one on p. 3) to give a sense of how the issues we discuss are played out in cutting-edge contemporary research. Some of these points are quite advanced, but nevertheless they should give you a sense of the sorts of issues that research psychologists are currently discussing, and where the field as a whole is heading. The chapter then concludes with a set of three or four Test Yourself questions that deal with the major issues covered in each chapter, as well as discussion questions and exercises. You can use

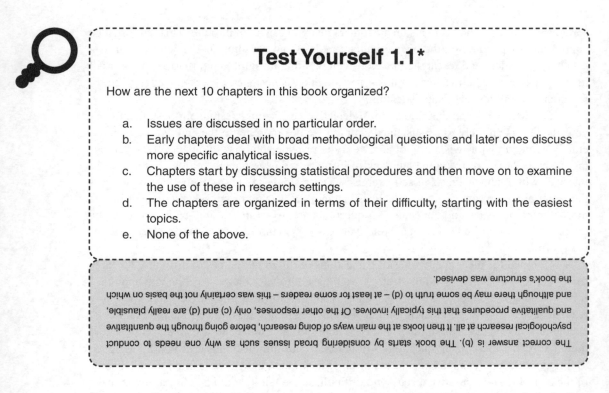

Test Yourself 1.1*

How are the next 10 chapters in this book organized?

a. Issues are discussed in no particular order.
b. Early chapters deal with broad methodological questions and later ones discuss more specific analytical issues.
c. Chapters start by discussing statistical procedures and then move on to examine the use of these in research settings.
d. The chapters are organized in terms of their difficulty, starting with the easiest topics.
e. None of the above.

The correct answer is (b). The book starts by considering broad issues such as why one needs to conduct psychological research at all. It then looks at the main ways of doing research, before going through the quantitative and qualitative procedures that this typically involves. Of the other responses, only (c) and (d) are really plausible, and although there may be some truth to (d) – at least for some readers – this was certainly not the basis on which the book's structure was devised.

these to reflect upon and assess your understanding of the chapter as a whole before moving on.

At the end of most chapters we have also provided a list of some key references that you may want to look at if you are interested in pursuing certain issues further. Generally, though, we have been quite miserly in our referencing. This is mainly because we were keen not to clutter up the text with citations that would do little to help us communicate the particular point we were making. It is also the case that many of the views we present are widely held, so to attribute them to any one person (or a small number of people) would not be particularly appropriate. Yet where our ideas clearly derive from the work of a particular person or group of people, we have (as is necessary in all scholarly writing) endeavoured to acknowledge their source.

The only other main point to note is that, throughout the text, key concepts and terms are marked in bold. Definitions of each are provided in a box at the end of each section. Cross-references within the same box are indicated by terms that are in bold and italicized. We chose to place the definition of terms here, rather than in a glossary at the end of the book, to consolidate the learning process in an ongoing way. We would urge you to make sure that you are thoroughly familiar with these terms as about 90% of them will represent *assumed knowledge* in many later-year courses. Indeed, we explicitly based our decision about which items to place in these boxes on a survey of second- and later-year psychology instructors.

The information in these boxes should also be useful if you are revising for an exam, or returning to the book after a long absence. So in many ways the boxes serve as the milestones with which our journey is marked out. Let us get on with it.

CHECKLIST
Revisiting the key goals for this chapter

☐ I understand the purpose of this book.
☐ I understand the book's structure and how to use it.
☐ I am motivated to engage with the book's goals and to read on.

Discussion/essay questions

a. Should the study of statistics and methodology be made optional in psychology courses?
b. Discuss the proposition that the key to successful research is a sound understanding of methodology.
c. Is the general public's limited understanding of research methodology and statistics a cause for concern?
d. What are the main things to be learned from studying psychology?
e. What general skills does a good psychologist need? To what extent are these skills related to an understanding of the research process?

Research in Psychology: Objectives and Ideals

Key goals for this chapter

- Explain the purpose of psychological research and psychological science.
- Explain the ways in which psychological science progresses.
- Outline the key principles of psychological research.

What is psychological research and why do it?

In the previous chapter we attempted to justify the study of research methodology and statistics by arguing that it will allow you to conduct and understand psychological research. But this raises another question. Why do that research in the first place?

In order to answer this question we need to consider what the academic discipline of psychology is and what differentiates it from other disciplines. Broadly speaking, 'doing psychology' involves examining aspects of mental life and their impact on behaviour. As we discuss in more detail below, such examination typically takes one of four forms:

- *description* in which researchers attempt to understand and map out patterns and regularities in relevant phenomena (e.g., 'What are the different types of human emotion?');
- *prediction* in which researchers attempt to work out what the precursors and consequences of a given phenomenon are (e.g., 'Is setting goals effective?');
- *explanation* in which researchers seek to understand why particular phenomena occur (e.g., 'Why do groups often make extreme judgements?'); and
- *application* in which researchers attempt to use their knowledge to address relevant issues in the world at large (e.g., seeking to reduce stress in the workplace).

Table 2.1 gives an indication of the different aspects of mental life that are examined by researchers in different fields of psychology. Importantly, though, the difference between psychology and other academic disciplines is not just something to do with the topics that psychologists investigate. Many of the core issues addressed by work in fields referred to in Table 2.1 will also be examined by students of philosophy, art, literature, history, sociology, and so on. This is true, for example, if someone is interested in the nature of sensation and perception, or in issues of self, consciousness and identity. Importantly, too, these other subjects provide significant and valuable insights into these topics. Indeed, one of our colleagues is fond of observing that anyone interested in learning about interpersonal relationships should start by reading a Dostoevsky novel.

Table 2.1   Fields of psychology

Different fields of psychology	Representative topics and issues
Biological psychology	The brain's control over human and other animal behaviour
Clinical psychology	The basis and treatment of mental disorders
Cognitive psychology	The nature and basis of complex thought processes and reasoning
Comparative psychology	Animals' evolutionary adaptation to their environment
Cross-cultural psychology	The impact of culture on social behaviour
Developmental psychology	Physical, intellectual and social development over the human lifespan
Educational psychology	Cognitive and social processes in a learning environment
Environmental psychology	The impact of the physical environment on psychological well-being
Forensic psychology	The psychological factors involved in criminal activity
Health psychology	The contribution of psychological factors to illness
Industrial/organizational psychology	Cognitive and social processes in the work environment
Neuropsychology	Brain mechanisms underpinning cognitive processes
Perception	Processes that give coherence and unity to sensory input
Personality psychology	Individual differences in patterns of behaviour and temperament
Political psychology	Political decision making, terrorism, voting behaviour
Psychophysics	Quantitative relationships between physical stimuli and individuals' experience of them
Social psychology	The impact of other people on individuals' thoughts, feelings and action
Sport psychology	The impact of psychological processes and states on human performance

What is customarily understood to differentiate psychology from these other disciplines is the *method* it uses to investigate these topics. In general, psychologists are committed to studying mental life and behaviour by using what is known as the **scientific method**. Just what the scientific method is, is itself a topic of great debate (particularly among philosophers of science), but in general terms it reflects *a commitment to test knowledge through observation and* (if possible) *experimentation*. In this sense it is an **empirical method** (i.e., an activity based on observing the world) that is used to discover truth, or at least *move towards* its discovery as we become more certain about what is true and what is false.

Psychologists, then, are not generally content to base their assertions – their descriptions, predictions, explanations and applications – simply on argument, opinion, gut feeling, or appeals to common sense or logic. Do not misunderstand this point, though. We are not saying that things such as argument, common sense and logic have no place in psychology. They do, and their role is absolutely central. But this role relates largely to empirical evidence and its interpretation.

There are some heavy words in the preceding few paragraphs, and it is certainly true that the claims of anyone who uses concepts such as *science*, *knowledge* and *truth* should be closely examined to see if they deliver as much as they promise. It is worth noting, too, that on the basis of such examination some people have argued that these terms are really quite hollow and are used only to make particular views and practices sound serious and important. For example, Paul Feyerabend has argued that in modern Western society people who look up to science do so out of a quasi-religious faith that is blind and misdirected (e.g., Feyerabend, 1975). Others have argued that all truth is relative and that the quest for absolute scientific truth is therefore meaningless and futile.

Nevertheless, these complaints have had relatively little impact on what scientists do (or think they are doing). Moreover, some researchers have argued that these objections merely point to aspects of human behaviour that psychologists (and other social scientists) need to account for. One way in which they set about doing this is by trying to identify all the factors that contribute to truth and trying to understand their role.

These rather lofty (and really very complex) debates aside, though, there are three essential reasons for wanting to conduct psychological research using the scientific method:

- *discovery* – the desire to find out more about human behaviour and the mental processes associated with it;
- *verification* – the desire to ensure that those findings are correct; and
- *understanding* – the desire to ensure that our interpretation of those findings is correct.

To make this a little clearer, think of something that everyone reading this book has probably thought about at some stage or other – the effect that separation from a loved one will have on a relationship. As a casual observer or as someone who is keenly interested in the question (perhaps because your partner is about to go overseas on a long trip), you will probably think about lots of things that bear upon this issue (How long have we known each other? How much do we love them? How much do they love us? How many presents are they going to bring back?). Based on these observations you may conclude that 'absence makes the heart grow fonder'. The question, though, is whether this conclusion is really appropriate.

Of course in one sense it is, because we all come to conclusions like this all the time in forming our opinions and deciding what to do in different situations. But the fact of the matter is that the same information inevitably leads different people to different conclusions. Indeed, we ourselves may reach different conclusions depending on our circumstances (our mood, our options, our state of inebriation). So, informal observation leads some people to conclude that 'absence makes the heart grow fonder', but others may lean towards the proverbial wisdom that 'absence leads the heart to wander'. Going back to the three points listed earlier, in order to understand *which* of these conclusions is true or *when* each is true we need to adopt a more systematic approach to the question. For example, is it the case – as another version of the saying has it – that 'absence (only) makes the faint heart wander'? In short, we need to take a systematic approach in order to understand exactly what is going on here – to answer the all-important question of *why* separation has these different effects.

Test Yourself 2.1*

Which of the following is not associated with use of the scientific method in psychological research?

    a.   A commitment to producing knowledge through observation and experiment.
    b.   A commitment to basing knowledge exclusively on common sense and opinion.
    c.   A commitment to basing knowledge on empirical evidence.
    d.   A commitment to discovering truth.
    e.   A commitment to ensuring that findings are correctly interpreted.

The correct answer is (b). Common sense and opinion play an important role in psychological research and its interpretation, but they are not all that is important. In particular, this is because use of the scientific method is associated with the attempt to base knowledge on systematic observation and measurement. The word 'exclusively' is therefore what makes statement (b) suspect. Both (a) and (c) are statements of what the scientific method *is*, at least in part; (d) is the objective of all research using the scientific method and (e) is an important aspect of that objective.

empirical method A procedure for obtaining information on the basis of observation.

scientific method A procedure for acquiring and testing knowledge through systematic observation or experimentation (e.g., through use of empirical methods).

How does psychological research progress?

When we say that the key goal of psychological research is to understand *why* mental processes and behaviour have particular effects, we are essentially saying that we want to *explain* those phenomena. Ideally, psychologists achieve this by developing psychological **theory**. A theory is a set of explanatory principles used to make sense of and integrate a range of empirical findings. Theories can vary in specificity from broad explanatory frameworks comprising abstract principles to sets of concrete hypotheses about particular structures and mechanisms. Not all psychologists actually use the word 'theory' to describe the forms of explanation they develop (some prefer terms like 'model', 'analysis', 'account', or – as we will discuss below – 'hypothesis'), but almost all use some form of explanatory system with similar properties.

Importantly, then, psychological research should not simply be conducted in an attempt to uncover more and more *facts* about relevant topics. As an example, research on a topic such as memory does not just involve getting lots of different people to complete lots of different memory tasks.

RESEARCH BITE 2.1
The rise of the short report

In recent years a number of new psychology journals have started up that aim to publish short reports of exciting findings rather than more dense reports of findings from multiple studies. Alison Ledgerwood and Jeff Sherman (2012) note that this has both positive and negative consequences. On the plus side it draws attention to 'sexy' findings that may grab the attention of a broad audience (e.g., journalists and people outside psychology). But on the minus side it may serve to devalue basic science that relies on the careful accumulation of knowledge over time. It may also work against the process of theoretical integration through which a deep understanding of psychology is advanced.

Reference
Ledgerwood, A., & Sherman, J. W. (2012). Short, sweet, and problematic? The rise of the short report in psychological science. *Perspectives on Psychological Science*, 7, 60–66.

Of course research using the scientific method *can* be conducted in this way (and in fact some of it is, particularly where the researchers' goal is one of description). But as the French philosopher of science Henri Poincaré originally observed at the end of the nineteenth century, in the same way that a house is more than just a pile of bricks, so science is more than just the accumulation of facts. Similarly, in a book on astronomy and astrophysics, Gribbin and Rees (1990) open their discussion by noting that if science were only to comprise facts, it would have ground to a halt years ago. This is because it would have been weighed down by the burden of too much data. Instead Gribbin and Rees suggest that:

> Science proceeds because of our ability to discern patterns and regularities in the natural world. As we come to see how previously unconnected facts hang together, we fit more data into laws of greater scope and generality, and we need to remember fewer independent basic facts, from which the rest can be deduced. The astonishing triumph of modern science ... is its ability to describe so many of the bewildering complexities of the natural world in terms of a few underlying principles. (p. 3)

What is true of the laws of physics is also true of psychological theories. What perhaps separates psychologists from physical scientists is that they often disagree much more with each other about what these principles actually are. But this is not really the point. Even if they *disagree* about which theory is right, most psychologists still believe that their goal is to resolve these disagreements and settle upon one correct explanatory framework – a process that also goes on in many 'newer' areas of the physical sciences (e.g., debate on the role of 'cold dark matter' in the formation of galaxies).

In psychology, then, theory serves the same two important purposes that it does in other sciences – both of which are dealt with in the above statement by Gribbin and Rees. First, it should be capable of accounting for *multiple facts*. Second, it should allow researchers to generate predictions about what will happen in *novel* situations. The purpose of most psychological research is to test these predictions using scientific methods.

These predictions are often presented in the form of **hypotheses**. Hypotheses are statements about the **causal relationship** between particular phenomena (although, as we will see in Chapter 8, the term 'hypothesis' has a slightly different meaning when it relates to certain aspects of statistical tests). In other words, they are statements of *cause and effect* that say how one thing affects another. Broadly speaking, all psychological research is conducted in order to establish whether particular hypotheses are true or false. Often these hypotheses are derived from (or used to develop) psychological theory, but they do not necessarily have to be. They will often be tentative statements, too, particularly in the early stages of theory development.

To illustrate this process, we can think back to the case of someone contemplating the effects of separation on a relationship (let us call her Susan). We noted before that in contemplating this problem Susan could call to mind a whole series of cases where couples have been separated. She may remember that when Michelle went away to Greece her boyfriend left her, but that when Rita went to Bali her boyfriend missed her so much that he asked her to marry him the night she returned home. Furthermore, Susan may decide to observe some future separations very closely (perhaps monitoring a range of different kinds of relationship) to gather even more information about this topic. If she does she will clearly obtain a lot of data or facts and perhaps at the end of the process she will feel qualified to make a decision about whether or not she should go away. Perhaps she will conclude that absence really does make the heart grow fonder and decide to journey to Patagonia after all.

We noted before that Susan's strategy will be of limited use if it is unsystematic (if it is not based on the scientific method). But even if Susan *did use the scientific method*, her research would still be severely limited if it were simply concerned with data gathering. For one thing, when would she have enough data to know that she was right? Would it be enough to base her judgement on five relationships, or 50, or 5000? This is actually an intractable question for any scientist who wants to make conclusions only on the basis of raw observation (through a process known as **induction**). Even if every single relationship Susan observed (between couples of every conceivable type) survived separation, could she be sure that hers would?

A key feature of Susan's problem here is that her research is taking place in a theoretical vacuum – she does not have a theory to guide and structure her investigation (a theory that would suggest particular hypotheses to test). If she did, she could gather data that were *particularly* relevant to it. Alternatively, she could consider two competing theories and gather data that tested between them.

Photo 2.1 Karl Popper, the Austro-British philosopher of science who argued that science progresses through a process of falsification. As he saw it, science progresses when theories that are shown to be false are replaced by new theories that have superior explanatory power (© Getty Images).

In this way, the advantage of having a theory is that it tells us *where to look* for evidence. For example, if Susan has a theory that predicts that 'absence makes the heart grow fonder', it may be more profitable to test this among people who have shaky relationships than among those who have strong relationships. This is because often the most useful way to examine a theory is to test it in a situation where it is least likely to be supported (though in practice most scientists do this quite rarely).

Progress in psychology is thus made not only by collecting evidence that supports a theory or hypothesis, but also by collecting evidence that *contradicts* it. When a theory is contradicted in this manner (through a process referred to as **falsification** or **refutation**), it generally has to be rejected or at least refined. According to Popper, this is how most scientific progress is achieved (Popper, 1968; see also Magee, 1974).

In order to provide a critical test of her theory that predicts that 'absence makes the heart grow fonder', Susan may therefore want to see what happens to Martina (a friend with a very shaky relationship) when she is separated from her boyfriend. If Martina's boyfriend leaves her, this should force Susan to reject the simple version of her theory. At the very least she should modify it, perhaps by adding a *qualifying statement*, so that the revised theory (or hypothesis) becomes 'absence makes the heart grow fonder, but only if the initial relationship is already strong'.

One other point to note about Susan's theory is that it does not actually *explain* anything about the relationship between separation and feelings. The statement 'absence makes the heart grow fonder' is actually a **redescription**, not an explanation. Strictly speaking, a psychological theory should explain and not just describe the findings from psychological research. It has to say *why* absence makes the heart grow fonder and not just *that* it makes the heart grow fonder. Related problems arise when psychological theory involves **circular argument** or **reification**, in which an empirical finding is wrongly believed to be explained simply by a process or state responsible for producing that finding. If, for example, a researcher attempts to explain students' good performance in a maths exam by saying that they have a high level of inherent mathematical ability, we can see that the (so-called) explanation does not necessarily tell us very much. Similarly, if we attempt to explain evidence that absence makes the heart grow fonder with reference to a 'separation-induced attachment mechanism' we run the risk of contributing more to psychological jargon than to psychological knowledge. Nonetheless, such strategies often prove tempting both for researchers and for their audience. Among other things, this is because they have the seductive capacity to explain *all* the available empirical data.

In Susan's case, then, a better theory might propose that 'separation strengthens attraction to someone you have a high opinion of (and weakens attraction to someone you don't) because memory preserves only the most salient (i.e. the most important or prominent) features of a person (or object)'. To avoid having to repeat the details of this explanation every time the theory is referred to, the theory will probably be identified by an abbreviated title. So this explanation might be referred to as 'salient feature theory'.

The advantage of this type of theory is that it allows researchers to examine *processes* and not just particular products or events. To illustrate this point, think about how people understand the operation of a car. Here we can formulate two kinds of theory: those of the type typically developed by drivers, and others of the type typically developed by engineers. As a driver you may develop (through empirical observation, i.e., driving) a descriptive understanding of the form 'if I depress the accelerator, then the car will go faster'. But an engineer may develop an explanatory theory of the form 'if I depress the accelerator, then the car will go faster because it increases the flow of oxygen to the engine and the engine then burns more fuel which in turn makes the engine go round faster'.

The advantage of the engineer's theory is that because it offers an explanation of the observed relationship between the accelerator and the car's speed, engineers are not only able to drive a car but also to understand (and design) *other* machines where this principle operates. Clearly this is something that most drivers cannot do. So, going back to our relationship example, if it really is true that memory preserves the salient features of objects, then this may allow a psychologist not only to predict when separation will have a bad effect on a relationship, but also to understand why it does and to apply this understanding to other things. For example, it might help us understand why as people grow older they start to think that summers were more pleasant when they were young, that milk used to taste better, or that the police used to be more honest.

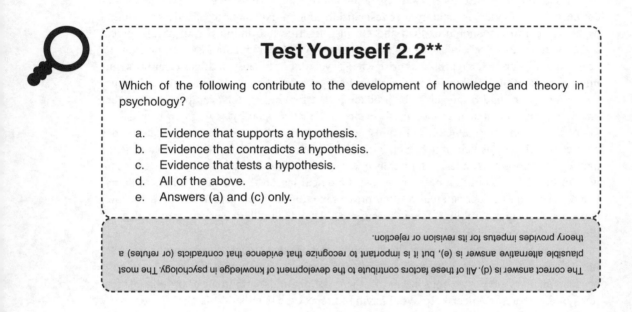

Test Yourself 2.2**

Which of the following contribute to the development of knowledge and theory in psychology?

a. Evidence that supports a hypothesis.
b. Evidence that contradicts a hypothesis.
c. Evidence that tests a hypothesis.
d. All of the above.
e. Answers (a) and (c) only.

The correct answer is (d). All of these factors contribute to the development of knowledge in psychology. The most plausible alternative answer is (e), but it is important to recognize that evidence that contradicts (or refutes) a theory provides impetus for its revision or rejection.

causal relationship An association between two or more things, such that one causes the other (i.e., makes it happen).

circular argument An argument in which the thing to be explained is presented as the explanation (e.g., where memory ability is used to explain memory performance).

falsification The process of rejecting conclusions and theories on the basis of evidence that is inconsistent with them. A commitment to carrying out research with this objective is referred to as 'falsificationism'.

hypothesis Formally, a statement about the *causal relationship* between particular phenomena (i.e., in the form 'A causes B'). This is usually derived from a particular *theory* and designed to be tested in research. In statistics and in informal usage, a hypothesis can also be a statement of the expected results of a study.

induction The process of drawing conclusions and developing theories on the basis of accumulated observations.

redescription The process and outcome of attempts to explain an empirical finding by restating that finding (e.g., where fear of confined spaces is used to explain claustrophobia).

refutation Another word for *falsification.*

reification Treating an abstraction as if it were a real concrete thing. In psychology this refers to the process and outcome of treating an empirical finding as if it were the straightforward expression of an underlying psychological process (e.g., seeing performance on intelligence tests as the expression of intelligence).

theory A system of explanation used to make sense of, and integrate, a number of empirical findings. A theory can vary in specificity from a broad explanatory framework comprising abstract principles to a set of concrete hypotheses about particular structures and mechanisms.

Principles of good research

Although many of the ideas discussed in the previous two sections would be endorsed by a wide range of psychological researchers, they are often in the background when research is actually being done.

For this reason, most researchers would probably prefer to comment on research *products* rather than the research *process*. In their own research they would then strive to achieve the best product by adhering to some relatively down-to-earth principles that are widely endorsed by other researchers (e.g., Ray, 1993; Sternberg, 1995). In this section we will focus on five principles. These suggest that psychological research should be (a) reliable, (b) valid, (c) cumulative, (d) parsimonious and (e) public.

Two qualities that all psychologists strive for in their research are **reliability** and **validity**. These terms are easily confused with each other and with other things, but it is essential to have a clear grasp of both. Put simply, *reliability relates to our confidence that a given empirical finding can be reproduced* again and again and is not just a 'freak' or chance occurrence. If a finding is reliable it will be easy to reproduce through **replication**. A good way to remember what reliability refers to (and to avoid confusing it with validity) is to think about what it means to advertise a second-hand car as 'reliable'. If it really is reliable the engine will not just start once in a blue moon, it will start every time you turn the ignition. If after you buy the car you find that it only starts occasionally, you will think that you have been duped – and what is more, you will be right. Similarly, if some psychologists suggest that a given finding is reliable but no one else can ever reproduce it, their research will be called seriously into question.

The concept of validity is slightly more difficult to grasp, largely because it can take a number of different forms. In the simplest terms, validity relates to our confidence that a given finding shows what it purports to show. Examining the validity of a **study** therefore

RESEARCH BITE 2.2
Replication: An ideal honoured in the breach?

The idea that a given finding can be replicated is central to its reliability and is a corner-stone of all science. Yet how often does this occur in psychology? According to research by Matthew Makel, Jonathan Plucker, and Boyd Hegarty (2012), not very often. They found that only 1.6% of psychology articles used the word 'replication' or variants of it, and that, of these, only around two-thirds actually involved replication. Interestingly too, these replications were much more likely to be successful if they were performed by a researcher who was an author of the original study. They do note, though, that in recent years there has been a marked increase in the number of reported replications and see this as a positive development.

Reference
Makel, M. C., Plucker, J. A., & Hegarty, B. (2012). Replications in psychology research: How often do they really occur? *Perspectives on Psychological Science, 7*, 537–542.

involves seeing whether its findings have been correctly interpreted. If they have not then the research is invalid. Continuing with our car example, a car without an engine (and that there-fore *never* starts) is actually *reliable* (because the same result is continually reproduced), but it is not a *valid* car because it is not what it seems or purports to be – if you like, it has been misinterpreted as a car when it is actually something else (perhaps a very cumbersome piece of modern art or a heap of scrap metal).

As a more psychological example, think of a study in which some researchers send a person overseas to see whether this makes that person think more favourably of their partner. Let us assume that it does (again and again, i.e., it is a reliable finding). If on this basis the researchers conclude that 'absence makes the heart grow fonder' their conclusion may not be *valid*. The study may show something else – and almost certainly does. It may just show that holidays make people feel better about things in general (including their partners).

Discussions about the validity of findings are some of the most common (and most heated) in psychological research. They contribute to many of the disagreements between researchers that we have alluded to already, partly because establishing the validity of research findings tends to be much more difficult in psychology than in other scientific fields (such as physics or biology). This is mainly because the things in which most psy-chologists are interested – mental processes or states – can *never* be observed or measured directly. It is never possible for psychologists to read someone's mind or know exactly what is going through it. We will discuss the implications of this point further in the next two chapters.

Disagreement about validity generally relates to assertions that findings which are said to show one thing can be *reinterpreted* in a way that suggests that they actually show something completely different. Debates about the validity of IQ testing are a good example. Some researchers have argued that studies using IQ tests 'show' that there are racial differences in intelligence. Their critics, however, argue that these studies only 'show' that IQ tests are culturally biased – that their construction reflects the values and prejudices of the test designers (see Gould, 1981).

A belief that research should be *cumulative* relates to the discussion of progress in the previous section. The basic idea here is that at any given time research into a particular issue or problem needs to be guided by research that has been conducted on it previously and to move forward by building on its insights. To the extent that it is cumulative, research should develop from a sound knowledge base in which researchers learn from and avoid the mistakes of the past. It was to such a process that the physicist Isaac Newton attributed his own success when he remarked, 'if I have been able to see further than others it is because I have stood on the shoulders of giants'.

Just how researchers choose what particular problem to address is itself a very important issue, and could be the topic of a whole book. In practice, though, the agenda of psychological research is governed by an array of factors including (a) the work of other researchers in the field of interest, (b) the questions that are defined as important by both the general and the scientific community, and (c) the social, economic and political climate. All these factors actually affect each other. This can mean that sometimes the issues addressed by researchers will change dramatically in a very short period of time – a process that the philosopher Kuhn (1962) referred to as 'scientific revolution'. Nevertheless, during periods of stability (or what Kuhn called 'normal science'), groups of psychologists interested in a given topic will typically be engaged in the process of striving (both collaboratively and competitively) to explore and explain one particular issue as comprehensively as possible.

In thinking about this process of research development, one problem that may occur to you is how a researcher's ideas can ever be conclusively rejected. As we saw before, even when a hypothesis is refuted by a particular piece of evidence it is still possible to cling to the theory from which it was derived simply by continuing to add qualifying statements to the theory. So if the evidence from people who do not have strong relationships contradicts the theory that 'absence makes the heart grow fonder', then a researcher can propose a new theory such as 'absence makes the heart grow fonder, but only if the initial relationship is strong'. But what if this is true only of heterosexual relationships? And what, then, if it is only true for couples without children? Exactly

Photo 2.2 Thomas Kuhn, the American philosopher of science who argued that science progresses through processes of scientific revolution. Such revolutions involve sudden dramatic changes in thinking within a particular research field (© Getty Images).

how long can researchers cling on to a theory (or another explanatory principle) before they are forced to give it up?

One answer is that they should hang on to the theory until a better one comes along. The question is, though, what makes a competing theory *better*? One commonly accepted answer appeals to the principle of **parsimony**. This asserts that the best theory (or other explanatory structure) is the one that provides the simplest, most economical and efficient explanation of the evidence. In these terms, the goal of psychology (and of science in general) is to *explain the largest number of facts in terms of the smallest number of principles*.

To illustrate this point, we could develop three theories that might be used to explain the relationship between separation and attraction. Theory A (let us call it 'motivated nostalgia theory') might assert that separation from an object causes us to exaggerate the object's worth, because we are motivated to have positive memories of things encountered in the past (this explains the finding that 'absence makes the heart grow fonder'). Theory B ('physical reinforcement theory') could suggest that separation from an object causes us to devalue it because attraction has to be maintained by constant physical reinforcement (this explains the finding that 'absence leads the heart to wander'). Finally, Theory C ('salient feature theory') might argue that separation from an object causes us to exaggerate that object's qualities (whether good or bad) because memory tends only to preserve the most salient features of an object (this explains why 'absence makes the heart grow fonder' when we like someone and why 'absence leads the heart to wander' if we dislike them). According to the principle of parsimony, of the three theories, C should be preferred because it explains more empirical facts but still only involves one principle. So, in cases where researchers have to choose between two or more theories, if they apply this principle, they should favour the one that explains either more evidence or the same amount of evidence (or more) with fewer principles.

All the above principles relate to how good research is done, but a final question concerns what one should do with good research. The short answer to this is that good research needs to be *public*. It is clear that keeping research findings secret will do nothing to advance scholarly debate. If Galileo had kept his observations to himself, the study of astronomy as a whole would have suffered. Similarly, it is important that research psychologists contribute to the scientific (and, where relevant, the general) community.

This participation takes many forms. Nowadays many psychologists are keen to discuss their research on television and radio, in newspapers and popular books. Here they have to justify their work to the general public. Just what qualifies as success here is quite a moot point, but the researchers would probably conclude that they had been successful if their research had become widely known, if it had had some impact on the policy of relevant bodies (e.g., government agencies) or if they had benefited commercially (e.g., by selling a lot of books).

Researchers also commonly present their ideas and findings at conferences. These vary in terms of the composition both of the audience and of the speakers: from the most general (e.g., a conference on 'violence in the general community' that attracts people with different reasons for being there and from all walks of life) to the most specific (e.g., a workshop on 'cognitive development in early childhood'). Here the quality of the research might be gauged by the applause of the audience, the tone of the questions asked of the presenter, or the extension of an invitation to return next year. In some cases, too, the proceedings of these conferences are published, either formally or informally.

For most academic psychologists, however, the most important benchmark (or 'performance indicator') is their ability to publish their research in scholarly journals and books. The contributions to the more prestigious of these are handled by academic editors and the merits of the research are evaluated (often anonymously) by other experts in the field. On the basis of those experts' judgement the editor will either reject the research or, usually only after revision, accept it for publication. Many journals publish less than 10% of the papers that are submitted to them.

This process of public exposure allows psychological research not only to be communicated, but also to be checked, both by the researchers' peers and by other scientists and members of the general public. This process of public scrutiny is a way of seeking to ensure that research satisfies the principles of good research that we have discussed above. For example, it allows other people to challenge the interpretation of research findings or to attempt to reproduce them themselves – thereby testing both the validity and the reliability of the research. This scrutiny can be uncomfortable and sometimes even humiliating, especially when it involves criticism. But opening up research to the *possibility* of such criticism is generally considered to be an important way of ensuring its integrity.

RESEARCH BITE 2.3
All science relies on honesty and trust

In the wake of a number of highly publicized cases of academic fraud in psychology, Wolfgang Stroebe, Tom Postmes, and Russell Spears (2012) conducted a systematic review to establish whether fraud was more of a problem in psychology than in other disciplines and whether it reflected a particular problem with psychology's process of peer review. The researchers found no evidence that either of these things were true. However, they did observe that, across all sciences, fraud is rarely brought to light as a result of the peer review process – largely because this is not what reviewers are looking for. All science, they conclude, necessarily relies on trust, and there is always a possibility that this will be exploited by unscrupulous researchers.

Reference
Stroebe, W., Postmes, T., & Spears, R. (2012). Scientific misconduct and the myth of self-correction in science. *Perspectives on Psychological Science*, 7, 670–688.

Finally, in an era when accountability (to both the public and the scientific community) is seen as an important means of justifying research funding, it is likely that researchers who are not prepared to make their work public will receive less support for doing research in the future.

Test Yourself 2.3**

Which of the following statements is true?

  a.   If a finding is reliable it should be easy to replicate using the same procedures.
  b.   If a finding is reliable it will also be valid.
  c.   If a finding is reliable it will be important.
  d.   If a finding is reliable it must be an example of good scientific practice.
  e.   If a finding is reliable it has been correctly interpreted.

The correct answer is (a). Reliability relates to the ability to reproduce or replicate a finding. Many reliable findings are incorrectly interpreted (i.e. invalid), so (b) and (e) are wrong. Reliability is also different from (though sometimes confused with) importance (a point we will discuss in more detail in later chapters), so (c) is wrong. Many examples of bad scientific practice produce findings that are reliable, too, so it is important not to fall into the trap presented by (d) – though many researchers do.

parsimony The goal of accounting for the maximum number of empirical findings in terms of the smallest number of theoretical principles. The most parsimonious theory is the one that accounts for the most findings using the fewest principles.

reliability The extent to which a given finding will be consistently reproduced. A reliable finding is one that is consistently reproduced.

replication Both (a) the process of attempting to reproduce a previously obtained finding and (b) a research finding which reproduces another that has been obtained previously.

study A piece of empirical research.

validity The extent to which a given finding shows what it is believed to show. A valid finding is one that has been logically and correctly interpreted.

Some notes of caution

In writing this chapter we have tried to make it clear that few (if any) of the practices we describe would be subscribed to by all researchers in psychology. Most would agree with many of the criteria identified above and with the use of the scientific method, but many would also question the role of theory and other explanatory frameworks in the discipline, or suggest that these serve very different purposes than those we have outlined. Moreover, even if researchers *believe* that they adhere to many of these principles, it is possible to argue that they do not in practice.

In the case of parsimony, for example, many researchers have argued that there are actually competitive pressures in the 'industry' of psychological research that lead researchers to develop mini-theories that address quite specific phenomena in preference to grand theories with broader applicability (e.g., Aronson, 1997). One reason for this is that mini-theories allow researchers to work in their own well-defined territory and to have the prestige that goes with it, with less pressure from rival theorists. On the other hand, grand theories (and grand theorists) can be quite threatening and are often seen to be unnecessarily imperialistic.

So – as the title of this chapter suggests – the scientific principles we have discussed are, at the very best, *ideals*. And even then they are ideals that not all psychologists would endorse. Nevertheless, they are ideals that most psychologists would *recognize* and as such they play an important part in researchers' attempts to understand what they do and to represent that understanding to other people. At the heart of this point is a recognition of the fact that all science is a profoundly *human* enterprise. In spite of attempts to represent science as utterly impartial and objective, it is always shaped by the world in which it takes place – a world of politics, economics, ideology and history.

The impact of the Second World War on the things psychologists studied and the kinds of explanation they developed makes this point clear (a point that can also be made by thinking about the things that physicists were doing around this time). In the wake of the Holocaust, in which millions of people from different groups were exterminated by the Nazis, researchers became much more concerned to investigate issues of prejudice and group hatred. Indeed, the war was the stimulus for a range of 'classic studies' in social psychology that sought to demonstrate how tyranny and oppression could be sustained by the actions of

Photo 2.3 Psychology, like all science, is shaped by a desire to answer questions that society considers important. This can also lead to certain questions not being asked. Among other things, these protesters outside St Paul's Cathedral in London were interested in the causes and consequences of the 2008 economic crisis. Within psychology (and other disciplines, such as economics) there is greater interest in such questions today than there was 10 years ago.

Photo 2.4 The events of the Second World War were the stimulus for a range of 'classic studies' in psychology that sought to understand what would turn civilized decent people into agents of tyranny and oppression.

ordinary people with no history of psychological disorder or psychopathology (Smith & Haslam, 2012).

Curiously, then, the processes that contribute to people's belief in a theory or that lead them to test a particular hypothesis (and overlook others) are actually affected by many of the things that psychologists themselves study. For example, they may depend on how committed researchers are to the theory, their perceptions of the other people who endorse the theory, what makes sense to them, and their own self-interest. Many would argue that what psychologists believe (and what they do not believe) is as much to do with these human factors as it is to do with abstract principles such as parsimony and validity. However, we raise this point more to urge you to think broadly and openly about the principles we have discussed in this chapter than to open the door on further debate.

CHECKLIST
Revisiting the key goals for this chapter

☐ I understand the purpose of psychological research and of psychological science.

☐ I understand the ways in which psychological science progresses (at least in ideal terms).

☐ I understand the key principles of psychological research.

Further reading

A large number of books provide useful discussions of the nature of research in psychology and the scientific status of that research. Valentine's (1982) book is typical of these and deals with a large number of important issues from the nature of explanation to the role of computer simulation in psychology. Chalmers (1978) provides an engaging discussion of the philosophy of science that has very broad relevance – not just to psychologists. Goldacre's (2008) book offers a highly readable account of the ways in which people often make false claims in the name of science in order to promote particular ideas and products. His column by the same name in *The Guardian* (available online at www.guardian.co.uk/science/series/badscience) is also well worth reading on a regular basis.

Chalmers, A. F. (1978). *What is this thing called science?* Milton Keynes: Open University Press.

Goldacre, B. (2008). *Bad science.* London: HarperCollins.

Valentine, E. R. (1982). *Conceptual issues in psychology.* London: Allen & Unwin.

Objective and ideals: A checklist for research evaluation and improvement

Table 2.2

Potential problem	Question to ask	Potential improvement
Empirical weakness	Do researchers have sufficient empirical evidence to back up their claims about particular psychological processes or states?	Consider carefully the relationship between the claims that researchers make and the empirical evidence they use to back up those claims. In particular, try to identify empirical gaps and to consider assumptions that are implicit in the arguments presented. Where gaps exist, or assumptions appear questionable, consider conducting empirical research that clarifies matters and advances understanding of the relevant processes and states. The decision to conduct this research should be tempered by the importance of any problems you identify and of the research question as a whole.
Theoretical weakness	Have researchers integrated their empirical findings within a sufficiently broad and sufficiently plausible explanatory framework?	Consider how well researchers have succeeded in reconciling the range of empirical findings on a given topic and whether any integrated analysis they provide allows predictions to be made which extend beyond existing empirical work. Where necessary, seek to develop an appropriate theory that performs these functions and devise novel empirical studies that enable it to be tested.
Inductive reasoning	Have researchers developed an understanding of a particular issue simply by generalizing on the basis of prior empirical observations (i.e., without developing an appropriate theory)?	Develop a theory that explains previous findings and allows novel predictions to be tested.
Redescription; circular argument	Does a given psychological theory simply redescribe particular empirical findings rather than explain them?	Examine the content of psychological theory closely. If redescription is being presented as explanation, develop a critique along these lines and attempt to develop an alternative theory that explains why particular empirical findings arise and that can be tested in further empirical research.

(Continued)

Table 2.2 (Continued)

Potential problem	Question to ask	Potential improvement
Reification	Does a given psychological theory suggest that particular empirical findings are the unmediated expression of an underlying psychological process?	Examine the content of psychological theory closely. If you find evidence of reification, develop a critique along these lines and consider alternatives to the explanation provided. Devise research that tests between these alternative explanations and the one proposed in the original research.
Limited reliability	Can a particular empirical finding be replicated?	If the reliability of an empirical finding appears questionable, attempt to replicate it before proceeding to more elaborate tests or extensions of a theory.
Limited validity	Does a particular empirical finding show what researchers believe it to show?	Try to develop an alternative explanation of the empirical finding in question. If this alternative explanation appears plausible, devise empirical research that tests it competitively against the explanation proposed in the original research.
Non-cumulativeness	Does a particular piece of research draw from and attempt to develop existing knowledge?	Where a particular piece of research appears to have overlooked previous research or to have failed to draw connections with a relevant body of the literature, point this out. If necessary, conduct additional research that clarifies the nature and importance of these links.
Lack of parsimony	Does a particular theory appear to be unnecessarily complicated or to contain too many qualifying statements?	If a theory appears to be unparsimonious, try to devise a simpler theory (one that contains fewer explanatory principles but explains as many, or more, empirical findings). Having done this, devise a study that subjects the two theories to a competitive test.
Lack of scrutiny	Has a researcher subjected his or her findings and conclusions to peer review?	If research has not been subjected to stringent peer review (e.g., by relevant psychological journals) it is prudent to treat it with some scepticism. When commentators on a particular topic assert that 'research has shown …', ask whether this is really the case and whether this is all that research has shown. Where you identify an error, attempt to correct it on the basis of evidence that is empirically and theoretically sound, but do so in a manner that you would find acceptable if you were the person making the supposed error.
Lack of accountability	Has a researcher endeavoured to promote an understanding of his or her research in the broader community?	Where relevant, psychologists have a responsibility to contribute to public debate by communicating their research findings to a non-academic audience. Consider ways of doing this that promote informed debate rather than reinforce popular myths or prejudices.

Test Yourself 2.4*

Which of the following statements is true?

a. The major goal of science is to identify as many facts as possible.
b. The major goal of science is to develop as many theories as possible.
c. The major goal of science is to explain as many facts as possible with the smallest number of theoretical principles.
d. The major goal of science is to do as much research as possible with as little money.
e. Both (a) and (b).

Test Yourself 2.5**

Which of the following is not a widely accepted feature of good research?

a. It should be public.
b. It should be cumulative.
c. It should be valid.
d. It should be reliable.
e. It should support a theory.

Test Yourself 2.6***

Which of the following statements is true?

a. All research in psychology is concerned with the development of explanatory theory.
b. All research in psychology shows commitment to the scientific method.
c. All research in psychology uses the scientific method even if researchers do not believe in it.
d. The interpretation of all research in psychology is open to question, as with all scientific research.
e. None of the above.

Test Yourself 2.7***

After reading some research on the topic of students' attitudes to university courses, Mark does some research to find out what students' favourite subject at university is. In this he finds that final-year psychology students prefer studying psychology to any other subject. On this basis he concludes that psychology is the most popular subject. However, Jane

(Continued)

(Continued)

argues that this conclusion is wrong as the research actually shows that students prefer the subject they end up studying. What is the basis of her objection to Mark's research?

a. The research is invalid.
b. The research is unreliable.
c. The research is non-cumulative.
d. The research is unparsimonious.
e. None of the above.

The correct answer to 2.4 is (c). This is the essence of the point made by Gribbin and Rees (1990) – and of the statement by Einstein that 'the grand aim of all science is to cover the greatest number of empirical facts by logical deduction from the smallest number of hypotheses or axioms'. If science were only concerned with generating more and more information (whether in the form of data or theory) it would grind to a halt under the burden – so (a), (b) and (e) are incorrect; (d) may be true for some scientists (and those who fund them), but it is not the major aim of science.

The correct answer to 2.5 is (e). Research should be public, cumulative, valid and reliable, but in order to be these things it does not necessarily have to support a theory. It may in fact contradict one or more theories and possibly stimulate the development of new theories.

The correct answer to 2.6 is (d). We noted at the end of this chapter that the conduct of psychological research is a human enterprise and that as such its output is always interpreted by people with particular values, beliefs and expectations. As these change, so too may the interpretation of even the most widely accepted wisdom. This is true of all science, so this fact does not make psychology any less scientific than, say, physics (although physical scientists are usually very keen to affirm the objectivity of what they do). Answers (a), (b) and (c) are true of much psychological research, but certainly not all of it. As we noted in the last section of the chapter, at best (a) and (b) are ideals to which many (but not all) researchers aspire.

The correct answer to 2.7 is (a). Jane is arguing that Mark's research does not show what he thinks it shows (i.e., that it is invalid). There is no reason to think either that if Mark did his research again he would not get exactly the same results, or that his research did not build on the previous research he had read about. So neither the reliability of his work nor its cumulative basis is being called into question. Jane's analysis is also no more parsimonious than Mark's – it still explains the findings in terms of one explanatory principle.

Discussion/essay questions

a. What is the role of theory in psychological research?
b. Is psychology a science or a pseudo-science?
c. Does the scientific method unnecessarily restrict psychological enquiry?
d. Can psychological research ever be completely valid?
e. What role does the principle of parsimony play in psychological research and in science in general?

Exercises

a. From the material you have studied in other psychology courses to date, identify an explanation of a phenomenon that has been proposed in the literature, and ask the following questions:

    i. Is the explanation a theory?

    ii. How many principles are involved in this explanation?

    iii. Are there competing explanations that represent alternatives to this explanation?

    iv. What form does the public evidence in favour of the explanation take?

    v. Does the research conform to the ideals identified in this chapter?

b. A widely replicated phenomenon is the 'cocktail party effect'. This refers to the fact that people can be listening to one conversation in a crowded and noisy room but nevertheless hear their own name mentioned in another conversation – even though they have no awareness of that conversation.

    i. Write down in 25 words or less an account of why you think this happens. Then look up 'selective attention' in the index of a psychology textbook to see what explanations have been proposed by previous researchers.

    ii. Does your account bear any resemblance to any of these explanations? What are the key differences between your account and the textbook explanation?

Research Methods

Key goals for this chapter

- Explain the purpose of psychological measurement and the different forms it can take.
- Outline the major methods used in psychological research.
- Understand the key strengths and weaknesses of different research methods.

In the previous chapter we asked why researchers do research in psychology and what they are looking for when they do. If a researcher has decided to go ahead and conduct research, the next obvious question is 'What different research strategies are available?'.

Our response to this question starts with an examination of the things that psychologists measure and of the basic types of psychological measurement. We then look in turn at the four major research methods that psychologists employ in order to conduct research: (a) experimental, (b) quasi-experimental, (c) survey and (d) case study. The strengths and limitations of each of these methods are considered in separate sections in which we also discuss the basis on which researchers choose among them. This choice can be difficult to make and quite controversial. But as we shall see, it is often affected by factors over which the researcher has limited control.

Psychological measurement

In the previous chapter we noted that one of the things that differentiates psychology from other sciences is the fact that the things in which psychologists are typically interested – mental states and processes – can never be directly observed or measured. You cannot touch or see a mood, a thought, a disposition, a memory or an attitude. Instead, you can only observe things that are associated with these phenomena. This does not mean that the phenomena themselves are any less real, it simply means that they can be hard to get a handle on.

Of course the difficulty of observing and measuring phenomena of interest also exists in other sciences, such as astronomy and chemistry, but in these fields this problem has often been addressed by making relevant technological advances. For instance, difficulties that are caused by an inability to observe distant stars have led to the development of more powerful telescopes. Technology in psychology and related fields has made significant advances, too. It is now possible to monitor blood flow through the brain and a range of electrical signals within it. Similarly, technology exists to test reaction times and various other subtle and non-conscious responses. But these still only allow psychologists to study the *outcomes* of mental activity, or things that are *associated* with it – never the activity itself.

You might think that this constitutes such a serious impediment to research that it makes the whole enterprise of trying to study psychology futile. Indeed, just such a belief underpinned the emergence of **behaviourism** as a major approach to psychology in the 1920s. Proponents of this view (notably J. B. Watson and later B. F. Skinner) asserted that human behaviour could be understood without the need to examine, or even posit the existence of, internal states such as thoughts or emotions.

Nevertheless, the fact that something cannot be seen does *not* mean that hypotheses about its nature cannot be put forward and tested. Physicists have never seen subatomic particles or black holes, yet scientific analysis of their effects has been crucial to theoretical and practical advances in that field. The same is true in psychology, in which researchers generally use different forms of measurement to inform them about two types of psychological phenomenon: **stable psychological characteristics** (such as intelligence, personality or certain types of belief), and **dynamic mental processes** (such as memory, mood or judgement).

Both of these aspects of mental life are examined using similar measurement **instruments**. The primary difference is that when researchers examine dynamic processes they are usually interested in obtaining an on-the-spot measurement which they will compare with others obtained under different conditions. In contrast, to examine characteristics researchers usually administer particular **psychological tests**. These will either already exist or be devised by the researchers. The tests generally seek to make judgements about any one individual by comparing their responses with those of the general population. They do this to make statements about an individual's relative position on the **dimension** in question (e.g., IQ, verbal reasoning, neuroticism, depression). In the case of widely used clinical and educational tests, the process of developing these tests in order to establish their reliability and validity is usually very extensive.

In conducting research into mental processes and characteristics, researchers have three main measurement options available to them. First, they can use **behavioural measures**. These study particular forms of behaviour and make inferences about the psychological phenomena that caused or contributed to them. These measures come in a wide range of forms and are usually tailored to the specific question in which the researcher is interested. For example, the type of toy that children play with when given a choice

RESEARCH BITE 3.1
The science of behaviour?

By one definition, psychology is the science of behaviour. However, in their review of the field, Roy Baumeister, Kathleen Vohs, and David Funder (2007) note that, over time, psychologists have studied less and less actual behaviour in their research. Instead, they have increasingly come to rely on methods and measures that are assumed to relate to behaviour but which do not demonstrate this link directly (e.g., self-reports of attitudes, feelings and memories). They observe that one reason why this occurs is that studying behaviour can be hard work and very messy. However, when researching a given topic it is worth reflecting on what is lost by *not* going to the trouble of studying 'real' behaviour.

Reference
Baumeister, R. F., Vohs, K. D., & Funder, D. C. (2007). Psychology as the science of self-reports and finger movements: Whatever happened to actual behavior? *Perspectives on Psychological Science*, 2, 396–403.

(e.g., whether it is a gun or a teddy bear) can be used as a measure of their aggressiveness (Bandura, Ross, & Ross, 1961). Alternatively, finding out whether a person can recall more words that start with a 'k' than words that have 'k' as their third letter can tell a researcher something about the processes involved in the operation and organization of memory (Tversky & Kahneman, 1974). As a final example, discovering whether young children can imagine what a three-dimensional scene looks like from someone else's perspective might enable inferences to be made about the role which the self plays in the process of organizing and representing visual information (Piaget, 1952). By the same token, the performance of any individual child on this task may tell a researcher something about the state of the child's intellectual development.

A second measurement option is to use **self-report measures**, which ask people about their thoughts, feelings or reaction to a given issue. Providing that it is possible for people to reflect consciously on the relevant thoughts or behaviours, the responses they make can be used either to supplement other behavioural measures or as data in themselves. Again these can be used to gain insight into both processes and states. So, the fact that people evaluate another person more favourably if they believe that that person belongs to the same group as themselves may tell us something about the process of stereotyping (Tajfel, 1970). On the other hand, people's responses to a large number of questions about their lifestyle and personal habits can be used to make inferences about their personality (e.g., Hathaway &

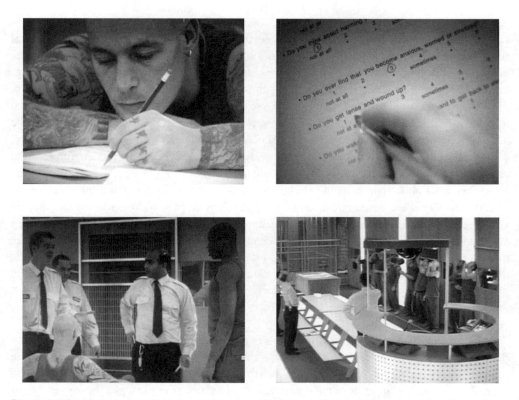

Photos 3.1–3.4 Different methods can be used to assess the same psychological state or process. In the top pictures a participant in the BBC Prison Study completes self-report measures of stress. These were supplemented by behavioural observation that involved monitoring and filming the participants around the clock. Stress was also assessed by taking daily measures of the cortisol in participants' saliva (as seen in the bottom right picture; Haslam & Reicher, 2006; Reicher & Haslam, 2006).

McKinley, 1943). Here the unusual nature of a person's beliefs may lead a clinician to suspect that the person is psychologically disturbed (e.g., Eysenck & Eysenck, 1985).

Finally, researchers can use **physiological measures** to examine things that are believed to be directly associated with particular forms of mental activity. These can be thought of as measures of mental traces (i.e., of things associated with mental activity, whether conscious or not). For example, measures such as heart rate or galvanic skin response (GSR, a measure of the electrical conductivity of the skin) can serve as measures of anxiety or arousal (e.g., as associated with different emotional states such as anger, happiness or disgust; Ekman, Levenson, & Frieson, 1983). Similarly, measures of blood flow or electrical activity in the brain may tell us about the neural structures that are involved in particular forms of mental activity (e.g., reading aloud; Lassen, Ingvar, & Skinhoj, 1978). These same data can also inform researchers about a person's enduring mental state – for example, informing them that they have generally low arousal levels or are suffering from a particular form of brain damage.

Although they are used primarily (but not exclusively) to make inferences about behaviour rather than psychological states or processes, it is worth adding here that **behavioural trace measures** are also widely employed in some areas of psychology (e.g., environmental, consumer and organizational). These involve obtaining physical traces of people's behaviour to inform researchers about what people are currently doing or have done in the past. Again, these measures take many different forms. For example, the amount of electricity being used in a town might be used to infer whether its residents are asleep or awake. Similarly, the sales of a particular edition of a newspaper could tell researchers something about the level of interest in a particular topic. More mundanely, an examination of people's garbage could provide information about their lifestyle or eating habits.

Decisions about which of the above measures to use will be dictated by a number of factors. Many of these are practical and will be linked to other methodological choices that we will discuss in the following sections. For example, self-report measures are relatively cheap and easy to administer, and so lend themselves to survey-based research examining large numbers of people in naturalistic settings. On the other hand, physiological measures can be difficult and expensive to obtain and so they are usually used only in experimental research involving very few participants. However, decisions about which of these measures to use are guided as much by the particular question a researcher wants to address as by these pragmatic considerations.

Whatever choice a researcher makes, one point to emphasize about all these measurement options is that *none of them provides a pure or direct measure* of the variables in which researchers are interested. In all cases it is possible that the measures will be contaminated by other things, and that this may cloud interpretation of the data. For example, the toys that children play with may be a reflection of the aggressiveness of their parents, rather than their own aggressiveness. People's responses to a questionnaire may give insights into prevailing social norms (i.e., what people think is appropriate) rather than their personality. Skin conductance may measure people's excitement when it is intended to measure their anxiety.

These 'other things' in which the researcher is not immediately interested are referred to as **extraneous variables**. Because they adversely affect researchers' ability to interpret their findings correctly they can pose serious threats to the validity of a study or an entire research programme. This is a point to which researchers need to be continually alert. It is often dealt with by using *multiple measures* or – as we will discuss below – by conducting controlled experiments to rule out the influence of a particular variable.

One feature of psychological measurement that distinguishes it from measurement procedures in some other sciences is that it normally involves taking multiple observations. This might mean measuring more than one person or measuring the same person more than once. Some of the reasons for doing this are easy to see. If we were to base knowledge on one person's response to a single question or task, our research finding might tell us something about the particular characteristics of the person we chose to measure but very little about the **population** in general. For this reason we would probably be quite worried about the *reliability* of the finding.

To make the ramifications of this point clearer, imagine that you were concerned to find out how much reading ability 10-year-old children have. If you measured just one girl's ability you might get a distorted picture because you selected a child who had very high or very low ability. For reasons that we will explain in much greater detail in later chapters, you would want to guard against these possibilities by selecting a large sample of children to participate in your research. In order to get an accurate picture you would also want to avoid systematically selecting children of high or low ability.

You might argue that although you need to measure quite a few children to get an accurate picture of 10-year-olds' reading ability, a single measure of one child's ability would be sufficient to tell you what that particular child's ability is. In fact, though, were you to do this, the problem of reliability would come up again. Perhaps the child was having a bad day, or was ill on the day of the test, or was bad at the particular test chosen (but good in general), so that her score was not a good measure of her true ability. To guard against these possibilities there is no alternative but to take multiple measures.

In short, variability in responses means that psychological measurement normally involves taking large samples of observations from a population to reduce uncertainty about the conclusions we should draw. We also normally want to ensure that the sample is drawn from a population in a way that does not bias the results.

The easiest and best way to get an unbiased sample from a population is to draw a **random sample** from that population. One of the things that this means is that we need to select people to participate in our research in such a way that everyone in the population has an equal chance of being included. Often this procedure will also necessitate obtaining participants from a *sub-population* that is available to be studied. If we wish to **generalize** the results of our research to another situation we need to ensure that the sample we study is a random sample of any sub-population we have drawn it from, and that the sub-population is *representative* of the broader population on characteristics that we want to make generalizations about.

The extent to which we can do this varies from issue to issue. If we want to establish how colour perception works in humans then we need to sample from a sub-population that we believe has similar perceptual characteristics to the one we ultimately want to generalize to (the population in general). For example, a perceptual psychologist may believe that first-year university students are a close match to the general population in terms of their ability to perceive colour (we use the symbol $\approx$ to denote 'approximately equal to'). Under this assumption the sampling procedure works in this way:

$$\text{sample characteristics} \approx \text{sub-population characteristics}$$

$$\approx \text{population characteristics}$$

This is represented in Figure 3.1. The proportions of grey and white rectangles in the sample are the same as in the specific sub-population and in the population in general. If white squares represent people with good colour vision and grey squares represent people with poor colour

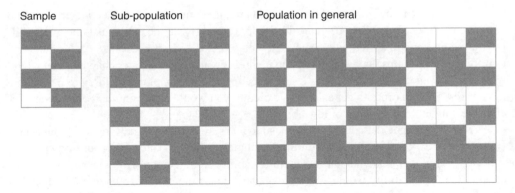

Figure 3.1 A sample with characteristics similar to those of the sub-population and the population

vision, then we can see that the proportions of people with good and poor colour vision are the same in all three groups. In other words, the sample characteristics are approximately the same as those of the specific sub-population that are approximately the same as those of the population in general.

This strategy is reasonable providing we can assume that the sub-population is similar to the population in general. This seems a plausible assumption for colour vision and until somebody provides a plausible theory that would explain why the colour vision of university students should be different from the population in general, it makes sense for perceptual psychologists to continue to obtain research samples in this way.

For a researcher interested in estimating a population's attitudes to the environment or IQs, however, this assumption would probably not hold. In particular, this is because university students might have more favourable attitudes to the environment and higher IQs than the population in general. For the example of attitudes to the environment, the following model would hold (where $\approx$ means 'approximately equal to' and $\neq$ means 'not equal to'):

$$\text{sample characteristics} \approx \text{sub-population characteristics}$$

$$\neq \text{population characteristics}$$

If the grey rectangles in Figure 3.2 represent negative attitudes to the environment, we can see that the prevalence of these negative attitudes is greater in the population than in the sub-population or the sample. Thus although the sample has similar characteristics to the sub-population, it is quite different from the population in general. The implication is that if we want to find out about the nature of attitudes to the environment in the population then we need to study people from a sub-population that is more representative of the population in general. In fact the best strategy here is to take a random sample directly from the population.

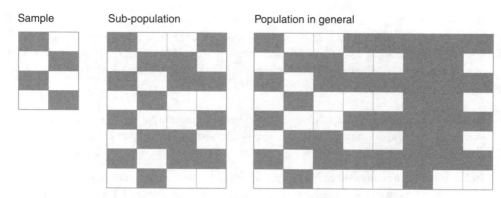

Sample   Sub-population   Population in general

Figure 3.2   A sample with characteristics similar to those of the sub-population but different from those of the population

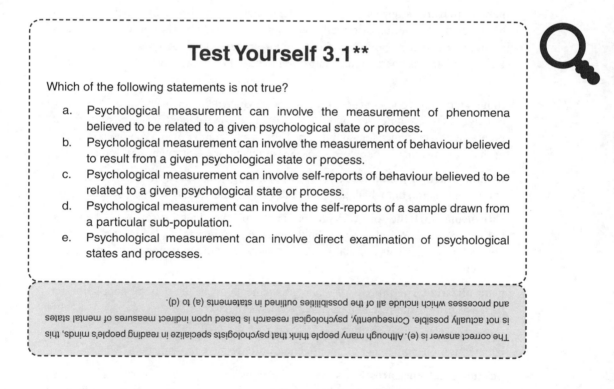

Test Yourself 3.1**

Which of the following statements is not true?

a. Psychological measurement can involve the measurement of phenomena believed to be related to a given psychological state or process.
b. Psychological measurement can involve the measurement of behaviour believed to result from a given psychological state or process.
c. Psychological measurement can involve self-reports of behaviour believed to be related to a given psychological state or process.
d. Psychological measurement can involve the self-reports of a sample drawn from a particular sub-population.
e. Psychological measurement can involve direct examination of psychological states and processes.

The correct answer is (e). Although many people think that psychologists specialize in reading people's minds, this is not actually possible. Consequently, psychological research is based upon indirect measures of mental states and processes which include all of the possibilities outlined in statements (a) to (d).

The next question that one might ask is whether it is ever possible to generalize results about things such as IQ or attitudes from a sample drawn from a sub-population that differs from the population in general. The answer is 'yes', but only where the population is similar in *relevant* ways. So although we might not be able to estimate the IQ of the general population from a sample drawn from a particular sub-population, we *might* be able to estimate the effect of Wonder Drug X on the general population's intelligence by measuring the effect of the drug on a sample of university students. We are only able to do this, however, if we assume that the drug has the same *effect* on university students (or very intelligent people) as it does on everybody else. Clearly, these are quite complex issues and we will deal with them more thoroughly as we progress through the book.

behavioural measures Measures designed to gain insight into particular psychological states or processes that involve recording performance on particular activities or tasks.

behavioural trace measures Measures designed to gain insight into behaviour that examines phenomena associated with that behaviour. For example, footprints in the sand could provide a behavioural trace of where people have walked, and this could be used to measure people's preference for particular parts of a beach.

behaviourism An approach to psychology that asserts that human behaviour can be understood in terms of directly observable relationships (in particular, between a stimulus and a response) without having to refer to underlying mental states. Behaviourism was the dominant approach to psychology for most of the first half of the 20th century.

dimension Any property of people or things on which they can differ (e.g., intelligence or height). Different people and things can therefore be situated or placed at different points along any dimension and it is possible to differentiate between them in terms of the positions they occupy (e.g., for measurement or assessment purposes).

dynamic mental processes Aspects of psychology that are seen to be common to people in general, but which are changeable over time (e.g., mood and judgement).

extraneous variable Any variable that is not of immediate interest to a researcher but which may pose a threat to validity because it compromises the interpretation of research findings. This is usually because it obscures the measurement of processes of interest.

generalization The process of making statements about the general population on the basis of relevant research (e.g., experiments or surveys).

instrument Any procedure or device used to assess or measure psychological or behavioural phenomena (e.g., intelligence, attitudes, eye movements).

physiological measures Measures of physiological states or processes (e.g., skin conductance and blood flow) used in psychological research to gain insight into particular psychological states or processes.

population The complete set of events, people or things that a researcher is interested in and from which any sample is taken.

psychological tests Measurement procedures used to identify a person's mental state relative to other people (or population norms). These typically involve large numbers of questions or tasks. Test reliability and validity are established through extensive research.

random sample A sample in which each member of the population has the same probability of being included. This is ensured by random selection methods (e.g., by drawing lots).

sample Either the group of participants from which a particular set of responses is obtained or that set of responses itself.

self-report measures Measures designed to gain insight into particular psychological states or processes that ask participants to reflect on their own mental processes or behaviour.

stable psychological characteristics Aspects of psychology that are seen to be relatively enduring over time and to be properties of particular individuals (e.g., personality and intelligence).

The experimental method

Using any or all of the above measurement strategies, psychologists often choose to investigate particular research questions by conducting **experiments**. These attempt *systematically to manipulate theoretically relevant variables and to examine the effect of these manipulations on outcome variables*. In order to clarify the meaning of the jargon in this statement (in particular, the terms **variable** and **manipulation**), we can state slightly less technically that experiments are attempts to change some aspect of a person's situation or mental state which is both of interest to the researcher (i.e., an aspect that is theoretically relevant) and capable of being altered (i.e., an aspect that is variable). The experimenters then look at the effect of this change on an aspect of the person's behaviour that can vary and on which the first aspect is believed to have some impact.

The most important point here is that experiments usually involve active intervention on the part of the researcher. Experimenters do not just sit back and watch what is going on in the world; instead they attempt to make some change to the world and then monitor the impact of that change. If a male friend of yours is feeling unhappy and you want to find out how to make him more cheerful, you could do one of three things. You could wait for him to cheer up and then see if you can infer what was responsible for his mood change, or you could ask him directly what would make him feel better. Alternatively, you could *intervene*. That is, you could actually do something to change your friend's circumstances (perhaps by taking him out for a meal) and see whether this intervention has any effect. This third strategy closely resembles the one that researchers adopt when they conduct experiments.

To examine what experiments involve more closely, we can refer back to the 'physical reinforcement theory' that we talked about in the previous chapter. As you may recall, this theory proposed that attraction to a person requires constant reinforcement if it is to be sustained. If a researcher were interested in human relationships, he or she might very well want to explore this idea in more depth. An experiment with this aim might involve manipulating the amount of physical reinforcement that a person received from someone else. The researcher would then look at the effects of different amounts of reinforcement on the person's feelings of attraction. In this example, then, physical reinforcement is the *theoretically relevant variable which is manipulated* and attraction is the *relevant outcome variable*.

To flesh out this example in more detail, one way in which such an experiment could be conducted would be to take a sample of 100 people who are in relationships from a given population and stop 50 of them seeing their partners at all for a given period (perhaps a month). These 50 people are an **experimental group** because they have been subjected to the relevant experimental **treatment** (in this case withdrawal of physical reinforcement). The other 50 people would not be deprived of their partner's company in this way, but would be allowed to continue interacting as normal. Because they are not subjected to experimental treatment,

RESEARCH BITE 3.2
National psychological associations

Below is a list of some of the main national psychological associations and societies. These are ordered by the date of their foundation.

1892 American Psychological Association (APA)

1901 British Psychological Society (BPS)

1904 German Psychological Society (Deutsche Gesellschaft für Psychologie, DGPs)

1938 Dutch Association of Psychologists (Nederlands Instituut van Psychologen, NIP)

1939 Canadian Psychological Association (CPA)

1944 Australian Psychological Society (APS)

1947 New Zealand Psychological Society (NZPsS)

1970 Psychological Society of Ireland (PSI)

1994 Psychological Society of South Africa (PsySSA)

Reference

American Psychological Association. (2013). *Directory of national associations of psychology*. Washington, DC: Office of International Affairs.

these 50 people represent a **control group**. Another way of describing the design of this study is to say that it has two **conditions** – that is, two different *levels of treatment*, in this case an experimental condition and a control condition. It should be noted, though, that an experiment does not necessarily have to incorporate a control group – it can consist of two experimental groups instead.

You may have noticed that the terms we have introduced here are also commonly used in other areas of scientific research. For example, in medical drug trials patients who receive a new treatment are referred to as the experimental group and patients who receive conventional treatment or no treatment are called the control group. Note, too, that the people who take part in an experiment (indeed, in any form of research) are usually identified by a special term that distinguishes them from members of the general population who do not take part. Traditionally such people were referred to as **subjects**. However, because it is seen to be less demeaning to the people it refers to, the term **participants** is now recommended by most professional bodies (in particular, the **American Psychological Association, APA**). Accordingly, this is the term used by most contemporary psychologists and hence the term that we use in this book.

Going back to our experiment, after the experimental manipulation (i.e., separation) had been implemented and given time to have some effect (in this case after a month in which the experimental group had undergone separation but the control group had not) the researchers would be interested in looking at how attracted to their partners all the participants in this study were. In other words, they have to measure attraction. They could do this in lots of ways – for example, by asking participants to fill in a questionnaire (a self-report measure) or by seeing how much time they wanted to spend together (a behavioural measure). A range of physiological measures could also be employed.

Let us say that on the basis of theory and past research the experimenters decided to measure attraction by monitoring how much time participants spend with their partners at weekends (by asking them to keep diaries). Here the researchers would be particularly interested to see whether the behaviour of participants in the experimental group differed from the behaviour of participants in the control group. Specifically, they would want to see if participants in the experimental group were less attracted to their partners, as this is what 'physical reinforcement theory' predicts – that a reduction in actual contact should reduce attraction to a partner (that 'absence leads the heart to wander').

In this example, then, there are two variables in which the researcher is interested. In fact *all* experiments include these two different types of variable and each is given a different name. The variable that is systematically manipulated (in this case physical reinforcement)

Photo 3.5 Wilhelm Wundt is generally credited with conducting the first formal experiments in psychology in his laboratory at Leipzig University in Germany. Note, though, that experiments are defined by method rather than by things such as place or technology. That is, what matters is how research is done rather than where or what with. Thus all experiments involve manipulation of a variable of interest (the independent variable), but they need not be conducted in a laboratory or involve complex apparatus.

is referred to as the **independent variable** (or **IV**). This can also be thought of as the treatment variable. The outcome variable that is measured after the manipulation has been carried out (time spent together) is called the **dependent variable** (or **DV**). Because they involve measurement of outcomes, dependent variables are sometimes called 'dependent measures'.

It is important to have a clear grasp of these terms and what they mean, because they are recurrent features of research terminology. People often get the two terms confused (largely because they sound so similar), but one way to think about the difference between them is to remember that the dependent variable is measured *after* the independent variable has been manipulated. So the dependent variable *depends* on the experimental manipulation. The letter 'd' is also a useful memory aid as the *d*ependent variable provides the experimental *d*ata.

In experiments, independent variables are manipulated by the experimenter. In general, independent variables are *causal* variables and dependent variables are *effect* variables. In other words, change in the independent variable is expected to cause change in the dependent variable.

This point about the causal impact of the independent variable goes to the heart of why researchers actually conduct experiments. This is because in any experiment where there is a substantial change in the dependent variable, this allows the researcher to make the logically appropriate **causal inference** that this change *must* be due to manipulation of the independent variable. It also follows from points made in the final section of the previous chapter, that if we can correctly *interpret* the reasons for this change (i.e., if we can say exactly why the independent variable had the effect it did), then our interpretation of the experiment will be *valid*.

Test Yourself 3.2*

A researcher conducts an experiment that tests the hypothesis that 'anxiety has an adverse effect on students' exam performance'. Which of the following statements is true?

a. Anxiety is the dependent variable, exam performance is the independent variable.
b. Anxiety is the dependent variable, students are the independent variable.
c. Anxiety is the independent variable, students are the dependent variable.
d. Anxiety is the independent variable, exam performance is the dependent variable.
e. Students are the dependent variable, exam performance is the independent variable.

The correct answer is (d). In the experiment, the experimenter will be concerned to examine the impact that manipulations of anxiety have on students' exam performance. The independent (manipulated) variable is therefore anxiety and the dependent (outcome) variable is performance. This is because performance is hypothesized to be dependent on anxiety. Note, too, that students are not variables in this (or any other) study, they are the participants.

If an interpretation of what causes change in any dependent variable is correct, the experiment as a whole will have what is referred to as **internal validity**. We will discuss these points in more detail in the next chapter.

There is only one point that qualifies the above statements about our ability to draw causal inferences from experimental methods. However, this point is *extremely* important. It is that in order to have complete confidence in the correctness of a causal inference, conditions *must be identical in every respect* except for differences in the treatment (i.e, the independent variable). To be at least reasonably confident we must therefore take steps to equate the conditions.

Why must we equate the conditions in this way? The answer is that unless we know that the groups were similar *before* we manipulated the independent variable we cannot be sure that any differences between the groups that we observe later are due to that experimental manipulation. So, unless we equate the groups in this way, we cannot conduct a proper experiment.

The next obvious question is 'How should we equate the groups?'. There is one very good way. This is to allocate participants randomly to different conditions – through a procedure known as **random assignment**. Why randomly? The long answer appeals to a knowledge of some statistical principles that we will talk about in later chapters.

The short answer is that this procedure ensures that the experiment does not *build in differences* between groups – either on significant dimensions (their sex, wealth, age, intelligence or personality) or seemingly trivial ones (their eye colour, hair length or length of surname). Accordingly, randomization involves *strictly unsystematic* assignment of participants to conditions (e.g., based on the toss of a coin or the roll of a die).

We can use an extreme example to help make it clear why this is important. Imagine that in our separation and attraction experiment all the participants we assigned to the experimental condition were men and all the participants we assigned to the control condition were women. In this case if we found that participants in the experimental condition were less attracted to their partners than those in the control condition, this would not *necessarily* arise from the fact that participants in the experimental condition had been starved of company. Instead, it could be due to the fact that these participants were men and that men in general like their partners less than women do.

Even the most trivial systematic difference can undermine a researcher's ability to make an appropriate causal inference. For example, a researcher might place people into different conditions on the basis of their position on a roll: putting people whose names are late in the alphabet in the control condition and those with names early in the alphabet in the experimental condition. But by doing this the researcher may inadvertently build ethnic differences into the two groups – so that people from one geographical region (perhaps where names starting with Y and Z are common) are in one condition and people from another region in the other. In this case any difference observed on the dependent variable might therefore be due to differences in ethnicity rather than differences in physical reinforcement. It may, for example, reflect the fact that people of one ethnic group (whose names may generally start with letters early in the alphabet) are more attracted to their partners than members of another ethnic group. However, ethnicity is just one of the many dimensions on which people with different last names *may* differ and it is impossible to say that none of these will have any impact on attractiveness.

The primary strength of the experimental method, though, is that, *providing participants are randomly assigned to conditions*, researchers can be sure that effects observed on the dependent variable are due to one of two things: their manipulation of the independent variable or chance. In this way, it gives researchers **experimental control** over both what they investigate and the causal interpretation of their findings. Furthermore, as we shall see in later chapters, through appropriate use of statistics (which quantify chance) and by using sufficiently large experimental samples we can ensure that experimental research findings will generalize to the population at large.

As we discussed earlier, in order to generalize, the researcher must ensure that the participants in an experiment are *representative* of that general population on relevant dimensions – that they constitute a **representative sample**. For example, in our study of separation and attraction we might need to ensure that the social skills and physical attractiveness of the participants were similar to those of the general population. We will return to this point in the next chapter.

Yet while experimental findings allow researchers to be confident that there is something to explain, experiments do not always allow researchers to know how to interpret their findings. In other words, it can often be hard to establish an experiment's internal validity. This is because it is much easier to ascertain *that* an independent variable has had an effect than it is to ascertain *why* it has had an effect.

Problems in establishing an experiment's internal validity often occur when experimenters do not really manipulate what they think they are manipulating but actually manipulate something else. Thinking about our experiment on separation and attraction, it should be relatively easy to establish that separating participants from their partners reduces attraction to them, but it is much harder to conclude with certainty that this is due to a lack of physical reinforcement (the independent variable we wanted to manipulate). What we may have manipulated instead is just the participants' *opportunity to meet new people*, and it may be this variable that leads to the effects we observe. That is, participants in the experimental group may have become less attracted to their partners because – unlike participants in the control group – they were able to meet lots of new people. Where alternative explanations of experimental outcomes such as this are identified it is often because the experiment involves an *unintended* manipulation of an extraneous variable. The technical term for unintentionally manipulating variables is **confounding**, and this is quite common in experimental research. It is certainly true that many disagreements between researchers are based on differing views about the existence of confounds and about what exactly experimenters have manipulated in their experiments.

We can use another example to reinforce this point. Imagine that some researchers are interested in the effect that a lack of space has on psychological distress. To investigate this they may put 50 people in a small room for two hours and 50 people in an open field for the same amount of time. As they expect, they may find that the people in the room get more distressed. The researchers may therefore want to conclude that crowding makes people distressed. However, a confound in this study may be the heat generated by having a lot of people in one room. So it may be the heat, not the crowding, that is producing effects on the dependent variable (distress). Another way of putting this is to say that in this study the two variables, space and temperature, are confounded.

Beyond these problems in establishing internal validity, one further reason why researchers may choose not to conduct experimental research is that they are interested in things that are unique to a particular individual. Experimental research is generally very useful in helping researchers test general theories about mental processes and human behaviour, but it does not necessarily help understand *idiosyncrasy*. So, coupled with the use of statistics, experiments enable us to say quite a lot about the behaviour of people *on average* and *as a general rule*. The same tools may be less useful in helping to understand the specific behaviour of one particular person at one particular point in time.

Test Yourself 3.3***

An experimenter conducts a study in which she wants to look at the effects of altitude on psychological well-being. To do this she randomly allocates people to two groups and takes one group up in a plane to a height of 1000 metres and leaves the other group in the airport terminal as a control group. When the plane is in the air she seeks to establish the psychological well-being of both groups. Which of the following is a potential confound, threatening the internal validity of the study?

a. The reliability of the questionnaire that she uses to establish psychological health.
b. The size of the space in which the participants are confined.
c. The susceptibility of the experimental group to altitude sickness.
d. The susceptibility of the control group to altitude sickness.
e. The age of people in experimental and control groups.

The correct answer is (b). In answering this question it is important to remember that a confound is an unintended manipulation of an extraneous variable. So the question here is 'What has the researcher manipulated as well as altitude?' There are many confounds here, but one answer to this question is that she has also manipulated the participants' personal space. It may be the case that just being in a confined space adversely affects well-being so that the effects that the experimenter ultimately observes have nothing to do with altitude at all. Note, too, that none of the things mentioned in the other answers (i.e., (a), (c), (d) and (e)) have actually been systematically manipulated in the experiment, so these could not represent confounds. Random allocation controls for possible differences in these and other variables (so long as the sample size is sufficiently large; see Chapter 7).

In practice, though, this last problem is less important than it might appear. This is because very few research psychologists are actually interested in drawing conclusions about individual people. Even if researchers were interested in the psychology of eccentricity, it is unlikely that they would only be interested in making statements about just one individual, at one point in time, and in one place. It is much more likely that they would be interested in understanding what eccentrics have in common and what makes them different from other non-eccentric people – and experimental research could play an important role in examining these issues.

Nevertheless, even if researchers are totally committed to experimental research, in some situations experimental methodology will not be an option. This is because some variables are impossible (or almost impossible) to manipulate. People's age and height cannot be changed, and the same routinely applies to their sex, cultural background and parents' birthplace. But even if a variable can be manipulated, it may not always be ethical to do so. For example, it may be highly inappropriate to conduct an experiment in which you attempt to manipulate people's physical and psychological health (points we will return to in Chapter 13). In such situations, psychologists usually have to resort to other research methods.

American Psychological Association (APA) The main professional body for psychologists in North America. With over 130,000 members organized into 54 divisions, this body is widely seen to define 'best practice' for psychologists (not only researchers, but also clinicians and other practitioners) around the world. Most countries have similar bodies and there are also a range of bodies that oversee activity in specific fields of research and practice.

causal inference Either the process of reaching conclusions about the effect of one variable on another, or the outcome of such a process.

condition A situation in which *participants* are all treated the same way (i.e., exposed to the same level of *treatment*) and where that treatment relates to something being investigated by the researcher.

confounding Unintended or accidental manipulation of an extraneous *variable* that occurs because that variable (called a confound) is associated with an *independent variable* in an experiment. A confound is thus a special case of extraneous variable.

control group *Participants* in an *experiment* who are not subjected to a relevant *treatment* (as distinct from an *experimental group*).

dependent variable (DV) The outcome variable on which a researcher is interested in monitoring effects.

experiment A piece of research in which one or more independent variables are systematically manipulated and all others are controlled. Experiments assess the impact of manipulated (independent) variables on relevant outcome (dependent) variables.

experimental control The process of holding particular variables constant across different conditions of an *experiment* so that they have no impact on the results.

experimental group Participants in an experiment who are subjected to a particular level of a relevant *treatment* (as distinct from a control group).

independent variable (IV) The *treatment* variable manipulated by the experimenter in an experiment, or more generally the causal variable that is believed to be responsible for particular effects.

internal validity The extent to which the effect of an independent variable on a dependent variable has been correctly interpreted.

manipulation The process of systematically varying an *independent variable* across different experimental conditions. This is sometimes referred to as the 'experimental treatment'.

participants The people who take part in a particular piece of research.

random assignment The process of assigning participants to conditions on a strictly unsystematic basis. When this occurs every participant has the same chance of being placed in any experimental condition.

representative sample A sample of research *participants* that is similar to the general population on characteristics that are relevant to the research question.

subjects Another word for *participants*, but now not widely used to describe human beings as it is seen to be demeaning.

treatment The experimental intervention that is the basis of the *independent variable* and therefore differentiates between *participants* in different conditions or phases of an *experiment*.

variable An aspect of a person, animal, subject or situation that can change.

The quasi-experimental method

In situations where an independent variable is difficult or impossible to manipulate (such as the participants' age or sex), researchers sometimes choose to employ quasi-experimental methodology (Cook & Campbell, 1979). Quasi-experiments are identical to experiments, apart from one major difference: participants *are not randomly assigned to conditions* on one or more variables. So, as with proper experiments, **quasi-experiments** have both independent and dependent variables and the researcher is interested in observing the effect of differences in the independent variable on the dependent variable. However, the independent variable is not actually manipulated. Instead, participants are assigned to different conditions explicitly on the basis of differences in that variable.

To illustrate this point, we can imagine some researchers who are interested in the effects of separation on attraction, but have developed a theory that suggests that separation has different effects on the relationships of young and old people. Perhaps they believe that for old people 'absence makes the heart grow fonder', but for young people 'absence leads the heart to wander'. In order to test this idea experimentally, the researchers clearly cannot assign some participants randomly to one experimental condition and *make them* old and assign some participants randomly to another experimental condition and *make them* young. So rather than manipulate the independent variable (age), they will probably just *find* some older people (e.g., 70-year-olds) and *find* some young people (e.g., 18-year-olds) and then compare the two age groups.

The process of conducting this quasi-experiment would be very similar to that of the experiment considered previously. Indeed, for this reason the researchers themselves would almost certainly refer to their study as an experiment rather than as a quasi-experiment. So, in the quasi-experiment the researchers might separate both groups of participants from their partners for an extended period and at the end of it see whether the two groups differ in their attraction towards their partners. Specifically, they would want to know if there was any support for the hypothesis that old people have stronger bonds with their partners. (Ideally, the experiment would also include two control groups who would not be subjected to separation, one made up of young people and one made up of old people.)

Although this strategy mimics that of proper experiments described in the previous section, it follows from our discussion of the importance of random assignment that the quasi-experimental method has a significant drawback compared with its experimental counterpart. As you may have foreseen, the systematic assignment of participants to different levels of the independent variable interferes with the researchers' ability to make conclusive causal inferences. In other words, where experiments involve systematic assignment of participants to conditions it *may not be valid* to conclude that any variation that is ultimately observed in the dependent variable has been caused by variation in the independent variable.

This point can be illustrated by referring back to our example. Imagine that the researchers find, as they predicted, that after a month of separation old people are more attracted to their partners than young people. Could they conclude that this is due to the fact that physical reinforcement is a more important component of younger people's relationships? Is it appropriate to conclude that this difference is due to the different age of the two groups of participants?

The answer to both questions is definitely 'no'. The reason for this blunt response is that although the age of the two experimental groups is different, so are a lot of other things which are associated with age but which the researcher was not able to control. Old people not only are older than young people, but may also be wealthier, more cautious, more conservative, happier, less restless, less healthy, less mobile, and so on – and any one of these uncontrolled differences *could* be responsible for the observed effects.

Any factors like this which are not (or cannot be) controlled for, and which impinge upon the researchers' ability correctly to interpret their findings and make valid causal inferences, are another form of *extraneous variable*. In this case the only way their influence can be fully controlled (and therefore ruled out) is by strictly random assignment of participants to conditions – that is, by use of fully experimental methodology. We will discuss this point further in the next chapter.

Test Yourself 3.4*

What distinguishes the experimental method from the quasi-experimental method?

- a. The scientific status of the research.
- b. The existence of an independent variable.
- c. The existence of different levels of an independent variable.
- d. The sensitivity of the dependent variable.
- e. The random assignment of participants to conditions.

The correct answer is (e). Quasi-experiments are like experiments in every respect but one – the fact that participants are not randomly assigned to conditions. They therefore contain independent variables with different levels (though level is not fully 'manipulated' for each participant) as well as dependent variables. Although experimental studies have the advantage of allowing researchers to draw conclusions about cause and effect, they are no more scientific than quasi-experiments.

It follows from these points that quasi-experiments have one less advantage than experiments. However, because this deficit relates to the researcher's ability to make causal inferences (the single most important feature of experiments), it constitutes a serious drawback. Yet as we noted at the start of this section, random assignment of participants to conditions is often impossible. This fact alone makes quasi-experimental methods quite common.

> **quasi-experiment** A piece of research with the same features as an experiment but that does not involve the random assignment of participants to conditions on one or more variables.

The survey method

When people are not able to manipulate a given variable experimentally (or do not want to), the quasi-experiment is not the only option available to them. Indeed, the quasi-experiment can also be considered a special case of a methodology that is used extremely widely in psychological research – the **survey method**. This method is common to a lot of social scientific research and most of us encounter **surveys** quite frequently and in a number of different forms. These include opinion polls, market research, performance evaluations and censuses. They come in a range of guises – from structured telephone interviews to open-ended questionnaires.

Survey methodology typically *obtains information about a number of different variables in which the researcher is interested and identifies the relationship between those variables*. In other words, the methodology is used to identify the extent and nature of any association (or **correlation**) between different variables. For this reason what we have termed the survey method is often called the **correlational method**. The method does not necessarily require a response from participants at all. Instead, as with an experiment, it may merely involve *observations* of relevant variables on the part of the researcher.

Using surveys does not require a given variable to be examined outside its natural setting through manipulations conducted in a laboratory (a procedure common in experiments). On the contrary, one of the primary advantages and attractions of the survey is that it is usually quite easy to administer *anywhere*. In this manner, researchers can examine the relationship between variables that would be extremely difficult to isolate experimentally, such as wealth, age, socio-economic status, health, physical attractiveness and sexual preference. And while experiments are typically concerned with a limited number of different levels of a given variable, surveys usually include variables on which participants vary considerably and in many different ways.

In this way, using a survey to look at how age affects the relationship between separation and attraction is a clear alternative to using the quasi-experiment we discussed earlier. Researchers might include in such a survey participants who had undergone (or were actually undergoing) different amounts of separation – perhaps by studying scientists stationed in Antarctica. The survey might therefore involve participants of all ages rather than just the two ages of participants in the different conditions of the quasi-experiment (18 and 70). As well as asking participants how long they had been separated from their partner and how psychologically close they still felt to that person, the researchers might look at the relationship between these two variables and others that might be of theoretical interest – such as participants' health, intelligence and personality. Is attraction associated with good health or intelligence or introversion?

The clear benefit of this research strategy is that it allows researchers considerable scope to investigate many aspects of phenomena at the same time in the environment where they occur. For a number of reasons (ethical, financial, logistical) it can be extremely difficult to conduct experiments in people's place of work, on holiday, while they are waiting to see a doctor, or in other natural settings. It is usually easier, though, to administer a questionnaire or ask a series of questions in an interview. For this reason survey methodology is often used by researchers who want to examine important issues in the places in which they arise (perhaps before seeking to explore them further in controlled experiments).

A further important feature of surveys is that, coupled with appropriate statistical methodology, they allow researchers to make and test *predictions* about the relationship between particular variables. For example, if researchers discover through a survey that older people feel more attracted to their partners, then they will be able to predict (with a quantifiable amount of uncertainty) both how attracted someone is to their partner if they know that person's age, and how old someone is if they know how attracted that person is to their partner.

This sort of descriptive and predictive information can be very useful for a range of people. This is one reason why surveys are so widely used by makers of social policy, consumer organizations, advertising agencies, government departments, prospective employers, and so on. Information from our separation and attraction survey could, for example, prove invaluable to someone who has to decide how to distribute counselling resources among people of different ages. Similarly, surveys that identify relationships between people's lifestyle and various health risks can identify problems that require further investigation. They can also play a part in the development of advertising campaigns, intervention strategies and the training of health care professionals.

A key problem with all research, however, is that the applicability of the findings may be limited to the group of people that is actually studied. As with an experiment, it is therefore important that the participants in a survey are a representative sample of the population to which the survey will be generalized. Even so, it is likely to be the case that the relevance of the responses obtained will be restricted to a particular place and time. A survey conducted in the United States in the 1960s to examine the relationship between separation and attraction may have little to say about the relationship between these variables in Australia in the year 2015.

Yet by far the most severe limitation of survey methodology is that it does not allow researchers to draw causal inferences from their findings. This is the same problem that we have already discussed in relation to quasi-experimental methodology. Again, knowing that a relationship exists between two (or more) variables does not allow the researcher to say *what caused* that relationship.

In the case of the survey this can be a big problem because researchers are often extremely keen, or put under a lot of pressure, to provide *explanations* and not just descriptions. Journalists, grant-awarding bodies and the public in general often push researchers to explain what is going on in their research. And even if the researchers are unwilling to do so, others may jump to their own conclusions. If we hear that people's level of stress can be used to predict whether or not they will get a heart attack, we may conclude that 'stress causes heart disease'. But these statements are not justified and are often extremely misleading. This is because other explanations are just as likely to be true. For example, it may be that heart disease causes stress or that both stress and heart disease are caused by something else (such as diet).

The point here is that *correlation is not causation*. This is an extremely important point and it needs to be driven home because it is routinely overlooked by researchers in a wide range of fields (not just by psychologists). Accordingly, we will return to this point several times in later chapters.

The fact that survey (and quasi-experimental) research is limited in its ability to address causation, however, does not mean that researchers should conduct experiments at every available opportunity. Experimentation is not a substitute for careful observation and description of behaviour. In psychology, as in all sciences, there is an important place for *both* descriptive *and* explanatory research procedures.

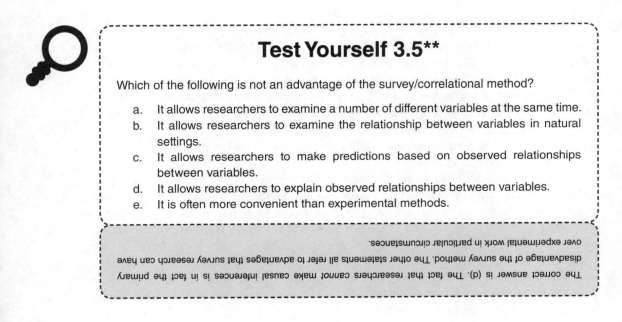

Test Yourself 3.5**

Which of the following is not an advantage of the survey/correlational method?

a. It allows researchers to examine a number of different variables at the same time.
b. It allows researchers to examine the relationship between variables in natural settings.
c. It allows researchers to make predictions based on observed relationships between variables.
d. It allows researchers to explain observed relationships between variables.
e. It is often more convenient than experimental methods.

The correct answer is (d). The fact that researchers *cannot* make causal inferences is in fact the primary disadvantage of the survey method. The other statements all refer to advantages that survey research can have over experimental work in particular circumstances.

correlation A measure of the nature and strength of the relationship between two variables.

correlational method See *survey method.*

survey A research tool which obtains information about people's behaviour, mental states or environment.

survey method A procedure (also known as the correlational method) involving the collection of information about different variables in order to measure those variables and the relationship between them.

The case-study method

One of the things common to the three methods we have discussed so far is that they all typically involve quite a few participants. For reasons that we outlined at the start of the chapter, it is rare for fewer than half a dozen people to participate in an experiment and some surveys have thousands of respondents. Yet in some areas of psychological enquiry participants are extremely hard to come by. At one extreme a neuropsychologist may need to test theories of memory organization using participants who suffer from a very rare memory disorder, and at the other extreme researchers who want to investigate the social psychology of rioting may have trouble finding even one group of rioters in the city where they do research.

Photos 3.6 and 3.7 Henry Gustav Molaison (left) – better known as HM – had surgery for epilepsy that left him with almost no ability to create long-term memories. Together with other researchers, Brenda Milner (right) studied HM extensively over a period of years, and this case study played a key role in advancing theories of memory function. These in turn contributed to the emergence of cognitive neuropsychology as a major field of research. (Photo 3.6 © Suzanne Corkin, used by permission of The Wiley Agency LLC. Photo 3.7 © Pierre Charbonneau).

The questions addressed by these researchers may be extremely important, but any methodology that requires lots of participants is out of the question. Does this mean that these phenomena cannot be investigated? Thanks to the **case study**, it does not. Indeed, many of the most important insights gained by psychologists have come from researchers observing a single person or group. Freud's (1933/1964) analysis of Little Hans (a boy who had an intense fear of horses), Milner's (1966) work with HM (a patient with no apparent long-term memory) and Festinger, Riecken, and Schachter's (1956) studies of Mrs Kietch's religious cult (and how it dealt with the fact that the world did not come to an end when it said it would) provide a few of the best-known illustrations of this point.

Investigation of small samples is possible because the case study is simply a special instance of the methods that we have already considered. It is possible to apply experimental techniques to the investigation of a single case by experimentally manipulating a given variable *over time*. So, for example, over a period of days or weeks a neuropsychologist may vary the amount of practice a patient is allowed before being asked to recall a list of words, in order to see if this affects the patient's recall of those words. Similarly, a social psychologist may vary the task that a group has to perform to see if this affects the group members' mood. There are some precautions that need to be taken to eliminate particular confounds (in particular, the influence of time and prior exposure – points we will discuss more in the next chapter). However, essentially the same principles (and precautions) apply to case studies as to studies involving large numbers of participants. Nevertheless, one of the common complaints about case-study research is that the findings it produces can be unreliable because they are peculiar to the particular case being studied. For this reason researchers who base their conclusions on single cases are generally keen to replicate their findings wherever possible.

As with large-scale studies, sometimes manipulations of a given variable will be impossible or problematic. An experimenter may not be able (or want) to manipulate the behaviour of police at a riot or the treatment given to a patient suffering from a stroke. Accordingly, any study that is conducted may be based on the researcher's own *observations* of the participant's behaviour and environmental features. This scenario in effect corresponds to the survey method, where the researcher is able to monitor a large number of variables (the behaviour of the police, the crowd's mood, the physical conditions).

As one would expect, these two types of case study have broadly similar strengths and weaknesses to those that we have already identified in experiments and surveys. Experimental case studies allow the researcher to make appropriate inferences about causality, but the types of manipulation that are possible may be very limited. Observational case studies provide a good opportunity for detailed examination of a significant psychological phenomenon or event, but do not allow the researcher to make conclusive statements about cause and effect.

For these reasons case studies can generate data that are every bit as useful as those obtained in their full-scale counterparts. In particular, they often provide the opportunity for an in-depth exploration of theoretical ideas where the real-life manifestations of the phenomena in which a researcher is interested are either rare or complex (or both). In this capacity case studies play a key role not only in supporting theoretical predictions, but

Test Yourself 3.6*

Which of the following statements is true?

    a.   Case studies have played no role in the development of psychological theory.

    b.   Case studies have all of the weaknesses and none of the strengths of larger studies.

    c.   Case studies have none of the weaknesses and all of the strengths of larger studies.

    d.   Case studies should only be conducted if every other option has been ruled out.

    e.   None of the above.

The correct answer is (e). The essential point to note about case studies is that most of their properties (including their weaknesses and strengths) are the same as those of larger studies. The primary difference is therefore one of sample size (i.e., the number of cases upon which conclusions are based). As a general statement, case studies are not universally superior or inferior to studies based on larger samples. They have played a major role in the advancement of psychological knowledge, and many researchers actually consider them to be a primary source of information rather than a 'last resort'.

also in *refuting* theories. You may remember from the previous chapter that a *single* piece of information that contradicts a theory can be enough to bring the value of that theory seriously into question. In a well-designed case study, such refutation can be achieved by the one case that demonstrates that something a given theory predicts ought not to happen does happen.

> **case study** Research (usually quite intensive) that involves a single participant or group of participants.

Overview

One of the points that emerges from this chapter is that despite the array of topics and issues that research in psychology can cover, researchers themselves actually have quite a limited number of tools available to them in order to conduct that research. The way these tools are used varies enormously, depending on both the topic itself and the underlying objectives of the researcher. Nevertheless, almost all psychological research could be classified as falling into one of the four categories we have discussed. The number of categories reduces to just two if quasi-experiments and case studies are seen merely as special cases of the other methods.

As we have seen, exactly which of these methods a researcher eventually decides to use depends on many things. Some of these relate directly to the applicability of the method to the topic at hand. In some situations it is not possible to manipulate a variable (e.g., abnormality or medical status) experimentally and in others it is not possible to examine a variable (e.g., reaction time or processing capacity) by using a survey. Other factors that influence a researcher's choice may be more a question of personal preference or established practice (either among a particular group of researchers or in the investigation of a particular issue).

Contrary to popular belief, choices about research location and research participants do not necessarily constrain the researcher's choice of methodology. Experiments do not have to be conducted in the laboratory and laboratory work need not be experimental. In fact many of the most significant psychology experiments have been **field studies**, using members of the general community in their natural environment. Similarly, a great deal of survey work is conducted on first-year psychology students in laboratory classes.

Regardless of the orientation researchers adopt, they should be aware of both the strengths of that approach *and* its limitations. This is important because researchers ultimately tend to classify themselves either as experimentalists or as survey-based researchers and then are inclined to emphasize the strengths of their preferred methods and the weaknesses of others. This will often be entirely appropriate as some methods are much more suitable for investigating certain topics than others. But no one method is *universally* superior. Part of any research psychologist's role is therefore to be able to make judgements about the appropriateness of any given method based on its suitability for investigating the issue at hand. Being a good researcher is not a question of *whether* you do experiments or surveys; it is more a matter of *when* and *how* you do them.

It is fair to add that many of the advances made in psychological knowledge have been gained through *innovation* at the methodological level – by researchers who were willing to explore old questions in new ways. Two cases in point would be Sherif's (1956) experimental field studies in which experiments on group conflict were conducted using young boys who were attending summer camps in the United States, and de Groot's (1965) quasi-experimental studies of chess experts' and novices' ability to encode and remember the positions of pieces on a chessboard.

In view of the potential limitations of any one method, many researchers use (or at least consider using) *multiple* research methods in order to explore the same issue in many different ways. In practice this is how knowledge in many areas of psychology has progressed over time – with the strengths of one approach correcting for the limitations of another. For this reason, the fact that psychologists have to make methodological choices should be seen more as an asset than as a basis for conflict. In the final analysis, the challenge faced by researchers is to demonstrate the merits of their own work by exploiting that asset appropriately.

field study A piece of research that is conducted in a natural (non-artificial) setting.

CHECKLIST
Revisiting the key goals for this chapter

☐ I understand the purpose of psychological measurement, and the different forms it can take.

☐ I know what the major methods used in psychological research are.

☐ I understand the key strengths and weaknesses of different research methods.

Further reading

Readings specific to the various methods covered in this chapter are provided in the following chapters. However, Leong and Austin (1996) and Sansone, Morf, and Panter (2004) are advanced texts that provide detailed discussions of all of these methods as well as discussions of a range of practical issues that confront researchers (e.g., designing a research programme, applying for grants).

Leong, T. L., & Austin, J. T. (1996). *The psychology research handbook: A guide for graduate students and research assistants.* Thousands Oaks, CA: SAGE.

Sansone, C., Morf, C. C., & Panter, A. T. (Eds.) (2004). *Handbook of methods in social psychology.* Thousand Oaks, CA: SAGE.

Research methods: A checklist for research evaluation and improvement

Table 3.1

Potential problem	Question to ask	Potential improvement
Poor or limited choice of measure	Have researchers used an appropriate measure to investigate the psychological process or state in which they are interested?	Consider the different types of measure that could be used to investigate the issue at hand (e.g., behavioural, self-report, physiological). Consider the advantages and disadvantages (as well as the practicalities) of using different types of measure or different measures of the same type. If appropriate, design and conduct research that involves these alternative measures.
Extraneous variables	Are research findings contaminated by factors that are not of immediate concern to the researchers?	Think broadly about factors that are not addressed in the research but which may be affecting the findings (and their interpretation). Take steps to eliminate these (for more detail, see Chapters 4 and 5) or to compensate for them by using multiple methods.
Unrepresentative sampling	Is the experimental sample representative of the sub-population from which it is drawn and is the sub-population representative of the general population of interest?	Consider the implications of any unrepresentative sampling that has occurred. If necessary, take steps to improve the sampling procedure (e.g., by using random sampling; for more detail see Chapter 5) and then attempt to replicate the research findings.
Confounding	Is assignment to experimental conditions associated with an additional variable that is not of immediate interest to researchers (and which they had not intended to manipulate) but that could be having an impact on the findings?	Take steps to eliminate the impact of confounding variables by controlling for them. This is typically done by manipulating the independent variable of interest under conditions where the level of the confound is held constant.
Lack of experimental control (in quasi-experiments and surveys)	Is the interpretation of a relationship between an IV and a DV compromised by a failure to manipulate the IV experimentally?	Consider ways in which it might be possible to manipulate an IV experimentally. If none is feasible, and an IV has not been manipulated experimentally, try to generate alternative explanations of the relationship and be careful to avoid the correlational fallacy of implying that the IV caused the DV (for more detail, see Chapter 10).
Poor or limited choice of method	Have the researchers used an appropriate method to investigate the psychological process or state in which they are interested?	Consider the different types of method that could be used to investigate the issue at hand (experimental, quasi-experimental, survey, case study). Consider the advantages and disadvantages (as well as the practicalities) of using alternative methods to supplement and extend the research. If appropriate, design and conduct research that involves these alternative methods.

Test Yourself 3.7*

An experimenter, Tom, conducts an experiment to see whether accuracy of responding and reaction time are affected by consumption of alcohol. To do this, Tom conducts a study in which students at university A react to pairs of symbols by saying 'same' or 'different' after consuming two glasses of water and students at university B react to pairs of symbols by saying 'same' or 'different' after consuming two glasses of wine. Tom predicts that reaction times will be slower and that there will be more errors in the responses of students who have consumed alcohol. Which of the following statements is *not* true?

a. The university attended by participants is a confound.
b. The experiment has two dependent variables.
c. Reaction time is the independent variable.
d. Tom's ability to draw firm conclusions about the impact of alcohol on reaction time would be improved by assigning participants randomly to experimental conditions.
e. This study is actually a quasi-experiment.

Test Yourself 3.8*

What is an extraneous variable?

a. A variable that can never be manipulated.
b. A variable that can never be controlled.
c. A variable that can never be measured.
d. A variable that clouds the interpretation of results.
e. None of the above.

Test Yourself 3.9*

Which of the following statements is true?

a. The appropriateness of any research method is always determined by the research question and the research environment.
b. Good experiments all involve a large number of participants.
c. Experiments should be conducted in laboratories in order to improve experimental control.
d. Surveys have no place in good psychological research.
e. Case studies are usually carried out when researchers are too lazy to find enough participants.

Test Yourself 3.10**

A piece of research that is conducted in a natural (non-artificial) setting is called:

a.   A case study.
b.   A field study.
c.   A quasi-experiment.
d.   A survey.
e.   An observational study.

The correct answer to 3.7 is (c). The independent variable in this study is alcohol consumption. The university that participants attend (A or B) has actually been manipulated along with alcohol consumption so, as (a) suggests, this is a confound. The experiment examines the impact of the independent variable on two dependent variables: reaction time and correctness of response, so (b) is true. As stated in (e), the fact that participants were not randomly assigned to conditions makes this a quasi-experiment. The problem of the confound could have been dealt with (and the study improved) by randomly assigning participants to conditions – thereby making this a proper experiment rather than a quasi-experiment (so (d) is also true).

The correct answer to 3.8 is (d). An extraneous variable is a variable that is not of immediate interest to a researcher, but which poses a threat to validity because it compromises the interpretation of research findings. This usually occurs because the variable's impact upon the dependent variable has not been controlled for and so its influence upon that dependent variable cannot be ruled out. So if in a quasi-experiment participants are assigned to conditions on the basis of their intelligence, their wealth and socio-economic status may be extraneous variables that are confounded with intelligence. In this case the researcher cannot conclude that the effects that he or she wants to explain in terms of intelligence are not in fact due to these other variables. Under certain circumstances, extraneous variables of this type can be controlled (through random assignment of participants to conditions) and usually they can be studied in their own right, so answers (a), (b), (c) and (e) are all false.

The correct answer to 3.9 is (a). One of the points we have tried to emphasize in this chapter is that no one method is suitable for all occasions and for the investigation of all research questions. The choice of method must be tailored to the researchers' needs and circumstances. Despite the fact that all of the other statements here have probably been made by researchers at some time or other, they are actually false. Large samples and laboratory conditions do not guarantee good research and experiments are not always better than survey-based research.

The correct answer to 3.10 is (b). The term 'field study' refers to any piece of research that is conducted in its natural setting 'in the field'. Such research is not restricted to any one method and can take the same form as any other piece of research. Accordingly, field studies can be experiments, quasi-experiments, surveys, case studies or observational studies.

Discussion/essay questions

a. Compare the advantages and disadvantages of experimental and survey methodologies.
b. Why does so much psychological research use quasi-experimental methodology?
c. Are the benefits of experimental control overrated?
d. Does an overreliance on survey methodology compromise the scientific status of psychology?
e. What are the strengths and limitations of case studies?

Exercises

a. Choose two topics that are covered in an introductory psychology textbook. Examples might be 'modelling of aggression in children' and 'long-term memory'. Classify the references used to explore each topic as (i) experimental studies, (ii) quasi-experimental studies, (iii) surveys, (iv) case studies or (v) presenting too little information for classification.

   i. Are there differences in the distribution of references into these categories for each topic?
   ii. If so, what factors do you think have contributed to these differences?

b. In dealing with these topics, do the authors of the textbook question the internal or external validity of any research reviewed? [Hint: This could be reflected in statements like 'the conclusions of this research have been challenged on methodological grounds' or 'it is difficult to know whether these results can be generalized to other settings'.]

   i. Is the validity of research on the two topics criticized on different grounds?
   ii. If so, what factors do you think contribute to the different forms that criticism takes?

Experimental Design

Key goals for this chapter

- Identify the key components of an experiment, and go through the decisions involved in putting them together in order to design a good experiment.
- Identify factors that interfere with one's ability to interpret the findings of an experiment.
- Identify factors that limit one's ability to generalize from the findings of an experiment to the world at large.

In the previous chapter we noted that the experiment is one of the main research options available to people who want to do psychological research. We also dealt with some of the factors that dictate whether or not researchers decide to conduct experiments. However, we did not deal in any detail with the issues that confront them if they do. These details are the substance of this chapter.

Because we are going to deal with the *details* of designing experiments, we will tackle a number of quite difficult issues. Some of these are more fundamental than others and hence more immediately relevant to the first pieces of psychological research that you are likely to encounter or conduct. However, as you progress to more advanced courses and are exposed to a range of research articles, you will need to have a good understanding of all these concepts.

In essence the issues we are going to address are those of **experimental design** and **operationalization**. They concern the choices that the experimenter has to make about how to construct experiments in order to test hypotheses effectively. This effectiveness has two main bases: experimental components and experimental validity. We will treat these bases as if they were independent, but, as we will see, each actually exerts a strong influence on the other.

The first key to the effectiveness of experiments is an appropriate choice of experimental *components*. So, among other things, a researcher needs to select (a) an independent variable, (b) a dependent variable, (c) a participant sample and (d) a method and criterion for establishing that the effects of manipulating the independent variable are sufficiently large to be taken seriously and of sufficient practical and theoretical interest. The first three of these components will be dealt with in the first half of this chapter and the fourth will be covered in Chapters 7 and 8.

Although participants and variables constitute the crucial ingredients of an experiment, their quality does not guarantee that the experiment will be effective. As with a cake, they have to be assembled appropriately – usually on the basis of a tried and tested recipe. And as any cook will attest, it is here that many of the secrets of their success (and failure) lie. Accordingly, a large part of any experiment's effectiveness derives from an experimenter's ability to construct a study in a way that allows its findings to be correctly interpreted. To do this the experimental design needs to avoid a number of potential threats to *internal validity*. Appropriate experimental design should also enable the researcher to *generalize* experimental findings to other non-experimental settings. However, this process is jeopardized by threats to **external validity**. In the latter part of this chapter we discuss some of the main forms that threats to these two types of validity take and some of the most common strategies that are employed to overcome them.

> **experimental design** Both (a) the process of constructing experiments and (b) the resulting structure of those experiments.
>
> **external validity** The extent to which a research finding can be generalized to other situations.
>
> **operationalization** The process of deciding how to manipulate and/or measure independent variables and how to measure dependent variables.

Choosing an independent variable

As we discussed in the previous chapter, in any experiment the independent variable (IV) is the variable that the researcher manipulates. On the basis of a theory or hypothesis, this variable is predicted to have a causal effect on a relevant outcome measure (the DV). The goals in selecting an independent variable to manipulate in an experiment are quite straightforward: to identify a variable that *can* be manipulated; and to ensure that this variable corresponds as closely as possible to the theoretical variable in which the researcher is interested. Satisfying these objectives can be quite difficult – partly because there is often an inherent tension between them.

To explain these points, we can develop a new example based on research into the cognitive aspects of depression (e.g., Abramson, Seligman, & Teasdale, 1978; Seligman & Maier, 1967). A researcher interested in depression may have a general theory that whether or not people become depressed by failure depends upon how they explain that failure to themselves.

The way in which people explain events can be thought of as their 'attributional style', so the theory suggests that depression depends upon people's attributional style. The theory might suggest that if people *internalize* failure (e.g., by saying to themselves 'it's my fault') they become depressed, but if they *externalize* it (e.g., by saying 'it's someone/something else's fault') they do not.

In this case, the key theoretical variable is attributional style. The goal of any experiment designed to test this theory would therefore be to manipulate people's attributional style to see whether it has any effect on their depression. But how can we manipulate attributional style *directly*? It is not possible to open up people's heads and turn a dial that changes 'attributional style' from 'external' to 'internal'. Even if it were, it would be ethically unacceptable to do so (and, as we noted in the previous chapter, such ethical considerations contribute considerably to many researchers' decisions to conduct correlational research).

The problem here is one that we first noted in Chapter 2 when we discussed the general issue of research validity and on which we elaborated when discussing psychological measurement in Chapter 3. It arises from the fact that psychological research is generally concerned with making statements about theoretical variables – usually mental states or processes – that are not directly observable. This means that psychologists often have to manipulate theoretical variables *indirectly*, by using independent variables that they believe will have a specific impact upon a given mental process or state. In other words, they have to make decisions about how to *operationalize* the independent variable.

Photo 4.1 At least 20% of people in developed countries experience depression at some point in their lives and it is the leading cause of disability worldwide (Lopez, Mathers, Ezzati, Jamison, & Murray, 2006; World Health Organization, 2012). For these reasons, a growing body of experimental research has sought to understand the psychological processes that underpin its development and effective treatment. However, this presents a range of practical and ethical challenges that researchers need to negotiate in order to advance our understanding of the condition.

To manipulate people's mood a researcher may play them happy or sad music or ask them to think about something good or bad that has happened to them recently. We cannot just change their mood by flicking a switch. We have to manipulate variables that can be expected to change their mood. Similarly, in our example the researcher may attempt to manipulate attributional style by exposing people to failure (e.g., in an exam) and then asking some of them to answer questions like 'Have you always been stupid?' or 'Can you explain why you did so much worse than everyone else in identical circumstances?' – questions that encourage them to reflect on their own contribution to their performance (i.e., to internalize). The researcher may ask other participants questions like 'Do you think that the fact that you weren't allowed to revise for the exam affected your performance?' or 'You were very unlucky, weren't you?' – questions that encourage them to reflect on the contribution of other factors to their performance (i.e., to externalize). We should note, however, that there would still be ethical concerns about aspects of this manipulation (concerns we will return to in Chapter 14).

Having performed indirect manipulations of this sort, it is often necessary for researchers to show that those manipulations have had the desired effect on the relevant theoretical variable. This demonstration is achieved by something referred to as a **manipulation check**. A manipulation check is a dependent variable. But unlike other dependent variables, it checks that manipulation of the independent variable has had an effect on a theoretically relevant *causal* variable. For this reason, obtaining an effect on this type of measure is a *prerequisite* in an experiment rather than an end in itself.

So, after making people listen either to Chopin's 'Funeral March' or to Beethoven's 'Ode to Joy', a researcher may ask them how they feel in order to check that the people who listened to Beethoven were in a better mood. Likewise, in our main example, having attempted to manipulate participants' attributional style by asking questions about their exam performance, the researcher could ask them a question like 'How much are you personally responsible for your failure?' (perhaps getting them to circle a number on a seven-point **scale** with end-points labelled 'not at all' (1) and 'completely' (7)). If participants who were asked 'internal' questions tended to mark higher numbers, then this suggests that the manipulation is working. Indeed, we can see that by this process the experimenter has successfully got to 'first base' and thereby overcome a major hurdle in psychological experimentation.

Researchers are usually keen to obtain very big effects on manipulation checks. If they do not they will probably be inclined to strengthen the manipulation of the independent variable. This might involve increasing its duration or intensity, reinforcing it with additional manipulations or simply using a different (superior) manipulation. Such steps are often necessary because it is a general rule of experiments that in order for them to have the best chance of working (i.e., for the manipulation to lead to an effect on the dependent variable), the researcher needs to ensure that the manipulation of the independent variable is *as strong as possible*.

In our examples so far we have often referred to experiments where one group of participants is exposed to one level of a particular independent variable and another group of participants is exposed to another (e.g., where the study contains two experimental groups or an experimental group and a control group). For example, we have discussed studies in which one group of participants is asked questions that lead them to externalize while another is asked questions that lead them to internalize; or where an experimental group of participants is separated from their partners and a control group is not. When the independent variable is manipulated in this way it is a **between-subjects manipulation** (better referred to as a between-participants manipulation in research involving human beings). This is because levels of the independent variable differ between participants in different conditions.

The manipulation of independent variables does not have to involve different groups of participants, however. It is also possible to conduct experiments where the *same* participants are exposed to different levels of the independent variable but at different times.

For example, one could conduct an experiment where the same group of participants were induced to internalize their failure at one point in time but to externalize it at another. When the independent variable is manipulated in this way it is referred to as a **within-subjects (within-participants) manipulation**. This is because levels of the independent variable differ *within* the same participants.

A number of factors determine whether the independent variable is manipulated within or between subjects. Two of the principal advantages of within-subjects manipulations are (a) that they reduce by at least 50% the number of people needed to participate in any given experiment, and (b) that they remove all of the differences between the participants in different conditions that are produced by chance as a result of the random assignment of different participants to different conditions. This is because the same people participate in each condition and their responses are directly compared across the two conditions. For this reason we say that each participant is being used as 'their own control'. This means that the differences between conditions that arise because different people are being measured (in between-subjects designs) are eliminated or controlled.

As we will see below, however, within-subjects procedures can involve a number of quite serious threats to internal validity. This is mainly because other variables can change systematically between different phases of an experiment.

Test Yourself 4.1**

What is a manipulation check and what is its purpose?

a. A dependent measure used to check that manipulation of an independent variable has been successful.
b. An independent variable used to check that measurement of a dependent variable has been successful.
c. A measure used to check that an experiment has an independent variable.
d. An independent measure used to check that the operationalization is relevant.
e. A dependent measure used to check that an independent variable is sufficiently relevant.

The correct answer is (a). A manipulation check cannot check or ensure the relevance of any variable, so (d) and (e) are incorrect. It is a dependent measure used to check that the independent variable has actually been manipulated and so is operating in the experiment. Therefore (c) is incorrect because the experiment includes an independent variable in the first place, a manipulation check is meaningless – indeed, without an independent variable there is no experiment; (b) is wrong because it completely reverses the logic of experimental design.

between-subjects manipulation Systematic change to an independent variable where different participants are exposed to different levels of that variable by the experimenter.

manipulation check A dependent measure (that is not the primary dependent measure of interest) that checks that manipulation of the independent variable has been successful (i.e., it has changed the theoretically relevant causal variable that the experimenter wants to manipulate).

scale A system for deciding how to arrange objects or events in a progressive series. In this way scales are used to assign relative magnitude to psychological and behavioural phenomena (e.g., intelligence or political attitudes).

within-subjects manipulation Systematic change to an independent variable where the same participants are exposed to different levels of that variable by the experimenter.

Choosing a dependent variable

Of course, the main 'prize' in any experiment is not to find effects on manipulation checks, but to find out whether there are effects on the main dependent variables – ones upon which the independent variable is hypothesized to have particular effects. So, in our depression experiment, the researcher is not going to be satisfied with the knowledge of having changed people's attributional style, but will want to know whether this change in attributional style has had any effect on the participants' mood. In order to do this, the experiment has to include dependent variables – in this case measures of mood – on which such effects might emerge.

As with independent variables, the operationalization of these dependent variables can involve a trade-off between theoretical relevance and practical considerations. When they choose independent variables, experimenters often have to choose between what they would *like to manipulate* and what they *can manipulate*. Similarly, in the choice of dependent variables, there is sometimes a conflict between what experimenters would *like to measure* and what they *can measure*. This conflict creates what we call the **relevance–sensitivity trade-off**. This means that when the dependent variable is highly relevant to a given issue, it may be less sensitive to changes in the independent variable.

As an example, we can think of a team of researchers interested in studying the effect of drivers' mood on the safety of their driving. In an effort to understand the phenomenon of 'road rage', the researchers might hypothesize that drivers who are in a bad temper are more dangerous. One way of manipulating the independent variable (mood) would be to ask people to perform either very rewarding or very frustrating tasks. The experimenters could put some people in a good mood by asking them to complete an easy puzzle and others in a bad mood by asking them to solve an impossible one.

RESEARCH BITE 4.1
Choose dependent variables with care

In an editorial in the *Journal of Sports Sciences*, Simon Jobson, Alan Nevill, and Greg Atkinson (2009) make a plea for researchers to choose outcome variables with care. They argue that this has become even more important over time because the proliferation of possible measures, and an associated sense that measurement must be as sophisticated as possible, have meant that many researchers end up not being able 'to see the forest for the trees'. Their main recommendation is for researchers to ask themselves, before they conduct their research, what the key outcome they are interested in is. Focusing narrowly on those measures in which they are directly interested is then not a limitation of their study but a strength.

Reference
Jobson, S. A., Nevill, A., & Atkinson, G. (2009). Choose your primary outcome variables with care. *Journal of Sports Sciences*, 27, 313–314.

The most dramatic demonstration would then be to show that drivers in bad moods caused more accidents. We can see that there are serious ethical problems with this research, but even if they did not exist, one can imagine that it would be unlikely that any manipulation of the independent variable (mood) could ever be strong enough to bring about sizeable change in this dependent variable (number of road accidents) unless the study was going to include a massive number of drivers and be conducted over a very long period of time. The point here is that the dependent variable is not sensitive enough. To deal with this problem the researchers would have to design a study with a much more sensitive dependent variable.

For example, they could see whether drivers who were put in a bad mood drove faster or looked in their rear-view mirror less often. Although the dependent variable might now be sensitive enough to detect changes in the independent variable, its link to the theoretical variable of interest is

Photo 4.2 If you wanted to conduct an experiment to understand the causes of 'road rage' – in order to establish the causal status of a variable in which you were theoretically interested – how would you do this? In particular, how would you ensure that the dependent variable was both sufficiently sensitive to the manipulation you introduced and sufficiently relevant to the issue you were addressing? Answering this question involves resolving a relevance–sensitivity trade-off.

less direct. Clearly, people might argue about whether accidents are really caused by fast driving or by not looking in the rear-view mirror. So in this case it could be argued that the researchers have simply replaced one research question with another.

This same point could be applied to our depression example. It is unlikely that any manipulation of an independent variable would ever produce really big differences in the number of participants who showed signs of clinical depression. On the other hand, the manipulation may produce differences in less dramatic dependent measures such as participants' responses to questions like 'How often do you feel sad?'.

The way in which researchers usually seek to deal with the tension between relevance and sensitivity in their choice of dependent variables is to select variables on which they can obtain effects (which are sensitive enough) and seek to ensure that these are as relevant as possible. However, in some cases this strategy opens up their work to a charge of *non-relevance* – and these charges are commonly made against experimentalists in all areas of psychology (educational, cognitive, social, clinical, etc.). This is particularly apparent where researchers justify their work in terms of variables that they never actually investigate. In the above examples the researchers might make claims about the relevance of their work to the

Test Yourself 4.2**

Which of the following statements is true?

a. Dependent variables that do not measure the most relevant theoretical variable are pointless.
b. A study that employs dependent variables that are sensitive enough to detect variation in the independent variable is a quasi-experiment.
c. Unless dependent variables are sufficiently sensitive they will not reveal the effects of manipulating an independent variable.
d. Unless dependent variables are sufficiently relevant they will not reveal the effects of manipulating an independent variable.
e. None of the above.

The correct answer is (c). Dependent variables that are not sensitive enough to reveal the effects of manipulating the independent variable can obviously tell you nothing about what those effects are (or may be) – so (e) is wrong. Dependent variables do not have to be the most theoretically relevant to have any purpose, as this relevance can be established by additional research – so (a) is wrong. Indeed, often the sensitivity of dependent measures can only be established after an experiment has been conducted. An experiment that uses dependent variables that are not sufficiently sensitive is still an experiment (it just will not reveal any effects of manipulating the independent variable) – so (b) is wrong. Relevance also has no bearing on the dependent variables' ability to respond to change in the independent variable – so (d) is wrong.

reduction of road deaths and clinical depression (and obtain research funding on this basis), but never actually establish the link between their dependent variables and these phenomena.

Just how big a problem lack of relevance is for experimental research is a matter of some debate. Most researchers would agree that it is important to try to establish the relevance of an experiment's dependent measures to any phenomenon in which they are interested. This being the case, debate often arises because many researchers shy away from the task of establishing relevance, not because the task is an impossible one.

The main strategy for establishing the link between measured variables and variables more relevant to the issue being addressed is to back up experimental research that produces effects on a given dependent variable with additional research demonstrating a causal (not just a correlational) relationship between that variable and one of greater relevance. In the driver example, having found that mood affects driver speed, researchers could then conduct another experiment to address the question of whether speed affects safety. Indeed, ideally they (or someone else) would have established the relevance of speed to issues of safety *before* they conducted the experiment into the effects of mood on speed.

> **relevance–sensitivity trade-off** The principle that the more relevant a dependent variable is to the issue in which a researcher is interested, the less sensitive it may be to variation in the independent variable.

Choosing an experimental sample

As well as needing to decide what they are going to manipulate and measure in an experiment, researchers also need to decide who is going to participate in it. In many cases the choice of a sample is unproblematic. For example, if researchers are interested in looking at the impact of psychological therapy on anxiety, they will probably want to conduct their research on people who are anxious. Similarly, if researchers are investigating the impact of a given teaching method on the classroom learning of young children, then they will want to work with young school children in their study.

But what if a researcher is interested in examining normal psychological processes in the general ('normal') population? If you are a student of psychology, you will probably have been encouraged (or required) to participate in research of this nature. Testifying to this point, investigations by a number of researchers in a number of different sub-fields (experimental, social, personality) indicate that in around 80% of published research papers the participants in psychology experiments are first-year undergraduates (Cochrane & Duffy, 1974; Smart, 1966; West, Newsom, & Fenaughty, 1992). In these cases the choice of experimental participants appears to have been pretty straightforward.

However, first-year students themselves are often less willing to take their participation in experiments for granted. Quite reasonably, they often ask 'How can you possibly hope to make statements about human psychology in general when you only study a select subset of human beings in your research?'. This question (and the criticism it implies) appears more compelling when students learn that the researcher is interested in issues such as

RESEARCH BITE 4.2
The problem of WEIRD samples

In an opinion piece in *Nature*, Joseph Henrich, Steve Heine, and Ara Norenzayan (2010) draw attention to the fact that participants in around 96% of the experiments that are published in leading psychology journals are WEIRD. That is, they are members of Western, Educated, Industrialized, Rich and Democratic societies. Yet the authors note that this is true of only around 12% of the world's population. They argue, though, that 'evidence that basic cognitive and motivational processes vary across populations has become increasingly difficult to ignore' (p. 29). Nevertheless, few articles allude to this possibility, and the authors argue that this is a significant problem both for generalization and for psychological theorizing.

Reference

Henrich, J., Heine, S. J., & Norenzayan, A. (2010). Most people are not WEIRD. *Nature*, *466*, 29.

prejudice, depression or phobia. Such questions are asked even more forcefully when it is noted that student populations are usually studied in the laboratory rather than in the situations they encounter in their everyday lives. How can laboratory-based studies of people who are generally intelligent, healthy, assertive and tolerant tell us anything about the psychological make-up of the general population whose actions take place in a world of politics, poverty, oppression, struggle and intolerance?

Many non-experimental psychologists ask this same question, and go on to argue that the conclusions inferred from most experimental samples are necessarily flawed. Many experimentalists, too, would argue that research should not be based *solely* on student samples. Most would certainly encourage a researcher to conduct experiments using other samples wherever possible. However, the fact is that samples of certain types of participant (e.g., the chronically depressed, phobic, prejudiced or uneducated) are few and far between. Moreover, when they have been located there may be particular problems associated with studying them (e.g., it may be difficult for them to participate in the research).

More importantly, though, experimentalists generally argue that it *is* possible to gain significant insights into human nature on the basis of samples and situations that are not representative of the breadth of human society and experience. The arguments marshalled to support this point are quite complex, but they rest on two main points.

The first was noted in the previous chapter when we introduced the concept of a *representative sample*. We made the point there that in order to be able to apply research findings to a particular population (e.g., most 'normal' people), experimental samples and situations do not have to be representative of that population in *every* respect. Instead, the experimental sample only has to be representative of that population in *theoretically relevant* respects.

For example, if a perceptual psychologist is interested in how people with normal eyesight are able to locate objects in space, it would be appropriate to base his or her research on the perceptions of people with normal eyesight but not on those of people with a squint or astigmatism. However, it does not matter if those people are wealthier, taller or smarter than most other people. Similarly, if researchers are interested in how people form first impressions of other people and theorize that they do so on the basis of physical appearance, it only matters that their sample is representative of the population to which the research will be generalized on dimensions that relate to judgements of physical appearance. For example, they need to be able to detect differences in physical appearance and to be able to communicate those perceived differences.

The second point that is absolutely critical here is that researchers *have to have a theory* in order to make judgements about what is (and what is not) a relevant dimension of the experimental sample and the experimental situation. This also applies when the sample is directly relevant to the issue being studied. For example, in an educational study of pre-schoolers, researchers may need to ensure that those young children are representative of the population to which they wish to apply their research in terms of their intelligence and maturity.

If researchers do not attempt to ensure that their experimental sub-population is representative in this way, and they attempt to generalize any empirical findings they obtain straight to the larger world, then they are guilty of **naive empiricism**. For example, if a researcher conducts a study with some students and finds that their judgements of physical appearance are based primarily on hair colour, then he or she may be tempted to (and often will) suggest that all people make judgements on this basis. However, this strategy is very dangerous largely because it is merely a form of *induction* – a form of scientific reasoning we discussed in Chapter 2.

Experimentalists argue that theory offers the scientific solution to this problem because it means that experiments can test theoretical ideas on any sample and in any situation where theoretically relevant variables can be manipulated (e.g., Turner, 1981). In this way we could test the theory that people's first impressions of others are based on their physical attractiveness by exposing *any sample* to people who differ in *what the sub-population from which that sample is drawn* defines as physical attractiveness (one aspect of which may be hair colour in a particular Western society, and neck length in a particular African society) and see if these different people are evaluated differently. Such a theory might predict that only Westerners would be more attracted to people with blond hair. In this way we would generalize our research to the larger world not on the basis of the experimental data themselves (which would almost certainly vary across samples, situations and cultures), but *on the basis of the theory* that they support. As we discussed in Chapter 2, it is then up to further research either to endorse or to challenge that theory.

Yet as we have already indicated, if they can, researchers often want to conduct experiments using specialized samples that are particularly relevant to the phenomena they are investigating. For example, if you were interested in studying the efficacy of treatments for depression, it would make sense to conduct research using people who have being diagnosed with, or who are believed to be particularly susceptible to, depression. Indeed, in this and other cases, it may be impractical to manipulate a given variable (e.g., type of treatment) using a non-specialized sample.

In this case, the researcher may also resort to quasi-experimental methodology (e.g., looking at the recovery rates of people who have been given different treatments). However, as we noted in the previous chapter, this strategy creates problems in establishing causality because participants in different experimental conditions may differ on more than just the independent variable of interest. One way in which researchers often try to deal with these problems is by **matching**. Matching involves ensuring that different experimental groups do not differ appreciably on dimensions that could be implicated in any effects obtained on the dependent variable (i.e., ensuring that they are *matched* on theoretically relevant variables).

Matching is very common in some areas of research (e.g., educational and clinical psychology) where it is almost impossible (as well as unethical) to manipulate theoretically relevant variables such as intelligence, mental illness or particular forms of brain damage. Researchers systematically assign participants to groups based on differences in the variable of interest (e.g., intelligence or mental illness), but seek to ensure that they do not differ systematically on other key variables such as age, sex or socio-economic background.

Matching is also used in some fields to establish relevant *baselines* against which performance can be appraised. For example, in clinical studies a researcher may seek to obtain controls matched on variables such as age, sex and years of education, in order to gauge more accurately the amount of impairment in the performance of someone with brain injury or a particular clinical syndrome. This procedure allows the researcher to eliminate the variables on which the participants are matched as potential causes of differences in performance.

When we discussed the idea of randomly assigning participants to conditions in the previous chapter, you may have thought that matching was another quite reasonable strategy that we ought to have considered as a means of eliminating systematic differences between groups. Yet although it sounds promising, matching is never as effective a means of removing differences between groups as randomization. This is partly because it is very difficult to do successfully, especially if the researcher is attempting to match participants on more than one or two variables.

For example, in our depression experiment, if the researcher thinks it would be too hard to manipulate participants' attributional style, then he or she may decide to identify two sub-groups of participants: one of 'internalizers' and one of 'externalizers'. Yet by doing this the experimenter loses control over the independent variable. Perhaps internalizers are more intelligent, less imaginative, have unpleasant parents or received fewer Christmas presents as children. It may be any one of these factors – not attributional style – that is responsible for the greater depression that they ultimately display. The strategy of matching could eliminate some

Test Yourself 4.3**

A team of researchers is interested in conducting an experiment in order to test an important theory. In order to draw appropriate conclusions from any experiment they conduct, which of the following statements is true?

  a.   The experimental sample must be representative of the population to which they want to generalize the research on dimensions of age, sex and intelligence.
  b.   The experimental sample must be representative of the population to which they want to generalize the research on all dimensions.
  c.   The experimental sample must be representative of the population to which they want to generalize the research on all dimensions that can be measured in that population.
  d.   The experimental sample must be representative of the population to which they want to generalize the research on all dimensions relevant to the process being studied.
  e.   None of the above.

The correct answer is (d). In experimental research the concept of sample representativeness relates to the correspondence between the sample and the population to which the research is to be generalized on dimensions relevant to the processes the research addresses (rather than on all dimensions or a predetermined set of them). Thus (a), (b) and (c) are wrong because it is not necessary for a sample to be representative of the relevant population on all dimensions (measurable or not) or on a universal subset of those dimensions.

of these differences (e.g., if the researcher selected internalizers and externalizers of similar intelligence), but it could never eliminate them all.

matching The process of attempting to remove systematic differences between experimental groups on variables not of primary interest but considered likely to produce differences in a dependent variable.

naive empiricism The process of directly generalizing research findings to other settings and samples, without basing that generalization on a theory or explanation of the research findings.

Threats to internal validity

So far we have talked about the ingredients and purpose of experiments, but we have not really dealt with how experiments are put together and conducted. As in any science, assembling and running experiments are essential aspects of the experimental process – not least because it is very easy to construct bad experiments and to conduct experiments badly. In particular, there are a number of features of design that can compromise the experiment's *internal validity*, leading researchers to interpret incorrectly the effects they obtain. The seven main forms that threats to internal validity take were originally identified by Campbell and Stanley (1963), and we will discuss each in turn, as well as the main ways to deal with them.

One of the main things that can cause problems in experiments is *the passage of time*. This is a big problem in experiments that have within-subjects designs where participants make a number of responses. As an example, imagine a team of researchers who want to conduct an experiment in order to look at the effects of a particular psychological therapy on anxiety. One obvious way of doing this would be to obtain some clinically anxious participants, see how anxious they are, then administer the therapy and see if their anxiety is reduced. This experimental design thus involves two observations and an intervening experimental treatment.

If we were to represent the experiment schematically, one way to do so would be as an O_1–X–O_2 design, where the Os indicate the observations, the X represents the experimental treatment or manipulation, and the order (from left to right) and the subscripts indicate the passing of time.

Now if in this study the experimenters find that the participants are less anxious at the second observation (the **post-test** observation, O_2) than at the first observation (the **pre-test** observation, O_1) they will probably want to conclude that this was due to the effects of the treatment. However, this conclusion is not necessarily valid because between the two observations other things *apart from the manipulation* will have occurred. Basically both the participants and their circumstances will have changed – and these changes, *not the treatment*, may be responsible for the change between the two observations. The participants will all have grown older and greater maturity may itself serve to reduce anxiety. Time may also make people more uncertain, more sceptical or less healthy, and so on. Any such changes in the participants that occur simply as a result of time passing are generally referred to as instances of **maturation effects**.

Two forms of maturation effect are particularly important. Both relate to the fact that by the time they complete the post-test, participants have already had some experience of the task they have to perform because they have completed the pre-test. So, on the one hand, any change in their performance over time may be due to the *practice* that they gained from doing the pre-test. If people do better the second time they take a particular test, their improvement may reflect the fact that they have done more work, but it may also reflect the fact that they know what is on the test. On the other hand, by the time they come to the post-test, participants may have become bored or tired, and this *fatigue* may contribute to a falling off in their performance. These **practice effects** and **fatigue effects** are of particular interest to psychologists because they relate to the important topics of learning and motivation.

Maturation refers to the direct effects of time on the participants in experiments. However, time also exerts indirect effects on participants because it is associated with changes occurring in the world that those participants inhabit. So, between any two observations participants may be affected by any number of things going on in the world – change in the weather, the economy, the political climate, and so on. For example, while our researchers were conducting their anxiety experiment the likelihood of nuclear war may have diminished (perhaps because an international peace treaty has been signed) and this may have reduced the participants' anxiety. More mundanely, the participants might have started watching a self-help video that had nothing to do with the treatment, or they may all have signed up for alternative therapy. Any changes to the participants' circumstances that take place over the course of a study are referred to as **history effects**.

Maturation and history effects pose threats to internal validity because they result in the participants not being completely identical at pre-test and post-test phases of an experiment. Indeed, they can lead to *systematic differences between observations* at different phases of a study. This is one reason why participants exposed to different levels of a within-subjects variable are not perfectly matched. And as we noted in the previous chapter, this fact clearly compromises our ability to interpret the results of an experiment correctly.

Other factors to do with the *experimental situation itself* may also mean that participants are systematically different at different phases of an experiment. For one thing, when participants are observed or asked to respond for a second time (i.e., at the post-test, O_2) they *already have experience* of being observed or having to respond (at the pre-test, O_1). Problems of this nature are referred to as **testing effects**. As an example of how these might adversely affect the interpretation of some results, think of an experiment in which researchers are interested in the effects of mnemonics (strategies for remembering things) on memory. They might hypothesize that teaching participants to use mnemonics to help them remember letter strings will improve their recall (e.g., to develop a mnemonic like 'Every Good Boy Deserves Favour' to remember the notes on the line of the treble clef in music – EGBDF). To investigate this idea they could conduct an experiment with a pre-test–treatment–post-test design (i.e., O_1–X–O_2). In this the participants could first be asked to remember some letter strings and have their memory measured, then be taught how to develop mnemonics, then come back a week later and have their ability to remember letter strings measured again.

As in the anxiety study, if the participants' memory has improved at the second phase of testing, the researcher will probably want to attribute this to the effects of their mnemonic training. However, this may have had no effect at all. Perhaps the participants who did poorly in the first phase were so ashamed of their performance that when they came back a second time they were much more motivated to do well (perhaps this had also led them to develop alternative memory strategies before they were tested again).

Testing effects are actually one aspect of the more general issue of experimental **reactivity**. This refers to the fact that participants will often *react* to features of an experiment so that the process of *making observations can change observations*. As an everyday example, think what would happen if someone you disliked asked you 'Are you doing anything special tomorrow night?'. You might say 'I'm not sure', even though you knew full well that you planned to do absolutely nothing. The response you give to the person is therefore not an accurate reflection of your intentions, but a reaction to the question and its assumed purpose (perhaps you fear the person wants to come round and bore you to death with some holiday photographs). Clearly, if reactivity affects participants' responses on dependent variables in experiments, it can cause serious problems of interpretation.

One of the best examples of reactivity at work was provided by a series of famous studies conducted in the Hawthorne Works of the Western Electric Company from 1924 onwards (e.g., Roethlisberger & Dickson, 1964). These studies were designed to investigate the effects that changes to working conditions had on the productivity, health and job satisfaction of the workers employed to perform a range of fairly unexciting tasks at the factory. To investigate these things the researchers set about trying to manipulate a number of features of the working environment. Among other things, they manipulated the illumination in the assembly rooms as well as their temperature and humidity. The experimenters went on to manipulate things such as the management style of the supervisors, the control exerted over workers and the size of the work groups.

What the researchers expected was that these manipulations would have systematic effects. For example, they expected that workers would complain more about eye-strain and become less productive as the lighting in the factory was dimmed. What they found, however, was that *every* change in working conditions led to an increase in productivity and worker satisfaction. So, when the lighting was made brighter productivity went up and the workers felt happier, but workers were also more productive and happy when the lighting was reduced to a level similar to moonlight (for a more detailed discussion of these studies, see Haslam, 2004).

As you might expect, the researchers were perplexed by these results. Eventually, though, they figured out what was going on. They discovered that their findings were attributable not to the nature of the change in the work environment, but to *change itself*. The workers in the factory were so used to being bored, ignored and taken for granted that they responded positively to the simple (but, for them, remarkable) fact that someone was paying attention to them and doing something different for a change. In other words, the participants' behaviour was changed by the process of participating in research and being made to feel important, rather than by the variables being deliberately manipulated. This effect is called the **Hawthorne effect** (after the factory where the above research took place) and it arises in any research where responses are affected by participants' sensitivity to the fact that they are participating in research.

Another way in which reactivity commonly manifests itself is through **order effects**. These arise if the responses to treatments change depending on the order in which the treatments occur. In the example of memory training, if all the participants were asked to remember letter strings using both multiple-choice questions and by writing down all the words they could remember (i.e., free recall), one might expect that participants would be better at the free-recall task if they did this after the multiple-choice task rather than before. This is because doing the multiple-choice task first would prepare them for the free-recall task.

Photos 4.3 The Hawthorne works of the Western Electric Company in Chicago. In the 1920s it was found that the behaviour of workers in the factory changed as a consequence of taking part in research. Specifically, they became more productive because, among other things, the research made them feel that the work they were doing was important. As a result, the factory gave its name to the Hawthorne effect – a form of reactivity in which behaviour changes when people know they are participating in research. (Source: Mr Harman, Wikipedia)

Other features of the experiment may also change between any two observations, and these **instrumentation effects** undermine validity in much the same way. Instrumentation refers to *any* feature of the experiment related to the collection of data – for example, who they are collected by, where they are collected and the methods used for collection. So, in the earlier study of memory, if the data from the post-test were collected by a different experimenter than the one who collected them at the pre-test, this could have unforeseen effects on the participants' responses. For example, if the experimenter at the post-test was more attractive or pleasant than the experimenter at the pre-test, the participants might be motivated to perform better. By the same token, if the experimenters measured memory by different methods at the two phases this could have similar effects (e.g., if they used free recall at the pre-test and multiple choice at the post-test).

A final set of threats to internal validity relates to strategies for selecting participant samples and the effects of those strategies. The first of these are **selection effects**, and we have met and dealt with these before in our discussion of quasi-experimental designs. These effects arise when participants are assigned to different levels of an independent variable on the basis of some specific criteria (e.g., their age or their score on a particular test). So here any differences between groups on the dependent measures may exist *before* the manipulation occurs because different sorts of people have been selected for the groups.

As we have noted several times already, the basic problem posed by selection effects is that when participants are not randomly assigned to conditions, any change in the dependent variable may be due to things *associated with* the independent variable rather than due to the independent variable itself. So, in the example where participants were selectively placed into experimental groups on the basis of being externalizers or internalizers, if internalizers became more depressed after failure this may be due to things associated with their attributional style rather than due to their attributional style itself. Perhaps internalizers have generally experienced more failure in the past than externalizers, and this past experience of failure makes them more depressed when they confront it again. This, however, is only one of a large number of alternative explanations of such an outcome and, because the independent variable is not directly manipulated, all or none of these explanations *could* be valid.

A more subtle problem arises when an independent variable is manipulated within subjects and the participants are selected because of their extremity (or peculiarity) on the variable of interest. Imagine that the researcher who was investigating the effects of mnemonics on memory used participants who had performed particularly poorly on a previous memory test (imagine that none of them remembered more than 1 letter string out of 20). The problem here is that, *without any treatment taking place at all*, the likelihood of observing such poor performance again is very slight. This is because the performance is so bad it cannot get any worse. Therefore, any change can only be an improvement. As a result 'improvement' is quite likely to occur regardless of whether or not any experimental intervention occurs. This is due to a statistical phenomenon known as **regression to the mean**.

An example of how regression to the mean can cloud the interpretation of research data was provided by Tversky and Kahneman (1974). They noted the case of flight instructors who found that trainee pilots who made an excellent first landing generally performed less well on their second landing. The instructors thought that this deterioration in performance was a result of over-confidence on the part of these pilots. The instructors may have been right, but whether they were right or wrong, worse performance on average was almost *inevitable* as a result of regression to the mean. Pilots who are already performing extremely well cannot improve, so if there is any change in their performance at all they must do worse. Regression to the mean will occur whenever researchers attempt to compare scores from a sample that is extreme on one variable with scores from the same sample on another variable that is not perfectly related to the first. This point is quite complex but it will be easier to understand when you have read more about correlation, a topic we cover in Chapter 9.

One final threat posed by sampling strategies again arises where a variable is manipulated within subjects. This is the problem of participant **mortality effects**. It relates to the fact that in the time between any two observations, *particular* participants may withdraw from a study. In extreme cases (e.g., in animal and medical studies) this is because participants die, which is where the term 'mortality' comes from. More commonly, mortality arises from people choosing to drop out of the study. For example, in the study examining the effects of a psychological therapy on anxiety, it is quite possible that some participants will not turn up for the post-test (O_2) – possibly because they are too anxious. Clearly, though, if anxious participants were to drop out of the experiment, or only those who feel the therapy is working turn up to be tested again, any conclusion about the effectiveness of therapy might be very misleading.

The problem posed by all of the above threats to internal validity is essentially the same. That is, they all produce systematic differences between different experimental observations

RESEARCH BITE 4.3
Why psychological effects sometimes 'wear off'

In an editorial in the *Journal of Child Psychology and Psychiatry*, Sally Ozonoff (2011) discusses a well-documented phenomenon whereby the effects that psychologists study tend to become weaker over time, such that they appear to 'wear off'. Why might this be? One factor that contributes to this is regression to the mean because researchers are more motivated to write up research findings that are very exciting and newsworthy than those that are less obviously interesting. Journals are also more likely to publish those same findings. However, the exciting finding will sometimes prove to be a statistical aberration that is subsequently corrected by further research.

Reference
Ozonoff, S. (2011). Editorial: The first cut is the deepest: Why do the reported effects of treatments decline over trials? *Journal of Child Psychology and Psychiatry*, 52, 729–730.

over and above those caused by manipulation of the independent variable. It can be seen that in many cases these effects are quite subtle and, for that matter, quite intriguing. We should also add that, armed with an awareness of these problems, you will be in a position to identify faults in much of the research that you hear about every day – for example, a news item describing the latest medical 'breakthrough', or one which trumpets the new-found cause of a particular social problem. Faced with this list of potential experimental problems, you may also wonder if it is ever worth going to the trouble of trying to conduct valid experiments.

Well, the good news is that despite the subtlety of many of the problems we have identified in this section, all can be addressed (in many cases quite easily) by appropriate experimental design. Going through the details of all the possible ways in which this can be achieved would be a long and arduous task, so we will not. In fact, the ways in which researchers set about dealing with these problems differ enormously as a function of the type of research they are doing.

However, the basic principle used to eliminate these threats to validity is one that we have already talked about at length: *experimental control*. As we have pointed out, the main way in which experimental control is achieved is through randomization and/or matching. For example, an effective way of dealing with order effects, practice effects and fatigue effects is (a) to randomize the order in which participants complete dependent measures, or (b) to make participants in both an experimental and control group complete all dependent measures in the same order, or (c) systematically to vary the order in which items are presented, through **counterbalancing**.

The point of the latter strategy can be demonstrated by thinking of an experiment in which participants have to perform two tasks, A and B. Imagine that they all perform Task A *then* Task B and their performance is found to be superior on Task A. This effect could occur because the participants have greater aptitude for Task A (or because Task A is easier), but it could also arise from the fact that participants were tired or bored by the time they came to do Task B. However, the second interpretation could be ruled out if the same effect emerged after counterbalancing such that half of the participants were randomly assigned to perform Task A first and the other half to perform Task B first. Counterbalancing is a simple strategy that allows researchers to neutralize or quantify any effects associated with the order in which tasks are completed.

These points about experimental control can be demonstrated by describing one of the main forms of what Campbell and Stanley (1963) call a *true experimental design*. This is a design that deals effectively with all of the above threats. It involves supplementing the basic pre-test–treatment–post-test design described earlier (i.e., O_1–X–O_2) with an additional pre-test–post-test control (i.e., O_1–O_2). This control condition involves different participants but a pre-test and post-test that are identical in every respect (e.g., including exactly the same measurement procedures and the same experimenters). This can be represented schematically as follows:

condition	time $\longrightarrow$		
experimental	O_1	X	O_2
control	O_1		O_2

If participants are randomly assigned to these two conditions, we can compare the results obtained at the post-test (O_2) in the experimental condition with those obtained at the post-test (O_2) in the control condition (as well as the change between pre-test and post-test in both cases). If there is a big enough difference, then this *must* be a result of the experimental treatment (manipulation of the independent variable) rather than any of the seven threats to internal validity described earlier.

As an example, in the case where researchers were interested in establishing the efficacy of a particular anxiety therapy they could randomly assign participants to experimental and control conditions and start by measuring the anxiety of each group of participants (due to random assignment there should not be any substantial difference between them). They could then treat one group of participants using the therapy but leave the other group alone (this constitutes the manipulation of the independent variable). Later they could measure the anxiety levels of both groups again. If the post-test shows that anxiety is much lower in the experimental group than in the control group (and there had been no difference between the groups before), then the researchers can correctly attribute this difference to the effects of the therapy. Similarly, if anxiety is now clearly greater in the experimental group than in the control group, they would have to conclude that the therapy is having a harmful effect.

Test Yourself 4.4***

An experimenter conducts a study examining the effects of television violence on children's aggressiveness. To do this she asks 40 schoolboys who display normal levels of aggressiveness to watch one violent video a week for 40 weeks. On a standard measure of aggressiveness, which she administers both before and after each video over the 40-week treatment, she finds that the boys are much more aggressive in the last 10 weeks of the study. Without knowing anything more about this study, which of the following can be ruled out as a threat to the internal validity of any conclusions she may seek to draw?

  a.   History effects.
  b.   Maturation effects.
  c.   Mortality effects.
  d.   Regression to the mean.
  e.   Testing effects.

The correct answer is (d). Regression to the mean could not contribute to the effects, because the boys participating in the study were selected on the basis of their being normal rather than extreme. This would not have been true, though, if the experimenter had selected as participants the 40 most aggressive boys in the city where the study was conducted. The other factors could all be responsible for the effects she observed. For example, the boys could have become more aggressive because they dislike a new government education policy initiative or because someone has told them what the study is about (*history effects*) or because boys in general may get more aggressive as they grow up (a *maturation effect*). Less aggressive boys may have withdrawn from the study because they did not enjoy watching violent films (a *mortality effect*). Finally, the boys may have become more aggressive because they were angry at being repeatedly tested (a *testing effect*).

counterbalancing Systematic variation in the order in which participants respond to dependent measures or receive treatments. This is designed to neutralize or help quantify order effects in within-subjects designs.

fatigue effects A special case of *maturation effects* where performance on a post-test deteriorates as a result of boredom or tiredness associated with having already completed a *pre-test*.

Hawthorne effect A threat to internal validity posed by people's awareness that they are participating in research. As a result of this awareness, findings arise from the fact that research is being done, rather than from the nature of research manipulations. The effect is a special case of *reactivity*.

history effects Threats to internal validity posed by events occurring between two experimental observations. These events can be of both major import (e.g., the outbreak of war) or relatively mundane (e.g., participants reading a newspaper article relevant to the research).

instrumentation effects Threats to internal validity arising from changes in dependent variables and materials used to record them.

maturation effects Threats to internal validity posed by the capacity for the passage of time to produce changes in the participants between two experimental observations.

mortality effects Threats to internal validity created by the selective withdrawal of participants from an experiment.

order effects Experimental effects that result from the sequencing of experimental treatments or the completion of dependent measures.

post-test An observation made after an experimental treatment.

practice effects A special case of *maturation effects* where performance on a *post-test* is improved as a result of the practice gained from performing a *pre-test*.

pre-test An observation made before an experimental treatment.

reactivity Change in dependent variables caused by obtaining responses on those dependent variables. This threat to internal validity is often posed by participants' reactions to particular experimental procedures or measures (e.g., feeling that they are being observed).

regression to the mean The tendency for observations and responses that are extreme on one measure to be closer to the mean on another measure. If this problem is not recognized it constitutes a threat to internal validity (see also Chapter 9).

selection effects Threats to internal validity posed by assigning participants to conditions on a non-random basis.

testing effects Threats to internal validity that arise when responses on one dependent measure affect responses on another.

Threats to external validity

In the previous section we discussed how the addition of a between-subjects manipulation to a within-subjects experiment resulted in an almost perfect basic experimental design. There is only one real problem with the strategy we outlined, and this is that the effects of testing across the two observations (O_1 and O_2) may **interact** with the experimental manipulation, so that participants who are exposed to a particular level of a treatment react to the first phase of testing differently than those who are exposed to another level (e.g., in a control condition where they receive no treatment). This reactivity does not undermine the experiment's internal validity because the effect is still due to the experimental manipulation, but it does still constitute a problem. The problem is that the results of the study may only generalize to situations where people have been given the pre-test (O_1). In other words, the pre-test–post-test design can compromise *external validity*.

For example, in our anxiety study it may be the case that when participants receive therapy they become less anxious about being tested, so they perform less anxiously at the post-test (O_2). The results of this research would thus only tell us about the effectiveness of therapy as a means of reducing anxiety about testing. The results would not necessarily tell us anything about the effectiveness of therapy for the treatment of anxiety in general.

For this reason, one modification to the above design involves getting rid of the first observation, so that there is no pre-test for the experimental treatment to react with. This design can be represented as follows:

This design in fact represents the basic building block of most experimental research. This is largely because it is simple, neat and effective.

Experimental pre-tests are not the only things that threaten an experiment's external validity, however. You may remember that we discussed the issue of generalization both in the previous chapter and earlier in this chapter. We made the point that in order to generalize from an experimental sample to another population, the sample has to be representative of the population on theoretically relevant dimensions.

A related question concerns the process by which researchers seek to generalize from experimental situations to situations beyond the experiment. How, for example, can the effects of separation on attraction be studied in an experimental situation that manipulates features of relationships quite crudely and one at a time? Surely this is a complex phenomenon shaped by the *interaction* of multiple factors (the many different things that contribute to any human relationship) so that each separation ends up having a more or less unique effect?

This is another complex issue, and one on which a multitude of opinions exist. Broadly speaking, though, debate centres around a number of features of experimental design which are seen to have the potential to compromise external validity. These include the *reactivity* of participants both to features of experimental design (as noted above) and to the experimenter's hypothesis, and the *artificiality* of experimental settings.

Commonly cited research by Rosenthal (e.g., 1966) is particularly relevant to problems of participant reactivity. Rosenthal's research suggested that even if researchers believe they are testing a hypothesis in an even-handed way, they may lead participants to behave in the way that the experimenters want. This can be because participants respond to cues in the experiment that tell them what is expected of them. For example, a question like 'Do you *really* want to do that?' may lead participants to assume that the correct answer is 'No' and to respond accordingly. These cues are known as the experiment's **demand characteristics** (Orne, 1962), and they can be thought of as *norms* that participants conform to because they appear to be appropriate guides to behaviour in the situation they confront. We are all motivated to seek out and act upon information of this sort in our everyday lives (indeed, these processes are routinely studied by social psychologists), so it is not surprising that normative information can exert a profound influence on people's behaviour in experiments.

Behaviour by the experimenter in the form of **experimenter bias** can have a similar effect. Experimenter bias is any behaviour by the researcher that prevents a fair test of the experimental hypothesis. As an example, the experimenter may react more positively to responses that are to his or her liking (e.g., by nodding or smiling). Less subtly, the researcher may 'prod' participants so that they behave in the desired way. Indeed, in a famous experiment where rats had to learn how to run through a complex maze, some experimenters were observed literally prodding the rats that they wanted to do well in order to make them run faster (Rosenthal & Fode, 1963).

The first point to make here is that the value of any research (experimental or non-experimental) will always be destroyed by any form of *cheating*. In practice, cheating can take any number of forms – from overtly prodding participants to fabricating data. If experimenters cheat it will be a lot easier for them to confirm their hypotheses, but such confirmation is meaningless.

Cheating is a very serious problem in all science. But the problems it creates in psychology are moral and not methodological in origin, and so they cannot be remedied by improving research designs. This is mainly because if scientists cheat they are not really conducting research at all.

However, the issue of *unintentional* experimenter bias can often be attended to quite straightforwardly – simply by using an experimenter who is **blind** to the condition in which participants are placed (a procedure that is very common in drug trials). Indeed, even if experimenters are not made blind in this way, there is some doubt as to whether experimenter bias is an especially serious problem (e.g., Barber & Silver, 1968). This is partly because it appears that even when participants are aware of an experimenter's hypothesis and so are sensitive to the experiment's demand characteristics, they may be at least as likely to seek to disconfirm that hypothesis as to confirm it.

Clearly, though, participants' awareness of an experimental hypothesis can jeopardize the external validity of findings. For this reason many researchers go to considerable trouble to conceal the purpose of any experiment they conduct. This can be done by means of **deception** – either misinforming participants about the purpose of an experiment or using **concealment** to avoid telling them the whole truth. Often this involves presenting participants with a plausible (but misleading) **cover story** that informs them that an experiment is about one thing when really it is about another.

Yet probably the most important threat to external validity concerns the ability of researchers to generalize on the basis of experiments that deliberately study psychology in laboratory situations. When researchers conduct experiments they try to manipulate theoretically relevant variables while holding all others constant. The question that arises is whether this inevitably deprives those variables of their meaning and richness.

The arguments that experimentalists use to defend their practices are similar to those that we presented in discussing the meaning of representative sampling. Most would agree that experiments simplify situations that confront people in their everyday lives. Indeed, the experimental control that produces this simplicity gives experimental research its explanatory power (as we noted in Chapter 3). But whether or not in any given case this practice constitutes *over*-simplification is an empirical and theoretical issue. In other words, it is something that can only be established by considering each case on its merits and doing additional research if necessary.

So, for example, if researchers argue that experimental research into separation and attraction has over-simplified the effects of separation by not looking at how it is affected by age (or any other variable, such as wealth or power or gender), they can conduct experimental research that supports this point and leads to a revision of the original researcher's theory. The examples we use in this book usually describe simple experiments involving only one independent variable, but in fact few experiments examine variables in isolation. Instead they usually explore complex interactions between *multiple psychological and situational* features. If a theoretical principle is challenged by the findings that such research produces, researchers can reject or modify that theory or principle accordingly. This should lead to a better theory on the basis of which it is more appropriate to generalize.

It is worth noting here that there is little or no research that has ever suggested that the operation of psychological processes and the impact of psychological states necessarily differ in experiments and in the so-called real world. This is because experimental settings – even those in a laboratory – are still a part of that real world. So, effects produced in experiments can be reproduced in the real world and real-world phenomena can be reproduced in experiments. As Turner (1981) puts it, there is no Great Wall of China between the two.

Indeed, it is possible to turn the argument about the irrelevance of psychological experiments on its head. In most sciences experiments are used for the purpose of creating ideal circumstances that would not otherwise occur in real life. In psychology, too, experiments are useful *precisely because* they control for the influence of extraneous variables that cloud the analysis of everyday behaviour. On this basis, some researchers have argued that the problem with many psychology experiments is that they are too uncontrolled and therefore too similar to everyday life, not that they are too artificial (e.g., Dawes, 1996).

Test Yourself 4.5*

Which of the following can increase a researcher's ability to generalize findings from a particular piece of research?

a. Cheating.
b. Experimenter bias.
c. Deception and concealment.
d. Participants' sensitivity to demand characteristics.
e. The use of unrepresentative samples.

The correct answer is (c). A researcher's ability to generalize a given set of research findings to other settings will often be *enhanced* by the use of deception (e.g., use of a cover story), because this can reduce the likelihood of participants reacting to the experimental hypothesis and deliberately behaving in a way that supports or undermines that hypothesis. Deception and concealment might sound like cheating (i.e., (a)) but they are specific methodological strategies that can be used in research with ethical approval. Thus (a) and (b) are wrong because the same is not true of any conduct by the experimenter which wittingly (e.g., in the form of cheating) or unwittingly (e.g., in the form of experimenter bias) contributes to support for an experimental hypothesis. Behaviour by the participants which is affected by their knowledge of the hypotheses (i.e., demand characteristics) may also make the research findings specific to that experimental situation – so (d) is wrong; (e) is wrong because the use of unrepresentative samples will also make research findings specific to that experimental sample.

Looked at in this way, where there is a problem with generalizing from experimental research to the real world it will often arise not from the fact that the research is invalid, but from the fact that it is *irrelevant*. One of the main problems with experimental research is that researchers can easily be led to examine the impact of particular variables *because they can*, rather than because they should. For this reason, the relevance of experiments in psychology can be compromised more by a researcher's motivation than by his or her method. If topics are only studied because they are easy to investigate or because the findings are easy to publish, it will often be the research *questions* that are at fault, not the *conclusions*.

blind (experimental) A control for *experimenter bias* achieved by ensuring that the experimenter is unaware of the condition to which participants have been assigned. This is often called a *double blind* if the participants are also unaware of which condition they are in (i.e., the level of treatment they are receiving).

concealment A research strategy similar to deception that involves giving participants limited information about a study (rather than misleading them with false information).

cover story Information about the supposed purpose of a piece of research which conceals its actual purpose.

deception The strategy of misleading participants in order to conceal the purpose of some research and thereby reduce *reactivity*.

demand characteristics Cues that convey an experimental hypothesis to participants.

experimenter bias A threat to external validity that arises when experimenters construct or conduct an experiment in such a way that it unfairly tests (and usually is more likely to support) an experimental hypothesis.

interaction A situation where the effect of one independent variable depends on the level of another. If the effect of people's wealth on their happiness also depends on their intelligence (e.g., so that only intelligent wealthy people are happy), there is an interaction between wealth and intelligence (see Chapter 10).

CHECKLIST
Revisiting the key goals for this chapter

☐ I know what the key components of an experiment are, and what decisions I need to make when putting them together to design a good experiment.

☐ I understand the factors that interfere with my ability to interpret the findings of an experiment.

☐ I understand the factors that limit my ability to generalize from the findings of an experiment to the world at large.

Further reading

As indicated earlier, Campbell and Stanley's (1963) book represents a classic contribution to the field of experimental design and is well worth reading. Our chapter in Sansone, Morf, and Panter's (2004) very comprehensive handbook builds on the ideas discussed in this chapter, but uses examples from current research in social psychology and is pitched at a more advanced level.

Campbell, D. T., & Stanley, J. C. (1963). *Experimental and quasi-experimental designs for research*. Chicago: Rand McNally.

Haslam, S. A., & McGarty, C. (2004). Experimental design and causality in social psychological research. In C. Sansone, C. C. Morf, & A. T. Panter (Eds.), *Handbook of methods in social psychology* (pp. 237–264). Thousand Oaks, CA: SAGE.

Experimental design: A checklist for research evaluation and improvement

Table 4.1

Potential problem	Question to ask	Potential improvement
No manipulation check	Have the researchers taken steps to ensure that a variable has been manipulated effectively?	If the efficacy of an experimental manipulation is in doubt, include a manipulation check to help clarify matters.
Insensitivity of the DV	Is the manipulation of the IV strong enough to produce discernible effects on the DV?	If the manipulation of the IV is too weak, try to identify ways of strengthening it or of making the DV more sensitive (bearing in mind how any changes may impact upon the theoretical relevance of the DV).
Irrelevance of the DV	Is the DV relevant to the phenomenon in which the researchers are interested?	If the DV is not relevant enough, try to identify ways of making it more relevant (bearing in mind how any changes may impact upon the sensitivity of the DV).
Sampling bias	Are the research participants representative of the population of interest on theoretically relevant dimensions?	If the sample is not representative of the population, conduct a replication with a more representative population.
Naive empiricism	Are the researchers seeking to generalize from experimental evidence without recourse to theory?	Work on theory development before conducting an experiment to ensure that experimental manipulations (and subsequent generalization) are informed by theory.
Maturation effects	Are responses affected by the fact that time has passed (and participants have matured) since previous responses were obtained?	
Practice effects	Are responses affected by the fact that participants had more practice at performing a task as a study progressed?	
Fatigue effects	Are responses affected by the fact that participants became more tired as a study progressed?	
History effects	Are responses affected by the fact that things have happened in the world since previous responses were obtained?	Consider whether effects attributable to maturation, practice, fatigue, history, testing, reactivity, order, instrumentation or mortality may be implicated in

Potential problem	Question to ask	Potential improvement
Testing effects	Are responses affected by the experience of previous testing?	experimental findings. If this is the case, consider the relative merits of studies in which (a) the order of measures and/or treatments is randomized, (b) the order of measures and/or treatments is counterbalanced or (c) different participants are randomly assigned to conditions in which they complete different measures and/or respond to different treatments (including a control condition).
Reactivity	Are responses affected by the fact that participants know they are taking part in research?	
Order effects	Are responses affected by the order in which responses are made?	
Instrumentation effects	Are responses affected by changes to features of the testing environment since previous responses were obtained?	
Mortality effects	Are responses affected by an inability to collect data from participants who took part in a previous phase of research?	
Selection effects	Are responses affected by the researchers' decision to assign particular participants to particular conditions?	If assignment to conditions is non-random, consider whether any differences in the populations from which participants in different conditions are drawn may be contributing to the observed effects. If this is the case, consider if it is possible to assign participants randomly to conditions. If it is not, consider the merits of matching conditions or using statistical procedures (beyond those covered in this book) to control for differences.
Regression to the mean	Are responses affected by the fact that in a previous phase of research participants were selected on the basis of their extremity on a dimension of interest to the researcher?	Consider using a between-subjects design where extreme participants are assigned randomly to treatment and control conditions. Alternatively, conduct research using a random sample of participants.
Interaction between pre-test and IV	Are the effects of an experimental treatment restricted to situations in which this is coupled with a particular pre-test?	If validity is compromised by a pre-test (or there

(Continued)

Table 4.1 (Continued)

Potential problem	Question to ask	Potential improvement
Unnecessary pre-test	Is internal or external validity compromised by the use of a pre-test?	is no clear need for one) simplify the experimental design by removing it.
Demand characteristics	Are particular responses encouraged by the researchers or by features of the research environment?	If responses are affected by participants' or researchers' awareness of (or beliefs about) experimental hypotheses, consider (a) keeping participants blind to the conditions to which they have been assigned and/or to the hypotheses (e.g., through concealment or deception), (b) making the experimenters blind to the conditions to which participants have been assigned, or (c) conducting a double-blind study in which both participants and researchers are unaware of the conditions to which participants have been assigned.
Experimenter bias	Is the researchers' behaviour preventing a fair test of an experimental hypothesis?	
Over-simplification; artificiality	Does an experimental design promote an over-simplified understanding of a psychological process or phenomenon?	If the conclusions drawn from experimental research appear to be over-simplified, develop a critique along these lines and design research (experimental or otherwise) which tests and promotes a more complex analysis.
Irrelevance	Are the processes examined in a particular experiment irrelevant to the broader issues in which the researchers purport to be interested?	If experimental research appears to be of questionable 'real-world' relevance, develop a critique along these lines and design research (experimental or otherwise) that is relevant.

Test Yourself 4.6**

A researcher conducts an experiment to investigate the effects of positive mood on memory. Mood is manipulated by giving participants a gift. In the experiment, before they are given a memory test, half of the participants are randomly assigned to a condition in which they are given a box of chocolates, and the other half are given nothing. Which of the following statements is *not* true?

    a.   Mood is a between-subjects variable.
    b.   The experiment has two conditions.
    c.   The experiment includes a control condition.
    d.   The independent variable is manipulated within subjects.
    e.   Experimental control eliminates potential threats to the internal validity of the experiment.

Test Yourself 4.7*

Which of the following is a researcher's overall objective in using matching?

- a. To control for extraneous variables in quasi-experimental designs.
- b. To increase participants' enjoyment of correlational research.
- c. To ensure that participants are randomly assigned to conditions.
- d. To ensure that groups of participants do not differ in age and sex.
- e. To ensure that groups of participants do not differ in intelligence.

Test Yourself 4.8**

Which of the following threats to validity is the most difficult to control by improving experimental design?

- a. Maturation effects.
- b. Cheating by experimenters.
- c. History effects.
- d. Sensitivity to demand characteristics.
- e. Experimenter bias.

Test Yourself 4.9**

Some researchers decided to conduct an experiment to investigate the effects of a new psychological therapy on people's self-esteem. To do this they asked all their clients who were currently receiving treatment for low self-esteem to continue using an old therapy, but treated all their new clients with the new therapy. A year later they found that clients subjected to the new therapy had much higher self-esteem. Which of the following statements is true?

- a. The greater self-esteem of the clients exposed to the new therapy resulted from the superiority of that therapy.
- b. The greater self-esteem of the clients exposed to the new therapy resulted from the fact that the new clients were more optimistic than those who were previously receiving treatment.
- c. The greater self-esteem of the clients exposed to the new therapy resulted from the fact that the new clients were less disillusioned with therapy than those who were previously receiving treatment.
- d. The greater self-esteem of the clients exposed to the new therapy resulted from the fact that the new clients were more intelligent than those who were previously receiving treatment.
- e. It is impossible to establish the validity of any of the above statements based on the results of this study.

(Continued)

(Continued)

The correct answer to 4.6 is (d). This experiment has two conditions: an experimental condition designed to create good mood; and a control condition. As (a) suggests, mood is manipulated between subjects as participants are assigned to either the control condition or the experimental condition. Only if the same participants were exposed to different levels of the mood manipulation and completed a memory test after each one would the independent variable be manipulated within subjects – so (b) is wrong. Note, however, that a within-subjects manipulation would pose a number of threats to internal validity. In particular, this is because the two tests would have to be different in order to rule out effects due to *reactivity*, and then any difference could be due to *testing effects*. As answers (c) and (e) suggest, these threats are eliminated in this design by the addition of an experimental control group.

The correct answer to 4.7 is (a). Matching is a procedure used to ensure that when participants have been assigned to groups on the basis of differences in an independent variable (e.g., age), they do not differ systematically on other variables which could plausibly lead to their being different on the dependent variable (i.e., extraneous variables such as wealth and level of education). Any variable other than the independent variable is extraneous, so these are not confined to differences in age, sex or intelligence as answers (d) and (e) suggest. Matching is normally carried out precisely when random assignment is not possible – so (c) is wrong; (b) is wrong because matching does not have any systematic impact on participants' enjoyment of research.

The correct answer to 4.8 is (b). Experimental design, however good, can never overcome dishonesty on the part of the experimenter because the experiment ceases to be research and becomes instead an exercise in fraud. Maturation effects (a) and history effects (c) can be controlled by use of a control group to check for any spurious effects that arise from the passing of time. Participants' sensitivity to demand characteristics (d) may be eliminated through the use of an appropriate cover story, and experimenter bias (e) can be eliminated by not informing the experimenter of the experimental condition to which participants have been assigned (i.e., making them blind).

The correct answer to 4.9 is (e). The problem with establishing the validity of any interpretation of these results arises from the method of participant *selection*. This study is actually a quasi-experiment, and because the participants were not randomly assigned to treatment conditions, it is possible that the difference between groups arose from differences *associated* with the therapy they received, not from the therapy itself. It is quite possible that the clients who were receiving treatment before the experiment started and who continued receiving the old therapy were more jaded, more fatigued, less intelligent, more depressed and so on than the new clients assigned to receive the new therapy. They may even have had lower self-esteem to start with. Any one of these differences may have been responsible for the difference between the groups' self-esteem at the post-test. In other words, any of (a), (b), (c) and (d) *could* be true, but by the same token they could all be false.

Discussion/essay questions

a. What factors govern the choice of an independent variable?
b. What factors govern the choice of a dependent variable?
c. How can experimental data obtained from students contribute to our understanding of the general psychological process?
d. What are the main problems associated with experiments that use within-subjects designs?
e. What role does counterbalancing play in experimental research?

Exercise

a. John wants to conduct an experiment to assess the effect of a new teaching technique (the treatment, X) on 4-year-old children. In planning his research, he considers the designs below. What are the primary problems, if any, with each (assume participants are assigned randomly to conditions)?

i.	O_1	X	O_2
			O_2
ii.	O_1	X	O_2
		X	O_2
iii.		X	O_2
			O_2
iv.	O_1	X	O_2
v.	O_1	X	O_2
			O_2
		X	O_2
vi.	O_1		O_2
			O_2

Survey Design

Key goals for this chapter

- Explain the differences between surveys and experiments, and the implications of these for the research process.
- Identify the key components of a survey, and go through the decisions involved in putting them together in order to design a good survey.
- Explain the different types of survey and the issues that surround their use.

Many people are familiar with opinion polls or surveys, and just about everyone who reads this book will have participated in such a survey at some time or other. In an opinion poll the opinions of members of a sample are measured in order to estimate the amount of support for particular opinions in the general community. For example, pollsters might randomly select a sample of 2000 voters from around a country and try to establish which political parties and policies those people support. In this case the researchers conduct the poll not because they are more interested in the views of this sample of people than in the views of the rest of the population, but precisely because they want to use these people's responses to estimate what the opinions of the rest of the population are. In a political opinion poll, the aim is often to predict which candidate or party will win a forthcoming election.

The term 'survey' is therefore one that most people will have come across before. However, in this chapter we want to work with a precise definition that distinguishes surveys from experiments. The definition rests on the idea that in any piece of research you have to *measure* variables but you do not necessarily have to *manipulate* them. If you measure dependent variables *and* manipulate independent variables you are doing an experiment; if you measure both then you are doing a survey.

RESEARCH BITE 5.1
Surveys as tools of power and democracy

In a fascinating exploration of the rise of the survey as a research tool in the twentieth century, Jean Converse (2009) notes that, over time, this became an indispensable tool of both power and democracy. On the one hand, various elites (e.g., political and scientific) found surveys essential for understanding the sentiments of citizens that they wanted to influence, predict and control. On the other hand, the capacity for surveys to gather information from large representative samples of citizens also allowed people to participate more fully in the democratic process. For this reason, the survey can be thought of as a tool that proved to be every bit as important for industrialization and social progress as other forms of technology and communication.

Reference
Converse, J. M. (2009). *Survey research in the United States: Roots and emergence 1890–1960*. New Brunswick, NJ: Transaction.

In this chapter we start by considering the differences between surveys and experiments in more detail. We then look at the sorts of questions that surveys are used to answer. After that we examine the process of finding a sample or selecting participants to help answer research questions. Finally, we discuss some of the different types of survey technique available.

The differences between surveys and experiments

If they were asked to make a general observation about the difference between surveys and experiments, a lot of people would say that surveys involve doing research in the community and that experiments involve doing research in the laboratory. This is often true, but it is not always the case. We have already noted that surveys can be done in places that have the words 'Psychology Laboratory' on the door, and that experiments can be done in the field.

The main differences between experiments and surveys relate to the sorts of question that surveys and experiments can answer. As we discussed in Chapters 3 and 4, experimental research tends to be concerned with establishing causal relationships between variables. Experimenters typically do this by comparing different groups that have been equated by randomization. If the differences between groups are big enough, they conclude that the difference arises from the manipulation of the independent variable.

In contrast, surveys tend to be concerned with measuring naturally occurring *relationships* between variables. The results from the sample surveyed are generalized to the population; that is, they are used to estimate the characteristics of the population of interest. It is important to note that any statement about the population is always an *estimate* and therefore statements about observed relationships are always made with some *uncertainty*.

Let us compare two studies of the same question to see how the experimental and the survey methods would treat them differently. We will look at the effect of televised violence on aggressiveness in children – a question of interest to social, developmental and personality psychologists. Some researchers would address this question using the experimental method. They might take a sample of 100 children, randomly divide them into two groups (experimental and control) and then show the experimental group a television programme containing some violence. The control group could be shown an episode from the same series that did not include violence. After the children had watched the programme the experimenters could measure the amount of violence that the children displayed in a specified period (e.g., the next hour).

Taking a rather different tack, survey researchers might measure (rather than manipulate) the amount of violent television that children watch and then measure the aggressiveness of the children. This research procedure might involve selecting a random sample of 1000 children and then giving their parents a **questionnaire** that asks them to list the television programmes that their children normally watch. The questionnaire would also ask the parents to describe their children's behaviour. The researchers would **code** the level of violence in the television programmes that each child watches and the parents' descriptions of the aggressiveness of their children's behaviour. There could be lots of variations on this research that would improve the methodology of the study, but this is a fair example of how this question could be addressed by survey techniques.

This example illustrates two key differences between experiments and surveys. First and foremost, the experiment allows researchers to manipulate variables and to use experimental control. Second, surveys tend to involve many more participants (often more than 10 times as many). This means that survey research can be much more expensive to conduct.

The fact that surveys require more participants is hard to get around. A major reason for this is that survey and experimental research often have different objectives. One key difference is in what they aim to generalize. As we noted in Chapter 3, survey researchers often try to generalize from the sample directly to the population in order to make statements about the relationships observed in everyday life between psychological, behavioural and environmental characteristics. In order to do this they need to ensure that their sample is a **representative random sample** of the population.

Experimenters, on the other hand, try to establish controlled conditions where they show the immediate effect of some independent variable on a dependent variable. As we discussed in Chapter 4, they seek to establish controls so that they can generalize observed *processes* to a population where the same conditions are found. In contrast, much survey research tries to generalize a particular result to the population.

Experiments are therefore well suited to investigate things that are believed to be changeable. In particular, they are used to examine the dynamic mental processes that we talked about in Chapter 3. Surveys are more suitable for studying things that are believed to be constant and enduring – like intelligence or personality.

We can illustrate these points by referring back to the example of research into televised violence. Let us imagine that the experimenters found that children in the experimental group were more likely to go out and hit another child than were children in the control group. The researchers might seek to generalize this finding by saying that their research shows that watching televised violence makes children more likely to commit *aggressive acts*. Survey researchers, however, might find that children who watched violent television programmes were more likely than those children who did not watch violent programmes to be rated as aggressive by their parents. They might then seek to generalize this finding by saying that *aggressiveness* is associated with watching violence on TV.

Survey techniques thus lend themselves to examination of stable long-term states or conditions, while experiments are more suited to studying the immediate effects of psychological processes on behaviour. So, in the above example the survey and the experiment actually address related but subtly different questions. The experiment addresses the immediate effects of one television programme, and the survey addresses the long-term effect of televised violence on aggressiveness as a stable characteristic of the child.

As we also noted in Chapter 3, the main feature that distinguishes surveys from experiments is that the experiment allows us to infer causal relationships. In our example, the most that the survey researchers can hope to demonstrate is that watching violent television programmes is or is not associated with aggressive behaviour. Survey research never allows us to say that violent television causes aggressive behaviour because there are always other uncontrolled variables that could have produced any observed effect. Perhaps aggressive children like to watch violent programmes, or perhaps boredom leads people both to be aggressive and to watch violent programmes. That is, if children who watch more violent programmes are more aggressive it need not be the case that watching violent programmes *causes* aggressiveness. Again, the point here is that correlation is not causation. The fact that two things are associated with each other does not mean that one causes the other.

In (well-designed) experiments we can be much more confident about causal inferences. If we find a difference in aggressiveness between the experimental and the control conditions then this difference can only be due to one of two things: random error or the manipulation of the independent variable. This is because we have *controlled* everything else. In Chapters 7 and 8 we will discuss how we make the decision as to whether chance or the manipulation is the most plausible cause.

Given this enormous advantage that experiments offer the psychological scientist, one might reasonably ask why researchers bother doing anything other than experiments. The answer is that sometimes scientists are only interested in observing relationships. This is especially true in the initial stages of research where it is often useful to observe what is going on before launching into experimental manipulations – not least because we may have no detailed idea as to which variables to manipulate. Even if people do not conduct formal surveys before they do experimental research on the issue, they will often at least attempt to make some observations relevant to the process in which they are interested. Also, there are circumstances under which scientists are not allowed or not able to conduct experiments.

These issues apply to all sciences, not just psychology. Astronomers and geologists rarely do experiments, simply because it would be difficult or impossible to manipulate the independent variables of interest (such as the position of certain stars or the depth of the earth's crust). Instead they rely largely on the same logic of controlled observation that underpins psychological surveys. Clearly, this does not mean that astronomy and geology are unscientific. Similarly, an epidemiologist (who studies the spread of a disease) would not be allowed to release a disease into a human community. All the epidemiologist can do is study diseases that have already occurred. Psychologists often confront the same problem – one of the main reasons why they are unable to manipulate some important variables is that such manipulation would be unethical (something we will discuss further in Chapter 14).

There are two complications in this overview of the differences between surveys and experiments. Some surveys actually involve manipulations (e.g., those that use **split-ballot techniques** in which different people complete different versions of the survey), and if these involve full experimental control then they are really experiments. Some surveys also incorporate manipulations without randomization and, as we discussed in Chapter 4, these are called quasi-experiments.

Test Yourself 5.1*

Surveys are preferred in some areas of psychology for which of the following reasons?

- a. They are usually cheaper.
- b. They allow researchers to infer causal relationships.
- c. They are more scientific because similar methods are used in astronomy and geology.
- d. It is often impossible to manipulate the independent variables the researchers are interested in.
- e. They use randomization to achieve random sampling.

The correct answer is (d): (a) is wrong because surveys are often more expensive than other forms of research; (b) is wrong because surveys do not involve manipulations or experimental control and cannot establish cause; (c) is wrong because science involves both experimental and survey methods; and (e) is wrong because, although they sound the same, *randomization* and *random sampling* are quite different ideas. Random sampling relates to the procedure for selecting the sample; randomization is the process for assigning participants randomly to different conditions.

Another question you might reasonably ask is how surveys can have independent variables when no variables are actually manipulated. The answer is that in surveys independent variables are variables the researcher *believes to be* causal. If researchers do not manipulate variables they cannot prove that they *are* causal variables. They can, however, prove they are *not* causal variables. Understandably, there is quite a lot of confusion on this point: correlation cannot prove causation, but a lack of a correlation can disprove causation. If our television survey found no relationship at all between the amount of violent television watched and aggressive behaviour (using valid and reliable measures), then aggressive behaviour cannot be caused by violent television. Thus, under certain conditions, survey methods can allow researchers to falsify causal hypotheses.

> **code** A scheme for converting responses into numerical values. Researchers might write something such as 'Sex was *coded* 1 = male, 2 = female'. All this means is that, when describing the results, numbers are used rather than words. This is a useful thing to do for the purpose of analysing data.

> **questionnaire** A set of questions to be answered by a research participant. These questions could be printed and given to the participant, completed by participants online, or asked by the researcher in an interview.

> **representative random sample** A random sample of the population that has the same characteristics as the population.

> **split-ballot technique** A survey research procedure whereby experimental manipulations are included. The most obvious form involves randomly selected participants receiving different questionnaires. In effect, split-ballot techniques are not surveys but experiments.

Setting the question

Many surveys are designed to estimate the level of one or more variables in the population. This is true of political opinion polls, for example. Psychological surveys are more commonly concerned to estimate relationships between variables. Just about any issue in psychology can be addressed in a survey design if a researcher has enough time and resources. As noted above, survey researchers normally try to establish the relationship between variables. The question might be what the relationship is between gender and verbal reasoning, or between personality disorders and homelessness, or between age and level of understanding of emotion. In each case we want to know if one of the variables is related to the other – whether gender differences are linked to differences in verbal reasoning, whether personality disorders are associated with homelessness or whether children's understanding of emotion changes as they grow older.

In all of these cases we cannot manipulate the relevant variables. We cannot make people belong to different sexes, we cannot give people personality disorders or make them homeless, we cannot make children become older. Nevertheless, we can often *eliminate* the possibility that some relationships are causal if it is the case that one thing can only cause another if it occurs *before* the other. Children's eye colour could be caused by their parents' eye colour (in fact children do inherit eye colour from their biological parents), but parents' eye colour cannot be caused by their children's. Similarly, it is silly to think that improving children's understanding of emotion will increase their physical age.

Researchers decide which relationships to investigate in their surveys by a complex process (along the lines outlined in Chapter 2). The actual questions they address are determined by events that occur within scientific communities and within the general community. In this way theoretical development and pressing social issues often come together to determine the precise questions that survey researchers investigate.

Finding a sample

Once we have decided what research questions we want to address we need to find some participants to help us answer them. That is, we need to decide what population to sample from (Chapter 4). Most survey researchers want to control sampling for two reasons. They want to reduce the amount of uncertainty about their sample so that it is as small as possible (see the discussion of sampling error at the end of Chapter 6), and they want to be able to generalize the results of their study to the relevant population.

A good example of this process is a political opinion poll where a sample of people is asked which political candidate they are going to vote for. Ethical researchers do not aim to produce a change in such opinions, they want to find out what those opinions really are. They want to eliminate uncertainty about whether the opinions really are what they appear to be and they want to know that the methods they use are *reliable* and that the opinions expressed are *valid* reflections of people's real voting intentions (in fact, we can never be totally sure about this latter point). In this case, the poll is only useful if it can be generalized to the entire population of voters (in other words, the poll needs to have *external validity*).

When researchers are interested in any large population, if the sample they study is not representative of that population it does not matter if they have two dozen, two thousand or two million people in their survey. If the sample is not representative, the only thing a bigger sample does is lead researchers to draw the wrong conclusions more confidently.

One of the best examples of this point was provided by the *Literary Digest* survey of voter preference for the 1936 US presidential election. This magazine conducted what was one of the largest ever political opinion polls. Its researchers contacted every US voter who was listed in the telephone directory or who was registered as owning a car. The researchers obtained over 2 million responses (a typical opinion poll of the US population today will involve between 1000 and 2000 people). Despite their prodigious effort the pollsters got the result completely wrong. The poll said that the Republican candidate, Landon, would win by a landslide when in fact President Roosevelt was re-elected. The apparent reason for this failure to predict the correct outcome was that the researchers had limited their sample to the wealthier segments of the population who owned cars and telephones. This population was not the same as the US voting population

Photos 5.1 and 5.2 In the 1936 US presidential election, pollsters predicted that the Republican candidate, Alfred Landon, would win. However, these polls were flawed because the sampling frame was biased, and Landon lost the election to the Democrat Franklin Roosevelt (pictured in the left picture here) by 8 electoral votes to 523. In contrast, in 2012 pollsters using far superior sampling techniques were able to predict Barack Obama's Democratic victory with an impressive level of precision.

in 1936 (though it would be far more representative now). So although the researchers had a big sample it was a very biased (i.e., unrepresentative) sample. Similar problems would have occurred in the last US presidential election if pollsters had limited their sample to male voters, white European American voters or voters who were members of a golf club.

It is therefore essential that a survey sample is representative of the population of interest. If it is not, then the sample is useless for any purpose. We noted in Chapter 4 that for many psychological experiments the population in which researchers are interested is *all* human beings who display the psychological process they are investigating. For research into visual perception, the population of interest is usually people with normal vision. So for research in this area just about anybody with normal vision who can communicate what he or she sees and understands the experimenter's instructions can be part of the sample. No matter how narrowly people are chosen, they should be representative of people with normal vision. Similar sampling considerations are true for many other areas of psychology. This sampling procedure is called **convenience sampling**.

The alternatives to convenience sampling are **systematic sampling** methods, which can be divided into **probability sampling** and **non-probability sampling** techniques. Probability sampling involves drawing people from the population so that any member of the population has a specifiable probability of being sampled. This sounds complex, but all it means is that when we select a probability sample we have to know what each population member's chance of being included in the sample is. In **simple random sampling** (a special case of probability sampling) every individual has exactly the same probability of being sampled.

Simple random sampling involves obtaining a complete listing of the population of interest, whether that is a class list, the voter roll, a telephone directory or something else. This listing is called a **sampling frame**. For the *Literary Digest* survey the telephone directory and the list of car owners constituted the sampling frame (the problem was that the sampling frame did not list the entire population of interest). To draw a simple random sample from the population the researchers would then attach a number to each person in the listing and if that number were chosen by a random process (e.g., pulling numbers out of a bucket, or using a table of random numbers) that person would be included in the sample. Simple random sampling is one method that makes it possible to obtain a representative random sample of the population.

Non-probability sampling includes all techniques where there is not an identifiable probability of each member of the population being included in the population. Convenience sampling is one form of non-probability sampling; another is **purposive sampling**. Purposive sampling involves obtaining a sample of people who all have a particular characteristic. For example, researchers who are interested in the effects of televised violence on children might take a random sample of the whole population and then exclude households where there were no children. But it might be more sensible just to go out and try to find a group of children. These children would suit the researchers' purpose but would not have been drawn randomly from the population. The same point applies if researchers are interested in studying mental illnesses and personality disorders. If they want to find out what the level of the mental illness schizophrenia is in the community, it makes sense to sample the entire population. However, if they want to find the relationship between schizophrenia and other mental illnesses (such as depression) it makes sense to restrict their sample to schizophrenics.

The general rule is that non-probability samples are not useful for estimating the level of a phenomenon in a population. If we want to know whether young people who watch more television eat more junk food than those who watch less television then we cannot find out how much junk food people eat or how much television they watch simply by going to the local junk food outlet and interviewing young people (a purposive sample). Their answers may be honest but they may still mislead us in the same way as the *Literary Digest* survey misled people in 1936. Perhaps the people who watch a lot of TV are having their food home delivered. Despite this limitation, non-probability samples can be useful in mapping out the range of possibilities. A survey in the junk food outlet may give us clues about the relationship between variables. If the hypothesis is true we would expect to find the relationship between the variables in our local outlet unless we are unlucky or there is something odd about that outlet. A single non-probability sample on its own cannot resolve this matter but it is a piece of evidence that can add to one's understanding of a given phenomenon in a useful and meaningful way.

Once researchers have decided on a sampling procedure they need to make a decision about the **sample size**. If the researchers eliminate systematic bias from the sample, then the bigger the sample, the better it will reflect the population and so the better it will be for the research. This is because, for reasons we will discuss in Chapter 7, a larger sample size reduces uncertainty about what conclusions it is appropriate to draw on the basis of data obtained from the sample.

The size of the chosen sample will be reduced by **non-response**. This occurs, for example, where people do not feel like participating in or forget to participate in the research, or their responses are lost in the mail. This is a problem because a smaller sample size reduces the ability of researchers to draw conclusions from the research. More importantly, though, it can also introduce threats to both internal and external validity. For example, if people choose not to respond because they are offended by the **survey instrument** then the sample will be unrepresentative of the population. For example, if a questionnaire sent to married women in North America is called 'A Study of Housewives' Attitudes' then it might be the case that women who object to the term 'housewife' will refuse to fill in the questionnaire. This problem is one of *reactivity* – a threat to both internal and external validity that we discussed in the previous chapter. Similarly, it is conceivable that only highly motivated people will respond to the survey and not those who are too busy or too lazy (this is a problem of mortality). In both cases the survey might therefore systematically exclude a relevant part of the population (e.g., feminists or the unmotivated) and, as in the case of the 1936 *Literary Digest* survey, this would lead to biased results.

RESEARCH BITE 5.2
When do people respond to surveys?

When people fail to respond to a survey this can introduce sampling bias because non-responders may be unrepresentative of the population as a whole. Taking steps to increase survey response rates is therefore very important. Julia Cook, Heather Dickinson, and Martin Eccles (2009) examined 350 studies to identify factors that increase the likelihood of medical staff responding to postal surveys. Among other things, they found that people were more likely to respond to relatively small surveys than to big ones (those with more than 1000 people) and if they were sent a reminder. These patterns fit with other evidence that people are more likely to respond to surveys when they feel that researchers are interested in them personally and that their responses matter.

Reference
Cook, J., Dickinson, H., & Eccles, M. (2009). Response rates in postal surveys of healthcare professionals between 1996 and 2005: An observational study. *BMC Health Services Research*, 9, 160.

Test Yourself 5.2***

A television news programme shows a murder case including video footage of the grieving parents of the victim. The television station then conducts an opinion poll in which it asks viewers to phone in and vote for or against the death penalty for murder. The results of the survey show that 83% of the 20,000 viewers who ring in are in favour of the death penalty. Which of the following statements is true?

a. The results of this study can only be generalized to people who watch news programmes.
b. The results of this study can only be generalized to people who own a television.
c. The results of this study can only be generalized to people who care about the death penalty.
d. The results of this study can only be generalized when we know much more about the sampling method.
e. The results of this study can only be generalized if the bias created by showing the grieving parents is eliminated.

The correct answer is (d). Unless we know more about the way the sample is selected we cannot draw any conclusion about the true level of support for the death penalty in the community. In this case the sample selects itself from those who are watching the programme and who have access to a telephone. Nevertheless, we cannot say that (a) or (b) is true because only a subset of those who watch the programme or have access to phones will ring in. We do not know how that sample selects itself so we cannot conclude that it is a *representative* sample. It is likely that of the people who watch the programme, only those people who care a lot about the issue will phone in, but we cannot be sure. Perhaps only people who have faith in phone-in polls take part. Some people might also phone in several times. Answer (c) sounds plausible but it is only a hunch about a possible source of bias. Answer (e) also sounds plausible, but it is only a guess and not necessarily true. In short, people are well advised to treat the results of phone-in polls with a great deal of caution.

convenience sampling A sampling procedure where a sample is chosen from the people who are available to participate in research. Often just about any person who can understand the instructions and complete the task is acceptable. This is the technique used in many psychological experiments (often involving undergraduate students).

non-probability sampling A sampling technique where there is not a specifiable probability of a member of the population being sampled.

non-response The failure to obtain responses in circumstances where a person is selected from the population but does not actually participate in the survey.

probability sampling A sampling technique where there is a specifiable probability of each member of the population being sampled.

purposive sampling Selecting those members of a population who have a definable characteristic. For example, a study of depression might sample only those members of a population who are clinically depressed.

sample size The number of participants in a study. This is represented by the symbol N.

sampling frame A listing of all members of the population of interest.

simple random sample A random sample in which every member of the population has the same probability of being included.

survey instrument A means of collecting data from the sample. This could be a questionnaire form, a web page or an interview.

systematic sampling Sampling where participants are selected according to a specific plan or method (either *probability* or *non-probability sampling*).

Types of survey

So far we have talked about survey design in very general terms. In fact there are many different survey methods and the wide choice reflects the many different interests, approaches and objectives of psychologists. We cannot, for example, expect that the same techniques would be applicable to studying adults and children, or for answering questions in cognitive and clinical psychology. It is difficult to say that one method is always better than another, though some techniques are certainly better than others for particular purposes.

Questionnaires are normally printed booklets with instructions and questions. These can be administered by researchers (i.e., handed out and then collected), mailed out to potential participants, or distributed by other means such as electronic mail or in a magazine.

Interviews are really just questionnaires where the questions are asked by researchers in person or over the phone. The interviewer writes down or records the response as he or she asks each question.

Computer-aided interviewing is used for telephone surveys. The computer assists the interviewers by telling them which question to ask next. Computer-aided interviewing allows researchers to conduct split-ballot surveys. That is, they can help to turn surveys into experiments by introducing manipulations. The computer achieves this because it is programmed either to produce different questions depending on previous responses or to ask different people different questions (randomly assigning them to different conditions).

Naturalistic observational studies are widely used in both human and animal research and involve the observation of behaviour without any attempt to interfere with it. So, for example, comparative psychologists might study the behaviour of animals by observing them in the wild, or environmental psychologists might study the movement of people through a shopping centre or the flow of traffic through an intersection. In none of these cases would any intervention take place (e.g., in the form of an experimental manipulation).

These observational studies can take many forms. One possibility is direct public observation where the participants are fully aware that they are being observed. This is normally true in *case studies* (as discussed in Chapter 3). For example, organizational psychologists might want to know how corporate boardrooms really work. Suppose they want to examine the hypothesis that male board members have more power than female members. The psychologists might obtain permission to attend a company's boardroom meetings for a few months in order to get a picture of what is going on. While attending meetings they would attempt to measure the amount of control over decisions that was exerted by males and females. To do this they might record the amount of time male and female board members spent talking during meetings, the number of times their suggestions were agreed to by other members, or the number of times males and females were interrupted.

Obviously, there are other possible research strategies that could be used in this case. For example, the researchers could give a questionnaire to the board members. The problem is that what people write down on their questionnaires would not necessarily correspond to their behaviour in their everyday lives. If the researchers ask male board members whether they give fair consideration to the proposals of female board members then they may well say that they do. They may say this because it is true, or they may say it because it is **socially desirable** (i.e., they think it is the right thing to say), or because they do not remember how they actually behave (can you remember which shoe you put on first every day?). The point here is that people do not have perfect memories and they are not always totally honest.

This problem is illustrated by attempts to establish the popularity of television programmes using questionnaires (ratings booklets). These usually obtain different results from those obtained by electronic devices attached to television sets (called 'people meters'). One interpretation of this discrepancy is that when people fill in the questionnaires at the end of the week they forget, or lie about, what they have actually watched. Because of this it has been argued that questionnaires are an unreliable measure of viewer preference. Questionnaires may also be invalid measures if responses are biased. This could occur if people reported that they had watched particularly desirable or popular programmes. For example, it is easy to imagine that adolescents might not wish to report everything they had seen if they thought their parents would see the ratings book.

So, as in much psychological research, we are caught between two problems: that if we ask people to tell us what they think they may not be accurate (because they cannot tell us the truth or they do not want to tell us); and that if we simply observe behaviour we may also make mistakes (possibly due to experimenter bias). Another big problem is that if people know that they are being observed they may act differently. Think again of the case of the boardroom. Would male members be prepared to act in an aggressive or dominating manner if they knew their behaviour was being observed by outsiders? Perhaps not, because this behaviour would look bad to the observers.

These problems to do with the social desirability of responses apply to many types of research including experiments, questionnaires and observational studies. Again the problem reflects the more general issue of *reactivity* that we discussed in the previous chapter.

One way around this problem is to use **non-obtrusive measures**. These are research procedures that ensure that the participants are *not aware* that they are being involved in the research process (these methods are also called **non-reactive techniques**). The logic of such research is that people cannot change their behaviour in response to being observed if they do not actually know they are being observed. In observational studies this could be done by making audio recordings, by using secret video cameras or one-way mirrors, or by infiltrating organizations with researchers who pretended not to be researchers. There are serious ethical issues associated with conducting this sort of research (that we will discuss in Chapter 14) because the participants have not given their consent to be observed. Such hidden observation is always considered to be acceptable by scientists where the participants are animals (i.e., it is always acceptable to observe animals in their natural habitat, providing that that habitat is not disturbed by the research). Hidden observation is also acceptable where human participants are unable to give consent but someone else is legally able to (such as the parent or guardian of young children). However, a hidden camera in a boardroom or living room is extremely unlikely to be considered acceptable (however interesting the results might be).

Another alternative open to researchers who want to conduct non-reactive research is to use **archival records** or *behavioural trace measures* (see Chapter 3). Archival studies involve checking through records of behaviour such as books, videos, Internet sites, and so on. These are non-reactive because the behaviour has occurred in the past so the participants cannot change it as a reaction to being observed. Rather than watching what goes on in a corporate boardroom, the researchers may obtain evidence of what has happened in boardrooms in the past (e.g., minutes and other records of meetings, the autobiographies of chief executives, and so on). The researchers might operationalize dominance as the number of times proposals brought by male and female board members were accepted. This technique is exactly the same as the methods that historians often use in their research.

Research examining physical traces of behaviour attempts to use evidence of a previous behaviour to define some dependent variable. These techniques are identical to the techniques used by archaeologists.

The researchers might look at which seats the female board members were assigned, perhaps assuming that more dominant board members would occupy seats closer to the chairperson of the meeting (naturally, they would need to establish that this was a valid and reliable measure of dominance). If females were allocated less dominant seats then this evidence would be consistent with the researchers' hypothesis (although it would not establish a causal relationship between gender and dominance).

As we noted earlier, a lot of survey research is concerned with variables that have long-term effects. Often it is not possible or appropriate for experimenters to control people's lives for extended periods of time, so it can be difficult to investigate variables that have long-term effects using experimental techniques. Thinking back to the example of televised violence, it is obviously the case that very few parents would allow experimenters to control the television watching of their children over a period of weeks or months. Surveys deal with these issues more effectively.

Research that examines long-term effects of ageing and maturation uses **developmental surveys**. A common type of developmental survey is the **cross-sectional study**. In this type of study a cross-section or slice of the population is taken at a particular point in time. If psychologists want to know whether the number of years of education has any effect on IQ scores then they need to study people who differ in the years of education they have received. Obviously they cannot *manipulate* the length of education. One possibility would be to take a sample of people with (say) 10 years of education and compare them with a sample with 12 years of education. A problem would arise, however, in the internal validity of this study. If a difference in IQ were found, we could not be sure that the difference was due to the number of years of education rather than some other difference between the samples. Any such differences are *confounds*, and this example can again be used to make the point that correlation does not establish causation. Perhaps people with higher IQ scores tend to stay at school longer (i.e., IQ could cause years of education and not the other way around).

The main alternative to the cross-sectional design is the **longitudinal study**. A longitudinal study involves taking a sample of participants and following them over a period of time. As an example, a longitudinal study into the effects of education on IQ might measure the IQs of a sample of students with 10 years of education and then measure them again 2 years later. Using the terminology that was introduced in Chapter 4, the difference between cross-sectional and longitudinal designs is that cross-sectional studies are conducted between subjects and longitudinal studies are conducted within subjects. The advantage of the longitudinal study is that it allows the researchers to use each participant as his or her own control and this serves to reduce uncertainty involved in deciding whether key variables are really having an effect (see Chapter 7).

Longitudinal studies of this type, however, can fall victim to a number of additional threats to internal validity in the form of testing, mortality and maturation effects (Chapter 4). In our example, the effects of all three problems can be seen quite clearly. First, it is apparent that *repeated testing* may produce changes in the participants. People may get better at doing IQ tests through practice. Alternatively, they may start to do worse on the tests because they become bored or lose interest. *Mortality* effects might be a problem because, due to the passage of time between measurements, it is quite likely that a number of people would drop out of the study (perhaps those who were least intelligent or least motivated). Finally, in this example education is actually confounded with *maturation*. Accordingly, IQ could increase with age rather than with education.

Most of these problems can be dealt with through appropriate controls of the form discussed in the previous chapter. However, in relation to the final point, it is worth noting that in developmental research *maturation* is often the independent variable of interest. So rather than wanting to control for maturation, developmentalists actually want to examine it in its own right. This points to something that happens all the time in psychological research: what one researcher sees as a crucial variable, another sees as an undesirable confound.

Yet another alternative to these cross-sectional and longitudinal strategies is to conduct a **successive cross-sectional study**. That is, rather than following the same sample (called a **cohort**) over time, the researchers would draw a different sample from the population at different times. This is the procedure normally used in opinion polling. It overcomes the problem of testing effects, but because it has a between-subjects design more participants are needed to draw conclusions with the same certainty. The differences between longitudinal, cross-sectional and successive cross-sectional studies are summarized in Table 5.1. The longitudinal design involves measuring the same sample twice, the cross-sectional study involves measuring two

Table 5.1   Types of developmental survey

	Time 1	Time 2
Longitudinal	Select and measure sample	Measure sample again
Cross-sectional	Select and measure Sample A Select and measure Sample B	
Successive cross-sectional	Select and measure Sample A	Select and measure Sample B

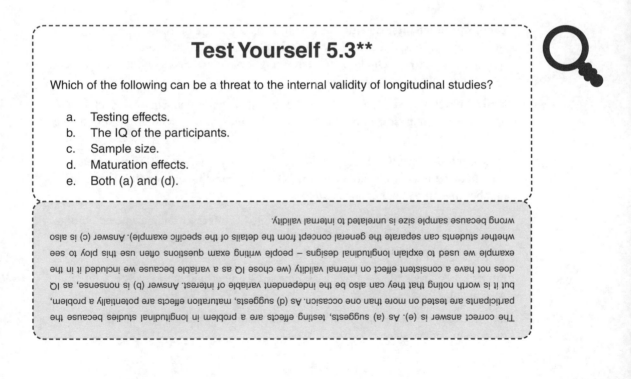

Test Yourself 5.3**

Which of the following can be a threat to the internal validity of longitudinal studies?

a.   Testing effects.
b.   The IQ of the participants.
c.   Sample size.
d.   Maturation effects.
e.   Both (a) and (d).

The correct answer is (e). As (a) suggests, testing effects are a problem in longitudinal studies because the participants are tested on more than one occasion. As (d) suggests, maturation effects are potentially a problem, but it is worth noting that they can also be the independent variable of interest. Answer (b) is nonsense, as IQ does not have a consistent effect on internal validity (we chose IQ as a variable because we included it in the example we used to explain longitudinal designs – people writing exam questions often use this ploy to see whether students can separate the general concept from the details of the specific example). Answer (c) is also wrong because sample size is unrelated to internal validity.

different samples at the same time, and the successive cross-sectional study involves selecting two different samples at two different times. Of course, these principles can be applied to studies that involve more than two observations.

Although this chapter (like those before it) has focused on procedures that all involve attempts to quantify mental states and behaviour, there are also observational studies that do not attempt to *measure* variables in the way that is implied throughout most of this book. This research uses techniques called **qualitative research methods**, and we will discuss these in more detail in Chapters 12 and 13. These methods are often similar in appearance to the observational techniques used in certain types of case study, and they are becoming increasingly popular in some areas of psychology. The techniques (especially those that we will discuss in Chapter 13) typically involve reporting behaviour and commenting on it, without attempting to quantify the behaviour – that is, without attempting to express it in numbers. These techniques are often used by **critical psychologists** who challenge conventional approaches to psychological research. In turn, many mainstream psychologists are critical of qualitative methods. Again, we will explore the basis and nature of this debate in later chapters.

archival records Written or other records that are stored and are available for study. Sometimes these are stored in institutions called archives, but any record that is not in current use is also called an archive.

cohort A group of participants who take part in a particular piece of research at the same time.

computer-aided interviewing A research procedure where the researcher is prompted by a computer to ask questions over the telephone in a particular order. The order of questions is set by the chief researchers. Many surveys are now administered entirely by computer using dedicated web pages.

critical psychologists Psychologists who are critical of the conventional methods and approaches of mainstream psychology. For this reason, they tend to use alternative methods.

cross-sectional studies Studies that sample a cross-section of the population at a particular time. In developmental psychology the sample normally comprises a number of different age groups (*cohorts*).

developmental surveys Surveys conducted into the effects of ageing and maturation. Such surveys may be conducted by developmental psychologists or others interested in changes in psychological processes and behaviour over time.

interview A series of questions asked by a researcher and answered by a research participant.

longitudinal studies Studies where the same sample of participants is measured on more than one occasion.

naturalistic observational studies Non-experimental studies in which the researcher observes behaviour and makes no attempt to interfere with the participants.

non-obtrusive measures Measurements that are obtained without the participants being aware that they are participating in research.

non-reactive techniques Research procedures that use *non-obtrusive measures* to reduce the reactivity of participants' behaviour.

qualitative research methods Procedures for studying psychological and behavioural phenomena that do not involve their quantification.

social desirability The extent to which people's behaviour appears acceptable to other people. If behaviour is affected by people trying to behave in ways that they perceive to be desirable to the researcher then this threatens both the internal and external validity of research.

successive cross-sectional studies Studies that take repeated samples from a cross-section of the population at different times. These combine the features of *cross-sectional* and *longitudinal studies*.

Constructing a questionnaire

We noted earlier that questionnaires are one of the most common forms of survey instrument.

It is worth noting, too, that the use of questionnaires is not restricted to survey research. For example, in many of the experimental designs we have discussed, the effect of an independent variable would be assessed by using a questionnaire to collect data on relevant dependent variables. In light of the questionnaire's importance as a tool in psychological research, it is therefore worthwhile outlining some general principles of questionnaire design.

Perhaps the most important feature of a questionnaire is that it needs to be user-friendly and welcoming. Remember that the respondents are doing you a favour by responding, so you want to do everything you can to make their task as easy and pleasant as possible. You should start by providing a clear introduction to the questionnaire that explains what it is about and why it is worthwhile, and provides key information that the participants need to know (e.g., who is going to use the information and what it will be used for) and which may reassure them (e.g., that their responses are anonymous and will be confidential).

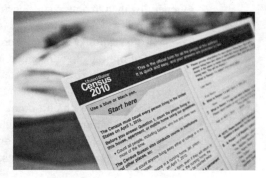

Photo 5.3 Completing surveys is close to being an inescapable part of life in contemporary Western societies – not least because citizens are required to complete a census at regular periods (typically every 5 or 10 years). These provide a mass of data that is indispensable for those who want to understand society: governments, organizations, researchers. It is essential that such surveys are well designed, and knowing how to do this is an incredibly useful skill. (© Charlie Litchfield/AP/Press Association Images).

The questionnaire as a whole then needs to be set out clearly and to ask questions in as straightforward a way as possible. In particular, avoid using jargon and avoid asking two things in the same question (using what are known as **double-barrelled questions**). It should be easy to read, pleasing on the eye and create a positive impression (e.g., it should not contain typographic errors or bad grammar). It should not be any longer than it needs to be, because the longer it is, the more off-putting it is likely to be. Moreover, even if someone goes to the trouble of completing a long questionnaire, it is likely that by the time they get to the end, their concentration will have lapsed and hence the responses they give will be less valuable. This is especially true if you are asking for their opinion rather than for factual information (which is another reason for asking for demographic information at the end of a survey).

Nonetheless, sometimes a questionnaire needs to be long and in such cases it is worthwhile paying careful attention to the way it is structured. In particular, the questionnaire as a whole should be organized so that the process of responding makes as much sense as possible. Sub-headings can help in this process, and, as far as possible, there should be a logical sequence to the questions.

The fact that people's attention can wander while completing a questionnaire is also a factor to bear in mind when thinking about the order in which questions are asked. For this reason it is often best to put the most important questions towards the start of the questionnaire, and to place open-ended questions towards the end (as these take longer to complete and are often more fatiguing). Questions that ask for demographic information (e.g., about a person's age and sex) are also usually placed at the end of a questionnaire because they can be quite *reactive*. For example, if you ask people whether they are heterosexual or homosexual, this may lead them to believe that the research is 'about' sexuality and hence affect their responses. Generally, then, reactive and sensitive items are placed at the end of a questionnaire.

It is also very common for researchers to ask respondents to provide answers to questions using **response scales**, where the nature of a response is indicated by selecting one of a number of options that are sequentially ordered on a scale. An example of this was provided in Chapter 4, where we discussed a manipulation check in which participants were asked to respond the question 'How much are you personally responsible for your failure?' on a seven-point scale with end-points labelled 'not at all' (1) and 'completely' (7). When using such scales it is important to attach meaningful labels to the numbers. This can be done either by providing *anchors* in which only the end-points are labelled (as in this example), or by attaching labels to all scale points, as in the following example:

Was this year's exam more difficult than last year's?

1	2	3	4	5
much less difficult	slightly less difficult	the same	slightly more difficult	much more difficult

Indeed, here the numbers need not be included at all, and can simply be added by the researchers when they set about performing quantitative analysis at a later stage.

Labelling all scale points reduces some of the ambiguity in a scale and makes it easier for participants to understand what a particular response means. However, this procedure takes up more space and can create problems if the labels do not correspond to the particular response that the participant has in mind. A general principle of scale labels is that they need to be non-overlapping and discrete, and this can sometimes be hard to achieve if all points are given separate labels.

It can also be a mistake to use a response scale with too many points. There is little to be gained by using more than nine, and five- or seven-point scales are the norm. Note that scales typically have an odd number of points because this means that they have a clear mid-point. On the other hand, under certain circumstances, using a scale with an even number of points can be useful, as the absence of a clear mid-point makes it impossible for respondents to 'sit on the fence'. At their simplest, such scales take the form of two-option **forced-choice responses** (e.g., 'yes–no').

If a questionnaire contains a large number of such scales, this may also increase the likelihood of a respondent simply making an identical response to each scale. To check for and to discourage response bias of this form, it can be useful to measure the same

Test Yourself 5.4**

Which of the following statements is true?

a. Questionnaires should not ask people to provide personal information.
b. Questionnaires should aim to obtain as much information from people as possible.
c. The order of items in a questionnaire is not particularly important.
d. Questionnaires should contain a mixture of open-ended and forced-choice items.
e. None of the above.

The correct answer is (e). All of these statements are false. Answer (a) is incorrect because, in some sense, all questionnaires require people to provide personal information. Note, however, that steps need to be taken to deal with sensitive personal information appropriately (e.g., by assuring respondents that their responses are anonymous and confidential, if this is true) and the broad ethical implications of a particular questionnaire need to be addressed *before* it is administered (see Chapter 13). Answer (b) is incorrect because it is important to ensure that a questionnaire only collects information which is of use to the researcher. There is no justification for simply collecting information 'for the sake of it', and it is likely to be counterproductive (e.g., in inducing response fatigue). Answer (c) is incorrect because the order of questionnaire items is very important. For example, more reactive items need to be asked last. And (d) is incorrect because there is no formula for the type of items questionnaires contain – the mix of items depends on a number of factors, including the nature of the research question; see Chapter 12).

psychological state using multiple items where some items require **reverse scoring**. This involves asking questions so that a person with a given psychological state would answer some by marking a higher score and others by marking a lower score. For example, a questionnaire to measure depression might include the normally scored item 'Do you ever feel low or depressed?' as well as the reverse-scored item 'Do you feel positive about the future?'. On the second item a higher score would indicate *lower* depression, and so responses on it would need to be reversed when creating a single depression score. However, in constructing reverse-scored items, it is important to avoid the need for double-negative responses (e.g., the response 'not at all' to the statement 'Are you never happy?'), as these are very confusing.

> **double-barrelled questions** Questionnaire items that ask two (or more) questions at the same time (e.g., 'Do you believe in climate change and does this upset you?).
>
> **forced-choice responses** Questionnaire items where a respondent has to select one response from two or more options.
>
> **response scale** An ordered sequence of responses to a particular questionnaire item. These responses can be numbered in the questionnaire, or numbers can be attached to them prior to quantitative analysis.
>
> **reverse scoring** The practice of having some of the items that measure a particular construct worded so that a *higher* score is associated with a *lower* level of the construct. For example, on a scale designed to measure happiness, if a question asked 'Are you sad?' higher agreement would indicate less happiness. So, before calculating an overall score for the construct, scores on these particular items are transposed so that on all measures a higher score is associated with a higher level of the construct. This is done by (a) subtracting the participants' responses from the scale mid-point and (b) adding the resulting score, including the + or − sign, to the scale mid-point to provide a new score.

Conducting research online

If you do decide to conduct a survey early in your research career then, unless you are part of a large research team or you have access to relatively large amounts of research funding, there are two main methodological possibilities that you are likely to choose. Both strategies involve convenience sampling. If your target population is people in school classrooms, or you have access to people who belong to a particular organization or who work or live at a particular location, then you will probably be using a pen-and-paper survey. This will involve asking people whether they wish to participate in the survey and, if they do, handing them a questionnaire and waiting for them to return it to you.

In many other circumstances the best available option will be to conduct a non-probability survey via the Internet. The steps to follow here involve creating a questionnaire in very much the same way that you would for a pen-and-paper survey. When you have the list of questions you need a platform to administer the survey and a way of recruiting people to complete it.

The platform to administer the survey might belong to a university or private company, but in either case it will have procedures (computer programs) for turning your questionnaire into web pages and for recording and storing the responses. Many computer programs for doing this are relatively easy to use.

After the survey has been created you also need to bring your survey to the attention of the people you wish to recruit. This may involve using a commercial service to advertise the survey or making people aware of the survey via email, social media, or through an organization. The critical issue here is that you need to avoid spamming. It is highly likely that you are already being sent lots of junk email that is of no interest to you. Some people will regard your request for them to participate in the same way. If you do use an email list or organization to send your request then you need to make sure that you have permission to use it in this way. This relates to your ethical duty as a researcher (see Chapter 14) and it is an important professional responsibility.

The other issue that you will face is that, unless you use a reliable commercial or university service, then you may be unable to confirm that your participants are who they say they are. For example, if you are looking for a sample of women who have experienced domestic violence and you receive 100 completed surveys, then how can you be sure that the participants are women, or that they have experienced domestic violence, or that the same person has not completed the survey 100 times? The same issue applies with other methods, but it is more likely to be perceived to be a problem in the case of Internet-based research. However, Birnbaum (2004) argues that this problem is likely to be more apparent than real – not least because people generally have no interest in lying or in wasting their time. He also suggests a number of ways in which researchers can reduce the risk of this problem. These include having procedures to ensure that no more than one set of responses can be submitted from the same computer, and being able to corroborate some findings with data drawn from other sources.

Photo 5.4 Online surveys are becoming increasingly popular in psychology. They have at least four important advantages over pen-and-paper surveys. First, they are easy and cheap to distribute. Second, the data are entered directly into a computer program ready for analysis, saving you the trouble of having to do this and eliminating errors in this process. Third, they can be constructed so that respondents have to answer every question, so you are less likely to have gaps in your data set. And fourth, they save paper and storage space.

RESEARCH BITE 5.3
Blind trust? Problems of privacy in online surveys

Surveys are often extremely effective at getting people to disclose personal information. For example, there are many things that people prove willing to reveal in responding to a questionnaire from an unknown psychologist that they would never dream of telling their closest friend. For this reason it is vital that researchers do not violate respondents' trust and take steps to ensure their privacy (see also Chapter 14 later). As Hyunyi Cho, and Robert LaRose (1999) observe, this is an especially sensitive issue with online research because, in comparison with other forms of survey, it is typically harder for participants to assess the credentials of researchers and, at the same time, typically harder for researchers to guarantee data security.

Reference
Cho, H., & LaRose, R. (1999). Privacy issues in Internet surveys. *Social Science Computer Review*, *17*, 421–434.

Overview: Designing a survey

One thing that is clear from this chapter is that there are many options open to researchers who wish to use survey methods. Despite this, we should add that our coverage of survey strategies has been far from exhaustive and we have only hinted at the richness of possible survey designs. However, most of the strategies that we have not dealt with build upon the core principles and practices outlined above. In order to summarize these, it is instructive to highlight the main steps involved in designing a survey:

1. *Formulate the research question.* Before researchers can begin to collect data they must be clear about the question they want answered. In survey research the question is often about the relationship between two (or more) variables. Survey methods cannot be used to tell us whether one variable causes another. However, they can be used to falsify causal relationships by showing that certain variables are not related. This is because one variable cannot cause another if it is not related to it.

2. *Decide on the measurement of dependent and independent variables.* Measuring the variables often involves complex steps of operationalization (Chapter 4). The variables

should be both relevant and sensitive and every effort should be made to eliminate extraneous variables (Chapter 3).

3. *Decide on the population of interest.* This involves deciding exactly to which population the results will be generalized.

4. *Decide on the sample size.* Other things being equal, the larger the sample size, the less uncertainty there will be about what is going on in the population from which the sample is drawn. This is because large surveys have a greater probability of revealing relationships between variables that exist in the population. However, increasing the sample size does not increase the validity of a survey if there is any bias in the methods or the sampling. In this case a large sample will only increase the chance of drawing the wrong conclusions.

5. *Decide on the sampling method.* The key choice of sampling method is between a probability and a non-probability sample. In order to obtain a representative random sample of the population, appropriate probability sampling methods have to be used.

6. *Decide on the technique.* There are many ways of administering a survey. These include observational, questionnaire, interview, archival and other techniques. Choices of which to use will be dictated by a number of factors, including the ease and likelihood of obtaining appropriate responses and established practice in the research area.

7. *Consider possible experimental manipulations.* Researchers should always consider the possibility of using some experimental manipulations in surveys (the split-ballot technique). Experimental manipulations allow researchers to make causal inferences, and help them to be more certain about the reasons for any effects they obtain. These are massive benefits that are sometimes overlooked by survey researchers. One possible reason for this is that when some researchers conduct surveys, they believe they are collecting pure measures of psychological variables and thus do not feel there is a need to complicate the research with experimental manipulations. Some researchers also believe that such manipulations are artificial. This cuts to the heart of the distinction between surveys and experiments in psychology. Of course, many interesting variables cannot be manipulated experimentally (for ethical or other practical reasons), but that is not a reason to rule out experimental manipulations if they are possible. Even if it is not possible to manipulate the main independent variable of interest it may still be possible to control experimentally for some confounds (e.g., order effects).

In conclusion, we should note that none of the above decisions can be made in isolation, and that it is not always possible (or necessary) to make decisions in the order they are presented here. Researchers may decide that they will measure the dependent variable using a particular psychological test and then find that the test is too long to include in a telephone interview and that they have to change the measure. For this reason, we often liken designing any piece of research (whether it be an experiment or a survey) to a juggling act. As you get further into the act you pick up new balls. Each step in the design of the research is like a new ball that has to be worked seamlessly into the act, lest everything comes crashing down around your ears. Because of this, when dealing with a new problem, even the most experienced researchers often need to conduct preliminary **pilot studies** before they get their research procedures to work well.

> **pilot study** A preliminary piece of research designed to 'road-test' various design elements (e.g., independent variables, dependent variables, details of procedure), in order to establish their viability and utility prior to the investment of time and money in a full study.

CHECKLIST
Revisiting the key goals for this chapter

- [ ] I understand the differences between surveys and experiments, and the implications of these for the research process.
- [ ] I know what the key components of a survey are, and what decisions I need to make when putting them together to design a good survey.
- [ ] I understand the different types of survey and the issues that surround their use.

Further reading

There are a number of very good volumes dedicated to issues of survey design. However, the book chapter by Schuman and Kalton (1985) provides an accessible, comprehensive and relatively succinct treatment of the topic. Fraser and Lawley's (2000) text is also very user-friendly and provides multiple worked examples of appropriate survey practice. Birnbaum (2004) provides a useful treatment of Web-based research – although we do not endorse his arguments about institutional review boards.

Birnbaum, M. H. (2004). Methodological and ethical issues in conducting social psychology research via the Internet. In C. Sansone, C. C. Morf, & A. T. Panter (Eds.), *The SAGE handbook of methods in social psychology* (pp. 359–382). Thousand Oaks, CA: SAGE.

Fraser, L., & Lawley, M. (2000). *Questionnaire design and administration*. Brisbane: Wiley.

Schuman, H., & Kalton, G. (1985). Survey methods. In G. Lindzey & E. Aronson (Eds.), *The handbook of social psychology* (3rd ed., Vol. 1, pp. 635–697). Reading, MA: Addison-Wesley.

The original publication of the *Literary Digest* article that we discussed above is also available at: http://historymatters.gmu.edu/d/5168/

Survey design: A checklist for research evaluation and improvement

Table 5.2

Potential problem	Question to ask	Potential improvement
Unrepresentativeness; sampling bias	Have the researchers collected data from a sample that is representative of the population of interest?	Think about the characteristics of people included in the survey and of those not included. If they differ, this suggests the sampling process was not representative (and was not random). Reflect on the impact that this may be having on the research findings. If this impact is significant, take steps to improve the sampling process (e.g., by making it truly random).
Limited consideration of options	Could the research have been improved by conducting a split-ballot survey?	Think of ways in which it may have been possible to investigate the impact of a relevant variable by systematically varying the form and content of the survey instrument.
Inappropriate sampling	Is the researchers' sampling strategy appropriate?	Think about the range of sampling options available to the researchers in addition to the one that they have chosen (e.g., convenience sampling, purposive sampling). If any of these options would have had appreciable benefits (e.g., in saving time without compromising external validity) consider implementing it.
Inappropriate sample size	Is the sample size large enough?	If a sample is too small to reduce uncertainty about a particular finding to a tolerable level, then (providing that the sampling strategy is appropriate) increase the sample size.
Reactivity	Has the nature of the survey instrument affected who responds or the way they respond?	Think about ways in which the nature or content of the survey may be encouraging participants either to respond in particular ways or to avoid responding. Reflect on the impact that this may be having on the research findings. Consider trying to assess the extent of this impact by conducting a split-ballot survey. If the impact is significant, modify the survey instrument appropriately (e.g., by rewording the rubric or particular questions).
Inappropriate survey choice	Have the researchers used the appropriate type of survey?	Think about the survey techniques that the researchers might have used but did not (e.g., archival, observational, non-reactive). If any of these have obvious advantages, design a study that incorporates them.
Poor questionnaire design	Is the questionnaire polished, clear, and in a form suited to obtaining information that will allow researchers to address the research question(s) in which they are interested?	Think about how the questionnaire will appear to potential respondents. Why might they not want to complete it? What might they misunderstand? Also, think about the nature of the information the questionnaire will yield. Will it allow you to answer your research question? Make changes in light of your reflections on these questions.

Test Yourself 5.5**

In a survey where the results are obtained from a representative random sample of a population, which of the following is true?

a. The results can be generalized to that population.
b. The sample can only be obtained by simple random sampling.
c. The sampling procedure is similar to that used in most experimental research.
d. Both (a) and (b).
e. None of the above.

Test Yourself 5.6**

Which of the following statements about convenience sampling is true?

a. It should always be avoided.
b. It is appropriate providing the sample size is extremely large.
c. It can be used under some circumstances.
d. It is a non-probability sampling technique.
e. Both (c) and (d).

Test Yourself 5.7***

Which of the following is likely to be a problem for non-reactive studies that use non-obtrusive measures?

a. Social desirability effects.
b. Defining the probability of maturation for each member of the population.
c. Appropriate operationalization of variables.
d. Behavioural traces.
e. Both (c) and (d).

Test Yourself 5.8**

A team of researchers conducts a study in which they ask boys and girls from a local high school to complete a battery of psychological tests that investigate their social skills and levels of sociability. Ten years later they ask boys and girls from the same school to perform the same tests. Which of the following statements is *false*?

a. The study has a successive cross-sectional design.
b. The research is invalid because developmental studies should not include psychological tests.
c. Testing effects are eliminated by using a between-subjects design.
d. Mortality effects are eliminated by using a between-subjects design.
e. Maturation effects are eliminated by using a between-subjects design.

The correct answer to 5.5 is (a); (b) is not correct because there are other probability sampling techniques that will produce representative random samples, and (c) is wrong because representative random samples are rarely used in experiments. Because (a), and only (a), is correct, both (d) and (e) must be wrong.

The correct answer to 5.6 is (e). If (a) were correct only a very small proportion of published research in psychology (and almost no experiments) would ever have been conducted. Answer (b) is not true, as the 1936 *Literary Digest* survey shows; (c) must be true if (a) is not true. Convenience sampling makes sense where you can generalize the findings from a convenience sample on the basis of a theory to a population of interest (e.g., all people with normal vision). Answer (d) is correct because there is not a definable probability of being sampled for each member of the population.

The correct answer to 5.7 is (c). Appropriate operationalization of variables is always a major problem in any research. In non-reactive, non-obtrusive studies social desirability and other reactive effects are eliminated because the participants do not know that they are being observed – so (a) is incorrect; (b) is a meaningless string of jargon. Behavioural traces are not problems as such, instead they are a potential source of the dependent variables. Because (d) is therefore wrong, (e) must also be wrong.

The correct answer to 5.8 is (b). Developmental studies and surveys can involve any form of measurement instrument (as outlined at the start of Chapter 3), and certainly are not restricted to questionnaires or interviews. Answer (a) is true because this study includes a different sample of participants at the two stages of testing. Because of this between-subjects design, (c), (d) and (e) are all true, too – noting that problems arising from testing, mortality and maturation effects are all associated with within-subjects designs.

Discussion/essay questions

a. What are the main differences between the surveys typically used in psychological research and opinion polls?
b. Under what conditions should researchers consider using non-obtrusive measures?
c. Discuss the strengths and limitations of the various sampling strategies available to researchers using surveys.
d. Is the inability to draw causal inferences an insurmountable limitation of the survey method?
e. Discuss the strengths and limitations of telephone-based survey techniques.

Exercises

a. Researchers want to find out whether men and women have the same level of colour vision. They select 100 men and 100 women by giving volunteers a test of colour vision in a shopping centre.

(Continued)

(Continued)

    i.   What sort of sampling method have the researchers used?

    ii.   Is the sample likely to be representative of the population in general?

    iii. Is the sampling method appropriate given the research question?

b. An economic psychologist, Maisie, conducts a survey into people's spending habits and financial plans. The questionnaire she designs contains the following items. What are the problems with these, and how might they be improved?

    i.   How much do you earn?

    ii.   Do you ever worry that you haven't got enough money? (tick one) yes no

    iii. Are you in a pension plan and a superannuation scheme? (tick one) yes no

    iv. Do you have an ISA? (tick one) yes no

    v.   On the scale below indicate your level of agreement with the following statement (circle one number)

        I do not always organize my finances as well as I might
        agree 1 2 3 4 5 6 7 disagree

    vi. How much do you agree with the following statement? (circle one)

        I organize my finances quiet well
        disagree completely 1 2 3 4 5 6 7 agree completely

Descriptive Statistics

Key goals for this chapter

- Outline the different forms that psychological data can take.
- Explain the different ways in which (a) a typical data point and (b) the spread of data points can be described statistically.
- Explain the difference between samples and populations.

So far in this book we have looked at a number of the processes that go on behind the scenes in psychological research. We have discussed why people conduct research, what they want to achieve when they do, and how research is designed in order to achieve particular objectives. In doing this we have tackled some of the most complex issues that a researcher can ever confront. One thing we have not done, however, is actually talk about the process of *handling and making sense of research data*. If you like, we have dealt with executive and managerial issues, but we have not actually got our hands dirty at the data coal-face. To do this we need to enter the domain of **statistics**.

Although in some fields researchers are able to keep their hands relatively clean by leaving statistical problems to other people, no research psychologist will ever be able to avoid them completely. This is because a large amount of psychological training is focused explicitly on providing psychology students with statistical skills, and an understanding of statistics is essential to the appropriate interpretation of any research finding. A research psychologist cannot get by simply with a knowledge of psychological principles for the same reason that an artist cannot get by simply with a knowledge of artistic principles. Psychologists need to know how to deal with data in their many forms in the same way that artists need to be familiar with the properties of different paints.

Two forms of statistics are essential to the appropriate handling of research data. **Descriptive statistics** enable a researcher to *describe* the properties of a particular **data set** (e.g., responses to an experiment or survey). **Inferential statistics** enable a researcher to make appropriate *inferences* from those descriptions in order to decide whether those descriptions can also be applied to a population from which the sample is drawn. We will deal with the main forms of inferential statistics that are used to examine experimental and survey data in Chapters 7, 8 and 9.

In this chapter we will look at how we can appropriately summarize the properties of a given data set using descriptive statistics. Our discussion focuses on two key properties: the description of a *typical* piece of data; and the description of the *spread* of data. However, before we can address these issues we need to discuss the different forms that the data obtained from psychological research can take.

> **data set** A specified body of numerical information obtained from a given piece of research.
>
> **descriptive statistics** Numerical statements about the properties of some data.
>
> **inferential statistics** Numerical statements that represent conclusions about populations on the basis of sample data.
>
> **statistics** Numerical statements about data from a sample, and the scientific discipline associated with making and understanding those statements.

Different forms of research data

In Chapter 3 we noted that there are three types of psychological measure: behavioural, self-report and physiological. Having decided upon which one (or which combination) of these measures to use, the actual measure employed by researchers can vary immensely. A behavioural measure could be the number of times a person has visited a doctor in the last year or the amount of money that the person spends on food. A physiological measure could be the volume of blood flow in a particular region of the brain or a person's skin conductance. A self-report measure might be a person's response to a statement on a rating scale or a stated preference for one of three candidates in an election.

Despite this vast array of possible measures, the data from any piece of psychological research always take one of four different forms. **Nominal measures** simply identify the category or class of events to which a particular response belongs. As the term suggests, they involve giving different levels of a variable different names. Nominal variables describe people and their behaviour in terms of *categories* – as male or female; young or old; depressed or non-depressed; Australian, French or American; or as occupying a particular position in a soccer team. Nominal data such as these can still be coded numerically (e.g., Australian = 1, French = 2, American = 3; goalkeeper = 1, left-back = 2, centre-back = 3; etc.), but the numbers here do not express a quantity, they simply serve as convenient tags. In this way the levels of nominal variables differ in kind or type, not in degree or amount.

Ordinal measures place responses on a single measurement continuum where different values indicate the relative magnitude (i.e., the strength or amount) of a particular response. In other words, they involve a relative *ordering* of responses. The position students come in a class exam (i.e., their rank in the class) is an ordinal variable, as is the grade they get in a course (e.g., A, B, C). Unlike nominal variables, the levels of ordinal variables differ in degree and amount, and they can be numerically coded in a way that reflects this (e.g., by giving an A grade a score of 4, a B grade a score of 3, and so on).

Ordinal measures only represent an ordering or ranking of responses, however. Nothing at all is implied about how far apart the various responses on that measure are. For example, the difference between an A grade and a B grade need not be the same as the difference between a B grade and a C grade. The same is not true of interval measures, where there is a *specific and constant quantitative relationship* between the various outcomes that are measured. In the case of interval measurement, the various scores or responses obtained correspond to an equal quantity of the measured variable (like marks on a ruler). As a result, the distance between any two points that are a given number of scale positions apart will be equivalent to the distance between any other two points the same number of scale positions apart (in the way that the amount of time or difference between 1 o'clock and 4 o'clock is the same as the difference between 8 o'clock and 11 o'clock). However, there is no true zero point and therefore we cannot compare ratios of variables. It makes little sense to say that 2 o'clock is twice as late as 1 o'clock and it is just wrong to say that 40°C is twice as hot as 20°C. This is because 0°C is not a true zero point, it is an arbitrary point chosen for convenience.

The distinguishing feature of ratio measures is that they clearly specify a zero point (such as absolute zero on the Kelvin temperature scale). Measures such as weight, height and speed are all ratio measures. They have the same properties as interval measures (so that the difference between 10 kilometres per hour and 20 kilometres per hour is the same as the difference between 40 kilometres per hour and 50 kilometres per hour), but they can be directly compared as ratios. That is, it is possible to say that 20 kilometres per hour is twice as fast as 10 kilometres per hour.

It is very common for psychology textbooks to include this system of classifying measures and this is partly because the mathematical operation one can perform on data depends on the form that those data take. In practice, however, it is often more convenient to distinguish between just two types of measure. One form (nominal) involves placing observations (e.g., scores, responses) into distinct categories that have no quantitative relationship to each other. Other measures (ordinal, interval and ratio) differentiate between observations along a numerical dimension. These non-nominal measures can take the form of either discrete variables, where responses fall into a limited number of separate categories measured in whole numbers (e.g., the number that a person circles on a rating scale), or continuous variables, where any response can be treated as if it were measured in terms of an infinite number of points on a continuum and there is no clear gap between positions on the scale (e.g., a person's weight or reaction time).

It is worth noting that the investigation of most psychological phenomena can involve either discrete or continuous measures and that the type that is employed depends upon the researcher's objectives and circumstances. For example, reaction time, intelligence and

Test Yourself 6.1**

A researcher conducts an experiment in which she assigns participants to one of two groups and exposes the two groups to different doses of a particular drug. She then gets the participants to learn a list of 20 words and 2 days later sees how many they can recall. In the experiment the dependent measure is simply the number of words recalled by each participant. What type of dependent measure is this?

    a.   Nominal.
    b.   Ordinal.
    c.   Interval.
    d.   Ratio.
    e.   None of the above.

The correct answer is (d). The number of words recalled is a ratio measure, because all the possible scores that it is possible to obtain (0, 1, 2, 3, ..., 20) are separated by equal intervals and there is also a true zero. The dependent variable could be made into a nominal measure if the participants were scored only as having good or poor memories (e.g., if they remembered 10 or more words, or less than 10 words, respectively). It could also be made into an ordinal measure if participants were simply ranked in terms of the number of words they remembered (so that the person who remembered the most words was given a ranking of 1 etc.).

personality can all be measured either along a single continuous quantitative dimension (milliseconds, IQ scores, level of extroversion) or in terms of discrete categories (such as fast or slow, intelligent or unintelligent, extroverted or introverted). Nevertheless, most of the statistical principles that we are going to discuss in the remainder of this chapter (and in the following chapters) apply to the analysis of non-categorical data where responses are *quantitatively differentiated* on either a continuous or discrete dimension. It is also fair to say that this is by far the most common form of data encountered in psychological research.

continuous variable A variable that can be treated as if there were no breaks or steps between its different levels (e.g., reaction time in milliseconds).

discrete variable A variable with clear breaks or steps between its different levels (e.g., responses on a rating scale).

interval measure A measure on which the obtained scores are numerically related to one another so that adjacent scores are separated by an equal interval, but where there is no true zero value.

nominal measure A measure reflecting distinct categories that have different names but the categories are not numerically related to one another.

ordinal measure A measure on which the obtained values reflect the ordering of responses on a continuum, but where the intervals between scores are not necessarily equal.

ratio measure A measure on which the obtained values stand in a numerical relationship to one another so that adjacent scores are separated by an equal interval and where there is a true zero value.

Describing a typical score: Measures of central tendency

To provide a concrete example around which to structure our introduction to statistics, let us go back to one of the studies we described a few chapters ago where a researcher was interested in looking at the impact of attributional style on depression. Conceivably, before the researcher examines this issue in any depth he or she might want to find out how a control group of students responds to failure in an exam. The researcher might want to do this to see whether students generally attribute their failure to internal factors (such as their lack of intelligence or motivation) or to external factors (such as bad luck or the exam conditions). To do this, the researcher might ask a number of students (say 25) to respond to the question 'How much was your failure due to things beyond your control?' by getting them to circle a number on a seven-point scale with end-points labelled 'not at all' (1) and 'completely' (7). Let us imagine that the numbers circled by the 25 participants in this study were as follows:

5, 4, 2, 6, 7, 4, 5, 3, 4, 5, 3, 5, 5, 5, 3, 4, 5, 6, 1, 2, 6, 4, 6, 7, 3

These scores constitute the data set in this study, and when presented in this untreated form they are often referred to as the **raw data**. However, it makes sense that in trying to manage these data the researcher would try to organize them in some way. With this in mind, the first obvious thing to do is to put the numbers in some sort of order (either ascending or descending) as follows:

1, 2, 2, 3, 3, 3, 3, 4, 4, 4, 4, 5, 5, 5, 5, 5, 5, 5, 6, 6, 6, 6, 7, 7

This ordering begins to tell us how the data are *distributed* across the range of possible responses.

The data could be summarized further by noting the frequency with which the different responses were made. So, in this case there is one response of '1', two of '2', four of '3', five of '4', seven of '5', four of '6' and two of '7'. For ease of presentation, this information about the **distribution** of responses could be presented in a table that would summarize the data in numerical form. In particular, a **frequency table** reporting the number of times each different response was made would take the form shown in Table 6.1.

Alternatively, the response distribution could be represented pictorially in a graph. One common way of doing this is to use a **frequency graph**, where the area of each bar or column

Table 6.1 Frequency table for attributional style study data

Response	Frequency
1	1
2	2
3	4
4	5
5	7
6	4
7	2

is proportional to the frequency of any given response (or group of responses). These are called **bar charts** for discrete variables and **histograms** for continuous variables. The bar chart for our exam data is shown in Figure 6.1.

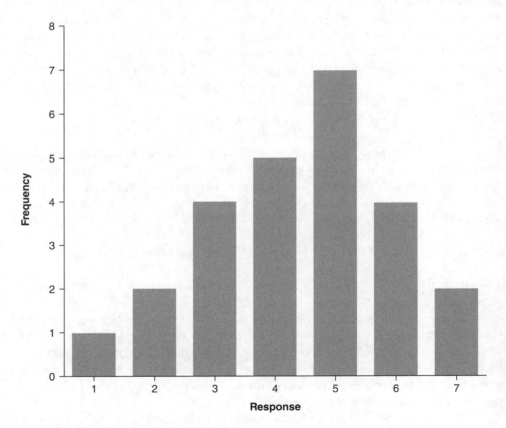

Figure 6.1 Bar chart for data in Table 6.1

All of the above methods offer very useful ways of representing *all* the data that the researcher has obtained in the study. But if researchers had to reproduce data in one of the above forms every time they wanted to communicate what they had found, this could be quite a time-consuming task. It might also be completely impractical if the data set were much larger (with many more different levels of response) or if researchers had multiple sets of data to report.

The same would be true if a friend were to ask us a question like 'What do your colleagues think about the government?'. In response we could provide a very detailed answer to the question. We could, for example, reply that three of our colleagues are enthusiastic about the government, eight are relatively neutral, four are opposed to its policies and two are vigorously opposed. However, by doing this we would risk missing the point, and it might easily detract from our friend's ability to get a clear indication of what our colleagues thought in general. Indeed, our friend might think that we were trying to be funny or being deliberately evasive.

What our friend would probably be looking for, then, is some statement of what our colleagues *typically* thought about the government. Similarly, in dealing with the above data on attributional style, the researcher may want to know what constitutes a *typical response* to failure. The descriptive statistics that provide answers to this sort of question are known collectively as **measures of central tendency**.

In everyday interaction when someone asks us to describe any typical thing, this can have three distinct meanings. A typical reaction to the government, for example, could be (a) the *average* reaction, (b) the reaction of an *average person*, or (c) the most common reaction. These three distinct meanings of typicality are also reflected in the three main descriptive statistics used to measure central tendency.

The first and most commonly used of these statistics is the **mean**. The mean is a measure of the average score. It is calculated by adding up all the different scores and dividing this total by the number of scores. So in the case of the data from the attributional style study (on p. 132), the sum of the 25 responses is 110 and the mean, or average response, is therefore 110 divided by 25. This comes to 4.40 exactly. In other words, the mean is the *arithmetic average* of a given set of numbers, whether those numbers be responses, scores or values (terms that we will use more or less interchangeably in what follows).

We should also point out in passing that when a computation does not work out to be an exact number, the number of figures reported after the decimal point depends on the amount of accuracy that is possible given the measurement taken. In this way the reported result generally depends on the number of **significant figures** that it is appropriate to report – that is, the number of digits that are accurately measured and therefore provide meaningful information.

On the basis of this principle, when a calculation produces more numbers after the decimal than are warranted, researchers usually report a value with a specified number of digits after the decimal place – the value that is closest to the one obtained. As an example, 1807 divided by 21 comes to 86.047619, but this would be written as 86.05 if the researcher had decided to report just two digits after the decimal place. This procedure is known as

rounding. If the obtained number falls exactly half-way between two such numbers the higher number is normally reported (this is known as **rounding up**). As an example, 100 divided by 32 comes to 3.125, but when reporting this figure you would round it up to 3.13. The strategy of reporting just two digits after the decimal place – 'rounding to two decimal places' – is one that is widely used by research psychologists and journals. However, it is worth noting that this can introduce error into measurement (known as **rounding error**) and so this procedure needs to be used judiciously (Bakker & Wicherts, 2011).

Something else that we need to alert you to is that as this chapter progresses it will get increasingly difficult to describe the mathematical operations we are performing by using words alone. For this reason we are going to start introducing some statistical notation. This may make you feel slightly nervous. However, the reasons for doing this are much the same as the reasons for introducing specialized terminology and jargon in previous chapters (terms such as independent variable, reactivity and between-subjects manipulation). First, statistical notation is so widely used by other researchers that if we did not introduce you to it a large amount of what other people have to say on important issues would remain completely incomprehensible. Second, it should be emphasized that although statistical notation is often difficult to master at first, once it is understood and learned it allows researchers to communicate very complex ideas succinctly and efficiently. This book would be about twice as long (and far more exhausting to read) if at every relevant point we had not used jargon but instead substituted the definition that is provided in the boxes at the end of each section. The same point is true for statistical notation.

RESEARCH BITE 6.1
The dangers of rounding

A paper by Marjan Bakker and Jelte Wicherts (2011) looked closely at the process of rounding up in psychological research. Taking a random sample of nearly 300 research articles, they found two things. First, that researchers often reported the results of rounding inaccurately. Second, that inaccuracies were not random, but tended to be in directions that were consistent with the researchers' hypotheses. They concluded that researchers need to follow professional guidelines more closely and report key results (in particular, p-values; see Chapter 8 later) to two decimal places.

Reference
Bakker, M., & Wicherts, J. M. (2011). The (mis)reporting of statistical results in psychology journals. *Behavior Research Methods*, *43*, 666–678.

So, if we wanted to represent the formula for the mean in words, we could do so as follows:

$$\text{mean score} = \frac{\text{sum of all scores}}{\text{number of scores}}$$

However, this formula could also be written using the following statistical notation:

$$\text{mean score} = \frac{\text{sum}(X)}{\text{number}}$$

If we replace the words 'mean score', 'sum' and 'number' with the symbols $\bar{X}$, $\sum$ and N we get

$$\bar{X} = \frac{\sum X}{N}$$

Each of the terms in this formula relates to the corresponding phrase in the longhand version above. More specifically, X refers to the scores on the variable we have measured (i.e., responses on the rating scale – in this case, 1, 2, 2, etc.). $\bar{X}$ (pronounced 'X-bar') refers to the mean value of that variable X. $\sum$ (the Greek letter sigma or S) means that everything that is referred to in what follows needs to be added together or summed. So $\sum X$ is shorthand for 'the sum of all the scores' (i.e., $1 + 2 + 2 + \cdots + 7$). Finally, N refers to the number of scores obtained (i.e., the sample size).

As we have suggested, however, the mean is not the only way to represent central tendency. A second way to represent a typical score in a given data set is simply to identify *the middle score* (equivalent to the score obtained by the average person). The technical term for this is the **median**. Where scores are ordered sequentially (ranked from either lowest to highest, or highest to lowest) this is the value that has an equal number of values above and below it. So, in the attributional style data (on p. 132) the median response is 5 as this has 12 responses above it and 12 below it.

In fact, in any data set where the scores are ordered sequentially, the median value can be worked out by adding 1 to the number of scores (N) and halving it (dividing ($N + 1$) by 2) and then identifying the score that falls at this point in the sequence. In the attributional data there are 25 responses, so the median is the 13th value in the sequence (because half of $(25 + 1)$ is 13). Expressed in mathematical terms, the median score in a sequence of a given number of scores (N) is the $((N + 1)/2)$th value. Note that the positioning of the brackets in this or any other formula is vital, because *we must complete all the computations inside the brackets before we do anything else*.

Returning to our discussion of how to calculate a median value, the only slight complication in the procedure outlined above arises when there is an even number of scores in

Photo 6.1 Have you ever watched the TV program 'Deal or No Deal'? If you have, you will know that the drama hinges on the contestants' decisions to accept or reject a banker's offer of money to withdraw from the game rather than continue. If they continue they win an amount of money from a range of amounts that are listed on a board (a list from which amounts are randomly removed). These decisions are based partly on whether or not the banker's offer seems fair and reasonable. However, whether or not this is the case is hard to judge (hence the show's drama). One key reason for this is that fairness can be defined in terms of either the mean amount of money the contestant expects to win or the median, and these two things are typically very different. So in this example, Aideen could expect to win £1000 if she based her decision on the median of the sums on the board, but £20,420 if she based that decision on the mean. So what should she do? In this case Aideen accepted an offer of £9000 – which suggests she (like the show's producers) had a pretty good understanding of statistics.

a data set. In this case the median is simply a score that falls exactly half-way between the *two* middle values. Let us imagine, for example, that the research into attributional style yielded only 24 responses because one of the highest responses (a '7') had not been collected. Here the median value (the $(24 + 1)/2$)th or 12.5th value) would fall between the 12th and 13th values (4 and 5, respectively) and so it would be 4.5 (even though 4.5 does not correspond to an actual or possible response).

The third and final measure of central tendency corresponds simply to the *most common value* in a particular data set. This is referred to as the **mode**. In any given set this is the response or score that occurs most frequently, so it will always correspond to the tallest column in a frequency graph. In the attributional style data, the modal response is 5, as this response was made by more participants than any other. Of course, sometimes it will happen that two or more scores are observed with equal highest frequency. In this case all modes are reported.

We can use a computer program such as IBM SPSS Statistics software (SPSS) to help us calculate these measures of central tendency. To start with, open up the application SPSS on your computer. The application will give you an option to enter new data by clicking on the button 'Type in Data', as shown in Figure 6.2. This will bring up a new window (called a data editor) into which you can type values.

Type in the data exactly as shown in Figure 6.3. Include one row for each participant with the participant number in the first column (VAR00001) and the score in the second column (VAR00002). This is a very common pattern used in data analysis in psychology and other human sciences where we have rows representing a set of scores for a participant and columns representing variables. In this case the first variable (VAR00001) is not real data, it is simply a record-keeping variable that we create for the purpose of keeping track of which participant has which score. Note too that, as with all the examples in the chapters that follow, this data file is also available in the Supplementary Online Material [Chapter6_Descriptives.sav].

When you have done that it is a very good idea to give each variable an informative name instead of the forbidding and meaningless computer names used by SPSS (if you use these SPSS names in your assignments we can pretty much guarantee that your instructors will take marks off, so it is worth getting into the habit of using meaningful names from the outset).

So let us change 'VAR00001' to 'Participant' and 'VAR00002' to 'Response'. To do this click on 'Variable View' at the bottom of the window which changes the data window so that we see

Figure 6.2

Figure 6.3

information about each variable in a row. In the first column labelled 'Name' double click on 'VAR00001' and then type in 'Participant'. Do the same for 'VAR00002' and change it to 'Response'. You can also add more detailed descriptions of your variables in the column entitled 'Label' and adjust the type of measurement in the column labelled 'Measure' (neither of these steps is essential for the analysis). For these data the variable 'Participant' is a 'Nominal' measure and the variable 'Response' is a 'Scale' measure, as in Figure 6.4.

Figure 6.4

We are now actually ready to use SPSS to calculate the measures of central tendency, but just before we do there is a critical step. We need to save the data file to make sure we do not have to do the same work all over again. Choose a helpful name (such as '2013_Exam_ Results') and save the data file somewhere you will be able to keep it safe (e.g., a personal work folder or USB drive).

When you have done that go to the 'Analyze' menu and drag down to 'Descriptive Statistics' and then select 'Frequencies'. You should see something like Figure 6.5.

Figure 6.5 Frequencies

Select 'Response' on the left and then click on the arrow in the middle to drag it to the box on the right beneath 'Variable(s)'. Now press 'Statistics' on the right and the window shown in Figure 6.6 will appear.

Figure 6.6

On the right-hand side select 'Mean', 'Median' and 'Mode'. If you then press 'Continue', SPSS will take you back to the previous screen. If you now press 'OK' SPSS will display the three measures of central tendency for that variable and these should look like Figure 6.7.

Statistics

Response

N	Valid	25
	Missing	0
Mean		4.4000
Median		5.0000
Mode		5.00

Figure 6.7

Below that SPSS also displays a useful table (Figure 6.8) that shows the breakdown of the values (so that we can see, for example, that only 8% of participants had a response of 7 from the column labelled 'Percent', and that 48% had a score of 4 or less from the column labelled 'Cumulative Percent').

Response

		Frequency	Percent	Valid Percent	Cumulative Percent
Valid	1.00	1	4.0	4.0	4.0
	2.00	2	8.0	8.0	12.0
	3.00	4	16.0	16.0	28.0
	4.00	5	20.0	20.0	48.0
	5.00	7	28.0	28.0	76.0
	6.00	4	16.0	16.0	92.0
	7.00	2	8.0	8.0	100.0
	Total	25	100.0	100.0	

Figure 6.8

bar chart A *frequency graph* for discrete variables in which the length of bars or columns indicates the frequency with which different levels of a variable have been observed.

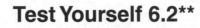

Test Yourself 6.2**

A researcher conducts a study to find out how many times people had visited a doctor in the previous year. Five people participated in the study and the numbers of visits they had made were 2, 5, 7, 4 and 2. Which of the following statements is true?

a. The mean number of visits is 2.
b. The median number of visits is 2.
c. The median number of visits is 4.
d. The modal number of visits is 4.
e. The modal number of visits is 7.

The correct answer is (c). The median number of visits (i.e., the ((5 + 1)/2)th, the third in sequence) is 4, not 2 as (b) suggests. Answer (a) is wrong because the mean number of visits is equal to the total number or sum of visits (20) divided by the number of scores (5) which also equals 4. And (d) and (e) are wrong because the mode refers to the most common number of visits, and this is 2.

distribution The spread of scores across levels of a variable.

frequency graph A graph that shows the number of times that the different levels of a variable have been observed. Among other things, this can take the form of a *bar chart* or *histogram*.

frequency table A table that reports the number of times that the different levels of a variable have been observed.

histogram A *frequency graph* for continuous variables in which the area of bars or columns is proportional to the frequency with which different levels of a variable have been observed.

mean The average of a set of scores ($\bar{X}$). It is equal to the total of all the scores ($\sum X$) divided by the number of scores (N).

measures of central tendency Statistics that describe a typical score.

median The middle score of a set of scores. It is equal to the $((N + 1)/2)$th value, where N is the number of scores in the data set.

mode The most commonly occurring score in a data set.

N Statistical notation for the number of scores obtained on a given measure and also the total number of respondents to a measure (i.e., the sample size).

raw data Data that have not been summarized or transformed in any way.

rounding (up) The procedure for reducing the number of digits reported after a decimal point where a calculation produces more digits than necessary. Rounding up involves increasing the last reported digit by 1 when the first deleted digit is greater than or equal to 5 (e.g., so that 3.665 becomes 3.67).

rounding error The inaccuracy that is introduced through the process of *rounding*. This can be considered to be a form of measurement error.

$\sum$ **(sigma)** Statistical notation indicating summation (i.e., 'the sum of …').

$\sum$**X (sigma X)** Statistical notation for the sum of all the scores of a given variable (X).

significant figures The number of digits that are accurately measured and that are considered to convey meaningful information about a numerical value.

X Statistical notation for (a) the scores on a given variable and (b) the variable itself.

$\bar{X}$ **(X-bar)** Statistical notation for the mean of X. The mean of Y would be $\bar{Y}$.

The relationship between measures of central tendency and a response distribution

It is clear from our calculations of the mean, median and mode for the attributional style data that these three statistics can differ. You may recall that the mean was 4.40, but the median and mode were both 5.00. For this reason, one question that you may have asked yourself is which measure we should use. For many statistical purposes, the mean is the preferred measure of central tendency. Consequently, it is perhaps more appropriate to ask under which circumstances we should not use the mean as a measure of central tendency.

To start with, we can see that the mean is of no use when we are dealing with nominal data. For example, there is no way that we can meaningfully say what a mean surname or town is. The mean can also be of dubious value for ordinal data, like the mean level of education in a country (primary, secondary or tertiary) or people's ranking on an aptitude test. If we have an interval or ratio scale, however, we can set about answering this question by looking at how measures of central tendency vary depending on the shape of a response distribution. The important point is that this variation is *systematic*, so that if we know how a given set of scores is distributed we will also know which of the three measures will have the highest value without having to work them all out.

The first thing we need to do, then, is to describe the different shapes that a set of scores (or what we can call a response distribution) can have. If we return to consider the data presented in Figure 6.1, you will recall that the columns of the bar chart were based on the *actual* responses of our experimental sample of 25 participants.

Now just by looking at this distribution of responses we can see that it is off-centre or **skewed**. In fact it is clear (both from this figure and our previous calculations) that the mode is displaced to the right, or towards more positive responses. When this is the case a distribution is said to be **negatively skewed**. This is because the direction of skew (positive or negative) refers to the position of the tail of the distribution – its longer end.

At first this description will probably strike you as being a bit odd. It seems counter-intuitive because you might assume that the direction of skew would refer to the position of the distribution's peak (i.e., its mode) rather than its tail. However, the terminology reflects the fact that *when a distribution is skewed the mean often provides an ambiguous measure of central tendency*. More specifically, when the peak of a distribution is displaced towards higher values (as it is in this case), the mean will tend to be an unduly *negative* measure of central tendency. By the same token, when the peak of a distribution is displaced towards lower values, the mean will tend to be an unduly *positive* measure of central tendency, and so in this case the distribution will be described as **positively skewed**.

When a distribution is skewed the mean is an ambiguous measure of central tendency as it will tend to differ (sometimes quite considerably) from the mode and from the median. This is true, for example, if a researcher wants to make a statement about typical salaries or personal wealth in a given country. The distributions of wealth and wages are both positively skewed, because in all countries a very small proportion of people earn exceedingly large amounts of money. Accordingly, mean wage and mean salary levels are often misleading statistics because they tend to exaggerate wealth and earnings (which is one reason why these statistics are normally preferred by governments and employer groups).

By the same token, people's self-evaluations tend to be negatively skewed as most people tend to have quite a high opinion of themselves (e.g., Svenson, 1981). We chose to reflect this in the data in our attributional style example where the participants prefer not to blame themselves for their failure. In such a case the mean will tend to underestimate people's sense of their self-worth and the extent to which they deflect blame away from themselves.

In cases of severe skewness the median will usually be a more appropriate measure of central tendency than the mean because it will tend to fall *between* the mean and the mode (because skewness is all about the mean and mode being different from each other). The median is also the best measure of central tendency if we do not know the shape of a distribution. However, the mean, median and mode will be identical when the distribution of data is symmetrical (providing there is only one mode), and of the three the mean is usually the preferred measure.

In order to clarify the above points, the three types of distribution we have discussed are represented in Figure 6.9. This also indicates the relative position of the mean, median and mode for each distribution.

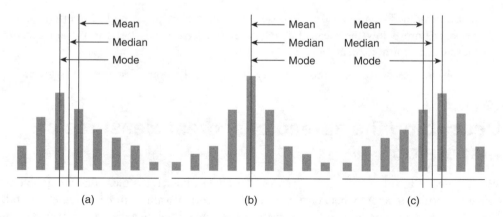

Figure 6.9 Relative position of mean, median and mode in (a) positively skewed distribution; (b) symmetrical (non-skewed) distribution; (c) negatively skewed distribution

Test Yourself 6.3*

Which of the following statements is most likely to be true if the distribution of a variable is severely skewed?

a. The mean will be the best measure of central tendency.
b. The median will be as misleading as the mean.
c. The mode will no longer be the most common response.
d. The median will be the best measure of central tendency.
e. The mode will be the best measure of central tendency.

The correct answer is (d). If the distribution of some data is severely skewed both the mean and the mode can be misleading statistics. If a distribution is positively skewed (so that scores tend to be relatively negative) the mean will tend to be too positive a measure of central tendency and the mode will be too negative. On the other hand, if a distribution is negatively skewed (so that scores tend to be relatively positive) the mean will tend to be too negative a measure of central tendency and the mode will be too positive. Thus statements (a), (b) and (e) are incorrect. As (d) suggests, in both cases the median will fall between these values and so will often be a more appropriate measure. Answer (c) is incorrect because, regardless of skew, the mode is always the most common score or response.

negative skew The shape of a response distribution in which a high proportion of responses are above the mean. In such cases the mean tends to be too negative a measure of central tendency.

positive skew The shape of a response distribution in which a high proportion of responses are below the mean. In such cases the mean tends to be too positive a measure of central tendency.

skewness The degree of non-symmetry in the distribution of scores on a given variable.

Describing the spread of scores: Measures of dispersion

When we want to summarize the properties of a given data set it is clear that being able to convey information about what constitutes a typical score or value will be extremely useful. However, in many ways it is only half the story. Knowing the average height of people in a basketball team will be useful, but we would consider a team in which every player was almost exactly the same height to be very different from one in which some players were extremely tall and others extremely short. Similarly, we would consider the psychological health of people in two cities to be very different if the people in one city were all moderately happy, while in the other city a large proportion were extremely happy but the remainder were clinically depressed.

The point here is that knowledge about the *distribution of data around a typical value* can be every bit as important as knowledge of that value itself. For a start, if the data are tightly clustered around a central value this will make it much easier to make a reasonably accurate prediction about what any one value is likely to be, compared with a situation where the data are more scattered. For this reason researchers generally use *two* summary statistics to characterize a given data set: a measure of central tendency and a measure of *dispersion*. However, researchers are sometimes guilty of neglecting dispersion and concentrating too much on central tendency.

One of the most obvious statistics that could be used to measure dispersion is the **range** of scores contained in a data set. This is simply the difference between the maximum and minimum scores in any given case. So, for our attributional style data (see p. 132) the range is 6.00 as this is the difference between the highest and lowest observed responses (7 and 1, respectively).

However, it is not hard to see that range could be an extremely misleading statistic in certain circumstances. For example, imagine we measured the height of people who lived in two towns (Blacktown and Greytown), and found that 50 people in Blacktown were 1.20 metres tall and 50 were 1.80 metres tall, but that in Greytown one person was 1.20 metres tall, one was 1.80 metres tall and the other 98 were 1.50 metres tall (Figure 6.10). The range and mean are the same in both towns (i.e., range = 0.60, $M = 1.5$) but, as we can see by comparing the frequency graphs, the height of Blacktown residents is generally quite different from the mean, while the height of Greytown residents is generally quite similar to the mean. If we want to convey more information about important differences of this type, we need to use a

Figure 6.10 Heights of (a) Blacktown residents and (b) Greytown residents

more sophisticated measure of dispersion, which would allow us to say how certain we were that a typical score describes the sample.

One of the first things that we should note here is that scores that lie a long way from the typical value for a distribution will contribute a great deal to the dispersion of a distribution. Such scores are called **outliers** and they can have a profound – sometimes unduly profound – impact. We can see this from the above example for the distribution of Greytown residents' heights. Here, if we were to remove the outliers from the distribution (the person who is 1.2 m tall and the one who is 1.8 m tall) there would actually be no dispersion at all. In order to reduce spurious dispersion, researchers often take steps to eliminate outliers. This can be done either through **transformation** of the entire data set (e.g., taking the square root of every score) or by dealing with each outlier individually (e.g., by deleting or recoding them; see Tabachnick & Fidell, 2012). The decisions as to what to do about outliers are often difficult, but before we can make those decisions we need to find out whether they are present.

In order to quantify dispersion more precisely, the first thing that we could do is measure *the average distance of all the scores from the mean score*. However, the average difference between any set of scores is always going to be equal to zero (because the negative differences below the mean exactly cancel out the positive differences above the mean).

One of the best ways to get round the problem caused by minus signs is to *square* all the deviations from the mean – in other words, to multiply each deviation by itself. This gets rid of negative values because a negative number multiplied by a negative number always results in a positive number. So, for example, $-3.48 \times -3.48 = 12.11$.

The **variance** of a given variable incorporates this procedure of squaring deviations from the mean rather than computing **absolute differences**. This statistic is therefore calculated by summing together the squared deviations of each score from the mean and dividing this sum by the number of scores. Variance, then, is the *average squared deviation from the mean*.

The procedure for calculating the variance of any variable (X) is summarized in the following formula:

$$\mathrm{Var}(X) = \frac{\sum (X - \bar{X})^2}{N}$$

What the formula essentially says, then, is that the variance of any variable (X) is equal to the sum of the squared differences between each score and the mean, divided by the total number of scores (though in practice, as we will see later, we need to use the number of scores minus one, or $N - 1$, to get a more accurate, or unbiased, estimate).

To calculate variance we can put all the values (1, 2, 2, 3, etc.) in one column (under the heading X), put the mean in a column to the right of them (under the heading $\bar{X}$), then subtract the numbers in the left column from those in the right column and put the resulting values in a third column (under the heading $X - \bar{X}$). Finally, in a fourth column (under the heading $(X - \bar{X})^2$)

Figure 6.11

we can square each of the values in the third column (i.e., multiply them by themselves). Having done all this, the values in this fourth column can then be added together and divided by the number of rows (25) to provide the variance.

We can use SPSS to calculate variance using the 'Frequencies' command (Figure 6.11) and selecting 'Variance' from the 'Dispersion' statistics on the lower left side (and, at the same time, if we wanted, we could also request statistics which assess skewness and **kurtosis** – the degree to which a distribution is peaked – by clicking on these boxes from the 'Distribution' statistics on the lower right side).

When we do, we get the output in Figure 6.12, telling us that variance (calculated using $N - 1$ as the divisor) is 2.417.

Statistics

Response

N	Valid	25
	Missing	0
Variance		2.417

Figure 6.12

The variance is a very commonly used measure of dispersion. Like the mean, its primary advantage over alternative measures is that it is useful when working with inferential statistics.

Although we have noted some of the advantages of variance as a measure of dispersion, this statistic in fact has one drawback. This arises from the fact that its calculation is based on squaring the difference between individual scores and the mean. Because of this, the variance of any variable (X) is represented in *squared units* of X (i.e., X^2). If we wanted to know the dispersion of the height of people in a basketball team, calculating the variance would therefore give us that measure in terms of centimetres squared (cm^2) rather than just centimetres. However, centimetres squared is actually a measure of *area* rather than *height*, so it does not give us exactly what we are looking for.

The way that we can get around this problem is to compute the square root of the variance. Like the mean deviate, this statistic is measured in the same units as the variable in which we are interested and we can refer to it as the *root mean square deviate*. This statistic has everything we are looking for in a measure of dispersion. Accordingly, it is the statistician's and the research psychologist's measure of choice. It is called the **standard deviation** (or **SD**) and it can be selected from SPSS in the same way as variance (by selecting 'Std. Deviation' in the box above 'Variance').

In the case of our attributional style data, the standard deviation of responses is simply equal to the square root of the variance (2.417) which is 1.555. The only difference between the formula for standard deviation and the one for variance is that for standard deviation the whole variance formula is qualified by a square root sign ($\sqrt{\ }$) as follows:

$$SD(X) = \sqrt{\frac{\sum(X - \bar{X})^2}{N}}$$

Test Yourself 6.4**

If X is a variable, which of the following is *not* measured in the same units as X?

a. The mean of X.
b. The range of X.
c. The standard deviation of X.
d. The variance of X.
e. The difference between minimum and maximum values of X.

The correct answer is (d). Variance is measured in units of X^2 as it is the average *squared* difference between a set of scores and the mean of those scores. Other measures of dispersion (range (b), the difference between minimum and maximum values of X, (e) and standard deviation (c)) as well as all measures of central tendency (including the mean ((a)) are measured in units of X.

absolute difference The unsigned difference between two scores. It is the score that is obtained if the smaller of two values is subtracted from the larger value (so that no negative scores are produced).

kurtosis A measure of the degree to which a given distribution is peaked. Measures of kurtosis indicate departure from the smooth peak associated with a standard normal distribution.

outliers Scores that are very different from the typical value for a distribution. Because they are very different from the central tendency of a distribution they contribute a great deal to the amount of dispersion in the distribution.

range The difference between the maximum and minimum scores of a given variable.

standard deviation (*SD*) The square root of variance. It is expressed in the same units of measurement as the variable.

transformation A systematic arithmetic change to a variable that alters its distribution (e.g., the process of taking the square root of each score in a sample).

variance The average squared difference between a set of scores and the mean of those scores.

Observed distributions and theoretical distributions: The difference between samples and populations

Up to this point we have been talking about statistics for samples. These relate to observations or measurements of things that have taken place at particular times in particular places. Although these observations are vital, scientists are often more interested in things *in general* than they are in just the observed details of the sample. This is true for two reasons that relate to the issues we discussed in Chapters 2, 3 and 4. First, the observations we make are more interesting if they generalize to a population – that is, if we are confident of their external validity. But perhaps even more fundamentally, knowing something about things in general enables us to say something about the particular sample. For example, knowing about things in general allows us to say whether our observations are unusual and interesting.

Working with statistics is thus a two-way process because we are trying to do two different things. We are trying to say something about things in general (the population) on the basis of the sample, and we are trying to say something about the sample based on what we know about things in general. We will discuss how we do these two things more in the next chapter. For present purposes we need only accept that we need to be able to describe things in general, as well as particular samples.

Even if you have never studied statistics before you already know quite a bit about the difference between the distribution of things in general and particular observations. We can illustrate this with the example of rolling a fair six-faced die. You know that if you were to roll a die like this many times then you would tend to get approximately equal proportions of 1s, 2s, 3s, 4s, 5s and 6s. More specifically, about one-sixth of your throws would be 1s, one-sixth would be 2s, and so on.

You also know that you would not always get exactly equal proportions. If you roll a die 12 times you are unlikely to get two of each number. Think, for example, of the times that you have waited for what seems like hours before throwing a 6 to get started in a board game. This difference between what we expect and what we find in any given case is the difference between **observed** and **theoretical distributions**.

The problem is that we only very rarely measure the entire population because to do so would take too much time and effort. The scientific solution to this problem is to theorize. That is, if we do not know what the characteristics of the population are and we are unable to obtain these characteristics empirically (i.e., through observation or measurement), what we have to do is to estimate these characteristics on the basis of a set of plausible and public assumptions. We assume that if certain conditions hold then the population will be expected to have particular properties. In this way we create a theoretical distribution of the population to go along with the empirically observed distribution of the sample. When we do this we find that we can use concepts that describe our observed distributions (e.g., central tendency, dispersion and skewness) to describe the likely shape of the theoretical population distribution. However, we also find that we need to develop some new terms and concepts.

The first of these terms and concepts is **expected frequency**. We discussed what a frequency is when we talked about frequency graphs earlier in this chapter. If we assume that any sample is drawn randomly from a given population then we would *expect* the *frequency* of responses in the sample to match the proportions of those responses in the population. In our die-rolling example we would expect the distribution of a sample of 12 throws to be similar to the distribution of all throws that have ever been made. For

Photos 6.2 and 6.3 Probability is an important part of life's richness – and a constant focus for human fascination. Understanding how it works, and how to work with it, is central to most sciences. Certainly, this is an important part of training in psychological science, and it is a very valuable part of a psychology student's developing skill set. For example, this fascination is part of the allure of both the stock market and the slot machine.

example, about one-sixth of our throws should be 6s and about one-sixth of all the die rolls ever made should have been 6s. In our sample of 12 rolls the expected frequency of 6s is therefore 2 (i.e., 1/6 × 12).

An expected frequency such as this is directly related to the concept of **probability**. Probability refers to the likelihood of events under certain conditions (e.g., the likelihood of throwing a 6 under conditions where a die is thrown once and that die is unbiased and has six sides). As we have seen, if we know what the probability of an event is we can convert this into an expected frequency by multiplying the probability by the sample size. On the other hand, if we know what the expected frequency of an event is we can convert this into a probability by dividing the expected frequency by the sample size, and thereby generate a number between 0 and 1.

So, returning to our experiment on attributional style, if the probability of a response of '5' on a rating scale were .4, this would mean that in a sample of 25 people we would have an expected frequency of 10 such responses (i.e., 25 × .4) and in a sample of 40 people an expected frequency of 16 (i.e., 40 × .4). In this case, though, you may be wondering exactly how we originally identify either probabilities or expected frequencies. In the die-rolling example it is relatively easy to see that the probability of throwing a 6 is 1/6 (or .167), but it is not so obvious how we could generate the same sort of figure for psychological data. We deal with the answer to this question in Chapter 7 when we discuss the concept of the statistical model.

All that we need to know for the present is that it is often very useful to estimate the expected frequencies of the various outcomes from some research – that is, to develop an estimated frequency distribution. This distribution represents estimations about the population of all the similar people that might have been included in any piece of research with a given sample size. In contrast to frequency distributions obtained from actual data (which are presented in frequency graphs), this distribution is typically represented as the area under a curve. This in effect represents the outline of a fine-grained histogram. Returning to the attributional style data, if we assume (a) that our responses are in fact drawn from a continuous dimension so that fractional scores (e.g., 1.1, 1.2, 1.3, etc.) are included within each category (e.g., '1') and (b) that the population's responses mirrored those of our sample (a big assumption that may in fact be unjustified), then the estimated frequency distribution of the population – known as the *population distribution* – would be represented by the area under the curve in Figure 6.13.

As well as being able to estimate how a variable is likely to be distributed in a population, researchers often need to be able to estimate the central tendency and dispersion of that variable. Usually they want to estimate its mean and standard deviation. Such characteristics are referred to as **population parameters** rather than population statistics. To distinguish between sample statistics and population parameters, the latter are usually identified by Greek letters. So we use the symbol SD or s_x to identify the *sample* standard deviation, but the Greek letter σ (sigma) for the *population* standard deviation. Similarly, we use the symbol $\bar{X}$ for the *sample* mean but the Greek letter μ (mu) for the *population* mean.

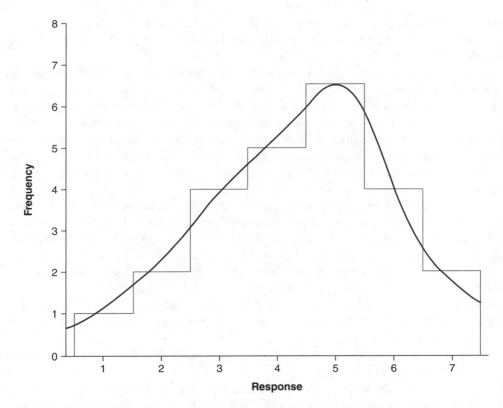

Figure 6.13   Frequency and population distributions for the attributional style study

If we do not know what the population mean is (and we usually do not), the best estimate of it is the sample mean. Similarly, if we do not know what the population standard deviation is, then the best estimate we have available is the sample standard deviation. So, if we have sampled randomly from the population (then for a reasonably large sample size for reasons that we will discuss in Chapter 7), the mean and standard deviation of our sample data will provide a reasonable estimate of the population mean and standard deviation.

However, there is one complication with the formula we gave for the standard deviation above as a means of estimating the population standard deviation. This is that the sample standard deviation is a *biased* estimate of the population standard deviation. In fact it can be shown that the sample standard deviation is an *underestimate* of the population standard deviation. In other words, the sample standard deviation tends to be smaller than the population standard deviation. To correct for this, we need to make a slight adjustment to the statistic. We do this by dividing the numerator (i.e., the top half) of the equation by $N - 1$ rather than N.

Having made this correction, the formula for population standard deviation can therefore be written as follows:

$$s_X = \sqrt{\frac{\sum(X - \bar{X})^2}{N-1}}$$

You will notice that the only difference between this equation and the one for the sample standard deviation is that there is an $N-1$ term on the bottom line of the equation (the denominator) rather than an N.

Calculating the values in this way will tend to give an unbiased estimate of the population standard deviation, providing that sampling is random. Note that whenever we refer to or need to calculate standard deviation in the remainder of this book, this is the formula we will apply.

We now have some useful tools for describing the shape and parameters of theoretical distributions. We can use these concepts of expected frequency and population mean and standard deviation to describe the shapes of such theoretical distributions. By knowing the shapes of these distributions we can examine the observed data from a sample and compare them with what they should look like if the sample is drawn from a specific population.

To illustrate how this process works we can think back to the example where we throw a die many times and record the number. The theoretical distribution for this case is called a **uniform** or **flat-rectangular distribution**. For such a distribution every outcome has an equal probability of one-sixth or .167 (see Figure 6.14).

Imagine now that we decide to toss two dice and add the scores together. Instead of having six possibilities we now have 11 possibilities. What is more, these possibilities are not equally likely. In fact you have a much better chance of getting a combined score of 7 (1 chance in 6) than a combined score of 12 (1 chance in 36). This is shown in Figure 6.15.

What happens as we add more and more dice to the theoretical distribution is that we start to get a particular form of bell-shaped curve. This curve is almost certainly the most useful and important of all the distributions observed in psychological research and is known as the **normal distribution**. The normal distribution is reasonably common in psychological data. It is observed, for example, in the distribution of such things as people's IQ scores, their height and pulse rate. The distribution is symmetrical about its mean, so its mean, median and mode are all equal (see Figure 6.16).

The question you are probably asking yourself here is why this distribution is so common. Why do so many theoretical distributions of variables follow a bell-shaped curve? There are at least three answers to this. The first can be seen in our dice example. Most things in life are not decided from a few discrete alternatives such as the faces of a die. Instead they are based on a complex sum of lots of different factors. Most of us do not lead our lives by tossing coins or rolling dice. Instead most of our decisions and actions are determined by the

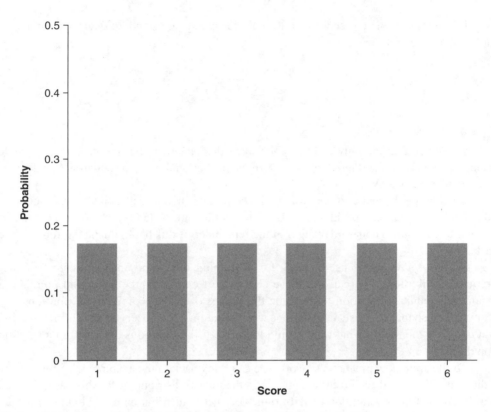

Figure 6.14   Theoretical distribution for the score from a single die

interaction of many different factors, each one of which might be reduced to a simpler set of choices. Adding all of these complex events together will tend to produce a range of events that vary in their likelihood, so that extreme occurrences that rely on the conjunction of many specific events will be very unlikely indeed.

In the case of rolling two dice and adding the scores together, a 12 can only be obtained by rolling a 6 on the first die (die A) *and* a 6 on the second die (die B). However, a 7 can be obtained by rolling any one of six different combinations: (die A = 1, die B = 6); (2, 5); (3, 4); (4, 3); (5, 2); (6, 1). Similarly, people may only grow up to become extremely tall if they have an unusual genetic make-up *and* their mothers have good health during pregnancy and they have good nutrition and health during childhood. If height does depend on this simple model (the full explanation is of course much more complex than this) then it will be approximately normally distributed because relatively few people will meet *all* these conditions. To think of something more psychological in nature, extreme behaviours such as reacting violently to somebody might also be determined by a complex interaction of different factors. Perhaps people only react violently when they are very angry *and* they do not fear retaliation *and* they

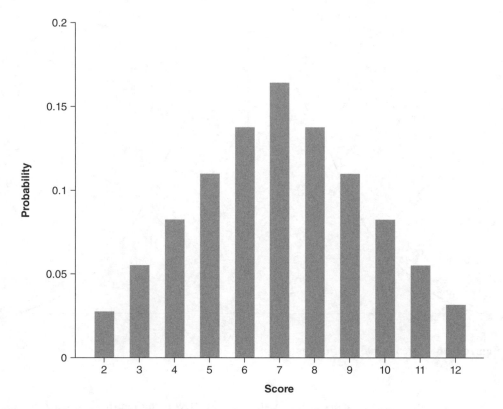

Figure 6.15   Theoretical distribution for the score from two dice

have previously been exposed to violent role models. If violent behaviour follows this very simple model then there is quite a good chance that it too will be normally distributed. This is the case with many variables that relate to individual differences (such as intelligence and some personality traits).

The second, related, answer to the question of why so many phenomena are normally distributed is that most measurements in psychology are associated with a degree of uncertainty. That is, most measurements actually involve **measurement error**. These measurement errors can be seen as deviations from the true value that would have been obtained if we could have measured a value with perfect accuracy. These deviations from the true score can arise for a large number of reasons – including the fact that data sometimes get corrupted or lost, creating a problem of **missing data**. In this, though, deviations from accurate measurement are likely to reflect complex processes like those that we have discussed in the previous paragraph. Accordingly, generally speaking, they should be normally distributed. And if the deviations are normally distributed then there is a good chance that the measurements themselves will be normally distributed.

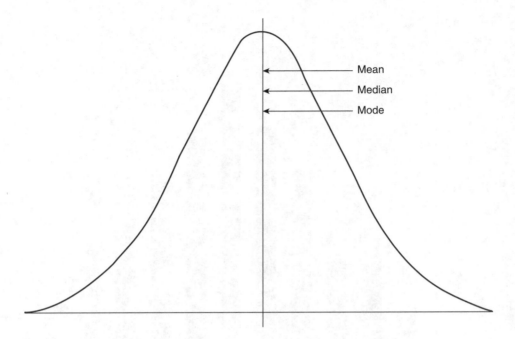

Figure 6.16   The normal distribution

These measurement errors occur in all sciences. If you studied the published height of the tallest mountain in the world (Mount Everest) over the last 100 years you would find that the height has changed as measuring techniques have changed. We would also expect that if a team of researchers set out to measure the height of Mount Everest on a number of different occasions using an unbiased measuring technique they would produce a number of different results and that these would be normally distributed about the true height of the mountain. Similarly, if psychologists were to measure a person's IQ using many different unbiased measuring techniques they would expect that the measurements would be normally distributed about the true IQ score. This variation between different tests of the same thing is quite distinct from variation between different people's IQs (individual differences) and is also distinct from variation within the same person's IQ (e.g., variation due to maturation). In fact, though, it is often hard to distinguish between these things empirically. For this reason, individual differences, measurement error and maturation get rolled into one measure of dispersion.

One important way in which error is introduced into measurement is via **sampling error**. Let us imagine that statisticians want to find out what the level of unemployment in a country is (as they regularly do in most developed countries). They could survey the entire population of that country and find out whether each person is employed or not. However,

RESEARCH BITE 6.2
What to do with missing data

Unsurprisingly, this book focuses on analysing data that are available to analyse. However, researchers often need to analyse data that are not available – because they are missing. For example, if you had to say what the mean age of people in a class of 20 people was, how would you do this if you only had data from 19 (e.g., because someone was away when data were collected, or refused to reveal their age)? This is a complex issue about which there is considerable debate. As John Graham (2009) explains, much depends on which data are missing, how much is missing, and why. On the basis of such information, he notes that modern statistical techniques offer ways for generating 'best estimates' of missing data that make this less of a problem than it might first appear.

Reference
Graham, J. W. (2009). Missing data analysis: Making it work in the real world. *Annual Review of Psychology*, *60*, 549–576.

statisticians find this takes too long and costs too much. So instead what they do is take a representative random sample of the population and measure the level of unemployment in that sample. When you hear the unemployment rate reported in the news this is the figure that is actually being used. But of course, even if the sampling is done perfectly we can never be sure that the sample corresponds to the population exactly – and it rarely will. However, if the sample is representative and randomly selected, the differences between the sample and the population will be due to complex processes that are normally distributed around the true value.

The third reason why so many variables are normally distributed is perhaps more surprising. Normal distributions are so mathematically useful that, even if variables are not actually normally distributed to begin with, it is worth using mathematical procedures to make them normal. This is something that psychologists often do.

We will consider issues to do with population parameters and normal distributions in a lot more detail in Chapter 7. For now, though, we will only note that if we are interested in a variable (e.g., the responses of our control sample on the attributional style response scale) and we know (a) the *mean* of that variable together with (b) its *standard deviation*, and we also know (c) that that variable is *normally distributed*, then armed with this knowledge we can make a number of incredibly powerful statements about the behaviour of that variable in

Test Yourself 6.5**

If scores on a variable are normally distributed, which of the following statements is *false*?

a. All scores on the variable will have been observed with equal frequency.
b. The distribution of scores is symmetrical about the mean.
c. Similar distributions are commonly observed in data obtained from psychological research.
d. There will be relatively few extreme scores.
e. The mean, median and modal scores will be equal.

The correct answer is (a). When every score on a variable is observed with equal frequency, the distribution of scores on that variable will be uniform (i.e., flat and rectangular), not bell shaped. As statement (d) suggests, when a variable is normally distributed, the more extreme a score is, the less likely it is to be observed. Statements (b) and (e) are true because a normally distributed variable is symmetrical about its mean, and its mean, median and mode are equal. As (c) suggests, the normal distribution is commonly observed in data obtained from psychological research. In part, this is because many psychological variables are normally distributed (e.g., IQ scores, personality variables).

the population. For example, we can confidently make statements about (a) the proportion of scores on that variable that will fall within a given range (e.g., above a certain value), (b) how unusual any given observation is, and (c) the difference between this sample and others with which we want to compare it and for which similar information is available. It should be clear from the material we have covered in previous chapters that these are precisely the sorts of thing that research psychologists want to know.

expected frequency Formally, the *probability* of some event multiplied by the sample size. That is, it is the likely total number of events of a particular type resulting from a random process (e.g., drawing a random sample of a given size from the population). For example, the expected frequency of heads when you toss an unbiased coin 10 times is 5 (i.e., 0.5×10).

flat-rectangular distribution Another name for a *uniform distribution*.

measurement error Deviations between a true score and an observation produced by inaccuracies in measurement. This can arise from inaccuracies in the measurement instrument or from other sources.

missing data Data that are relevant to a particular piece of research and that the researcher intended to include in his or her analysis but which (for a range of possible reasons) are not available for analysis.

normal distribution The symmetrical spread of scores that is obtained when scores on a variable are randomly distributed around a mean in a bell-shaped curve. The term is applied to *observed* and *theoretical* distributions.

observed distribution A distribution obtained by empirically observing a set of scores (a sample). It is assumed that the *observed distribution* is drawn from a theoretical distribution of scores in a population.

population parameter Some characteristic of the population that is estimated on the basis of data from a sample.

probability (*p*) The likelihood of an event. Probabilities are expressed as a number between 0 and 1, where 0 indicates that an event definitely will not occur and 1 indicates that an event definitely will occur. The sum of all probabilities (corresponding to all possible events) equals 1, and any given probability corresponds to a fraction of this total. Under certain circumstances, probability can be thought of as the sample size divided by the *expected frequency*.

sampling error Differences between a sample and the population. It is therefore error associated with estimating the true value of some characteristic of a population.

theoretical distribution An expected or hypothesized distribution of what scores should be like in general. Population distributions are usually theoretical distributions (except where every member of the population has been measured with perfect accuracy).

uniform distribution A distribution where there is an equal frequency (or equal expected frequency) of each possible event. Also known as a *flat-rectangular distribution*.

CHECKLIST
Revisiting the key goals for this chapter

- ☐ I understand the different forms that psychological data can take.
- ☐ I understand the different ways in which (a) a typical data point and (b) the spread of data points can be described statistically.
- ☐ I understand the difference between samples and populations.

Further reading

A number of excellent texts deal with the consequences of not mastering the concepts in this chapter – pointing, in particular, to the ways in which statistics can be misused and misinterpreted. The short books by Huff (1993) and Paulos (1990) are particularly good examples of this genre and they are both well worth reading.

Huff, D. (1993). *How to lie with statistics*. New York: Norton.
Paulos, J. A. (1990). *Innumeracy: Mathematical illiteracy and its consequences*. New York: Vintage Books.

Descriptive statistics: A checklist for research evaluation and improvement

Table 6.2

Potential problem	Question to ask	Potential improvement
Inappropriate measurement of central tendency	Have the researchers used an appropriate measure of central tendency (in particular, is the use of the mean appropriate)?	Because the mean is often used as a default measure of central tendency, it can be useful to consider whether use of this measure is unjustified or misleading. This is most likely to be the case if the distribution is highly skewed, in which case you should consider the implications of reporting an alternative measure (usually the median).
Inappropriate measurement of dispersion	Have the researchers used an appropriate measure of dispersion (in particular, is the use of standard deviation appropriate)?	Because standard deviation is often used as a default measure of dispersion, it can be useful to consider whether using this measure is unjustified or misleading. This is most likely to be the case if a data set includes outliers (a problem that can also contaminate other measures).
Outliers	Have the researchers looked for the presence of outliers?	Examine the distribution to see if it contains outliers. If it does, see if this can be corrected by an appropriate statistical transformation of the data. If this is not possible, consider (a) removing individual outliers or (b) recoding them to the same value as the nearest non-outlier. Ensure you report any transformations that you make.

Test Yourself 6.6*

Which of the following is not a measure of central tendency?

a. The mean of a distribution.
b. The mean squared deviation of some data.
c. The modal value of a set of values.
d. The median response on a scale.
e. An average score.

Test Yourself 6.7***

The shaded bars in the histogram in Figure 6.17 represent the times (rounded to the nearest 10 milliseconds) that 50 people take to react to a loud noise. Which of the following statements is *not* true?

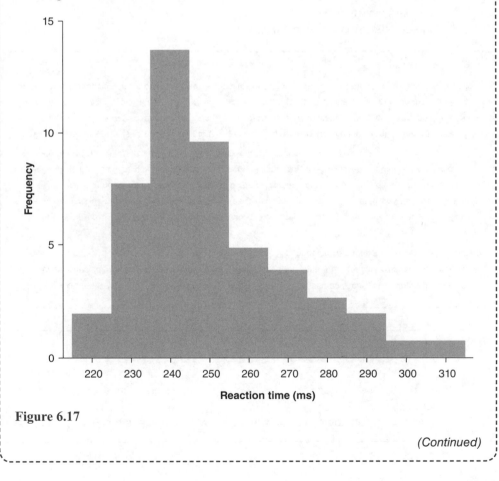

Figure 6.17

(Continued)

(Continued)

a. The distribution of reaction times is negatively skewed.
b. The modal reaction time is 240 ms.
c. The median reaction time is greater than 240 ms.
d. The mean reaction time will be greater than the modal reaction time.
e. The mean is an ambiguous measure of central tendency.

Test Yourself 6.8*

'Root mean squared deviate' could be used as another name for which measure of dispersion?

a. Range.
b. Skewness
c. Variance.
d. Standard deviation.
e. Squared deviation from the root.

The correct answer to 6.6 is (b). The mean, median and mode are all measures of central tendency (i.e., attempts to describe a typical value), and average is just another word for central tendency. However, mean squared deviation is a measure of dispersion (it is the average absolute difference between a set of scores and the mean of those scores) and is another name for variance.

The correct answer to 6.7 is (a). This distribution is actually positively skewed. Because of this the mean will tend to be an ambiguous measure of central tendency (as (e) suggests). Both the median and the mean will also be greater than the mode (which, as (a) suggests, is the most common reaction time of 240 ms). Note that by understanding the relationship between measures of central tendency and a response distribution we can deduce that statements (c) and (d) are correct without having to compute these measures.

The correct answer to 6.8 is (d). The answer to this question is given away by the term 'root'. Standard deviation is the square root of the variance, and is the mean squared deviation from the mean (the average squared difference between a set of scores and the mean of those scores). Range is just the difference between the highest and lowest scores. Skewness is a measure of the shape of the distribution. There is no such term as squared deviation from the root.

Discussion/essay questions

a. What are the advantages and disadvantages of different measures of central tendency?
b. What are the advantages and disadvantages of different measures of dispersion?

c. Which descriptive statistics would you use to summarize information about wage levels in different countries? Discuss the reasons for your answer.

d. Why does the normal distribution play such an important role in psychological research?

Exercises

a. Draw a frequency graph for each of the following data sets (from scores on a response scale):

  i. 7, 6, 5, 1, 5, 5, 6, 4, 7, 5, 3, 2, 4, 6, 4
  ii. 1, 2, 4, 3, 5, 3, 5, 3, 2, 3, 6, 7, 3, 4, 2, 2, 1, 2, 4, 2

b. Are these distributions skewed at all? If so, in what direction?

c. Work out the mean, median and mode for each of the above data sets.

d. Work out the range, mean deviation, variance and standard deviation(s) for each of the above data sets.

e. One of the factors that often leads to distributions that would otherwise be normal being skewed is the existence of a floor or a ceiling at one end of a distribution. A ceiling is a point that scores cannot exceed and a floor is a point that all values must exceed. For example, in the case of reaction time, the floor is 0 milliseconds because a person cannot respond before a stimulus is presented.

  i. Based on the principles we have discussed in this chapter, what should be the impact of floors on the relative position of mean, median and modal values for a distribution?
  ii. Why do floors have this impact?

f. Having answered the previous question:

  i. Would you expect the mean number of cars owned by people in the Unites States to exceed the median number of cars owned? Why?
  ii. Would you expect the mean score on a very easy exam to exceed the median score on the same exam? Why?

g. In his book *Life's Grandeur*, Stephen Jay Gould (1997) notes that over the past century the performance of the *best* baseball hitters has declined (so that the batting averages of the best players are lower than in the past). Does this imply that the overall performance of baseball batters has decreased? Why (or why not)?

Some Principles of Statistical Inference

Key goals for this chapter

- Identify two forms of uncertainty in psychological data – one relating to our capacity to describe phenomena (descriptive uncertainty), one relating to our capacity to describe the significance of those phenomena (inferential uncertainty).
- Explain why and how we address inferential uncertainty by understanding and making probability statements based on the likelihood of observed events occurring by chance.
- Outline principles for making inferences about individual data points and about sets of data points.

As we outlined in Chapter 2, a major part of research in psychology involves making decisions about how confident we should be in the conclusions we draw from research data. Statistics allow us to express this degree of confidence in numerical terms. This is a useful thing to do because it allows us to say clearly when we have great confidence in the pattern of findings we observe and when we are not so sure about them.

In this chapter we are concerned with how we go about making those decisions. Imagine that you have done a piece of research where you have followed all the steps we have outlined in the book so far. The research might be an experiment with a control condition and a theoretically interesting experimental condition and you have randomly assigned participants to those conditions. Imagine you have eliminated all confounds and have a dependent variable that is both relevant to the question in which you are interested and sensitive to changes in the independent variable. You have collected the data and calculated the means and standard deviations, and you now want to know if the theory you set out to test is supported or not. If there is a difference between the mean scores obtained for the experimental and control groups, you will want to know whether you should take that difference seriously, or just consider it as a chance event. So, the critical question is 'Exactly how confident should we be that the difference between the groups is big enough to take seriously?'.

Alternatively, the research you conducted could have been a survey investigating the relationship between two variables. Imagine you have drawn a representative random sample from the population of interest, you have measured the variables in a valid and reliable manner and now you want to know whether the variables are related in the sample. If they are related in the sample you want to be able to draw a conclusion about the relationship between the variables in the population. In both the experiment and the survey, you want some way of expressing your confidence that what you have found is interesting or unusual, and not just some uninformative random event.

Why is this necessary? Why is it that psychologists cannot just accept the results they observe, without resorting to statistical analysis in order to make statements about confidence? In fact, when they use statistics to make statements about confidence psychologists are no different from anybody else. Before they decide whether they should believe that something is true, they simply want to know what the evidence for that belief is. For example, most people will choose not to carry an umbrella unless they are reasonably sure that it could rain. Similarly, if the share price of a company drops slightly, the shareholders do not immediately rush off and sell all their shares in the company, unless they believe that the fall in price is a sign of further falls to come. Perhaps neither the umbrella-holder nor the shareholder will perform a statistical test before making their decisions (though many stock purchasing decisions are now made by computers following statistical rules programmed by human beings). However, both will definitely base their decision on the evidence available and will take steps to reduce any uncertainty they may have about that evidence (e.g., by listening to weather forecasts or stock market reports). The fact that psychologists use statistics to make these decisions is simply a reflection of the controlled and systematic manner in which, as scientists, they make observations and draw conclusions in their work.

Even without statistical training we can all make quasi-statistical decisions in everyday life. Imagine you go to a casino and play a game of chance where you win if any tails are tossed and the house wins if every coin toss comes up heads. If a coin is tossed 10 times and heads comes up 10 times, you will be left with two possible conclusions. Either something funny is going on and the game has been rigged (e.g., because the coin is biased) or the casino has been very lucky. *This is exactly the same type of decision as those we make in statistics.* If we find a difference between the means of an experimental and control condition then we have to decide between two possibilities: either there really is something going on (and the independent variable is having an effect) or the difference is due to chance.

There is yet another reason why we cannot just say that any observed difference between means is 'big enough' for us to be interested in it, or that any observed relationship between variables is a 'big enough' relationship. The reason is that, if we use accurate measuring techniques, we will almost always find a difference between means or a relationship between variables. If you were to measure the IQs of a sample of 20 males and a sample of 20 females you would almost certainly find a 'difference' between the mean IQs of your male and female participants. Let us imagine that you find that the males have an IQ that is one point higher than that of the females. How confident would you be in concluding that males are more intelligent than females? While you are thinking about that, let us also imagine that you measured the heights of 20 males and 20 females, and found that the mean height of the males was 10 cm more than that of the females. How confident would you be that males are taller than females? We suspect that most people would be happy to say that the first data set does not *prove* that males are more intelligent than females, because the difference is so small. Others would say that evidence from just 40 people proves nothing. Yet most people would accept the difference in heights as evidence that males are taller than females. Indeed, if someone tried to tell you that males *were not* taller than females you might seriously question their powers of observation. As a scientist you might well tell the person to have a good look around and measure the heights of the people they see.

But what if this troublemaker were to follow your advice and measure the heights of 20 men and 20 women, and come back to you and simply say 'Here are the data. I have calculated the means and standard deviations as per the instructions in Chapter 6. I want to know, what *makes you so sure* that men are taller than women?'. What possible answer could you give?

It would be unsatisfactory to say 'Look, I just *know* that men are taller than women'. Doing research is not so much about reaffirming what we already know, as about adding to that knowledge by enquiring into what we do not know. If we restrict our enquiries to what we already know with absolute certainty then there is no point in doing research. It is also true that few of the interesting statements we can make about psychological processes can be made with *absolutely no uncertainty*. When we say that 'men are taller than women' or 'males and females are of equal intelligence', we acknowledge some uncertainty in those statements. We know that some women are taller than some men and that some men are more intelligent than most women and that some women are more intelligent than most men. That being the case, we try to make statements that are true on average, on the balance of evidence available to us. What inferential statistics help us to do is decide how confident we should be that some statement is true *on average*.

What of the question posed by our height-measuring troublemaker? How can we be sure that men really are taller than women? Although it might be tempting to tell the person to go away and stop bothering us, it would actually be well worth attempting to grapple with the substance of such questions. This is because they actually touch on the key concepts in inferential statistics that we confront in psychology, and the next time you are confronted by similar questions might be when you are doing research or a class test. The aim of this chapter is to help you answer questions of *exactly* this form.

Statistical inference

Throughout this book so far we have suggested that a key objective of research is to reduce uncertainty so that we can confidently draw conclusions. If we are not sure about something we need to collect evidence that will enable us to be more certain. It is always worth looking first to see whether somebody else has already answered the question we are interested in (by searching the literature), but in practice we often need to collect new data.

In this chapter we want to distinguish between two types of **statistical uncertainty**. The first is the type of uncertainty that we talked about in the previous chapter when we discussed *dispersion*. We call this **descriptive uncertainty**. A normally distributed variable can be expressed as a mean plus a certain amount of variability around that mean. In this case the mean will be the best summary of the scores for a given sample. If most of the scores are close to the mean then this will be reflected in a small standard deviation – that is, the mean will be a good indicator of each score and there will be relatively little uncertainty about the position of the score. But if the other scores are spread out a long way from the mean, there will be quite a lot of uncertainty about where each score lies. Thus descriptive uncertainty is uncertainty in our ability to know, or to predict, individual scores on the basis of a measure of central tendency.

The idea of uncertainty about whether the mean is a good summary of the scores contains within it the notion of **random error**. As we discussed in Chapter 6, theoretically speaking, random error arises from two main sources: imprecision in the measurement instrument and other kinds of measurement error; and sampling error. There are important differences between these two things, and researchers who are concerned to reduce random error will take different steps to deal with each of them. For example, to deal with measurement error they may try to devise a more reliable dependent measure, and to reduce sampling error they may take a larger random sample from the population. In practice, however, none of these things can be eliminated completely, and in a great deal of psychological data there are also differences between individual people that cannot be removed by accurate measurement or representative sampling.

For practical purposes, as we noted in the previous chapter, measurement and sampling error are therefore usually lumped together with individual differences because they are all things over which the researcher does not have total control.

The other type of statistical uncertainty relates to the conclusions we draw from research, and this is our primary focus in the present chapter. This sort of uncertainty arises from not knowing whether the patterns we observe in the data (e.g., a difference between means) are *informative* because they reflect some process of interest or whether they are due to a series of **chance** events. We call this **inferential uncertainty**. If we eliminate all alternative explanations of experimental results through good research design, there are still always two possibilities: the results could reflect the impact of the independent variable and hence provide meaningful information, or they could be due to sampling error. If we can reduce or control uncertainty in the form of random error then we can reduce inferential uncertainty about our conclusions. Although inferential uncertainty and descriptive uncertainty are related to each other – inferential uncertainty will be higher when descriptive uncertainty is high – they are actually quite different concepts.

We can see the difference between the two types of uncertainty in the following example. Imagine that you had conducted the study where you measured the heights of 20 men and 20 women. If you wanted to answer the question 'How tall are men?' then the best answer you could give would be the mean height for your sample of men. However, there would be some uncertainty in your response because not all men are the same height (if they were the standard deviation would be zero). This type of uncertainty is descriptive uncertainty. On the other hand, if you wanted to answer the question 'Are men taller than women?' then the obvious thing you need to do is to compare the mean height of the men with the mean height of the women. If you were to answer this question 'yes' or 'no' there would still be inferential uncertainty because you could never be entirely sure that the results were not due to chance rather than due to a real difference. The difference may reflect the fact that there just happened to be a (random) difference in the heights of the particular samples of men and women that you selected. Thus descriptive uncertainty and inferential uncertainty are different because they reflect uncertainty about the answers to quite different questions.

As we will see, however, the amount of inferential uncertainty does depend upon the amount of descriptive uncertainty (or variability). To take the most extreme example, if the standard deviation of two groups in a study were zero (so that there was no descriptive uncertainty) then there would be no inferential uncertainty. However, it is possible for descriptive uncertainty to be low, but for inferential uncertainty to be high. This would occur when the standard deviations were small but the means of two groups *were very similar*. It is also possible for descriptive uncertainty to be high and for inferential uncertainty to be low, and this is more likely to be the case when the sample size is very large.

The other key difference between these forms of uncertainty is that they are measured in different ways. Random error – descriptive uncertainty – is measured in terms of dispersion or variability (e.g., standard deviation). Uncertainty about whether our results are due to chance – inferential uncertainty – is normally thought of as a probability. When the probability that our results could have been produced by chance or random error is very low then our uncertainty about our conclusions is low. That is, inferential uncertainty will be low.

In fact, though, we can *never* calculate the probability that our results are due to chance. Instead what we can do is calculate the probability that a **random process** (such as coin tossing) could

Photo 7.1 How likely do you think it is that these five dice were thrown fairly (rather than placed by the photographer)? Intuitively, you probably think they were placed because you know that the chances of throwing five 6s are very low indeed. What is more, you would be correct. Indeed, you would only expect to throw five 6s once in every 7776 throws. More formally, what you have done in this case is reject the hypothesis that this was a random event. Exactly the same logic underpins decisions about the significance of findings in psychological research.

produce results as dramatic as the ones we have obtained. If this probability is very low then we can conclude that it is unlikely that our results are due to chance. This is a fine technical point, but it is a mistake for researchers to lose sight of the fact that the statistics they use express uncertainty in this form (Tukey, 1991). If we want to make a decision about whether our results are due to chance or to some meaningful process, we need to work out the probability that a random process could have produced results like ours. Once we know how plausible it is that our results are due to chance, we can decide whether we think they *are* due to chance or to the meaningful process. In other words, although we can never tell whether our results have been produced by a random process, we can decide how *plausible* that possibility is. Inferential uncertainty relates to precisely this sort of decision.

Sometimes we can calculate this probability exactly, but most of the time in psychology it is necessary first to work out a **test statistic**. Once we have calculated that statistic we can then determine the probability of a random process producing a result as dramatic as that which we have obtained. The two possible conclusions – that something is going on (representing meaningful *information*) and that the results are due to chance or random *error* – are related to inferential statistics that we calculate using equations of the following form:

$$\text{test statistic} = \frac{\text{information}}{\text{error}}$$

What this sort of equation tells us is that as the ratio of information to error gets larger, the calculated statistic will be larger. Also, as the statistic becomes larger, the probability that chance or random error could have produced results of this size becomes smaller. This means that if we want to reduce uncertainty about our conclusions, we need good evidence to support the conclusion (i.e., high information) and/or a very small amount of random error. To understand statistical equations we recommend that you always think about what the **information term** and the **error term** are in each equation. You will find the expression 'error term' in many statistics books. The idea of an 'information term' is less widely used. But by introducing this term we can express the key idea of inferential statistics quite succinctly: to the extent that the information term is much larger than the error term, the probability that results of the observed size (or greater) could have been due to chance will be low. Thus uncertainty about inferences will be low.

It is worth returning to the example of a game of chance in order to see how these random processes work. Remember that the casino employee tossed the coin 10 times and obtained 10 heads. This is a simple example where we are able to calculate exactly the probability of a random process producing an outcome that unusual (without needing to calculate an information and error term to estimate the statistic). We suggested that if you saw this happen you could explain this in one of two ways, concluding either that the coin was biased or that the casino had just been very lucky. If we conclude that the result is due to a biased coin then we are saying that the behaviour of the coin is both meaningful and important. If we say that the casino was just lucky we are saying that the behaviour of the coin was due to random error or chance. The best way to make this decision in a systematic way is to imagine how an ordinary, fair coin would behave in the same circumstances.

This process of imagining how an ordinary coin would behave over a run of 10 tosses is called creating a **statistical model** of coin tossing. In this case we use a simple but reasonable statistical model that assumes that there is an equal chance of getting a head or a tail. We say that the probability of a head or a tail is .5. This model also allows us to calculate what is called the **expected value** of the distribution. The expected value is really just another name for the *mean* of a population. For a sample of 10 coin tosses with a probability of .5 the expected value for the number of heads is 5 (i.e., $10 \times .5 = 5$).

Can we now make the decision as to whether the casino has cheated? Well, we could compare the expected value of 5 with the obtained value of 10. These outcomes are obviously different but we still do not know *how* different. After all, it is *possible* (but unlikely) to obtain 10 heads from 10 tosses of a fair coin. In order to decide how confident we can be that the coin is biased we need to extend our statistical model a bit to consider not just the expected value of the distribution, but also the uncertainty or variability associated with that distribution. What we need to do is map out all the probable outcomes that we could obtain from tossing that coin. Fortunately, mathematicians have already done that by creating the **binomial distribution**. This allows us to calculate the probability of any possible outcome when we toss a fair coin 10 times. This binomial distribution tells us that the chance of obtaining 10 heads is $.5^{10}$, that is .0009765. In other words, there is less than a 1 in 1000 chance of a fair coin doing what the one in the casino did. It is your decision as to whether you would say the casino was cheating on the basis of this evidence, but it might be unwise to keep betting in that casino (bear in mind that casinos make most of their money not from cheating, but by having a better understanding of probability than their customers do).

The binomial distribution for 10 coin tosses is shown in Figure 7.1. You can see that the distribution is symmetrical around five heads (which is the mean, median and modal response) and that the probability of this outcome is .246. This distribution is chunky like a frequency graph rather than smooth like a normal distribution because there is a small and discrete set of outcomes (11 in fact). If there were a thousand possible outcomes the distribution would be a lot smoother.

All other statistical inferences involve a similar process to this. In order to decide whether we have observed a chance event or a meaningful event we create a statistical model of what *could* happen by chance. This statistical model describes the likelihood of each of the events that could occur if there is nothing special going on – that is, when we are observing a random process such as tossing a fair coin. The statistical model takes into account the variability and uncertainty in the situation, and tells us what the chance of obtaining an effect as large as the one we have observed would be if the process were random. If this probability is very small then we can be more confident that something is going on, in the same way that we can be reasonably certain that something funny is going on in the casino.

In the previous chapter we showed you how to calculate means and standard deviations. We also suggested that, compared with other measures of central tendency and dispersion, means and standard deviations are especially useful in inferential statistics. This is mainly

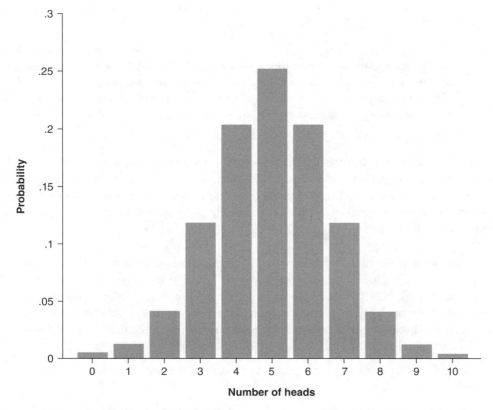

Figure 7.1   Theoretical distribution for 10 fair coin tosses

Test Yourself 7.1**

Imagine a coin-tossing experiment in which a coin is tossed 10 times and the researcher records the number of heads obtained. Which of the following statements is true?

a.   The binomial distribution helps provide a statistical model for this coin-tossing experiment.
b.   The binomial distribution gives the probability that the coin is biased.
c.   Very rare events are always random.
d.   The information term of the statistic used in this experiment will be a measure of chance, or random error.
e.   Both (a) and (b).

(Continued)

due to the properties of the normal distribution. So, if we know that a variable is normally distributed with a given mean and standard deviation, then we know just about everything we need to about that variable. This is especially true when we want to make inferences about relationships between variables, because we can create detailed statistical models about how random variables behave.

binomial distribution The distribution of the possible outcomes from a *random process* where there are two possible events (event *p* and event *q*) so that the probability of one or other occurring is 1 (and the probability of *p* occurring is 1 minus the probability of *q* occurring, i.e., $p = 1 - q$). An example would be the process of tossing an unbiased coin, where the probability of getting heads is .5 and the probability of getting tails is .5.

chance Another word for events occurring due to random processes or, less formally, luck.

descriptive uncertainty *Statistical uncertainty* arising from variation in observations around any measure of central tendency for which the researcher proposes no explanation. It is uncertainty in knowing or predicting individual scores on the basis of a measure of central tendency. This uncertainty is quantified by dispersion measures (e.g., standard deviation, variance, range).

error term In an equation for a test statistic, the mathematical expression that estimates how much *random error* there is in the data.

expected value The mean value of a probability distribution. For example, the expected value for the number of heads when a fair coin is tossed 50 times is 25.

inferential uncertainty *Statistical uncertainty* relating to the possibility that an observed result is due to *random error* or *chance*. This uncertainty is estimated by a probability value, where a low probability indicates low uncertainty.

information term In an equation for a *test statistic*, the mathematical expression that tells us how much evidence there is that the results are not due to *chance* or *random error*.

random error The amount of *descriptive uncertainty* or *chance* variation associated with statistical statements and observations.

random process A process that generates a range of different events which are independent of each other. When this is the case the occurrence of one event is not dependent on the occurrence of another.

statistical model A detailed statement about the likelihood of a particular set of events.

statistical uncertainty Doubt about statistics arising from the presence of *random error*. Generally speaking, such uncertainty is easier to estimate than to reduce.

test statistic A numerical statement about a population based on sample data.

Inferences about individual scores

When we conduct research, what sort of inferences can we make from the results we obtain? Most importantly perhaps, if we know the mean and standard deviation of a variable and that it is normally distributed, we can say how likely some individual score or event is. An example of just such a variable is IQ. This is because IQ scores are actually constructed so that they are normally distributed and have a mean of 100 and a standard deviation of 15.

Let us say someone does an IQ test and obtains a score of 120. We might want to know if that is a high or average score compared with the rest of the population. By knowing the shape of the normal distribution we are able to say exactly where that score lies in relation to the rest of the population. What we are able to do is express the difference between that score and the population mean in terms of **standard deviation units**. In this case 120 is 20 IQ points away from the population mean of 100. More informatively, we can say that it is 20/15 or 1.33 standard deviation units away. This process of converting scores into units that express differences from the mean in standard deviation units is called **standardization**. This is done to make different scores comparable. To standardize a score all you need to do is subtract the mean from the score and divide by the standard deviation.

As a student, you may have already encountered the term 'standardization' in relation to test scores. It is very common for instructors to standardize the results of class tests. This can be puzzling for students when they find that the scores that they have obtained on a test have gone up or down. If you are a student and you are not already clear what standardization is, then the next few paragraphs are probably worth paying particularly close attention to.

The reasons for standardizing scores are quite easy to grasp, but it is harder to understand why standardization involves the particular mathematical operations that it does. Let us take an example of two students who take tests at the start of two different classes (that have been created by random assignment so there are no differences in ability) where one teacher is a much harder marker than the other. Both students obtain 75% (i.e., they both have the same raw score of 75 out of 100), but Student A is in a class where the class mean is 50 (with a standard deviation of 10) while the mean for Student B's class is 80 (also with a standard deviation of 10). Which performance would you be more impressed by? Most people would say Student A because this person is performing at a level 25 points better than the class mean, while Student B is actually five points worse than the class mean. Unless we have some reason to believe that Student B's class is of higher ability than Student A's class we should conclude that Student A has performed better.

The main point about standardization is therefore that it is useful to express individual scores in terms of a difference from a mean in order to compare them. This explains the mathematical operation of subtracting the mean from the score. Why do we then divide this difference by the standard deviation? The answer is that if we want to know how well a person has done relative to the class on average, it is helpful to express the difference from the mean relative to the amount of dispersion (of which the standard deviation is one measure). This difference can be thought of as a *statistical difference* or distance. Dividing the difference by the standard deviation tells us how distinctive or remarkable a score is. We know that Student A has done better than the class mean, but we would also like to know what proportion of the class was doing that well. Is it the case that 10% or 5% (or even less) of the class have done as well as this student? Ideally we would want a score that tells us this information without having to remember what the distribution of all the scores was. This is what standardization allows us to do. It gives us a single number that expresses the difference from a mean, relative to the standard deviation (which is related to average deviation from the mean).

So, in the examples above, Student A has a standardized score of 2.5 (i.e., $(75 - 50)/10$) and Student B has a standardized score of -0.5 (i.e., $(75 - 80)/10$). Providing that they believed that the classes were of equal ability (and this is crucial), most people would be much more impressed with Student A's performance.

For this sort of purpose, standardization is a useful procedure that has a sound statistical basis. This is not to say that standardization has always been used sensibly and well. Indeed, on occasion it has been seriously misused by educators and social policy-makers. It is fair to say, though, that it is much more likely to be misused by those who do not understand its statistical rationale.

Standardizing scores will create a distribution of scores with a mean of 0 and a standard deviation of 1. A normal distribution with a mean of 0 and a standard deviation of 1 is called a **standard normal distribution**. A score that has been subtracted from the mean and then divided by the standard deviation is called a *z*-score. A variable whose values have been converted to *z*-scores has a mean of 0 and a standard deviation of 1. Putting these ideas into the form of an equation,

$$Z_x = \frac{\text{score}_x - \text{mean}}{\text{standard deviation}}$$

In this equation the top line on the right is the information term and the bottom line is the error term. To work out the z-score associated with an IQ of 120, we would do the following calculation:

$$Z_{120} = \frac{120 - 100}{15}$$
$$= 1.33$$

To set these standard scores to another mean and standard deviation, all you need to do is multiply them by the new standard deviation and then add the new mean. The order in which you do these calculations is very important. For example, if you wanted to create a new 'height quotient' with a mean of 100 and a standard deviation of 15, you would multiply people's standardized heights (which would have a mean of 0 and standard deviation of 1) by 15 and then add 100.

Another reason for wanting to describe scores in standard deviation units is that if we know the variable is normally distributed then we know exactly what proportion of scores will be greater than any given z-score. We can get an insight into how this works by referring to Figure 7.2, which shows a standard normal distribution.

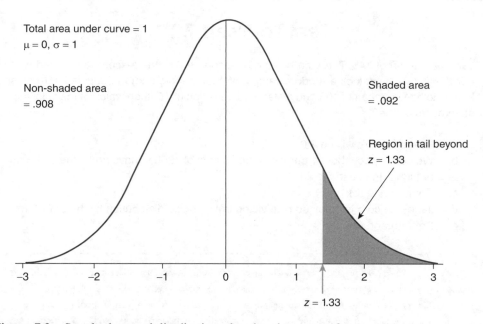

Figure 7.2 Standard normal distribution, showing the z-score for $z = 1.33$

In a figure such as this any z-score corresponds to a point on the horizontal axis of the graph. As you can see, if we draw a vertical line through the distribution at that point we divide it into two regions or areas (shaded and non-shaded), so that the line cuts off a certain part of that distribution. Remember that the distribution is actually a representation of what the total population of everybody's IQ would look like. So when we divide the curve into two areas we divide this population into two groups, those who lie at 120 or below and those who lie above 120.

We can use this distribution to work out exactly what proportion of people have scores above or below any particular value. So, in this case we can work out what proportion of people have IQs above and below 120. This is because different z-scores correspond to points that cut off different, *specifiable* proportions of the population.

The way we work out the area under the curve to one side of the line cut through it by a z-score is complex. The good news is that you do not have to do any of the complicated calculations. The areas under the curve have already been worked out and are given in Appendix B Moreover, in most statistical analyses these values will be provided by means of a computer program such as IBM SPSS Statistics software (SPSS).

To use this table look down the left-hand column (labelled z) for the z-score 1.33. The area under the curve that lies in the tail beyond this z-score is then provided by the value in

Test Yourself 7.2**

Jane has an IQ of 145. The area beyond a z-score of 3.0 (the z-score associated with her IQ) is .001. If we took a random sample of 1000 people from the population (that is known to have a mean of 100 and a standard deviation of 15) then which of the following statements is true?

a. Jane's z-score will be 3.0.
b. We can expect about 1 person in the sample of 1000 to have an IQ the same as or higher than Jane's.
c. Both (a) and (b).
d. Jane's z-score is obtained by dividing the binomial distribution by the error term.
e. Both (a) and (d).

The correct answer is (c). The z-score is given in the question as 3.0, so (a) is correct; (b) is also correct because the proportion of the normal curve beyond Jane's z-score is also the proportion of the population with her IQ or higher. If it is a random sample we should expect .001 of the sample (or 0.1%) to have an IQ this high (i.e., 1 person in 1000). (d) is incorrect because the binomial distribution has nothing to do with this case. The z-score is obtained by dividing the difference between the score and the mean by the standard deviation.

the 'Area in tail beyond z' column. In this case the value associated with a z-score of 1.33 is .092. Because the total area under the curve corresponds to all the events that could occur, this total area equals 1, the sum of all probabilities. The value associated with the area of the curve beyond any particular z-score therefore indicates the probability (between 0 and 1) of obtaining a score above this value. In this example the probability of a score greater than 1.33 is .092. Another way of putting this is to say that 1.33 cuts off .092 × 100% of the total area under the curve. Accordingly, we can say that 9.2% of the population have an IQ of 120 or more and 90.8% have an IQ of less than 120.

standard deviation units The units in which *z-scores* are expressed.

standard normal distribution A normal distribution with a mean of 0 and a standard deviation of 1. *z-scores* correspond to different points of the horizontal axis of the standard normal distribution, cutting off regions of different sizes.

standardization Setting the mean and standard deviation for a variable to new values that are useful in a particular setting. In order to do this, we subtract the original mean from each value and divide it by the standard deviation, then multiply this value by the new (or desired) standard deviation and add the new mean.

z-score The difference between a score and the mean divided by the standard deviation. These scores have very useful properties when they are drawn from a normally distributed population.

Inferences about means

It seems reasonably easy to find out where an individual lies in relation to the rest of the population when we know that the population is normally distributed with a specified mean and standard deviation. Can we make similar statements about groups? Imagine we gave an IQ test to a class of 30 children and obtained a mean IQ for the class of 120. Could we find out whether the class mean differed from the expected population mean? The answer is 'yes', but, as you can probably imagine, things now start to become a bit trickier.

Things become trickier as a result of a statistical principle that just about everybody understands and uses in their everyday life. It is called the **law of large numbers**. For those who have not studied statistics in the past, it may seem strange that we say that you already understand something that you have never heard of. Part of the reason for this is that statistical ideas often sound more complex when it becomes necessary to express them technically.

The principle with which you are already familiar is that, other things being equal, uncertainty is reduced by taking many measurements of the same thing. We are more confident about something that we have lots of evidence for than about something we have little evidence for. This is why the mean score will be a more reliable indicator of what is going on in a sample than any individual score: the mean is the position in the sample that describes the sample with the least uncertainty because it is the average of many observations.

Photo 7.2 There are about 70 people in this photograph. How surprised would you be to discover that the person holding a towel in the bottom left-hand corner has an IQ over 120? Perhaps not very. Indeed, about 1 in every 11 people has an IQ this high. But how surprised would you be if you found that the average IQ of all the people in this picture was over 120? Extremely. Indeed, the likelihood of this being true is so small that it is almost inconceivable that it could occur by chance alone. Accordingly, if you did discover this to be the case, then you would make the inference that something very unusual is happening here. In this, your thinking would be informed by your intuitive understanding of the law of large numbers, and this is a key principle that underpins inferential statistics more generally.

Thus, although around 9% of the population have IQs over 120, far fewer than 9% of classes of 30 randomly selected students will have a *mean* IQ over 120. We claimed a moment ago that you already understand this principle. To illustrate this, suppose that we offered you two choices: $20 if you could toss a fair coin five times and obtain five heads, or $20 if you could toss a fair coin 10 times and obtain 10 heads. Most people would take the first option (especially if they have been reading this chapter carefully so far). What if we offered you $200 if you could toss 10 heads? You would still be better off taking $20 for tossing five heads. By calculating the values from the binomial distribution we can show that you have 31 in 1000 chances of winning the $20 prize but only a 1 in 1000 chance of winning the $200. To make the offers of equal value we would have to offer you about $620 for tossing 10 heads.

Thus, obtaining the same extreme proportion of 100% heads with a small sample happens fairly regularly, but obtaining an extreme proportion with a larger sample is very rare if the process is truly random. We know that if we toss a coin 1000 times we can be reasonably confident that there will be something like 500 heads and 500 tails, even though we do not know what any given coin toss will yield. If we ask what the outcome of tossing a coin 10 times will be, then we can still expect there to be around 50% heads, but the variation in the proportion of heads will actually be much larger than with 1000 tosses. If you repeatedly perform the experiment of tossing a coin 10 times you will eventually have an example of all 10 tosses being heads (you can expect one every 1024 trials or so). On the other hand, we can expect that you will be tossing a coin a very long time before you get 50 out of 50 heads (at two minutes per 50 coin tosses you could expect to get 50 heads out of 50 tosses once every 4 billion years or so – so get tossing). We know it sounds a bit paradoxical, but this is the good thing about random processes: even though each **random event** is unpredictable we can have a pretty good idea of how random processes will behave in the long run, providing that we know what the probability of a relevant event is. This long-term predictability is what makes random processes useful in statistical models.

Non-random processes are quite different in this respect. Suppose that instead of tossing a coin 1000 times we asked a person to *place* a coin on a table 1000 times. Now we might *hope* to do a better job of predicting how the person will place each coin than of predicting a random coin toss, but the possibility also exists that we could do *far worse* than chance. It is so unlikely that the possibility is not even remotely worth considering that someone could toss a fair coin 1000 times and obtain 1000 heads, but it would be a trivially simple exercise for

RESEARCH BITE 7.1
The dangerous allure of the law of small numbers

In a very highly cited 'classic' article, Amos Tversky and the Nobel Prize-winner Daniel Kahneman (1971) showed that most people – including well-trained psychologists – apparently believe in the law of small numbers. That is, they mistakenly believe that small samples should be as representative of an underlying population as large samples. Among other things, this can lead researchers to have undue confidence in their ability to replicate findings obtained with small samples, and then to be unduly disappointed when those attempts at replication fail. The best remedy is to be wary of this problem and capitalize on the law of large numbers by conducting research (including replications) with large samples.

Reference

Tversky, A., & Kahneman, D. (1971). Belief in the law of small numbers. *Psychological Bulletin, 76*, 105–110.

somebody to place a coin heads up 1000 times. This illustrates what we mean about random processes being predictable (even though random events are not).

Let us take another example to explore some additional issues related to the law of large numbers. Imagine that the mean height of the men from a city is 175 cm and the standard deviation is 10 cm. If we were to take random samples of 10 men from the population and also take random samples of 100 men from the same population we would find that a larger proportion of the 10-man samples would have high means such as 185 cm. We would also find that a larger proportion of the 10-man samples would have low mean heights such as 165 cm. This is because there is greater variability in smaller samples as fewer scores need to be extreme in order to make the mean extreme. In other words, the process of dividing up exactly the same population in different ways provides a different distribution of means. More specifically, the law of large numbers implies that the *means* of large samples will be more tightly clustered around the population mean than the *means* of small samples. In other words, there will be less random error with large samples because the means will be less spread out. Of course, the overall population mean would not change, nor would the population standard deviation. It is the *same* population being divided up in each case – all we are doing is dividing it up randomly into samples of different sizes. However, the larger random samples provide more reliable **estimates** of the *population parameters*. In other words, they are more likely to provide summary statistics (e.g., means and standard deviations) that are close to those of the population the sample is drawn from.

The law of large numbers is a fundamental principle on which the inferential statistics that we use in psychology are based. We will not have too much difficulty in finding one person who has an IQ of 120 (as we have seen, about 9% of people have an IQ of over 120), but we will be looking for a long time before we randomly draw a sample of 30 people from the general population who have a *mean* IQ of 120.

This statistical knowledge makes us more confident that if we *do* find a class (i.e., a sample) of 30 students with a mean IQ of 120 then this is unlikely to be a chance event (though it is always possible that it could be). In other words, we can be reasonably sure that we have discovered an intelligent group of students, and that there is probably some reason, other than chance, for their being so intelligent on average (perhaps particularly intelligent students have all been put in one class). It will be easier to decide whether or not the sample is a random sample from the population if the sample size is large, because extreme events such as randomly drawing a sample with a very high or very low mean will be more unlikely. The law of large numbers suggests that larger sample sizes should reduce uncertainty in the form of random error and consequently reduce uncertainty about our decision as to whether observed patterns are due to chance.

To calculate how confident we can be about such decisions we need to introduce some new ideas. The first of these is the idea of a **sampling distribution**. A sampling distribution is a theoretical distribution similar to those we discussed in Chapter 6. Its shape is derived from our understanding of the statistical model we are using. What we do is determine theoretically what would happen if we drew a sample of a particular size from a population. For example, we determine what the distribution of IQ scores in a sample of 30 people drawn randomly from the general population might look like based on knowledge that the population of IQ scores has a mean of 100 and a standard deviation of 15. Of course, in practice any sample is unlikely to have exactly this mean and standard deviation, and its exact mean and standard deviation will depend on the people that are sampled.

The sampling distribution we use does not exist in reality because it is not based on actual observations. However, we can specify what the sampling distribution would look like if it did exist. This is where our knowledge of the properties of the normal distribution becomes really useful. If the sampling distribution is a normal distribution then we know pretty well exactly what it would look like, so long as we know the population mean and standard deviation.

This might sound a bit mystical, in so far as we are relying on a sampling distribution that we have never actually seen, but we believe that we know what it would look like if we could see it. Nevertheless, these ideas work. What we are doing is no different from what we did with the binomial distribution for the coin-tossing example. To create the sampling distribution for some normally distributed variable we simply calculate what would happen if we drew a sample of a particular size from the population. We could do that empirically (e.g., by going out and collecting the data from different groups), but we do not need to do that if we have a good statistical model (in the same way that we have a good model of how a fair coin behaves over a long run of tosses).

The second concept we need to introduce is the **sampling distribution of the mean**. This is the sampling distribution that would be obtained if we repeatedly sampled from the population and calculated the means. In the coin example we could compute such a sampling distribution for the number of heads obtained for sample sizes of 10 and 20. They are shown in Figure 7.3.

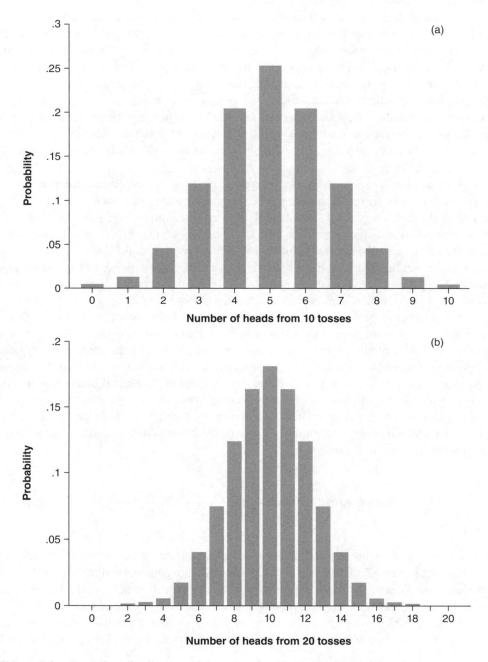

Figure 7.3   Sampling distribution of the mean for (a) 10 and (b) 20 fair coin tosses

We can see that the sampling distribution for 20 coin tosses is much more steeply peaked about the mean than that for 10 coin tosses. This is another way of saying that the sampling distribution for 20 coin tosses has less variance.

We could also construct a theoretical sampling distribution of the means from a normally distributed population of men with a mean height of 175 cm and a standard deviation of 10 cm (assuming random sampling). We have not actually done this, but instead have approximated the sampling distribution by generating some random data where the population is divided first into samples of 10 men and then into samples of 100 men (Figure 7.4). What this involves is selecting a random sample of a given size (10 in Figure 7.4(a), 100 in Figure 7.4(b)) and calculating the mean for each sample. The histograms therefore do not show distributions of heights; instead they show distributions of the *means* of heights. About 300 samples were taken in each case. If we did this exercise again we would obtain distributions with slightly different shapes.

There are two things to note about Figure 7.4. First, we can see that the distributions are shaped rather like a normal distribution (even though they are not smooth, we can say that they are approximately normally distributed). Second, as the sample size gets larger the mean of these distributions stays the same, but the amount of dispersion of these sampling distributions decreases (even though the population standard deviation of the original sample must remain the same). In Figure 7.4 it can be seen that when the sample size is 10 the means range from 167 to 183, but that when the sample size is 100 the means only range from 172 to 177. In effect this is a statistical demonstration of the law of large numbers.

Two extremely useful properties of the sampling distribution of the mean are that it has a mean equal to the population mean, and a standard deviation equal to the population standard deviation divided by the square root of the sample size. Furthermore, for very large samples the sampling distribution of the mean will tend to be normally distributed. The last of these properties is a statement of a statistical principle called the **central limit theorem** and it tends to hold for large sample sizes even if the distribution that we are sampling from is not normally distributed. The standard deviation divided by the square root of the sample size is called the **standard error**. The **standard error of the mean** is the standard deviation of the sampling distribution of the mean:

$$\text{standard error of the mean} = \frac{\text{standard deviation}}{\text{square root of sample size}\,(N)}$$

Now we know that all this jargon sounds very confusing. However, do not panic. We are still working with just two statistical principles, the law of large numbers and the idea of random sampling. Just about everything else follows from these relatively simple points. This is not to say that it will not take some hard work to get these ideas clear in your own mind.

What we think we do need to do at this point is convince you it is worth doing that hard work. The ideas that we are discussing here are extremely useful for answering questions such

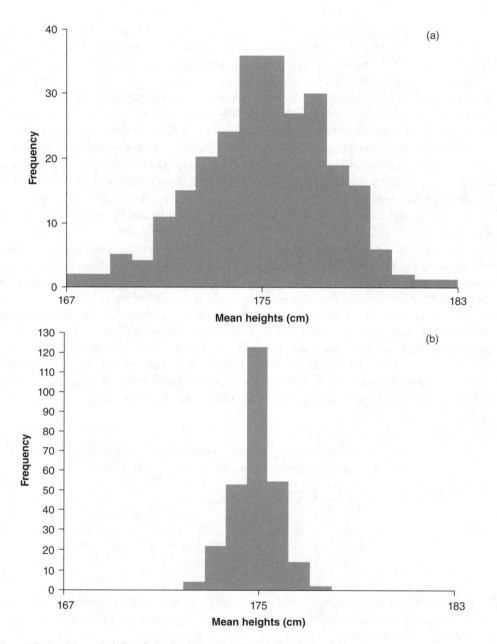

Figure 7.4 Mean heights for samples of (a) 10 and (b) 100 men

as 'When is an observed difference worth taking seriously?' and 'Can we be confident about decisions based on our data?'. This makes them intriguing and interesting in themselves (or at least when compared with many other statistical concepts). By using these theoretical sampling distributions we are able *to go beyond the data given* and say something about certainty (or uncertainty). That is, by comparing our data with what we would expect to happen by chance, we are able to answer questions such as 'How sure are you that men *are* taller than women?' or 'How sure are you that a class of 30 people with a mean IQ of 95 really is below average?'.

The statistical principles outlined above thus put us in a very strong position when it comes to answering interesting questions of this form. Let us take the case of the school teacher who gives an IQ test to her class of 30 students and finds that their mean IQ is 95. Should the teacher draw the conclusion that the IQ of her class is lower than the population mean?

There are two answers to this. First, there is the obvious answer that it is lower – in fact, five points lower. We do not need inferential statistics to tell us that. The more interesting answer, however, is somewhat more sophisticated, and draws on the concepts that we have been introducing here. We can tell the teacher where her class of 30 students lies in comparison with other samples of the same size drawn randomly from the population. That is, we can do for her class scores what we did previously for the individual score of 120.

From the discussion above we know a number of things about the theoretical sampling distribution of the mean. We know that samples of size 30 drawn from a population with a mean of 100 and a standard deviation of 15 will have a mean of 100 and standard deviation of $15/\sqrt{30}$. That is, they will have the population mean as their mean and the standard deviation of the sampling distribution of the mean as their standard error (which is the population standard deviation divided by the square root of the sample size). In this case, the standard error of the mean = $15/\sqrt{30}$ = 2.74.

$$Z = \frac{\text{sample mean} - \text{population mean}}{\text{standard error of the mean}} \quad \begin{matrix}\text{(information term)} \\ \text{(error term)}\end{matrix}$$

$$Z_{class} = \frac{95-100}{15/\sqrt{30}}$$
$$= \frac{-5}{2.739}$$
$$= -1.83$$

With this information we can calculate the value of z for the entire class in the following way. In essence, what we want to know is how many **standard error units** the class mean of 95 is from the population mean.

The mean of 95 is five points from the population mean, and 5/2.74 is 1.83 standard error units *below* the mean, which gives us a z-score of −1.83. From Figure 7.5 we can see that 1.83 standard error units cuts off a small amount of the population. Indeed, from Table B.1 in Appendix B we can see that the area beyond a z-score of 1.83 is .034 (i.e., 3.4% of the population). What this

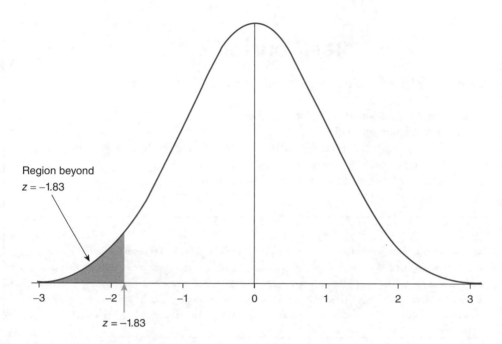

Region beyond
$z = -1.83$

$z = -1.83$

Figure 7.5 Standard normal distribution, showing the z-score for $z = -1.83$

is telling us is that if we were to repeatedly draw random samples of 30 people from the population and measure the IQ of each group, only 3.4% of those groups would have a lower mean IQ than the class in question. Put another way, around 96% of all the other samples of the same size in the world can be expected to have a higher mean IQ than this class.

The thing to point out here (the law of large numbers again) is that around 37% of all the individuals in the world have IQs of 95 and lower. So, although it is not at all unusual for an individual (a sample of one) to have an IQ of 95, it is much more unusual for a sample of 30 (drawn from the general population) to have an IQ this low. In this case the teacher can be fairly confident that her class has a lower IQ than the population average.

We can use this example to illustrate how the process of inferences for individual scores is actually a special case of inferences about groups. It is just that inferences for individual scores are based on a sample size of one. We said that when comparing one individual's score with the population mean we express the scores in standard deviation units and when we compare a group's score we express it in standard error units. In fact, we use standard error units in both cases, but when $N = 1$, the standard error is the same as the standard deviation because the square root of 1 is 1 and dividing a quantity by 1 does not have any effect on the quantity.

We can summarize the process here as one of deciding where the sample mean lies in relation to the population mean. If there is a very low chance of sampling that mean from the population we conclude that the sample is probably not drawn from that population but

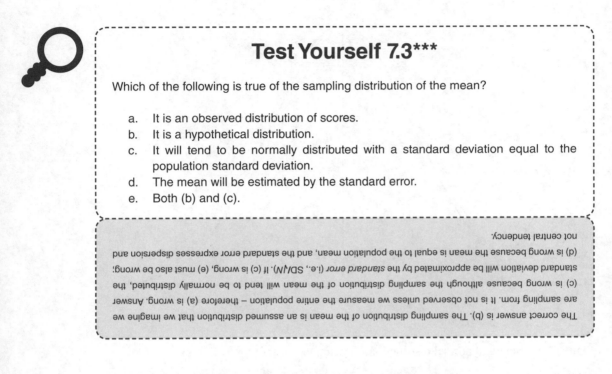

Test Yourself 7.3***

Which of the following is true of the sampling distribution of the mean?

a. It is an observed distribution of scores.
b. It is a hypothetical distribution.
c. It will tend to be normally distributed with a standard deviation equal to the population standard deviation.
d. The mean will be estimated by the standard error.
e. Both (b) and (c).

The correct answer is (b). The sampling distribution of the mean is an assumed distribution that we imagine we are sampling from. It is not observed unless we measure the entire population – therefore (a) is wrong. Answer (c) is wrong because although the sampling distribution of the mean will tend to be normally distributed, the standard deviation will be approximated by the *standard error* (i.e., $SD/\sqrt{N}$). If (c) is wrong, (e) must also be wrong; (d) is wrong because the mean is equal to the population mean, and the standard error expresses dispersion and not central tendency.

instead belongs to another population. Perhaps less intelligent students were assigned to that teacher's class by the school authorities. We cannot be sure *what the explanation is*, but we can be confident that *there is something to be explained* and this is the purpose of conducting statistical tests. The tests can reduce inferential uncertainty but they cannot directly reduce methodological uncertainty – a point we will return to in Chapter 15.

In these examples we know the population mean for IQ and we know the population standard deviation. This is a very unusual case because most of the time we do not know the population parameters. Although we know the population mean and standard deviation for IQ we do not know what they are for other variables such as height unless we go out and measure the entire population. When we do not know the population mean and population standard deviation we have to estimate them. To do this we have to use a different sampling distribution. We will consider this case in the next chapter.

central limit theorem The statistical theorem that for large samples the *sampling distribution of the mean* will be approximately normally distributed.

estimate A statistic used to approximate a population parameter on the basis of the sample data. For example, the sample standard deviation is often used as an estimate of the population standard deviation.

law of large numbers The idea that the average outcomes of random processes are more predictable with large samples than with small samples. In other words, large samples are associated with less uncertainty in their estimates of population parameters.

random event An event that is an outcome of a random process.

sampling distribution A hypothetical distribution of the values of some statistic (e.g., the mean). This provides information about the pattern of values that would be expected to arise from repeated sampling from a particular population.

sampling distribution of the mean A sampling distribution obtained by calculating the means for samples of a given size. Where the sample size is large, it has a mean that is equal to the population mean and a standard deviation that is equal to the standard error of the mean.

standard error The standard deviation of any *sampling distribution*. This is an estimate of random error in estimates of population parameters.

standard error of the mean The standard deviation of the *sampling distribution of the mean* (i.e., the standard deviation divided by the square root of the sample size).

standard error units Units that quantify random error in estimates of population parameters. If we calculate the difference between two scores and divide this difference by the standard error the result is expressed in standard error units.

Overview

There are a lot of important points in this chapter, and we think that you will almost certainly need to read it several times before they all make sense. You will also probably find that in years to come you need to come back and refresh your understanding of these very important principles. We hope that when you engage in this process of revision the following summary is useful.

Doing inferential statistics is all about making decisions about how confident you should be in conclusions made on the basis of data. There are two major factors that help us to make decisions about confidence: the information we have obtained and the amount of descriptive uncertainty about that information (random error). If the information is pretty clear despite the descriptive uncertainty, then we can be confident in the conclusion (there is low inferential uncertainty). The inferential statistics used in psychology tend to involve comparing the evidence that 'something is going on' with a measure of uncertainty or random error. Where the ratio of information to error is very large we are more confident that something is going on.

Thus, the statistics that we will describe in the next two chapters of this book are of the form:

$$\text{test statistic} = \frac{\text{information}}{\text{error}}$$

Where information is large and error is small, the ratio of information to error will be large and the corresponding probability that a random process could have produced results like the ones obtained will be small. Where this probability is small we can be relatively confident that our results are not due to chance.

The next question concerns how we obtain the information and error terms. The process by which we go about deciding how confident to be about our observations involves creating a model of what would happen if there were no information and only uncertainty. This is another way of saying that we create a model that describes what would happen if the process we are observing were random. The main advantage in treating the process as random is that random processes are highly predictable *in the long run*. If we know something behaves as a random variable then we will have a good idea of what its distribution will look like, even though we almost never really have all the information about each member of the population (if we did we would not have to do research).

The model we create is represented by a *sampling distribution*. The *sampling distribution of the mean* is what we would obtain if we kept on taking random samples of a particular size from a population for ever and calculated the mean for each sample. The sampling distribution of the mean has a mean that is equal to the population mean, but it has a standard deviation that is equal to the population standard deviation divided by the square root of the sample size. The sampling distribution of the mean will tend to be normally distributed even if the population distribution is not normally distributed. A consequence of dividing the standard deviation by the square root of the sample size is that the sampling distribution of the mean involves less uncertainty than the population of individual scores, and this is particularly true when the sample size is large. This follows from the law of large numbers, as it is far less common to select random samples with extreme means (either high or low) if you have a large sample rather than a small one.

In statistical inference the law of large numbers is reflected in the fact that the standard deviation is divided by the square root of the sample size to obtain the *standard error*. The larger the sample size, the smaller the standard error will be. Standard error is a measure of random error. The effect of the division by the square root of the sample size is to reduce random error (uncertainty about the values of parameters), and by reducing this error we reduce uncertainty relating to the question of whether the sample is a random sample of the population.

What the sampling distribution of the mean enables us to do is compare our obtained mean with the expected value of the sampling distribution. From this comparison we work out the probability that, for a sample of a given size, we could have obtained a mean at least as big by taking a random sample from the population. This probability is *not* the chance that our results are due to random error, but is our best guess of this probability. If this probability is very small then we can be more confident that the results reflect something of interest and not just random error.

In other words, constructing ratios of information to error allows us to *compare models* or to *test hypotheses*. These two approaches to statistical inference are presented in more detail in the next chapter.

Obviously, there are many difficult ideas in this summary, but the really important thing is to make sure that you (a) understand the difference between the two types of uncertainty we have discussed (descriptive uncertainty and inferential uncertainty), and (b) remember that everything else follows from the principles of random sampling and the law of large numbers.

CHECKLIST
Revisiting the key goals for this chapter

☐ I understand the two forms of uncertainty in psychological data – one relating to our capacity to describe phenomena (descriptive uncertainty), one relating to our capacity to describe the significance of those phenomena (inferential uncertainty).

☐ I know why and how we address inferential uncertainty by understanding and making probability statements based on the likelihood of observed events occurring by chance.

☐ I understand the principles for making inferences about individual data points and about sets of data points.

Further reading

Most statistics textbooks that are pitched at a more advanced level than this one include a more elaborate discussion of statistical inference than we have provided here. However, if you are looking for such a discussion, Smithson's (2000) book in this series is a place to start.

Smithson, M. (2000). *Statistics with confidence*. London: SAGE.

Statistical inference: A checklist for research evaluation and improvement

Table 7.1

Potential problem	Question to ask	Potential improvement
Descriptive uncertainty	Is the researchers' ability to describe a given population compromised by the amount of variation in their sample data?	Examine the data and try to ascertain (or hypothesize about) the cause of any unduly high levels of variation. This may be a true reflection of the population(s) from which the sample data are drawn. However, if the variation appears to reflect empirical limitations (e.g., measurement inaccuracy, uncontrolled extraneous variables) you may be able to reduce this through appropriate refinements (e.g., better measurement, improved experimental control).

(Continued)

Table 7.1 (Continued)

Potential problem	Question to ask	Potential improvement
Inferential uncertainty	Is the researchers' ability to make statistical statements about a given population compromised by the amount of random error (relative to information) in their sample data?	Examine the data and try to ascertain (or hypothesize about) the basis of the high ratio of random error relative to information. This may be a true reflection of the population(s) from which the sample data are drawn, but it may also arise from either (a) measurement and other problems (e.g., associated with high descriptive uncertainty) that can be addressed through empirical refinement or (b) a lack of statistical power that can be addressed by conducting a study with a larger sample.
Inferential uncertainty about individual scores	Do the researchers want to compare scores or to understand how a single score stands in relation to a population with a known mean and standard deviation?	Standardize scores by subtracting the population mean from them and dividing by the population standard deviation. This procedure turns raw scores into z-scores and Table B.1 in Appendix B can be used to provide information about the proportion of scores in the population that would be expected to be larger than any obtained z-score.
Inferential uncertainty about sample means	Do the researchers want to compare means or to understand how a sample mean stands in relation to a population with a known mean and standard deviation?	Standardize means by subtracting the population mean from them and dividing by the standard error of the mean (the population standard deviation divided by the square root of the sample size). This procedure turns raw means into z-scores and Table B.1 in Appendix B can be used to provide information about the proportion of scores in the population that would be expected to be larger than any obtained z-score.

Test Yourself 7.4**

Which of the following statements about descriptive uncertainty and inferential uncertainty is true?

a. Both are types of statistical uncertainty.
b. Only descriptive uncertainty is a form of statistical uncertainty.

c.   They are unrelated.
d.   Both are measured by the information term of any statistic.
e.   They provide different answers to the same questions.

Test Yourself 7.5*

Which of the following statements about z-scores is true when they are used to make inferences about individual scores?

a.   They are produced by random processes.
b.   They are calculated by dividing the difference between the score and the mean by the standard deviation.
c.   They can only be used to make inferences about groups.
d.   They follow the central limit theorem.
e.   None of the above.

Test Yourself 7.6***

Which of the following statements about statistical inferences in psychology is *false*?

a.   Statistical inferences usually involve calculating a statistic that is obtained by dividing an information term by an error term.
b.   Statistical models allow us to calculate the probability that our results are due to chance.
c.   The sampling distribution of the mean is a useful concept for making inferences about groups.
d.   Statistical inferences about the mean can often make use of the z-distribution when the population standard deviation is known.
e.   The law of large numbers implies that, other things being equal, it is easier to be confident when making inferences using large samples.

Test Yourself 7.7***

Which of these options follows from the law of large numbers?

a.   If you are unlucky in roulette you should stick with the same number because it has to come up eventually.
b.   The mean of a small random sample of the population is more likely to be a reliable estimate of the population mean than that of a large sample.
c.   In the long run we can expect similar numbers of heads and tails from a fair coin.

(Continued)

(Continued)

d. The mean of a large sample will be larger than the mean of a small sample.

e. The standard deviation of a large sample will be smaller than the standard deviation of a small sample.

The correct answer to 7.4 is (a). If (a) is true, (b) must be wrong. Answer (c) is wrong because inferential uncertainty actually arises as a result of descriptive uncertainty. Answer (d) is wrong because descriptive uncertainty is reflected in the error term, not in the information term. Answer (e) is wrong because, although the two are related (because inferential uncertainty increases with descriptive uncertainty), they are not the same thing. Indeed, descriptive and inferential uncertainty reflect uncertainty about the answers to quite different questions. Descriptive uncertainty is uncertainty about the extent to which the sample is accurately described by a measure of central tendency (e.g., the mean). Inferential uncertainty is uncertainty about whether a relationship between variables or a difference between means is meaningful.

The correct answer to 7.5 is (b). z-scores involve the standard deviation and not the standard error. Answers (a) and (d) are nonsense answers based on other terms used in the chapter, and (c) is wrong because z-scores are also used for inferences about individual scores.

The correct answer to 7.6 is (b). This statement is false because statistical models actually allow us to calculate the probability that a random process (or chance) could have produced results as dramatic as ours. Statistical models cannot tell us whether a random process is actually operating. The former is our best way of estimating the probability that the results are due to chance, but it is not the same thing. All of the other statements are true and are explained in this chapter.

The correct answer to 7.7 is (c). Answer (a) is wrong because, if the game is fair, then random events are independent and do not depend on what has occurred in the past. Answer (b) is wrong because the statement is the wrong way around – the mean of a large random sample will be a more reliable estimate – and (d) is wrong because if both samples are drawn from the same population then their means should be estimates of the same population mean. There is no reason for one to be larger or smaller than the other (though the larger sample will tend to have a mean that is closer to the population mean). Answer (e) is wrong, but would be correct if we replaced 'standard deviation' with 'standard error'.

Discussion/essay questions

a. How does knowledge of random processes contribute to our ability to make statistical inferences?

b. Why is standardization a useful statistical procedure?

c. What is the law of large numbers? Discuss some everyday situations that demonstrate people's general awareness of the law.

d. What is the difference between a sample statistic and a population parameter? What are the implications of this distinction and why is it important?

Exercises

a. Janet obtains a score of 18 in an exam where the population mean level of performance is 15.2 and the standard deviation is 2.6 and the distribution of scores is normal. What is her standardized score in this test?

b. What percentage of exam-takers would be expected to obtain a score higher than Janet's?

c. A lecturer observes that his current class of 190 students obtains a mean score of 15.6 in this exam. How many standard error units is the class mean from the population mean?

d. What percentage of similar-sized classes would be expected to obtain a higher mean exam score than that of this particular class?

e. The sports teacher at a school randomly divides students into two teams for a sports day. The red team has 100 students and the blue team has 900 students. The prize goes to the team with the 10 fastest runners in the 1500 m race (i.e., for a team to win, its 10th fastest runner must beat the 10th fastest runner on the other team). The school population mean time for the 1500 m is known to be 7 minutes and the standard deviation is known to be 1 minute (60 seconds). All students enter the 1500 m race, and the running times are normally distributed.

  i. How many runners from the blue team would you expect to finish in the top 20 places?

  ii. Why is question (i) a trick question?

  iii. In what time would you expect the 10th fastest member of each team to complete the race?

  iv. What principle tells us that the contest is unfair? What should we infer if the red team wins the prize?

f. Gina is trying to find the best candidate to fill a vacancy in her architecture office in New York. She is given information about a field of three overseas applicants. Unfortunately, they all took their architectural exams in different places. Adam obtained a score of 145 in his exam in Adelaide (where the mean score in the test was 110, with a standard deviation of 15), Brenda obtained a score of 240 in her exams in Birmingham (where the mean score in the test was 180, with a standard deviation of 30), and Charles obtained a score of 50 in his exam in Christchurch (where the mean score on the test was 35, with a standard deviation of 7).

  i. Assuming that the population of candidates for the exams in the three cities is normally distributed and of equivalent ability, who appears to be best qualified for the job?

  ii. What percentage of architecture students would perform better than the best candidate for this job?

  iii. If Gina randomly selected three architects from the cities and standardized their scores, what proportion of those groups would have standardized means that were greater than the lowest standard score of any of the present applicants?

  iv. What does this tell us about the field of applicants for this job?

Examining Differences between Means: The *t*-test

Key goals for this chapter

- Introduce the *t*-test – a statistical procedure that allows researchers to establish how likely it is that observed differences between two means would have arisen by chance.
- Show how different types of *t*-test are used to examine different types of data.
- Explain the process of interpreting the results of *t*-tests, and the different ways that this can be done.

In the previous chapter we dealt with some statistical inferences under conditions where we knew quite a few things about the dependent variable. We used two examples: coin tossing and IQ test scores. At the risk of revealing trade secrets, we should point out that these two examples are pretty common in this sort of book.

The reasons for the popularity of these examples are worth looking at: the example of coin tossing is widely used because it relates to people's experiences in their everyday lives, but it is also an example where we can directly calculate an *exact* probability for each possible outcome. However, this state of affairs is pretty rare in psychological statistics. As we made clear in Chapter 7, most of the time we first have to calculate a test statistic (involving dividing an information term by an error term) and then identify the probability associated with that statistic by working it out or looking it up in a table.

The example of IQ scores is also widely used in books such as this one, in order to provide an introductory example of statistical inference. In part this is because IQ is a psychological variable that most people will have heard of before, but an even better reason is that we know that in the population the mean IQ is 100 and the standard deviation is 15. How do we know this? You might think that there is a mysterious process at work here, but in fact we know these things because the people who design IQ tests actually go to some trouble to ensure that IQ tests yield a mean of 100 and a standard deviation of 15. Once the test designer has ensured that the test is a valid and reliable measure of intelligence through extremely extensive sampling of the population and rigorous comparison with other measures, the mean of the test is reset to 100 and the standard deviation is set to 15 (following the process called *standardization* that we explained in Chapter 7). When all this is done the results of the test are then said to be IQ scores.

But this is actually quite an unusual set of circumstances. This extensive process of measurement and validation has been carried out for only a limited number of psychological variables, and in many cases there are still residual disputes about the validity of these measures. This means that, most of the time, psychological researchers do not know the population parameters of the measures they use. Instead they have to *estimate* these parameters. Along these lines, you will remember that we discussed how to estimate the population standard deviation in Chapter 6.

If we can estimate the population standard deviation we are in a position to conduct a *t*-test. A *t*-test is a test for differences between means under conditions where the population standard deviation is not known and therefore has to be estimated. In this chapter we first discuss the case where we are comparing the mean of a single sample with a known value. This is very similar to the case in the previous chapter where we compared the mean IQ of a sample of children in a particular class with the population mean of 100. We then deal with within-subjects experiments where we compare the mean response of a sample at one point in time, or on one measure, with the sample's mean response at another time or on another measure. Finally, we discuss the two-sample or between-subjects *t*-test. Here we compare means of two different samples of people. At that stage we will finally be able to answer the sort of question that we posed at the start of the previous chapter: How certain can we be that the scores for two groups of people on some psychological variable are really different?

> *t*-test A test for differences between means under conditions where the population standard deviation is not known but has to be estimated.

Student's *t*-distribution

The *t*-distribution describes a sampling distribution used to test the difference between means when the population standard deviation (σ) is unknown. It has a mean, or expected value, of 0. The reason why the expected value is 0 is that the **sampling distribution of differences between means** is based on a statistical model where we imagine that we are continuously drawing *two* random samples from the same population and comparing their means. Because the two samples are drawn from the same population, their means should both be estimates of the same population mean. Thus, saying that the expected value of the sampling distribution of the difference between the means is 0 is just a technical way of saying that we would expect no difference between the means if they are in fact estimates of the same population mean. If we find a large enough difference between the means of the two samples we draw, we start to question whether both means are actually estimates of the same population mean. We would go through the same process if we saw a coin come down heads or tails too many times and started to wonder if the coin was fair.

Put simply, the *t*-distribution describes the statistical model of what happens when you take random samples of a certain size from the population and subtract one mean from the other and divide the result by an estimate of the standard error. We are able to compare empirical results with the results we obtain from this statistical model and, what is more, the *t*-distribution tells us how likely the observed difference between means would be if that *t*-distribution's statistical model did apply. In the same way that the binomial distribution can tell us how likely a run of heads is with a fair coin, the *t*-distribution can tell us what the chance is of drawing two random samples from the same population with a difference between them of a certain size or bigger. However, what the model can never do is tell us whether the two samples are from the same population or from different populations. That is a decision researchers have to make for themselves, guided by the results of the statistical test.

The shape of the *t*-distribution changes as the sample size increases. This is once again a consequence of the law of large numbers. As we take larger and larger samples we obtain a statistic that actually becomes closer and closer to the normal distribution. This is largely a result of the fact that as samples become larger we obtain better estimates of the unknown population standard deviation. Indeed, with infinitely large samples *t* becomes normally distributed and equivalent to *z*.

There is thus a different *t*-distribution for every different sample size. Each *t*-distribution shows what the probability of any given difference between means is, expressed in standard error units. For example, if we found a difference between mean heights for a sample of three men and a sample of three women of 10 cm and a standard error of 5 cm then this would correspond to 2.0 *t*-units (i.e., 10/5). This would cut off the region of the *t*-distribution that is marked in Figure 8.1(a). We can see that only a small proportion of all the possible differences between the means lies beyond this point.

What this distribution does is map out all the possibilities that could occur if you were to calculate the mean for random samples of three people from the population and subtract the means for another random sample of three people, and express the differences between the means in standard error units. We can contrast this to the *t*-distribution for two samples of 30 people (Figure 8.1(b)).

The overall shapes of these distributions are pretty similar, but you can see that the tails of the sampling distribution as a whole are much smaller with the larger sample size. This is reflected in the fact that the area beyond 2.0 *t*-units is even smaller than it was in Figure 8.1(a), so that it contains an even smaller proportion of possible differences between means.

Rather than corresponding to sample size exactly, however, the sampling distribution of *t* depends on something called the **degrees of freedom**. The degrees of freedom are the

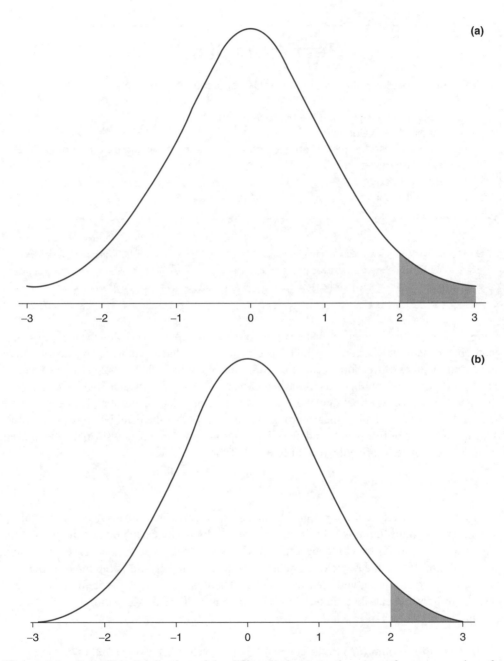

Figure 8.1 Sampling distribution of the difference between the means for two samples of size 3 (a) and 30 (b)

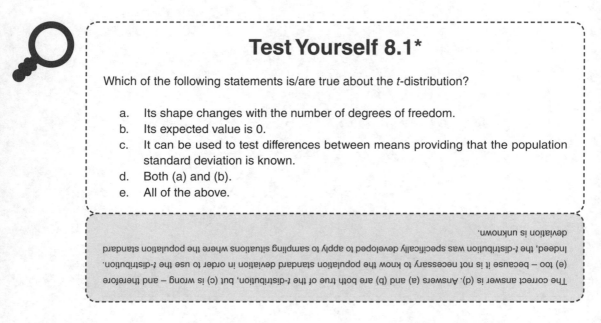

Test Yourself 8.1*

Which of the following statements is/are true about the *t*-distribution?

a. Its shape changes with the number of degrees of freedom.
b. Its expected value is 0.
c. It can be used to test differences between means providing that the population standard deviation is known.
d. Both (a) and (b).
e. All of the above.

The correct answer is (d). Answers (a) and (b) are both true of the *t*-distribution, but (c) is wrong – and therefore (e) too – because it is not necessary to know the population standard deviation in order to use the *t*-distribution. Indeed, the *t*-distribution was specifically developed to apply to sampling situations where the population standard deviation is unknown.

number of scores in a given set that are free to vary. To explain what this means, think of a waiter in a restaurant who forgets which customer ordered what at a table of five people. Here he has four degrees of freedom because if he can remember what four people ordered, he must get the fifth right. Put another way, if the waiter just guesses which meal to hand to one person after another he is only 'free' to make mistakes to a certain degree and that degree is four (if he gets the first four people's meals wrong then he knows that the meal belongs to the fifth). If he has one table of five people and one of two – providing that he knows which table placed the orders – then he has five degrees of freedom. That is,

$$df = (N_{table1} - 1) + (N_{table2} - 1) = 4 + 1$$

Returning to Figure 8.1, the top figure is actually the *t*-distribution for 4 degrees of freedom and the bottom figure is *t* for 58 degrees of freedom. The calculation of the number of degrees of freedom varies a bit depending on what sort of *t*-test you are doing, so we explain the calculation for each case below. The issue of degrees of freedom is the major difference between the *z*-distribution and the *t*-distribution. There is only one *z*-distribution for *z*-tests, the standard normal distribution, but for *t*-tests there is a different distribution for each different number of degrees of freedom.

degrees of freedom (*df*) In the calculation of a given statistic, the number of scores that are free to vary.

sampling distribution of the difference between means The hypothetical distribution of differences between the means of two random samples drawn from the same population. It has a mean of 0 and a standard deviation that decreases with the square root of the sample size.

t-distribution The hypothetical distribution of expected differences between the means of randomly chosen samples drawn from the same population divided by an estimate of the standard error.

Comparing the results for a single sample with a specific value

Often psychologists collect a set of data from a sample and then want to know whether the results are greater or less than some specified value. Let us imagine that 10 students do a multiple-choice test in psychology. Imagine, too, that the mean number of correct responses is 25 out of 100 and that there are five choices for each question. We might want to decide whether the students are performing better on the test than they would if they had just randomly chosen an answer. Given that there are five choices, the expected number of correct answers is 20. Some example data are shown in Table 8.1.

Table 8.1 Exam scores

Participant	Exam score
1	18
2	22
3	30
4	28
5	25
6	22
7	24
8	25
9	27
10	29

To judge whether students are performing better than chance we construct the test statistic *t* as a ratio of information over error (in fact we could do an exact probability calculation in this case as we did in the coin-tossing example, but we chose not to do that here).

We can use a computer program such as IBM SPSS Statistics software (SPSS) to help us make this judgement. To start with, open up the application SPSS on your computer and choose the option to type in new data.

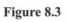

Figure 8.2

Figure 8.3

Type in the data exactly as shown in Figure 8.2. Include one row for each participant with the participant number in the first column and the score in the second column. This is a very common pattern used in data analysis in psychology and other human sciences where we have rows representing a set of scores for a participant and columns representing variables. In this case the first variable is not real data, it is simply a record-keeping variable that we create for the purpose of keeping track of which person has which score. Note too that, to enable you to check your work, these data are also provided in the Supplementary Online Material [Chapter8_OneSamplettest.sav].

When you have done that let us rename 'VAR00001' by changing it to 'Participant' and 'VAR00002' to 'TestScore' (with no space before 'Score'). We are now actually ready to use SPSS to perform the statistical analysis, but before starting choose a helpful name and save the data file somewhere you will be able to keep it safe (noting that the habit of saving data files carefully and using logical names to identify them is a very good one to get into).

After saving the data go to the 'Analyze' menu of SPSS and select 'Compare Means → One-Sample T Test'. When you do you should see the display shown in Figure 8.3.

The variable that we want to test here is called TestScore. We want to be able to judge whether exam scores are higher than the expected (chance) value of 20. Thus, our test variable is 'TestScore' so we need to drag that variable from the left to the right in order to select it for the analysis. We also have to enter the test value of 20 into the text box labelled 'Test Value'. The window should now look like Figure 8.4.

Figure 8.4

If it does, click on 'OK' and you should see the display in Figure 8.5.

T–Test

[DataSet1] /Users/20062061/Documents/SPSSInc/PASWStatistics18/OneSampleBookexample.sav

One-Sample Statistics

	N	Mean	Std. Deviation	Std. Error Mean
TestScore	10	25.0000	3.68179	1.16428

One-Sample Test

	Test Value = 20					
					95% Confidence Interval of the Difference	
	t	df	Sig. (2-tailed)	Mean Difference	Lower	Upper
TestScore	4.294	9	.002	5.00000	2.3662	7.6338

Figure 8.5

SPSS here provides us first with some descriptive statistics that tell us that there are 10 participants ($N = 10$) with a mean exam score of 25.0 and that the standard deviation is 3.68 and the standard error of the mean is 1.16 (this is just the standard deviation divided by the square root of the sample size).

The next table contains the actual results of the analysis (or inferential statistics). Here we have compared a mean score of 25.0 with the test value of 20. We want to know if that difference is big enough to be taken seriously or so small that it can be treated as a chance variation. In other words, is this class of 10 students good or are they just lucky?

The results of the analysis give us a value for t of 4.294. This has been calculated by dividing the difference between the mean (25; $\bar{X}$ in the equation below) and the test value (20; value in the equation below) by the standard error of the mean (1.16; $s_X/\sqrt{N}$ in the equation below). This division involves the ratio of information to error. Here the information term tells us that the mean is five points bigger than the test value and the error term tells us that the average amount of variation expected in the mean – for a sample of 10 people drawn from a population with that standard deviation – is around 1.16 points.

$$t(9) = \frac{\bar{X} - \text{value}}{S_X/\sqrt{N}} \quad \text{(infomation term)}$$
$$\text{(error term)}$$
$$= \frac{25 - 20}{3.68/\sqrt{10}}$$
$$= 4.29$$

Is this t-value big enough for us to decide one way or another? If the t-value were 0 then that would tell us that there was absolutely no difference between the sample mean and the test value, and even if the *t*-value was 1 that would still be indicating that the difference between the mean and the test value is still so small that we would routinely expect differences of that size if we were just to draw samples of 10 people from a population with that mean. That is, it looks like a run-of-the-mill everyday occurrence. As the value of *t* becomes much bigger than 1, however, the picture changes. In this example the difference between the mean and test value is 4.29 times as large as the differences we would routinely expect. When it comes to deciding if the class is lucky or good then we need to be leaning towards thinking that if they are lucky then they have been really, really lucky.

If they were of average ability, how lucky have they been? To answer this we need the other information in the table. This includes the number of degrees of freedom (*df*) for the test (which in this case is $N - 1 = 10 - 1 = 9$) that tells us the shape of the *t*-distribution and allows SPSS to calculate that a *t* of 4.29 is associated with a *p*-value of .002. This is telling us that if we took samples of 10 people from a population with a mean of 20 and a standard deviation of 3.68 then we should expect differences as big as five points only twice in every thousand occasions. That result does not prove that the students were good, but it really encourages us to doubt that they were simply lucky (we therefore have low inferential uncertainty).

Test Yourself 8.2***

The mean height of a sample of 100 men in 2014 is 180 cm, with a standard deviation of 10 cm. The mean for the same population in 1914 was 170 cm. Imagine that we want to use the 2014 sample to test whether the height of the population has changed over the intervening 100 years. Which of the following statements is true?

a. The number of degrees of freedom for the test in this case is 99.
b. The *t*-value is 10.0.
c. The *t*-value corresponds to a very small probability that a random process of taking samples of 100 men from a population similar to the 1914 population would produce a sample of 180 cm or taller.
d. All of the above.
e. Answers (a) and (b) only.

The correct answer is (d). Answers (a), (b) and (c) are all correct here. The degrees of freedom are equal to $n - 1$ = 99, so (a) is correct. The *t*-value is $(180 - 170)/(10/\sqrt{100})$ = 10, so (b) is correct. A *t*-value of 10.00 far exceeds the *t*-value for 99 degrees of freedom associated with a probability level of .001, so (c) is correct. In other words, there is less than a 1 in 1000 chance that a random process of taking samples from the 1914 population would produce a difference this size or larger.

The table puts the same information in another way by showing us the confidence intervals for the difference. We will come back to confidence intervals later in the chapter, but for now just think of confidence intervals as a range of expected values.

Within-subjects *t*-tests

The within-subjects *t*-test is used when we are comparing means based on sets of data that are collected in pairs from the same participants. Let us go back to the example used in Chapter 2 where we talked about the process of testing a 'physical reinforcement theory'. This simple theory explained the observation that 'absence leads the heart to wander' by proposing that attraction to another person is dependent on physical reinforcement achieved through interaction with them. Let us imagine we do an experiment to test this theory where participants have to make attractiveness ratings of two people – one with whom they have interacted (Person I, for Interaction) and one with whom they have not (Person N, for No interaction). In this experiment physical reinforcement has been manipulated *within subjects* because all participants are in both conditions. Our theory predicts that attraction will be greater for ratings of Person I than Person N. The dependent variable is ratings of the attractiveness of these two people on a nine-point scale from 1 to 9 (where 1 = 'do not like at all' and 9 = 'like a great deal'). Suppose our data were as in Table 8.2.

Table 8.2

	Target person	
Participant	**I**	**N**
1.00	7.00	6.00
2.00	6.00	6.00
3.00	5.00	2.00
4.00	6.00	4.00
5.00	5.00	3.00
6.00	7.00	5.00
7.00	3.00	5.00

Note that these are *pairs* of data. For example, Participant 1 responded '7' when rating the person he or she had interacted with (Person I) and '5' when rating the person he or she had not interacted with (Person N).

Just by looking at these results we can see that the pattern of data is generally consistent with our hypothesis, but the question is whether the ratings of *I* and *N* are *sufficiently different* to infer that they reflect a real underlying difference. As we have already noted several times, inferential statistics cannot answer this question directly, but they can tell us how likely it is that two sets of responses as different as this would have been drawn randomly from the same population. To find out, we can use the skills with SPSS from the earlier example:

Figure 8.6

1. Open SPSS and create a new data file (the Type in Data choice).
2. Create three variables in the data file named 'Participant', 'RateI' and 'RateN' and enter the data as in Figure 8.6 (this is also provided in the Supplementary Online Material [Chapter8_WithinSSttest.sav]).
   Click on 'Variable View' and then 'Variable Label' so you can give the variables meaningful labels such as 'Rating of Person I' and 'Rating of Person N'.
3. After saving the data file in a personal folder or on a USB drive go to the 'Analyze' menu of SPSS and select 'Compare Means → Paired-Samples T Test'. When you do you should see the display in Figure 8.7.

Figure 8.7

The variables we want to compare are 'Rating of Person I' and 'Rating of Person N'. So drag 'Rating of Person I' to be 'Variable 1' in 'Pair' '1' and 'Rating of Person N' to be 'Variable 2' and then click on 'OK'.

The first table that is generated gives us the descriptive statistics, in the form shown in Figure 8.8.

Paired Samples Statistics

		Mean	N	Std. Deviation	Std. Error Mean
Pair 1	Rating of Person I	5.5714	7	1.39728	.52812
	Rating of Person N	4.4286	7	1.51186	.57143

Figure 8.8

The second table (Figure 8.9) gives us another descriptive statistic that tells us the strength of the (linear) relationship between the variables. We discuss this more in the next chapter, but for the time being we simply want to know if the value in the correlation cell is greater than .3 (if it is not then we are not using the best method to answer the question).

Paired Samples Correlations

		N	Correlation	Sig.
Pair 1	Rating of Person I & Rating of Person N	7	.338	.458

Figure 8.9

The third table (Figure 8.10) gives us the result of the *t*-test. The value tells us that the mean difference between the ratings of Person I and Person N is 1.14 (I is rated higher than N) and that the variability in these differences can be expressed as a standard deviation of 1.67616 or a standard error of the mean of .63353. This corresponds to a *t*-value with 6 degrees of freedom (*df*) of 1.804 that is associated with a *p*-value of .121.

Paired Samples Test

| | | Paired Differences | | | | | | | |
| | | | | | 95% Confidence Interval of the Difference | | | | |
		Mean	Std. Deviation	Std. Error Mean	Lower	Upper	t	df	Sig. (2-tailed)
Pair 1	Rating of Person I – Rating of Person N	1.14286	1.67616	.63353	-.40734	2.69305	1.804	6	.121

Figure 8.10

SPSS has calculated the *t*-value using the following formula:

$$t = \frac{\bar{D}}{S_D / \sqrt{N}} \quad \begin{array}{l}\text{(information term)}\\\text{(error term)}\end{array}$$

So, substituting relevant values from the above tables, we can see this was calculated as follows:

$$t = \frac{1.14285}{1.67616/\sqrt{7}} \quad \begin{array}{l}\text{(information term)}\\\text{(error term)}\end{array}$$

$$= \frac{1.14285}{0.617}$$

$$= 1.804$$

The corresponding *p*-value tells us that if there really were no differences between the measures (i.e., they were both measuring the same thing), then a difference as large as that which has been obtained could be expected 121 out of every 1000 times. That is, it is quite unlikely but not extremely unlikely.

Between-subjects *t*-tests

The above case dealt with a situation where we had two sets of data from the same sample of participants. So, by using difference scores, we could use one mean and one standard deviation to represent both sets of scores. Let us now consider a between-subjects case where we are comparing means obtained from *different* groups of participants. In essence, our decision as to whether those means are likely to have been drawn from the same population comes down to a statement about the difference between two means *relative* to the variation of scores around each of those means and the number of responses on which the means are based.

This may sound complex, but the underlying logic is quite simple and can be illustrated in the following scenario. In this diagram each 'e' is a response on a scale from 1 to 7 by a person in an experimental condition, and each 'c' a response on the same scale by a person in a control condition; the sample size varies between the three cases:

In which of these cases would you be most confident that the responses of people in the two conditions reflected a real underlying difference between groups? Your confidence should be greatest in Case 3. This is for two reasons. First, in Case 3 the dispersion of the two sets of responses is smaller than in Case 1 (and the **overlap** in the response distributions is smaller). Second, Case 3 provides more evidence of a real difference than Case 2 because it is based on more data (i.e., the sample size is larger). So here, even though the means are the same in each case, we would be more confident that the population mean for the experimental condition really was greater than that for the control condition in Case 3 because the *difference in means relative to the amount of error* is greater.

Going back to our example of research on 'physical reinforcement theory' that was exploring the basis of attraction between people, let us consider a new experiment. In this experiment, instead of each participant rating two target people (the within-subjects case), let us imagine that some participants in an experimental condition interact with and then rate a target person and that *other* participants in a control condition do not interact with the target person they are asked to rate. Participants might then rate their attraction to the target person they are asked to consider on a nine-point scale (where 1 = 'do not like at all' and 9 = 'like a great deal'). Here we would obtain two independent sets of 'attractiveness ratings', one from participants in the experimental condition and one from participants in the control condition. Let us imagine that the data looked like Table 8.3.

Our physical reinforcement theory predicts that participants in the experimental condition should like the target person more. This would appear to be the case: the mean rating of the target's attractiveness is higher in the experimental condition ($\bar{X}_1 = 6.4$) than in the control condition ($\bar{X}_2 = 4.4$).

Table 8.3

Participant	Attractiveness rating	Condition
1	4	Experimental
2	5	Experimental
3	7	Experimental
4	8	Experimental
5	6	Experimental
6	9	Experimental
7	7	Experimental
8	8	Experimental
9	5	Experimental
10	5	Experimental
11	4	Control
12	4	Control
13	6	Control
14	5	Control
15	7	Control
16	3	Control
17	4	Control
18	2	Control
19	5	Control
20	4	Control

The question, though, is whether this difference is big enough to allow us to conclude that the two means are unlikely to have been drawn from the same population. In other words, what we really want to know is whether the two samples are drawn from the same population (with the same population mean) and are just different by chance or whether the samples are drawn from two different populations. As you may be sick of reading by now, we can never tell this exactly. So instead we determine the chance that a difference this large could be obtained by drawing random samples from the same population. To do this we can go back to SPSS and create a new data file entering the numbers from the table above (again, this is also available in the Supplementary Online Material [Chapter8_BetweenSSttest.sav]).

This time, in addition to scores we have a categorical variable, condition, that has two levels: experimental condition and control condition. We need to tell SPSS which of our participants are in each condition. Let us use the coding '1 = Experimental' and '2 = Control'.

We now need to put some labels on the values to help us understand the output and so that we remember how we coded these variables the next time we look at them. After entering the data as shown above, go to 'Variable View' and click on 'VAR00003'. First of all rename this 'Condition' and then click on 'Value Labels'. Type in 'Experimental Group' for the value '1',

Research Methods and Statistics in Psychology

and 'Control Group' for value '2'. After renaming 'VAR00001' as 'Participant' and 'VAR00002' as 'AttrScore' and giving it a clear variable label such as 'Attractiveness Rating' and then saving the data file, we are ready to go.

Now select 'Compare Means → Independent-Samples T Test'. Select 'AttrScore' as the 'Test Variable' and 'Condition' as the 'Grouping Variable', and then select 'Group 1' to have the value '1' and 'Group 2' to have the value '2'. Click on 'OK' and SPSS will produce two tables. The first of these (shown in Figure 8.11) contains descriptive statistics. The second (shown in Figure 8.12) contains the inferential statistics.

Group Statistics

	Condition	N	Mean	Std. Deviation	Std. Error Mean
Attractiveness Rating	Experimental Group	10	6.4000	1.64655	.52068
	Control Group	10	4.4000	1.42984	.45216

Figure 8.11

Independent Samples Test

		Levene's Test for Equality of Variances		t-test for Equality of Means					95% Confidence Interval of the Difference	
		F	Sig.	t	df	Sig. (2-tailed)	Mean Difference	Std. Error Difference	Lower	Upper
Attractiveness Rating	Equal variances assumed	.799	.383	2.900	18	.010	2.00000	.68961	.55119	3.44881
	Equal variances not assumed			2.900	17.653	.010	2.00000	.68961	.54915	3.45085

Figure 8.12

SPSS gives us two versions of the t-test, one assuming that the samples are drawn from populations with the same variance and one that relaxes that assumption. We will come to this later, but in this case the results are the same for the two methods so we will choose the method assuming equal variance.

SPSS has calculated a t-value of 2.900 based on 18 degrees of freedom that is associated with a p-value of .010. SPSS has calculated this t-value using the following formula:

$$t = \frac{\bar{X}_1 - \bar{X}_2}{\sqrt{S^2_{pooled}\left(\frac{1}{N_1} + \frac{1}{N_2}\right)}} \quad \text{(information term)} \atop \text{(error term)}$$

In this case:

$$t = \frac{6.4 - 4.4}{\sqrt{2.38\left(\frac{1}{10} + \frac{1}{10}\right)}} = \frac{2.0}{0.69} = 2.90$$

The *p*-value of .010 implies that there is 1 chance in 100 that a random process could have produced a difference between means this large.

Before moving on, it is worth noting that one of the most confusing things about *t*-tests is the wide variety of different terms that are used to describe the different types of tests. If you were to read another textbook after this one, you might be forgiven for thinking that there are lots of different types of *t*-test. In fact there are only two types that you really have to worry about – the within-subjects *t*-test and the between-subjects *t*-test. We have chosen to use these names because they relate directly to the methodological terms that psychologists use, and because they match the usage of these terms in other statistical tests (in particular, analysis of variance, an advanced procedure for comparing more than two means, also referred to as ANOVA; see Chapter 10).

Table 8.4 is intended to help you work out what the different types of *t*-test are when you see the terms used in other books and in the research literature.

Table 8.4 Terms used to describe *t*-tests

Terms for within-subjects t-tests	Terms for between-subjects t-tests
Dependent *t*-test	Two-sample *t*-test
Related-samples *t*-test	Independent-groups *t*-test Independent-
Paired samples *t*-test (this is what SPSS calls it)	samples t-test (this is what SPSS calls it)
Repeated-measures *t*-test	
Correlated-samples *t*-test	

Test Yourself 8.3*

Which of the following is *not* relevant to a between-subjects *t*-test?

a. The pooled variance estimate.
b. A difference score *D*.
c. An information term.
d. A sampling distribution of the differences between means.
e. A probability that a difference of the same size or larger could be obtained by a random process.

The correct answer is (b). The difference score *D* is used in the within-subjects *t*-test where we deal with the difference between pairs of the scores from the same participant. The features referred to in answers (a), (c), (d) and (e) are all aspects of between-subjects *t*-tests discussed in this chapter.

Test Yourself 8.4***

If an experimenter conducts a *t*-test to see whether the responses of participants in a control group differ from those of an experimental group, which of the following outcomes will yield the highest *t*-value?

  a. If there are 10 participants in each condition and the difference between the mean responses of the control group and the experimental group is 2 and both have standard deviations of 1.
  b. If there are 10 participants in each condition and the difference between the mean responses of the control group and the experimental group is 2 and both have standard deviations of 2.
  c. If there are 20 participants in each condition and the difference between the mean responses of the control group and the experimental group is 1 and both have standard deviations of 1.
  d. If there are 20 participants in each condition and the difference between the mean responses of the control group and the experimental group is 2 and both have standard deviations of 1.
  e. If there are 20 participants in each condition and the difference between the mean responses of the control group and the experimental group is 2 and both have standard deviations of 2.

The correct answer is (d). The value of *t* is largest when you have small standard deviations, large samples and a large difference between means. All of these conditions apply in answer (d). The largest samples contain 20 participants per condition, the smallest standard deviation is 1, and the largest difference between means is 2. Based on these principles, we can conclude that the value of *t* will be greater in (a) than in (b), greater in (d) than (a), greater in (d) than (c) and greater in (d) than (e). Of course we could actually calculate the *t*-values for each of the alternatives, but this would take quite a bit of time. The point of this question is to get you thinking about what the formula for *t* actually means.

overlap of distributions The degree to which two distributions share the same range of values. The overlap of the two distributions in Figure 8.13 is shown by the shaded region.

pooled variance estimate An estimate of the variance of the population made by averaging the variances of the two samples to provide the error term for the between-subjects *t*-test.

weighted average An average where the result is modified to take account of differing sample sizes. A weighted average tends towards a given sample mean in

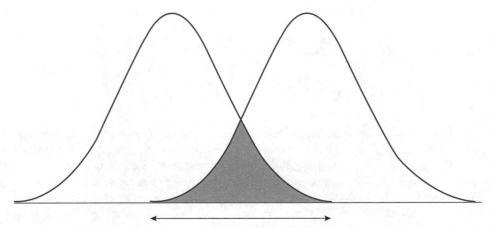

Overlap of distributions

Figure 8.13

proportion to the sample's size relative to the size of other samples being compared. If one group of 10 people has a mean score of 10 and another group of 100 people has a mean score of 20, the weighted average will therefore be much closer to the mean of the larger sample. In this case it is not 15 but $[(10 \times 10) + (100 \times 20)]/110 = 19.09$.

The controversy about what to do with *t*-values

At this stage you might be feeling that the process of statistical inference is a bit clumsy. After all, we are interested in two possibilities: whether the results we have obtained are due to chance or whether they represent a real difference between two means. These possibilities seem pretty obvious to most people when they are explained, but confusion arises because inferential statistics never allow us to reach either conclusion with complete certainty. Statistical tests never allow us to say that our results are due to a random process. All they can ever do is tell us how likely they would be if they *were* due to a random process. Similarly, the results of statistical tests can never tell us that our findings are not due to chance.

The inability of statistics to answer particular questions can be confusing and frustrating for both students and experienced researchers – not least because in order to convey accurately the truth of what statistical tests are telling us we have to use very awkward forms of expression. Indeed, you probably encountered some frustration while reading the preceding pages. Consider the way we described the results of the within-subjects *t*-test: 'That is, it is quite unlikely but not really unlikely.' We can hear you saying 'Can't you just tell me whether it is one or the other? Is it unlikely or not? Or could you at least tell me whether it is unlikely enough?'.

RESEARCH BITE 8.1
The prudence of a Bayesian approach

One major limitation of the hypothesis-testing approach is that it does not allow researchers to test the plausibility of the null hypothesis or to weigh evidence in favour of this against that in favour of the alternative hypothesis. One approach that can do these things involves using Bayesian statistics. Although beyond the scope of this text, these are becoming increasingly popular in many areas of psychology. A recent study by Ruud Wetzels and colleagues (2011) also shows that in around 70% of cases where a hypothesis-testing approach would lead one to conclude that there is positive evidence against the null hypothesis, a Bayesian approach would characterize that evidence as relatively weak.

Reference
Wetzels, R., Matzke, D., Lee, M. D., Rouder, J. N., Iverson, G. J., & Wagenmakers, E. J. (2011). Statistical evidence in experimental psychology: An empirical comparison using 855 *t*-tests. *Perspectives on Psychological Science*, 6, 291–298.

Photo 8.1 Did this card player cheat, or is he just lucky? It is important to remember that statistics cannot answer such questions. In this case they could only allow us to say exactly how lucky this person was if they were playing fair – and then to base our judgement on this information.

However, *attempts to simplify the way we express statistical ideas lead to inaccuracy.* Because the temptation to simplify statistical test results is quite strong, many psychologists and statist-icians have argued that statistical tests are poorly understood and poorly used. This problem can be traced back to the fact that statistical tests do not answer *exactly* the questions that research scientists want to answer. They only answer *related* questions.

When you decided where to study or which mobile phone to buy you may have asked other people about their experiences or have read reviews. You may have used this information to make your decision, but your decision is not the same as that information.

Doing a statistical test is more like getting the advice of a trusted friend ('yep, that's a good phone') than actually making a purchase decision.

Another useful analogy might be an election result and a public opinion poll a month before the election. The question that everybody wants to know the answer to is who will win the election. We cannot answer that question until the election but, as we saw in Chapter 6, if an opinion poll is conducted properly, we can use its results as a guide upon which to base our expectations. Statistical tests play the same role. They cannot tell us if there is a real difference but they give us a basis for making a reasonable decision about whether there is a difference.

Problems with reporting and interpreting statistics have been around for a long time. But recently in psychology there has been a great deal of argument about exactly how to use inferential statistics (e.g., as reflected in the initial report of the Task Force on Statistical Inference of the Board of Scientific Affairs of the American Psychological Association, released December 1996, 1998). For the purposes of this chapter, the controversy relates to what to do with t-values once we have obtained them. The next few sections offer *choices* to students and instructors about how to conduct statistical tests and make statistical inferences. *We suggest that all students should be familiar with the hypothesis-testing approach and with the alternative approaches.* This follows the advice of many psychological statisticians who argue that we should compensate for the limitations of the hypothesis-testing approach by employing (or at least considering) other methods (Cohen, 1994, 1995; Hammond, 1996; Judd, McClelland, & Culhane, 1995; Syvantek & Ekeberg, 1995; Wilkinson et al., 1999).

Handling the results of *t*-tests: The hypothesis-testing approach

Once we have obtained the value of t and worked out the corresponding probability value we have some more decisions to make. What we have effectively done so far is turn an observed difference between means into a probability value. We then have to decide whether that probability is small enough for us to conclude that the two means were unlikely to have been drawn from the same population. You might reasonably ask whether this process has got us very far. After all, we only did the t-test so that we could make a definitive statement about whether the difference between the means was large or small, and now it seems that we have to decide whether the **p-value** is big or small.

The answer is that we have indeed made some progress because, rather than simply talking about differences between means, we now have a probability value that is comparable across research situations. The probability value is comparable because it depends on both the difference between the means and the amount of dispersion or random error in the sample.

The **hypothesis-testing** or **significance-testing** approach to t-tests is an attempt to come up with definitive answers to the question of whether we have observed an informative difference between means or not. The logic underpinning this approach is to develop a statistical model that assumes that both means are based on random samples from the same population (i.e., the samples share the same population mean and standard deviation). The sampling distribution provided by the *t*-distribution is just a mathematical way of expressing this statistical model of no difference between means, and, as we have discussed, the expected value of the *t*-distribution is zero. That is, if the means are both drawn from the same population then there *should be* no difference.

This statistical model that there should be no difference between the means is called the **null hypothesis**. In all psychological research the null hypothesis is really a statement about what we would expect if there is nothing dramatic going on in our research (and in the population to which it relates). That is, it is a statement of what should occur if we are simply observing a random process. The null hypothesis is often called H_0 (pronounced 'H nought').

When testing for a difference between means using a *t*-test, the null hypothesis is

$$H_0: \mu_1 = \mu_2 = \mu$$

What this says is that the null hypothesis assumes that, μ_1, the population mean associated with Sample 1 (in the between-subjects case) or with Variable 1 (in the within-subjects case), is the same as μ_2, the population mean associated with Sample 2 or Variable 2, and that they are both equal to the same value (μ). This model also assumes that the standard deviations of each sample are estimates of the population standard deviation (and should therefore be similar).

The model is just like imagining that we have programmed a computer to repeatedly produce means for pairs of samples of a given size from a population with a certain mean and standard deviation. Imagine that we then get the computer to calculate the *t*-values obtained and draw these differences as a frequency graph. If the null hypothesis is true then our data should look like a typical distribution of *t*-values randomly generated by the computer (i.e., a normal distribution). In fact, because random variables are so well behaved in the long run, we do not need to write such a computer program to do statistics – we can use equations and look up values in a table.

When we use a hypothesis-testing approach to test for differences between means we contrast this null hypothesis model with the alternative that there actually *is* a difference between the means. This is called the **alternative hypothesis** or H_1 and is a statement to the effect that something dramatic *is* going on in our research – reflecting something going on in the population from which our samples are drawn. In this case we assert that the two means are really drawn from two different populations with different means. When testing for a difference between means using a *t*-test, the general form of the alternative hypothesis is therefore

$$H_1: \mu_1 \neq \mu_2$$

This says that the alternative hypothesis is that μ_1, the population mean associated with Sample 1 (in the between-subjects case) or with Variable 1 (in the within-subjects case), is *not* the same as the population mean associated with Sample 2 or Variable 2. An alternative hypothesis like this is normally based on a theory which provides the rationale for our research.

The logical process of the hypothesis-testing approach involves testing between the null hypothesis and the alternative hypothesis. We do not accept the null hypothesis when inferential uncertainty is high, but we reject it and accept the alternative hypothesis when inferential uncertainty is low. *In other words, we never say that the null hypothesis is true, but under certain circumstances we conclude that it is probably false, and so accept the alternative hypothesis.* Researchers and students often forget the fact that, regardless of the results of statistical tests, we can reject or not reject the null hypothesis but we are never entitled to accept the null hypothesis. Again, this is because statistics can never *prove* that a random process has produced the results. We do not know whether the null hypothesis is actually true or whether our study was just not sensitive enough to detect a real difference between means.

In order to make the decision about whether we will reject the null hypothesis or not, we take our *t*-distribution and divide it into three regions. A large region in the middle contains most possible values of *t* and two small regions in the tails of the distribution contain only a few extreme values of *t*. These small regions are called the **rejection regions**. If the obtained value of *t* falls in one of these rejection regions then we say that the difference between means is **statistically significant**. In other words, statistical significance is another way of saying that inferential uncertainty is low. The process is shown in Figure 8.14.

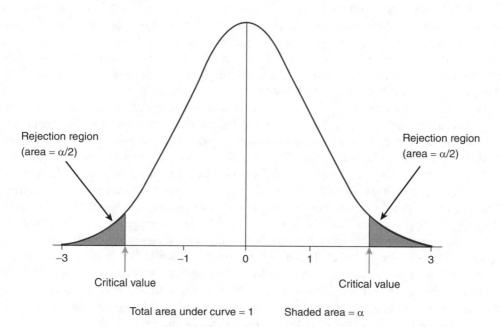

Figure 8.14 The *t*-distribution showing rejection regions

You will note that for each tail there is a value that cuts off the rejection region. These values are called **critical values**. If the obtained *t*-value falls in the tail beyond either critical value, it falls in the rejection region. Under these conditions we *reject* the null hypothesis (hence the name 'rejection regions') and conclude that the difference between means is significant – thereby accepting the alternative hypothesis.

How large should these rejection regions be? Well, that depends on how much inferential uncertainty you are prepared to live with. Those psychologists who use significance levels tend to follow the suggestion that a 5% or less chance that a random process could produce the same results is sufficiently low to conclude that the results were not produced by a random process. This figure is commonly used in psychological research, but people also use 1% and .1% chances. We call these values **alpha levels** (or, to use the Greek letter for alpha, α levels). Alpha levels correspond to the size of the rejection region, and because we can never be completely sure that our results are not due to chance, an alpha level is essentially just a researcher's statement about the level of inferential uncertainty that he or she is prepared to live with. Rather than use percentages as alpha levels we quote them as probability values, so a rejection region of 5% corresponds to an alpha level of .05. When the obtained t-value exceeds the critical value and the value falls in the rejection region, we say 'p is less than α' where α is an alpha level such as .05 (so here we would write $p < .05$).

As an analogy to the process of working with alpha levels, imagine that you and a friend want to drive to a town 500 kilometres away. Your car is not particularly new and lately you have heard a few rattles coming from somewhere near the engine. Your natural inclination is to assume that the rattles mean nothing, that they are just randomly generated noise that you need not pay attention to. This, in effect, is a null hypothesis – a statement of the view that the noise does not amount to much. On the other hand, you at least entertain the possibility that there may be something to the noise after all. Maybe the engine is about to self-destruct. This, in effect, is an alternative hypothesis – a statement of the view that the rattle is *not* just a random noise, but a signal that you should pay attention to and probably do something about.

Faced with these two possibilities (the only logical alternatives) you then have to decide which one to go with. It is not an easy decision to make, but one way to do this would be to decide on an alpha level for your car before you set out on your trip. This amounts to a statement of the amount of uncertainty about whether the car is fit for the journey that you are prepared to accept – a statement of when you are going to take the mysterious noise seriously. The alpha level you set will depend on a large number of factors including the importance of the journey, the cost of a breakdown and the weather. You might be prepared to start the journey if you thought that the chance that there was really something wrong with the engine was less than 10% (an alpha level of .10). However, your friend might only be prepared to travel with you if there was no more than a 1% chance of the engine breaking down (an alpha level of .01). Obviously, in everyday life we do not go around quantifying uncertainty like this in numbers. We express our everyday doubts by saying things like 'I'm pretty sure we'll make it' or 'I don't want to seem rude, but I'd feel happier taking the bus'.

In reflecting on this process, it is important to point out that alpha levels are criteria that researchers set *before* they conduct research in much the same way that high jumpers set the height of the bar before they run up and make a jump. If their obtained result yields a value that falls in the rejection region associated with a given alpha level then they reject the null hypothesis. How much they exceed the critical value by is not particularly important. On the other hand, if their obtained value falls outside the rejection region then they do not reject the null hypothesis. Again this decision should not be affected by the distance between the obtained and critical values. The point here is that if you adopt the hypothesis-testing approach then you either clear the bar (the critical value associated with your alpha level) or you do not.

There are just two further complications to the process we have described so far. You will note that there are two rejection regions in Figure 8.14. This is because t-values can be positive or negative. This occurs because the first mean can be larger than the second, or the second can be larger than the first. Because the obtained value of t can fall in either tail, we call this a **two-tailed test**.

The total rejection region is divided into two tails. If $\alpha = .05$ (5%) then each of the two rejection regions will be 2.5% (i.e., $\alpha/2$) of the total distribution. Under some circumstances, however, we can take a slightly different approach where we test a different alternative hypothesis. Think for a moment about H_1:

$$H_1: \mu_1 \neq \mu_2$$

This can be re-expressed in the following way:

$$H_{1a}: \mu_1 > \mu_2$$

and

$$H_{1b}: \mu_1 < \mu_2$$

That is, if the two means are not equal then one has to be larger than the other. Sometimes we might want to test both those possibilities, but under other circumstances this does not make sense. If we compare the heights of men and women we might want to know whether men are taller or not, but it is not particularly useful or relevant to test the idea that men are shorter than women. Thus, under some circumstances we only have

$$H_1: \mu_1 > \mu_2$$

That is, we hypothesize that one mean will be greater than the other. If this is the case, rather than using two rejection regions, it can be appropriate to use a single rejection region at one end of the distribution, as shown in Figure 8.15. You will note that the critical value cutting off the rejection region is closer to zero (i.e., smaller) in this case. This test with only one rejection region is called a **one-tailed test** or a **directional test**.

Opinions about when one-tailed tests should be used vary, but they are most appropriate under circumstances where researchers know that one mean cannot possibly be larger than the other. So unless they have a good reason not to, researchers should use the two-tailed test described above, where there is a rejection region in each tail. Using one-tailed tests to make non-significant results become significant is particularly inappropriate – this is equivalent to high jumpers lowering the height of the bar when they have just failed to clear it with their one and only attempt.

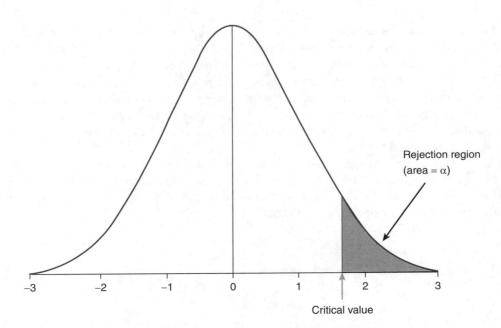

Rejection region
(area = α)

Critical value

Figure 8.15 The *t*-distribution showing rejection region for one-tailed test

A second complication is that sometimes when we make a statistical inference we find that we have made a mistake. Either we have said that there is a difference between means when there is not really a difference, or we have said that there is no difference when there is. When we say there is a difference between means when there is none – in other words, when we *reject the null hypothesis when it is actually true* – this is called a **Type I error**. The second type of error – where we *do not reject the null hypothesis when it is false* – is called a **Type II error**.

In the language that we have been using to deal with issues of statistical inference, these two types of error relate to the *appropriateness* of a researcher's certainty. A Type I error occurs when researchers are wrong in saying that something is going on. A Type II error occurs when researchers are wrong in saying that something is not going on.

As you can probably see, these two types of error are actually interrelated. This is because as researchers seek to reduce the likelihood of making a Type I error (by reducing their alpha level and being prepared to tolerate less inferential uncertainty), their chances of making a Type II error are increased. In fact both errors arise because we make all-or-none decisions about information which is not clear cut but is based on probability. However, as we have been at pains to point out, if the data were clear cut we would not need to use statistics in the first place.

The chance of making these errors is something that we have to take very seriously. An acute problem arises where certain statistical tests or methodological circumstances are more likely to lead to one type of error than the other. Because we are always liable to make some errors we need to know whether those errors will be of a particular kind so that we can correct them. Furthermore, some types of error are more undesirable than others in particular circumstances. For example, if clinical psychologists were testing the effectiveness of a therapy that has the possibility of harmful side-effects, they would want to avoid Type I errors because they would not want to expose clients to these risks if the therapy did not actually help.

We are more likely to make Type II errors when the sample size or the effect is small, when we are investigating effects of a small size, where there is a lot of random error, or where the alpha level is very small. It is worth looking at the terms in the equation for the t-statistic to see why this is the case. Type II errors can only occur when the obtained test statistic is smaller than the critical value of t – that is, when we do not reject the null hypothesis. Type II errors are therefore associated with factors that reduce the value of the calculated t-value and with those that increase the critical t-value. A small value of calculated t will be obtained when there is a small sample size, a large error term or a small information term (i.e., a small difference between means). A large critical value of t will be obtained when the alpha level (not the p-value) is very small.

When the likelihood of making a Type II error is inflated for one or more of these reasons, the t-test will be unlikely to reveal any relationships that may be present in the data. This is analogous to looking at stars with a very weak telescope. To avoid these problems we can use a more powerful test, in the same way that an astronomer would use a more powerful telescope. Powerful tests have a greater ability to reveal relationships that are present in the data. It is thus possible to distinguish between tests in terms of their **power**. Saying that a test is powerful is the same as saying that the test has a low chance of producing a Type II error. Formally, we can therefore define power as $1 - \beta$, where β (the Greek letter beta) is the probability of a Type II error.

In general, we should use the most powerful test of a hypothesis that is appropriate for the data we are dealing with (a point we will return to later when we discuss the assumptions of statistical tests). A test that is not powerful is called a *conservative* test. In the example of testing the effectiveness of a therapy with harmful side-effects, we would probably wish to use a conservative test. However, in order to identify those side-effects in the first place, we should definitely use a powerful test. We can summarize the process of hypothesis testing as follows:

1. Decide on an alpha level before you commence the research. This is the amount of inferential uncertainty that you see as acceptable.
2. Calculate the t-statistic and obtain the corresponding probability value using SPSS.
3. If the probability value is less than the alpha level then reject the null hypothesis and conclude that the difference between means is statistically significant. If the probability value is greater than the alpha level you should conclude that the result is not statistically significant and should make no inferences about differences between the means.

When you report the results you should do so in the following way (assuming an alpha level of .05). To report a significant result:

The difference between means was significant, $t(18) = 2.90$, $p = .010$

To report a non-significant result:

The difference between means was not significant, $t(6) = 1.804$, $p = .121$

Obviously in these examples the values of t and p and the degrees of freedom vary. When doing your own research you need to use the values that you have calculated for the data you are working with.

Note here that you should report the p-value that corresponds to the highest t-value in the relevant row of the table that has been exceeded (or the exact p-value if, for example, it is available from a computer program). Some textbooks advise researchers simply to report whether the obtained p-value is less than the alpha level (e.g., with an α of .05 to report '$p <$ .05' even when p is much smaller than .001). However, we advise against this practice simply because it reduces the amount of information available to the reader about the inference that is being made.

The whole process of using the hypothesis-testing approach to conduct t-tests is summarized in Online Appendix B. Examples of how to write these tests up formally are presented there, too.

Test Yourself 8.5**

Which of the following must be true of a statistically significant result of a t-test?

a. The probability that a difference at least as large as the observed difference could be produced by a particular random process will be less than the alpha level.
b. The obtained value of t will exceed the alpha level.
c. The rejection regions must be significantly different from each other.
d. Both (a) and (c).
e. Alpha must be set at .05.

The correct answer is (a). A significant t-test yields a p-value that is less than a predetermined alpha level. Answer (b) is wrong because the value of t must exceed the critical value, not the alpha level. However, if t is greater than the critical value then p will be less than the alpha level. Answer (c) is a nonsense answer – we want the means to be significantly different from each other, not the rejection regions. If (c) is wrong, (d) must be wrong. Although an alpha of .05 is a popular alpha level, it is only one possible choice, so (e) is wrong.

alpha level The largest probability that the researcher is prepared to accept in order to reject the *null hypothesis*. The probability of a random process producing a result as big as the one obtained has to be smaller than this for a statistical test to be significant. It is equal to the probability of making a *Type I* error and should be set before research is carried out.

alternative hypothesis The hypothesis that the research reveals an effect (e.g., that two samples are drawn from different populations and that there is an informative difference between their means). Also referred to as H_1. This is normally the hypothesis that the research was designed to test.

critical value The value associated with a statistical test (e.g., t) that cuts off the *rejection region*. If the obtained value exceeds this value then the test result will be significant. This is because the probability of the obtained value will be less than the *alpha level*.

directional test A *one-tailed* statistical test, where the *alternative hypothesis* specifies the direction of any effect (e.g., hypothesizing that one particular mean will be greater than another).

H_0 The *null hypothesis* that the research reveals no effect.

H_1 The *alternative hypothesis* that the research reveals an effect.

hypothesis-testing approach The process of making decisions as to whether the pattern of obtained results (e.g., differences between means) is due to chance (H_0) or to significant effects (H_1).

null hypothesis The hypothesis that the research reveals no effect (e.g., that two samples are drawn from the same population and that there is no informative difference between their means). Also referred to as H_0. This is the hypothesis that statistical procedures allow researchers to reject.

one-tailed test A *directional test* with a single *rejection region*. Such a test has a rejection region whose area is twice as large as that for a *two-tailed test*, and is based on the *alternative hypothesis* being *directional* (e.g., hypothesizing that one particular mean is larger than the other).

***p*-value** The probability, as revealed by a statistical test, that a random process (involving taking random samples of a particular size from a particular population) could produce some outcome.

power The ability of a statistical test to reveal effects that exist in the data. Increasing power reduces inferential uncertainty. Formally, power is equal to $1 - \beta$, where β is the probability of a *Type II error*.

rejection region The area of the sampling distribution associated with a statistical test (e.g., the t-distribution) that is cut off by the *critical value(s)*. The size of these regions depends upon the ***alpha level***. For example, an alpha level of .05 corresponds to a rejection region (or regions) taking up 5% of the total distribution.

significance-testing approach Another name for the *hypothesis-testing approach*.

statistical significance An outcome where the probability that an effect at least as large as that observed could be produced by a random process is less than a predetermined ***alpha level***. Where a result is statistically significant it is implausible that a random process could have produced the effect.

two-tailed test A test with two ***rejection regions*** that is based on the ***alternative hypothesis*** that research reveals an effect (e.g., that two means are different). The nature of any departure from randomness (e.g., which mean will be larger) is not specified.

Type I error Making the statistical inference that an effect exists (e.g., that there is a difference between means) when the effect is actually due to a random process. Here the ***null hypothesis*** is rejected when it is actually true.

Type II error Making the statistical inference that there is no effect (e.g., that there is no difference between means) when the effect does actually exist. Here the ***null hypothesis*** is not rejected when it is actually false.

Other ways of handling the results of *t*-tests: Probability-level, confidence-interval and effect-size approaches

Despite its popularity, the hypothesis-testing or significance-testing approach is only one way to make decisions about inferential uncertainty. There are several alternatives that are preferred by statisticians who do not like the all-or-nothing nature of the hypothesis-testing approach. In this section we present three alternative methods for dealing with inferential uncertainty. All of them are acceptable in different areas of the psychological research literature. However, different instructors will have preferences about which one they want students to use in their work.

The probability-level approach

The **probability-level approach** is the technique that we presented in the sections earlier where we first explained how to do a *t*-test. This involves simply calculating and reporting both a *t*-value and an associated probability level. If this approach is taken, the results are not described as being significant or non-significant – or at least hard-and-fast significance levels are not used. Instead the researcher simply states the probability that a random process could have produced a difference as large as the one obtained. The disadvantage of this method is that it is a bit clumsier to express in words. One advantage is that other people can look at your results and use another approach if they choose, so it is best where possible to provide an exact p-value (e.g., writing '$p = .014$' rather than '$p < .05$') even if you adopt the hypothesis-testing approach. If the p-value is very small (i.e., less than .001) it is best to write '$p < .001$', rather than '$p = .000$', just to capture the idea that the value is not exactly zero.

The confidence-interval approach

When we estimate parameters we can do one of two things. We can estimate a parameter by suggesting a particular value. This is called a **point estimate**. However, when we do this we still have a degree of uncertainty about the correspondence between this point estimate and the true parameter value. To deal with this uncertainty we could therefore specify a range of values around the point estimate within which we expect the true value to lie. Such a range of possible values is called a **confidence interval** (or sometimes an interval estimate). Confidence intervals can be constructed for a variety of parameters, including the mean and the difference between means.

When examining differences between means, the **confidence-interval approach** involves reporting a probable range of differences between population means. This is the likely range of differences that would be obtained by taking random samples from the same population and subtracting one mean from the other.

The size of the confidence interval depends on the amount of inferential uncertainty that researchers are prepared to accept and the amount of random error present. The less uncertainty they are prepared to live with, the larger the confidence interval will be. As a result, more and more of the possible differences between means that would be obtained from a random process will lie within the confidence interval.

The probability of including the true value in the confidence interval is used to name the confidence interval. A 95% confidence interval for the sample mean would contain the true population mean 95% of the time if many samples of the same size as the empirical sample were drawn randomly from that population. A 95% confidence interval for a difference between means would contain the true difference between means 95% of the time.

We can set the size of the confidence interval in SPSS by clicking on 'Options . . .' (Figure 8.16) and then setting the 'Confidence Interval Percentage' (Figure 8.17).

In the SPSS examples here we have confidence intervals for differences between means. These are obtained by taking the t-value that corresponds to the proportion of the sampling distribution that we wish to exclude. A 95% confidence interval excludes 5% of the possible differences between means so we want the t-value that corresponds to that proportion for the given number of degrees of freedom. We can look these up in a set of statistical tables, and for the example of the between-subjects t-test with $df = 18$, the critical value for a 95% confidence interval is 2.101. When we multiply this number by the standard error of the difference between the means we obtain the amount we have to add and subtract from the observed difference (i.e., 2) to create the confidence interval. This value is $2.1009 \times 0.68961 = 1.44881$. The lower bound (limit) of the 95% confidence interval is thus $2 - 1.48881 = 0.55119$ and the upper bound is $2 + 1.48881 = 3.48881$.

Figure 8.16

Figure 8.17

In other words, if we repeatedly took a sample of 10 people from one population and another sample of 10 people from a population with the same variance and a mean score two points higher we would expect (i.e., be confident) the obtained differences between the samples to be between (i.e., within the interval) 0.55119 and 3.48881 on 95% of occasions. We write this (rounded to two decimal places) as $CI_{.95} = [0.55, 3.49]$.

Why is this range of values useful? The answer is that knowing what to expect gives us some basis for deciding whether the results we obtained are remarkable or surprising. The confidence interval does not contain the value 0.0. That tells us that if two samples did come from the same population with the same mean then this is a remarkable result.

The last of these steps is contentious because many would argue that it simply reproduces the logic of the *t*-test (see Frick, 1995). This is because there is a simple relationship between these confidence intervals and *p*-values. A difference with a *p*-value of less than .05 will lie outside the 95% confidence interval, a difference with a *p*-value of less than .01 will lie outside the 99% confidence interval, and so on. For this reason confidence intervals can be seen as a means of rewriting statistical tests, because if a difference is significant with $p < .05$ then it will also lie outside the 95% confidence interval. This is because the *t*-test and the confidence interval involve the same three terms: the difference between the means, the standard error and the critical value. However, the two approaches use these terms in different ways. As Figure 8.18 illustrates, the confidence interval corresponds to the region of the *t*-distribution that is between the tails that would be cut off by the critical values. So, a 95%

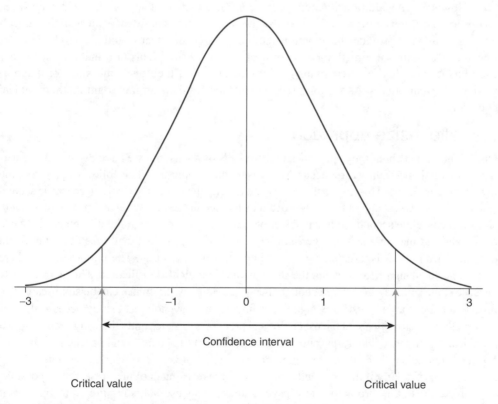

Figure 8.18 The *t*-distribution showing confidence interval

confidence interval includes all the possible outcomes that would lead us not to reject the null hypothesis at an alpha level of .05.

For these data any difference between the means that is greater than 1.45 or less than −1.45 will lie outside the 95% confidence interval. Here the difference between means was 2.0, so this difference lies outside the 95% confidence interval. In other words, we can conclude that 95% of differences between means produced by a random process would not be this large.

Confidence intervals are a very good way of making the level of inferential uncertainty associated with a given test clear. By alerting the researcher to the range of possible outcomes associated with the process of doing the research, the calculation of a confidence interval puts results in perspective by comparing our obtained result directly with a range of possible results that would be produced by a random process. This avoids the trap that can occur when researchers using the hypothesis-testing approach lose sight of the idea that their results are being treated as one possible sample from a specified population and are being used to estimate parameters of that population. Nevertheless, most of the thorny issues associated with statistical inference are as evident in the use of confidence intervals as they are when using the hypothesis-testing approach.

However, one additional benefit of the confidence-interval approach is that even when an observed difference between means lies within a specified confidence interval, the confidence interval itself provides information about how large an effect would need to be in order to make us certain that something was going on in our research. This information can be very useful as it may give researchers insight into the ability of their tests, measures or manipulations to reveal effects. As we discussed in Chapter 4, this is an important methodological consideration.

The effect-size approach

One of the things about the approaches to the results of *t*-tests that we have discussed so far is that inferential uncertainty is reduced by increasing the sample size. This follows again from the law of large numbers. This means that we can do exactly the same study twice (where the second study is a *replication*) and obtain a significant difference in the first study and not in the second, simply because the second study has fewer participants – even though the differences between the means and the variances are the same in each case. So, the fact that a result is significant does not mean that it is large enough to be important or interesting. The important point here is that statistical significance is not the same as **psychological significance**. This is true partly because if the sample size is large enough then just about any difference can be significant. The mistaken belief that a statistically significant finding in a psychological study necessarily tells us something important about the psychological processes or states under investigation (i.e., that statistical significance *implies* psychological significance) can be referred to as the **significance fallacy**. This fallacy is made all the more potent because it is one to which researchers easily succumb – particularly if they are under pressure to make as much of their research as possible.

To address this problem many psychologists who use statistics prefer to base their interpretation of results on an **effect-size approach**. **Effect sizes** are not affected by the sample size and simply tell us whether the difference between the means is large compared with the amount of dispersion (or descriptive uncertainty). These effect sizes help us to compare results across studies.

A number of proposals have been made about how to measure effect size. One measure is d. This is essentially the difference between means divided by the standard deviation. Unlike the t-statistic, the standard deviation is not divided by the square root of the sample size, so the size of d does not depend on the sample size. The measure of effect size that we will use here is r, largely because we use this statistic again in the next chapter. The formula for r is

$$r = \sqrt{t^2/(t^2 + df)}$$

This value of r can vary between 0 and 1. And as with all measures of effect size, the value of r can be compared across studies. It is very important to do this, but in areas where there is no prior research we can follow the 'rule of thumb' used by Cohen (1988): if r is at least .1 it can be considered to be a weak effect, if it is at least .3 it is a moderate effect, and if it is at least .5 it is a strong effect. In the examples we used previously, the size of the effect for the between-subjects t-test in the 'physical reinforcement theory' experiment would be presented as follows:

$$
\begin{aligned}
r_{between} &= \sqrt{t^2/(t^2 + df)} \\
&= \sqrt{2.90^2 / (2.90^2 + 18)} \\
&= \sqrt{8.41/26.41} \\
&= .56
\end{aligned}
$$

This is a strong effect. In the within-subjects example used to examine the same theory, the effect size would look like this:

$$
\begin{aligned}
r_{within} &= \sqrt{t^2 / (t^2 + df)} \\
&= \sqrt{1.43^2/(1.43^2 + 6)} \\
&= \sqrt{2.04/8.04} \\
&= .50
\end{aligned}
$$

This too is a strong effect.

Our use of these examples makes it clear that the different approaches to statistical tests lead to different conclusions about the importance or interest of studies – remember that the hypothesis-testing approach would have suggested that the within-subjects test results yielded no effect (by any conventional choice of alpha level). Results can be highly statistically

RESEARCH BITE 8.2
When small effects are a big deal

When researchers use the effect-size approach to assess the impact that an independent variable has on a dependent variable there is a general assumption that bigger effects are better. Indeed, where the effect is small, readers may conclude that the experimental effect that has been demonstrated is trivial and unimpressive. However, in an influential paper, Deborah Prentice and Dale Miller (1992) argue that this need not be the case. In particular, this is because small effects can be very impressive if the manipulation of the IV was quite minimal or if the DV is hard to influence. They therefore argue that information about effect size always needs to be evaluated relative to the specifics of a particular experimental design.

Reference
Prentice, D. A., & Miller, D. T. (1992). When small effects are impressive. *Psychological Bulletin*, *112*, 160–164.

Test Yourself 8.6**

Researchers conduct a *t*-test and obtain a *p*-value of .0012. Which of the following is an appropriate conclusion on the basis of the information provided?

  a. The result is significant.
  b. The effect size will be large.
  c. Both (a) and (b).
  d. A 99% confidence interval for the differences between the means will include the observed difference.
  e. A 95% confidence interval for the differences between the means will not include the observed difference.

The correct answer is (e). We cannot say whether a result is significant or not unless an alpha level is specified, so (a) is wrong (although this is a point that even seasoned researchers often forget), and (b) is wrong because a small *p*-value does not necessarily correspond to a large effect size. If (a) and (b) are wrong, then (c) must be wrong. Answer (d) is wrong because if the *p*-value is less than .01 the 99% confidence interval cannot include the observed difference. The confidence interval would have to be 99.9% before it included the observed difference. Answer (e) is correct for the reasons that make (d) incorrect.

significant but of small size, or of large size but not significant. This is because effect sizes are not estimates of inferential uncertainty. They do not tell us whether the results could have been due to chance, they simply tell us the size of those results relative to error but ignoring sample size. To address the issue of inferential uncertainty, effect sizes need to be accompanied by other measures. Before taking the results of a piece of research that showed a large effect size too seriously, most researchers would want to be confident that the results were not a chance occurrence. In other words, effect sizes are very useful but they complement rather than replace the other approaches. Our advice is that the results of *t*-tests should always be accompanied by measures of effect size.

confidence interval An estimated range of values for a population parameter. The size of the confidence interval is expressed as a percentage. If sampling is random, a 95% confidence interval has a 95% chance of containing the population parameter.

confidence-interval approach An approach to inferential statistics based on the use of *confidence intervals* rather than *point estimates*.

effect size A measure of the size of an effect that ignores the sample size.

effect-size approach An approach to inferential statistics based on the calculation of *effect sizes* rather than probability levels.

point estimate A single value used to estimate a population parameter. For example, the sample standard deviation is a point estimate of the population standard deviation.

probability-level approach A procedure whereby the researcher calculates the probability that a random process could produce a difference as big as that observed. No hard-and-fast inferences about statistical significance are made.

psychological significance An outcome of research which produces important knowledge about psychological processes or states. This should not be confused with statistical significance.

significance fallacy The mistaken belief that a statistically significant result in a psychological study constitutes a *psychologically significant* finding.

Some notes of caution

All of the procedures described in this chapter are based on statistical models. Statistical models allow us to make inferences so long as the principles they are based on are applicable. These principles are called **assumptions**. Assumptions are the foundations upon which everything else we do with statistics is based. If the assumptions do not hold (where we say there is a **violation of assumptions)** then the process of doing inferential statistics can be very risky because we can make the wrong inferences.

Given that assumptions are so important, you may well ask why we are talking about them now, towards the end of the chapter. That is a very good question, and the answer is that we have, in fact, been talking about assumptions all the time up to this point, without calling them assumptions. This may become clearer when we point out that the assumptions of the between-subjects *t*-test are that our samples are *independent* random samples from a population with a normal distribution, and that the standard deviations of both samples are estimates of the same underlying population standard deviation.

Let us go through these assumptions one at a time. There is only one new term that has been introduced here, and that is 'independent'. **Independence** refers to things being separate and standing on their own. Events are independent if the occurrence of one has no effect on the probability of the other. Coin tosses are independent events. If we toss a coin and obtain a head then the chance of the next coin toss being a head is the same regardless of what has occurred in the past. This point is often misunderstood. One way in which it is misunderstood is in the **gambler's fallacy** – the belief that luck has to change (see Question 7.7 at the end of the previous chapter). Samples are independent if the probability of one participant's inclusion in the sample is not affected by the probability of any other person being sampled. In other words, the samples are selected randomly from the population.

Whenever researchers do anything to bias the selection procedure – for example, if they deliberately select participants to be in one particular group (rather than randomly allocating participants) or if they use the same participants twice in a between-subjects *t*-test – the

RESEARCH BITE 8.3
The skewing effects of neglecting skew

Many statistical tests rely on variables being normally distributed. However, many variables that psychologists study violate this assumption. Winnifred Louis, Ken Mavor, and Deborah Terry (2003) make the point that this is true in the case of extreme behaviours because strong norms mean that few people engage in these. When norms are strong and behaviours are skewed to be very common (e.g., wearing clothes) or very rare (e.g., joining a hate group), analyses which include norms as predictors of behaviour tend to produce misleading results. Specifically, they underestimate the norms' importance relative to factors that are more normally distributed (e.g., personality). This can lead to faulty theoretical conclusions.

Reference
Louis, W. R., Mavor, K. I., & Terry, D. J. (2003). Reflections on the statistical analysis of personality and norms in war, peace, and prejudice: Are deviant minorities the problem? *Analyses of Social Issues and Public Policy*, 3, 189–198.

assumption of independence is violated. Under these conditions *t*-tests can give misleading results. For within-subjects *t*-tests the assumption of independence is relaxed. This is for the obvious reason that if the same sample is used for both measures these samples *cannot* be independent. However, the participants that comprise the sample still need to be independent of each other.

The use of *t*-tests also assumes that the samples are drawn from a normally distributed population. This is known as the **assumption of normality**. This is a very important idea in those areas of psychological statistics that rely on **normal theory tests**. We will provide no detailed justification for this idea here, but just point out that the mathematical solutions to statistical problems become much easier if we are able to assume that the variables are normally distributed. It is easy to see why this would be the case given the advantages of a normal distribution that we have already identified. If we know that a variable is normally distributed and we know its mean and variance, we know a great deal about it. Not surprisingly, it is easier to develop statistical tests for variables that are well understood in this way.

Finally, a third assumption is that the samples must both have standard deviations that are estimates of the same population standard deviation. This is called the **assumption of equal variance**. Where this is not true we cannot be sure that our procedures for deciding the level of inferential uncertainty will be accurate. If the standard deviations are not equal then we should treat the results of the *t*-test with caution. In fact, there are correction procedures that can be used under these circumstances involving the transformation of variables (see Chapter 6).

When we do between-subjects *t*-tests, SPSS provides Levene's test of the equality of variance as shown in Figure 8.19. If the probability (marked 'Sig.') is very small it is worth considering using the version of the *t*-test that does not assume equal variances in the line below.

Independent Samples Test

		Levene's Test for Equality of Variances		t-test for Equality of Means						
									95% Confidence Interval of the Difference	
		F	Sig.	t	df	Sig. (2-tailed)	Mean Difference	Std. Error Difference	Lower	Upper
Attractiveness Rating	Equal variances assumed	.799	.383	2.900	18	.010	2.00000	.68961	.55119	3.44881
	Equal variances not assumed			2.900	17.653	.010	2.00000	.68961	.54915	3.45085

Figure 8.19

As we mentioned in Chapter 6, one thing that can contribute a great deal to the amount of variance in a distribution is the presence of one or more outliers. This means that if we have outliers in one sample and not in the other, the assumption of equal variance is likely to be violated. The effect of this will normally be to reduce the power of the test. The only way to check whether outliers could be affecting your results is to look at your data. This could involve constructing a frequency graph.

For example, the bar charts for the between-subjects *t*-test that we used as an example earlier are shown in Figure 8.20. If instead the distribution of data from the experimental condition had been like that in Figure 8.21 (i.e., if the response of Participant 1 had been '1' rather than '4'),

Figure 8.20 Bar charts for the between-subjects *t*-test carried out above (see p. 209): (a) control condition; (b) experimental condition

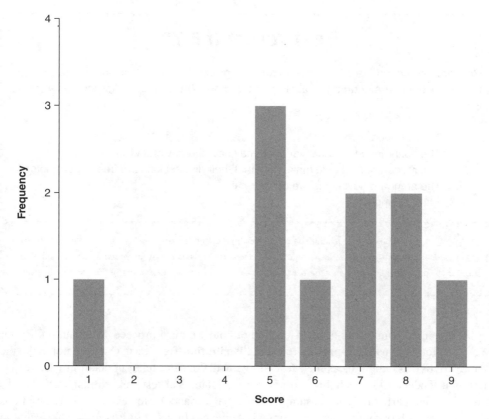

Figure 8.21   Bar chart showing evidence of outlier

we would have evidence of an outlier. The presence of this outlier increases the standard deviation of the data in this condition from 1.65 to 2.28. As a result, the assumption of equal variance could be violated and, if it were, the power of a *t*-test would be dramatically reduced. That is because a larger standard deviation makes it more difficult to demonstrate differences between the means. Outliers like this can be present for all sorts of reasons, including mistakes in recording the data. As we noted in Chapter 6, outliers can sometimes be corrected by appropriate statistical transformation, but sometimes it is better to remove or recode individual outliers.

Another point that we glossed over earlier concerns the advantages that we get from using the various types of tests. The within-subjects *t*-test is especially useful because it is a very powerful test: it is good at finding differences where they exist. The power of this test comes from using the same people on two different measures. More specifically, because each person is used as their own baseline for assessing the difference, this rules out a lot of the random variation that comes from using different people. This has the effect of reducing the amount of error so that any information is more likely to be revealed. However, if the correlation between the variables is less than .3 (see Chapter 9) then the power advantage of the within-subjects *t*-test disappears.

Test Yourself 8.7*

Researchers conduct a t-test to compare two groups and find that one of the groups has a much larger standard deviation than the other. Which of the following statements is true?

a. The variances are robust.
b. The assumption of equal variance may have been violated.
c. The researchers should make sure that their distributions are free of parameters.
d. The standard deviations are not normal.
e. Both (b) and (d).

The correct answer is (b). Answers (a), (c) and (d) are all nonsense involving mixing up other terms from this section. In particular, with respect to (a), *tests can be robust, not variances*, and with respect to (d), *distributions are normal, not standard deviations*. If (d) is wrong, then (e) must also be wrong.

Where the assumptions of the t-test do not hold we must proceed with caution. By far the best option is to use **non-parametric** and **distribution-free** tests. These do not make the same restrictive assumptions as the t-test and we will consider them in detail in Chapter 11. There is a tendency in psychology to assume that statistical tests are **robust** to violations of assumptions (particularly the assumption of equal variance). However, these assumptions are considerably less robust than is commonly believed. In general, it is *highly desirable* to look for violations of assumptions in your data – for example, by using a frequency graph to explore its distribution. One of the major benefits of this inspection process is that problems or other interesting features of the data are likely to reveal themselves. There is little to lose and much to gain from looking carefully at data before subjecting them to statistical tests.

assumption of equal variance An assumption of the t-test procedure that the variances of the samples that are compared are both estimates of the same population variance and thus are similar.

assumption of independence An assumption of the t-test procedure that sampling of the underlying population is independent and can be treated as random.

assumption of normality An assumption of the t-test procedure that the samples are random samples drawn from a normally distributed population.

assumptions The conditions that must be satisfied before we can use a statistical test with confidence. The assumptions of the t-test are that the samples are independent and randomly sampled from a normally distributed population that has the same variance for all samples.

distribution-free tests Tests that make no assumptions about the theoretical distribution of variables in the population from which a sample is drawn (i.e., the sampling distribution).

gambler's fallacy The mistaken idea that random events are not independent. A gambler may believe that a long run of good or bad luck has to change. The gambler's fallacy arises from a misunderstanding of the law of large numbers. The idea that a random process will behave in a predictable way on average over a long run of observations can be misunderstood to imply that there is 'a law of averages' that serves to *change* the probability of random events based on past events. However, coins, dice and other things that generate random outcomes do not have memories.

independence A term with numerous meanings in statistics. Two events are independent where the probability of one occurring does not depend upon the probability of the other occurring.

non-parametric tests Generally similar to *distribution-free* tests, but, technically speaking, these tests do not involve hypotheses related to a population parameter.

normal theory tests Statistical tests, such as the *t*-test, that assume that samples are drawn from a population that is normally distributed.

robust test A statistical test that tends to yield valid results even when the assumptions underpinning that test are violated.

violation of assumptions Threats to interpretation of the results of statistical tests that arise when the conditions required for the test to work properly do not hold.

Overview

This chapter began with a consideration of how to compare means when the population standard deviation is unknown. We covered three situations where the *t*-test can be used: for testing the difference between the mean of a single sample and some hypothesized population mean; for testing the difference between the means for a single sample on two different variables; and for testing the difference between two samples on a single variable.

In each case we find a value for *t* that corresponds to a probability that the results are due to random error. This probability corresponds to the level of inferential uncertainty. However, once we have obtained that probability we have some additional decisions to make.

Having found a *t*-value and a probability level, there are several choices as to how to treat, interpret and use these. The traditional approach has been to perform significance tests. To understand much of the literature that has already been published in psychology you will need to have some familiarity with this approach. Nowadays, however, important alternatives are available. These techniques include the use of confidence intervals and effect sizes.

CHECKLIST
Revisiting the key goals for this chapter

☐ I understand how to conduct a *t*-test – a statistical procedure that allows me to establish how likely it is that differences between two means of the size we have observed could be produced by a random process (drawing random samples of specified size from a specified population).

☐ I know how different types of *t*-test are used to examine different types of data.

☐ I understand the process of interpreting the results of *t*-tests, and the different ways that this can be done.

Further reading

Wilkinson and colleagues (1999) summarize the findings of the American Psychological Association's Task Force on Statistical Inference, and we recommend that you read this (it can be found online at: www.apa.org/science/leadership/bsa/statistical/tfsi-followup-report.pdf). Smithson's (2002) book also provides a detailed explanation of various alternatives to the hypothesis-testing approach, focusing in particular on confidence intervals and effect sizes.

Smithson, M. (2000). *Statistics with confidence.* London: SAGE.
Wilkinson, L., & The Task Force on Statistical Inference (1999). Statistical methods in psychology journals. *American Psychologist, 54,* 594–604.

t-tests: A checklist for research evaluation and improvement

Table 8.5

Potential problem	Question to ask	Potential improvement
Inferential uncertainty about an individual sample mean	Do the researchers want to compare a sample mean with another score when the population mean and standard deviation are unknown?	Subtract the comparison score from the sample mean and divide by the standard error of the mean (the sample standard deviation divided by the square root of the sample size). This procedure creates a *t*-score and – having calculated the degrees of freedom (the sample size minus one) – statistical tables or a computer program such as SPSS can be used to provide information about the probability of observing by chance a *t*-score as large as the one obtained.

Potential problem	Question to ask	Potential improvement
Inferential uncertainty about means from the same sample	Do the researchers want to compare means associated with data that have been obtained from the same sample on two occasions when the population mean and standard deviation are unknown?	Following the procedures described in this chapter, use a statistical package such as SPSS to conduct a within-subjects t-test. This will generate a t-score and provide information about the probability (p) of observing by chance a t-score as large as the one obtained.
Inferential uncertainty about means from different samples	Do the researchers want to compare means associated with data that have been obtained from two independent samples when the population mean and standard deviation are unknown?	Following the procedures described in this chapter, use a statistical package such as SPSS to conduct a between-subjects t-test. This will generate a t-score and provide information about the probability (p) of observing by chance a t-value as large as the one obtained.
Significance fallacy	If the researchers are using a hypothesis-testing approach to t-tests, have they distinguished appropriately between psychological and statistical significance?	Consider significance levels in conjunction with effect sizes (e.g., compare p and r). Be alert to the dangers of making too much of statistically significant t-values when effect sizes are low.
Violation of the assumption of independence	Do the means that are being compared relate to independent sets of observations?	If sample scores are not independent (and dependent scores are not being compared in a within-subjects t-test) it can be misleading to compare them using a t-test (or any other statistical test) if, in effect, the same piece of data is being counted more than once. Accordingly, if possible, any source of dependence (e.g., the fact that the same participant responded twice) should be removed before collecting data. If this is not possible, the nature of the violation should be noted and results treated with caution.
Violation of the assumption of normality	Do the means that are being compared relate to observations that are normally distributed?	If the distribution of sample scores is non-normal (e.g., severely skewed or U-shaped) and the cell sizes are unequal, or there are reasons to believe that the mean is a misleading indicator of central tendency, you should seriously consider using a non-parametric test (Chapter 11) or correct the distribution by transformation (see Chapter 6).

(Continued)

Table 8.5 (Continued)

Potential problem	Question to ask	Potential improvement
Violation of the assumption of equal variance	Do the means that are being compared relate to samples that have equal variance?	If sample variances are unequal (e.g., one is more than four times bigger than the other) you should seriously consider using a non-parametric test (see Chapter 11). This is only worth doing if the size of one sample is much larger than the other.
Outliers	Is the distribution of scores (especially its shape and variance) dramatically affected by the presence of outliers?	Examine the distribution of scores to see if it contains outliers. If it does, see if this can be corrected by an appropriate statistical transformation of the sample data. If this is not possible, consider (a) removing individual outliers or (b) recoding them to the same value as the nearest non-outlier. Ensure you report any transformations that you make.

Test Yourself 8.8*

If an experimenter were to conduct an experiment in which participants were randomly assigned to either a control condition or an experimental condition, which of the following statements would be true?

    a. It will be appropriate to analyse results using a between-subjects t-test.
    b. Any statistical analysis will be based on pairs of responses.
    c. If a t-test is performed to analyse the results, it will have $n - 1$ degrees of freedom.
    d. The experiment involves two related samples.
    e. Both (a) and (c).

Test Yourself 8.9**

John, a second-year psychology student, is using the hypothesis-testing approach and an alpha level of .05 to examine a difference between two means. He discovers that this difference is associated with a t-value of 3.46. If the critical t-value with $\alpha = .05$ is 2.056 what should he conclude?

    a. That the difference between the means is statistically significant.
    b. That the alpha level is too high.
    c. That the alpha level is not high enough.
    d. That the experiment did not contain enough participants to draw a strong conclusion.
    e. That no conclusion can be made about the nature of the underlying populations.

Test Yourself 8.10**

Which of the following suggests that the assumptions underlying a between-subjects *t*-test have been violated?

a. Evidence that the dependent variable is normally distributed.
b. Evidence that the samples being compared have unequal variances.
c. Evidence that the manipulation of the independent variable had no effect.
d. Evidence that sampling was random, and that scores were independent.
e. None of the above.

Test Yourself 8.11***

Which of the following increases the likelihood of a Type II error when conducting a *t*-test?

a. A high alpha level.
b. A large sample size.
c. High power.
d. Low random error.
e. A small difference between means.

The correct answer to 8.8 is (a). Between-subjects *t*-tests are used for between-subjects designs such as this. Answer (b) is wrong because pairs of responses are used in within-subjects *t*-tests; (c) is wrong because there will be $N_1 + N_2 - 2$ degrees of freedom; and (d) is wrong because the two samples are independent and not related. Because (c) is wrong, (e) must also be wrong.

The correct answer to 8.9 is (a). There are no grounds to support any of the other conclusions. Answers (b) and (c) are wrong because the alpha level is a criterion that is set before the research is carried out. The alpha level quantifies the amount of inferential uncertainty the researcher is prepared to tolerate and is a decision to be made by the researcher (as always, these decisions should be influenced by an evaluation of past practice in that area of research). In short, decisions about the appropriate size of alpha levels are not made on the basis of the results of the study they are applied to. Answer (d) is wrong because the test has yielded a significant result. We would only suspect that (d) were correct if a significant result were not obtained with a small sample size. Answer (e) is wrong because if the result is significant the experimenter should conclude that the means belong to samples drawn from different populations.

The correct answer to 8.10 is (b). Evidence that the samples being compared have unequal variances violates the assumption of equal variance. Other assumptions of the *t*-test are that the variable under investigation is normally distributed (as a) suggests) and that scores on that variable are independent (as (d) suggests). The outcome of a *t*-test cannot tell us about the appropriateness of that statistical procedure — so (c) is wrong.

(Continued)

Discussion/essay questions

a. Why is the hypothesis-testing approach to statistical inference controversial?
b. Has a reliance on hypothesis-testing techniques had a detrimental impact on the study of psychology?
c. Discuss the relative advantages and disadvantages of a confidence-interval approach to statistical inference.
d. In what way does the presence of outliers affect the results of *t*-tests?

Exercises

a. An experimenter conducts a study in which participants try to remember a number of digits. Some participants do this after consuming a litre of full-strength beer, others do it after drinking a litre of full-cream milk. The data from the study were as follows:

   i.   What form of *t*-test is appropriate to analyse these data?
   ii. What value of *t* does the appropriate test yield?
   iii. Is this effect statistically significant with α set at .05?

b. Imagine that the data in Table 8.6 were obtained from examination of the same participants under different conditions (i.e., that the researcher collected pairs of data from each participant).

Table 8.6

	Participant number									
	1	2	3	4	5	6	7	8	9	10
Milk	7	6	7	7	8	8	9	5	6	7
Beer	6	5	6	7	5	3	7	6	7	5

    i. What form of *t*-test is appropriate to analyse the data?

    ii. What value of *t* does the appropriate test yield?

    iii. Is this effect statistically significant with α set at .05?

c. A parapsychologist wants to know whether a person claiming to have psychokinetic powers can produce higher numbers throwing red dice than throwing blue dice. The results are analysed by *t*-test. Why is it more appropriate to test this hypothesis by comparing scores obtained when the person throws many dice at the same time and adds them up, rather than just comparing the scores when a single die is thrown? [Hint: What shape would the distributions of scores be in each case?]

d. A psychotherapist consults you (as an expert psychological statistician) to see whether an expensive new therapy she has developed is working and whether it has any side-effects. For this purpose she provides you with two sets of scores for 200 patients. One set of scores measures psychological functioning pre- and post-treatment and the other measures the presence of self-reported side-effects pre- and post-treatment.

    i. What form of *t*-test is appropriate to analyse these data?

    ii. What alpha levels would you recommend?

    iii. In the course of your discussion with the therapist, you find out that the therapy was administered in groups. Why does this make it problematic to analyse the data using a *t*-test?

e. A personality researcher asks you whether 10 students in his class have a mean score significantly greater than the population norm on a standard personality test (with alpha set at .05). The population norm on the test is 100, and the students' scores are 111, 101, 94, 131, 120, 98, 114, 113, 132 and 109. What answer would you give him?

243

Examining Relationships between Variables: Correlation

Key goals for this chapter

- Introduce correlation – a procedure for examining relationships between variables.
- Introduce Pearson's *r* – a statistic that quantifies the nature and strength of the linear relationship between two variables.
- Explain how the results of correlational analysis should be interpreted, with particular reference to the difference between correlation and causation.

A lot of what we have talked about in the last two chapters relates to comparisons between means, and comparing means is what psychologists typically do when they use experimental methodology. However, in a great deal of research investigators confront another interesting question: What is the *relationship* between two variables? For example, how is stress related to heart disease? How is socio-economic status related to intelligence? How is personality related to the judgements people make?

This type of question can be addressed by experiments (as in the previous chapter, where we used an example of the relationship between the amount of physical contact and attraction), but is more typically examined in surveys. In surveys the researchers collect information about variables where there may be many different values for each variable (in the attraction study, for example, lots of different levels of contact, not just two, and lots of different levels of attraction). Surveys also often measure two or more variables, each with multiple levels. We can contrast this with the case of a *t*-test where we have an independent variable with just two levels (a categorical variable) and a dependent variable with multiple levels.

In survey research we often want to know whether two variables vary *together*. In other words, we want to determine whether there is an association between the variables. This is quite different from the example of the with-in-subjects *t*-test, where we are interested in the question of whether there are informative differences between participants' scores on different measures. In this chapter we want to look at pairs of scores to see whether high scores are consistently associated with high scores (and low scores with low scores) *or* whether high scores are consistently associated with low scores. Where there is a relationship between variables that takes either of these two forms we say there is a *correlation* between the variables.

For any given participant in a correlational study we do not just have that participant's responses on one dependent measure (*X*). These would be **univariate** data. Instead, we have participants' responses on *pairs* of measures (*X* and *Y*). The technical term for this type of data is

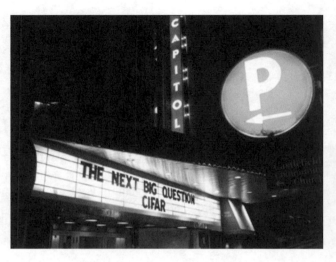

Photo 9.1 At this public lecture in Toronto, researchers associated with the Canadian Institute for Advanced Research attempted to answer the question 'What makes people happy?'. Their answers were based partly on an examination of correlations between happiness and variables like wealth, health and number of social connections.

bivariate. The idea of correlation is useful because it helps us make **predictions**. Knowing that there is a relationship between two variables enables us to predict (with some degree of uncertainty) the score on one variable if we know the score on the other variable. This reason for doing statistical analysis is quite different from those we considered in Chapter 8.

Nevertheless, while *t*-tests and correlations are used to address different questions, they can also be seen to be closely related. In fact a between-subjects *t*-test and a correlation can be used for exactly the same purpose. This makes sense if we think of the *t*-test as a way of examining the relationship between an independent and dependent variable – trying to see if variation in the independent variable is associated with variation in the dependent variable.

As an example of some data that we might conduct correlational analysis upon, we can imagine research where we recorded both people's reaction time and the amount of alcohol they consumed in the last three hours. If there is a relationship between these two variables in the sample, then it is possible to predict the score on one variable as long as we know the score on the other variable.

When discussing the relationship between these variables, we would be interested in knowing whether increasing alcohol consumption (*AC*) is related to longer or shorter reaction times (*RT*), or whether there is no discernible relationship between these variables. If there is no relationship, then we cannot predict reaction time from knowledge about the amount of alcohol a person has consumed (or vice versa).

bivariate Involving the relationship between two variables (roughly speaking, 'variate' is another word for variable).

prediction A common statistical purpose or goal of correlational analyses. The aim is to be able to estimate (with some uncertainty) a person's score on one variable by knowing that person's score on another variable (or variables).

univariate Involving a single variable.

Some basic principles of correlation

One useful way to set about looking at the relationship between any two variables is to draw a **scatterplot.** This is a two-dimensional graph displaying each pair of observations (e.g., each participant's *RT* and *AC*). So, let us say our data were as shown in Table 9.1 (where *AC* is standard units of alcohol consumed in the last three hours and *RT* is reaction time in milli-seconds). These data can be represented graphically as in Figure 9.1. Note, too, that we could also draw the relationship as in Figure 9.2.

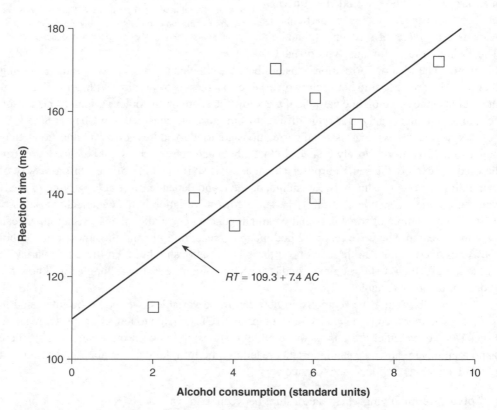

Figure 9.1 Graph of reaction time against alcohol consumption based on data in Table 9.1

Table 9.1   Observations from reaction-time study

Participant	AC	RT
1	9	172
2	2	112
3	4	132
4	6	163
5	3	139
6	5	170
7	6	139
8	7	157

$$AC = -7.34 + 0.085\ RT$$

Figure 9.2   Graph of alcohol consumption against reaction time based on data in Table 9.1

Now just by looking at either of these graphs we can see that there is an obvious relationship between alcohol consumption and reaction time: the higher one of these variables is, the

Test Yourself 9.1

Which of the following statements is true?

a. A negative correlation is the same as no correlation.
b. Scatterplots are a very poor way to show correlations.
c. If the points on a scatterplot are close to a straight line there will be a positive correlation.
d. Negative correlations are of no use for predictive purposes.
e. None of the above.

The correct answer is (e). All of the other alternatives are nonsense answers: (a) is wrong because a negative correlation involves one variable decreasing as the other increases, which is very different from no relationship; (b) is wrong because a scatterplot is in fact an excellent way to show a correlation; (c) is wrong because a correlation (or even no relationship) is also possible where points fall on a straight line; and (d) is wrong because negative relationships are just as useful for predictive purposes as positive ones. The amount people smoke is a predictor of their general physical health, but the relationship between smoking and health is negative.

higher the other is. We call this a **positive correlation**. A **negative correlation** is obtained where the values of one variable decrease as values of the other increase.

These sorts of relationship are **straight-line relationships**. A straight-line relationship is one where it is possible to draw a straight line through the scatterplot showing how the variables are related on average. For this purpose, a straight line and its equation are shown in Figures 9.1 and 9.2 (although the two lines are different, as we will see, there is only one value for the correlation).

Two points are important to note here. First, the stronger a positive or negative relationship is, the less the various points will depart from the straight line. Second, the smaller such departures are, the more confidently we can estimate or predict one variable on the basis of the other. So if a perfect positive correlation were found between *RT* and *AC*, the points on the graph would all lie on a straight line going upwards and we would be able to know from someone's reaction time *exactly* how much that person had drunk. If we knew how much a person had drunk, we would also know *exactly* what that person's reaction time would be.

> **negative correlation** A relationship between variables where high scores on the first variable are associated with low scores on the second variable, and low scores on the first are associated with high scores on the second. Spelling ability and number of spelling errors are negatively correlated because the more spelling ability a person has, the fewer spelling mistakes they will make.

positive correlation A relationship between variables where high scores on the first variable are associated with high scores on the second variable, and low scores on the first are associated with low scores on the second. Reading ability and IQ are positively correlated.

scatterplot A graph plotting the scores on one variable against the scores on another.

straight-line relationship A relationship between two variables that can be described by a straight line. The equation for such a line is $y = a + bx$, where b is the slope of the line (its gradient) and a is the y intercept (where it cuts the vertical axis). In Figure 9.1, the equation for the straight line is $RT = 109.3 + 7.4AC$. Accordingly, you can see that the line cuts the vertical axis at 109.3 and that for every two standard units of alcohol consumed, reaction time increases by about 15 milliseconds (i.e., about 2×7.4).

The measurement of correlation

Correlations are generally measured in terms of statistics called **correlation coefficients** and the most commonly used of these is the **Pearson product-moment correlation coefficient**. This usually goes by the more user-friendly label **Pearson's r**. The value of r indicates how strong a correlation is, and it can vary between -1.00 (a perfect negative correlation) and $+1.00$ (a perfect positive correlation). If there is no correlation the value of Pearson's r will be close to 0.

As with t-tests, computation of Pearson's r involves going through a series of standard steps. In essence, these allow us to establish the extent to which high scores on one variable are associated with high scores on the other, and low scores on one variable are associated with low scores on the other.

The formula for Pearson's r is

$$r_{xy} = \frac{\sum(X - \bar{X})(Y - \bar{Y})}{\sqrt{\sum(X - \bar{X})^2 \sum(Y - \bar{Y})^2}} \quad \begin{array}{l} \text{(information term)} \\ \text{(error term)} \end{array}$$

This is called the mean-deviation version of the formula for correlation. The terms on the top line of this formula, the information term, express **covariance**. Covariances reflect how much scores vary in the same way. As you can see by inspecting the top line of the equation closely, the covariance term is the sum of the product of differences between each participant's score and the mean score for each variable.

Each participant's contribution to covariance will therefore be close to zero when the difference between each score and the mean is close to zero for both variables. The contribution to covariance will have a large positive value when scores on both variables are well above the mean or when scores on both variables are well below the mean (because multiplying two negative numbers gives a positive number). The contribution to covariance of a pair of scores will have a large negative value when the participant has a score on one variable that is well below the mean and a score on the other variable that is well above the mean.

The sum of all these contributions to covariance for the sample will be a large positive number when there are lots of positive contributions, and will be a large negative number when there are lots of negative contributions. It will be close to zero where there is a balance of positive and negative contributions or where there are lots of small contributions.

The bottom line of the equation is an error term relating to the variances of the two variables (remember from Chapter 6 that variances are related to the sum of the squares of the deviation). Correlation is therefore an expression of *covariance relative to dispersion*. In effect, correlation is a *standardized* covariance. If there is large positive or negative covariance we can still have a correlation coefficient that is close to zero if the amount of random error (descriptive uncertainty) is large. Note also that the error term does not contain a $\sqrt{N}$ term. For this reason the law of large numbers or sample size does not affect the size of the correlation.

Although this appears quite complex, we can summarize the 'message' of the mean-deviation formula for correlation as follows. The correlation coefficient will have a large positive value when *both* scores for a participant tend to be above the mean or below the mean, and the size of the deviations relative to the mean is large compared with the standard deviations for the variables. On the other hand, the correlation coefficient will tend to have a large negative value when participants tend to have a score that is below the mean for one variable and a score that is above the mean for the other variable, and the size of the deviations is also large relative to the standard deviations.

It is useful to illustrate these points with some data. Let us imagine that we ask three women how many times they went to the theatre last year (variable X) and how many hours they spent watching television yesterday (variable Y). Imagine that their responses were respectively 11 times and 1 hour, 6 times and 5 hours, and once and 6 hours. The mean for X ($\bar{X}$) is 6.0 times and the mean for Y ($\bar{Y}$) is 4.0 hours. The other calculations we need to carry out are shown in Table 9.2.

Table 9.2

Participant	X	$(X - \bar{X})$	$(X - \bar{X})^2$	Y	$(Y - \bar{Y})$	$(Y - \bar{Y})^2$	$(X - \bar{X})(Y - \bar{Y})$
1	11	5	25	1	−3	9	−15
2	6	0	0	5	1	1	0
3	1	−5	25	6	2	4	−10
$\Sigma =$			50			14	−25
Mean =	6			4			

From the final column in this table, we can see that Participant 1 contributes negative covariance because her score on Variable X (i.e., 11) is larger than the mean for X (6) and her score on Variable Y (1) is lower than the mean for Y (4). Similarly, Participant 3 contributes negative covariance because her score on Variable X (1) is smaller than the mean (6) and her score on Y (6) is greater than the mean (4). On the other hand, Participant 2 contributes zero covariance because although there is a positive difference between her score on Variable Y and the mean for Y (in this case, $5 - 4 = 1$), her score on Variable X is equal to the mean for Variable X (both 6). Zero multiplied by any number yields zero. However, as a result of the high negative contributions to covariance yielded by Participants 1 and 3, and providing that random error is small for the sample, the overall data for the three women will yield a sizeable negative correlation.

Although it is possible to work out Pearson's r by comparing each score on a variable with the mean score on that variable, as with t-tests, nowadays people normally calculate it using a computer program. We can illustrate this by putting the data from Table 9.1 (denoting alcohol consumption as X and reaction time as Y) into IBM SPSS Statistics software (SPSS). Create a new data file that looks like the one in Figure 9.3 (with the variables renamed in this way) – noting that this file is also provided in the Supplementary Online Material [Chapter9_Correlation.sav].

Figure 9.3

But let us now add another feature of SPSS to give the variables AC and RT meaningful labels. Go to 'Variable View' and enter 'Alcohol Consumption' in the 'Variable Label' space for 'AC' and 'Reaction Time' for 'RT'.

Save the data file in a safe place with a meaningful name and then select the 'Analyze' menu and below that select 'Correlate' and then 'Bivariate'. You should see a window like Figure 9.4.

Figure 9.4

In this window select 'Alcohol Consumption' and 'Reaction Time' and then drag them across to the right side of the window (we will also deselect 'Flag significant correlations'). The boxes 'Pearson' and 'Two-tailed' should automatically be selected as defaults, so if you now click on 'OK' the program will perform our correlation analysis. This will generate the output shown in Figure 9.5.

Correlations

		Alcohol Consumption	Reaction Time
Alcohol Consumption	Pearson Correlation	1	.792
	Sig. (2-tailed)		.019
	N	8	8
Reaction Time	Pearson Correlation	.792	1
	Sig. (2-tailed)	.019	
	N	8	8

Figure 9.5

Test Yourself 9.2**

If a calculation of Pearson's r yields a value of −.96, which of the following statements is *false*?

    a. The observed correlation between variables is negative.
    b. There is a small amount of negative covariance between variables relative to random error.
    c. A high score on one variable is associated with a low score on the other.
    d. This correlation is useful for predictive purposes.
    e. Points on a scatterplot would resemble a straight line.

The correct answer is (b). As (a) indicates, the observed correlation between variables is negative (as the sign indicates). This means, as (c) suggests, that high scores on one variable are associated with low scores on another. The maximum absolute value r can have is 1.00, and as this correlation is quite close to this maximum it will be very useful for predictive purposes (i.e., (d)) and clearly resemble a straight line on a scatterplot (i.e., (e)). Furthermore, the high value of r indicates that the information to error ratio is *high* – in other words, there is a *large* amount of negative covariance between variables relative to random error.

From this output, you can see that we have now obtained a value for a correlation coefficient (r) of .792 and this is associated with a *p*-value of .019. The further away from zero this value is, the more highly correlated two scores are. The maximum value the correlation can have is 1 and the minimum value is −1. The obtained value of *r* is a descriptive statistic like a mean or standard deviation. The only difference is that, whereas the mean and standard deviation describe a single variable, the correlation coefficient describes the relationship between two variables. In the next section we discuss how to interpret this statistic.

Although in this section we have only discussed the product-moment correlation coefficient, it is worth noting that there are in fact many other types of correlation. Some of these are special cases of Pearson's *r* and produce the same results, so we have not discussed them for reasons of brevity and clarity. Others are useful where particular assumptions associated with this form of correlation are violated or where the data take a different form (e.g., where they are nominal or ordinal). We will talk about these assumptions later in this chapter.

correlation coefficient A measure of the degree of linear association between two variables.

covariance The degree to which scores above the mean on one variable are associated with scores above the mean on another variable. A negative covariance arises where scores above the mean on one variable are associated with scores below the mean on the other variable. *Correlation coefficients* are standardized covariances: that is, correlation coefficients also take random error into account.

Pearson's product-moment correlation coefficient A commonly used measure of association between variables that involves the ratio of the *covariances* of scores and the product of the standard deviations of the variables.

Pearson's r Another name for Pearson's product-moment correlation coefficient.

Interpreting and making inferences about correlations

We have already noted that an *r*-value of +1 indicates a perfect positive correlation, and an *r*-value of −1 indicates a perfect negative correlation. In both these cases the value of one variable can be predicted precisely for any value of the other variable. On the other hand, an *r*-value of 0 indicates there is no reliable relationship between the variables at all. These points are demonstrated in Figure 9.6.

Figure 9.6 Graphs showing *r*-values of (a) +1.00, (b) −1.00 and (c) 0.00

As in Chapter 8 when we discussed the interpretation of effect sizes, Cohen's (1988) overview provides a useful guide for interpreting correlations with absolute values that lie between 0 and 1. If *r* has an absolute value between .1 and .3 then the effect can be said to be of small size. If the absolute value of *r* is between .3 and .5 it is of moderate size, and if it is greater than .5 it is of large size. With a reasonable number of participants (e.g., more than 100), correlations of .3 and greater should be apparent to the naked eye in a scatterplot.

As well as allowing us to say how strong a relationship between two variables is, correlations also provide us with additional information about the proportion of variance in one variable that is associated with variation in the other variable. This is illustrated in Figure 9.7, where the total amount of variation in each variable is represented by a circle. The overlap of these circles represents correlation between the variables.

This representation makes sense when we think about what a relationship between the variables means. If two variables are correlated then that means they are varying in the same

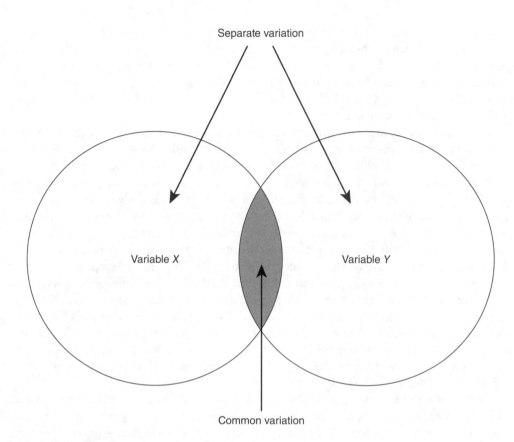

Figure 9.7 The common variance between two variables

way. This is the same as saying that if you know the value of one variable you know something about the value of the other. This is true of both positive and negative correlations. The degree to which two variables vary in the same way is called **common variance**. In fact, the square of the correlation (r^2) provides a measure of the common variance in two variables. This is the amount of overlap between the variables in Figure 9.7.

Because r is squared we have a measure of common variance that works for positive and negative correlations (because r^2 is always positive). We can then multiply this by 100 to express it as a percentage. For the example above, using the alcohol consumption/reaction-time data, a correlation of .79 is associated with $.79^2 = .63$ or 63% of the common variance. What this tells us is that variation in the number of alcoholic drinks a person has consumed in the last three hours is associated with 63% of the variation in the person's reaction time.

A correlation of this size is large enough to be very useful in many circumstances. In the hypothetical study of alcohol consumption and reaction time the researchers knew how much each participant had drunk. But imagine that they did not have this information and wanted to estimate how much alcohol a person had consumed when the only thing they knew was the person's reaction time. This is exactly the situation that a police force might find itself in if it were developing a test to discover whether drivers had consumed too much alcohol. The test would only be useful if it could be shown that it was associated with a high proportion of the variation in alcohol consumption.

On the other hand, low correlations mean that variation in one variable is only associated with a very limited amount of the variation in the other variable. Put another way, if the correlation between two variables (say, shoe size and IQ) is less than .1 then variation in one variable is associated with less than 1% of the variation in the other. This means that more than 99% of changes in the value of one variable will be associated with things *other than* change in the second variable. Similarly, a correlation of .3 between two variables means that they have less than 10% of variance in common (because $.3^2 = .09$ or 9%), implying that more than 90% of the variation in one variable is associated with things other than variation in the second variable. In these two examples the percentages 99% and 90% represent separate variation. One way of thinking about what these numbers mean is to note that they represent the amount of variation in one variable that would still be observed if the other variable were held constant (i.e., fully controlled). So if you conducted research with people of identical shoe size, those people's IQ would still vary almost as much (99% as much) as it would if you sampled from the entire population (when shoe size was not controlled). However, if two variables are perfectly correlated (i.e., $r = \pm1$) then when one variable is held constant there will be no variation in the other at all.

Under some circumstances, as well as wanting to know how large a correlation is, we will want to make inferences about correlations. These inferences are similar to those we seek to make when conducting *t*-tests. In particular, if we are using a hypothesis-testing approach like that outlined in the previous chapter, we will want to know whether any relationship we observe is a chance event (the null hypothesis) or whether it represents a relationship so strong that it is unlikely to have occurred by chance (the alternative hypothesis).

In other words, we want to make an inference about the correlation coefficient for the *population* (this coefficient is denoted by the Greek letter ρ, pronounced 'rho'). Following the logic outlined in the previous chapter, the null hypothesis is that there is *no* relationship between the variables in the population (i.e., H_0: $\rho = 0$), and the two-tailed alternative hypothesis is that there *is* a relationship (H_1: $\rho \neq 0$). A one-tailed alternative hypothesis would be either that there is a positive correlation (i.e., $\rho > 0$) or that there is a negative correlation (i.e., $\rho < 0$).

In order to see whether the obtained value of *r* is significantly different from one produced by chance we first calculate the degrees of freedom. For correlations, the degrees of freedom are equal to the number of observations minus two (i.e., $df = n - 2$). In the example above, the obtained correlation of .792 with 6 degrees of freedom is associated with a *p*-value of .019. So in this example, the correlation would be significant – and we would reject the null hypothesis that there was no relationship between the variables in the population – if our alpha level were .05 or .02. However, it would not be significant – and we would not reject the null hypothesis – if our alpha level were .01.

Test Yourself 9.3*

As part of a psychology assignment Kate has to calculate Pearson's r to measure the strength of association between two variables. She finds that $r = -.2$ and that this is significant at her selected alpha level of .05. What should she conclude?

a. That there is a significant but small relationship between the two variables.
b. That there is a non-significant but large relationship between the variables.
c. That there is a significant and moderate relationship between the variables.
d. That the two variables are unrelated.
e. That variation in one variable is associated with most of the variation in the other.

The correct answer is (a). A correlation with an absolute value between .1 and .3 is a small relationship by Cohen's (1988) criteria, but the relationship is also significant (by the criterion of $\alpha = .05$). It follows, then, that (b) is wrong. Answer (c) is wrong because a moderate correlation needs to have an absolute value greater than or equal to .3 (and less than .5). Answer (d) is wrong because the reasons that make (a) correct, and (e) is wrong because the amount of variation in one variable associated with variation in the other is only .2² (i.e., .04). Therefore the common variance between variables is associated with only 4% of the total variance. In other words, 96% of the variation in one variable is associated with factors other than variation in the other variable.

Following common usage, we recommend that the results of these significance tests should always be assessed alongside their effect sizes. To be useful, correlations normally need to be of at least moderate size (i.e., with an absolute value of at least .3) and unlikely to have arisen from random error (in other words, they should be statistically significant). In itself, statistical significance is not really sufficient. This is because with large sample sizes a very small correlation will be statistically significant. For example, with a sample size of 1000 an r greater than .081 in absolute value will be significant at an alpha level of .01, even though, for reasons we have already outlined, this correlation is associated with less than 1% of the total variance. The whole process of using hypothesis-testing and effect-size methods to deal with correlations is summarized in Online Appendix B.

common variance The amount of variation in one variable associated with variation in another variable (or variables). In the bivariate case this is given by r^2.

Some notes of caution

When we calculate correlations there are quite a few things that we need to be wary of. This is partly because, as with t-tests, the process of making inferences from correlations involves *assumptions*. If these are violated it will be imprudent to proceed without first taking steps to rectify the problem (if that is possible). The values you obtain for correlations are also affected by the sizes of the variance and the range of scores that are included in the analysis. Similarly, when we do research using correlation we must always be wary of the **correlational fallacy**.

An assumption of correlation is that there is a straight-line relationship between y and x of the form $y = a + bx$ (where a is the y intercept and b is the slope of the line). These straight lines are called *regression lines* and the slopes of these lines are called **regression coefficients**. An associated assumption is that the variables will jointly have a **bivariate normal distribution**. In practice, this means that a scatterplot of the relationship between the variables will have a cigar-shaped (i.e., elongated oval) form like that in Figure 9.8.

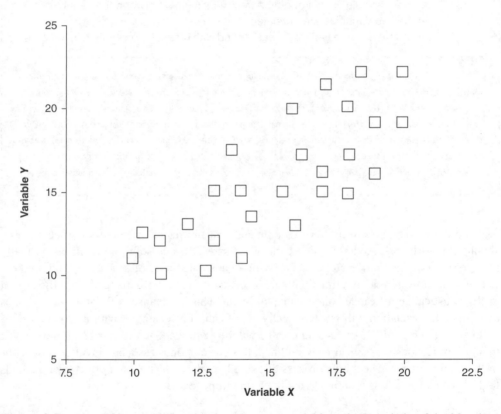

Figure 9.8   Cigar-shaped relationship between two variables, characteristic of the bivariate normal distribution

A particular problem arises when the overall pattern of the data is distorted by a few points that are very different from the others. These points are *outliers*, and in scatterplots we refer to them as *bivariate outliers* (because they are outliers in a plot of two variables and not just one). These outliers can have a disproportionate influence on the size of the correlation coefficient. In particular, if the outliers do not fit the straight-line relationship then a lower correlation coefficient will result – essentially because the outliers increase the amount of variance in the data.

Bivariate outliers are best detected by plotting the data. Indeed, the need to check that outliers are not present is another reason for starting any correlational analysis by drawing a scatterplot. The black square in Figure 9.9 gives an example of a bivariate outlier that would result in a lower correlation coefficient.

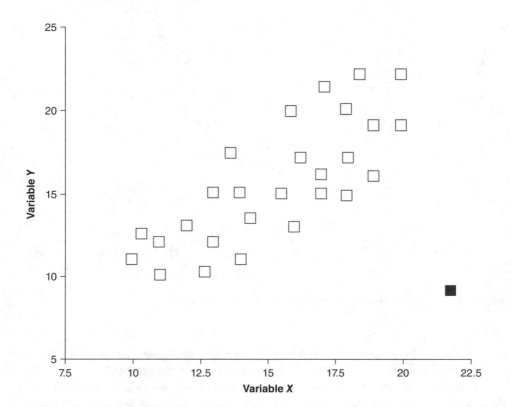

Figure 9.9   A bivariate outlier

The bivariate normal distribution will not apply, and therefore this assumption of the correlation procedure does not hold, where there is a *non-linear* relationship between the two variables. What happens, then, when variables are not related to each other by a function of the form $y = a + bx$ but instead $y = a + bx^2$? As you may recall from high-school mathematics, this is a simplified version of the equation for a parabola that results in a curve like that in Figure 9.10.

Where we encounter a **curvilinear relationship** like this, our procedures for computing the product-moment correlation coefficient break down. If a curvilinear relationship exists in the scatterplot then it is inappropriate to compute the correlation coefficient. Sometimes it is

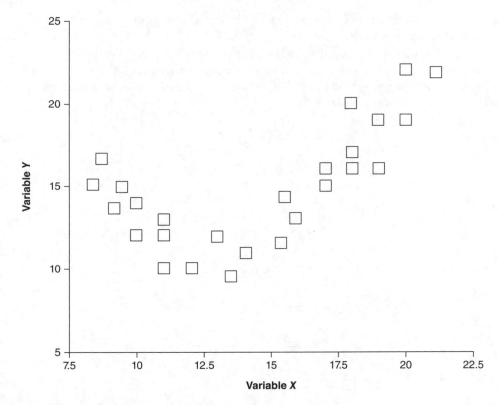

Figure 9.10   A non-linear relationship between two variables

possible to transform one of the variables (e.g., by taking the square root of all the *Y*-values) so that the relationship becomes linear. Having done this, we can compute *r*.

Another case where the relationship between variables will not yield a scatterplot with the desired cigar-shaped distribution occurs where we sample only a narrow band of participants from a wide population. Even though the bivariate normal distribution may apply to the relationship between the variables in the population in general, the relationship may not be shown in our particular sample. This is because correlations can be greatly changed if participants are sampled from a *restricted part* of the range of the scores.

This principle of **restricted range** is illustrated in Figure 9.11. This shows a hypothetical correlation between the number of hours of study for a statistics test (Variable *X*) and the mark obtained (Variable *Y*) for a sample drawn from the entire class (the whole graph) and for a sample restricted to those who studied less than 15 hours (the left portion of the graph). In the whole graph there is a very strong correlation of .87. However, when we restrict the sample to participants who studied for 15 or fewer hours (those to the left of the vertical line), we find that the correlation is now .53, and this is much harder to detect just by looking at the graph.

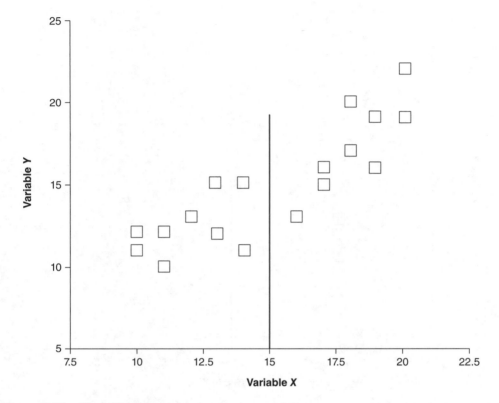

Figure 9.11 The effect of restricted range on correlation

What is happening in the second case is that the sample is restricted to a small part of the population – those who did less work. The relationship between hours of study and the mark obtained is very strong for the entire class, but for those who studied only a relatively small amount the relationship is much weaker. The point here is that even though a bivariate normal relationship can exist for the entire population, that relationship need not be evident for all sub-populations. Similarly, what looks like a linear relationship for a restricted range could really be a curvilinear relationship for the entire population. This applies in Figure 9.12, where the relationship across all values of X is curvilinear, but becomes linear if we restrict the sample to those with scores over 15. The only way to deal with these potential difficulties is to sample over as wide a range of the population as possible.

One of the consequences of making predictions based on the linear approach is that when we sample a restricted range of scores on one variable we may forget the effect of that restriction. Let us say that we took a group of people with a full range of scholastic achievement at high school and sent them all to a local university. After a semester at university we would probably find that the top 10% at university were not the same as those who were in the

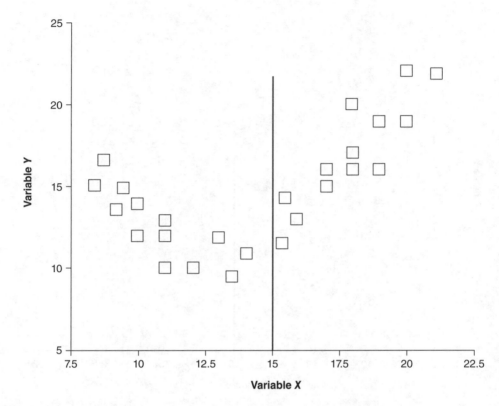

Figure 9.12   Two restricted sub-samples showing strong linear correlations, where the relationship across both samples is curvilinear

top 10% at school. On average, relative to the rest of the class, the ranking of those who were in the top 10% at school would have declined. The good news, however, is that the people in the bottom 10% at school would have improved (on average) relative to the rest of the class.

Having obtained such results it would be tempting to think of possible explanations for these changes in performance. Perhaps the top 10% were over-confident and did not try as hard at university, or perhaps university and school performance are based on different skills. These and other explanations are quite plausible, but they are more specific versions of a more general phenomenon – the phenomenon of *regression to the mean* that we discussed when dealing with issues of sampling and experimental design in Chapter 4.

This problem rears its head in this case because the top 10% in the class at school *cannot do any better* at university than the top 10% of positions that they already have. If there is any variation whatsoever, then it can only lead to their doing worse on average (if there is absolutely no variation their performance will only stay the same). The effect of this is that mean performance on the second measure – in this case, university performance – will be closer to

RESEARCH BITE 9.1
Voodoo correlations

There has recently been considerable controversy in the field of neuroscience around the topic of so-called 'voodoo correlations'. Specifically, it is claimed that taking multiple measures from a very specific brain region and correlating these with behaviour can generate misleadingly high correlations – primarily because this form of 'over-sampling' takes place within a restricted range. However, Klaus Fiedler (2011) makes the point that this issue is pertinent to psychological research more generally, because researchers often collect data from a limited sampling domain that is favourable to their hypotheses. He argues that reflecting on issues of restricted sampling is an important way to increase validity and refine theory.

Reference
Fiedler, K. (2011). Voodoo correlations are everywhere – not only in neuroscience. *Perspectives on Psychological Science*, 6, 163–171.

the mean for the sample. This applies to extreme scores wherever variables are not perfectly correlated. If it affects extreme scores at the top of the scale it is an example of one type of **ceiling effect** (referring to the fact that scores cannot get any higher) and if it affects scores at the bottom of the scale it is an example of a **floor effect** (referring to the fact that scores cannot get any lower; see Chapter 6, Exercise e, p. 163).

Regression to the mean will occur wherever we take extreme scores from a sample and examine the participants' scores on correlated variables. As we noted in Chapter 4, if proper controls are not in place, this comprises a serious threat to internal validity.

One of the ways in which restricted range affects correlations is by changing variance. Correlations are very sensitive to changes in variance. If you look back at the main equation for the correlation coefficient you will see that the error term (the bottom line) contains terms for the standard deviations of each variable. This relationship will be weaker if the standard deviations of the variables are larger. For example, this can occur if measurement in one setting is less reliable than in another. Therefore, before comparing correlations across situations you should be certain that the variances are comparable.

Moving beyond issues of how to conduct correlational procedures, we return to the most common mistake made by researchers when they come to *interpret* correlations. This is the *correlational fallacy* that leads researchers and consumers of research to assume that, because two variables are highly correlated, one must be *responsible* for variation in the other. The important point to reassert is that *correlation does not imply causation*.

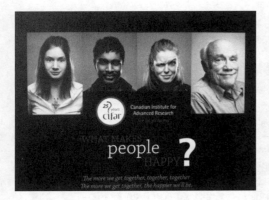

Photo 9.2 At the start of this chapter, below the photograph on p. 245, you may recall that we said that researchers had based their answer to the question 'What makes people happy?' partly on an examination of correlations between happiness and variables like wealth, health and number of social connections. Why only 'partly'? The answer is that correlational analysis can only show that there is a relationship between these various things and happiness (and that things such as number of social connections are more highly correlated with happiness than things like wealth; Helliwell & Barrington-Leigh, 2011). It cannot show that these things cause happiness. Accordingly, it is not possible to answer this question – or any other question of this form – with correlational research alone.

To drive this point home, imagine that researchers have conducted a study that reveals a strong positive correlation between the consumption of chocolate and aggressiveness. On this basis it *cannot* be concluded that chocolate causes aggressiveness. This is because the causal relationship between these variables may be *reversed* (aggressiveness may cause people to eat more chocolate), or the relationship may be the product of a *third factor* such as a person's upbringing. That is, certain styles of upbringing (e.g., a totally permissive style of parenting) may encourage chocolate consumption *and* aggressiveness, without each having a direct effect on the other.

There are many examples of spurious correlations that arise from the influence of a third factor like this. One example is the old story about researchers who found that there was a high correlation between the presence of 'spongy tar' in children's playgrounds and the incidence of polio. On this basis the researchers misguidedly claimed that 'spongy tar' caused polio. They urged the schools to dig up their playgrounds to get rid of the offending tar. However, this was a complete waste of time and money, because the researchers' causal analysis was wrong. In fact both spongy tar and polio were caused by a third factor: temperature. Excessively high temperature led to an increase in *both* polio and the sponginess of the tar. To reduce polio, schools needed to control the effects of temperature and not the type of tar in their playgrounds.

This inability to draw strict causal inferences (and the associated temptation to do so) is by far the most serious problem associated with correlational and survey methodology. Even if you learn nothing else from this book, by understanding this vital point you will have learned something that is sometimes forgotten by even the most eminent researchers.

bivariate normal distribution A straight-line relationship between two variables with a cigar-shaped dispersion.

ceiling effect A barrier to the correct interpretation of results that arises when the range of scores is limited because they are clustered in the region of the maximum scale value.

correlational fallacy The mistaken belief that because two variables are related one variable must cause the other.

curvilinear relationship A curved relationship between variables that is not well described by a straight line.

floor effect A barrier to the correct interpretation of results that arises when the range of scores is limited because they are clustered in the region of the minimum scale value.

regression coefficient The slope of a regression line (b in the equation $y = a + bx$). For a two-variable case, the standardized regression coefficient (β) will be equal to the correlation coefficient. This means that the correlation between two variables will be the same regardless of the regression line.

restricted range Selecting part of the sample so that there is not a full range of scores on a variable being measured.

RESEARCH BITE 9.2

The glass cliff: An example of reverse causation

In 2001 Michelle Ryan and Alex Haslam read a newspaper article that observed that companies with more women in leadership positions performed badly on the stock market. The article concluded that women leaders were 'wreaking havoc'. Ryan and Haslam (2007) pointed out that this evidence was correlational and that the causal direction might be in the opposite direction to that claimed in the report. Rather than women leaders causing companies to perform badly, poor performance could cause companies to appoint women to senior positions. This analysis was confirmed by archival and experimental research, leading the researchers to uncover a phenomenon they referred to as 'the glass cliff'.

Reference

Ryan, M. K., & Haslam, S. A. (2007). The Glass Cliff: Exploring the dynamics surrounding the appointment of women to precarious leadership positions. *Academy of Management Review, 32,* 549–572.

Conclusion

In this chapter we have only scratched the surface of the uses and possible forms of correlational analysis. We have, however, mapped out the basic principles necessary for calculating and interpreting correlations. We have also suggested some of the pitfalls that correlational

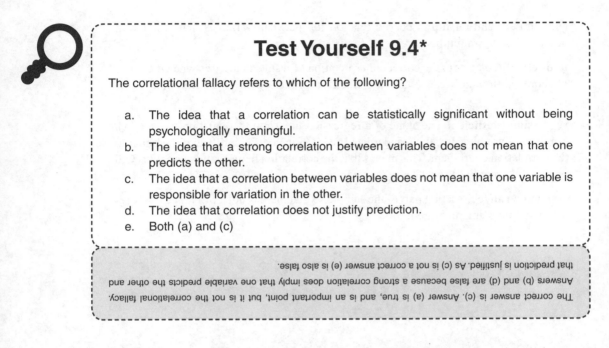

Test Yourself 9.4*

The correlational fallacy refers to which of the following?

a. The idea that a correlation can be statistically significant without being psychologically meaningful.

b. The idea that a strong correlation between variables does not mean that one predicts the other.

c. The idea that a correlation between variables does not mean that one variable is responsible for variation in the other.

d. The idea that correlation does not justify prediction.

e. Both (a) and (c)

The correct answer is (c). Answer (a) is true, and is an important point, but it is not the correlational fallacy. Answers (b) and (d) are false because a strong correlation does imply that one variable predicts the other and that prediction is justified. As (c) is not a correct answer (e) is also false.

research needs to avoid, such as changes in variance, restricted range, regression to the mean, and the correlational fallacy.

The last of these things is by far the most important. It is easy to overlook, but when designing your own research and evaluating that of other people you should always look to see whether causal inferences are being made on the basis of correlational evidence. You should do this regardless of whether the research under consideration is referred to as a survey or an experiment – remembering that many experiments are really quasi-experiments.

CHECKLIST
Revisiting the key goals for this chapter

☐ I understand the logic of correlation – a procedure for examining the relationship between variables.

☐ I know how to compute Pearson's *r* – a statistic that quantifies the nature and strength of the linear relationship between two variables.

☐ I understand how the results of correlational analysis should be interpreted, with particular reference to the difference between correlation and causation.

Further reading

Over the past few years correlation and regression techniques have become much more popular as a means of analysing psychological data. Cohen's (1988) book provides a very good introduction to this area, which underlines the importance of looking beyond statistical significance. Miles and Shevlin's (2001) text provides a good user-friendly introduction to the possibilities of such analysis and to the various ways in which it can be conducted.

Cohen, J. (1988). *Statistical power analysis for the behavioral sciences* (2nd ed.). Hillsdale, NJ: Erlbaum.
Miles, J., & Shevlin, M. (2001). *Applying regression and correlation: A guide for researchers and students*. London: SAGE.

Correlations: A checklist for research evaluation and improvement

Table 9.3

Potential problem	Question to ask	Potential improvement
Inferential uncertainty about a relationship between variables	Do researchers want to examine the relationship between scores on one variable and those on another variable when the population parameters are unknown?	Following the procedures described in this chapter, use a statistical package such as SPSS to calculate an r-score and to provide information about the probability (p) of observing by chance an r-score as large as the one obtained.
Significance fallacy	If the researchers are using a hypothesis-testing approach to correlation, have they distinguished appropriately between psychological and statistical significance?	Consider significance levels in conjunction with effect sizes (e.g., compare p and r). Be alert to the dangers of making too much of statistically significant correlations when effect sizes are low.
Bivariate outliers	Have the researchers tested for the presence of bivariate outliers that might be affecting the correlation?	Draw a scatterplot to identify bivariate outliers. If any are present and they appear likely to have an undue influence on the correlation, consider either removing them or recoding them so that they have the values of the nearest non-outlier. Ensure you report any transformations that you make.
Non-linearity	Is the relationship between variables linear?	Draw a scatterplot and see if data fall on a straight line. If they do not, be alert to the limitations of tests for linear relationships.

(Continued)

Table 9.3 (Continued)

Potential problem	Question to ask	Potential improvement
Restricted range	Have the researchers sampled across a full range of potential values for a given variable?	Consider values of variables that have *not* been sampled and consider whether the study is compromised by failing to include these.
Ceiling effects	Is a relationship between variables affected by the fact that scores on one or both variables cannot get any higher?	Try to understand what is constraining responses on the affected variables. If possible, suggest alternative measures.
Floor effects	Is a relationship between variables affected by the fact that scores on one or both variables cannot get any lower?	Try to understand what is constraining responses on the affected variables. If possible, suggest alternative measures.
Correlational fallacy	Have the researchers implied that one variable causes another on the basis of a correlation?	Suggest alternative interpretations of the correlation. Consider conducting experimental studies that might address issues of causality.

Test Yourself 9.5*

A group of researchers conducts some research in which they identify a significant positive correlation ($r = .42$) between the number of children people have and their life satisfaction. Which of the following is it *inappropriate* to conclude from this research?

a. That having children makes people more satisfied with their life.
b. That someone who has children is likely to be happier than someone who does not.
c. That the causes of life satisfaction are unclear.
d. That the consequences of having children are unclear.
e. That it is possible to predict someone's life happiness partly on the basis of the number of children they have.

Test Yourself 9.6**

Which of the following statements is true of the problem of restricted range?

a. Restricted range can reduce the size of correlations.
b. Restricted range can lead to a violation of the assumption of bivariate normality.

c. Restricted range can produce regression to the mean.
d. All of the above.
e. Answers (a) and (b) only.

Test Yourself 9.7**

If an experimenter observes a correlation of −1 between two variables, which of the following is *false*?

a. One variable is completely predictive of the other.
b. One variable is completely responsible for variation in the other.
c. Knowledge of the value of one variable allows one to know with certainty the value of the other.
d. A higher score on one variable is associated with a lower score on the other.
e. All the variation in one variable is associated with variation in the other.

Test Yourself 9.8**

If the correlation between people's wealth and a measure of their psychological well-being is .40, how much of the variation in their scores on the well-being measure will be associated with variation in their wealth?

a. 60%
b. 40%
c. 16%
d. 4%
e. It is impossible to say without information about how psychological well-being is defined.

The correct answer to 9.5 is (a). This statement is an expression of the correlational fallacy. Answers (c) and (d) are true because they recognize that correlation does not imply causation. Answers (b) and (e) are true because they merely point out that the existence of a correlation can be a basis for making predictions.

The correct answer to 9.6 is (d). Answers (a) and (b) are correct because restricted range can lead to violations of the assumption of bivariate normality and the effect of this can be to reduce correlations. This is primarily because the cigar shape across the entire distribution can be lost over a shorter range. Answer (c) is correct because although regression to the mean is often thought of as a different sort of problem, if the range is restricted to the extreme end of the population then scores on a second measure will be closer to the mean. If (c) is correct, (e) must be incorrect.

(Continued)

(Continued)

The correct answer to 9.7 is (b). This statement is false because it implies that correlation (even when it is perfect) allows researchers to infer causality. Although perfect correlation does not allow people to make causal inferences, it does allow them to know, with absolute certainty, scores on one variable on the basis of scores on the other (as suggested by statements (a) and (c)). In other words, 100% of the variation in one variable is associated with variation in the other (as suggested in statement (e)). Because the correlation is negative, a high score on one variable will be associated with a low score on the other – so statement (d) is true.

The correct answer to 9.8 is (c). The square of the correlation coefficient (r^2) is a measure of the common variance between two variables. This gives a direct indication of the amount of variation in one variable that is associated with variation in the other. In this case $r^2 = .4^2$, which comes to .16, or 16% of the total variance. It is certainly true that a researcher might want to question the validity of a particular measure of psychological well-being, but this does not affect the correlation between that measure and another and thus does not affect their amount of common variance – so (e) is not an appropriate answer.

Discussion/essay questions

a. Why is it helpful to create scatterplots in preliminary analysis of correlations?
b. What is the difference between a statistically significant and a psychologically significant correlation? Is this distinction important?
c. If correlations allow researchers to say nothing about causation, why are they of any interest?
d. In the wrong hands, few statistics are more dangerous than a correlation. Discuss.

Exercises

a. The data in Table 9.4 following were obtained from 12 participants in an experiment. The participants were of different ages, and scores were obtained on three dependent variables (speed, attention and accuracy). Draw scatterplots and calculate the correlation between the participants' age and each of these three dependent variables.

Table 9.4

Age	Speed(m/s)	Attention	Accuracy
10	150	2	2
11	160	1	3

Age	Speed(m/s)	Attention	Accuracy
11	165	1	2
12	155	2	4
12	140	4	1
12	130	3	5
13	120	4	3
13	135	1	7
14	130	3	3
14	115	3	5
15	110	2	6
16	120	3	5

b. Use the hypothesis-testing method to establish whether each of the above three correlations is statistically significant at the .01 level.

c. Based on Cohen's criteria, how would you describe the effect size of each of the above three correlations?

Table 9.5

Participant	Age	
	9 years	**12 years**
1	10	13
2	10	15
3	11	12
4	11	9
5	14	17
6	15	18
7	12	17
8	14	16
9	11	15
10	9	12

d. Based on these data, how much of the variation in a child's response speed is associated with variation in his or her age?

(Continued)

(Continued)

e. A researcher conducts a longitudinal study and administers a test of reading ability to 10 children at age 9 and then three years later at age 12. The data are as follows:

  i. The researcher wishes to find out whether there has been a change in the reading ability of the children as they have grown older. She expects a large change. Is she correct?

  ii. She also wishes to know whether there is a relationship between reading ability at age 9 and age 12. She expects the two reading ability scores to be highly correlated. Again, is she correct?

  iii. How is it possible for reading ability to change over time but the scores of the children at the different ages to be correlated?

10 Comparing Two or More Means by Analysing Variances: ANOVA

Key goals for this chapter

- Outline analysis of variance – a statistical procedure that allows researchers to establish how likely it is that observed differences between two or more groups would have arisen by chance.
- Show how different types of analysis of variance (ANOVA) are used to examine data that are structured in different ways.
- Explain the process of interpreting the results of analysis of variance.

In Chapter 8 we saw how it was possible to compare two means. The statistical procedure that we addressed in some detail was the *t*-test. We saw in that chapter, though, that this procedure is limited to comparing just two means at a time. The *t*-test is fine for giving us an insight into whether the mean scores of two groups are plausibly different or whether the mean scores of the same group on two variables are different, but it has its limits.

In particular, what should we do when we need to compare more than two means? The typical case where we might need to do this is where we have conducted an experiment involving many conditions. Participants in each group have been randomly assigned to a particular condition of an experiment. The conditions (representing different levels of the experimental **factors**) can be considered as levels of a categorical independent variable (or variables) and we want to know whether this variable (or variables) has affected some dependent variable which we have measured. That is, does our independent variable have an effect on the dependent variable – in other words, does the treatment make a difference?

One solution that might occur to you is that because you have lots of means to compare you could perform lots of *t*-tests. Thus, if we had the means for three groups (we can call them groups A, B and C) we could do three *t*-tests comparing A with B, A with C, and B with C.

This approach has two problems that we can address here, the first of which is quite easy to see. Each of the three *t*-tests combined gives us a clue as to whether two means are different (e.g., that memory is better with high practice than with low practice), but no single test helps us to establish whether there are differences between the three conditions in general. Often it is helpful to try to reach one overall conclusion about whether there are such overall differences.

The second problem is much less obvious, and it relates to the logic of significance testing. As we have been at pains to point out, significant results are never open-and-shut cases for the simple reason that they do not directly answer the questions we are interested in. Instead they only give us clues to those answers. They involve making decisions one way or the other on the basis of fuzzy evidence. This means that sometimes results are significant when they should not be (remember from the previous chapter that this is called a Type I error) and sometimes they are not significant when they should be (Type II errors). The problem is that when you do lots and lots of significance tests the chance of making a Type I error increases.

If we use an alpha level of .05 then the probability of a Type I error if we only do one test is also .05. Now think of a Type I error as one bad apple in a constantly replenished fruit bowl that always contains 20 apples. Each statistical test is like drawing an apple from the bowl. If we only draw one apple then our chance of getting a bad one on that draw is .05. However, as we do more tests then the chance that at least one of them will be significant increases. If we draw enough apples then, unless we are really lucky, sooner or later we are going to get a bad one. Similarly, if we did lots of *t*-tests on means sampled from the same distribution then we would find that some of them would be significant purely by chance (equivalent to a bad apple – and, as with apples, one bad test can spoil all the others). Now we could protect against this possibility by reducing our alpha level (e.g., from .05 to .01), but this creates the opposite problem – we may miss detecting differences that should be significant.

This is quite a tricky problem and we will return to it later in the chapter. In order to get to that point, however, we need to explain some procedures for comparing more than two means that get around these problems. These procedures involve analysing variance.

> **factors** Another term for independent variables. The term is used to describe design features of studies whose data are subjected to analysis of variance. The different levels of an experimental design together can comprise a factor, so that if we have a control group and two experimental conditions we have a factor with three levels.

Analysing variances

If we are interested in comparing means, why do we need to analyse variances? The answer is that variances are highly informative about the way variables behave. After all, they are called 'variables' and not 'meanables'.

Why are variances so informative then? Remember that the variance is the square of the standard deviation and reflects the amount of dispersion in the variable. There is more dispersion when the scores all tend to be quite different from the mean and there is less dispersion when the scores are all similar to the mean. Another way of saying this is to refer to variance as the descriptive statistical uncertainty in the variable (which can be considered to be due to random error). The mean is simply the position that describes scores on the variable with the least uncertainty. This way of thinking of the relationship between the mean and the variance makes most sense when the variable is normally distributed.

The previous paragraph gives us a hint as to one reason why we might want to compare variances. We might be interested in knowing whether one variable has a bigger variance than another. That is, is variable X associated with more dispersion, error and descriptive uncertainty than variable Y?

Imagine that we wanted to compare the variances of two variables. One obvious way to compare them is to form a ratio. To do this all we need do is divide the variance of one variable by the variance of the other. It is convenient to divide the larger variance by the smaller one. A ratio of this form gives us information about whether one variance is larger than another and by what amount. Values close to 1.0 tell us that the variances are about equal, and values much bigger than 1.0 tell us that one variance is much bigger than the other.

As usual, we have the problem that we need to know how big the statistic has to be before we can conclude that it is big enough to be meaningfully different. And again, as usual, statistics are unable to tell us what we would really like to know: 'Is one variance really bigger than the other?' However, statistics might be able to answer another question that gives us a clue to the answer to the question we are interested in.

The related question in this case is this: How plausible is it that the variances we have observed are really estimates of the same population variance? That is, can they be treated as if they were two different samples drawn in the same way (i.e., randomly) from the same population? If the variances are both estimates of the same population variance then they should both be pretty similar and any difference between them will be due to chance variations. That is, if one variable has a higher variance it might be because a few more observations that were quite different from the mean happened to occur on one variable and not the other (just as when digging for gold in the same hole we might turn up dirt one day and a gleaming nugget the next).

In order to examine this issue further we need to know how this ratio-based statistic behaves. More specifically, we need to know more about its sampling distribution. In fact, virtually all of the decisions we make in life are based on our knowledge of sampling distributions, and statistics just formalizes this fact. For example, the fact that you know something about the sampling distribution for gold digging (if you dig in most places you are likely to find a lot of dirt and very little gold) explains why you are currently reading this book rather than digging up your backyard. In the case of comparing variances, we need to know about the sampling distribution of the ratio of variances. As it happens, the behaviour of this sampling distribution is quite well understood, and providing that certain assumptions hold, it follows a particular pattern. This pattern is called the **F-distribution**.

Unlike the normal and the t-distribution, the F-distribution is not symmetrical. It is positively skewed, so that it has a tail at the right-hand end. If you think about it, it is easy

RESEARCH BITE 10.1
The man behind the F-word

Daniel Wright (2009) makes the point that when learning about techniques like ANOVA it is easy to have the impression that 'these were brought down from some statistical mount only magically to appear in SPSS' (p. 587). This, he argues, is far from the case. Statistics is a vibrant discipline populated by colourful characters who engage in passionate debates about the issues their work addresses. One example is Ronald Fisher, after whom the *F*-statistic is named. Fisher is often blamed for psychologists' fixation with the *p*-value of .05, but Wright notes that in fact this only gained prominence because, before the advent of programs like SPSS, researchers had to make statistical tables based on a limited set of *p*-values.

Reference

Wright D. B. (2009). Ten statisticians and their impacts for psychologists. *Perspectives on Psychological Science*, 4, 587–597.

to see part of the reason why the distribution has this shape: it is impossible to have a ratio of variances that is less than zero (a variance is an average sum of squares and a square of a number cannot be negative).

As with the *t*-distribution, the *F*-distribution varies in shape with the number of degrees of freedom. However, there is another complexity here: because the *F*-distribution involves the ratio of two variables we have to worry about degrees of freedom for both the numerator (the top line) *and* the denominator (the bottom line) of the ratio. The degrees of freedom for the numerator and denominator are here both equal to the number of people in the group minus one (i.e., $df = n - 1$). To compare the variances of two samples each containing 10 observations, the *F*-distribution we need has 9 degrees of freedom in the numerator and 9 in the denominator.

If both variances are equal then *F* will have a value of 1.0, but if that value differs from 1 we might be able to make an inference that the two distributions have different variances. Consider the data from Chapter 8 where we computed the variances for two different groups (control and experimental) to conduct a between-subjects *t*-test. The variance of the experimental group was 2.71 and the variance of the control group was 2.04 (which can be shown by squaring the standard deviations in Figure 8.11 on p. 210). We can turn these two variances into a ratio and obtain the *F*-value 1.33. We write *F*-values in the form $F(df_1, df_2)$, where df_1 refers to the numerator degrees of freedom and df_2 to the denominator degrees of freedom, so here $F(9, 9) = 1.33$.

If we assume that these two samples are drawn from a population with a normal distribution, what we now need to do is check what proportion of the F-distribution is cut off by this value. In this case, if we were to consult a table of values or use a computer program (e.g., www.danielsoper.com/statcalc3/calc.aspx?id=7) we would find that we would expect a ratio of variances this big or bigger around one-third of the time. This suggests that this ratio would not be a particularly unusual one to obtain if the samples really were both drawn from a population with the same variance. It is certainly not implausible that they are estimates of the same population variance.

This procedure has allowed us to compare variances. In doing so it gives us some guidance about the extent to which the assumptions that we made in Chapter 8 about doing the t-test hold. That is, there is no reason to believe that the variances are unequal (though, having said that, the actual test for inequality of variances that we used in this case is itself over-sensitive to the assumption of normality that we discussed in Chapter 8, and if we were really interested in answering this question we would use a more sophisticated test such as Levene's test of homogeneity of variance that is available in IBM SPSS Statistics software (SPSS) in the independent samples t-test command).

But having followed all this, you may still be wondering why a discussion of comparing variances is helpful when this chapter is supposed to be about comparing means. The answer is that we can use the F-distribution to compare means if we do something rather clever. This clever thing is to recognize that variances are simply average squared deviations. If we choose the right average squared deviations and form the F-ratio from them, then this ratio can be very informative.

F-distribution The hypothetical distribution of the expected ratio of variability between group means divided by variability within group means.

Comparing multiple means using one-way analysis of variance

In order to use the F-distribution to compare means we need to construct a ratio of two variances. Remember that variances are just the average of a sum of squares of the difference between a mean and some observations. So what we want to do is to transform the variances of these two variables into the classic ratio that underpins test statistics. Again, this is of the form

$$\text{test statistic} = \frac{\text{information}}{\text{error}}$$

But what exact ratio do we want to examine here? The short answer is that we want to compare the differences between groups (information) with the differences within groups (error; see the scenario on p. 208). If that ratio behaves in an unusual way then we may have something interesting to talk about.

Photo 10.1 As we have observed in previous chapters, all test statistics assess the ratio of information relative to error, such that one can be more confident that something significant is 'going on' to the degree that the information that this is the case outweighs random noise. In fact this is a basic principle of signal detection that we use to make judgements all the time (McNicol, 2004). For example, over time you would become less confident that this is the gravestone of Margaret Evans as the information contained in the carving becomes outweighed by the noise produced by erosion of the stone.

In analysis of variance, though, we do something even more cunning than usual. We actually create a ratio of two estimates of the *same* population variance. If a certain assumption holds true then these estimates should give us similar answers. However, if these estimates are very different then we really have to doubt whether our assumption was correct.

The assumption in question is a null hypothesis that there are no differences between means (in other words, that they are all estimates of the same population mean). If this assumption is correct then we can estimate the population variance in two ways. The first estimate is quite straightforward and involves an assumption that the population variance should be equal to the pooled variances of the **cells** we are comparing (remember that we saw how to calculate the pooled variance in Chapter 8).

The second estimate requires more subtlety. If the null hypothesis is true then the samples are drawn from the same population and any differences between means reflect chance variation. If this is true then all of the means should be estimates of the same population mean (and any differences between them reflect random error). If that is the case the central limit theorem that we discussed in Chapter 7 tells us what this distribution of means should look like.

This distribution of means will have a mean that is equal to the population mean and a variance that is equal to the population variance divided by the sample (cell) size (*n*). Remember, it is the variance we are trying to estimate here. So, if

$$s_x^2 = s^2/n$$

then if we multiply both sides of the equation by *n* we see it is also true that

$$s^2 = ns_x^2$$

What this tells us is that if we find the variance of the sample means and multiply it by the sample size we will have an estimate of the variance in the population means.

Providing that there is the same number of observations in each group it is reasonably straightforward to come up with this estimate. The variance of the sample means is based on the deviations between means of the groups we are comparing. We find the sum of the squared deviations between the mean for the entire sample and the mean of each group, and divide by the number of groups (less one to obtain an unbiased estimate) and then multiply by the number of people in each group.

We can then compare this estimate of the population variance with the estimate of the population variance obtained from pooling the within-cells variances by forming an F-ratio. If the ratio is close to 1.0 we have no reason to reject the null hypothesis, but if the number is much bigger than 1.0 we may be confident in rejecting the null hypothesis and conclude that the means are more variable than they should be if they are indeed drawn from the same population.

Clearly, though, the logic behind the above ideas is quite difficult to follow, so let us make this more concrete with an example. In this case we will work through the detailed calculations by hand and then perform the analysis within SPSS. This is because the calculations, although complex, are particularly helpful for understanding what analysis of variance is really all about. If you persevere in following these through this should help (a lot) at examination time and when you tackle more challenging forms of analysis in the future.

To start off let us stay with the example we used to discuss the between-subjects t-test in Chapter 8. These data are given in Table 10.1.

Table 10.1

Control group	Experimental group
4	4
4	5
6	7
5	8
7	6
3	9
4	7
2	8
5	5
4	5
$\bar{X}_i = 4.40$	6.40
	(Grand mean $\bar{X} = 5.40$)
$s^2_x = 2.04$	2.71

We will first look at a very simple way to calculate the F-ratio. We need to estimate the variances of two things (variables) and form a ratio of these variances. The first thing we need to estimate is the variance estimated from the means. We can construct such an estimate by taking the average deviations between the overall mean – generally referred to as the **grand mean** – and the cell means.

The unbiased estimate of the variance of the means (with equal cell sizes) is

$$\Sigma(\bar{X}_i - \bar{X})^2/(k-1)$$

where k is the number of cells, $\bar{X}_i$ is the mean for each group and $\bar{X}$ is the grand mean.

The only problem with this (as noted above) is that the variance of the means will tend to be smaller than the actual variance of the deviations as implied by the central limit theorem (the law of large numbers again). To correct for this we simply need to multiply this variance by the cell size n. Such variance estimates are also called **mean squares** or **MS** because the sums of squares are averaged. The mean square we calculate here is called the **between-cells mean square** (the shorthand is MS_B):

$$MS_B = \Sigma n\,(\bar{X}_i - \bar{X})^2/(k-1)$$

In this case the mean for the control group is 4.40 and the mean for the experimental group is 6.40. Here we can work out that the grand mean pooled across the two groups is 5.40 (because the cell sizes are the same, the grand mean is just the average of the cell means – try it and see). So

$$MS_B = \left\{10 \times \left(4.40 - 5.40\right)^2 + \left[10 \times \left(6.40 - 5.40\right)^2\right]\right\}/1$$
$$= \left((10 \times 1^2) + (10 \times 1^2)\right)/1$$
$$= 20$$

This value is associated with df_B degrees of freedom:

$$df_B = k - 1$$

where k is the number of cells.

As we noted above, when calculating an F-statistic the bottom line is an error term involving the average difference *within* groups. This is known as the **within-cells mean square (MS_W)**. We can work this out by pooling the variances we obtained previously. In Chapter 8 we saw that this value was 2.38. It is associated with degrees of freedom df_W:

$$df_W = N - k$$

This is the total number of participants minus the number of cells. Where we are only comparing two groups it is the same number as the degrees of freedom used in the between-subjects t-test. In this case

$$df_w = 20 - 2 = 18$$

The F-ratio is now found by dividing MS_B by MS_w:

$$F = 20/2.38 = 8.41$$

In order to evaluate this F-ratio we can compare it with the F-distribution with 1 and 18 degrees of freedom – which we could find in an online calculator (e.g., www.danielsoper.com/statcalc3/calc.aspx?id=7). We can see that this value is larger than the tabulated value for $F(1, 18)$ with $\alpha = .05$ of 4.41, so the probability of obtaining an F-ratio this large is less than .05. Indeed, the F-value is larger than the value with $\alpha = .01$ (the online calculator tells us that $p = .00954539$). In other words, if there really were no difference between the groups then we would expect to find a difference this big on less than 1 in 100 random selections of two samples of that size.

Referring back to Chapter 8, we see that this gives us a similar answer to the between-subjects t-test. Indeed, providing that there are only two groups to be compared (i.e., the numerator has 1 degree of freedom) there is an exact relationship between t and F in that $F = t^2$ (squaring the t-value of 2.90 gives us 8.41, which is the same value as we obtained from the F-ratio).

It is reassuring that F and t tell us the same thing under these circumstances, but the F-ratio really comes into its own when we want to compare data from more than two groups. So let us imagine that there were another two groups in our design and then go through the same process again. The new groups involve increased interaction between the participant and the target person they are rating, with the result that our extended (four-condition) study is now helping us to see not just whether interaction increases attraction, but whether the amount of interaction increases attraction. If we assume that our standard experimental condition involves a single session (and is renamed the 'one-session condition') then we can see that we now have two more conditions, one in which the participants have two interaction sessions and the other in which they have three interaction sessions (Table 10.2).

In this case, because the cell sizes are all the same, the grand mean of 6.525 is obtained by averaging the four condition means (4.40, 6.40, 7.80 and 7.50). For the same reason the pooled variance is obtained by averaging the four variances (2.04, 2.71, 2.40 and 1.61).

We now have an experimental design that involves four different conditions. Each of these conditions is made up of a group of participants who have been randomly allocated to that condition. And each condition or cell can be thought of as a level of our independent variable (or factor).

In order to compute the F-ratio we need a top line (the numerator or information term) and bottom line (the denominator or error term). Again, our top line here (MS_B) is based on

Table 10.2

	Exposure to target				
	No sessions (control)	One session (experimental)	Two sessions	Three sessions	
	4	4	5	9	
	4	5	8	6	
	6	7	9	9	
	5	8	9	7	
	7	6	5	6	
	3	9	8	6	
	4	7	8	7	
	2	8	9	9	
	5	5	8	8	
	4	5	9	8	
Mean $\bar{X}$	4.40	6.40	7.80	7.50	Grand mean = 6.525
Variance s^2_x	2.04	2.71	2.40	1.61	Pooled variance = 2.19

the deviations between each of the cell means and the grand mean multiplied by the number of observations in each cell, divided by the number of groups minus one. Thus

$$MS_B = \left\{ 10 \times \left[(4.4 - 6.625)^2 + (6.4 - 6.525)^2 + (7.8 - 6.525)^2 + (7.2 - 6.525)^2 \right] \right\} / 3$$
$$= \left[10 \times (4.52 + 0.02 + 1.63 + 0.95) \right] / 3$$
$$= (10 \times 7.11)/3$$
$$= 23.69$$

The within-cells variance estimate (MS_W) is simply equal to the pooled variance (i.e., 2.19). Hence

$$F = MS_B/MS_W = 23.69/2.19 = 10.81$$

Remember that if the variances are equal then the F-value will be 1.0, so 10.81 seems a lot bigger than that. Indeed, if we were to look up the probability that an F-value with 3 degrees of freedom in the numerator and 36 degrees of freedom in the denominator we would see that that probability would be very small (less than .001). This suggests that it is implausible that differences between cells as big as those we have obtained would be generated by taking random samples from the same population.

However, as promised, now that we know what we are doing, we can also run the analyses in SPSS. To do that, create a new data file that has three variables named 'Participant' (an identifying code), 'Exposure' (the number of sessions they interacted with the other person) and 'AttrScore' (the participants' rating of the target) and enter the data from the table above. Make the 10 people in the control condition (no exposure) participants 1 to 10, the 10 people with one exposure session participants 11 to 20, and so on. The first 16 of the 40 rows of data will look like Figure 10.1 (noting that the full data file is available in the Supplementary Online Material [Chapter10_OnewayANOVA.sav]).

1 : AttrScore	4.00		
	Participant	Exposure	AttrScore
1	1.00	.00	4.00
2	2.00	.00	4.00
3	3.00	.00	6.00
4	4.00	.00	5.00
5	5.00	.00	7.00
6	6.00	.00	3.00
7	7.00	.00	4.00
8	8.00	.00	2.00
9	9.00	.00	5.00
10	10.00	.00	4.00
11	11.00	1.00	4.00
12	12.00	1.00	5.00
13	13.00	1.00	7.00
14	14.00	1.00	8.00
15	15.00	1.00	6.00
16	16.00	1.00	9.00

Figure 10.1

After you have saved that file go to the 'Analysis' Menu and select 'Compare Means' and then 'One-Way ANOVA'. Drag 'AttrScore' to the 'Dependent List' and 'Exposure' to 'Factor' so that it looks like Figure 10.2.

Figure 10.2

Press on 'OK' and you should see the display in Figure 10.3.

Oneway

[DataSet2] /Users/20062061/Documents/Work folder/RMSiP 2nd ed folder/Chap10Oneway.sav

ANOVA

AttrScore

	Sum of Squares	df	Mean Square	F	Sig.
Between Groups	71.075	3	23.692	10.810	.000
Within Groups	78.900	36	2.192		
Total	149.975	39			

Figure 10.3

This output is called an ANOVA table, and you can see that it produces exactly the same values as the calculations that we conducted by hand. Hopefully, though, you now know what all these values refer to. This is important, because if you continue to study psychology you are going to encounter a lot more of these tables, and it is important that you know what their various contents tell you.

between-cells mean square (MS_B) This is an estimate of variance between cells and provides the numerator of an F-ratio.

cells The independent conditions in an experiment. The data in a given cell are thus based on responses from people who are all exposed to an identical experimental treatment, and whose treatment differs in some way from that administered to people in other cells.

grand mean The mean response across all the cells in a given experiment.

mean squares (*MS*) The average of the sums of squares.

within-cells mean square (*MS*$_w$) A measure of variance within groups that is equal to the pooled variance. This is an estimate of population variance and provides the denominator of an *F*-ratio.

Test Yourself 10.1***

Which of the following is a pooled variance estimate that constitutes the denominator of an *F*-ratio?

- a. The between-cells mean square (*MS*$_B$).
- b. The mean of the sampling distribution.
- c. The sum of the deviations from the grand mean.
- d. The grand mean.
- e. The within-cells mean square (*MS*$_w$).

The correct answer is (e). Population variance is estimated using within-cells mean squares (*MS*$_w$) and between-cells mean squares (*MS*$_B$), but it is *MS*$_w$ that constitutes the denominator. Answer (a) is wrong because the between-cells mean square (*MS*$_B$) that is equal to the sum of the squared deviations (*SS*$_B$) multiplied by mean cell size and divided by the degrees of freedom for the numerator constitutes the *numerator* of an *F*-ratio. Answer (c) is wrong because variances are means not sums, and in any case deviations from the grand mean are involved in the numerator. The most obvious reason why (b) and (d) are wrong is that *F*-ratios are ratios of *variances*, not means.

Another way to explain analysis of variance: Sums of squares and mean squares

In the previous section we explained analysis of variance as a way of making comparisons between means. Indeed, given the complexity of the material covered, you may be surprised by the claim that we have only introduced one genuinely new concept in this chapter so far, and that is the idea of the *F*-distribution.

This sort of explanation is slightly unusual in a book like this one. Most texts start with a treatment of ANOVA in terms of sums of squares and then move to mean squares (which are the variance estimates we have been talking about). However, we need to cover this terminology too (and not just so that you can have something interesting to say at parties when conversation strays onto the topic of sums of squares in ANOVA). This is because sums of squares have interesting properties and the idea of sums of squares has an extremely wide application in statistics.

A sum of squares is just that. It is the sum of all the squared deviations between a relevant mean and a set of scores. To see what this implies, we can express every score in our data set as the deviation between the score and the overall mean of all the scores. As we saw above, this mean is referred to as the grand mean, and the grand mean is the position that describes the whole set of scores with the least uncertainty.

Why would we express the data in this way? The answer is that once we have identified the grand mean then all of the variability in the data set can be understood as deviations from the grand mean. This gives us a new way of thinking about the score. It is not just a single number with a certain value, but it is a deviation from the average position. It is true that thinking about numbers as a mean plus a deviation makes them more complex, but it also allows us to do things with those numbers, in particular to calculate variances.

Where we sum the squares of all the deviations from a grand mean we get a single number that expresses all of the variability that exists in our data set. This single number is the **total sum of squares (SS_T)**. If the data contain lots of values that are smaller than and/or larger than the grand mean then the total sum of squares will tend to be large.

The total sum of squares is useful primarily because it can be divided up in a number of ways. This process is called **partitioning the sum of squares**, and ANOVA can be thought of as a set of procedures for deciding how to do this.

The method for partitioning sums of squares involves deciding on the types or **sources of variation** that we are interested in and then breaking up the total sum of squares into these types. Once we have done this we turn the sums of squares into variance estimates by dividing them by the degrees of freedom. As we saw above, we refer to these new qualities as *mean squares* and we can conduct statistical tests by forming ratios of these mean squares (which, after all, are variances).

In one-way ANOVA we are normally interested in partitioning the total sum of squares into two main sources of variation. The first of these is the **sum of squares between cells (SS_B)**, also referred to as the *treatment source*, and the second is the **sum of squares within cells (SS_W)**, also referred to as the *error source*.

In fact, the total source (SS_T) is exactly equal to the sum of the between-groups source and the within-groups source so that

$$SS_T = SS_B + SS_W$$

It is easy to see that this is the case by asking what other sort of variation there could be. We have deviations between the scores and their individual group means and we have variations between those group means. What other source of variation could there be that was not completely included within these two? None.

Each of these effects is also associated with a certain number of degrees of freedom. These values are the numbers you divide the sums of squares by to turn them into variance estimates (mean squares). The degrees of freedom can be partitioned in exactly the same way as the sums of squares. Thus

$$df_{\mathrm{T}} = df_{\mathrm{B}} + df_{\mathrm{W}}$$

As noted earlier in the chapter, the between-cells degrees of freedom (df_{B}) are equal to the number of cells (minus one to make it unbiased). The within-cells degrees of freedom (df_{W}) are equal to the total number of observations (minus one per cell to make it unbiased).

To see how all this works, we will return to the two-group example used previously. We have already calculated the between-groups sum of squares ($SS_{\mathrm{B}} = 20$). The within-cells sum of squares is equal to the average squared deviation between each score and its own group mean. These need to be pooled across all the groups involved. Table 10.3 shows the calculation of these average deviations for this example.

Table 10.3

Control group, $\bar{X}_c = 4.40$			Experimental group, $\bar{X}_e = 6.40$		
X	$X - \bar{X}_c$	$(X - \bar{X}_c)^2$	X	$X - \bar{X}_e$	$(X - \bar{X}_e)^2$
4	−0.40	0.16	4	−2.40	5.76
4	−0.40	0.16	5	−1.40	1.96
6	1.60	2.56	7	0.60	0.36
5	0.60	0.36	8	1.60	2.56
7	2.60	6.76	6	−0.40	0.16
3	−1.40	1.96	9	2.60	6.76
4	−0.40	0.16	7	0.60	0.36
2	−2.40	5.76	8	1.60	2.56
5	0.60	0.36	5	−1.40	1.96
4	−0.40	0.16	5	−1.40	1.96
	Σ	18.40			24.40

In order to pool the two contributions to the sum of squares we compute the total sum of all the deviations from group means. The sum of the squared deviations within cells (SS_{W}) is the sum of the squared deviations within the control group (let us call it SS_{WCG}) and the sum of the squared deviations in the experimental group (SS_{WEG}). Expressed algebraically,

$$SS_{\mathrm{W}} = SS_{\mathrm{WCG}} + SS_{\mathrm{WEG}}$$

Here

$$SS_{\mathrm{W}} = 18.4 + 24.4 = 42.8$$

To turn this into an unbiased variance estimate we need to divide by the number of observations (minus one for each group that we are pooling a variance from). In the example there are 20 observations; subtracting 2 gives us 18 (which is the number of degrees of freedom in the error term). When we have done this we then have an estimate of variance within groups that we can use as an error term called MS_W:

$$MS_W = 42.8/(20 - 2) = 2.38$$

Notice that this is exactly the same as the pooled variance that we obtained in Chapter 8 for these data. We have just calculated that value by another method.

Once we have divided by the appropriate degrees of freedom, we have mean squares for both sources and can form the F-ratio to examine how plausible it is that between-group differences of this size would have been obtained by randomly sampling groups from a single population.

Test Yourself 10.2**

Which of the following statements is true?

a. In one-way ANOVA the total sum of squares comprises two main sources of variance: within-groups variance and between-groups variance. Each has the same number of degrees of freedom.

b. In one-way ANOVA the total sum of squares comprises two main sources of variance: within-groups variance and between-groups variance. Each has its own number of degrees of freedom.

c. In one-way ANOVA the total sum of squares comprises three main sources of variance: within-groups variance, between-groups variance and error variance. Each has the same number of degrees of freedom.

d. In one-way ANOVA the total sum of squares comprises three main sources of variance: within-groups variance, between-groups variance and information variance. Each has the same number of degrees of freedom.

e. In one-way ANOVA the total sum of squares comprises three main sources of variance: within-groups variance, between-groups variance and information variance. Each has its own number of degrees of freedom.

The outcomes of these various steps can be formally summarized in an **ANOVA table**. This has one row for each effect as well as a row for the total. It also has a column for the name of the effect (this is called the source of variation), as well as columns for the sum of squares, degrees of freedom, mean square and F-ratio. We can also include columns for the level of significance (p) and the effect size (eta-squared, η^2) that we will discuss below. An ANOVA table for the above example would look like Table 10.4.

Table 10.4

Source	*SS*	*df*	*MS*	*F*	*p <*	*R²*
Between cells (Condition)	20	1	20	8.41		
Within cells	42.8	18	2.38			
Total	62.8	19				

As we will find out later in this chapter, there are other ways to partition the total sum of squares, but for the time being this is sufficient. Any partitioning, however, is only useful to the extent that it allows us to evaluate models. We consider this in the next section.

ANOVA table A summary table that provides key information arising from analysis of variance. Its rows relate to the various *sources of variation* and columns relate to the corresponding sums of squares, degrees of freedom and mean squares, as well as values of F, p and R^2.

partitioning the sum of squares The process of dividing up the *total sum of squares* in order to identify *sources of variation* in a data set.

sources of variation Components of the *total sum of squares* that are associated with particular features of a research design and partitioned out on this basis. In one-way ANOVA the two sources of variation are within-groups variance (error) and between-groups variance (information).

sum of squares between cells (SS_B) The sum of the squared difference between all cell means and the grand mean multiplied by the cell size.

sum of squares within cells (SS_W) The sum of the squared difference between each individual score and its cell mean.

total sum of squares (SS_T) In analysis of variance, the sum of all the squared deviations between individual cell means and the grand mean.

How big does a difference need to be? Significance testing and effect sizes

In the case of one-way ANOVA the model that is being evaluated is one in which the total sum of squares is partitioned in a particular way as compared with the null model where all the variance can be treated as error variance. We will tend to be less convinced by this null model when our statistical tests reveal that it is implausible.

In general, the models we are comparing take the following forms. First, the null hypothesis model is

$$X = \mu + e_{ij}$$

This says that the score for participant j in group i is equal to the grand mean (μ) plus the deviation of that participant from the grand mean (assumed to be error). Where this model holds, the expected values of the ratio of mean squares (the ratio of the average level of the mean squares over a long run if we were to sample repeatedly) will be distributed according to the F-distribution and will tend to be around 1.0.

The alternative model that we can test asks whether our experimental treatment has an effect. That is, do the groups to which participants are assigned make sufficient difference for us to consider this to be worthy of comment, attention and explanation? If they do then the following model would apply:

$$X = \mu_i + e_{ij}$$

That is, the scores will be expressed by the mean for the condition i plus error. In this case the treatment effect is also expressed as a deviation from the grand mean. Where this model holds, the ratio of the expected value of the ratio of mean squares will tend to be greater than 1.0. If it is sufficiently large we conclude that it is not plausible that the different groups have all been sampled from the same population, and we can therefore be more confident that there are differences between groups.

The significance-testing approach to making these decisions involves comparing the support for an alternative hypothesis that there are differences between the means with a null hypothesis of no difference. These have the form

$$H_0: \mu_1 = \mu_2 = \mu_3 \text{ etc.}$$

That is, the null hypothesis is that the population mean for Group 1 is the same as that for Group 2 which is the same as that of Group 3, and so on. This is compared with the alternative hypothesis (called the **effects model**):

$$H_1: \text{not all the } \mu s \text{ are equal}$$

These hypotheses are evaluated by comparing the observed value of F with the critical value of F for a certain number of degrees of freedom in the numerator and denominator for a particular alpha level (such as .05).

If the observed value is greater than the critical value of F then we conclude that the test is significant and we reject the null hypothesis. In the case of the two-group example above, if we set α at .05, then the critical value of $F(1, 18)$ is 4.41. Our obtained value ($F = 8.41$) exceeds this, so we conclude that the test is significant and we reject the null hypothesis.

Indeed, our grounds for doing this are especially strong as the obtained F-value exceeds the critical F-value for an α of .01 (8.29).

Alternatively, the same statistics can be considered as placing a confidence interval around F (for a detailed exposition of this point see Smithson, 2000). The 95% confidence interval for F lies between 0 and $F_{.05}$. If the obtained value lies within this range we cannot reject the null hypothesis, but if the obtained value lies outside the range we can be confident in rejecting the null hypothesis.

However, this information is most useful if it is supplemented by information about the *size* of effects. For the case of ANOVA the information we are interested in here is the extent to which the effects model is superior to the null model. This can be measured by examining the degree to which differences between groups make up a large proportion of the total amount of variance in the data. It is estimated by comparing the between-subjects sums of squares with the total sum of squares. This yields a statistic called **eta-squared** (η^2) that we mentioned above (but did not explain):

$$\eta^2 = SS_B/SS_T$$

Remember that SS_B must be less than SS_T (because $SS_T = SS_B + SS_W$, and because SS_W and SS_B are squared values they must be positive). Thus, where this ratio is large (close to 1.0) this means that most of the variance in the data is actually *variance between groups*. Where the value of η^2 is close to 0 (it can never be negative, again because both SS_B and SS_T are always positive) this means that most of the variance is actually within groups and not between groups (because any variance not associated with SS_B must be associated with SS_W).

All of this means that η^2 is a measure of the degree to which the treatment makes a difference; that is, of whether it matters which experimental condition participants were placed in. The particular thing it makes a difference to is accounting for variance: η^2 tells us how much better we are doing than the null model by taking the conditions into account, and in particular it gives us an indication of the proportion of variance that is accounted for by taking groups into account (or, alternatively, the proportion of variance that we would have to treat as error if we did not take groups into account).

We can examine this in relation to the example of our four-group experiment. We have already calculated MS_B and found that it was 23.69. We multiply this by df_B to obtain SS_B, which is $23.69 \times 3 = 71.075$. To find SS_T we need to know SS_W. We know that

$$MS_W = SS_W/df_W$$

and therefore

$$SS_W = MS_W \times df_W$$

We previously calculated MS_W and we know that $df_W = 36$ (the total number of observations, 40, less one for each group), so

$$SS_W = 2.19 \times 36 = 78.9$$

$$SS_T = 71.075 + 78.9 = 149.975$$

$$\eta^2 = SS_B/SS_T = 71.075/149.975 = .4739$$

In other words, differences between groups account for 47% of the variance in this sample and only 53% is associated with variance within groups. So, as well as being significant, the effect is associated with a large proportion of the variance. Indeed, Cohen (1988) classifies an η^2 greater than .14 as a large effect, one between .06 and .14 as medium-sized, and one between .01 and .06 as small. This, then, is a large effect.

If we go through the same process with our two-group example, we can compute η^2 very quickly from the values in our ANOVA table. Here $SS_B = 20$ and $SS_T = 62.8$, so $\eta^2 = SS_B/SS_T = 20/62.8 = 0.32$. Again, then, not only is the effect significant but it is also of large size (i.e., $\eta^2 > .14$). This agrees with the conclusion we arrived at in Chapter 8. Moreover, we can now fill in the two empty spaces (for p and η^2) in the ANOVA table so that it looks like Table 10.5.

Table 10.5

Source	SS	df	MS	F	p <	η^2
Between cells (Condition)	20	1	20	8.41	.01	.32
Within cells	42.8	18	2.38			
Total	62.8	19				

It is important to report these measures of effect size along with any inferences made on the basis of statistical tests. We normally need to know not just whether it is plausible that the differences are due to chance, but that the differences are sufficiently large to be concerned about. Are first-born children more intelligent than their younger siblings? If we took a sufficiently large sample we may find that they are, but the difference in intelligence would be very small. Accordingly, this difference might be of interest to those who study the influence of birth order on intelligence, but it might be so small as to be irrelevant for most everyday considerations. As noted in the previous chapter, effect-size measures therefore play an important role in helping us to put our results in perspective.

effects model A hypothetical model in which mean responses *differ* across the conditions of an experimental design. This represents an alternative to the null hypothesis that the mean response is the same in all conditions.

eta-squared (η^2) A measure of effect size used in ANOVA. This is equivalent to R^2 in correlational analysis (as discussed in Chapter 9). Cohen (1988) suggests that an effect with an eta-squared of .01 is small, greater than .06 is medium and greater than .14 is large.

Test Yourself 10.3**

What is the point of calculating the value of η^2 in relation to particular F- and p-values?

a. η^2 is a hypothesis-testing measure that can tell us whether a particular F-value is significant.
b. η^2 is the square of α and can tell us whether a particular p-value is significant.
c. η^2 is a measure of effect size that can tell us whether a particular F-value is significant.
d. η^2 is a measure of effect size that can tell us whether a particular p-value is significant.
e. η^2 is a measure of effect size that can tell us how much variance a particular effect accounts for.

The correct answer is (e). η^2 is a measure of effect size that quantifies the amount of variance between conditions in an experimental design as a proportion of the total amount of variance. This information is used in conjunction with information about the probability of an effect of the observed size (i.e., a p-value), to give an indication of the effect's psychological (not just statistical) significance. All other answers are wrong because η^2 is not a measure of probability or statistical significance. Note too that (a) and (b) are particularly wrong because η^2 has nothing to do with hypothesis testing and the square of α is a completely irrelevant value (for any purpose).

What does analysis of variance buy us? Some notes on comparing individual means

Once we have calculated the F-ratio and made the inference that chance variation is not a plausible way to explain the pattern we have observed, and that the effect size is sufficiently large to be concerned about, we have a new problem. We are prepared to accept that there are differences between conditions, but we have no idea *which* individual means are different.

What? Why have we gone to this amount of trouble to calculate F-ratios if we still have not answered this very simple question? This is quite a complex problem and there are several answers; we will address three of them.

The first answer is that once we have calculated the F-ratio and found that it is indicative of a statistically significant effect, we can be confident that there is some relationship between our independent and dependent variables (i.e., the conditions make a difference or there are differences between conditions). Armed with this knowledge, we can then explore the data further to find out where the differences lie (paying close attention to the number of tests we do and the possibility of the inflation of alpha). However, we know that there is no point in going further if the F-ratio is not significant. Thus, a non-significant F-ratio is a stark 'Keep out!' sign, while a significant one is an invitation to explore further.

The second answer is that a significant F-ratio is indeed not all that useful when we are comparing many different means (i.e., in a multiple-condition experiment). Instead of worrying too much about the F-ratio, researchers should instead plan to make comparisons of *particular* means in advance of collecting the data (again taking account of the inflation of alpha). The trick here is to work out which means to compare and what differences between those means reflect. This then raises the important question of where exactly the plans that lead us to make the comparisons come from. The answer is that they are given by our experimental hypotheses and predictions. Where we expect in advance that two means should be different (or that they should not be different) then we should plan to compare them.

The third answer to our problem is really a combination of the first two. This view says that we should calculate the F-ratio and if it is significant then proceed to test any comparisons that we considered in advance and/or any other comparisons that might occur to us on the basis of a discovery of significant F-ratios. This view is actually fairly common in psychological research, but it should be avoided as it rests on a statistical misunderstanding (which we will explain further below). In this book we will briefly discuss the first two views here.

Using *F*-ratios with and without comparisons planned in advance

If you find a significant F-ratio and have no comparisons planned in advance you should now proceed to conduct all possible **pairwise comparisons**. This simply means comparing every mean with every other mean. If we have three means, for example, there are three possible comparisons (A with B, A with C, and B with C) and if there are four means there are six possible comparisons. Such comparisons are called **post hoc comparisons** (*post hoc* is Latin for 'after this') because they were not planned in advance. There are many methods available for doing these multiple comparisons. One of the best known is the Scheffé method. This uses the F-ratio obtained from the ANOVA, and details are provided in more advanced ANOVA texts (e.g., Keppel & Wickens, 2003; Maxwell & Delaney, 1990).

If we know in advance that we wish to compare particular pairs of means then we can conduct planned (also called **a priori) comparisons**. There are many methods for doing planned comparisons (such as orthogonal polynomial contrasts); one simple method is to perform t-tests, but to make an adjustment to the alpha level of the t-test to take account of the inflation of alpha and adjust the error term used in the t-test to take account of the full set of data available.

The first adjustment relates to the problem that we referred to at the start of the chapter. It is always possible that some differences that we find to be significant actually reflect chance variation (i.e., they are not really valid). If we draw random samples from the same population then the probability that two will be significantly different is equal to the alpha level (often .05). If we do lots of comparisons we are more likely to find significant differences by chance (for the same reason that we are more likely to choose at least one bad apple over a long run of choices). One way to deal with this problem is to adjust the alpha level to take account of the number of comparisons we need to do (this is called the family of comparisons). Doing this will allow us to maintain an **experimentwise alpha level** that is the same as our intended alpha level. Each comparison, however, will be conducted using a lower (protected) alpha level.

Protecting the alpha level is quite simple to do. First, you count up the number of comparisons that you plan to calculate. Then you simply divide your alpha level by the number of comparisons you need to perform. This gives you the new alpha level to be used for each comparison.

As an example, let us say that we hypothesized that one or two exposures to a target person would increase their attractiveness but that an additional session would have no effect. In the design above this would mean that we would need to compare the no-exposure condition with the single-exposure session, the single session with the two-exposure session and the two-session condition with the three-session condition. That is, we have three comparisons (A with B, B with C, and C with D). To find our protected alpha level we simply divide by 3 (the number of comparisons) and use this as our alpha level. This is called the **Bonferroni adjustment**.

We can then perform our *t*-tests using this protected level of .017. In order to do this, however, the error term (denominator) comes from the pooled variance across all our cells. To find this, calculate the square root of MS_w and then multiply this by the square root of $2/n$, where n is the number of participants in each cell.

Thus to compare the mean of group i with the mean of group j, subtract the first mean from the second and divide by the error term:

$$t = \frac{\bar{X}_i - \bar{X}_j}{\sqrt{MS_w \times (2/n)}}$$

Critical *t* is not shown in Online Table C.2 for this value, but it is close to the level of .02 for a two-tailed test. This indicates that for 18 degrees of freedom an observed *t* of around 2.6 will be significant.

There are some quick points to make here. To follow this method you do not actually have to conduct an analysis of variance. If somebody advises you to perform an analysis of variance and check to see whether that is significant before conducting **planned comparisons**, they are simply giving you bad advice (see Maxwell & Delaney, 1990, p. 200, for more detail). They are essentially advising you to reduce the power of your test to reveal what is going on in the data. It is also worth noting that the Bonferroni adjustment becomes very conservative when the number of comparisons is large, so it is a good idea not to conduct too many comparisons (as a rough rule of thumb, you should include no more comparisons between cells than there are cells in your design). At the same time, be aware that planned comparisons need to be planned *before* your research is conducted, or else the likelihood of making a Type II error increases dramatically. Indeed, the practice of 'planning' comparisons by *H*ypothesising *A*fter the *R*esults are *K*nown (**HARKing**; Kerr, 1998) is extremely problematic.

There is obviously quite a bit to do when conducting one-way ANOVA. To help summarize this process, Online Appendix B shows the steps to follow and presents a worked example.

RESEARCH BITE 10.2
The perils of false-positive psychology

Fabricating data contaminates the scientific literature and is clearly wrong. However, Joseph Simmons, Leif Nelson, and Uri Simonsohn (2011) identify a range of practices that can also distort the field, but which are not, strictly speaking, fraudulent. These include (a) conducting multiple studies but only reporting those that yield significant findings, (b) conducting studies that include multiple dependent variables but only reporting those that yield significant findings, and (c) collecting data up to the point that effects become significant and then stopping. The researchers refer to this as 'false-positive psychology', and it is now widely accepted that such practices are extremely problematic.

Reference

Simmons, J. P., Nelson, L. D., & Simonsohn, U. (2011). False-positive psychology: Undisclosed flexibility in data collection and analysis allows presenting anything as significant. *Psychological Science*, 22, 1359–1366.

Test Yourself 10.4*

A researcher, Isobel, conducts one-way analysis of variance in which she compares the final marks of students who have studied psychology at one of five different institutions, A, B, C, D and E. The study looks at the marks of 100 students, 20 from each institution. On the basis of a given theory, the researcher plans to make four comparisons: between A and B, A and C, C and D, and C and E. Three other researchers make the following observations:

X: 'If Isobel used an experimentwise alpha level of .01, a Bonferroni adjustment would mean that each of these tests had an alpha level of .0025.'

Y: 'If Isobel used an experimentwise alpha level of .05, a Bonferroni adjustment would mean that each of these tests had an alpha level of.0025.'

Z: 'If Isobel used an experimentwise alpha level of .05, a Bonferroni adjustment would mean that each of these tests had an alpha level of .0125.'

Who is correct?

a. Only X.
b. Only Y.
c. Only Z.
d. X and Y.
e. X and Z.

The correct answer is (e). In this case the Bonferroni adjustment simply involves dividing the experimentwise alpha by the number of comparisons (i.e., 4). Thus when this alpha is .01, adjusted alpha is .01/4 = .0025, and when it is .05, adjusted alpha is .05/4 = .0125. Therefore both X and Z make correct observations, and only Y is incorrect.

a priori comparisons Comparisons between cells that a researcher has planned to perform prior to a study being conducted. These constitute a subset of all possible comparisons and have usually been identified as important on the basis of a particular theory.

Bonferroni adjustment An adjustment to alpha that takes into account the number of comparisons that are being made (and hence the number of t-tests that are being conducted).

experimentwise alpha level The overall alpha level that informs hypothesis testing in a given study. When specific tests are conducted, this may be adjusted to take into account the number of comparisons that are being made.

HARKing The practice of hypothesizing after results are known. If this provides a spurious basis for conducting planned comparisons, it will inflate the likelihood of Type II error.

pairwise comparisons Comparisons between every pair of cells in a given experimental design.

planned comparisons Comparisons between cells in a given experimental design that were envisaged (on the basis of an experimental hypothesis) prior to research being conducted.

post hoc comparisons Comparisons between cells that a researcher has not planned to perform prior to a study being conducted.

An introduction to analysis of variance with two independent variables

So far we have dealt with techniques for examining differences between levels of a single experimental manipulation. The chief question that we can answer here is whether that manipulation makes a difference. If we reject the null hypothesis then we are expressing some confidence that there are meaningful differences between experimental conditions.

Both the null model and the effects model can be thought of as providing answers to questions. One key question that the models give different answers to is 'What is the best guess for the score of a participant in Group i?'. If we are convinced by the effects model, then the best guess will be the mean for Group i. If not, the best guess is the grand mean. A slightly different way to state the question is to ask 'What is the effect of the treatment on the scores participants obtain?'. The answer that the effects model gives is 'people in some groups tend to get higher scores than other groups'; the answer that the null model gives is 'people get roughly similar scores in different groups'. In even simpler terms, the effects model answers 'yes' to the question 'Does the treatment make a difference?' and the null model answers 'no'.

We all know that the world is not always quite as clear cut as this. In many situations we are unable to give straight answers to questions such as 'Does the treatment make a difference?'. Our answers often take the form 'That depends on some other factor' or 'Yes, but only in some circumstances'. Take the example we have been considering of the test of the physical reinforcement theory. The conclusion suggested by the effects model is that the treatment does make a difference – exposure to targets leads people to regard those people as more attractive. Here, though, we are more than likely to ask just how widely we would expect this conclusion to hold. Would we expect the same pattern to hold with target people we already knew, or if the people the participants were exposed to could not speak the same language?

Assuming that we do not expect exactly the same relationship, the sorts of hunch that we could have in those cases fall into three classes: 'no', 'yes, but not to the same degree' and 'yes, even more so'. Regardless of which of these we suspect, in any case we are doing something quite special. We are hypothesizing an *interaction* between the treatment variable and some other variable (see Chapter 4).

This sounds like a complex thing to do (and it certainly does lead to statistical complexities), but in everyday life we hypothesize interactions between variables all the time. Let us imagine that while writing this text one of us remembers that he needs to phone someone in another town about some pressing matter to obtain some information for a colleague here. Will I ring the person now or wait until later? One would hope that this would be determined by how pressing the matter was. If it was really urgent I would probably do it now, but there are other possibilities. Some of the answers you might give could be 'It depends on whether your colleague is really desperate for the information', or 'It depends on whether you think the person will be at their phone', or 'It depends whether you remember', and so on. All of these involve positing an interaction between the urgency of the matter and other variables.

Imagine a friend asks if you are likely to go to a party on Saturday night. If you give just about any answer other than 'yes' or 'no' you are proposing a statistical interaction (and in this example maybe even a social one). For example, if you say 'It depends who else is going' or 'It depends on whether I can get a lift there', then you are saying that your likelihood of going is not just determined by whether you want to go, but by other factors. One interesting thing about these everyday exercises of logic, which we can all perform, is that they only become difficult to grapple with when we put them into statistical and mathematical terms.

Analysis of variance involving more than one categorical variable basically exists to answer the question of whether there is statistical evidence of interaction. It can still answer other questions, about whether other variables have effects on their own, but these effects, known as **main effects,** follow exactly the same ideas as one-way ANOVA. Interaction is the tricky part, but we will deal with the main effects first.

Let us consider a straightforward example. Imagine we measured biscuit eating in four people, two of whom were hungry when they started eating and two who were not. We provide one of the hungry people with chocolate biscuits and one with plain biscuits and do the same with the people who are not hungry. We wish to find out the effect of hunger and type of biscuit (plain or chocolate) on the number of biscuits eaten in the pack. We can represent these data in a 2×2 table (Table 10.6), and we might do that by treating hunger as the **row variable** and flavour as the **column variable**. Each row will have its own **row mean** (the average of means in that row) and each column will have a **column mean.**

Table 10.6

	Plain	Chocolate	(Row means)
Not hungry	5	15	10
Hungry	10	20	15
(Column means)	7.5	17.5	Grand mean = 12.5

By examining this table we can work out the effect of flavour and hunger on biscuit consumption. By examining the difference between the column means we can see that chocolate increases biscuit consumption by 10 and that hunger increases biscuit consumption by 5.

There is another useful but less obvious way to think about these data, though. We can consider each row or column mean as a deviation from the grand mean of 12.5. Why would we do this? The answer is that in many cases we want to know not only how large some score is in absolute terms, but also whether it is bigger or larger than the average. This is especially important when we are trying to work out whether some variable or combination of factors has an effect; that is, whether it makes a difference. Thus

$$\text{chocolate coating} = \text{grand mean} + 5$$

$$\text{plain} = \text{grand mean} - 5$$

$$\text{not hungry} = \text{grand mean} - 2.5$$

$$\text{hungry} = \text{grand mean} + 2.5$$

If we are prepared to believe these data then they suggest a model to us. Note that the difference between hungry and not hungry biscuit consumption is the same for chocolate and plain biscuits (+5), and that the difference between chocolate and plain biscuit consumption (+10) is the same for hungry and less hungry people (these two statements are identical in this case). That is, even though the effect of flavour is stronger than the effect of hunger, the effect of flavour is the same for both levels of hunger. This need not always be the case (see below), but it is the case here. The model that these data suggest to us is called a **main effects model** and it holds that the cell means are given by the sum of the effect of the row variable and the column variable at that cell. Will a person who is not hungry eat more or fewer chocolate biscuits than the grand mean of all biscuit eaters? The answer is found by adding the effect for chocolate (+5) to the effect for not being hungry (−2.5). This gives us a score of 2.5, suggesting that the person will consume 2.5 more biscuits than average under these conditions.

We can write this model in the following way:

$$X = \mu_{ij} + e$$

where

$$\mu_{ij} = \mu + \alpha_i + \beta_j$$

That is, the score for a participant is given by μ_{ij}, the mean for the particular cell the participant belongs to, plus error, and this cell mean is given by the grand mean plus an effect α_i and an effect β_j, where α_i is the row effect for cell i and β_j is the column effect for cell j. The row and column effects can be thought of as the deviations from the grand mean that occur at a particular level of a factor. Under this main effects model we can find the effect of the row and column by just *adding* these together (it can also be termed the **additive model**).

The biscuit example we used involved observations of only a single participant in each cell and not cell means calculated for several participants. Now consider some more realistic psychological data. These data come from an imaginary experiment that involved measuring the amount of distress (rated on a scale with values between 0 and 10) experienced in a group of adults who were exposed to very loud or very soft noises that were controllable or uncontrollable (they could switch them off by pressing a button). Each cell mean is based on measuring the responses of 12 participants who were randomly assigned to conditions.

The data file is available in the Supplementary Online Material [Chapter10_TwowayANOVA.sav], so you can type it in from there or else simply download it. The first few rows look like Figure 10.4.

If you are downloading the file, follow the instructions on the website. If you are typing in the data be sure to enter value labels for the variables 'Intensity' and 'Uncontrollability'. To do this, click on 'Variable View' and then go across to the 'Label' column in the 'Intensity' row (see Figure 10.5).

Click on the '...' in that cell and the window shown in Figure 10.6 will come up. In the 'Value' space type '1' and then in 'Label' type 'Soft'. Click on the 'Add' button. Then go to

	Participant	Intensity	Uncontrollability	Distress
1	1	1	1	2.00
2	2	1	1	2.00
3	3	1	1	3.00
4	4	1	1	3.00
5	5	1	1	4.00
6	6	1	1	4.00
7	7	1	1	4.00
8	8	1	1	4.00
9	9	1	1	5.00
10	10	1	1	5.00
11	11	1	1	6.00
12	12	1	1	6.00
13	13	1	2	3.00
14	14	1	2	3.00
15	15	1	2	4.00
16	16	2	2	4.00

Figure 10.4

	Name	Type	Width	Decimals	Label	Values
1	Participant	Numeric	11	0		None
2	Intensity	Numeric	11	0		None
3	Uncontrolla...	Numeric	11	0		None
4	Distress	Numeric	8	2		None

Figure 10.5

Figure 10.6

'Value' and type '2', then to 'Label' and type 'Loud'. Click 'add' and then press 'OK'. We have now labelled the values of the factor 'Intensity'. Do the same for 'Uncontrollability' (using the labels 'Controllable' for '1' and 'Uncontrollable' for '2').

We now are ready to do a two-way ANOVA. In the 'Analysis' menu select 'General Linear Models' and then 'Univariate'. The window in Figure 10.7 will appear.

Figure 10.7

Drag 'Distress' to the 'Dependent Variable' and 'Intensity' and 'Uncontrollability' to the 'Fixed Factor(s)'. This requests a two-way ANOVA with Distress as the dependent variable. Then click on 'Options . . .', and this produces the window in Figure 10.8.

Figure 10.8

The options we would like here are the 'Descriptive statistics' and the 'Estimates of effect size' (means broken down by factors and interactions can also be requested where required). Press 'Continue' and then 'OK'. After the analysis has run it will produce four tables.

The first table (Figure 10.9) just shows how many people were in each level of the factor (condition).

Between–Subjects Factors

		N
Intensity	1	24
	2	24
Uncontrollability	1	24
	2	24

Figure 10.9

The next table (Figure 10.10) provides the descriptive statistics that we asked for.

Descriptive Statistics

Dependent Variable: Distress

Intensity	Uncontrollability	Mean	Std. Deviation	N
1	1	4.0000	1.34840	12
	2	5.0000	1.34840	12
	Total	4.5000	1.41421	24
2	1	5.0000	1.34840	12
	2	6.0000	1.34840	12
	Total	5.5000	1.41421	24
Total	1	4.5000	1.41421	24
	2	5.5000	1.41421	24
	Total	5.0000	1.48754	48

Figure 10.10

These are artificially constructed data so all the cells have the same standard deviation and the cell means are all nice round numbers. These means are reproduced in Table 10.7.

Table 10.7

	Uncontrollability		
Noise intensity	Controllable	Uncontrollable	(Row means)
Soft	4.0	5.0	4.5
Loud	5.0	6.0	5.5
(Column means)	4.5	5.5	(Grand mean) 5.0

Here there are two levels of noise intensity (soft and loud) and for each of these there are two levels of uncontrollability (controllable and uncontrollable). We will refer to noise intensity as the row variable and uncontrollability as the column variable. Such a setup is called a **2 × 2 factorial design**. In this notation each of the factors has two levels. In this book we will only consider **fully factorial designs**, where all levels of each factor occur within each level of the other factor.

In the above example the main effects model seems to hold. Uncontrollable noises are more distressing than controllable ones and loud noises are more distressing than quiet ones. We can compute the deviations from the grand mean (in this case 5.0) for each level of the two factors in exactly the same way that we did for the biscuits:

$$\text{Controllable} = \text{grand mean} - 0.5$$

$$\text{Uncontrollable} = \text{grand mean} + 0.5$$

$$\text{Soft} = \text{grand mean} - 0.5$$

$$\text{Loud} = \text{grand mean} + 0.5$$

The key question here is whether these differences from the grand mean are sufficiently large to be surprising. The ANOVA table (Figure 10.11) helps us answer this question.

Tests of Between-Subjects Effects

Dependent Variable: Distress

Source	Type III Sum of Squares	df	Mean Square	F	Sig.	Partial Eta Squared
Corrected Model	24.000[a]	3	8.000	4.400	.009	.231
Intercept	1200.000	1	1200.000	660.000	.000	.938
Intensity	12.000	1	12.000	6.600	.014	.130
Uncontrollability	12.000	1	12.000	6.600	.014	.130
Intensity * Uncontrollability	.000	1	.000	.000	1.000	.000
Error	80.000	44	1.818			
Total	1304.000	48				
Corrected Total	104.000	47				

a. R Squared = .231 (Adjusted R Squared = .178)

Figure 10.11

The table shows that the main effects for intensity and uncontrollability are both associated with F values of 6.600. This value (with 1 and 44 degrees of freedom) is associated with a p-value of .014. In other words, there is quite a small chance that we would obtain differences as large as these by randomly selecting people from a population with that level of variability.

The table also presents **partial eta-squared** for the effects – represented in statistical notation as η^2_p. This is a measure of effect size that is appropriate when there is more than one effect (it 'partials' out the other effects). It is calculated by taking the sum of squares for the effect and dividing by the total of that sum of squares and the sum of squares for the error term. A partial eta-squared of .13 – indicating that the effects for intensity and uncontrollability both account for 13% of the variance in the data – would be considered a moderately large effect in most contexts.

When the main effects model does not hold we have a statistical interaction. It is best to explain interaction in two ways: graphically and numerically. Obviously to get a graphical understanding of interaction we need to draw what the interaction looks like. We do this by plotting the interaction on a graph. The conventions for doing this in psychology rely on column graphs of the form that we introduced in Chapter 6. Unfortunately this convention is particularly unhelpful for explaining interaction. A better option is provided by the line graph, and this involves drawing one line for each level of one of the two factors we are interested in. We have done this in Figure 10.12 for a different set of means that do in fact suggest an interaction. We can see from the graph that very loud noises were associated with a higher level of distress, but only when they were uncontrollable. Thus, if we were to ask 'What is the effect of noise intensity on distress?' the answer would be 'it depends on whether the noise is controllable or not'.

Let us now consider one of a number of other possible patterns of results. Imagine that we found that the soft noise was more distressing when it was controllable (perhaps participants were distressed by the fact that they found the noises difficult to detect). In this case the data might look like Table 10.8.

When we plot these data in a line graph (see Figure 10.14) we can see that we still have an interaction, but the form of the interaction is what we call a **crossover interaction.** Whereas

Figure 10.12 Line graph showing interaction

Table 10.8

Noise intensity	Controllability		
	Controllable	Uncontrollable	(Row means)
Soft	8.0	5.0	6.5
Loud	6.0	8.0	7.0
(Column means)	7.0	6.5	(Grand mean) 6.75

in the previous case being uncontrollable made loud noises more distressing but had no effect on soft noises, we now see that being controllable makes soft noises more distressing.

The ANOVA table for the above data is shown in Figure 10.13. These data are also provided in the Supplementary Online Material [Chapter10_TwowayinteractionANOVA.sav]. We can see

Tests of Between-Subjects Effects

Dependent Variable: Distress

Source	Type III Sum of Squares	df	Mean Square	F	Sig.	Partial Eta Squared
Corrected Model	81.000[a]	3	27.000	14.850	.000	.503
Intercept	2187.000	1	2187.000	1202.850	.000	.965
Intensity	3.000	1	3.000	1.650	.206	.036
Uncontrollability	3.000	1	3.000	1.650	.206	.036
Intensity * Uncontrollability	75.000	1	75.000	41.250	.000	.484
Error	80.000	44	1.818			
Total	2348.000	48				
Corrected Total	161.000	47				

a. R Squared = .503 (Adjusted R Squared = .469)

Figure 10.13

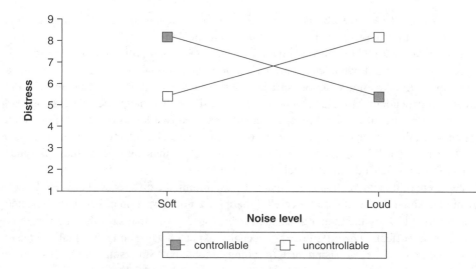

Figure 10.14   Line graph showing crossover interaction

Photos 10.2 and 10.3 Which of these two cars is the most useful? A sensible answer would obviously be 'Well that depends on what you want to use them for'. Any answer to a question that is conditional in this way (as indicated by the word 'depends') suggests that two or more factors interact to determine a relevant outcome (in this case the type of car and the intended use) rather than just one. A particular advantage of analysis of variance is that it provides a powerful way to examine – and establish the significance of – interactions of this form.

here that the interaction term (Intensity * Uncontrollability) is associated with an F-value (with 1 and 44 degrees of freedom) of 41.25. This is associated with a p-value that is smaller than .001. It is also associated with a very large effect size with partial eta-squared equal to .484.

  There are actually four logically distinct forms of interaction for a two-way factorial design like this one. All of them can be detected graphically as they involve different combinations of the main effects for the independent variables. In simple terms, though, an interaction exists whenever one of the lines we have drawn is not parallel to another line (as in

Figures 10.12 and 10.14). In each case we decide whether it is plausible that the interaction is sufficiently large to take seriously by conducting a statistical test.

How do we make that decision? Given that we know what an interaction would look like if we were to graph it, what sort of numerical or computational evidence would we need to be convinced to take an interaction seriously? The rough and ready answer is that for the case of two independent variables (such as the 2×2 design we have been discussing), an interaction exists when there is a bigger difference between two levels of one variable than there is between the corresponding two levels of another. This is the same as saying the lines representing the two different conditions are not parallel or that the size of the difference between two means depends on the level of the other factor.

The extent of this interaction is calculated by examining the differences between the cell means and the value that would be expected if there were no interaction effect. This expected value is the one given by the main effects model discussed above that says that the variables have independent effects. The difference between this expected value and the actual cell mean gives us our interaction effect. Using the terminology adopted by Smithson (2000), this can be thought of as the product of the row and column effect so that the relation

$$X = \mu_{ij} + e$$

still holds, but now

$$\mu_{ij} = \mu + \alpha_i + \beta_j + \alpha_i \beta_j$$

where $\alpha_i \beta_j$ is given by the deviation between the actual cell mean and the expected value for the cell mean based on the main effects model, that is

$$\alpha_i \beta j = \mu_{ij} - (\mu + \alpha_i + \beta_j)$$

We can write this again as

$$\alpha_i \beta j = \mu_{adj} - \mu$$

where

$$\mu_{adj} = \mu_{ij} - \alpha_i - j$$

The interaction term involves variance in the adjusted cell means. If the cell means adjusted for the row and column effects are highly variable (when compared with the variation within cells), then we have evidence of interaction. Thus, if the cell means adjusted for the row and column effects are pretty similar to the grand mean then we have little evidence of interaction. Another way of saying this is that where the cell means are quite different from the values we would expect given the rows and columns they belong to, then we have evidence of interaction. To return to our earlier biscuit example, given the main effects that people eat more chocolate than plain biscuits *and* eat more biscuits when they are hungry, to find then that the cell mean is somewhat higher than the grand mean when a hungry person is allowed to gorge themselves on chocolate biscuits is not surprising, and it is not evidence of interaction. We would expect it to be higher (due to the presence of these two main effects). However, if we find that the cell mean is substantially higher or lower than the grand mean that we would expect after adjusting for (i.e., adding) the row and column effects, then that *is* evidence of interaction.

Test Yourself 10.5***

An experimental psychologist conducts a study examining whether the speed with which two shapes can be identified as similar or different depends on whether the stimuli are (a) of equal or unequal size and (b) symmetrical or asymmetrical. The mean reaction times for the four cells of the design are as follows: equal symmetrical ($M = 132$ ms), unequal symmetrical ($M = 148$ ms), unequal asymmetrical ($M = 142$ ms), unequal asymmetrical ($M = 182$ ms). Which of the following is true?

a. A line graph in which these data are plotted suggests that there might only be a main effect for size.
b. A line graph in which these data are plotted suggests that there might only be a main effect for symmetry.
c. A line graph in which these data are plotted suggests that there might only be a main effect for size and an interaction between size and symmetry.
d. A line graph in which these data are plotted suggests that there might only be a main effect for symmetry and an interaction between size and symmetry.
e. A line graph in which these data are plotted suggests that there might be main effects for size and symmetry and an interaction between size and symmetry.

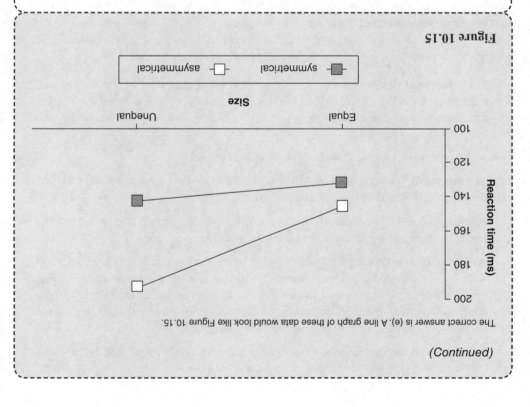

Figure 10.15

The correct answer is (e). A line graph of these data would look like Figure 10.15.

(Continued)

(Continued)

From this we can see that there is the suggestion of a main effect for size (such that equal-sized objects are judged faster than unequal-sized objects), a main effect for symmetry (such that symmetrical shapes are judged faster than asymmetrical shapes), and an interaction between size and symmetry (that means that the combined impact of these variables is not simply the sum of the two main effects). The interaction is suggested by the fact that the lines are not parallel. Answers (a), (b), (c) and (d) are wrong because they each overlook one or two of these three effects. Of course, we would be more confident in answering the question of whether there was an interaction after performing an analysis of variance.

In this case, then, the statistical inference we would therefore make is that it is implausible that the observed pattern of findings would be obtained by taking random samples from the same population. We can conclude (a) that the effect of noise intensity on distress probably does depend on whether it is uncontrollable or not, and (b) that the effect of uncontrollability of noises on distress depends on how loud the noise is.

Designs and interactions can involve many more cells as additional factors are added. Providing researchers design their experiments carefully, ANOVA can deal with these complexities (including repeated observations of the same participants). However, such considerations are well beyond the scope of this book. What is more important for present purposes is that you have some grasp of the underlying logic of ANOVA techniques, and have a sense of how SPSS manages this. If you have, you will be very well equipped to handle the issues that emerge from more complex experimental designs when the need arises.

2 × 2 factorial design A study with a *fully factorial design* in which each of two independent variables (factors) has two levels. An example would be an experiment that includes the factors' age (with two levels: young and old) and sex (with two levels: male and female).

additive model Another term for a *main effects model*.

column mean When mean scores from a two-factor study are represented in a table, the mean of all the mean scores in a particular column.

column variable When data from a two-factor study are represented in a table, the variable whose different levels are presented in different columns.

crossover interaction A pattern of two-way interaction in which, when a line graph is drawn, the lines connecting the means for different levels of the same factor cross over each other. This pattern indicates that at one level of one of the factors (A) the mean is higher for one level of the other factor (*X* will be greater than *Y*), but that at another level (B) this pattern is reversed (*Y* will be greater than *X*).

fully factorial designs Experimental designs in which all levels of each factor occur within each level of the other factor. If an experiment involves the factors' age (with two levels: young and old) and sex (with two levels: male and female), the old group will contain males and females, the young group will contain males and females, the male group will contain young and old, and the female group will contain young and old.

interaction sum of squares In a two-factor design, that part of the total sum of squares that is due to the interaction of column and row variables. In such a design this is the between-cell variance that is left over after accounting for column and row variance.

main effects Effects that reflect the impact of one independent variable averaged across all levels of other independent variables, rather than the impact of an interaction between two or more independent variables.

main effects model A hypothetical data model in which the combined effect of two or more independent variables results from their being added together.

partial eta-squared. This is a measure of effect size that indicates what proportion of the variance in a given data set is accounted for by a given effect. This is an appropriate measure to use when there is more than one effect (it 'partials' out the other effects) and it is calculated by taking the sum of squares for the effect and dividing by the total of that sum of squares and the sum of squares for the error term.

row mean When mean scores from a two-factor study are represented in a table, the mean of all the mean scores in a particular row.

row variable When mean scores from a two-factor study are represented in a table, the variable whose different levels are presented in different rows.

A final word

In this chapter we have only covered the basic procedures for conducting ANOVA. There is much, much more that can be done even with designs as simple as the ones we have discussed here, and designs that ANOVA can be applied to are often much more complex than these.

Indeed, even though ANOVA can become mind-numbingly complex, it is worth alerting you to the main ways in which this complexity presents itself. First, two-way designs can involve many more than four cells, and there can be more than two factors in a given design. Second, ANOVA can include within-subjects measures as well as between-subjects manipulations (noting that in this chapter we have only dealt with the analysis of between-subjects designs). Third, ANOVA can involve more than one dependent variable (this is called multivariate ANOVA or MANOVA). Fourth, the procedures for making planned and post hoc comparisons are enormously diverse. Fifth, there are many ways to partition sums of squares depending on the features of the design and the cell sizes (especially where these are unequal). Sixth, there are different procedures that need to be applied when the levels of the factors are not determined experimentally (i.e., where there is not random assignment to conditions).

In practice, it is likely that as you progress in your studies you will be introduced to these various complexities by learning to work more closely with programs such as SPSS.

Indeed, SPSS is a very good tool for this purpose and, as we have seen here, it is actually quite easy to use. However, this fact means that if you do not really know what you are trying to do, statistical packages can also be quite dangerous. For this reason, one very significant advantage of having introduced you to SPSS alongside a detailed account of the logic of ANOVA is that you are now far better placed to use such tools wisely and well.

Yet even without these complexities there are some points to be wary of. ANOVA is subject to the same assumptions as the *t*-test: homogeneity of variance, normality and independence. With equal cell sizes, ANOVA is quite robust to violations of the assumption of equal variances. It is also robust to violations of normality but the picture is more complex, because although ANOVA may still work well in comparing means, the decision to compare the means is dubious if the mean is a dubious measure of central tendency (due to extreme skewness). The assumption of independence is particularly important. Where these assumptions do not hold we face new choices, and we will consider some of these in Chapter 11.

CHECKLIST
Revisiting the key goals for this chapter

☐ I understand how to conduct analysis of variance (ANOVA) – a statistical procedure that allows me to establish how likely it is that observed differences between two or more means would have arisen by chance.

☐ I know how different types of analysis of variance are used to examine data that are structured in different ways.

☐ I understand the process of interpreting the results of analysis of variance.

Further reading

If you plan to do a lot of research using analysis of variance you would be well advised to read an advanced statistics text that deals with this and related techniques in much more depth than the present chapter. Of these, Maxwell and Delaney's (1990) volume is one of the most comprehensive. We also recommend Keppel and Wickens (2003). However, if you want an intermediate step up in complexity, we recommend Smithson's (2000) text that provides discussions of confidence intervals and other features not dealt with in this book.

Keppel, G., & Wickens, T. (2003). *Design and analysis: A researcher's handbook* (4th ed.). Upper Saddle River, NJ: Pearson Prentice Hall.

Maxwell, S. E., & Delaney, H. D. (1990). *Designing experiments and analyzing data: A model comparison perspective.* New York: Harper Collins.

Smithson, M. J. (2000). *Statistics with confidence.* London: SAGE.

ANOVA: A checklist for research evaluation and improvement

Table 10.9

Potential problem	Question to ask	Potential improvement
Inferential uncertainty about means from more than two different samples	Do the researchers want to compare means associated with data that relate to one independent variable and have been obtained from more than two independent samples?	Conduct one-way analysis of variance following the steps laid out in this chapter in order to provide information about the probability (p) of obtaining by chance differences between means as large as the ones obtained. Conduct any planned comparisons to identify the source of the difference.
	Do the researchers want to compare means associated with data that relate to two independent variables where data relating to each variable have been obtained from two or more independent samples?	Conduct two-way analysis of variance following the steps laid out in this chapter in order to provide information about the probability (p) of obtaining by chance main effects and interactions as large as the ones obtained. Conduct planned comparisons to identify the source of the difference.
Significance fallacy	If the researchers are using a hypothesis-testing approach to ANOVA, have they distinguished appropriately between psychological and statistical significance?	Consider significance levels in conjunction with effect sizes (e.g. compare p and R^2). Be alert to the dangers of making too much of statistically significant F-values when effect sizes are low.
Violation of the assumption of independence	Do the means that are being compared relate to independent sets of observations?	If sample scores are not independent it can be misleading to compare them using ANOVA (or any other statistical test) if, in effect, the same piece of data is being counted more than once. Accordingly, if possible, any source of non-independence (e.g., the fact that the same participant responded twice) should be removed before collecting data. If this is not possible, the nature of the violation should be noted and results treated with caution.
Violation of the assumption of normality	Do the means that are being compared relate to observations that are normally distributed?	If the distribution of sample scores is non-normal (e.g., severely skewed or U-shaped) and the cell sizes are unequal, or there are reasons to believe that the mean is a misleading indicator of central tendency, you should seriously consider using a non-parametric test (Chapter 11) or correct the distribution by transformation (see Chapter 6).
Violation of the assumption of equal variance	Do the means that are being compared relate to samples that have equal variance?	If sample variances are unequal (e.g., one is more than four times bigger than the other) you should seriously consider using a non-parametric test (see Chapter 11). This is only worth doing if the size of one sample is much larger than the other
Outliers	Is the distribution of scores (especially its shape and variance) dramatically affected by the presence of outliers?	Examine the distribution of scores to see if it contains outliers. If it does, see if this can be corrected by an appropriate statistical transformation of the sample data. If this is not possible, consider (a) removing individual outliers or (b) recoding them to the same value as the nearest non-outlier. Ensure you report any transformations that you make.

Test Yourself 10.6*

Which of the following statements is *false?*

a. One difference between ANOVA and *t*-tests is that ANOVA allows researchers to compare responses of more than two groups.
b. One difference between ANOVA and *t*-tests is that ANOVA does not make assumptions about homogeneity, normality and independence.
c. One difference between ANOVA and *t*-tests is that ANOVA can be used to examine simultaneously the impact of more than one variable.
d. One difference between ANOVA and *t*-tests is that ANOVA is based on analysis of the ratios of variances.
e. One difference between ANOVA and *t*-tests is that ANOVA uses two separate degrees of freedom (one for between-cells variance, one for within-cells variance).

Test Yourself 10.7**

A researcher conducts a study examining the impact of social support on depression in which he studies how four independent groups that each receive a different type of social support (financial, emotional, intellectual, none) react to a stressful experience. There are 20 people in each group. Which of the following statements is true?

a. There are 4 degrees of freedom for the between-cells variance.
b. There are 78 degrees of freedom for the within-cells variance.
c. If ANOVA yielded a between-groups *F*-value of −2.18 this would be significant with alpha set at .05.
d. If ANOVA yielded a between-groups *F*-value of 0.98 this would be significant with alpha set at .01.
e. None of the above statements is true.

Test Yourself 10.8***

Which of the following statements about the *F*-distribution is *false?*

a. The distribution is asymmetrical.
b. The distribution is one-tailed.
c. Higher values of *F* are associated with a higher probability value.

d. The distribution is positively skewed.

e. If the amount of between-cells variance is equal to the amount of within-subjects variance, the value of F will be 1.00.

The correct answer to 10.6 is (b). As noted at the end of the chapter, ANOVA requires exactly the same assumptions to be satisfied as a t-test: equal variances, the normal distributions, and independent observations. Answer (a) is wrong because the main feature of ANOVA is that it allows researchers simultaneously to examine data from more than two groups (something that cannot be done with a t-test); (c) is wrong because, unlike t-tests, ANOVA can be multi-factorial; (d) is wrong because ANOVA relies upon the F-distribution; and (e) is wrong because it involves a comparison of between-cells (treatment) variance and within-cells (error) variance, and each of these is associated with a different number of degrees of freedom ($N - k$ and $k - 1$, respectively).

The correct answer to 10.7 is (e). All of these statements are untrue: (a) is untrue because there are 3 degrees of freedom for the between-groups variance (i.e., $k - 1$); (b) is untrue because there are 76 degrees of freedom for the within-groups variance (i.e., $N - k$); (c) is untrue because F-values can never be less than 0; and (d) is untrue because an F-value of less than 1.0 can never be significant (it means that the between-groups variance is less than the within-groups variance).

The correct answer to 10.8 is (c). A higher value of F is associated with a lower probability value, so that the larger the ratio of between-subjects variance to within-subjects variance becomes, the less plausible it is that the ratio is the result of a random process. Answer (d) is wrong because it is in fact positively skewed – and if it is skewed it cannot be symmetrical, so answer (a) is wrong too. Answer (b) is wrong because, unlike the t-distribution, the F-distribution is not two-tailed (i.e., there is only one rejection region). Answer (e) is wrong because an F-ratio is the ratio of between-cells variance (the numerator) divided by within-cells variance (the denominator) and when these two are equal this ratio equals 1.

Discussion/essay questions

a. Why are procedures for examining statistical interactions so important in psychological research?

b. What are the advantages of performing ANOVA by hand rather than using a computer package?

c. Some people argue that the prevalence of ANOVA techniques as a basis both for designing research and for analysing data has led researchers to construct artificial models of human behaviour because phenomena tend to be simplistically understood in terms of main effects and interactions. Do you agree?

d. What problems of data analysis are encountered in studies in which two or more independent variables have two or more levels?

Research Methods and Statistics in Psychology

Exercises

a. A team of developmental psychologists measures the moral reasoning of children giving each a score from 0 to 100 (where 100 indicates a higher state of reasoning). The moral reasoning of 10 children in four age groups is assessed in this way and the scores are as given as follows:

Table 10.10

Age	10–11:	32	43	54	31	29	27	33	43	49	35
Age	12–13:	35	44	56	65	71	62	61	48	39	47
Age	14–15:	54	57	62	70	49	61	55	55	60	64
Age	16–17:	56	65	75	66	77	81	87	75	63	68

The researchers hypothesize that older children will have higher levels of moral reasoning, but before they can conduct specific tests of this hypothesis they want to conduct analysis of variance to see whether there is any evidence of an overall effect such that moral reasoning differs across age groups.

    i.   What would an ANOVA table for this analysis look like?

    ii. Would ANOVA provide the researchers with the evidence they require? (Base your answer on levels of p and η^2.)

b. Imagine that instead of being from four groups of different ages, the above data had been gathered from 10–11-year-olds and 12–13-year-olds from two different areas: one with a high crime rate (HCR) and one with a low crime rate (LCR) as follows:

Table 10.11

HCR	Age 10–11:	32	43	54	31	29	27	33	43	49	35
	Age 12–13:	65	64	56	75	71	68	63	68	69	77
LCR	Age 10–11:	54	57	62	70	49	61	55	55	60	64
	Age 12–13:	56	65	75	66	77	81	87	75	63	68

The researchers again hypothesize that older children will have higher levels of moral reasoning, but they also expect that there might be differences in the moral reasoning of children who live in areas with different crime rates, and that these might interact with children's age.

    i.   What would an ANOVA table for this analysis look like?

    ii. Would ANOVA provide the researchers with any evidence to support their hypotheses? (Base your answer on levels of p and η^2.)

Analysing Other Forms of Data: Chi-square and Distribution-free Tests

Key goals for this chapter

- Introduce the chi-square test – a statistical test that is used to analyse categorical data.
- Introduce a range of other statistical tests that can be used to analyse data without making assumptions about the distribution of data in the population from which they are drawn.
- Understand when and how to use these various tests.

So far in this book we have dealt with several methods for analysing quantitative data: these include within- and between-subjects *t*-tests, correlation and ANOVA. It should be obvious by now that different techniques are used in different circumstances (and this should be apparent even if you are not completely confident about what those circumstances are). To take an example, we know from Chapter 10 that you should use ANOVA (and not several *t*-tests) when you wish to compare three or more means.

The different circumstances that lead us to use different tests can be broken down in terms of three dimensions. The choice of technique depends upon (a) the form of data, (b) the question we are trying to answer and (c) the assumptions we are willing to make about the data we are dealing with.

By the *form of the data* we are simply referring to the number of levels of each variable. We are assuming that there are always one or two variables (i.e., that the data are univariate or bivariate) because **multivariate statistics** are beyond the scope of this book. For example, in previous chapters we have dealt with situations where we have either two variables with many levels (continuous variables as in the case of correlations and within-subjects *t*-tests), or one variable with a small number of levels (a categorical variable) and another with many levels (as in the case of between-subjects *t*-tests and ANOVAs). However, there is one other important form of data, and that is where both variables are *categorical.*

In the case of within-subjects *t*-tests (Chapter 8) and the Pearson product-moment correlation (Chapter 9) the form of the data is identical: we need two continuous variables. Nonetheless, *the question we are trying to answer* with the two statistics is very different. We use a correlation when we want to know whether the two variables are related, and a within-subjects *t*-test when we want to compare the means of the two variables.

However, there are many other questions that could be asked, and sometimes questions such as 'are the means of the two variables different?' do not make much sense. This is often because the form of the data does not lend itself to answering that kind of question. For example, it makes sense to calculate the mean age of the students in a class, but it does not make much sense to calculate the mean sex. Sometimes, too, we are not able to make the necessary assumptions about the data that would allow us to perform the test in which we are interested. For example, as we discussed in Chapter 6, it is not appropriate to compare means if the skewed distribution of our data makes the mean a misleading statistic.

To start our discussion, let us imagine, for example, that we wanted to know whether adolescent males or females were more likely to have eating disorders. Imagine that we had data from samples of 20 males and 20 females who were receiving therapy and that the data told us whether these clients had been diagnosed with an eating disorder by the clinical psychologist they were seeing. Some hypothetical data are shown in Table 11.1.

Table 11.1

	Male	Female
Do not have eating disorder	15	12
Have eating disorder	5	8

With these data we cannot ask whether the means are different. There are no scores from which to calculate means because both variables are categorical. Nevertheless, we could still ask whether the *proportion* of people with eating disorders is the same among the males and females. In this case 25% of the males have eating disorders, compared with 40% of the females. Clearly, a greater proportion of females have eating disorders. But we are faced with a familiar problem: Just how should we make sense of this difference? In this case we would like to know whether sex is related to the frequency of eating disorders. In particular, it would be helpful if there were a statistical test that could tell us how plausible it would be that proportions of eating disorder as different as this would be found if these samples of males and females were drawn from the same population (i.e., if there were no real differences between males and females in the level of eating disorders). As it happens, there is such a test – the χ^2 (chi-square) test of independence – and we will discuss this in some detail in this chapter.

Now imagine that instead of just a diagnosis of eating disorders we had a measure of the level of eating disorders for each participant. Let us assume that eating disorders were measured on an 11-point scale (from 0 to 10) but that the majority of participants scored 0 (indicating that they had no eating disorder at all). Reminding ourselves of the assumptions that should be satisfied before *t*-tests are performed (see pp. 231–235), under these circumstances it might not be safe to conclude that the scores for the two groups were drawn from a normally distributed population or that the variances of the two populations from which they were drawn were equal. If that were the case it might not be wise to use a between-subjects *t*-test because it would be questionable whether the assumptions of that procedure hold.

The question we would be left with here is whether or not there is a procedure that allows us to compare the scores of two groups when we are unable (or at least reluctant) to presume that these assumptions hold. As you might imagine from the fact that we are asking the question, there is such a test. Indeed, there are a number of them, and one example – the Mann–Whitney test – is discussed in this chapter.

To see the scope of the alternative situations that we need to be able to deal with, it is helpful to start by summarizing the relevant features of the procedures that we have already covered in previous chapters. This is the purpose of Table 11.2.

Table 11.2   Statistical tests and when to use them

Form of data	Question of interest	Assumptions about data*	Test used
One variable with many levels	Does the mean differ from some value (e.g., zero)?	(i) Population variances are unknown; (ii) observations are independent; (iii) the sample is drawn from a normally distributed population.	One-sample *t*-test
One variable with two categories; one variable with many levels	Are the means of the two categories different?	(i) Population variances are unknown; (ii) observations are independent; (iii) the two categories are drawn from populations with the same variance; (iv) the categories are drawn from normally distributed populations.	Between-subjects *t*-test
One variable with more than two categories; one variable with many levels	Are the means of the categories different?	(i) Population variances are unknown; (ii) observations are independent; (iii) the categories are drawn from populations with the same variance; (iv) the categories are drawn from normally distributed populations.	ANOVA
Two variables with many levels	Are the means of the two variables different?	(i) Population variances are unknown; (ii) observations are independent; (iii) variables are correlated; (iv) variables are drawn from normally distributed populations.	Within-subjects *t*-test
Two variables with many levels	Are scores on the two variables related?	There is a linear and bivariate normal relationship between the variables.	Pearson product-moment correlation coefficient

* We assume in each case that each observation of a different person is independent.

In this chapter we will deal with a range of other cases that are not covered in Table 11.2. Before we do, it is worth noting at the outset that these cases do not occur as commonly in the psychological literature as the other techniques that we have discussed in earlier chapters. This is one reason why they are located together in this chapter rather than each given separate chapters of their own.

At the same time, though, the fact that these alternative ways of analysing data are bundled together does not mean that they are inherently less relevant or important for psychological research. Instead, the fact that they are used relatively infrequently simply reflects features of the standard research training that psychologists receive and that orients them towards particular research designs and particular data management strategies.

Accordingly, when we outline these various alternative techniques, we think you will agree that it is important to be equipped to deal with the situations they relate to. When you conduct your own research in the future, we would also strongly encourage you to explore the limitations and possibilities of your data, to see whether or not the tests described below could be of any use to you. As with the jokers in a pack of cards, it may be the case that you use them only on special occasions, but when you do, they will be very useful indeed.

multivariate statistics Statistical procedures that simultaneously examine relationships between two or more variables. Bivariate statistics – that examine the relationships between two variables – constitute a particular class of these.

RESEARCH BITE 11.1
Myths about non-parametric tests

In an article in *Canadian Psychology*, Michael Hunter and Richard May (1993) note that, unlike psychologists, statisticians favour the use of non-parametric methods when analysing behavioural data. They argue that psychologists are reluctant to use non-parametric tests because they have been misled by five interrelated myths (or half-truths). These are that, compared with parametric tests, such tests are (a) less powerful, (b) less robust, (c) primarily to be used for non-interval data, (d) less direct and less clear as methods for testing null hypotheses, and (e) more restricted in their application. The authors argue that in fact the opposite is often true and that the perceived superiority of parametric methods is illusory rather than real.

Reference
Hunter, M. A., & May, R. B. (1993). Some myths concerning parametric and nonparametric tests. *Canadian Psychology*, *34*, 384–389.

Dealing with a single categorical variable that has two levels: The binomial test

The first case we will examine is one in which we have a single categorical variable with two levels (e.g., 'yes' or 'no'; 'present' or 'absent'; 'right' or 'wrong') and we want to get some insight into the different responses we have obtained. The only question that statistics can really help us with here is whether or not there are differences between the frequencies of the two responses that are large enough to be interesting.

In Chapter 7 we discussed the dilemma of being in a casino and trying to decide whether some game of chance was fair. That is, if we were playing such a game we would want to be confident that we are as likely to win as often as we should (which admittedly is probably less than we would like) given the rules of the game. We discussed briefly the way in which the binomial distribution could be used to help us decide how plausible it was that the game was fair. As we have been at pains to point out, statistics cannot tell us whether the game really is fair, they can simply give us a guide as to how confident we should be that it is not fair. In this section we give the barest taste of the possibilities involved in using the binomial test. The more advanced book in this series by Smithson (2000) provides a much more detailed treatment.

The binomial test involves calculating the expected outcomes or probabilities of two alternatives (such as winning and losing) and comparing these with the observed outcome. This is easy (but uninteresting) to do for a single trial or event. If the casino tosses a coin and it comes up heads then there is not much we (or anybody else) can say about it. The event (heads) had a probability of .5 and was just as likely as the other possible event (tails).

Things become more interesting if we observe the same process over many trials. If the casino kept tossing heads then it would be useful to know the chance of that run of events occurring. This is what the binomial distribution makes it easy for us to do. Among other things, it tells us that the probability of obtaining heads four times in a row with a fair coin is 1 in 16. That is, every 16 times you do the experiment of tossing a coin four times you can expect to get all four heads on one of those occasions (remembering everything we said earlier about the gambler's fallacy).

Let us call the outcome of getting four heads x, and the probability of this outcome $P(x)$. The value of this or any outcome based on the combination of multiple events, each with just two possibilities with known constant probabilities, is given by the formula for the binomial distribution:

$$P(x) = \frac{N!}{x!(N-x)!} p^x q^{N-x}$$

where a term such as 3! (pronounced '3 factorial') is equal to 3 multiplied by 2 multiplied by 1 (i.e., 6) and $N!$ is N multiplied by $N-1$ multiplied by $N-2$, and so on, down to 1 (with the special case that 0! is equal to 1), and p is the probability of one alternative and q is the probability of the other alternative (as these are the only two alternatives their probabilities must sum to 1).

In this case

$$P(x = 4\,\text{heads}) = \frac{4!}{4!(4-4)!}\,0.5^4 0.5^{4-4}$$

$$= 0.5^4$$

$$= .625 \text{ (which is 1 in 16)}$$

We can use this procedure for any set of circumstances where we want to compare an observed proportion with what we would have expected. Let us imagine that a school had a population with an equal number of boys and girls and the school offered an after-school special activity programme that attracted four boys and two girls. If we assume that boys and girls are equally likely to attend the programme, is this an unlikely outcome? Put another way, what is the likelihood that, if six people attend, four or more of them will be boys (assuming that boys and girls are equally likely to attend)? If this probability is very low, the school might conclude that it needs to investigate the reasons for girls' low interest in the programme (or the high interest of boys).

To calculate the probability, we simply calculate $P(x)$ for each of the cases we are interested in (four boys, five boys and six boys) and add these together. To do this we need a calculator and the formula for the binomial expansion. Here $p(\text{boy}) = .5$ and $p(\text{girl}) = .5$. Using the formula above, we find $P(4)$ to be .2344. We can easily calculate $P(5)$ and $P(6)$ as well, and sum them to find $P(\geq 4)$ to be .3438. That is, it is not very unlikely that the group would be made up of four or more boys. Certainly, the probability is not so small that we would describe it as statistically significant at conventional levels (e.g., $\alpha = .05$).

Let us imagine instead, though, that the school population did not contain an equal number of boys and girls but a majority of girls (80%). Now $p(\text{girl})$ is .8 and $p(\text{boy})$ is .2. Under these conditions, the combined probability of an outcome such as four or more boys is .0170.

This suggests that it is far less plausible that boys and girls are equally likely to attend. Accordingly, the reasons for boys' and girls' attendance patterns may be worth exploring.

The binomial test becomes tricky to calculate when there are multiple outcomes (we have to sum a large number of very small probabilities). Fortunately, however, there is a normal approximation that works very well when $n > 25$ and p (the probability of one alternative) and q (the probability of the other) are not very dissimilar in size (e.g., where both p and q are greater than .1). This is given by the equation

$$z = \frac{x - N_p}{\sqrt{Npq}}$$

This gives us the z-score corresponding to the probability that at least x cases are drawn from one category. Assume that the after-school programme attracts 30 students from a population with equal numbers of boys and girls, and that 19 are boys and 11 are girls. How plausible is an outcome like this if the programme is equally attractive to boys and girls? Using the formula

$$z = \frac{19-(30\times.5)}{\sqrt{30 \times .5 \times .5}}$$

$$= \frac{4}{\sqrt{7.5}}$$

$$= 1.46$$

we can see from Table B.1 in Appendix B that this z-score corresponds to a one-tailed probability of .072. However, if the same pattern had occurred in a school with 80% girls, the z-score would have been 5.93 (as an exercise, you may want to check this yourself). This z-score corresponds to a p-value much smaller than .001.

This normal approximation works less well when $n < 25$ or where the probability of one or the other alternative is close to 0 (e.g., less than .1). Nevertheless it gives us a powerful tool for making quick assessments about the likelihood of different events. If you invite an equal number of your friends and your partner's friends to a party and you find that more of their friends turn up than yours then you could calculate whether the assumption that both sets of friends are equally likely to turn up is plausible or implausible. More seriously, if a psychotherapist discovers that more cases treated by one common therapy have recurring problems than do cases treated by another, rarer therapy, the psychotherapist could assess the hypothesis that the two therapies are equally likely to produce the same rate of recurring problems.

In order to use these procedures sensibly, though, we need to bear one additional factor in mind – the **base rate** of the phenomena in question (i.e., those that constitute the independent variable). That is, we need to be aware of situations in which it is inappropriate to assume that two alternatives (p and q) are equally likely. We remember a (hard-drinking) comedian who used to observe that half of all road accidents were not caused by drunk drivers. His joke, of course, was 'Who's doing anything about all those sober drivers then, and what's their excuse?'. The humour (such as it is) rests here on equating the expected frequencies of sober and drunk drivers. The vast majority of drivers at any one time do not have excessive amounts of alcohol in their blood, so in order to decide whether it is dangerous to drive while drunk we need to compare the number of accidents for sober and drunk drivers *bearing in mind* the proportions of drunk drivers. If, for example, drunk drivers represent only 5% of the population but are involved in 50% of the accidents then that is clearly important.

We see how important expected frequencies are in the next case we consider. This also involves dealing with more than two levels of a variable.

> **base rate** The incidence of a particular phenomenon among a population of interest. Information about base rates is required in order to establish the significance of the incidence of the phenomenon within a subset of that population (e.g., people who have been subjected to a particular treatment).

Test Yourself 11.1**

A team of researchers conducts a large study looking at factors that predict poor health in the workplace. They find that more men than women have heart attacks at work. They plan to analyse their data using a binomial test, but are aware of the need to take into account relevant base-rate information. Which of the following constitutes relevant base-rate information for this purpose?

a. The proportion of people in the workplace who are men.
b. The proportion of people in the workplace who have heart attacks.
c. The proportion of men in the workplace who have heart attacks.
d. The proportion of women in the workplace who have heart attacks.
e. None of the above, as base-rate information is irrelevant here.

The correct answer is (a). Unless the researchers take into account the proportion of employees who are men, they will not be able to establish whether their results simply reflect the fact that men are more likely to work than women. This base-rate information is very important, so (e) is wrong. The other three answers are all incorrect because base-rate information is relevant to the independent variable (in this case, sex), not the dependent variable (incidence of heart attacks).

Dealing with a single categorical variable that has more than two levels: The chi-square test of goodness of fit

Imagine that instead of having one categorical variable with two levels (e.g., participants' sex with levels male and female) we had a categorical variable with three levels such as Therapy A, Therapy B and Therapy C. Imagine, too, that we conducted research in which we recorded the number of patients who were given a particular therapy and independently assessed as having had a successful outcome. If we did this research, the sort of data we might obtain are as shown in Table 11.3.

Table 11.3

Therapy A	Therapy B	Therapy C	Total (N)
35	27	13	75

Let us assume that all therapies have been used equally often. If this is the case, and if the therapies were equally effective, we would expect that the incidence of a successful outcome would be the same for each. This idea of the expected outcome or expected frequency (see Chapter 6) is critically important. If the **observed frequencies** (f_o) are clearly different from the expected frequencies (f_e) then this would be important evidence that the therapies differ in their effectiveness.

In this case, because the therapies are equally common, the expected frequency is simply the total ($n = 75$) divided by the number of therapies (3), giving us 25. Table 11.4 shows these expected frequencies as well as the difference between the observed and expected frequencies.

Table 11.4

	Therapy A	Therapy B	Therapy C	Total (N)
Observed	35	27	13	75
Expected	25	25	25	
Observed – Expected	10	2	−12	

We can see from this table that Therapy A is associated with more successful outcomes than expected, that Therapy C is associated with fewer successful outcomes, and that Therapy B does not differ much from the expected frequency.

Beyond this observation, though, it would clearly be useful if we were able to assess these differences to find out whether the observed outcomes are plausible in relation to a model that assumed that the rate of success was the same for every therapy. In doing this we are assessing how well the model *fits* these data. To use some statistical jargon, we are testing the **goodness of fit** of the model.

The **chi-square distribution** is extremely useful for testing goodness of fit. In order to use it in this way, we first need to calculate the χ^2 (chi-square, pronounced 'ky square') statistic by applying the following formula:

$$\chi^2 = \frac{\Sigma(f_o - f_e)^2}{f_e}$$

What this formula is saying is that the value of χ^2 increases to the extent that the sum of the squares of the differences between observed and expected frequencies (divided by expected frequencies) is greater than zero. So, in our example

$$\chi^2 = [(35 - 25)^2 + (27 - 25)^2 + (13 - 25)^2]/25$$

$$= (10^2 + 2^2 + 12^2)/25$$

$$= (100 + 4 + 144)/25$$

$$= 248/25 = 9.92$$

It can be seen that Therapy B has made almost no contribution to this value of 9.92 as 4/25 = 0.16 is only 1.6% of the total. Indeed, if all therapies had had an observed value equal to

25 then the value of χ^2 would have been 0. On the other hand, if all the cases with successful outcomes had occurred with one therapy then the value we obtained would have reached its maximum possible value for this sample size of 150. As a result, our obtained value lies somewhere in the range of 0 to 150, and we need to find some way of specifying where this position is and what meaning it has.

As with the techniques discussed in previous chapters, in order to assess the meaning of a calculated statistic we can compare it with a value of a theoretical distribution. In this case, as noted above, the distribution of interest is the chi-square distribution.

As with the t- and F-distributions, this distribution varies with the number of degrees of freedom. However, in the case of the chi-square distribution, the degrees of freedom (df) depend on the number of categories rather than n (the number of participants). In general $df = k - 1$, where k is the number of categories. In this example $df = 3 - 1 = 2$.

We can obtain values for chi-square by using an online resource such as www.quantpsy. org/chisq/chisq.htm. In this case, this would involve simply entering the frequencies for the three therapies in the top row of Figure 11.1 and pressing 'Calculate'.

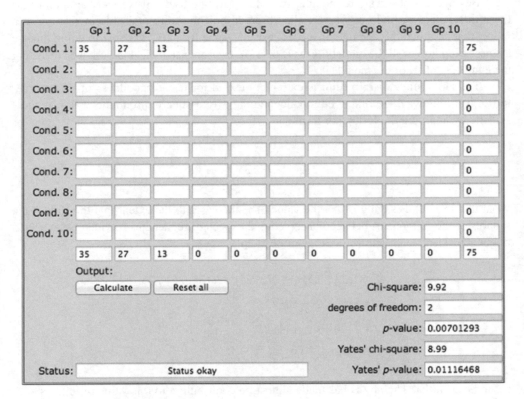

Figure 11.1 From Preacher (2001, April)

The output here shows us that the chi-square of 9.92 with 2 degrees of freedom is associated with a probability of .007. This tells us that if the three therapies are equally common and equally effective (so that the expected values were all 25) then it is quite unlikely that their success would follow the observed pattern. The logic of hypothesis testing would therefore lead us to conclude that the therapies have different success rates.

It is worth observing in passing that the maximum possible value of χ^2 was 150, but that our obtained value (9.92) was associated with a small probability even though it was relatively close to the minimum value of 0. This is a reflection of the fact that the chi-square distribution is not symmetrical but is skewed with a long positive tail (like the *F*-distribution).

It is also worth noting that the sorts of categorical outcome that make up the data set in this example are actually quite common in applied settings. Indeed, the example has a ring of truth about it in light of the fact that in clinical, health and organizational contexts a psychologist or other professional may not be able to obtain outcome measures that can be treated as continuous variables. Sometimes such data simply do not exist, and sometimes they do exist but cannot be obtained for ethical or practical reasons. Nonetheless, the example is an illustration of the point that very simple statistical techniques can be used to tackle quite substantial issues, and that they can be applied quickly and effectively in a variety of situations.

Test Yourself 11.2**

A researcher is interested in seeing whether families who go to a particular coastal town for their holiday are more likely to come from some towns than from others. In his research he looks at the visitors' books of three hotels and finds that together they have been visited by 1204 families over the past year. Of these, 261 are from Town A, 403 are from Town B, 312 are from Town C and 228 are from Town D. Which of these towns makes the greatest contribution to χ^2?

    a.   Town A.
    b.   Town B.
    c.   Town C.
    d.   Town D.
    e.   All make an equal contribution.

The correct answer is (b). To answer this question we need first to compute the expected frequency (f_e) for the number of visiting families. In this case this is $1204/4 = 301$. The town that makes the greatest contribution to χ^2 is then the town whose observed frequency (f_o) of visits is most different from this expected frequency. This difference between observed and expected frequency ($f_o - f_e$) is $261 - 301 = 40$ for Town A, $403 - 301 = 102$ for Town B, $312 - 301 = 9$ for Town C, and $228 - 301 = 73$ for Town D. The difference ($f_o - f_e$) is therefore greatest for Town B.

chi-square distribution (χ^2) The sampling distribution of the chi-square statistic (χ^2). The distribution varies as a function of the degrees of freedom, it can only have positive values and it is positively skewed. A larger value of the statistic indicates that a model based on expected frequencies has a worse goodness of fit, implying evidence against the null hypothesis.

goodness of fit An assessment of the correspondence between an observed pattern of data and a particular model of that data.

observed frequency The number of times that a particular outcome is observed. This is compared with the expected frequency in order to assess how well a particular model fits the data.

Examining the relationship between two categorical variables: The chi-square test of independence for 2 × 2 tables

The previous case dealt with a single categorical variable. Where we have two categorical variables then we can use very similar principles. In many ways this development is akin to moving from one-way to two-way ANOVA, but it is actually much simpler.

Let us look at the data on eating disorders again. Imagine we had 40 people, 20 of whom were male and 20 were female. We saw before that there was a different rate of eating disorders for males and females, but the question we would like to be able to answer is whether this is a remarkable event. A more formal way of asking this question is to imagine that males and females were equally likely to experience an eating disorder; that is, does the likelihood of an eating disorder *depend* on sex or is it *independent* of sex? Under such circumstances, how likely is it that a pattern as unusual as the one we have obtained would occur by chance? Recall that our data were as in Table 11.1, repeated here.

Table 11.1

	Male	Female
Do not have eating disorder	15	12
Have eating disorder	5	8

The format in which this data set is presented is called a **contingency table**. It shows the frequencies for a set of combinations of events or **contingencies**. This particular 2 × 2 table shows the frequencies of four contingencies: being male *and* having no eating disorder, being female *and* having no eating disorder, being male *and* having an eating disorder, and being female *and* having an eating disorder.

There are several ways in which we could try to make inferences about the data in this table. One thing we could do is compare the proportion of people with eating disorders for males and females using the binomial test (and its normal approximation). This procedure would be fine, but in this section we will consider another approach using the chi-square distribution. Our reasons for doing this are simply that the chi-square distribution can be applied to a much wider set of circumstances – including ones in which there are more than two levels of the variable in question.

To calculate a value of χ^2 we simply compare the expected frequencies with the observed frequencies as we did for one-way χ^2. The only slightly tricky feature of this task is the calculation of the expected frequencies. To do this we simply need to imagine for a moment what the table would look like if the *same* proportion of males and females had eating disorders. Put another way, we want to know how many people could be expected to have an eating disorder if sex was irrelevant (i.e., eating disorders are independent of sex).

You might think that the obvious way to do this would be to assume that the expected frequencies were all the same. However, we cannot do this because some contingencies are more common than others due to a higher base rate. To illustrate this, imagine that the contingency table looked like Table 11.5.

Table 11.5

	Male	Female
Do not have eating disorder	15	120
Have eating disorder	5	80

In this case there are obviously more women with eating disorders, but this is partly because there are more women in the sample. What we need to do therefore is calculate expected frequencies in a way that takes into account base-rate information concerning the overall preponderance of events in the categories that make up the table – in this case men versus women, and people who have eating disorders versus people who do not.

To calculate these expected frequencies we first need to compute the **marginal totals** for both the rows and columns. These are shown for the original data in Table 11.6.

Table 11.6

	Male	Female	(Row totals)
Do not have eating disorder	15	12	27
Have eating disorder	5	8	13
(Column totals)	20	20	$N = 40$

With these row and column totals we can compute the expected frequency (f_e) of each contingency. This is done for each contingency using the following formula:

$$f_e = (\text{row total} \times \text{column total})/N$$

For both males and females who do not have an eating disorder this expected frequency is as follows:

$$f_e = (27 \times 20)/40 = 13.5$$

And for both males and females who have an eating disorder:

$$f_e = (13 \times 20)/40 = 6.5$$

We can now elaborate on our initial contingency table by including the expected frequencies in brackets next to the four contingencies (Table 11.7).

Table 11.7

	Male	Female	(Row totals)
Do not have eating disorder	15 (13.5)	12 (13.5)	27
Have eating disorder	5 (6.5)	8 (6.5)	13
(Column totals)	20	20	$N = 40$

As we did with the previous case, we can then calculate the sum of squares of the differences between observed and expected frequencies for the four contingencies, dividing each one by the expected frequencies.

Again we can calculate this value readily using the www.quantpsy.org/chisq/chisq.htm website. Here just enter the frequencies for males in the first column and for females in the second column and press 'Calculate'. The program then shows us (Figure 11.2) that the obtained value of chi-square is 1.026 and that it is associated with 1 degree of freedom (the number of rows minus one multiplied by the number of columns minus one).

As you can see here, the associated probability is .311 and this suggests that it would not be surprising to obtain the pattern here if there really were no difference between men and women in the population. On this basis we therefore cannot conclude that our observed data are inconsistent with the assumption that the rows and columns are *independent*. In other words, the results provide no basis for rejecting the null hypothesis that a person's sex is unrelated to eating disorder.

As an interesting exercise, we can compare this result with the outcome of the binomial test in order to calculate the approximate probability that a sample of 13 people (the number of people with eating disorders in our contingency table) would include eight or more girls if the probabilities of including a boy or a girl were both .5. This is a slightly different question than the one we asked above, but it is clearly related.

	Gp 1	Gp 2	Gp 3	Gp 4	Gp 5	Gp 6	Gp 7	Gp 8	Gp 9	Gp 10	
Cond. 1:	15	5									20
Cond. 2:	12	8									20
Cond. 3:											0
Cond. 4:											0
Cond. 5:											0
Cond. 6:											0
Cond. 7:											0
Cond. 8:											0
Cond. 9:											0
Cond. 10:											0
	27	13	0	0	0	0	0	0	0	0	40

Output:

Calculate	Reset all

Chi-square: 1.026

degrees of freedom: 1

p-value: 0.31110001

Yates' chi-square: 0.456

Status: Status okay

Yates' p-value: 0.49949934

Figure 11.2   From Preacher (2001, April)

The binomial probability for this comparison is relatively large (.291). In other words, the event would not be particularly unlikely to occur if it were the result of a random process. Happily, then, we can see that these two statistical techniques would lead us to the same conclusion about our data.

There are a couple of important additional things to note. The first is that the chi-square procedure does not work as well if the expected frequencies are small. In particular, where the expected frequency of any contingency is less than five it is best *either* not to employ this procedure *or* to make adjustments to the data or to the calculation of the statistic. This can be done using the **Yates correction**, but this procedure is not recommended for general use, so we will not discuss it further here.

Second, in addition to the chi-square statistic, 2×2 contingency tables can also be used to obtain a measure of association between variables. This is done very simply by dividing χ^2 by N. This produces a value between 0 and 1 that we call **phi** or φ (pronounced 'fie'). This is a correlation coefficient and can be interpreted just like any other correlation coefficient (e.g., Pearson's r that we discussed in Chapter 10).

For the eating disorder data that we were working with above, this calculation would produce $\varphi = 1.03/40 = .026$. Indeed, we can use φ as an indication of effect size (in the way that we discussed in Chapter 8), and by squaring φ we obtain a measure of the amount of variance shared by our variables. In this case, then, the correlation is small, and the effect is very weak. Certainly, this analysis would indicate that the relationship revealed in these data is not sufficiently strong to warrant taking it too seriously as evidence of a difference in the incidence of eating disorders among males and females.

A further point to note is that when it comes to assessing the outcomes of contingency tables it can often be helpful to calculate **odds**. Odds represent a particular way of expressing the likelihood of some event and are widely used in gambling (but bear in mind that the odds offered by **betting** agencies do not reflect the true probabilities of events – if they did book-makers would not make a profit).

To convert probabilities to odds we subtract the probability of the event from 1 and divide by the probability of the event, thus:

$$odds = \frac{1 - p(e)}{p(e)}$$

A probability of .25 thus becomes $(1 - .25)/(.25) = 3$ (to 1).

As a further twist, in technical settings researchers usually drop the expression 'to 1' and invert these fractions. Odds of 3 to 1 would therefore be expressed as technical or **statistical odds** of .333.

For contingency tables we can also calculate **conditional odds**. These are statements of the likelihood of one event occurring given that another has occurred. They are calculated by dividing the frequency of one alternative by the frequency of the other alternative. For example, if we return to the eating disorders data, given that a person is female, the conditional odds of having an eating disorder are 8/12 or .666, and given that a person is male, the conditional odds of having an eating disorder are 5/15 or 0.333.

Once we have calculated conditional odds we can use them to create **odds ratios**. These are the ratios of the conditional odds of two alternatives, dividing the larger odds by the smaller odds (so that the ratio is capable of varying between ∞ [infinity] and 1). In this case

$$.666/.333 = 2$$

In other words, the odds of having an eating disorder for a female are double those for a male. Although this sounds like a large effect, the result of our χ^2 test gives us reason to doubt that the association is particularly remarkable.

Note, however, that if we had found the same relationship with a sample of 400 rather than 40 people we would have reached a different conclusion (Table 11.8).

Table 11.8

	Male	Female	(Row totals)
Do not have eating disorder	150 (135)	120 (135)	270
Have eating disorder	50 (65)	80 (65)	130
(Column totals)	200	200	N = 400

If you enter this into the same online program as before, you will see that in this case $\chi^2 = 10.26$ and that this is associated with a probability of .0013. Thus there is a small chance that a pattern as extreme as this would occur if males and females are equally likely to have eating disorders. Remember, though, that the φ coefficient will still be exactly the same (.026). So even though this pattern may now be considered to be statistically significant, it is still a very weak effect. Again, if we had real data suggesting effects of this small size then we would be very cautious in reading too much into them.

These calculations do show, however, that χ^2 depends heavily on the value of N. In line with our earlier discussion of the importance of information about effect sizes, φ and the odds ratio can therefore be seen as providing useful additional indicators to help interpret this statistic.

Finally, we should note that χ^2 can be calculated for tables with many more contingencies than the four shown for a 2×2 table. However, the principles of such analyses are exactly the same as those described above – they just involve more calculations. For more complex contingency tables, a set of procedures called **loglinear analysis** is also available, but these procedures are beyond the scope of this book.

> **conditional odds** Statements of the likelihood of one event occurring given that another has occurred. These are obtained from the data in specific rows or columns of *contingency tables*, and are expressed in terms of the frequency with which the event

Test Yourself 11.3**

The statistical odds of an event occurring are .25. Which of the following statements is true?

a. The probability of the event occurring is .25.
b. In four independent tests the expected frequency of the event is 1.
c. The probability of the event occurring is .2.
d. We cannot make a statement about probability or expected frequency, because odds are only ever calculated by bookmakers who are trying to make a profit.
e. None of the above.

The correct answer is (c). Statistical odds can be converted into probabilities by converting them into betting odds and then using the formula $p(e) = 1/(\text{betting odds} + 1)$. Statistical odds of .25 represent betting odds of 4 (to 1), so $p(e) = 1/(4 + 1) = .2$. The easiest mistake to make here is to confuse odds with probability and hence to select (a). If one does this, one might also mistakenly select answer (b) because an expected frequency of one event in four tests is equivalent to a probability of .25. Answer (d) is wrong because odds are frequently used by statisticians to make statements about probability or expected frequency.

occurs in a given row or column divided by the frequency with which it does not occur in the same row or column.

contingencies Events that are the combination of two or more categories of event. For example, the contingency of being a woman with an eating disorder is the consequence both of being a woman (vs. a man) and of having (vs. not having) an eating disorder.

contingency table Tables that present information about the frequencies of all possible contingencies associated with two or more categories of event.

loglinear analysis A statistical procedure for analysing data in complex contingency tables.

marginal totals The sum of the *contingencies* in a given row or column of a *contingency table*.

odds Statements of the likelihood of a given event occurring expressed as the ratio of the expected frequency of two alternatives: that the event occurs and that it does not occur.

odds ratios Ratios of conditional odds. These indicate the relative likelihood of one event rather than another occurring given that another has occurred.

phi (φ) A correlation coefficient that measures the association between two sets of dichotomous scores (e.g., male–female, yes–no).

statistical odds Statements of the likelihood of a given event occurring expressed in terms of the expected frequency of it occurring divided by the expected frequency of it not occurring. For example, if a die is expected to fall on a '3' one time out of six, the statistical odds of obtaining a '3' are $1/5 = 0.20$. Note that this is *not* the same as the probability of the event occurring.

Yates correction A statistical procedure used when calculating the chi-square statistic and the expected frequency of any *contingency* is very small. It was once very common to use this, but in fact it has been shown to be appropriate in only a very limited set of circumstances (where *marginal totals* are known in advance – which is rare).

Distribution-free tests

In previous chapters we have discussed tests that make reasonably restrictive assumptions about the shape of the population distributions that we sample from. For example, we assume in performing a between-subjects *t*-test that the samples are drawn from populations that are normally distributed and have equal variances. We noted before that it is customary (but not always correct) to believe that procedures like the *t*-test and ANOVA are robust to the violation

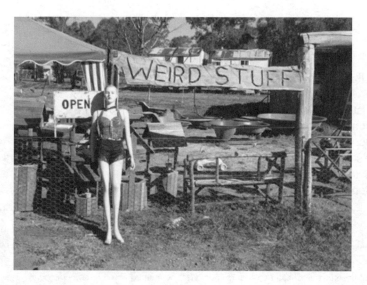

Photo 11.1 Sometimes we need to use distribution-free tests because we do not know enough about the population from which data are drawn to make assumptions about their distribution; sometimes we need to use them because we know the distribution is just plain weird.

of assumptions. In other words, it is widely believed that these tests produce similar results regardless of whether or not the assumptions hold.

Sometimes, however, it is neither convenient nor sensible to assume that these assumptions hold, and sometimes the violation of assumptions can compromise the inferences that we make about our data. As we noted earlier, if it can be true that the mean is sometimes a misleading statistic for describing a distribution, then it must also be the case that a test that compares the means of two distributions can be comparing two misleading indicators. Clearly, we need alternatives to deal with such situations. **Distribution-free statistics** provide such alternatives.

Roughly speaking, distribution-free statistics involve procedures that are relatively free from restrictive assumptions about the *shape* of the distribution of the population that the sample was drawn from. They still involve distributions (such as distributions of the test statistic and the observed sample distribution) and they still involve assumptions about the sampling distribution, but the assumptions they make about the shape of the population distribution are generally quite relaxed. Distribution-free statistics have many similarities to, and overlap with, a family of procedures called **non-parametric statistics**. The term 'non-parametric' refers to the fact that such statistics do not make assumptions about the parameters of particular distributions.

In what follows, we will stick with the term 'distribution-free' because, although the term 'non-parametric' is more common, it refers less obviously to the key feature of such tests: that they are free of restrictive assumptions about the shapes of distributions. The term **tests with relaxed assumptions** can also be used to convey this central idea more clearly.

335

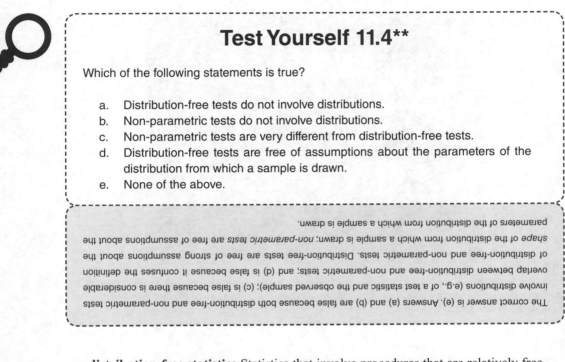

Test Yourself 11.4**

Which of the following statements is true?

a. Distribution-free tests do not involve distributions.
b. Non-parametric tests do not involve distributions.
c. Non-parametric tests are very different from distribution-free tests.
d. Distribution-free tests are free of assumptions about the parameters of the distribution from which a sample is drawn.
e. None of the above.

The correct answer is (e). Answers (a) and (b) are false because both distribution-free and non-parametric tests involve distributions (e.g., of a test statistic and the observed sample); (c) is false because there is considerable overlap between distribution-free and non-parametric tests; and (d) is false because it confuses the definition of distribution-free and non-parametric tests. Distribution-free tests are free of strong assumptions about the *shape* of the distribution from which a sample is drawn; *non-parametric tests are free of assumptions about the parameters of the distribution from which a sample is drawn.*

distribution-free statistics Statistics that involve procedures that are relatively free from restrictive assumptions about the shape of the distribution of the population that a sample is drawn from.

non-parametric statistics Statistics that do not make assumptions about the parameters of the distribution of the population that a sample is drawn from.

tests with relaxed assumptions Another term for *distribution-free statistics* that conveys more clearly the idea that such tests still involve distributions, but simply make relaxed assumptions about them.

Examining differences between two groups with relaxed assumptions: The Mann–Whitney test

In this chapter we discuss one distribution-free statistic in detail: the **Mann–Whitney test**. This is an alternative to the between-subjects *t*-test, but it has the great advantage that it can be used when the assumptions of the *t*-test do not hold or when the data are not measured in a form that allows direct numerical comparisons (i.e., where data are not obtained using ratio or interval scales).

A good example would be a case where our data represented the rankings of people from two groups. Let us imagine that some sports psychologists had developed a new coaching method for athletes and then entered the runners trained under traditional and new methods into a race. The dependent variable of interest here is not the time taken to complete the race but the placings or rankings of athletes in the race.

Imagine that the data for 26 athletes looked like Table 11.9. We can see from this table that athletes trained under the new method came 2nd, 3rd and 5th, and so on, and that athletes trained under the old method came 1st, 4th and 6th, etc. The mean rankings for each group and the sums of rankings are also shown as we will use these in the following calculations.

Table 11.9

Group	Ranking	
Old	1	
New		2
New		3
Old	4	
New		5
Old	6	
New		7
New		8
New		9
Old	10	
New		11
Old	12	
Old	13	
New		14
New		15
Old	16	
New		17
Old	18	
Old	19	
New		20
New		21
New		22
Old	23	
Old	24	
Old	25	
Old	26	
Σ rank	197	154
Mean rank	15.2	11.8

The question we would like to answer (but that a *t*-test cannot help us with) is whether the average ranking of one of the groups is better or worse than we would expect by chance. If one group does better than expected we know that the other must have done worse (as there are only two groups). In this case it is worth finding out whether the mean ranking obtained by athletes with the new training method is clearly better than we would expect if training method makes no difference. If training makes no difference then the mean rankings of both groups should both be estimates of the expected (i.e., mean) population ranking of both groups. As we noted when discussing the calculation of the median in Chapter 6, this mean rank is 13.5 (it is not a whole number because the total, 26, is even).

The Mann–Whitney test gives us information that helps us to answer the above question. For the sake of simplicity we will focus on the normal approximation of this test that can be used where $N > 25$ (or where the N for at least one group is 20). However, it is worth noting that if $N < 25$ then a slightly different procedure is used (one that involves using special statistical tables).

To calculate the normal approximation we compare the total (rather than mean) rankings of one of the groups with the expected total ranking of that group. If that total ranking is relatively small (when judged against the amount of error in estimating those rankings) then this would suggest that that group has done very well in the race (i.e., that it has more rankings near the top).

The expected sum of rankings is obtained by calculating

$$U_e = N_1 N_2 [(N_1 + N_2 + 1)/2]$$

where N_1 is the number of people in Group 1 and N_2 the number of people in Group 2. The standard error of the U-statistic is given by

$$S_U = \sqrt{\frac{N_1 N_2 (N_1 + N_2 + 1)}{12}}$$

We then calculate z in the following way:

$$z = \frac{U_1 - U_e}{S_U}$$

where U_1 is the sum of rankings for group 1.

Calculation of the Mann–Whitney test is straightforward, but it is convenient to do actual analyses in IBM SPSS Statistics software (SPSS). To do this, first enter the data as in Figure 11.3 (or use the data file provided in the Supplementary Online Material [Chapter11_MannWhitney.sav]). Now go to the 'Analyze' menu then 'Nonparametric Tests' and below that 'Legacy Dialogs', and then select '2 Independent Samples' (Figure 11.4).

Now drag 'Placing' into the 'Test Variable List' and 'Method' into the 'Grouping Variable'.

Figure 11.3

Figure 11.4

Then click on 'Define Groups' and enter '1' for 'Group 1' and '2' for 'Group 2' (Figure 11.5). Then click on 'Continue' and 'OK' and this will generate the output in Figure 11.6.

Figure 11.5

Mann–Whitney Test

Ranks

	Method	N	Mean Rank	Sum of Ranks
Placing	Old	13	15.15	197.00
	New	13	11.85	154.00
	Total	26		

Test Statistics[a]

	Placing
Mann–Whitney U	63.000
Wilcoxon W	154.000
Z	−1.103
Asymp. Sig. (2–tailed)	.270
Exact Sig. [2*(1–tailed Sig.)]	.287[b]

a. Grouping Variable: Method

b. Not corrected for ties.

Figure 11.6

This tells us that the average rank (placing) of athletes using the old method was 15.15 and for the new method was 11.85. This is associated with a Mann–Whitney U-value of 63, an associated z-value of −1.103 and a probability (p) of .270. Although the new method appeared to be associated with better performance (an average of three places higher), the difference in rankings would thus not be remarkably rare if it were the result of chance (i.e., if there were no real difference between the methods). Accordingly, we do not have a sound basis for concluding that type of training makes a difference to athletic performance.

In the example that we have just used we relied on data that already existed as rankings (placings in a race). However, it is worth noting that the Mann–Whitney test can also be used where our data exist as scores (e.g., as the times that the individual athletes took to complete the race). To use scores of this form we need to convert them into ranks and then use these in the analysis. As discussed in the previous section, this strategy is especially useful where we have scores but we do not want to make assumptions associated with a particular statistical procedure (e.g., a t-test) or have reason to believe that those assumptions have been violated.

One complication with the above procedure arises where two scores are identical (and therefore have equal rankings – these are called ties or tied rankings). Where this happens the calculation of the value of the statistic is problematic. The simplest, if not always the best, solution is to

RESEARCH BITE 11.2
The paradoxical popularity of non-parametric tests

Morten Fagerland (2012) observes that over the last 30 years the median size of the samples used in medical research has increased considerably. At the same time the use of t-tests has halved, while the use of non-parametric tests (such as the Mann–Whitney) has doubled. He notes that these trends appear to be paradoxical because parametric tests become more robust to violations of assumptions with larger samples. However, Fagerland argues that this has happened because with larger sample sizes non-parametric tests typically produce smaller p-values than their parametric counterparts. On this basis he cautions against overuse of non-parametric tests with large samples.

Reference
Fagerland, M. W. (2012). t-tests, non-parametric tests, and large studies – a paradox of statistical practice? *BMC Medical Research Methodology*, 12, 78.

Research Methods and Statistics in Psychology

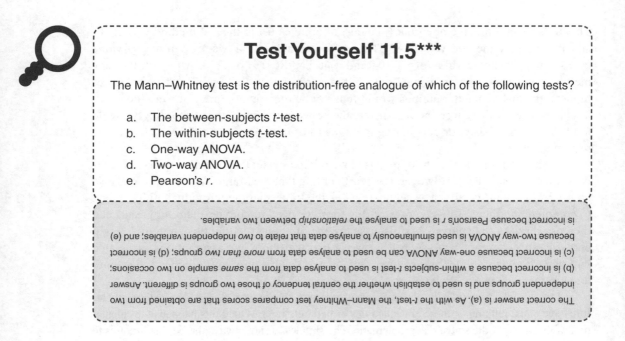

Test Yourself 11.5***

The Mann–Whitney test is the distribution-free analogue of which of the following tests?

a. The between-subjects *t*-test.
b. The within-subjects *t*-test.
c. One-way ANOVA.
d. Two-way ANOVA.
e. Pearson's *r*.

The correct answer is (a). As with the *t*-test, the Mann–Whitney test compares scores that are obtained from two independent groups and is used to establish whether the central tendency of those two groups is different. Answer (b) is incorrect because a within-subjects *t*-test is used to analyse data from the *same* sample on two occasions; (c) is incorrect because one-way ANOVA can be used to analyse data from *more than two* groups; (d) is incorrect because two-way ANOVA is used simultaneously to analyse data that relate to *two* independent variables; and (e) is incorrect because Pearson's *r* is used to analyse the *relationship* between two variables.

give both scores the same rank. The easiest way to do this is to give each their median rank. For example, if the 4th and 5th ranked scores are equal, both could be given a ranking of 4.5.

A more serious complication is that although the Mann–Whitney test is normally used to compare the central tendencies of two groups (and it is differences in the central tendencies that the test is most sensitive to), it also tests differences in the *dispersion* of the distributions.

Accordingly, it may be the case that the null hypothesis of no difference between the two groups is rejected because they have a different spread rather than a different mean (or mean rank). The test does not tell us whether this is the case and so this is clearly something to bear in mind when interpreting test results.

> **Mann–Whitney test** A distribution-free test that is usually used to compare the central tendency of two independent groups. In this regard it is the distribution-free analogue of a between-subjects *t*-test.

Some options for other cases

In this section we will briefly discuss some other cases that you might encounter and suggest options that you might take. However, because each of these tests is quite different we will not provide details or examples of how to calculate them. These can also be performed quite easily in SPSS, following steps similar to those that we have gone through above. More information is provided in specialist texts on distribution-free statistics (e.g., Siegel, 1956).

Examining differences between two related samples with relaxed assumptions: The Wilcoxon test

In the previous section we discussed the Mann–Whitney test for comparing two groups and noted that this was analogous to the between-subjects t-test. There are also analogues of the within-subjects t-test. These can be used when the samples are related (e.g., when comparing measurements of the same sample on two measures). The best known of these is the **Wilcoxon matched-pairs signed-ranks test**. This works in much the same way as the Mann–Whitney test in that it involves computing a sum based on ranks. However, unlike the Mann–Whitney test, the sum computed is the sum of the signed ranks of the differences between the two variables. If this sum has a large absolute value (either negative or positive) then we are more likely to conclude that there is a difference between the variables.

The Wilcoxon test also assumes that the differences in scores represent an ordinal scale. This assumption may not hold (and it is often difficult to tell whether it does). In this regard it is worth noting that alternatives such as the **sign test** and the **McNemar test** can be used in these circumstances, but that these are less powerful.

The sign test is a straightforward application of the binomial test presented at the start of this chapter. The signed difference between each pair of scores is calculated (i.e., the scores for the same participant on the two measures). If the proportion of positive or negative scores is very small when compared with the binomial distribution, then this is evidence against the null hypothesis of no difference.

> **McNemar test** A distribution-free test that is used to compare the central tendency of sets of data that are collected in pairs from the same participants. It is particularly applicable to 'before' and 'after' designs in which data are obtained from the same source on two occasions.
>
> **sign test** The binomial test when used to compare the central tendency of sets of data that are collected in pairs. The test is based on attaching plus and minus signs to differences between pairs of data. It makes no assumptions about the distribution from which those data are drawn.
>
> **Wilcoxon matched-pairs signed-ranks test** A distribution-free test that is used to compare the central tendency of sets of data that are collected in pairs from the same participants. In this regard it is the distribution-free analogue of a within-subjects t-test.

Examining differences between more than two groups with relaxed assumptions: The Kruskal–Wallis test

Distribution-free comparisons between groups are also possible when there are more than two groups. This is a direct analogue of one-way within-subjects ANOVA and it is called the

Kruskal–Wallis test. It works in much the same way as the Mann–Whitney test. Unfortunately, it is far more difficult to find distribution-free alternatives for testing statistical interactions. However, a **Friedman test** can be used to compare more than two related samples.

> **Friedman test** A distribution-free test that is usually used to compare the central tendency of more than two related groups. In this regard it is the distribution-free analogue of one-way within-subjects ANOVA.
>
> **Kruskal–Wallis test** A distribution-free test that is usually used to compare the central tendency of more than two independent groups. In this regard it is the distribution-free analogue of one-way between-subjects ANOVA.

Using ranked data in correlations

Many older statistics texts suggest that **Spearman's correlation (r_s)** should be used when judging whether ranked data are correlated. However, although the data take the specific form of ranks, this procedure is actually identical to the Pearson product-moment correlation that we discussed in Chapter 9 (and the **point biserial correlation**). As a result, it is not helpful to consider it further. However, it is worth noting that when dealing with ranked data, tied ranks still present something of a tricky issue. As we discussed in relation to the Mann–Whitney test, the easiest way to deal with scores that have the same rank is to assign them the same value (their median rank).

> **point biserial correlation** A correlation coefficient used to assess the degree of association between two variables when one is dichotomous (e.g., male–female; right–wrong).
>
> **Spearman's correlation (r_s)** A correlation coefficient used to assess the degree of linear association between two sets of ranked data.

Choosing the most powerful test

Given the wide variety of tests that are available for answering related questions, this implies a choice of test. It is important to have rules for making those choices as clear as possible.

As it happens, there is a reasonably straightforward rule that we can suggest. The test that should be applied is the most powerful test that can appropriately answer the question of interest. You will recall that by power we are referring to the ability of the test to reveal relationships if they actually exist. By 'appropriately answer' we mean that the assumptions of that test are not grossly violated in ways that threaten the interpretation of the test. As a simple rule of thumb, the classical or parametric tests that we have discussed in earlier chapters will be more powerful than the distribution-free alternatives that we have considered in this chapter and hence they will be more appropriate *provided that the assumptions of these tests hold.*

Overview and checklist

It is now possible to return to the table at the start of this chapter and present an extended range of alternatives. This is the purpose of Table 11.10.

Table 11.10 Statistical tests (including those with relaxed assumptions) and when to use them

Form of data	Question of interest	Assumptions about data*	Test used
One variable with many levels	Does the mean differ from some value (e.g., zero)?	(i) Population variances are unknown; (ii) observations are independent; (iii) the sample is drawn from a normally distributed population.	One-sample t-test
One variable with two categories; one variable with many levels	Are the means of the two categories different?	(i) Population variances are unknown; (ii) observations are independent; (iii) the two categories are drawn from populations with the same variance; (iv) the categories are drawn from normally distributed populations.	Between-subjects t-test
One variable with more than two categories; one variable with many levels	Are the means of the categories different?	(i) Population variances are unknown; (ii) observations are independent; (iii) the categories are drawn from populations with the same variance; (iv) the categories are drawn from normally distributed populations.	ANOVA
Two variables with many levels	Are the means of the two variables different?	(i) Population variances are unknown; (ii) observations are independent; (iii) variables are correlated; (iv) variables are drawn from normally distributed populations.	Within-subjects t-test
Two variables with many levels	Are scores on the two variables related?	There is a linear and bivariate normal relationship between the variables.	Pearson product-moment correlation coefficient
One variable with two levels	Is one level of the variable more common than the other?	None	Binomial test
One variable with more than two levels	Do the levels occur with the frequencies we would expect?	None	χ^2 test of goodness of fit

(Continued)

Table 11.10 (Continued)

Form of data	Question of interest	Assumptions about data*	Test used
Two variables with two or more levels	Are the two categorical variables related?	None	χ^2 test of independence
One variable with two categories; one variable with many levels	Do the two categories have different central tendencies?**	None	Mann–Whitney test
Two variables with many levels	Is the central tendency of the two variables different?	None	Sign test
One variable with more than two categories; one variable with many levels	Do the categories have different central tendencies?	None	Kruskal–Wallis test

*   We assume in each case that each observation of a different person is independent.

**   As noted in the text, this is the question of interest rather than the question the test is necessarily informative about, as the test also provides information about differences in dispersion.

Obviously the complexity of the range of matters that we can address has greatly increased. Indeed, armed with an understanding of the ideas contained in this table you are in a position to tackle a mind-boggling array of different situations. In many cases you will actually choose to proceed using a computer package such as SPSS to help you. Nonetheless, you can see that the simplicity of the tests we have dealt with in this chapter means that this can often be done just as effectively using a calculator and a sheet of paper.

There remains one final point to stress. Despite the diversity and sophistication of statistical tests, and the enormous lengths we all have to go to in order to understand how these tests work, they still do not normally answer the questions that we are interested in. A statistical test cannot tell us whether or not there is a real difference between groups or a relationship between variables; it cannot even tell us the probability that some relationship we have observed is true or due to chance. All the test can tell us is how likely the result we have observed would be if we made certain assumptions about the way the data were sampled from the population. This is why distribution-free statistics in particular are so important: precisely because they allow us to be somewhat more relaxed in our assumptions about the population (which we generally know very little about in most psychological research).

For this and other reasons, distribution-free statistics should really be used more widely in psychological research than they are. As we noted at the start of the chapter, the fact that we have spent so little time on them compared with the parametric alternatives is thus a reflection of the way the science of psychology is practised rather than a statement about the value of these procedures. Bear in mind, then, that the most complex statistical analysis is not necessarily the best. Sometimes, less is more.

Photo 11.2 In statistics, as in life, something does not have to be complicated to be good or useful. The beauty of distribution-free tests is that they are versatile, elegant and easy to use.

CHECKLIST
Revisiting the key goals for this chapter

☐ I know that the chi-square test is a statistical test that is used to analyse categorical data.

☐ I know that a range of other statistical tests can be used to analyse data without making assumptions about the distribution of data in the population from which they are drawn.

☐ I understand when and how to use these various tests.

Further reading

There is a long tradition of using non-parametric statistics to analyse data from psychological research. In testament to this fact, Siegel's (1956) book remains one of the classic texts in this area. It contains details of a large number of non-parametric tests that can be used to tackle a broad range of research situations. Smithson's (2000) text includes detailed discussions of a number of the statistics discussed here and also includes a treatment of confidence intervals. Also included is a reference to Preacher's website that is an excellent resource for calculating chi-square values.

Preacher, K. J. (2001, April). Calculation for the chi-square test: An interactive calculation tool for chi-square tests of goodness of fit and independence [Computer software]. Available from http://quantpsy.org.

Siegel, S. (1956). *Nonparametric statistics for the behavioral sciences*. New York: McGraw-Hill.

Smithson, M. J. (2000). *Statistics with confidence*. London: SAGE.

Other forms of data: A checklist for research evaluation and improvement

Table 11.11

Potential problem	Question to ask	Potential improvement
Inferential uncertainty (see Chapter 7) about the frequency of two events, where only two are possible	Do the researchers want to compare the frequencies?	Conduct a binomial test to compute the probability of observing frequencies as extreme as the ones observed if both events occurred with their expected frequency. If $n > 25$ use the normal approximation to this test.
Inferential uncertainty about the frequency of more than two events, where there is one independent variable		Conduct a χ^2 test of goodness of fit to compare observed frequencies with expected frequencies. Unless the base rate of events differs, expected frequency equals the frequency of observations divided by the number of events. χ^2 is computed by summing the squares of the difference between observed and expected frequencies and dividing by the expected frequency. Statistical tables or an online calculator can be used to provide information about the probability of observing by chance a χ^2 score as large as the one obtained.
Inferential uncertainty about the frequency of more than two events, where there are two independent variables	Do the researchers want to see if there is a relationship between the variables, such that one event is more likely to occur when another event has also occurred?	Conduct a χ^2 test of independence to see whether the observed frequencies differ from the frequencies that would be expected if the same proportion of events occurred in the two levels of both variables. χ^2 is computed by summing the squares of the difference between observed and expected frequencies and dividing by the expected frequency. Statistical tables or an online calculator can be used to provide information about the probability of observing by chance a χ^2 score as large as the one obtained.
Significance fallacy	In testing for independence, have the researchers distinguished appropriately between psychological and statistical significance?	Compute a phi-coefficient by dividing χ^2 by the total number of events, N. Consider significance levels for χ^2 in conjunction with effect sizes. Be alert to the dangers of making too much of statistically significant correlations when effect sizes are low.

Potential problem	Question to ask	Potential improvement
Inferential uncertainty about the central tendency of scores obtained from two samples, where assumptions about the distribution of scores are violated	Do the researchers want to compare the scores?	Conduct a Mann–Whitney test by ranking all scores and comparing the expected sum of rank scores (U_e) with the sum of rank of scores in one sample (U_1). If $n > 25$ use the normal approximation to this test in which a z-score is obtained by subtracting U_e from U_1 and dividing by the standard error of the ranks. Table C.1 can be used to provide information about the probability of observing by chance a z-score as large as the one obtained.
Inferential uncertainty about the central tendency of scores obtained from the same sample, where assumptions about the distribution of scores are violated		Conduct a sign test by computing the differences between the two sets of scores. Use the binomial test to evaluate the probability of observing frequencies of positive and negative scores like the ones you have observed if there is really no difference between the variables.

Test Yourself 11.6***

An organizational psychologist conducts a piece of research in which he tests the hypothesis that companies that have a pension plan retain more employees than companies that do not have a plan. To test this hypothesis he collects data from 60 companies recording (a) whether or not they have a pension plan and (b) what percentage of their employees are still working for the company after a year. However, on inspecting his data, the researcher finds that most companies retain a very high proportion of their employees and that scores on this measure are therefore very highly skewed. Which of the following tests would be most appropriate for comparing central tendencies?

a. ANOVA.
b. The χ^2 test of independence.
c. The χ^2 test of goodness of fit.
d. The Mann–Whitney test.
e. The between-subjects t-test.

(Continued)

(Continued)

Test Yourself 11.7*

Which of the following statements is *false*?

a. Distribution-free tests can be useful when the assumptions of other tests are violated.
b. Distribution-free tests are useful when handling categorical data.
c. Non-parametric tests are useful when handling categorical data.
d. Non-parametric tests have very few uses.
e. Non-parametric tests and distribution-free tests both make relaxed assumptions about the parameters of population distributions.

Test Yourself 11.8*

Which of the following is the main limitation of tests with relaxed assumptions?

a. Their assumptions are generally too relaxed.
b. They are usually very difficult to conduct.
c. They can only be used effectively in applied settings.
d. They provide information about odds rather than probabilities.
e. They generally have less power than parametric tests.

The correct answer to 11.6 is (d), though this is controversial. Because one of the variables of interest here is categorical (company has/does not have pension plan), and the other has many levels (proportion of employees retained), the two potential tests the researcher could use are the Mann–Whitney and the between-subjects *t*-test. However, (e) is wrong because the distribution of data violates one of the assumptions of the *t*-test (that data are normally distributed) and (a) is wrong because this same line of reasoning makes ANOVA inappropriate (noting too that this is identical to the between-subjects *t*-test where one variable has two categories). Both (b) and (c) are wrong because χ^2 tests require all data to be categorical.

The correct answer to 11.7 is (d). As we have shown in this chapter, non-parametric tests have a large number of uses and they are often both practical and easy to use. All of the other statements are true. As (a) and (e) suggest, non-parametric and distribution-free tests both make relaxed assumptions about population distributions, so they can be useful when the assumptions of other tests are violated. As (b) and (c) suggest, non-parametric and distribution-free tests are also both very useful when dealing with categorical data.

The correct answer to 11.8 is (e). The main limitation of tests with relaxed assumptions is that they tend to have less power than their parametric counterparts. Accordingly, *provided that the assumptions of parametric tests hold*, it is usually best to use these if possible. Having said that, tests with relaxed assumptions are generally very easy to conduct (so (b) is wrong), the fact that their assumptions are relaxed is one of their useful features (so (a) is wrong), and they can be used in a wide range of settings (not just applied ones, so (c) is wrong). Answer (d) is wrong because not all such tests involve the use of odds, and those that do still provide information about probability.

Discussion/essay questions

a. What reasons might a researcher have for using tests with relaxed assumptions?
b. Which research practices have contributed to distribution-free tests being used less widely than other statistical techniques in psychology?
c. Should psychologists use distribution-free tests more than they do?
d. What are the limitations of distribution-free and non-parametric tests?

Exercises

a. An organizational researcher looks at the composition of company boards and finds that although 40% of these companies' employees are female, only 44 of 138 board members are women.

   i. What is the expected frequency of female board members?
   ii. Do these data provide statistical support for the hypothesis that women are under-represented at this level?

b. A cognitive neuropsychologist conducts a study in which she investigates whether embedding words in song improves the memory of people who have amnesia. To do this, she gives 30 amnesiacs and 30 control condition participants (controls) a poem to remember and another 30 amnesiacs and 30 controls a song to remember in which the words of that poem are sung. She then tests each group's recognition by presenting participants with one segment that was in the poem and one segment that was not, and asking them to identify correctly which of the two segments was in the original material they had learned. The numbers of participants who identify the correct segment are as follows:

Table 11.12

	Poem	Song
Controls	28	29
Amnesics	16	27

   i. What is the expected frequency of correct identification in each sample of participants?
   ii. Is there any evidence that the amnesiacs' memory for poems is any better than chance?

(Continued)

351

(Continued)

    iii.   Is there any evidence that the amnesiacs' memory is better when they learn the material in song rather than poem form?

    iv.   Is there any evidence that learning the material in song rather than poem form has more impact on the amnesiacs' memory than on the memory of controls?

    v.   To the extent that there is a relationship between learning context (song or poem) and participant type (control or amnesic), what is its effect size?

    vi.   Do the data suggest that there may be problems interpreting the impact of the independent variable on the recognition of the controls in this study?

c.   Educational psychologists are interested in seeing whether students' scores in final-year school exams were higher in 2012 than in 2011. To examine this, they obtain the scores from a random sample of 15 students in each of the two years. These are as follows (each mark is out of 100):

2011: 27.1, 44.5, 58.9, 70.4, 73.2, 84.2, 85.1, 88.2, 89.3, 90.2, 92.2, 93.2, 94.0, 94.5, 95.2

2012: 59.3, 74.2, 86.4, 86.7, 90.3, 93.3, 94.4, 94.6, 94.7, 95.3, 95.7, 96.6, 96.7, 97.1, 98.8

The researchers initially conduct a *t*-test to examine these data, but some critics of their research point out that this procedure is inappropriate because the distribution of scores is very skewed and hence it is inappropriate to assume that they are drawn from a normally distributed population.

    i.   How should the researchers respond?

    ii.   Would they reach a different conclusion if they used a distribution-free test to analyse their data?

Classical Qualitative Methods

Key goals for this chapter

- Outline the logic of classical qualitative methods and the key principles that underpin their use.
- Introduce three classical qualitative methods: repertory grid analysis, content analysis and thematic analysis.
- Identify the strengths and weaknesses of classical qualitative methods.

Despite the many differences between the statistical techniques that we have discussed in the previous five chapters, it is clear that they all have one thing in common: they involve the collection and manipulation of *quantitative data*. This means that when we thought about potential research questions (e.g., 'Does absence make the heart grow fonder?'; 'Does attributional style affect psychological well-being?'), answers were provided that relied upon numbers rather than words and we had to devise scales or tests to measure things as varied as physical attraction, attributional style, anxiety, memory and intelligence.

Moreover, having collected data in this form, we can see that the methods for analysing them could be understood in terms of a series of well-defined decisions that led to readily interpretable outcomes. Among psychologists in general there is also a high degree of agreement about the nature of these decisions and the sorts of products they should lead to. For example, having asked two independent groups of participants to rate the attractiveness of their partners on nine-point rating scales, almost all researchers would recommend that the data be examined by means of a *t*-test (providing that certain statistical assumptions are not violated).

This is all well and good. However, it is possible to object to these practices on the grounds that they misrepresent the underlying subject matter of psychology. Indeed, criticism of this form may have already occurred to you. Thus you might be prepared to accept that quantitative methods are elegant and coherent, but still be troubled by a feeling that numerical solutions do not really capture the world as you (and the participants in psychological research) know it.

More specifically, you might point out that circling a number on a scale can never come close to capturing what it *means* to be in love, that a score on a test can never do justice to the *experience* of depression, or that when we say someone has a good memory we mean much more than that they can recall a lot of items from a meaningless list. In saying these things, you will be asking for examination of these phenomena that is *qualitative* rather than (just) quantitative and which does a better job of understanding them (a) as they are experienced by, and have meaning for, the people involved and (b) as they occur naturally 'in the real world'.

In this chapter and the next we will look closely at some of the alternative ways of doing research that represent an attempt to respond to this sort of objection. As we will see, beyond the details of the methods we discuss, a number of features distinguish this chapter from those that have preceded it. First among these is the fact that the choice of *which* qualitative method to use is made more difficult by the sheer variety of methods available. In an influential text, Tesch (1990) identifies over 40 such methods, and there are now many more. Related to this point, while the procedures for handling quantitative data are relatively circumscribed and easy to codify, those for handling qualitative data are much more indeterminate and varied. There is only one correct way to calculate a *t*-value, but an unlimited number of ways in which most qualitative methods can be deployed. And finally, for both of these reasons there is much less agreement among researchers about exactly how qualitative analysis should be conducted. So, although there is some dispute about how to perform quantitative analysis (e.g., about whether the hypothesis-testing approach is appropriate; see Chapter 9), this is relatively mild compared with the heated debates that surround many aspects of qualitative research. Indeed, it is not too much of an exaggeration to suggest that the only thing that really unites the various strands of qualitative research is a shared recognition among those who do it of the limitations of a purely quantitative approach.

For all the above reasons, our treatment of qualitative methods takes the form of an illustrative survey rather than an attempt to provide a comprehensive grounding in their many features and uses. To help focus these chapters we will consider approaches that differ considerably in the extent to which they depart from, and present arguments against, the various quantitative approaches we have discussed in previous chapters. However, before considering these methods and ideas in some detail, we will start by clarifying the basis of many of their proponents' misgivings about quantitative methods. This exercise has a dual purpose. On the one hand, it helps us to understand the basic motivations that underpin the various methods and to understand where those who use them are 'coming from'. On the other, it also raises a number of issues that *all* researchers need to consider carefully in developing a response to the challenge laid down by qualitative research. This is important because (as we suggested at the end of Chapter 5) there is a tendency for many researchers to advocate the exclusive use of quantitative methods and, in the process, to dismiss altogether the potential for qualitative approaches to contribute to psychological knowledge (usually on grounds that they are non-cumulative, non-generalizable, subjective, atheoretical and unscientific). This response is misguided, we suggest, because an appreciation of the issues raised by qualitative studies has the potential to enrich *all* psychological research – including that which has been exclusively quantitative. For this reason, far from being incidental to psychological enquiry or being on the wane, qualitative methods have played a major role in the development of *all* branches of the discipline and interest in them is very much on the increase. Bear in mind, though, that – at least to some degree – researchers are able to pick and choose among the methods on offer. A researcher does not need to accept every aspect of a particular critique in order to use most of the methods we describe.

A classical critique of quantitative approaches

The basis of what we can refer to as the classical critique of quantitative research is suggested by the introductory comments above and has probably already occurred to you either on reading the previous chapters or on exposure to research in lectures and laboratory classes. Stated simply, researchers who expose themselves to 'real-world' psychological processes and states, such as love, hate, attachment, pride, uncertainty, depression, intelligence, attention and memory, often come to the view that there is 'more' to these phenomena than can be conveyed by mere numbers and by crude attempts to manipulate discrete aspects of the environment one at a time. Thinking, for example, about our hypothetical study in which we tried to test between the theories that 'absence makes the heart grow fonder' and 'absence leads the heart to wander', we can see that it is possible to object to this at a number of levels. First, one can argue that the study is limited by the fact that feelings of the heart were transposed into numbers on a scale when, in reality, their positive and negative aspects encompass emotions as varied (and with distinctions as subtle) as fondness, pleasure, affection, love and lust as opposed to hate, dissatisfaction, distrust, pique, jealousy and boredom. On a scale ranging from 1 (do not like at all) to 9 (like a great deal), when a participant circles '6', we might treat this as if it communicated reasonably strong liking, but could it not also be an indication of mild attraction, mild passion, mild warmth or mild fondness? Or perhaps it signifies something altogether different – such as a sense of dutiful but ambivalent obligation. Did the person circle '6' because they really quite liked the target or because they felt some responsibility to express a certain degree of liking? Difficult as this question can be to answer, we can see that the problem becomes more serious if it is

Photo 12.1 A 2010 article in the magazine *Time* gathered together the observations of a range of commentators and concluded that 'shopping takes on meaning beyond a basic exchange of goods and currency, serving as therapy, entertainment, sport, drug, and sometimes torture' (Tuttle, 2010). The shops here all have names that allude to important constructs in psychology – memory and amnesia, happiness and stress, identity and madness. As with the experience of shopping, you might ask whether it is possible to capture the nuanced meaning of these constructs through quantitative research alone.

the case that circling a '6' means different things for different people. This is because these diverse meanings are necessarily conflated and unrecoverable when one makes a summary statement of the form 'the mean rating of participants in this condition was 6.40'. Moreover, dismissing this variation as statistical error or noise is problematic – not least because it does not actually show up as variation in the data set.

Beyond these problems with the dependent variable, a further problem relates to the practice of experimentally manipulating the independent variable. In our attraction study we did this by varying participants' exposure to a target and then measuring the impact of this manipulation on ratings of that target. Stop and think for a minute, though, about what the participants in the study were actually going through, and how they might have experienced this manipulation. Did they find the exposure pleasant, stimulating, or unusual? And did they find repeated exposure especially pleasant, increasingly tedious, or just plain weird? We discussed some of these issues in Chapter 4 when considering the problem of confounding – the fact that when an experimenter attempts to manipulate one thing (in this case interaction) he or she may actually be manipulating another (e.g., familiarity, boredom or weirdness). However, even if a researcher is sensitive to this issue, we can see that a more nuanced problem is that the same manipulation can mean different things to different people. So one person may have found repeated interaction with a stranger increasingly stimulating, while another found it increasingly bizarre.

One possible (and quite common) response to these observations is that while they pose problems for researchers in social areas of psychology that deal with 'warm and soft' phenomena such as emotions and feelings, they are of much less concern to experimenters in more cognitive areas who deal with 'cold and hard' questions of visual perception, verbal memory and the like. In fact, though, it is clear that this critique can be applied to these areas too.

Consider, for example, a cognitive experiment in which participants have to assign objects made of different shapes to different categories and the researcher measures the time it takes to complete the task as a function of stimulus complexity (e.g., by manipulating the number of different shapes that the object contains). While this dependent measure can be characterized as objective, it is nonetheless clear that it will be affected by the meaning that the task assumes for the participants. If they think the experiment is an intelligence test they may be motivated to respond quickly and in a way that is intended by the experimenter; but if they see it as 'another one of those pointless tasks designed to trick me' they may respond quite differently. In other words, the participants' *subjective orientation* to the task (i.e., the way they approach it) may vary and this will impact upon the meaning of both the independent and dependent variables. With one mindset the independent variable manipulates stimulus complexity and the dependent variable measures speed, but with the other mindset the independent variable may manipulate annoyance and the dependent variable may measure frustration or bloody-mindedness.

Faced with this dual problem relating to the indeterminate meaning of independent and dependent variables, one key recommendation of qualitative researchers is to adopt research practices that (a) focus on the meaning that particular behaviours have for participants themselves (this is commonly referred to as a **hermeneutic approach**) and (b) actively involve participants (and other interested parties) in the research process (a principle referred to as **participant involvement** or **user involvement**). Even where participants are required to complete quantitative measures, this usually means that they will be asked *individually* to discuss and explain *in their own words* what a particular response means and why they are making it. As a result, where quantitative approaches involve the cold, bare statistical analysis of numerical data, qualitative research focuses on words or other ways of capturing the warmer, richer elaboration of experience.

Differences of the above form constitute the classical critique of, and response to, quantitative research. Having said that, as we will see below, many of the actual methods in which these ideas are realized sit quite happily alongside the quantitative

Photo 12.2 The principle of participant involvement involves engaging participants in the research process rather than merely imposing research upon them. In this research with care home residents the researchers are interested in finding out what residents think about changes to the decoration in a communal lounge, as part of research which examined the impact of those changes on their well-being and cognitive functioning (C. Haslam et al., 2014).

methods we have already discussed in previous chapters and can be used for very similar purposes (Table 12.1). In this capacity qualitative methods can, for example, be used to embellish or question an empirical point, to demonstrate the relevance and utility of quantitative findings, or to formulate theoretical and empirical objections to a particular body of work. Indeed Gilbert and Mulkay (1984) make the point that researchers often adopt a hermeneutic approach when explaining why their results have not come out as expected, but a mainstream empiricist approach when dealing with results that they did expect.

Table 12.1 Distinguishing features of quantitative and classical qualitative research

Typical distinguishing features	Quantitative	Classical qualitative
Form of data	Numbers	Words
Method of data collection	Measurement	Observation (broadly defined)
Form of analysis	Statistical	Illustrative
'Feel' of analysis	Cold, bare, mechanical	Warm, rich, fluid

Test Yourself 12.1*

A hermeneutic approach to qualitative research involves which of the following?

a. Use of advanced statistical principles beyond the scope of this text.
b. Use of basic statistical principles similar to those that underpin distribution-free tests.
c. Attending to the meaning of particular phenomena for those who experience them.
d. A process of self-discovery in which the researcher reflects on his or her own role in the research process.
e. Spending a lot of time in isolation, quarantined from the outside world.

The correct answer is (c). Hermeneutic approaches focus on the experience of research participants and resist attempts to impose a particular understanding upon that experience. Answers (a) and (b) are wrong because, as the question indicates, this approach is qualitative and it does not rely on formal statistical tests to make claims about research findings. Answer (d) is wrong because, while much qualitative research does invite researchers to be reflexive and think about their own role, the point of a hermeneutic analysis is to reflect on the experience of those who are being studied. For this reason, spending a lot of time in isolation (i.e., a hermetic approach) is rather unhermeneutic, and so (e) is wrong.

hermeneutic approach An approach to research that focuses on the particular meaning that specific actions have for those who engage in them.

participant involvement Research practice that acknowledges the role that participants play in research and that seeks to involve them in as much of the research process as possible.

user involvement Research practice that acknowledges the need to do research that is of benefit to particular communities and that seeks to involve potential users in as much of the research process as possible.

Classical methods of collecting qualitative data

As suggested above, although quantitative methods are different from qualitative ones, the methods and principles that guide data collection are often very similar – especially in the case of what we refer to as 'classical' qualitative research. Indeed, almost all of the techniques that are typically used to collect quantitative data can also be used to collect classical qualitative data. This is particularly true of a number of the main methods of data collection that we have discussed in previous chapters – including interviews, case studies, archival studies and observational studies. In all of these settings, rather than seeking to gather numerical data (e.g., by using a survey instrument), a researcher can choose to gather verbal data from interviews (structured or unstructured), group discussion (e.g., using **focus groups** or **delphi groups**), written communication (e.g., letters, memos, public documents), recorded material (e.g., radio programmes, television interviews, documentaries, chat-shows), and a whole range of other sources (e.g., the Internet, transcripts of court or legislative proceedings).

As well as these generic methods for data collection, qualitative researchers have also devised a number of tools that enable them to collect data in specific forms. We will look at a few of these in more detail below, but some of the best-known tools are the **Q-sort,** the **verbal protocol** and the **repertory grid.** Each of these has particular features that allow researchers to abstract theoretically relevant forms of information from more complex material (in the same way that a mean summarizes particular information about a response distribution).

Considered as a whole, qualitative methods of data gathering vary in three key respects. First, the data can be structured or unstructured. Broadly speaking, the more structured the data are, the more likely they are to be handled in widely agreed ways after they have been collected. This is clearest in the case of the tools alluded to above where widely accepted practices exist for managing data and reporting the results of their analysis. Against this, data from less structured sources (e.g., open-ended interviews, websites) are much more likely to be handled in idiosyncratic ways that are tailored to the specific goals of the researcher.

Second, data can be gathered *explicitly for research purposes* or can exist *independently of research.* For example, a researcher who seeks to gain insight into processes of political leadership could either examine the content of politicians' television interviews or conduct interviews with them him- or herself (Reicher & Hopkins, 1996, 2001).

A third difference, related to the second, is that researchers themselves can either be internal or external to the data. For example, they can choose to conduct an interview themselves or to examine an interview that has been conducted by someone else.

In any of these scenarios the researcher will always be in control of the analytic process, but the researcher's proximity to the data and the purposes for which they were produced both have a bearing upon issues of *reactivity* (as discussed in Chapters 4 and 5). This is not because reactivity is an issue in some situations and not in others, but rather because the **reactive focus** of research differs across different data-gathering contexts. Specifically, where the researcher is internal to data gathering, the participant will generally be reacting directly to the researcher (and to his or her assumed agenda), but where the researcher is external to data gathering, the participant will usually be reacting to the perceived agenda of a different audience.

Although external agents may have interests that are independent of the researcher (and hence those data are less likely to be affected by participants' sensitivity to the researcher's goals), none of these options is inherently 'better' than any other. Instead, reactive focus represents one potential source of variation in the data. Indeed, this variation often becomes a *topic* for investigation, as may happen if a researcher compares the things that a person says to a researcher in private with those that they say to a public audience.

A good example of this strategy is provided by Gilbert and Mulkay's (1984) examination of biochemists' accounts of the scientific process. In their research articles and in descriptions of their own research activities the scientists drew upon what Gilbert and Mulkay refer to as an **empiricist repertoire**. This presented science as a completely objective activity in which progress was driven simply by the accumulation of critical data. However, in their private discussions with the researchers a **contingent repertoire** emerged in which the activities of competing scientists were dismissed for being driven by forces as varied as fashion, personal taste, luck, pig-headedness, blindness, prejudice and sheer stupidity. It is interesting to note, in passing, that the content of Gilbert and Mulkay's (1984) research is clearly relevant to the broad issues discussed in this chapter, as it is possible to argue that quantitative methods in psychology (and the products with which it is associated, e.g., empirical reports such as the one in Appendix A) are examples of the empiricist repertoire, while qualitative methods are generally more compatible with the contingent repertoire in serving to emphasize the subjective, human aspects of the research process (Potter, 1996; Woolgar, 1996).

contingent repertoire A way of accounting for scientific endeavour and progress that draws attention to the role played by subjective, human factors beyond the realm of the empirical phenomena under investigation.

delphi group method A method for collecting qualitative and quantitative data in which members of a group respond individually to questionnaires on a given topic, their responses are collated and discussed by the group as a whole, and members then complete a second questionnaire. The method is often used to generate and evaluate ideas in organizational and clinical settings.

empiricist repertoire A way of accounting for scientific endeavour and progress that focuses on the empirical phenomena under investigation and suggests that scientific activity serves as a neutral medium through which these are understood (i.e., that the data 'speak for themselves').

focus groups Methods for collecting qualitative data in which groups of participants discuss a series of questions pertaining to a particular topic. In this way, data emerge from the interaction of the participants rather than simple question-and-answer sequences. The technique is often used to see how people resolve differences and disagreement and how consensus about a particular issue emerges.

Q-sort A qualitative research tool in which participants sort cards containing statements into piles associated with different points on a response dimension. In its original form participants placed 100 cards with statements about personal characteristics into piles ranging from 'not characteristic of me' to 'very characteristic of me', and did so using a forced sort so that the number of cards in the piles corresponded to a normal distribution (i.e., so that 2 cards were placed in pile 0, 4 in pile 1, 6 in pile 2, 12 in pile 3, and so on).

reactive focus Those aspects of a situation to which a research participant is sensitive when engaging in a particular behaviour (e.g., responding to a question). Accordingly, these aspects constitute the basis for any concerns about reactivity that a researcher might have.

repertory grid A qualitative research tool used to gain access to participants' personal constructs. Participants are first asked to identify similarities and differences between elements that are relevant to an aspect of their life. Regularities in the content of these similarities and differences are then used to gain an understanding of the way in which the participants subjectively organize their world (see below for further detail).

verbal protocol A qualitative research tool in which participants introspectively comment on a particular topic and their responses are coded using pre-established guidelines. The most common of these is the 'thinking-aloud protocol' used to gain insight into participants' cognitive processes while performing particular tasks (e.g., playing chess or map reading).

Some general principles for collecting and analysing qualitative data

As we noted at the start of this chapter, one thing that is characteristic of qualitative researchers is their reluctance to adhere to a set of rigidly prescribed practices. Accordingly, there are some particular dangers in attempting to identify general principles that guide the collection and analysis of qualitative data. Indeed, this is because some researchers explicitly reject the idea that there might be any one way of approaching a research question that is inherently superior to others. For example, when discussing certain approaches to qualitative analysis (considered in more detail in Chapter 13), Potter remarks:

> If anything, there is even more variation of method than there is of theory. . . . For many of these approaches indeed, it is not clear that there is anything that would correspond to what psychologists traditionally think of as 'method'. (1996, p. 129)

Nonetheless, most handbooks of qualitative analysis do attempt to provide some guidelines to help researchers make certain sorts of decisions (or at least realize what sorts of decisions they have to make). For example, Yin (1994) discusses five steps for carrying out qualitative case studies and, with some minor adaptation, these can be seen as principles that could reasonably be used to guide most qualitative research. These steps are as follows:

1. *Develop appropriate research questions.* For obvious reasons qualitative research is not particularly useful if a researcher is seeking an answer to an essentially quantitative question (e.g., of the form 'How much?', 'How often?' or 'What proportion?'). Instead qualitative research is far better attuned to 'How do?' and 'Why do?' questions. The rationale for asking such questions also usually rests on

assumptions that (a) research participants are in a position to comment verbally on issues pertaining to the research topic, and/or (b) their comments are in some way relevant to understanding that topic. This would mean, for example, that qualitative research makes much more sense if one's research question is 'How do people feel about being separated from their partners?' rather than 'How do people repress unwanted thoughts?'.

2. *Identify key propositions for the study.* In Chapter 2, we discussed the idea that all research is driven (explicitly or implicitly) by a desire to test (or explore) a set of hypotheses that derive from a particular theory or approach to a topic. Although the focus may change over time (e.g., as a result of participant involvement), the same is generally true of qualitative research. This is because, even where it is exploratory, such research is usually conducted with some scientific purpose or outcome in mind. Stating the purpose of any study in advance is an important means by which its success can ultimately be judged. This is true even if the aims or goals of research are very minimal.

3. *Specify the unit(s) and context(s) of interest.* Although qualitative research typically focuses on the responses of individuals, the goal of research is rarely to find out more about those particular individuals or about individuals in general. Instead, research typically aims to make statements about *classes* of individuals (e.g., older daughters, scientists, chess players) or situations (e.g., organizational cultures, learning regimes, hospital wards). For example, in Reicher and Hopkins' (1996) studies of political leaders, the objective was to make statements about political leadership in general and about the way in which leaders tried to mobilize particular constituents (e.g., by appealing to shared national identity). Specifying the unit(s) and context(s) of interest (in this case political leaders discussing national identity) helps readers to understand the relationship between a particular piece of data (e.g., a response in an interview) and the research project as a whole.

4. *Establish the logic linking the data to the propositions.* Explaining how and why particular pieces of data help achieve particular research objectives is again a vital step in allowing the consumers of research to evaluate its success. The nature of these explanations will vary substantially as a function of the approach to research that is adopted (e.g., whether it is informed by a realist or constructionist philosophy). For example, in realist research a scientist's statement 'If you are an experimenter you know what is important and what is not important' might be used as an indication of the skills that experimenters are believed to have, but in constructionist research this statement could be used to make a claim about the situations in which scientists resort to an empiricist repertoire. Clearly, though, in order for a reader to know what status a particular piece of data has for the researcher, his or her analytical logic needs to be spelled out.

5. *Explain the criteria for interpreting the findings.* In previous chapters we discussed the idea of an alpha level as a benchmark that researchers use in order to decide

whether or not to reject a null hypothesis. Even though no such benchmark exists in qualitative research it is still necessary for researchers to indicate why they favour particular interpretations of their data and why they draw particular conclusions. Usually (but not always) these claims will rely on the detection of *regularities and patterning* within the data (e.g., repeated references to particular events, attempts to give indirect answers to questions under particular circumstances, the use of particular forms of sentence construction by particular groups). These regularities and patterns also usually rely on the detection of similarities and differences (e.g., within and between individuals and situations). In such circumstances the researcher should attempt to explain why any set of regularities and patterns has been singled out for attention. Among other things, this can help to offset claims that these patterns do not exist or that other interpretations of the data are more plausible.

Although the above steps play an important role in qualitative research, it is worth noting that each has a clear analogue in quantitative research. At the same time, as they are presented here, these steps appear to be much more indeterminate than those we have discussed in previous chapters. The idea of an alpha level, for example, represents an evidential criterion that runs through almost all quantitative research, but in the qualitative realm variation in the nature and form of interpretative criteria is immense. In order to illustrate this point, and to show how the above principles can be translated into different forms of research activity, it is therefore useful to consider in more detail some examples of different classical qualitative research methods.

Test Yourself 12.2*

Which of the following procedures would *not* be included in a programme of qualitative research?

a. Assessment of effect size.
b. Development of appropriate research questions.
c. Clarification of the logic linking the data to research propositions.
d. Explanation of criteria for data interpretation.
e. Identification of key propositions.

The correct answer is (a). As noted in Chapters 8, 9 and 10, measurements of effect size are used to make statements about the outcomes of statistical analysis and so they are quantitative rather than qualitative procedures. The other four answers are incorrect, not least because Yin (1994) identifies them as key steps in the process of conducting and reporting qualitative case studies.

Examples of classical qualitative research methods

Adapting schemes suggested by other reviewers (e.g., Henwood & Pidgeon, 1994), qualitative methods can be roughly classified as falling into two main groupings: (a) **classical methods** that generally embrace a philosophy of **realism** that shares many of the same objectives and assumptions as quantitative methods (Henwood & Pidgeon refer to these as *empiricist methods*); and (b) **contextual methods** that differ from quantitative methods in placing more emphasis on the subjective experience and goals of researchers and participants. Contextual qualitative methods will be the focus of Chapter 13 and there we will see that those who employ these methods also tend to endorse a more radical critique of quantitative methods than researchers who use classical qualitative methods. In this chapter, though, we focus on examples of classical research methods – where the research goals and philosophy are broadly compatible with those of the quantitative methods that we have discussed in previous chapters and where researchers bring to their research both a specified set of tools and an explicit framework for interpreting the data they produce.

> **classical qualitative methods** Approaches to qualitative psychological research that (a) accept the utility of the scientific method and (b) endorse – at least in part – the philosophy of realism that suggests that it is possible to detect and characterize accurately features of psychological reality.
>
> **contextual qualitative methods** Approaches to qualitative psychological research that are sensitive to the perspective and experience of participants and researchers as well as to the context in which research takes place.
>
> **realism** A philosophy that suggests that features of the world exist in an objective form that makes them amenable to measurement and definitive characterization.

Repertory grid analysis

The first method we will explore is **repertory grid analysis**. This shares with much other qualitative research a belief that it is important for psychological investigation in a range of domains to tap into the *subjective perspective* or **personal constructs** of participants. Indeed, the repertory grid was devised by the founder of personal construct theory, George Kelly (1955), in order to examine and try to understand how people feel about, and represent, themselves and key features of their world. This methodology has a range of applications that are pertinent to psychological research (and associated psychological interventions). For example, a counselling psychologist may want to understand the way a person feels about their family and friends in order to understand (and manage) family conflict; a social psychologist may want to know how a person feels about people from different cultures or ethnic backgrounds in order to understand (and reduce) prejudice; or an organizational psychologist may want to know how workers feel about various groups at their place of work in order to understand (and modify) aspects of organizational culture.

We can illustrate how these techniques work by considering the example of an organizational psychologist who wants to understand how clinical psychologists in a hospital represent that work environment.

Step 1: Grid construction

A first stage in the analysis requires construction of a grid in which (a) the various aspects of the psychologists' world that the researcher wants to focus on (referred to as *elements*) are listed on the left, (b) different combinations of three elements are identified in separate rows underneath, and (c) two blank columns on the right correspond to each row (these are then used to identify *constructs*). In our example this exercise involves five elements: clients, peers, managers, other health professionals and doctors, as in Table 12.2.

Table 12.2

Elements						Constructs	
Clients	Peers	Managers	Other health professionals	Doctors	row no.	Similarity	Contrast
□	□	□			1	....	....
		□	□	□	2	....	....
□		□		□	3	....	....
□	□		□		4	....	....
	□		□	□	5	....	....

Importantly, grids can be used to examine many different types of element (e.g., people, places, objects) but the elements that are included in any one grid all need to be of a similar type (e.g., all groups, as in this example). Note, though, that a normal grid would also contain about 10 elements and many more three-element combinations, so the example below is somewhat simplified.

Step 2: Identification of similarity and difference constructs in sets of three elements

Having created a grid in this fashion (where the boxes identify the elements in each combination of three), the participant, our clinical psychologist, is first asked to think about the three elements and indicate which two are most similar and which one is most different. For example, in the case of the Row 1 comparison between clients, peers and management, the psychologist might indicate that managers were the 'odd one out', with peers and clients being most similar. Having done this (and marked the responses in the appropriate cells of the grid, e.g., with a tick for the two similar elements and a cross for the one contrast element), the participant is asked to explain what makes the two elements similar to each other and what makes them different from the third element. These explanations can be given simplifying labels and these labels are then written into the blank spaces in the relevant columns on the right (one being the *similarity construct*, the other being the *contrast construct*). In this example, the psychologists might indicate that they think clients and peers are similar in having health-care goals, and that they differ from managers who have financial goals. This process could then be repeated for all the remaining sets of three elements, as in Table 12.3.

Table 12.3

Elements					Constructs		
Clients	Peers	Managers	Other health professionals	Doctors	Row no.	Similarity (✓)	Contrast (✗)
✓	✓	✗			1	Have health-care goals	Have financial goals
	✓		✗	✓	2	Aloof	Team-players
✗	✓			✓	3	Powerful	Powerless
✗		✓	✓		4	Professional	Non-professional
	✓		✓	✗	5	Equal	Superior

Step 3: Identification of similarity and difference in the remaining elements

When each of the three-element combinations has been used as a basis for eliciting constructs, the participant is then asked to indicate which of the two constructs (similarity or contrast) most appropriately describes each of the blank elements in each row (i.e., the elements not included in the original three-element combinations). In our example, the clinical psychologist might indicate that other professionals and doctors both share health-care goals (the similarity construct) and so a tick would be placed in both of these blank cells. This process can then be repeated for the remaining rows of the grid, as in Table 12.4.

Step 4: Grid organization

Having collected data in this way, the researcher's job is now to organize the grid in a coherent fashion. The first stage in this process is to see if there are any sets of rows in which either exactly the same or exactly the opposite pattern of ticks and crosses is found. This process of detecting similarity and difference can be assisted if all the contrast cells are shaded a dark colour as in the following grid. If we look at this, we can see that no two rows are identical but that Row 2 has the opposite pattern of ticks and crosses to Row 5. Effectively, then, these rows

Table 12.4

Clients	Peers	Managers	Other health professionals	Doctors	Row no.	Similarity (✓)	Contrast (✗)
	Elements					Constructs	
✓	✓	✗	✓	✓	1	Have health-care goals	Have financial goals
✗	✗	✓	✗	✓	2	Aloof	Team-players
✗	✓	✓	✗	✓	3	Powerful	Powerless
✗	✓	✗	✓	✓	4	Professional	Non-professional
✓	✓	✗	✓	✗	5	Equal	Superior

can be made identical by changing ticks into crosses and crosses into ticks and reversing the similarity and contrast constructs. We can perform this operation, and indicate that we have completed it by placing an '(R)' (for 'reversed') next to each construct.

The next task is to reorganize the rows *and columns* in the grid so that those that are adjacent to each other have as similar a pattern of crosses and ticks as possible. The result will be something like the grid in Table 12.5.

Table 12.5

Peers	Other health professionals	Clients	Doctors	Managers	Row no.	Similarity (✓)	Contrast (✗)
	Elements					Constructs	
✓	✓	✓	✗	✗	5	Equal	Superior
✓	✓	✓	✗	✗	2	Team-players (R)	Aloof (R)
✓	✓	✓	✓	✗	1	Have health-care goals	Have financial goals
✓	✓	✗	✓	✗	4	Professional	Non-professional
✓	✗	✗	✓	✓	3	Powerful	Powerless

If we look first at the columns in this grid we can see that on the left peers have all ticks and that they are most different from managers on the right (who have mainly crosses). Other health professionals, doctors and clients, with a mixture of ticks and crosses (but different patterns), are in the middle, but other health professionals are closest to peers because they share more identical cells or *matches* (four rather than three), and doctors are closer to managers as they share more matches (three rather than one). Turning then to the rows, those that share the smallest number of matches are at the top and bottom of the grid (i.e., Rows 2 and 5 versus Row 3). As we know, Rows 5 and 2 are in fact identical (after reversing Row 2) and these are at the top. Row 1 is next as it has most matches with Rows 5 and 2 (i.e., four rather than three or two). Row 4 follows as it has most matches with Row 1 (four rather than three). Finally, Row 3 (which has three matches with Row 4 above it) is at the bottom. This procedure leaves us with a grid that is coherently organized and that provides a readily interpretable 'map' of the clinical psychologist's understanding of the groups in his or her workplace. It may be the case, however, that there is some redundancy in this map – especially if multiple constructs appear to be structuring the elements in a very similar way.

Step 5: Grid simplification

As a final (optional) stage in grid analysis the researcher can therefore attempt to reduce the number of constructs by *combining* those which have a similar pattern of ticks and crosses across the various elements. In this example this would definitely seem to be warranted in the case of the constructs 'equal–superior' and 'team-players–aloof' (that share 100% of possible matches) and there might also be a case for combining the constructs 'professional–non-professional' and 'powerful–powerless' (which share 80% of possible matches). If we performed both combinations this would reduce the grid to three sets of constructs: 'equal/team-players–superior/aloof', 'have health-care goals–have financial goals' and 'powerful/professional–powerless/non-professional'.

Having seen how this process of grid reorganization works, you will probably not be surprised to discover that a well-defined set of mathematical operations can be used to guide you through it (these can also be performed using a computer program; Grice, 2002). Details are provided in Kelly's original book, *The psychology of personal constructs* (Kelly, 1955), and in more recent texts such as those by Stewart, Stewart, and Fonda (1981) and Jankowicz (2005). However, at least with simple grids like this, such formal operations can be approximated reasonably well by 'feel'.

It is also worth noting in passing that the procedures involved in structuring and simplifying the grid are conceptually very similar to those involved in a complex statistical procedure known as **factor analysis**. This is typically used as a method of **data reduction** – for example, when researchers want to combine those items in a psychological instrument (e.g., a survey or psychological test) that appear to be measuring similar things. Indeed, although we do not deal with factor analysis in this book, the process of reorganizing repertory grid data provides an excellent intuitive introduction to the operations that this involves (for more detail see Kline, 1994).

In any event, we can see from our example that repertory grid analysis has allowed us to achieve a number of interesting things. Most significantly, it has allowed us to explore some of the complexities of participants' subjective perceptions while at the same time making those complexities intelligible and manageable. In the case of our clinical psychologist we can see, for example, what affinities and oppositions he or she perceives between groups in his or

RESEARCH BITE 12.1
Limitations of repertory grid analysis

In a discussion of some of the challenges of using repertory grid analysis, Mildred Shaw (2011) argues that key problems relate to issues of scaling and simplification. Both arise from the fact that the method does not allow researchers to capture degrees of similarity and difference between constructs, with the result that important information is sometimes lost. She argues that this parallels issues that are encountered with quantitative data when ratings are turned into rankings and when assumptions of equal intervals between scale points are inappropriate. To address some of these issues, she outlines several alternative methods for handling this type of material – including one that involves hand-sorting data into clusters.

Reference
Shaw, M. L. (2011). The analysis of a repertory grid. *British Journal of Medical Psychology*, *53*, 117–126.

her workplace and the core dimensions on which those are defined. The potential uses of such information are considerable, and the repertory grid has a range of theoretical and practical applications. As examples, a researcher (or practitioner) could compare the data above with those obtained from (a) the same person at a different time (e.g., to assess the impact of some organizational intervention), (b) other members of his or her work group (e.g., to see if there is any consensus between personal constructs), or (c) members of other work groups (e.g., to try to characterize the hospital's culture as a whole).

Test Yourself 12.3**

Which of the following is *not* achieved through repertory grid analysis?

    a.   A formal representation of a person's understanding of aspects of their world.
    b.   A representation of reality from a given person's vantage point.

(Continued)

(Continued)

    c.   A structured map of an individual's subjective reality in relation to a phenomenon of interest to a researcher.

    d.   A grid that identifies perceived similarities and differences between elements that contribute to an individual's psychological experience of reality.

    e.   A factor analytic solution.

The correct answer is (e). All of the first four statements are characteristic of repertory grid analysis, and indeed all represent slightly different ways of saying much the same thing – that is, this analysis is a structured way of attempting to capture and map patterns of similarity and difference in a person's representation of an aspect of their experience that are important to them and relevant to a given research question. Although some of the mathematical procedures in analysing repertory grids are similar to factor analysis, the latter is a different (quantitative statistical) procedure.

data reduction The process of simplifying a data set by combining responses on one or more measures.

factor analysis A statistical method of ***data reduction*** that identifies and combines sets of dependent variables that are measuring similar things. The method relies on assessment of the correlations between all dependent variables and extraction of a small number of underlying factors that can be viewed as independent sources of relationships among those variables.

personal constructs The ways in which a person subjectively understands and represents important features of their world. These are typically elicited using ***repertory grid analysis***.

repertory grid analysis A method for summarizing aspects of participants' personal constructs. The core feature of this is a grid that identifies similarities and differences among elements that are judged with reference to dimensions (constructs) generated by the participant.

Content analysis

We can see that repertory grid analysis has a flavour that is not dissimilar to that of the quantitative methods addressed in previous chapters. In large part this is because the method relies on formal operations that are agreed upon by the people who use the method and which can be specified in textbooks like this one. As we noted earlier, the same is true of most other classical methods. In the case of **content analysis** – the method we will now consider – this quantitative flavour is enhanced further by the fact that it serves to *transform* qualitative data into quantitative data that (if desired) can then be subjected to formal statistical analysis.

Content analysis is a method for analysing communication after it has been produced. There are no boundaries to the forms of communication that can be studied – indeed, the method can be applied to the analysis of most forms of behaviour, as most behaviour has some communicative dimension. Importantly, though, records of the communication must exist in some concrete form. This means that if researchers are interested in map-reading ability they might want to examine verbal protocols in which novices and experts are asked to think aloud while performing a map-reading task (e.g., Green & Gilhooly, 1996); if they are interested in gender stereotypes they might want to examine the status and roles of men and women in television advertisements (e.g., Manstead & McCulloch, 1991); if they are interested in genius they might want to examine the memoirs or diaries of exceptional people (e.g., Howe, Davidson, & Sloboda, 1998); and if they are interested in racism they might analyse the websites of White Power and similar groups on the Internet (e.g., Douglas, McGarty, Bliuc, & Lala, 2005). Despite the differences between these various sources of data, there are several discrete steps that researchers need to perform in order to analyse their content (these steps change somewhat when people rely on automated computer programs for analysing content, such as Pennebaker and colleagues' Linguistic Inquiry and Word Count text analysis program; see www.liwc.net/).

Step 1: Specification of sampling domain

The first step is to specify clearly the **sampling domain** from which data are to be gathered. As noted above, the possibilities here are infinite, but a specific and theoretically relevant source of data needs to be identified before research can proceed. As an example, let us imagine that a research team is interested in establishing whether managers of hospitals and managers of industrial companies have different management styles. The researchers' hypothesis might be that hospital managers have a more democratic style and that industrial managers have a more autocratic style, but that these differences have reduced over time.

To investigate this issue the researchers might decide that it would be useful to examine a broad range of managers' communications: their emails or memos to staff, the messages they place on noticeboards, the things they include in the minutes of staff meetings, and so on. Whichever of these is selected, the *precise features* of the domain then need to be specified and justified on theoretical and methodological grounds. The considerations that guide this decision are much the same as those that we discussed in Chapters 4 and 5. In particular, the researchers must endeavour to ensure that the specification of a sampling domain does not introduce systematic bias into the research. If the researchers were to study managers' emails, for example, changes over time might be due to the novelty of the technology rather than management style per se. Some ingenuity is often called for here too. In this case, due to the availability of complete sets of recent and older data and the absence of obvious confounds, the researchers may decide to examine the articles that managing directors write in in-house company magazines. More specifically, they may decide to examine the articles appearing in the magazines of the 20 largest hospitals and the 20 largest industrial companies in the years 1990 and 2010.

Step 2: Development of coding system

The next important stage of analysis is the development of a *coding system*, This involves deciding upon categories or **coding units** that can be used to summarize key features of the data set. In written communication, coding units are typically specific words, phrases or themes. In communication more generally, they may relate to aspects of interaction such as its duration or intensity or the place and space in which it occurs. In this vein, you are probably familiar with the coding units that are used widely in the content analysis of professional sport. For example, analysis of soccer games includes categories such as 'assists', 'shots on goal' and 'passes completed'. Similarly, in our study of managerial style, relevant coding units might include 'favourable references to management decisions', 'favourable references to employee participation' and 'favourable references to teamwork'.

Again (and in contrast to the procedures involved in grounded theory), decisions about the nature of these categories will be devised *before* data analysis begins (but usually on the basis of preliminary examination of the material to be coded) and be driven by both theoretical and methodological considerations. On the one hand, the categories need to be relevant to the theoretical ideas being tested, but at the same time they need to be defined at an appropriate level of abstraction and not to introduce systematic bias into the analysis. For example, if our study of managerial style included the coding unit 'references to share price', it would not be surprising to find more instances of this unit in articles about industrial companies than in articles about hospitals, for the simple reason that hospitals are not normally listed on the stock market. In this case any variation in instances of the coding unit across the two types of organization would therefore not necessarily have anything to do with leadership style.

Step 3: Data coding

Having specified the sampling domain and the coding system, the next phase of content analysis involves the actual coding of data. Here the material in the sampling domain is systematically analysed, with instances of a given coding unit being recorded in a predetermined manner – typically through an entry (e.g., a tick) in the appropriate cell of a coding sheet. Where possible, coding is usually performed *blind* to reduce the possibility of experimenter bias (see Chapter 4). This means that information about the source of data is removed so that it cannot influence coding decisions, and where possible coders should be unaware of the specific hypotheses being tested.

In cases where coding systems are complex and the content of coding categories is open to multiple interpretations, coding will also usually be preceded by some form of *coder training*. During this the criteria for coding, decisions are clarified and potentially difficult decisions are discussed. In such cases it is also customary for *multiple coders* to perform the coding exercise independently before discussing and resolving any disagreement. The level of pre-discussion agreement between coders (generally the relative proportion of coding choices on which they agree or the correlation between their responses) can then be reported as an indication of the reliability of the coding process. Such measures are referred to as **inter-rater reliability** and, generally speaking, the higher this is, the better the coding system is seen to have been.

Step 4: Data analysis and presentation

Once the process of data coding is completed, its final outcomes can then be summarized in a range of ways. For example, in our study of leadership style the data might be presented in terms of either the proportion of companies in which there was at least one instance of a given coding category, as in Table 12.6(a), or the number of instances of a given coding category in each type of company, as in Table 12.6(b).

Table 12.6(a)

	Hospitals		Industrial companies	
	1990	**2010**	**1990**	**2010**
Percentage of articles including favourable references to:				
management decisions	35	65	50	60
employee participation	70	60	35	55
teamwork	15	40	25	45

Table 12.6(b)

	Hospitals		Industrial companies	
	1990	**2010**	**1990**	**2010**
Number of articles including favourable references to:				
management decisions	11	21	15	17
employee participation	32	25	17	28
teamwork	5	14	9	13

As with other quantitative measures (see Chapter 6), it is clear that each of these forms of presentation reveals slightly different patterns and hence serves to tell us slightly different things about the data. Moreover, based on material covered in previous chapters, we can also see that the patterns here can be described in language associated with quantitative analysis and could indeed be subjected to classical forms of statistical analysis. For example, if we look at the data in the top row of Table 12.6(b), there is evidence of a two-way interaction between organization type and year (a pattern discussed in Chapter 10) and the statistical

RESEARCH BITE 12.2
Twitter, 'infoveillance' and 'infodemiology'

Cynthia Chew and Gunther Eysenbach (2010) used content analysis of over 2 million Twitter posts ('tweets') to examine responses to the 2009 flu pandemic. Among other things, they show that use of the term 'N1H1' increased steadily over time (from 9% of tweets in May to 41% in December), and that around 5% of tweets contained misinformation. Tweets were also much more likely to be sent in response to a news story (23%) than to an announcement from a public health agency (2%). The researchers argue that this methodology offers an important and relatively cheap means of gathering 'real-time' information about responses to public health emergencies. Accordingly, they are strong advocates for this method of 'infoveillance' and the discipline of 'infodemiology'.

Reference
Chew, C., & Eysenbach, G. (2010). Pandemics in the age of Twitter: Content analysis of Tweets during the 2009 H1N1 outbreak. *PLoS One*, *5*(11), e14118.

significance of this could be formally established by performing a chi-square test of independence (Chapter 11). The results of content analysis will typically be presented in the body of standard empirical reports in much the same way as the results from the various quantitative methods that we dealt with in previous chapters.

Test Yourself 12.4**

A team of researchers wants to use content analysis to examine the behaviour of people in a crowd. Specifically, the researchers want to examine whether the number of times a person displays anger or frustration depends on the number of other people that are in close proximity. Which of the following statements is *false*?

a. The researchers would want to specify their sampling domain in advance.
b. The researchers might want to use multiple coders to ensure that coding is reliable.

c. The researchers might want to assess the level of inter-rater reliability in categorizing particular displays of emotion as anger or frustration.
d. The researchers would seek to clarify the nature of the coding categories 'anger' and 'frustration' after they have collected their data.
e. The researchers may want to perform statistical analysis on the data they obtain.

The correct answer is (d). This statement is false because in content analysis researchers seek to clarify the nature of coding categories *before* collecting data. In much the same way, as (a) suggests, they should determine in advance exactly where they will be collecting data. As (b) and (c) suggest, the researchers may want to use multiple coders to ensure that there is agreement in use of the coding categories, and then measure that agreement. After collecting their data the researchers are quite likely to want to analyse it statistically (e.g., using a chi-square test of association; thus (e) is true). Note that the activities suggested by (b) and (c) will be of limited use *unless* coding categories are specified in advance. Note, too, that although the data here do relate to an aspect of communication, they could quite easily relate to other forms of behaviour that are not communicative. Indeed, the principal elements of content analysis are very similar to methods used in behavioural observational studies that do not involve communication (e.g., as conducted by animal researchers).

coding units In qualitative analysis, the discrete features of any *sampling domain* (e.g., particular words or phrases) that form the basis of the coding system.

content analysis A method for abstracting meaningful quantitative data from qualitative data that relate to an aspect of communication.

inter-rater reliability The level of agreement between two or more raters when they use a particular coding system to code qualitative data. Examples of inter-rater reliability statistics include Cohen's kappa and Krippendorff's alpha.

sampling domain The sources from which qualitative data are collected and upon which analysis is performed.

Thematic analysis

As you progressed through the above description of the processes involved in content analysis, you may have started to have a sense that this method was not particularly 'qualitative' at all. That is, having being told that researchers typically engage in qualitative analysis so that they can get closer to the phenomena in which they are interested and to the perspective of participants on those phenomena, you may have been disappointed to discover that, in the end, content analysis (and, to a certain extent, repertory grid analysis) looked rather more cold, bare and mechanical than the warm, rich, fluid methodology you were promised. More particularly, you may have wondered whether it is always necessary when starting with material that is nuanced and textured to end up reducing this to some numerical or matrix-like form. Is it not possible to perform an analysis that retains something more of the feel of the original data?

The short answer to this question is 'yes'. Indeed, many qualitative researchers share a concern that methods like repertory grid and content analysis take them too far away from their raw data, deeming them to be further examples (like quantitative methods generally) of unhelpful **reductionism**. As a result, although they are used quite widely (especially content analysis), these are certainly not most qualitative researchers' method of choice. So what, then, is the most commonly used qualitative method? The answer is **thematic analysis**.

As with content analysis, the broad goal of thematic analysis is to take a given **data set** (that may be part of a larger **data corpus**) and abstract its core features for analytic purposes. More specifically (as the name suggests), the goal is to abstract core **analytic themes** – important patterns of information that are contained within a data set that are relevant to the research project at hand. However, rather than doing this with a view to then being able to subject the output to statistical analysis, the output of thematic analysis remains qualitative in form. This means, for example, that if one's data set comprises interviews with office staff about the design of their workspace, then thematic analysis will attempt to identify the key analytic themes that are present in those interviews (Knight, 2009). If one's data set is television and newspaper reports of a riot, then thematic analysis will attempt to identify the key analytic themes that are present in those reports (Reicher & Stott, 2011).

As with the methods we have discussed already, thematic analysis is a data reduction technique designed to render manageable and usable the large amount of information contained within a given data set. However, whereas many other methods can be seen to take the meaning out of this process, the goal of thematic analysis is to try to leave the meaning in (or as much of the meaning as possible) since this is the key reason for wanting to use the method in the first place – to the extent that some people describe thematic analysis as a method for abstracting meaning from data (Braun & Clarke, 2006).

In this regard, there are two key ways in which researchers can use thematic analysis. The first is a **top–down process**, in which they come to the data with a particular theory in mind, and then use that theory as a way of organizing information contained within the data. For example, a researcher may have a theory that suggests that issues of identity are at the heart of communication failure in organizations (Grice, 2005). He or she may then conduct interviews with a large number of people in organizations and seek to abstract a number of themes that speak to this point (e.g., identifying the many different ways in which identity concerns impact upon communication). Alternatively, a researcher may come to a topic with a relatively open mind and use a **bottom–up process** that seeks to let themes 'emerge' from the data (Boyatzis, 1998). For example, someone who is interested in understanding the function of documents in which organizations publicly spell out their purpose and goals (so-called mission statements) may examine a large number of these in order to identify common patterns within them. This may be done with a view to 'staking out' the field and formulating hypotheses that can then inform their own and others' future research (Morphew & Hartley, 2006).

As we will discuss more in the next chapter, a number of researchers have questioned the degree to which it is actually possible for themes to emerge in this way since all researchers come to a topic with assumptions and goals that will to some extent structure their own interpretative work. At minimum, they therefore argue that analysis should develop themes using a hybrid process that incorporates both top–down and bottom–up elements (e.g., Fereday & Muir-Cochrane, 2008). At the same time, it is fair to say that a great deal of thematic analysis treats this issue as largely unproblematic.

This difference in analytic approach speaks to the reality that, because it is employed so widely, thematic analysis assumes a very large range of forms. However, to give some general sense of the way in which it can be used, in what follows we summarize six steps that Braun and Clarke (2006) identify as central to all forms of thematic analysis. We will also illustrate these using a relatively simple example from work by Ryan and colleagues into perceptions of women in leadership positions (Ryan, Haslam, & Postmes, 2007).

Step 1: Data familiarization

The data upon which thematic analyses are performed can be drawn from virtually any source. However, regardless of the nature of the source, and whatever the form of the data, the researchers' first responsibility is to familiarize themselves fully with their content through a process of **immersion**. This involves engaging actively with the data and with their many potential meanings. One good way to start this is to engage in a process of **transcription** that involves turning research material (e.g., recorded interviews) into an accessible written form. Indeed, because the process of immersion is so important, one significant principle of thematic analysis is to ensure that one's capacity to collect data does not outstrip one's capacity to become familiar with the data. Certainly we are aware of many cases in which eager researchers have collected mountains and mountains of data (e.g., in the form of extensive interviews with a multiple participants), only to be faced with the daunting – and ultimately insurmountable – task of trying to get to grips with what they contain. Defining a data set with which one can become familiar is therefore a first priority.

In our example the data set in which we were interested took the form of open-ended responses to a target article on a BBC News website. The article discussed the phenomenon of 'the glass cliff' and described archival research showing that women were more likely to be appointed to leadership positions in companies when those companies were performing poorly than when they were performing well (Ryan & Haslam, 2004). Ryan and her colleague's primary interest was in identifying the various ways in which readers of the website responded to the question 'What do you think leads women to be appointed to "glass cliff" positions?' with a view to gaining insights into the psychology of this phenomenon. So the first phase of this process involved all the researchers reading the online comments (of which there were 164) several times. They then met with each other several times to talk through their reactions and to start distilling their thoughts.

Apart from anything else, this phase of the process helped to increase the researchers' enthusiasm for the project, since key comments were along the lines of 'This data set is really interesting' and 'There is some really good stuff in here.' Textbooks almost never mention the importance of such collective enthusiasm in helping to get research projects off the ground but, in practice, it often proves to be very important indeed. This phase may also yield equally important insights in the opposite direction. We may learn, for example, that we did not ask key questions or that important content is missing.

Step 2: Code generation

Having familiarized yourself with your data, the next step is to start finding ways of organizing the data so as to capture the meaningful features within them that are germane to your research question. In effect, this is a process of 'sorting' in which you try to identify features of the data set that define similarities and differences between the **data items** within it (along the lines of the constructs revealed by repertory grid analysis). If your analysis takes the form of a top–down process, then it is possible that you will have in mind a series of organizing principles (e.g., as suggested by previous theoretical analysis) that you bring to bear on the data and use as a preliminary basis for categorization.

This phase of the process involves identifying discrete examples that seem to exemplify a distinct feature of the data set. Elements with the same feature can then be given the same code, and those that are different can be given a different code. With written texts, this might be achieved by using different coloured pens to highlight different passages of text and then transcribing all those extracts that are highlighted in the same colour onto a card, or putting them on the same page of a word-processing document. Two key points here are that (a) all the data need to be subjected to this analysis, and (b) you need to work through the data carefully and systematically, so as to give every piece of data equal weight. It is also useful to start by identifying as many codes as possible, but then refine the number of these as you go, so as to keep the number of distinct codes manageable.

In Ryan and Haslam's research, this phase of the process was informed by a theoretical sense that participants' responses to the researchers' question were likely to vary along a dimension of perniciousness, such that at one extreme the glass cliff would be seen to reflect processes that were entirely pernicious (i.e., harmful responses such as those seeking to blame female leaders for poor performance due to prejudice against women) and at the other they would be seen to reflect processes that were entirely benign (e.g., women may make better leaders in times of crisis). Accordingly, the initial codes that the researchers developed organized responses into clusters that reflected different levels of perniciousness. As they went through the data, though, it became apparent that responses also differed along a dimension of intentionality. That is, some respondents saw the glass cliff as something that was the result of deliberate strategy (e.g., of discrimination), while others saw it as an accidental by-product of other things (e.g., company policy). This way of organizing the data initially suggested four codes (pernicious intentional; pernicious accidental; benign intentional; benign accidental), but as the process of working through the data progressed, new codes were generated that also reflected quite different forms of response (e.g., a belief that the glass cliff did not exist at all).

Step 3: Search for themes

The third phase of the analytic process involves translating the codes that emerged in the previous phase into discrete analytic themes. A key goal here is to try to *organize* those codes into a logical system of meaningful themes that help you to present a coherent picture of 'what is going on' in the data, and that is ultimately going to prove useful in 'telling the story of the data' to others. This is a step that has similarities with the process of grid organization (Step 4) in repertory grid analysis.

There are several points to bear in mind here. First, this phase involves actively exploring one's data, and so it can be helpful to use methods that help you to work with the data in suitable ways. This could involve putting data onto slips of paper and then putting slips that relate to the same code onto a small tray and then shuffling the trays around on a table. Alternatively one could do much the same thing by creating a table or a set of text boxes in a word-processing file (or in a dedicated qualitative research computer program) and then experimenting by moving those around in various ways. Second, in addition to major themes, material can also be organized into sub-themes. Third, one should aim to retain all data at this stage, and, if necessary, this may involve creating a 'miscellaneous' theme into which data that are too hard to categorize can be placed. Fourth, throughout this process it is important to keep a handle on what exactly the content of the themes is, and this may involve spelling it out in a sentence or two for your own benefit. This is where the initial phase of data immersion also really comes into its own, since the more familiar you are with your data, the easier it is to manipulate it in ways that will ultimately prove useful.

In the case of Ryan's glass cliff research, this process of abstracting themes from participants' comments led to the identification of the five themes in Table 12.7, two of which had sub-themes.

Table 12.7

Theme	Theme content	Sub-theme
Sexism	Sexist men give women bad jobs	
Group dynamics	Women get bad jobs as a by-product of differences in group status	Men given cushy jobs Women expendable Women lack support
Structural factors	Women get bad jobs due to structural realities	Women lack opportunity Women's appointment signals change
Implicit theories	Women get bad jobs because these suit them	
Scientific error	Women don't get bad jobs	

One can see here that the organization of themes retains something of the original coding structure, such that the first themes tend to explain the glass cliff as arising from pernicious processes (reflecting sexism), those in the middle are more neutral, while the last theme sees the research itself as pernicious (reflecting scientific error). Importantly too, in this case (where the researchers had a top–down as well as a bottom–up agenda) the themes also 'make sense' in terms of a range of factors that other researchers had previously identified as being important in this area.

Step 4: Review of themes

The next phase of the process involves looking over the themes that have been identified in the previous phase and critically assessing their capacity to capture the most important features of the data. Related to work in the field of categorization (McGarty, 1999), two important principles that guide this review are the simultaneous need for *intra-theme similarity* and *inter-theme difference* (analogous to what Turner, 1985, refers to as **meta-contrast**). That is, one needs to ask (a) whether there is sufficient similarity among the data that are illustrative of the same theme, and (b) whether there is sufficient difference between data that are illustrative of different themes. If the answer to one or both of these questions is 'no', then this suggests either that one needs to create additional themes (because intra-theme similarity is too low), or that some themes need to be merged (because inter-theme difference is too low).

At this stage of the process it is also useful to think about how one is going to organize the themes that have emerged in one's presentation of them. In this regard, two key options are to do this in the form of either a **thematic table** (like the previous one), or a **thematic map**. These maps themselves can be more or less complex, but the key goal is to communicate the nature of the themes one has identified, together with the nature of the interrelationship between them, in a way that is both accessible and interpretable.

Whether one chooses to create a table or a map depends largely on the requirements of one's presentation. Thus in the paper where they published their research (and where themes were revised from those identified in Step 3 above), Ryan and colleagues (2007) used a table (p. 188). However, in conference presentations they used a map of the form shown in Figure 12.1.

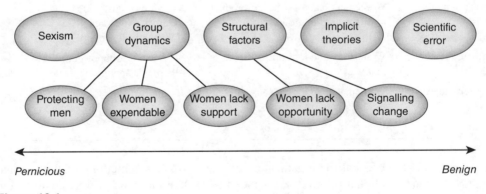

Figure 12.1

Step 5: Theme definition

What one can see as we progress through these steps is that the process of conducting them-atic analysis centres on a process of imposing structure and order on a body of material that can initially appear quite chaotic. As part of this process, the next step involves attempting to describe the content of each of the themes that one has identified in a way that not only captures its meaning, but also allows others to access that meaning as straightforwardly as possible. Together with other things, this will typically involve identifying a short, descriptive name for the theme that captures its content, as well as having a system of names that reflects one's overall analysis.

Among other things, the nature of this phase will depend on who is going to be read-ing your analysis. To take the research of Ryan and colleagues (2007) as an example, their published analysis was largely targeted at social and organizational psychologists who one would expect to be familiar with terms such as 'group dynamics' and 'implicit theories', and for whom these themes thus make sense. However, if one were presenting the analysis to an audience of lay people (e.g., a group of working women) one might want to give the themes more accessible names (e.g., 'women's status in society' and 'people's beliefs about women').

Step 6: Report production

Once one has gone through the previous five steps, the final task is obviously to write up the results of one's analysis in a way that allows readers to make sense of the themes that this pro-cess has identified, of the way that they relate to each other, and of their significance for the topic being investigated. As Braun and Clarke put it, this should 'provide a concise, coherent, logical, non-repetitive and interesting account of the story the data tell – within and across themes' (2006, p. 92).

There are three particularly important elements of this report. First, you must describe the process that you went through in arriving at your final analysis. This is important so that readers can assess for themselves whether that process seems reasonable, and so that, if they wanted, they could conduct the same analysis themselves (either for purposes of rep-lication, or in another piece of work that builds upon your own). Second, the account must be of a form that allows readers to understand how your analysis is relevant to, and helps advance understanding of, key issues in the field. In this sense it should not just *describe* the various themes you have identified, but also *explain* what they mean and why they are important. Third, it is useful to flesh out your analysis by providing **data extracts** that serve to exemplify each of the themes you have identified. Ideally, these extracts should be vivid, intelligible and to the point.

By way of example, this is how Ryan and colleagues discussed the theme of 'sexism' that they identified in their participants' explanations of the glass cliff:

> One of the most straightforward explanations for the tendency to place women in precarious leadership positions might suggest that it is a basic manifestation of sexism in the workplace. Indeed, when asked to generate possible explanations,

outright sexism was favoured by 20 per cent of respondents to the survey. For example, as one respondent wrote:

'I think the Glass Cliff is another form of the Glass Ceiling, intended to block women's passage up the ranks. Women will be put in Glass Cliff positions because there is a resentment of ambitious women who are often seen as threatening or difficult (not just by men) and also because it gives those who appoint them the excuse that they do allow women (superficially) equal opportunities and therefore allows them to avoid any charge of sexism' (Female student, 28). (Ryan et al., 2007, pp. 188–189)

These six steps give some general sense of the way that one can set about the business of conducting thematic analysis. It needs to be stressed, however, that there is no one idealized form that this analysis should take, and hence these steps (as with those that we identified for qualitative analysis more generally) should be taken as guidelines rather than actual rules. What is important, as with all research methods, is that the way you interpret these guidelines is suited both to the particular issue you are addressing and to the particular form of your data, and that it is aligned both with the particular theoretical and empirical goals that you have set yourself and with your general analytic philosophy.

RESEARCH BITE 12.3
Pitfalls of thematic analysis

In their influential review of thematic analysis, Virginia Braun and Victoria Clarke (2006) identify five potential pitfalls that those who use this method can easily fall foul of. These are (a) failing to analyse data thoroughly (or at all!) and simply cobbling together various data extracts; (b) confusing data questions with data themes; (c) performing a weak analysis in which themes lack clarity and coherence; (d) failing to match the content of analysis with the empirical and theoretical claims that are made; and (e) failing to match the form of analysis with the empirical and theoretical claims that are made. Although it can take many different forms, it is a serious mistake, they argue, to assume that this is an 'airy-fairy' method in which 'anything goes'.

Reference
Braun, V., & Clarke, V. (2006). Using thematic analysis in psychology. *Qualitative Research in Psychology*, 3, 77–101.

We will have more to say about this philosophy at the start of the next chapter, but at this juncture there are two further points that it is useful to make. The first is that in many ways thematic analysis is emblematic of, and foundational for, the forms of analysis that are most commonly encountered in qualitative research. The second is that, as we have presented it here, our treatment of thematic analysis is essentially 'classical', in the sense that it is informed by a realist philosophy that imagines that there are objectively knowable features of the world that it can capture and describe. In this it is aligned not only with the other two methods that we have discussed in this chapter, but also with the goals of quantitative analysis more generally. Indeed, again, this means that the outputs of thematic analysis can themselves be fed into quantitative analysis and explored using the various statistical techniques that we discussed in Chapters 6 to 9.

This in fact is what Ryan and colleagues did in their research when they went on to examine which of the themes they identified in respondents' explanations of the glass cliff were more likely to be encountered in the responses of men or women. This meant that the text above was followed by the results of a chi-square analysis:

> In this respect, it is also important to note that gender played an important role in people's explanations, as women were significantly more likely to favour sexist explanations (23.3 per cent) than men (6.5 per cent), $\chi^2(1) = 4.57$, $p = .04$. (Ryan et al., 2007, p. 189)

Nevertheless, thematic analysis does not need to take this quantitative form. Indeed, as we will see in the next chapter, it has spawned a number of variants that explicitly question whether it is appropriate to abstract themes from data in the relatively unproblematic way that we have described here.

Test Yourself 12.5*

Which of the following is *not* required for thematic analysis?

a. A data set.
b. A data item.
c. A data corpus.
d. A data management strategy.
e. Different coding categories for data extracts obtained from male and female participants.

(Continued)

---

analytic themes Within *thematic analysis*, the core patterns that a researcher abstracts from a given *data set* in order to capture the essence of that data set as it relates to the particular research project.

data corpus The entire body of material collected for a particular qualitative project.

data extract Part of a particular *data item*. Within *thematic analysis* this is typically used to illustrate a particular theme.

data item One particular piece of data from within a given *data set*.

data set Those parts of the *data corpus* that are used for a particular qualitative analysis.

immersion The process of engaging closely with a data set over a period of time, so as to become highly familiar with its form, structure and content.

meta-contrast The degree to which a given system of categorization captures both the similarity within categories and the differences between them.

reductionism An approach to scientific research that involves reducing a complex body of information (e.g., about psychological phenomena) to a simpler form.

thematic analysis A method for abstracting *analytic themes* from a given *data set*.

thematic map A diagram that presents a schematic representation of the themes that have emerged from thematic analysis and that organizes these in a coherent and readily interpretable way.

thematic table A table that presents the themes that have emerged from thematic analysis and that organizes these in a coherent and readily interpretable way.

transcription The process of turning research data (e.g., recorded interviews) into an accessible written form.

Critiques of classical qualitative methods

Despite the fact that we have considered details of only three methods, the previous section makes it clear that a broad range of options is available to the researcher who wants to collect and analyse qualitative data. For this reason it is misleading to speak of qualitative research as if it represented a homogeneous approach to data collection and analysis. Nonetheless, it is still quite common for researchers to present blanket objections to qualitative methods on a number of grounds. In this section we will briefly examine the basis and justification for such criticisms as they pertain to classical methods like those that we have just been looking at.

As we noted earlier, the criticism of qualitative methods that is probably encountered most frequently objects to them on grounds *that they are not scientific.* Researchers who hold this view typically argue that, compared with quantitative research, the procedures for quantifying and minimizing methodological and statistical uncertainty in qualitative research are vague and underdeveloped. For example, in experimental research it is possible to design studies that work within established experimental paradigms in which internal and external validity are maximized, and then to conduct statistical analysis through which the significance of those findings can be assessed. In the case of classical qualitative methods, however, it is not always clear how the reliability and validity of findings are established or what methods and criteria should be used to assess them. How do we know, for example, that the grids constructed through a particular repertory grid analysis, or the themes identified in a particular thematic analysis, are the 'right' ones?

In response to this objection, it is possible, first, to suggest that classical qualitative methods (and an associated logic that is invoked in most qualitative research) *would* allow us to answer these questions in ways that are directly analogous to other quantitative methods. For example, one might establish the reliability of a particular repertory grid or thematic analysis by showing that independent coders constructed very similar grids or abstracted very similar themes. Such an approach could also tackle issues of validity in much the same way as quantitative methods by eliminating confounds (e.g., associated with where or how the data were collected), and by having sufficiently large data sets. Issues of generalization could also be addressed through the development of appropriate theory (as argued in Chapter 4).

More generally, though, it is possible to argue that the model of psychological science against which qualitative methods are judged to be deficient is actually misinformed. Indeed, based on detailed analysis of the practices in which research psychologists engage, Woolgar (1988, 1996) suggests that psychological science (in common with all other branches of science) is a much less orderly and formalized activity than idealized versions suggest (e.g., as presented in research articles). So, rather than data 'speaking for themselves', it appears that the form and meaning of data are very much a product of social activity on the part of researchers and their collective decisions about what is important and what is not. Woolgar argues that by these practice-based standards, qualitative methods are no less scientific than quantitative ones.

A second critique of classical qualitative methods is that *they focus on the particular rather than the general* and that this undermines attempts to make far-reaching statements about psychology and behaviour. Human beings and other creatures understand many aspects of their lives by generalizing on the basis of repeated observation. For example, on the basis of experience, we

Photo 12.3 If your main reason for choosing to use qualitative methods is that you think they are quick and easy, then you are in for a nasty surprise.

know that it hurts more when you fall over on concrete than on carpet. As we saw in previous chapters, the quantitative approach is an extension of this approach to the domain of scientific enquiry, but it can be argued that qualitative researchers fail to capitalize on our potential to develop generalizations in this way. This is a reasonable point, but it is possible to make the counter-argument that many important behaviours are unique and generalization therefore risks misinterpretation. Against this, though, it needs to be acknowledged that most qualitative researchers *are* attempting to achieve generalization of some form, and that for this reason it is important that researchers take steps to ensure that their findings have more than just localized status and value. As with quantitative research (see Chapter 4), one way they do this is by developing appropriate *theory*.

A third and final critique of classical qualitative methods is that they are to be distrusted because *they involve taking an easy option*. According to this view, qualitative research is for losers. It is for those who are simply not up to the challenging task of conducting rigorously designed studies and analysing complex numerical data. Unlike the other two criticisms, this view is completely and seriously mistaken. Indeed, in almost every respect, the task of doing good qualitative research is every bit as demanding as that of doing good quantitative research. For example, it takes approximately 10 times as long to transcribe the dialogue from an interview as it does to conduct it, and this means that a typical study that requires this procedure demands over 100 hours of data entry. By comparison, the data from many experiments can be entered in a matter of minutes (or are already stored on computer). Similarly, where most quantitative data analysis can be conducted effortlessly and economically using step-by-step guides or computer programs, the analysis of qualitative data can be a drawn-out procedure that relies upon extensive collaboration with multiple parties (e.g., if independent coders are used in content analysis).

Having said this, it is certainly true that some students turn to qualitative methods because they harbour fears about quantitative techniques and succumb to the myth that a qualitative approach is an easy approach. This, however, is the very worst reason for doing qualitative research and it is destined to end in disappointment of one form or another: either the research process will prove much harder than expected or a fundamental lack of commitment will lead to substandard work.

In summary, then, we would suggest that all but the last of these criticisms have some substance, but that in the case of the first objection there are grounds for levelling similar objections against quantitative methods. While people sometimes fault qualitative research for being unscientific and affording limited psychological insight, it is thus wise to be aware that a great deal of quantitative work is open to the same criticism.

CHECKLIST
Revisiting the key goals for this chapter

☐ I understand the logic of classical qualitative methods and the key principles that underpin their use.

☐ I understand the principles that underpin three classical qualitative methods: repertory grid analysis, content analysis and thematic analysis.

☐ I understand the strengths and weaknesses of classical qualitative methods.

Further reading

In response to the growing interest in qualitative methods in the last few years, a number of edited texts have been put together to provide details and discussions of a range of key developments in this area. There is considerable overlap among these, but the following volumes are well worth reading, and cover methods discussed in this chapter and the next:

Richardson, J. T. E. (Ed.) (1996). *Handbook of qualitative research methods for psychology and the social sciences*. Leicester: BPS Books.
Silverman, D. (Ed.) (2011). *Qualitative research* (3rd ed.). London: SAGE.

The following readings also provide more detailed treatments of the three methods that we have focused on in detail in this chapter:

Braun, V., & Clarke, V. (2006). Using thematic analysis in psychology. *Qualitative Research in Psychology, 3*, 77–101.
Jankowicz, D. (2005). *The easy guide to repertory grids*. Chichester: Wiley.
Krippendorff, K. (2012). *Content analysis: An introduction to its methodology* (3rd ed.). London: SAGE.

Classical qualitative methods: A checklist for research evaluation and improvement

Table 12.8

Potential problem	Question to ask	Potential improvement
Descriptive uncertainty	Does quantitative analysis adequately capture features of the phenomenon that the researchers are investigating?	Consider using qualitative methods in addition to, or as an alternative to, quantitative analysis
Inter-rater reliability	How much correspondence is there in different raters' coding of qualitative data?	Measure inter-rater reliability using an appropriate index (e.g., the probability of agreement in the assignment of data to categories)

Test Yourself 12.6*

Consider the following two reports of a soccer match (from Dey, 1993):

  A: Wimbledon 0 Liverpool 0
  B: 'There was more excitement in the car park than on the pitch'

Which of the following statements is true?

  a. Report A is quantitative, Report B is qualitative.
  b. Both reports are qualitative.
  c. Both reports are quantitative (although one measures the score and the other measures excitement).
  d. Neither report could be used in psychological research.
  e. None of the above.

Test Yourself 12.7***

What is inter-rater reliability?

  a. A measure of the agreement between people coding a given set of qualitative data.
  b. A strategy for ensuring that people who code data are honest.
  c. A measure of the degree to which the personal constructs of researchers have affected their coding.
  d. A measure of the degree to which raters are reliable over time.
  e. The outcome of a process in which reflexive journals are inspected to ensure that researchers have taken account of the subjective meaning of phenomena for participants.

Test Yourself 12.8**

Which of the following statements is true?

  a. It is generally better for a researcher to use one method to collect and analyse data as this avoids confusion.
  b. Researchers who use different methods to examine the same issue are more likely to misrepresent features of the phenomena they are investigating.

c. Good researchers do not have methodological preferences as they are aware that these encourage disagreement and conflict.
d. Qualitative methods are interesting, but they have not had much impact on psychology.
e. None of the above.

The correct answer to 12.6 is (a). Indeed, as Dey (1993) observes, in many ways this simple example exemplifies the difference between quantitative and qualitative methods – since the score line tells one sort of story about a football match while the reporter's quip tells another. Both are informative and useful, but in very different ways, and hence (b) and (c) are wrong. It is certainly the case too that both could be useful for researchers, and so (d) is wrong. For example, the score line might be useful for someone wanting to look at the effect of anxiety on sporting performance (e.g., Rees et al., 2013), while the match report could be interesting to a researcher looking at the different ways in which people disparage groups they do not like (e.g., Holmes & Marra, 2002) or it may even alert us to the possibility that the statement was not ironic because interesting things happen in car parks (e.g., Tilley, 1993).

The correct answer to 12.7 is (a). Inter-rater reliability is used to assess the amount of agreement between coders of qualitative data. Answer (b) is wrong because it cannot measure whether coders are honest; (c) is wrong because the measure does not assess the factors that contribute to agreement or disagreement among coders; and (d) is wrong because the measure examines reliability between raters, not within the same rater. Answer (e) is a nonsense answer that sounds like a procedure that might be used by a grounded theory researcher (see Chapter 13) but is not.

The correct answer to 12.8 is (e). All of the other statements are false. Answers (a) and (b) are wrong because using different methods can actually be a way of eliminating confusion, as it allows researchers to develop a richer understanding of the issues in which they are interested and to reconcile apparently contradictory aspects of their analysis. At the same time, (c) is wrong because all researchers have methodological preferences, and the debate this leads to is often productive and healthy, and (d) is wrong because qualitative methods have always been influential in psychology and they are now more popular than ever.

Discussion/essay questions

a. Why have qualitative techniques increased in popularity in recent years?
b. What are the main reasons for choosing to conduct classical qualitative analysis?
c. Given the many different ways in which classical qualitative analysis can be performed, what factors determine a researcher's decision to use a specific technique?
d. What are the main problems with classical qualitative analysis? Can these be avoided?

Exercises

a. *Repertory grid analysis*

Conduct a repertory grid analysis to try to develop insights into the way that visitors to four different tourist attractions in the area where you live understand their experience. Here the different attractions will constitute the elements, and your goal is to develop an analysis that might be useful for the people who run those attractions in seeking to understand how visitors understand and interact with their 'brand'.

b. *Content analysis*

Obtain copies of all the major national newspapers that are published on a particular day and identify any articles which are related to the topic of mental illness. Your task is to perform content analysis on these in order to see whether there is a difference in the way in which mental illness is characterized (a) in different sections of the papers (e.g., news articles, court reports, feature articles), and (b) in different categories of paper (e.g., broadsheet, tabloid).

   i. What is the sampling domain here? How might it be improved?

   ii. What coding units would you use to code your data?

   iii. How would you ensure that your coding was reliable?

   iv. How would you analyse your data?

c. *Thematic analysis*

Find some people who are passionate supporters of different football teams. Interview them and ask them why they are so passionate about their particular team.

Conduct a thematic analysis to identify and abstract the main themes that run through these accounts going through the six steps identified by Braun and Clarke (2006).

Having done this, identify a series of research questions that are suggested by these themes, and that could form the basis for future research.

Contextual Qualitative Methods

Key goals for this chapter

- Outline the logic of contextual qualitative methods and the key principles that underpin their use.
- Introduce three contextual qualitative methods: grounded theory, interpretative phenomenological analysis (IPA) and discourse analysis.
- Identify the strengths and weaknesses of contextual qualitative methods.

In the previous chapter we examined methods that are premised upon the idea that it is hard to explore and represent the richness of psychological phenomena using numbers alone. In line with this sentiment, advocates of classical qualitative approaches have developed a range of tools that allow researchers to use various forms of analysis to describe and shed light on a range of different things in which psychologists are interested. Here, though, these are arrived at not through the gathering of numerical and statistical information about populations, but through analysis that focuses on trying to capture what people say about the world and how they say it. This clearly involves very different activities from those involved in quantitative analysis (not least because it cannot be conducted using programs such as IBM SPSS Statistics software (SPSS)), but the goal is generally still to identify general laws about human behaviour and the psychological processes and states that underpin it. But what if one considers this goal to be problematic? In particular, what method would you employ if you thought that the only way to understand behaviour was to produce analysis that remains closely tied to the contexts in which it occurred? The answer is that you would probably look to employ a more *contextualist* qualitative method.

A contextual critique of quantitative approaches

As we intimated in the previous chapter, contextualist qualitative methods are informed by a more radical position than the classical methods such as content analysis and repertory grid analysis. This suggests that qualitative researchers need to doing something altogether incompatible with quantitative goals and practices.

There are different components of this radical critique that not all researchers subscribe to, but three are widely discussed in various forms and arenas. First among these is an objection to the philosophy of realism (or **positivism**) that can be seen to underpin most quantitative research. As we touched on briefly in the previous chapter, realism reflects the view that is usually implicit in psychological research: that there is a set of objective psychological facts 'out there' awaiting 'discovery' by suitably trained researchers. For example, if a researcher sets out to test the theory that 'absence makes the heart grow fonder' or that 'memory declines with reduced attention', he or she implicitly assumes that there is something in the world that corresponds straightforwardly to 'fondness' or 'memory' (i.e., that these are DVs which can be measured objectively), and, by the same token, that there is something that he or she can do in the world that corresponds straightforwardly to a manipulation of 'absence' or 'attention' (i.e., that these are IVs which can be manipulated objectively).

Radical critics of quantitative methods reject these assumptions. In particular, they argue that features of the world only exist as a result of a set of meanings that are actively *constructed* by communities within it (e.g., scientists, students, Westerners). From this perspective, what 'counts' as 'fondness', 'memory', 'absence' or 'attention' can be seen to depend on who you are and where you fit into the social structure. Fondness, for example, might mean different things to a young person and an old person, and memory might mean different things to a cognitive psychologist and a person on the street. This means that fondness and attention are things that can be displayed and achieved in different ways by different communities, and that to understand whether or not they have been achieved one must understand and take the perspective of the particular community in question.

From this viewpoint, then, there is no such thing as an objective psychological fact, and the process of discovery is essentially one that involves conferring novel meanings on particular experiences. Having found that people react negatively to strong advertising campaigns, a researcher may claim to have discovered evidence of a 'rebound process', but one could actually argue that the researcher (and those who accept the discovery) has merely come to interpret a particular set of events in a new way and that other equally valid interpretations of this finding are possible (e.g., that it is an example of a 'threat process' or a 'denial process'). One can also suggest that these alternative interpretations have just as much claim to validity and indeed are just as likely to find favour at some time in the future – for example, if people from a different sector of the research community become powerful. Indeed, this argument is consistent with Kuhn's view that science moves forward through paradigm shifts, rather than progress-in-the-abstract, and through the development of *different* understandings, not necessarily *better* ones (see Chapter 2).

The above objections are consistent with philosophies of **idealism, constructionism/ constructivism, relativism** or (more loosely) **postmodernism**. Although these are all different approaches, broadly speaking, these are united by the view that no uniquely valid interpretation of the world is possible, for the simple reason that multiple interpretations of it exist and each appears equally valid when looked at from the perspective of the interpreter. If it is true that 'one man's meat is another man's poison', how can psychological reactions to a piece of pork be understood other than by reference to the subjective reality of the person who is asked to eat it? In other words, we cannot know whether pork is meat or poison without endeavouring to find out something about the cultural world of the would-be eater.

Arguments of this form contribute to a second component of the radical critique that involves a rejection of researchers' general drive to develop population-level laws of cause and effect. This is sometimes referred to as a **nomothetic approach** (a term introduced to psychology by Gordon Allport, 1937, who borrowed it from the German philosopher Wilhelm Windelband). Against this, and for reasons that follow from the above arguments, there are researchers who argue instead for an approach that attempts to understand the behaviour of individuals in the contexts where it occurs without seeking to elevate any such understanding to the status of a universal law (this is sometimes referred to as an **idiographic approach**).

We can illustrate this point with reference to a team of researchers who reject the 'classical' goal of striving to conduct studies that might ostensibly allow them to conclude that 'absence makes the heart grow fonder'. As a qualitative alternative, these researchers might conduct a study of two groups of people who were separated from their partners (e.g., overseas students and workers on an oil rig) and try (a) to identify the different meaning that separation assumed for each group (or sub-groups within them) and (b) to show how these different meanings are an aspect of different conceptions of what love is and what relationships are for. On the basis of such investigations, rather than concluding that absence makes the heart grow fonder (or that it does so only for a particular group in particular circumstances, as a more complex ANOVA design might suggest), the researchers might conclude instead that the ability to feel fondly towards one's partner when separated from him or her is dependent upon an ability to experience absence in a particular way, and that this ability is constructed or avoided within particular communities and by particular people in order to achieve particular objectives (e.g., to be seen to be 'doing romantic love' or 'doing masculinity'; Haule, 2010). Expressing a feeling that absence does or does not makes one's heart grow fonder (as one might do by circling either '7' or '2' on a questionnaire) might, for a male, be understood as a way of constructing oneself as a 'sensitive new-age guy' or a 'hard man' in order to have a particular sort of relationship with one's partner (which might then be used to legitimate or explain a whole host of other behaviours).

This, we can see, is an altogether different answer from that which emerges from standard quantitative research – in form, content and function. Among other things, it means that while a quantitative researcher might feel qualified on the basis of his or her research to give you a very short answer to the question 'If my partner goes overseas will she love me more or less when she returns?', a qualitative researcher is more likely to sit you down and start by asking 'Well, what exactly do you mean by love?'. The qualitative researcher might also want to move away from considering love as a variable and start thinking about the ways in which 'the idea of love' is used in everyday interaction.

RESEARCH BITE 13.1
(Re)populating psychological research

One of the key themes in the work of the British psychologist Mick Billig has been a concern with the 'depopulated' nature of psychology texts. In particular, he questions writing practices that treat participants as interchangeable voiceless entities. These, he argues, strip participants of agency and encourage researchers to imagine that the people who take part in their studies are merely passive consumers of research materials, rather than engaged contributors trying to make sense of their experience and to communicate nuanced points through their various responses. He also argues that this treatment – and the associated use of jargon – can reduce scientific understanding and precision rather than increase it.

Reference
Billig, M. (2011). Writing social psychology: Fictional things and unpopulated texts. *British Journal of Social Psychology, 50*, 4–20.

Developing these arguments further, a third and final point on which the radical critique argues against quantitative approaches is in its explicit recognition of the researcher's *involvement* in the research process and the interpretation of its outcomes, together with an associated belief that the products of scientific enquiry may only have *subjective*, not objective, validity. Such objections are targeted at a range of practices commonly associated with quantitative methods, but are most clearly expressed in an opposition to the standard practices for writing up research findings. If, for example, one reads the sample research report in Appendix A (entitled 'The Role of Children's Perceived Sex in Judgements of Their Emotions'), it is clear that it is written in a very detached style and tells the story of what was done and what was found in a dispassionate way. As a result, the facts appear to emerge as the consequence of a cold scientific process from which the wishes, beliefs and values of the researcher have been totally expunged. In fact, though, it seems reasonable to assume that these wishes, beliefs and values had a considerable role to play in the research and that, as aspects of the scientific process, they are just as important as the ones we conventionally report (and may be even more important; see Spears & Smith, 2001). For example, the fact that we chose to test a particular theory in a particular way might have depended upon our relationship with the proponents of that theory (do we see them as allies or opponents?), our personal ambitions (will doing this research help us to become famous or to receive more research funding?), and our political views (do we object to the theory on ideological grounds?). However, none of these issues is addressed in the report and a reader who was familiar with conventions in psychology would not expect them to be.

In important ways such factors mean that the outcomes of research *are* contingent upon researchers' own perspectives and objectives, and the apparent denial of this is something that many qualitative researchers object to. Among other things, this means that they are motivated to discover new ways of reporting psychological research that clearly identify their own role in the research process and which explicitly present their conclusions as *an* interpretation of the data, not *the only* interpretation. These points of divergence between quantitative and contextual qualitative research are summarized in Table 13.1.

Table 13.1 Distinguishing features of quantitative (and classical qualitative) and contextual qualitative research

	Quantitative (and classical qualitative)	Contextual qualitative
Distinguishing features		
Underlying philosophy	Positivist, realist	Relativist, constructionist
Goals of analysis	Nomothetic (oriented to discovery of universal causal laws)	Idiographic (oriented to understanding behaviour in its local context)
Products of analysis	Reliable, stable relationships between variables	Potentially variable meanings and rules
Application of findings	General	Particular
Stance assumed by researchers	Detached	Involved
Assumed status of analytical products	Objective	Potentially subjective

As presented in Table 13.1, the radical differences between quantitative (and classical qualitative) and qualitative research appear to be rather stark. However, it is important to note that in practice the distinction between the two is not so black and white. This is for at least three reasons. First, not all those who use contextualist qualitative methods endorse a radical critique (or, if they do, they only embrace certain parts of it). Second, many quantitative (and classical qualitative) researchers are sympathetic to the issues that this critique raises and try to display sensitivity to it in their research practice and theorizing (e.g., see Spears & Smith, 2001). And finally, as we discuss in the next sections, while contextualist qualitative methods are definitely different from both quantitative research and classical qualitative research, these differences are not always as marked as one might expect.

Test Yourself 13.1*

Which of the following is *not* associated with a postmodern approach to psychological research?

    a. Idealism.
    b. Realism.
    c. Constructivism.
    d. Relativism.
    e. Constructionism.

The correct answer is (b). In general, a postmodern approach to psychological research is *anti*-realist (and anti-positivist), which is to say it rejects the idea that science can produce objective knowledge about the world. In contrast, a postmodern approach can encompass idealism (suggesting that scientific activity and knowledge are subjective; so (a) is wrong), constructivism and constructionism (suggesting that meaning is actively constructed by members of a particular community; so (c) and (e) are wrong), and relativism (suggesting that there is no such thing as universal objective truth; so (d) is wrong).

constructionism/constructivism Philosophies that suggest that meaning and reality do not exist in a fixed form external to the perceiver, but rather are actively constructed by members of a particular community in order to achieve particular objectives. Although very similar, these two philosophies have slightly different nuances. In particular, constructivism can refer to an analytic approach that is based on examination of the way in which different realities are created.

idealism A philosophy that suggests that features of the world are created through the subjective act of perceiving the world and hence are not amenable to measurement or definitive characterization.

idiographic approach An approach to research that attempts to develop person-specific analyses of phenomena in the particular context in which they arise. This is not oriented to the discovery of universal causal laws (of the form 'A always leads to B').

nomothetic approach An approach to research that attempts to develop class-wide analyses of phenomena that apply generally to members of a given group or population. This is oriented to the discovery of universal causal laws (of the form 'A always leads to B').

positivism An approach to science that assumes that scientific activity produces (and should aim to produce) knowledge about objectively present and knowable features of the world.

postmodernism In popular (and rather loose) usage, a philosophy that embraces the tenets of idealism, relativism and constructivism in arguing that the constructs of value and worth are entirely dependent on the perspective of the judge and therefore that they are impossible to establish objectively.

relativism A philosophy which asserts that there is no such thing as universal objective truth. Instead it is asserted that different interpretative frameworks and perspectives create their own truths and that no absolute criteria exist for differentiating between these in order to establish their validity.

Examples of contextual qualitative research methods

A common feature of contextual qualitative methods is that in attending to the meanings that participants give to their own behaviour they are generally sceptical about the prospects of using *pre-existing tools* (e.g., as associated with the qualitative methods that we discussed in Chapter 12) to uncover that meaning. Instead, as a result of the idealistic philosophy they embrace, both approaches suggest that research methodology needs to be flexible and *participant driven*, rather than a prescribed formula or set of rules. At the same time, they also typically encourage researchers to display **reflexivity** by reflecting on their own role in the research process and the way in which they may contribute to the production of the particular patterns of behaviour that participants display (Henwood & Pidgeon, 1992; Wetherell, 2008).

Nevertheless, there are important differences between different contextual methods. Most particularly, following Henwood and Pidgeon (1994), one can differentiate between **contextualist methods**, which assume that theoretical understanding can be imposed upon, and abstracted from, the various contexts in which research is conducted, and **constructionist/constructivist methods**, which argue that meaning is contained within the context itself, and needs to be retained through attention to that context rather than abstraction from it.

constructionist/constructivist methods Approaches to psychological research which embrace a philosophy of constructionism/constructivism. Among other things, they (a) reject the scientific method as a means of developing psychological knowledge and (b) involve research and theorizing which attempt to understand, but not go beyond, the perspective and experience of participants.

contextualist methods Approaches to psychological research in which reliance on scientific method is tempered by an emphasis on developing theory that is sensitive to the perspective and experience of both participants and researchers as well as to the context in which research takes place.

reflexivity The process through which a researcher reflects on his or her own role in producing particular research outcomes.

Grounded theory

One of the ways in which constructionist approaches differ from conventional quantitative methods is in taking seriously the perspective of participants and in focusing on their under-standings of the world rather than seeking to impose the (often different) understandings of the experimenter on the data that those participants provide. Contextualist approaches share an emphasis on the perspective and interests of participants, but seek to *reconcile* this with the scientific goals of the researcher rather than to see the scientific process of theory develop-ment as inherently flawed or restrictive.

The clearest example of this is probably provided by **grounded theory**. In this (as the name suggests) researchers attempt to develop analyses of psychological topics that are *grounded* in participants' localized experiences of relevant phenomena. A particular concern of researchers who use this method is to attempt to lay bare the various processes through which psychological theory is developed. They attempt, in particular, to identify any biases, prejudices, predispositions or hunches that they bring into the experiment and to document how these are supported or challenged by particular research findings. In this way, analysis of a particular phenomenon is presented as it emerges through what Pidgeon and Henwood (1997, p. 255) describe as the dynamic '"flip flop" between ideas and research experience'.

It is worth noting that there are a number of different ways of working with grounded theory. These range from those that are more realist in treating participants' input as relat-ively unproblematic (and that are therefore very similar to thematic analysis, as discussed in the previous chapter) to those that are more constructionist in being sensitive to the multiple meanings and purposes that participants' input can have. In all cases, though, the research involves discrete phases of (a) data gathering, (b) data coding, (c) data organization and (d) data analysis. The last of these phases focuses on refinement, manipulation and manage-ment of the data.

To provide a concrete example of the method and the steps that involves, we can look at some pertinent aspects of a study by Pidgeon and Henwood in which they explored engineers' assessment and management of risk during a project that involved handling hazardous waste (for more detail, see Pidgeon & Henwood, 1997).

Step 1: Data gathering

Data gathering focuses on attempts to gather a rich and varied set of materials that relate to the issue in question. The core materials that Pidgeon and Henwood focused on took the form of semi-structured interviews with various people working on the hazardous waste project that were subsequently transcribed in detail. An example of a paragraph from one such transcript is as follows:

A. Paragraph from an interview relating to Hazardous Waste case-study Interviews, 27 April

Paragraph 8

I don't think there is any doubt that on this job I readily accepted the advice of the civil engineering consultant, L, and didn't have the experience to question that advice adequately. I was not aware of the appropriate site investigation procedure, and was more than willing to be seduced by the idea that we could cut corners to save money.

Step 2: Development of coding system

Having gathered data in this form, the researcher's next task is to develop an appropriate **coding system** for it. This involves identifying key concepts in the text that are perceived (a) to be relevant to the issue at hand and (b) to be useful for the purpose of cross-referencing ideas and ultimately abstracting key themes and ideas. In the above example such indexing might take the following form:

> B. Significant concepts identified within paragraphs
>
> Interview S
>
> Paragraph 8
>
> ACCEPTING PROFESSIONAL ADVICE
>
> CRITICIZING OTHERS' WORK
>
> CUTTING CORNERS
>
> EXPERIENCE

The most important feature of such concepts is that they should **fit** the data by providing an appropriate representation of it. Again, as with thematic analysis, this issue of fit can be seen to hinge in large part on abstracting concepts that have an appropriate amount of *meta-contrast* – being neither too specific nor too general. For this reason the concepts should not be predetermined, but be devised through a process of **open coding** as the research progresses.

Step 3: Development of concept cards

After multiple pieces of data have been indexed in this way, the researcher is then able to examine the different ways in which concepts (e.g., 'cutting corners') are used across the data set as a whole. This can be done on a **concept card** that lists *variants* of concept use across the data set as a whole. For this to occur, though, the concepts have to have been defined at an appropriate level of abstraction (not too specific, not too general), and, where necessary, the researcher has to go back to refine the coding system he or she has employed. In this case, a coding card (that need not be a card at all but could be a computer record) might have the following form:

> CARD 22 CUTTING CORNERS
>
> S Para 8   S said he was not aware of the appropriate site investigation procedures, and was willing to be seduced by the idea of cutting corners to save money.

T Para 12	G said he couldn't be bothered taking the time to do a neat job with the labels as nobody appreciated it anyway.
W Para 29	W's recollection of an instruction from a manager that he should save time by not checking whether concrete was permeable.

Precisely because this process of refining data handling is a subjective one (i.e., one that is based on the researcher's own interpretations of the data), and this subjectivity will clearly have a role to play in the conclusions that the researcher eventually draws, grounded theorists recommend that records be kept of the processes that guide data management and interpretation. These can take the form of memos or a **reflexive journal** that explains why particular decisions were made and allows these to be retrieved at a later date. An example of such a memo might be as follows:

MEMO

18 July 2002 by A. Researcher on Splitting CUTTING CORNERS

I decided to split the concept Cutting Corners into two concepts: Cutting corners due to external pressure (Card 232), and Cutting corners as a personal choice (Card 233) because the original concept was too cumbersome and broad. It also appeared that this distinction could be useful analytically because cutting corners due to external pressure seemed to be associated with decisions that related to core aspects of the project (e.g., chemical tests of concrete) whereas cutting corners due to personal choice seemed to relate to more superficial decisions (e.g., putting labels on neatly). This is seen in a comparison of T para 12 with T para 32 and W para 22 with W para 29.

Having completed a concept card (perhaps because adding more entries no longer adds any richness to the information it contains and the category it describes is said to have become *saturated*), the researcher then attempts to develop the analysis further by identifying the particular features that give a particular card its coherence. This can be done by attempting to define the coding concept itself, again in the form of a memo. In our engineering example, this might take the following form:

DEFINITION FOR CARD 232

CUTTING CORNERS DUE TO EXTERNAL PRESSURE

Many participants (particularly junior ones) refer to a perceived need to cut corners on vital parts of the project due to external pressure. This generally occurred in order to save either time or money. Pressure is usually implicit and only rarely explicit. Implicit pressure is seen to be part of a general culture of economy that the project managers reinforce in various ways (e.g., through timesheets, costings, budget meetings). It is also reflected in references to fear of being ridiculed (e.g., for being slow or fussy). External pressures are thus subtle, and hard to pin down but easy for managers to deny.

Step 4: Rationalization and analysis of concepts

Having attempted to summarize the data on one card (possibly by defining the concept that it relates to), advanced stages of analysis then involve the researcher attempting to draw links between cards and to integrate the emergent concepts at a higher level.

This can involve at least three things: (a) the identification of general themes that unite and distinguish between multiple concepts (as in thematic analysis; see Chapter 12); (b) the development of analytic **taxonomies** (i.e., classification schemes that help to organize concepts); or (c) the clarification of relationships among concepts. Again, a key goal here is to maximize *fit* by ensuring that any analysis retains its fidelity by imposing structure on it that, on the one hand, is not so general that it loses contact with the specifics of the data that you have gone to great pains to explore in detail, and, on the other hand, is not so specific that opportunities to abstract important generalities are overlooked.

Step 5: Report production

Having gone through this process, your final task is to produce a research report that allows others to benefit from your work. In many ways this will resemble the procedures for reporting the results of thematic analysis that were described in the previous chapter. However, in the case of grounded theory, two specific goals remain paramount: (a) *documentation* of decisions relating to the analysis that allow the research process to be interrogated and audited; and (b) sensitivity to issues of *reflexivity* that demonstrate awareness of the role that the researcher's subjective decisions played in the analysis. In other words, the report needs to remain faithful to the *grounded* nature of the method itself.

In relation to all of these activities and goals, a residual question that you may be asking yourself is 'How will I know when any analysis is good enough?'. In other words, when does any analysis contain enough documentation, enough reflexivity and enough fit? Partly because it incorporates some of the idealist philosophy of constructionists, these questions are hard to answer in the abstract (in the way that we could when performing a *t*-test, say). Nonetheless, grounded theorists do assert that the method has the potential to take researchers' understanding of psychological processes forward, and that whether or not it does can be established with reference to a number of criteria. Among other things, these can include assessment of whether the research (a) leads to the development of *novel* understanding of relevant issues, (b) helps develop understanding that is (to some extent) *transferable* from one content domain to another, and (c) is validated, and perceived to be useful, by the research participants themselves. For example, the study of risk management in engineering projects might be perceived to have been worthwhile if it suggests that a particular type of organizational culture is a major contributor to accidents, and this is perceived to be useful by engineers themselves and helps them to eliminate accidents across a range of industries in future.

Whether or not grounded theory achieves these various aims also depends in part on the degree to which one engages fully with its idealist philosophy. As Braun and Clarke (2006) note, in practice, many researchers use 'grounded theory lite' as a method for organizing data and abstracting its key themes – so that, in effect, they are really conducting a fancy form of thematic analysis (and potentially not that fancy). This is all well and good, but it needs to be recognized that 'full-cream' grounded theory research involves being wary of researchers' attempts to impose meaning on reality without a full interrogation of the processes this involves and of the damage it can do to participants' localized understandings of their world.

Test Yourself 13.2**

What is the role of a reflexive journal in grounded theory?

a. To record data that are collected in the field, but that need to be analysed at a later stage, once the researcher has had an opportunity to reflect on them.
b. To allow participants to record their own thoughts and feelings about the research process – in particular, aspects of it that they are uncomfortable with and that they can discuss with the researcher later.
c. To allow researchers to record their thoughts about the research process, so that the rationale for their decisions is recoverable at some later stage.
d. To allow researchers and participants to reflect upon each others' activity so that differences in their perspective can be reconciled by a third party.
e. To record specific features of the physical environment that reflect on the research process as a whole, but that might be omitted from quantitative analysis.

The correct answer is (c). Reflexive journals are used by researchers that the processes that lead them to collect and interpret data in particular ways are available for examination at a later stage. This is intended to ensure that decisions and activities that have a bearing on research outcomes (and which can help to explain why data have a particular form) are recoverable after data have been collected. Although they all sound plausible, each of the other answers is wrong: (a) is wrong because reflexive journals are not used to record data; (b) and (d) are wrong because they are not used by participants (though other forms of research journals or diaries may be); and (e) is wrong because, while it might discuss features of the environment that bear upon a researcher's decisions, those features are not its primary focus.

coding system In qualitative analysis, the categories used to summarize key features of a data set.

concept card A card that lists the various ways in which a concept (or theme) has been used within a given data set.

fit In *grounded theory*, the degree to which any aspect of analysis is an appropriate and recognizable description of the phenomena under investigation.

grounded theory A qualitative research practice in which understanding of a phenomenon is inductively derived from studying that phenomenon from the perspective of those to whom it is relevant. In this way, the researcher does not begin with a theory and then test it; instead, theory is discovered, developed and provisionally verified as it emerges from systematic examination of data.

open coding In *grounded theory*, the process of developing coding concepts and categories that fit the data as closely as possible. For this reason, such concepts are not predetermined but evolve over the course of the coding process.

reflexive journal A researcher's record of thoughts and activities that relate to the research process. Among other things, this is intended to provide insight into the decisions that guide data management.

taxonomy A classification scheme used to summarize and organize information.

Interpretative phenomenological analysis (IPA)

We noted in the previous chapter that qualitative researchers often adopt a hermeneutic approach, in which they seek to explore particular psychological phenomena by understanding the meaning that those phenomena have for people who encounter them. Another way of saying this is to observe that qualitative researchers are often interested in the **phenomenology** of psychological experience. What does it mean to be in love? What does it feel like to be depressed? Yet having asked such questions, concerns with issues of reflexivity might also lead to a secondary question – that is, how are researchers' understandings of the meaning that given phenomena have for people affected by the meaning that those phenomena have for the researchers themselves?

To return to one of the examples that has run throughout this book, as researchers, we may be interested in what 'love' means to you. And to investigate this question we may ask you lots of questions seeking to explore your thoughts about love – questions such as 'How does the way you love your mother differ from the way you love your partner?'. However, when one looks at this question, it is clear that there are a number of assumptions bound up within it that have led us to ask it in this way and which will therefore have consequences for the answers we get. Among other things, the logic of the question implies that there is a difference between these two forms of love (Grice, 1975), and in most contexts you would probably assume that we are not seeking to explore issues of incest. Clearly, though, this might depend on whether or not we were interested in Freudian processes of psychodynamic attraction (e.g., the Oedipus complex; Kulish & Holtzman, 2010), and whether or not you thought we were. Furthermore, the type of answer that you gave to such a question is likely to vary considerably depending on whether we asked it in a psychology class, in a counselling session, or on a bus where one of us just happened to be sitting next to you. In particular, in the former situation you might give us a relatively 'straight' answer, but in the latter case you might tell us to mind our own business – or worse.

The critical point to note here, then, is that the type of response you would give to the question (and your behaviour more generally) is bound up in both the meaning of the situation for you and the meaning of the situation for the researcher. This is what researchers refer to as a **double hermeneutic**, and a core goal of **interpretative phenomenological analysis** (which from now on we will refer as **IPA**) is to try to explore the ways in which these are involved in the meaning that experiences assume for research participants in the world at large. In this regard, the method is intimately concerned with the people's sense-making activities as they seek to understand the world around them and to act meaningfully within it.

As with all the other methods that we have discussed in this and the previous chapter, the process of performing IPA can be formalized in terms of a series of discrete steps, and we can illustrate these with reference to a particular research example. In this case, we will look at work by Clare (2003) that examined the way in which people who have been diagnosed with dementia experience changes in their sense of self as the disease advances and their memory starts to deteriorate.

Step 1: Definition of research question and sample

The process of conducting IPA focuses on the process of conducting in-depth interviews with a small number of research participants whose experiences are directly relevant to the topic that you want to research. The key goal is then to use these interviews as a means of trying to discover and understand how people make sense of a particular set of experiences within their social world. In this regard, the researcher is meant to try to approach the interviews – and the topic as a whole – with questions that are broad and open. Indeed, the method is perhaps best seen as a tool of hypothesis generation rather than hypothesis testing, and that is best suited to early phases of theory development in which relatively little is known about the issues under investigation.

Because, as we will see, the process of conducting IPA is intensive and time consuming, the method places an emphasis on interview quality rather than quantity. Also, rather than trying to find a broad, diverse or random population to study, the goal is to identify a small homogeneous sample that has direct experience of the topic in question. Indeed, some analyses take the form of single case studies, and very few involve more than a dozen. Building on the insights of Kelly's (1955) personal construct theory, Smith and Osborn (2003) have argued that three is an ideal sample size, since this allows researchers to explore similarities and differences within interviews in a manner akin to the process of examining sets of three elements in repertory grid analysis (see Chapter 12).

Clare's study in fact involved a relatively large sample of 12 Alzheimer's patients who were attending a memory clinic in the south of England. All were living at home with a partner or spouse, and all performed poorly on a standard test of cognitive functioning commonly used to inform dementia diagnosis.

Step 2: Data collection and transcription

The preferred method for collecting data upon which to perform IPA is the **semi-structured interview**. A **structured interview** is one in which a predetermined set of questions is asked in a predetermined sequence, and researchers endeavour to stay as close as possible to a given **interview schedule** in order to maintain consistency and hence increase the integrity and reliability of data. In effect, this involves taking a person through a survey like those that we discussed in Chapter 5, rather than having them complete it by themselves. In contrast, a semi-structured interview is considerably more flexible and should take the form of a conversation rather than an inquisition. Questions should thus be (a) open rather than closed (e.g., 'How are you feeling?' is preferable to 'Are you feeling sick?'); (b) asked one at a time rather than be double-barrelled (e.g., 'Has your memory changed?' followed, if the answer is 'yes', by 'How does this make you feel?', is preferable to 'Has your memory deteriorated and made you angry?'); (c) neutral rather than value laden (e.g., 'How has your personality changed?' is preferable to 'Have you become aggressive?'); and (d) couched in lay terms rather than jargon (e.g., 'Is the doctor giving you any drugs?' is better than 'Are you taking NMDA receptor antagonists?').

A key goal of early questions is to develop rapport with interviewees so that they feel comfortable and free to explore the topic in ways that they see fit. Rather, then, than positioning themselves as the authority on the topic in question, researchers are encouraged to see and treat the interviewee as the expert.

In preparing for the interview, the researcher needs to identify a number of key issues that he or she wants to explore and to organize these in some logical fashion. Typically this will start with relatively general and non-threatening questions that allow the interviewee to ease into the topic, but then delves deeper as the interview progresses. In this regard, the structure of the interview can be seen to resemble a funnel in which questions start at a relatively abstract level (e.g., 'How are you feeling?') but become increasingly specific ('Do you feel that your ability to remember things is changing?', 'Does this affect your relationship with your partner?', 'Does it affect your sense of who you are'?).

At every stage the goal is to probe the topic gently rather than to fixate on an explicit agenda. If the participant finds questions hard to answer, it is also useful to have thought about a series of prompts that might reframe the question and make it easier to answer. There is also no requirement for interviews to proceed in a linear fashion, and when digressions are initiated by the interviewee it can be useful to explore these and then return to prepared questions later, if necessary. You will also need to record your interview, so it is important to get the interviewee's permission to do this, and to ensure that he or she is comfortable about this and all other aspects of the interview process.

Once you have conducted your interviews, you then need to transcribe them. As we noted at the end of the previous chapter, this is a time-consuming and painstaking process, as it involves recording not only what the interviewee and an interviewer said, but also any other significant features of the interaction – for example, pauses, laughs or external interruptions. For example, part of the transcript in Linda Clare's research might have looked like this (where L = Linda and I = Interviewee; based on Clare, 2003, p. 1022):

L: Do you feel that your ability to remember things is changing?

I: Yes. Definitely. (looks away).

L: How do you think it is changing?

I: It's just getting a whole lot worse. . . . I mean sometimes I forget really stupid things. Daft things. Things I never used to forget. (pause)

L: How do these changes affect you?

I: The changes ... I think you're half aware of them and not quite sure what was going on, if anything was going on, maybe like when you're getting older that's well, so what? Um but then as it speeded up ... I'd think, I wish I wasn't like this ... and then my wife began to notice things as well and I thought, well there's something wrong even if she's not always right ... and that was the business where we said, OK, let's try and get down to it and see the doctor.

Step 3: Identification of themes in the first case

The process of data analysis involves trying to identify units and patterns of meaning in respondents' accounts of phenomena within their psychological world (that accounts for the P in IPA). However, this is an engaged interpretative act on the part of the researcher rather than a passive mechanical one (that accounts for the I), and there are many ways of setting about this task.

However, Smith and Osborn (2003) recommend that researchers start by working with one of their interviews and familiarizing themselves fully with what it contains through a process of careful reading and rereading. In the process of doing this, you should start to make notes on the text by remarking on things within it that seem to be worthy of comment. Again, there are no rules about what these notes should refer to: they might be comments on the use of language, on the way in which a person talks about themselves, or on internal consistencies and inconsistencies. Having done this, you should then work through the text again and try to identify themes that start to tie together some of these various comments, and to organize them in meaningful ways and at a higher level of abstraction – always bearing in mind that it is the participants' meanings you are trying to capture, not your own.

One can see here how a range of initial notes on the left have been transformed into concise phrases on the right that capture what appear to be key themes within the text. As with both grounded theory and thematic analysis, the skill here centres on identifying themes that have sufficient *meta-contrast*: being abstract enough to allow you to identify similarities

L: Do you feel that your ability to remember things is changing?

Shame   I: Yes. Definitely. (looks away).

L: How do you think it is changing?

Anger?   I: It's just getting a whole lot worse . . . I mean sometimes I forget really stupid things. Daft things. Things I never used to forget. (pause)

Starts to   L: How do these changes affect you?
notice

I: The changes… I think you're half aware of them and not quite sure what was
Validation   going on, if anything was going on, maybe like when you're getting older   *REGISTERING*
by close   that's well, so what? Um but then as it speeded up…. I'd think, I wish I wasn't
other   like this … and then my wife began to notice things as well and I thought, well
triggers   there's something wrong even if she's not always right … and that was the   *REACTING*
action   business where we said, OK, let's try and get down to it and see the doctor.

across different parts of the text, but specific enough to remain faithful to the meaningful differences within it.

Step 4: Organization of themes

Once you have been through the first interview and identified key themes within it, the next step involves trying to organize these in ways that do justice to what participants had to say about the topic in question, but which also impose structure and order upon their accounts. This will typically involve three distinct phases. The first involves *clustering* themes that appear to go together and, if it appears appropriate, combining them. The second involves *ordering* themes in ways that meaningfully communicate the logic of participants' experiences – for example, as these unfolded over time or across different settings. Finally, the themes should be presented in a table that presents the themes in a coherent fashion, and in a way that is amenable to interpretation by others.

In Clare's study she identified five key processes that older adults with Alzheimer's discussed in their accounts of their difficulties: registering, reacting, explaining, experiencing and adjusting. However, she also noted that the way respondents engaged with these varied, so that sometimes they tried to protect themselves from the threat that memory changes caused and at others they tried to engage with that threat. This meant that she was able to organize the themes as in Table 13.2.

Step 5: Examination of themes in subsequent cases

As noted above, it is possible to conduct IPA on a single case, in which case you could wrap up the analysis at this point. It is more common, though, to continue by working through

Table 13.2

Process	Self-maintaining theme	Self-adjusting theme
Registering	Uncertainty	Acknowledging
Reacting	Minimizing	Disintegrating
Explaining	Normalizing	Switching the wires
Experiencing	Putting on a protective coating	Spending time in the depths
Adjusting	Holding on, compensating	Fighting, accepting

subsequent cases (e.g., the second and third interviews in cases where you have conducted three) in order to both validate and refine your initial analysis. Smith and Osborn (2003) recommend that researchers do this by starting from scratch with each interview and repeating Steps 3 and 4 with each. When this is complete, you should then look for patterns of convergence and divergence across the cases as a whole, again with a view to organizing the themes that have been identified in meaningful ways. This can involve either reconciling the themes across the different cases (as Clare, 2003, did – so that the above table was seen to capture the experiences of all her participants), or else presenting an analysis that exposes variations in the themes and their structure across those cases.

Step 6: Report production

As with all the other methods we have discussed, the final step of IPA involves the production of a research report. In basic terms, this needs to document the process that you have gone through, to describe what you have found, and to discuss the significance of your findings for the topic in question. However, with IPA, as with grounded theory, special attention needs to be paid to the role of the researcher in the research process as a whole and to the process through which participants' experiences have been interpreted.

This sensitivity can be seen in the Discussion of the paper in which Clare (2003, p. 1025) reported her findings, where she concludes:

> The participants' accounts demonstrate the complex processes involved in the expression of awareness of memory problems and other changes in early stage AD. All participants acknowledged having problems with memory, and some were able to describe the gradual process of becoming aware of these; thus, none of the participants could be said to be entirely unaware. Participants made varying judgements, however, about the meaning or impact of their memory problems, expressed a range of emotional responses, and engaged in different strategies as they attempted to cope and adjust. . . . There were, in addition, indications of the way in which the interview context sometimes influenced responses. Contact with professionals had important implications, too; both a lack of information and a very blunt presentation of the diagnosis could result in self-maintaining strategies and thus apparent unawareness. Awareness was evident or not in participants' accounts of five multi-faceted processes ...

However, as with grounded theory, one nagging question that you may be left with concerns the degree to which the method can ever live up to its aspirations. Can researchers ever really come to a question with an open mind? Can this analysis (or any other) ever really disentangle the phenomenology of participants from the phenomenology of researchers? Is this really what they are trying to do when they write up their reports?

Regardless of how one answers such questions, an important contribution of IPA (and of grounded theory) is to bring these interpretative issues into play and make them a legitimate focus for psychological enquiry. Nevertheless, for many commentators – particularly those who embrace a hard-line constructionist philosophy – the approach simply does not go far enough. To really come to grips with the constructed nature of psychological reality, they argue, one needs to engage much more closely with the construction process itself.

> **double hermeneutic** A feature of the research process that reflects the fact that attempts to discover the meaning of phenomena for participants is necessarily bound up with the meaning that they have for researchers.

> **interpretative phenomenological analysis (IPA)** A research method that attempts to discover the meaning of phenomena for participants, but that also recognizes – and attempts to do justice to the fact – that this is necessarily bound up with the meaning that those phenomena have for researchers.

RESEARCH BITE 13.2
Double hermeneutic or half hermeneutic?

IPA has become increasingly popular in recent years, especially in the fields of clinical and health psychology. In a review of this work, Joanna Brocki and Alison Wearden (2006) identify 52 papers that have used IPA to explore the phenomenology of various medical conditions and other health-related issues. They note that an attraction of the method is that it allows researchers to delve into patients' experience of illness rather than to fixate on issues of cause and effect. But they also note that research papers pay scant attention to the researchers' own interpretative role in the research process. In this, sensitivity to the double hermeneutic appears to be more an ideal than a reality.

Reference
Brocki, J. M., & Wearden, A. J. (2006). A critical evaluation of the use of interpretative phenomenological analysis (IPA) in health psychology. *Psychology and Health, 21*, 87–108.

interview schedule The plan for an interview that provides details of the issues that a researcher wants to explore and the questions that the researcher wants to ask. It may also include details of prompts to be used in the event that a question proves difficult for an interviewee to answer.

phenomenology The meaning that a given phenomenon has for the people who experience it.

semi-structured interview An interview in which a researcher has a predetermined set of questions to ask, but where the interviewer does not necessarily stick to these or ask them in a particular sequence. Instead, the interview itself is conducted in a naturalistic and conversational manner that puts the interviewee at ease and facilitates rapport between interviewer and interviewee.

structured interview An interview in which a predetermined set of questions is asked in a predetermined sequence. The goal is to maximize consistency across interviews and ensure that all participants have a similar experience.

Test Yourself 13.3*

In devising an interview schedule for a study that will involve interpretative phenomenological analysis (IPA), which of the following should one try to include?

a. Double-barrelled questions
b. Jargon
c. Open questions
d. Value-laden questions
e. Offensive questions.

The correct answer is (c). A goal of the semi-structured interviews that are used as a basis for IPA is to explore the respondents' experience of a relevant phenomenon in a broad and open fashion. This is done by letting them take the lead and go where they want to – something that open (rather than closed) questions (of the form used in structured interviews) allow for. Answer (a) is wrong because double-barrelled questions should be avoided in all interviews (and surveys) because they make answers hard to interpret. Answer (b) is wrong because jargon will often create a sense of distance between interviewer and interviewee and this is something that IPA seeks to reduce. Answer (d) is wrong because value-laden questions can induce reactivity and lead the interviewee to answer in particular ways (e.g., to say what they think the interviewer wants to hear). If the interviewee does not share the interviewer's values this may also undermine rapport. Finally, (e) is incorrect because all interviews (and surveys) should avoid offensive questions. Apart from anything else, this is because interviews need to conform to ethical principles and show respect for participants (a point we will discuss in more depth in Chapter 14).

Discourse analysis

As suggested above, constructionist approaches are among the most controversial in psychology for the simple reason that they are founded upon a rejection of the scientific method as it is typically understood and applied in research. Indeed, rather than developing (or trying to develop) hypotheses about psychological states and processes and seeking to test these in empirical studies, constructionists see the empirical method itself as a medium for constructing particular meanings in order to achieve particular objectives – for example, to be seen as a scientist and to be seen to be 'doing science'. In this way, where another psychologist might seek to abstract meaning from quantitative or qualitative data in order to test and develop theory (so that the data are essentially a theoretical *resource*), constructionists see the process of abstracting meaning as a *topic* in itself. For this reason, constructionist methods focus very much on the fine-grained qualities of language itself, rather than seeking to abstract other forms of data from it.

Discourse analysis is possibly the clearest example of this practice. Among other things, it is commonly used to inspect the character of naturally occurring discourse in order to discover subtle (and typically undetected) features of it that allow people to achieve particular ends. Almost any form of language can be used for this purpose: conversations, discussions, speeches, advertising campaigns, the text of a dog licence, the instructions for using a food processor.

Where the analytical material takes the form of spoken language, this is usually reported using a standardized transcription system. Aspects of this system are illustrated by the following text reported by Potter (1997, p. 151) and transcribed from a famous BBC interview of Princess Diana by Martin Bashir:

Bashir:	Did you (.) allow your ↑friends, >your close friends,<
	to speak to °Andrew Morton°?
Princess:	Yes I did. [Yes I did.
Bashir:	[°Why°?
Princess:	I was (.) at the end of my tether (.)
	I was (.) <u>desp</u>erate (.)
	>I think I was so fed up with being< (.)
	seen as someone who was a bas:ket case (.)
	because I am a very strong person (.)
	and I <u>kn</u>ow (.) that causes complications, (.)
	in the system (.) that I live in.
	(1.0) ((smiles and purses lips))
Bashir:	How would a book change that?
Princess:	→ I ↑dunno. ((raises eyebrows, looks away))

> Maybe people have a better understanding (.)
>
> maybe there's a lot of women out there
>
> who <u>suff</u>er (.) on the same level
>
> but in a different environment (.)
>
> who are unable to: (.) stand up for themselves (.)
>
> because their esteem is (.) cut into two.
>
> → I dunno ((shakes head))

In this text (.) refers to a pause of less than 0.2 seconds, (1.0) refers to a pause of 1 second, ↑ indicates raised pitch, > and < surround talk that is noticeably faster, °s surround talk that is noticeably lower in volume, : indicates a lengthening of the preceding sound, [indicates where talk starts to overlap, underlining indicates stress or emphasis, (( )) surround transcriber's comments, and → points to lines that are referred to in the researcher's commentary on the text.

We can see that the transcription system makes the text relatively hard to read. At the same time, though, once the reader is reasonably familiar with transcription conventions, the system makes it possible to recover precise features of dialogue (e.g., intonation, pitch, speed) that would otherwise be unavailable for scrutiny. And in this particular case, the method allows the researcher (Potter) to make a detailed examination of the role that the two instances of 'I dunno' play for the person who uttered them.

Two points are relevant here. First, it is clear that the utterance 'I dunno' could easily pass without note if it had not been subjected to detailed transcription of this form. This would be particularly true if the researcher who was recording the dialogue was concerned only to note its substantive content, as an 'I dunno' could easily be seen as trivial and irrelevant. Second, though, even if the researcher did note the presence of 'I dunno', from a realist perspective it is likely that it would be interpreted as a *literal* representation of the speaker's cognitions. In effect, then, it could be treated in the same way as a response of '1' on a five-point scale which asked the question 'Do you know why this book would help your cause?' and 1 represented a response of 'not at all' and 5 a response of 'very definitely'.

Against such literal interpretations of data (whether qualitative or quantitative), discourse analysts note that any single response can have a range of potential meanings. For example, when asked the question 'Did you enjoy yourself?', the response 'Oh, absolutely!' (a '5' on a five-point scale perhaps) could be meant to be taken literally, but it could also be intended to be ironic, sarcastic, witty or half-hearted. How can quantitative (or empiricist qualitative) methods differentiate between these various meanings? Constructionists argue that they cannot and therefore insist that attempts at interpreting language and behaviour need to be tied firmly to the contexts of production. Their methods therefore focus on identifying those various features that ensure that responses and interaction have the particular meanings that they do.

Here, too, any hypotheses are intended to emerge *from* the data rather than to be *taken into* the data-gathering exercise. For example, in the case of 'I dunno' Potter suggests that this serves as a form of 'stake inoculation' in which the speaker expresses ignorance in order to deflect potential accusations that she engaged in particular behaviour (telling her friends to contribute to a book that was critical of the royal family) for self-serving or malicious reasons. Having made this assertion, the researcher can then examine other transcripts to find evidence (a) of the same construction ('I dunno') being used for the same purposes, (b) of the same construction being used for different purposes, or (c) of different constructions being used for the same purposes. Other aspects of the same or different transcripts – especially those that are contradictory or inconsistent – can also be used to shed light on the meaning and function of such a construction. For example, were Diana to indicate in some other discourse that she knew exactly why Andrew Morton's book would help her cause, this might suggest that her use of 'I dunno' in the interview transcribed above was not a reflection of genuine ignorance (although it is worth noting in passing that this logic in fact embodies some realist assumptions – specifically that ignorance, or anything else for that matter, can be authenticated as 'genuine').

The broad function of such analysis is to show how language is used actively and creatively by participants to achieve complex social goals (e.g., representing oneself positively and other people negatively), and, as a corollary, to show that an understanding of how those goals are achieved is impossible without detailed analysis of discourse. At a theoretical level it also serves to critique psychological (and other) research that treats language as a uniform, neutral and literal conduit for the transmission of information.

There is no finite set of ways in which discourse analysis can be performed and no prescribed set of methods by which means it should be conducted. For this reason it would be a foolhardy exercise to try to identify discrete steps that one should go through in order to conduct the analysis, in the way that we have with preceding methods. Indeed, some (but not all) of its proponents suggest that providing such prescriptions may lead them into the positivist trap of privileging one interpretation of a text or an interaction when many are usually possible and valid. For this reason, discourse analysts describe the method as a 'craft skill' akin to riding a bicycle: hard to learn and hard to describe (e.g., Potter, 1997, pp. 147–148). Nonetheless, like riding a bicycle, discourse analysis is seen as something that one can do badly or do well, and it is very definitely not a method where 'anything goes'. The question of whether this fact is incompatible with the idealist philosophy that often informs the approach is one we will return to later in the context of a broader philosophical reflection on the range of complex analytical issues that this chapter has brought to the fore.

discourse analysis A constructionist practice that involves the fine-grained analysis of language. By this means researchers focus on how language does more than merely describe the world or relay information, but is used instead to achieve complex social objectives in particular contexts.

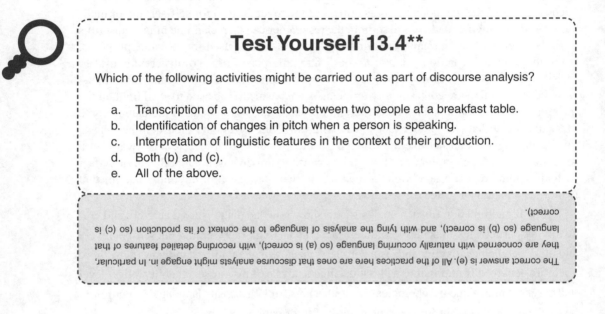

Test Yourself 13.4**

Which of the following activities might be carried out as part of discourse analysis?

a. Transcription of a conversation between two people at a breakfast table.
b. Identification of changes in pitch when a person is speaking.
c. Interpretation of linguistic features in the context of their production.
d. Both (b) and (c).
e. All of the above.

The correct answer is (e). All of the practices here are ones that discourse analysts might engage in. In particular, they are concerned with naturally occurring language (so (a) is correct), with recording detailed features of that language (so (b) is correct), and with tying the analysis of language to the context of its production (so (c) is correct).

Critiques of contextual qualitative methods

In the previous chapter we discussed three key criticisms that are often levelled against classical qualitative methods: first, that they are unscientific; second, that they focus on the particular rather than the general; third, that they are an easy option. These same three criticisms are often made in relation to contextual qualitative methods. For example, a critic may ask how we know that Princess Diana's use of 'I dunno' represents a stake inoculator rather than a statement of genuine ignorance, an habitual response to a difficult question, or a verbal tic. And he or she may also ask on what grounds we would use this finding as a basis for generalization to other contexts. Likewise, he or she might object that fine-grained attention to something like the Diana interview risks losing sight of general truths by attending only to those that are very specific. And, finally, he or she may say that because such data can be collected while watching television, this research is far too easy to conduct to be considered serious science.

It is possible to respond to all three of these criticisms in much the same way as we did in the previous chapter. First, one could make the point that, if one so desired, one could use contextualist qualitative methods in much the same way as other quantitative methods. Such analysis might, for example, show that Princess Diana used the phrase 'I dunno' much more commonly after a question in which her personal motives were questioned than when other types of difficult question were posed – and, indeed, such logic is often implicit in the sorts of research that discourse analysis and other contextual qualitative researchers conduct. Second, issues of generalization could also be addressed through the development of appropriate theory (as argued in Chapter 4), while at the same time observing that many phenomena of interest to psychologists are quite unique. After all, there will only ever be one Diana interview. Third, it is again a colossal mistake to imagine that the methods and techniques we have examined in this chapter are easy to apply and master. They are not. More generally too, one should also recognize that the model of science against which contextual qualitative methods are routinely contrasted is itself very limited – and indeed this is a point that the methods themselves have been used, with powerful effect, to demonstrate (e.g., see Gilbert & Mulkay, 1984; Woolgar, 1988, 1996).

There are, however, two additional criticisms of contextual qualitative methods that do not apply to the classical methods we considered in the previous chapter. The first of these is that *they do not tell us much about psychology*, but are really only useful as tools of philosophical, sociological or linguistic analysis. This criticism is targeted mainly at constructionist approaches such as discourse analysis, and it is one that many researchers in this tradition would themselves accept. However, as with debate about the scientific credentials of qualitative research, such researchers would also question whether quantitative and classical qualitative approaches are really exploring underlying psychological processes in the unproblematic way that their proponents suggest. Rather, because almost all windows onto psychological states and processes involve the use of language of some form (either in participants' responses or researchers' interpretations), constructionists would argue that psychological research is essentially a social activity that serves merely to favour and formalize particular *accounts* of psychological processes. For this reason, constructionists would argue that it makes a lot more sense to draw on ideas from other fields that are concerned with understanding language (e.g., sociology, linguistics, philosophy) than to focus on psychology as if it were a self-contained island of knowledge and wisdom.

A second particular criticism of contextual qualitative methods is that *they fall foul of their own logic*. Again, this criticism is focused mainly on constructionist methods, with critics here observing that, although they are not always perfect, quantitative methods at least lay down specific criteria by which research procedures and outcomes can be judged. In the case of the three methods we have discussed in this chapter, how would we know whether the method had been performed well or badly, successfully or unsuccessfully – especially if one contends that all understandings of psychological processes are equally valid? And to which guidelines could we appeal if we disagreed with another researcher's assessment of our work? We alluded to this point above when noting that discourse analysts sometimes compare the method with riding a bicycle – something for which the instructions cannot be spelled out but which nevertheless people clearly succeed or fail at (Potter, 1997). The problem here, though, is that this response appears to rely on a level of realism that the approach itself rejects. Certainly, in suggesting that meaning and validity are relative constructions that can be gauged only from the perspective of the participant, but that research products can (and should) be recognized as successful or unsuccessful, constructionists have been accused of wanting to have their cake and eat it.

Conclusion: The challenge of contextual qualitative methods

Although it is common for textbooks like this one to address quantitative and qualitative research techniques in different chapters, the above discussion points to some of the serious problems of this strategy. First among these is the fact that the distinction between quantitative and qualitative approaches is much less clear than one might imagine. Indeed, as we have seen, the differences between discourse analysis and other qualitative methods are in many ways much more pronounced than those between those qualitative methods and standard quantitative methods. For this reason any approach to psychological research that is informed by a conviction that quantitative research is uniformly good and qualitative research is uniformly bad (or vice versa) is very foolish. Instead, it seems more productive to recognize that the quality of one's research is not defined by the method one uses, but rather by one's ability to use a method appropriate to the question one is interested in answering. Hence, a researcher who has the capacity to use qualitative methods cleverly when they are suited to the research question at hand will always be a better researcher than one who cannot.

The benefits of being able to draw upon multiple methods are well illustrated by the work of Reicher and his colleagues on crowd behaviour. In order to develop a rounded theoretical analysis of this phenomenon, this research has involved experiments that manipulate key theoretical variables (Reicher, 1984a), observational studies of crowds (e.g., Reicher, 1984b), content analysis of participants' statements (e.g., Stott, Hutchinson, & Drury, 2001) and discourse analysis of such statements (Potter & Reicher, 1987). So, rather than falling prey to **methodolatry** (Reicher, 2000), Reicher's work speaks to the manifold advantages of **methodological pluralism**.

This is not to say that a researcher should not have a preference for one or other approach, or that most (or all) of one's research should not rely on a single method. There is nothing wrong with preferring quantitative to qualitative research (or vice versa), or in doing research that is mainly or exclusively quantitative (or qualitative). What we would suggest, however, is that it is a mistake to advocate one or another approach without considering both how your research might be enhanced by taking an alternative approach and how you would respond to criticism of your research that might be levelled against it by advocates of an alternative approach.

Formulating responses to potential criticisms of your own work is important for at least two reasons. First, this is because it is likely that at some stage in your career your work will be exposed to criticism from researchers who embrace philosophies and methodologies that differ from yours. At that time you will need to mount a thoughtful defence of your research strategy. But this will be difficult to do convincingly if you have not reflected critically on the issues raised in this chapter – thorny though many of these are. Second, these considerations are important because the process of conducting research to address criticisms of your work that are informed by the sorts of issues that we have discussed in this chapter is one of the best ways of taking that work forward.

Science does not progress because its practitioners cocoon themselves from ideas that they find threatening and hard to deal with. Instead it progresses when (and if) researchers are prepared to rise to the challenges created by productive intellectual tension. Qualitative research plays an important role in psychological science by creating tensions of exactly this form. For this reason alone, the challenges it lays down are well worth taking seriously and well worth responding to.

RESEARCH BITE 13.3
Experiments as paradigms of power

In a thought-provoking examination of the way experiments 'work', Russell Spears and Heather Smith (2001) argue that all experiments are 'paradigms of power' in which the production of particular results is to some extent contingent upon participants accepting the authority of the experimenter to define the experimental situation in particular ways. For this reason, results are likely to be affected by specific forms of accountability within a particular experiment (e.g., participants' sense of being under surveillance by the experimenter). The authors argue that when explaining experimental results, experimenters therefore need to take a more reflexive perspective on their own role in eliciting particular patterns of data.

Reference
Spears, R., & Smith, H. J. (2001). Experiments as politics. *Political Psychology*, 22, 309–330.

methodolatry A dogmatic approach to research methods that argues that one method (or set of methods, e.g., those that are quantitative) is inherently superior to all others.

methodological pluralism An approach to research methods that argues that researchers need to be able to use different types of research method in order to answer different types of research question.

CHECKLIST
Revisiting the key goals for this chapter

☐ I understand the logic of contextual qualitative methods and the key principles that underpin their use.

☐ I understand the principles that underpin three contextual qualitative methods: grounded theory, interpretative phenomenological analysis (IPA) and discourse analysis.

☐ I understand the strengths and weaknesses of classical qualitative methods.

Further reading

The following chapters provide reasonably concise (and highly cited) introductions to the three methods that we have covered in this chapter and to the various issues that they raise. These will also direct you to a range of more comprehensive texts if you are keen to explore a particular method in greater depth.

Potter, J. (2004). Discourse analysis. In M. Hardy & A. Bryman (Eds.), *Handbook of data analysis* (pp. 607–624). London: SAGE.

Smith, J. A., & Osborn, M. (2003). Interpretative phenomenological analysis. In J. A. Smith (Ed.), *Qualitative psychology: A practical guide to research methods* (2nd ed.) (pp. 51–80). London: SAGE.

Strauss, A., & Corbin, J. (1994). Grounded theory methodology: An overview. In N. K. Denzin & Y. S. Lincoln (Eds.), *Handbook of qualitative research* (pp. 273–285). Thousand Oaks, CA: SAGE.

Contextual qualitative methods: A checklist for research evaluation and improvement

Table 13.3

Potential problem	Question to ask	Potential improvement
Participant involvement	Do participants share and/or value the researchers' understanding of the phenomenon they are investigating?	Consider using qualitative methods in which the participants are more directly involved in the research process (e.g., grounded theory).
Positivism/realism	Is it the case that features of the world do not exist in a form that makes them amenable to decontextualized description and measurement?	Consider using methods that attend to contextual variation in phenomena (including qualitative methods such as discourse analysis).
Idealism/constructivism/ relativism/postmodernism	Is it the case that features of the world (including contextual variation) can be made amenable to description and measurement?	Consider using methods that involve description and measurement (including various qualitative methods such as content analysis and grounded theory).

Test Yourself 13.5*

A team of researchers investigating young people's attitudes to marriage favours a contextualist approach to qualitative research in which commitment to the scientific method places emphasis on the perspective of participants and researchers and features of the research context. Which of the following approaches is most likely to appeal to the researchers?

a. Content analysis.
b. Analysis of contextual variance.
c. Grounded theory.
d. Discourse analysis.
e. Repertory grid analysis.

(Continued)

(Continued)

Test Yourself 13.6**

Which of the following qualitative methods does not require coding categories (e.g., themes and concepts) to be defined at an appropriate level – such that they are neither too specific nor too general?

a. Thematic analysis.
b. Grounded theory.
c. IPA.
d. Discourse analysis.
e. None of the above (all incorporate this requirement).

Test Yourself 13.7**

Which of the following statements is true?

a. It is generally better for a researcher to use one method to collect and analyse data as this avoids confusion.
b. Researchers who use different methods to examine the same issue are more likely to misrepresent features of the phenomena they are investigating.
c. Good researchers do not have methodological preferences as they are aware that these encourage disagreement and conflict.
d. Qualitative methods are interesting, but they have not had much impact on psychology.
e. None of the above.

The correct answer to 13.5 is (c). Grounded theory is a contextualist approach that attempts to combine use of scientific method with sensitivity to human and environmental factors that bear upon the process of data collection and interpretation. Answer (a) is wrong because content analysis is a realist method that does not place emphasis on participants' own views; (b) is wrong because, although it has an authentic ring to it, there is no such thing as analysis of contextual variance; (d) is wrong because discourse analysis is a constructionist method that questions the utility of scientific method; and (e) is wrong because, while it tries to capture the participants' perspective on phenomena of interest (i.e., their personal constructs), repertory grid analysis is not generally used to place emphasis on the context in which such constructs are elicited.

The correct answer to 13.6 is (d). A key reason for this (and why (e) is wrong) is that discourse analysis argues that researchers should not seek to abstract categories from research data in the way that most other methods do. Answer (a) is wrong because, as we saw in the previous chapter, thematic analysis requires themes to be defined in such a way that they simultaneously maximize intra-theme similarity and inter-theme difference. Answer (b) is wrong because grounded theory incorporates a similar idea within its concept of fit, and (c) is wrong because IPA been influential in psychology and they are now more popular than ever.

debate this leads to is often productive and healthy. Answer (d) is wrong because qualitative methods have always

analysis. At the same time, (c) is wrong because almost all researchers have methodological preferences, and the

understanding of the issues in which they are interested and to reconcile apparently contradictory aspects of their

different methods can actually be a way of eliminating confusion as it allows researchers to develop a richer

The correct answer to 13.7 is (e). All of these statements are false. Answers (a) and (b) are wrong because using

and IPA all suggest that coding categories need to have an optimal level of *meta-contrast*.

general nor too specific. These answers can be summarized by observing that thematic analysis, grounded theory

also argues that researchers need to identify themes that organize their interpretations in ways that are neither too

Discussion/essay questions

a. What are the main differences between different forms of contextual qualitative analysis?
b. Do classical qualitative methods have more in common with quantitative analysis than they do with contextual qualitative methods?
c. Is the proliferation of contextualist qualitative methods a problem?

Exercises

a. *Grounded theory*

Conduct a search of national newspapers to find articles on the topic of health, and specifically the question of how health funds are allocated (e.g., in cases where particular patients require expensive treatment). Analyse these articles using grounded theory in order to characterize the nature of this debate.

  i. Use open coding to develop a coding system comprising coding categories that capture the ways in which this topic is treated. Stay very close to the meaning of sentences – avoid too much abstraction at this stage. Note also that at this stage the label for coding categories will only be provisional. As other examples of a concept come up, you may find you need to change the label in order to provide a better 'fit' to the data.

 ii. Identify links between the coding categories and concepts that provide structure to debate in this area.

iii. What conclusions emerge from this analysis concerning the way in which decisions about health care are represented in various sections of the media?

(Continued)

(Continued)

    iv. What implications do these representations have for academic analysis of economic decisions?

    v. How do representations of health-care rationing affect public understanding of this issue as a whole?

b. *Interpretative phenomenological analysis (IPA)*

Prepare a full schedule for a semi-structured interview in which you plan to explore the way that patients respond to a heart surgery. This should identify (a) general issues that you want to discuss, (b) specific questions that you want to ask, as well as (c) prompts to follow up on questions that prove hard to answer.

c. *Discourse analysis*

Photo 13.1 In 1998 President Bill Clinton had to give sworn testimony to a US grand jury about what he described as his 'improper physical relationship' with Monica Lewinsky. How might one use discourse analysis to explore the content and context of that testimony? (© AP/Press Association Images).

Consider the following text that is taken from President Clinton's testimony to the US grand jury, in which he was questioned about his relationship with Monica Lewinsky (from Hepburn, 2003, pp. 166–196). This is a response to questioning about a phone call with Lewinsky in which it has been suggested that Clinton asked her to lie about an impending court case.

(12.0)

Mister Wisenberg ((C raises an index finger at Q)) I remember that she came in to visit that day, (0.5) I remember that she was very upset.

(2.5)

I don't recall whether I talked to her on the phone before she came in to visit, (.) but I may well have.= I'm no- not denying that I did. I just don't recall that.

i.   Identify as many different features of this transcript as possible (e.g., the words, the pauses, the sequencing of ideas).
ii. Draw up a list of the various goals that Clinton appears to be trying to achieve in his statement.
iii. Reflect on whether particular features of his statement correspond to particular goals.
iv. Reflect on the way that these patterns shed light on the phenomenon of memory, and on their relationship to the analysis offered by researchers who study memory using different methodologies.

Research Ethics

Key goals for this chapter

- Explain why ethics are a central part of the research process.
- Identify the core ethical values that should inform psychological research.
- Identify the key forms of ethical risk associated with psychological research.

Science and society

Some time ago (indeed, before the authors had even started studying psychology) a man offered $1000 to anyone who could prove that smoking causes lung cancer in humans. Of course, nobody has ever claimed the prize. Based on the principles you have already read about in this book you could help design research that would have a chance of winning that prize. But we hope that after reading this chapter on **research ethics** you will understand why nobody will ever claim the $1000. The reasons all revolve around the ethics of running the experiment that would prove that smoking causes lung cancer.

The question whether smoking causes lung cancer is really one for medical research. So, instead, let us consider an issue that is just as important, but is one that psychologists are directly concerned with – patients' attitudes to their recovery from cancer. Most people have an opinion on this issue. Some believe that positive attitudes help patients recover from cancer (or to survive longer). Others believe that if you have cancer, that's that – you will either recover or not, regardless of your attitude. Still others believe that positive attitudes do not matter all that much, but that if you have negative attitudes you will tend not to recover. There is evidence to support all of these possibilities, and substantial research into the issue has been conducted by psychologists and medical scientists.

We have chosen this issue not just because it is something you probably have an opinion about, but also because it is an important question and one to which science has not yet provided all the answers. We could have chosen a trivial issue to explain research ethics, but to do so would have risked missing the point. Research ethics relates to *serious issues*, often issues that are deeply personal for many people. Two other features of this example are important too: the facts that most people have an opinion about recovery from cancer and that science has yet to answer all their questions. Research ethics often relates to *issues that people in many different communities have opinions about.* Moreover, if you asked us 'What are the effects of attitudes to cancer on recovery?', we would have to say 'The jury is still out'. There has been much progress, but nobody can confidently say 'The effect of a person's attitude to cancer on recovery is …' . This is partly because research ethics affects *the ability of the science to answer difficult questions* about sensitive issues.

Let us consider why the question of the effects of attitudes to cancer on recovery has not yet been resolved by science. The reasons are much the same as the reasons why nobody has ever claimed the $1000 prize for proving that smoking causes lung cancer. Suppose that you believe negative attitudes to cancer reduce a patient's chance of recovery. Several simple experiments could test this idea, but they are all so obnoxious that nobody has ever carried them out. For example, researchers could randomly allocate a large sample of cancer patients to two groups and thoroughly convince one group they were not going to recover (assuming that this could be done effectively), while having no contact with the control group. A few months later they would measure the condition of the patients.

Now it is true that research even more offensive than this has been conducted – for example, by scientists in Nazi Germany. But the vast majority of people who discovered that such research was going to be carried out where they worked or studied would be shocked. Many would go to rallies, sign petitions and write to politicians. Some of the researchers' colleagues might give media interviews and call for the researchers to be thrown out of their professional associations, and all this would occur in an effort to stop the research from going ahead. It is likely that the institution in question would forbid its researchers from carrying out the research, and if the research went ahead there could be an enormous legal quagmire, possibly leading to criminal charges.

Why would all this happen? It would happen because the science of psychology, like any science, is part of the society in which the scientists work. There are three reasons why society has a right to express opinions about how scientists should carry out their research. First, society pays the bills for research (through taxes and tuition fees). Second, members of society often participate in that research. Third, the research is usually *about* society. For all these reasons, the bogus experiment that we discussed above would never be carried out because society – in the form of governments, students, other researchers, lawyers, university administrations and community action groups – would say 'Find another way to answer this important question'.

In reality there are no researchers we know of who would want to carry out the study we have described. Universities and research centres are not full of crazy psychologists who want to do research that would harm participants. Researchers are not opposed to society, they are part of society, and they generally stick to the standards and values of the society they live in. In particular, this is because researchers have ethical standards, both formal and informal. Formal codes of practice are explicitly designed to limit harm to participants. For example, participants must generally be told enough about the research to enable them to decide whether they want to participate. If researchers do not follow the principles set out in these codes, they will not receive funds from research bodies and journals will not publish their research. Moreover, their research will almost certainly be forbidden by their institutional **ethics committee**.

How, then, could the researchers address the question about the effects of attitudes to cancer in another way? Not easily. One possibility would be to change the question. The researchers could run an experiment with an experimental group comprising people whose attitudes were manipulated so that they became more positive. They could then compare this group with a control group (who could be assumed to have more negative attitudes). However, there is a major problem with this study. It would actually be testing the hypothesis that *positive* attitudes improve recovery. At the end of the day, if the research showed that attitudes did not affect cancer recovery this might be because the researchers were studying the wrong attitudes.

Another possibility would be to use a correlational or survey approach (as discussed in Chapters 5 and 9). The researchers could find a sample of cancer patients, measure their attitudes to recovery, and then follow them up six months later to see how they were doing. They could then correlate attitudes to cancer with a measure of health. Alternatively, the researchers could conduct a quasi-experiment where a group of patients with positive attitudes was matched with a group of patients with negative attitudes on variables such as the severity of cancer. Six months later the health of people in the two groups could be compared.

If you have read the previous 12 chapters of this book you will be able to see what the problems with these various research strategies are. In the case of the quasi-experiment, any number of *extraneous* variables could compromise any interpretation of the findings. For example, matching people for severity of cancer may build in other differences between groups (such as amount of treatment or age). In short, there is no way that the researchers could *prove* that negative attitudes prevent recovery from cancer.

Thus, the often quite reasonable demands that society makes on researchers mean that important questions that could in principle be answered by simple research strategies are never addressed. Although this is most obvious for serious and controversial issues such as attitudes to cancer, in fact it applies to all areas of research in psychology. Whenever psychologists design research they have to consider the effects that the research will have on participants. We have argued that to design and understand research you need to know a lot about principles such as randomization, causal inference, and so on. Ethical principles are *every bit as important* to the real business of doing psychological research as any of the other ideas that we have discussed in this book.

You may think that the example we have used seems a bit far-fetched. Would researchers really ever do something that could have very serious effects on research participants? Would people really ever care enough about psychological research to organize angry protests and write letters to politicians? The answer to both questions is 'yes'.

A striking illustration of the first point is provided by research conducted by Berkun, Bialek, Kern, and Yagi (1962) in which the participants were soldiers who thought they were being shelled by artillery while they tried to repair a broken radio. The amount of time it took to repair the radio was the dependent variable. Certainly, this study was done some time ago, and it was done by psychologists working for the US defence forces, but the fact remains that the research was done, and unless society had intervened, it is possible that psychologists would still be doing similar things.

Are there cases of strong popular reactions against psychological research? There have been many examples. One is provided by research on racial differences in intelligence. This has been controversial for a long time and continues to cause heated debate (e.g., Fraser, 1995; Gould, 1981; Herrnstein & Murray, 1994). Some prominent researchers in the area have met angry protests in universities and other forums throughout the world when they have presented their views.

The area that provokes the greatest continuing controversy, however, is research that uses animals. We will consider the rights and wrongs of animal research in a later section, but research with animals is now so controversial and produces such strong feelings in segments of the wider community that many researchers find that they can no longer perform the research they feel they need to do. All we would say for now is that the conflicts here can be quite different from those that arise in other areas of psychology.

ethics committee A body set up by a research institution such as a university to review ethical principles relating to the conduct of research at that institution. Such

---

Test Yourself 14.1*

Which of the following is true about the relationship between scientific research and society?

a. Science exists outside society.
b. Ethical principles are generally imposed by governments on psychologists against their will.
c. Only scientists should decide what is ethical or not about research.
d. Decisions about research ethics are always a matter of personal choice.
e. None of the above.

The correct answer is (e). This is almost a trick question. The relationship between scientific research and society is so complex that anyone who tries to reduce it to a few simple statements is always going to risk making mistakes. Statement (a) is simply wrong: science is part of society. Statement (b) is sometimes wrong, as many ethical principles have willingly been *introduced* by psychologists. If (a) is wrong, (c) must also be wrong, as by most standards members of a society have a right to say what they think is unacceptable in their society. If scientists disagree it is up to them to explain why. Statement (d) is wrong because, although people have personal views, decisions about research ethics are often made by relevant groups in society, for example funding bodies and ethics committees.

committees usually contain representatives from groups for whom research ethics is important and relevant (e.g., researchers, lawyers, medical practitioners, ministers of religion, members of the general community).

research ethics The principles by which researchers decide the best way to balance the contribution of their research to human knowledge against potential damage to human welfare. Researchers are obligated to have a knowledge of any code of ethics that applies to their research.

Ethical values

In practice, when it comes to designing and conducting research in psychology, the task of trying to specify what is and what is not ethical proves to be enormously difficult. Researchers and ethics committees can (and do) spend an extremely long time discussing and arriving at decisions about whether the methods of a given study are moral, appropriate and defensible. For this reason, although they may have clear views about what is and what is not acceptable, few ethical committees will attempt to specify in advance what constitutes ethical and unethical research. Instead, they are likely to want to examine every study on its individual merits and to identify broad ethical principles that they endorse and that they want all researchers to uphold.

Indeed, recognizing this as an important goal, the International Union of Psychological Science in 2008 ratified a *Universal Declaration of Ethical Principles for Psychologists* that aimed to provide a moral framework and generic set of principles designed to inform the conduct of psychologists around the world (see Gauthier & Pettifor, 2012). This enshrined the following four core principles that relate not only to research, but to all forms of professional activity:

1. *Respect for the dignity of persons and peoples.* The core idea here is that psychologists need to respect the value of people as both individuals and members of different communities and cultures. They need to treat every person as having value regardless of such things as social status, ethnic background, education level and gender. Moreover, they need to take account of the fact that people have different backgrounds that will determine their sensitivity to particular practices and procedures. This means that just because something is not perceived to be offensive for members of one community (e.g., middle-class men), it cannot be assumed that this will be the case for everyone else. Special care also needs to be taken to protect the dignity of individuals and groups who, for one reason or another, are vulnerable – for example, children, older adults, members of cultural minorities.

2. *Competent caring for the well-being of persons and peoples.* As with the Hippocratic oath taken by medical doctors, the overriding principle here is that psychologists should strive to ensure that their work is beneficial to others, and, most particularly, that it does not cause them harm. Apart from anything else, this commits researchers to the goal of being well trained so that they know what they are doing. It also requires them to try to correct any harm that they may commit inadvertently.

3. *Integrity.* In the course of their work psychologists need to be open, honest and truthful. They should also avoid exploiting others for their own gain, and avoid putting their own interests ahead of others. There is a strong sense of balance present in this principle. Integrity involves being open and honest about the risks involved in research when recruiting participants, but it may well involve withholding information in publications in order to maintain the confidentiality of those participants.

4. *Professional and scientific responsibilities to society.* As we have noted at several points in previous chapters, psychological research is not set apart from the 'real world', it is part of it. In this regard, research psychologists have two broad responsibilities: first, to ensure that their work contributes to understanding of that world; and second, to ensure that, as far as possible, it improves it. Among other things, this means that it is important to ensure that one's research is as well designed and well informed as possible.

Even if they do not subscribe to this particular declaration, most professional bodies that govern the research activity of psychologists around the world embrace similar principles to these. To take just one example, in Australia the National Health and Medical Research Council builds its ethical guidelines for research with human participants around four key principles that correspond closely to those in the *Universal Declaration*: respect, beneficence, justice and research merit.

RESEARCH BITE 14.1
The cultural dimensions of respect

The New Zealand researchers Natasha Tassell and Andrew Lock (2012) note that the principle of 'respect' enshrined in the *Universal Declaration of Ethical Principles for Psychologists* can have different meanings for people in different cultures. In particular, they note that while in the West respect often involves treating people as individuals, in Maori culture respect is associated with treating a person in a way befitting their place within a particular family that has particular ancestors. For research to be properly ethical, researchers thus have to be sensitive to such cultural variation and understand that, when it comes to translating values such as respect into practice, there is no 'one size fits all'.

Reference
Tassell, N. A., & Lock, A. J. (2012). Cultural considerations for professional psychology ethics: Te tirohanga ahurea hei whakatakato tika, whakapakari te aro ki te tangata: Te ahua ki Aotearoa. *Ethics and Social Welfare*, 6, 56–73.

Nevertheless, the challenge of living up to these principles is not always easy. Among other things, this is because different principles can sometimes be hard to reconcile with each other and so much depends on which one is prioritized. For example, as we will see in the next section, this occurs when researchers see the goal of understanding a given phenomenon to be more important than the goal of being totally open in one's communication with participants. At the same time, the principles themselves are open to interpretation, and it is clear that good intentions do not always translate into good outcomes.

Ethical risks associated with participation in research

Many readers of this book will have already participated in psychological research. If you are doing an introductory psychology course you may have been asked to take part in research, often in exchange for course credit. Exactly the same thing is going on right now in universities and colleges all over the world.

For this reason research ethics is not a dry, abstract concern for other people, or something you can file away until the exam comes around. Most people who read this book will participate in psychological research and many will conduct research themselves. In fact much (perhaps most) of the research that is conducted in psychology is done by students – either advanced undergraduates or postgraduates. So when you participate in research there is a good chance that you are actually helping another student. In any case you will be helping to advance the sum of psychological knowledge, as well as observing how research is done by real researchers. Some would also argue that if you are studying psychology you are consuming psychological knowledge and so it is only fair that you help to add to this knowledge. However, these arguments are not reasons to make light of ethical concerns, and if you are asked to participate in research you should be aware of your rights as a participant.

It is extremely unlikely that anyone reading this book will experience actual harm from participating in psychological experiments – not least because, as we have seen, the minimization of harm is one of the core principles by which ethical approval for research is guided. Many of you will find that research participation is interesting, engaging and informative. Even if this is not the case, research participation in psychology is probably a lot safer than attending a class or catching a bus. Indeed, the biggest risk most participants face is that they might have to spend a few less than scintillating hours watching a computer screen or filling in questionnaires.

So what exactly are the main risks to participants in research? These fall into four main categories: (a) stress; (b) breaches of confidentiality; (c) deception; and (d) invasive procedures.

Some research may cause *stress* for participants. Sometimes this cannot be avoided – especially if stress is what the researchers are actually investigating. This is quite a plausible scenario as stress is a major topic addressed by a range of psychologists (e.g., in clinical, organizational and cognitive areas). As an example of such research, take the researcher who wants to examine the hypothesis that fear or anxiety impairs intellectual performance. Clearly, there is no way for this researcher to study these issues experimentally without creating some distress in the participants. However, the researcher must strive to ensure that the stress does not persist outside the experimental session, and the research in general must minimize unintended or unnecessary stress. The research that has probably generated the most concern about stress for participants is that by Milgram (1963, 1974) on obedience. We will look at his work in more detail shortly.

Confidentiality is important because participants often give sensitive information to researchers. Participants are remarkably willing to give researchers information about their relationships, religious beliefs, sexual orientations and political attitudes – information that they would not dream of giving to even their closest friends. This is part of a general inclination on the part of research participants to be cooperative and helpful. As Orne (1969) noted, if someone walked up to people in the street and asked them to do 10 push-ups, they would ask 'Why?'. But if a psychologist made the same request in an experiment, they would ask 'Where?'.

One reason why research participants are so helpful is that many of them are committed to the research process. They want to answer researchers' questions because they want to contribute to the advancement of the science. Whatever the reasons for participation, it is essential that researchers do not abuse the trust that is placed in them, and that they maintain the confidentiality of their participants. If someone tells a researcher something, that person should be able to assume that nobody else will ever know who gave the researcher that information, and this should be especially true for any sensitive or personal information. For example, this is why participants in clinical or neuropsychological research are identified by a pseudonym or their initials (as in the case of HM, the patient with no apparent long-term memory, whom we mentioned in Chapter 3). The only exception is where participants give the researcher explicit permission to reveal their identity. This is very rarely necessary.

Deception is one feature of psychological research that contributes to more than its fair share of ethical debate – primarily because it can be seen to be inconsistent with the principle of *integrity* discussed earlier. As we discussed in Chapter 4, deception involves giving participants information that is false. You may wonder why it is necessary for researchers to deceive participants. The reason is that many experiments, especially in social psychology, involve elaborate setups where participants think that one thing is happening but actually something else is happening. This is because most social psychologists believe that people's behaviour is influenced not so much by what is actually happening as by what people *think* is happening. Deception is therefore used to control *reactivity* (Chapter 4).

Let us illustrate this point with an example. Imagine that we want to know whether people respond differently to emergency situations when they are alone rather than in a group. Latane and Darley (1970) investigated this important question by asking participants to complete a questionnaire in a small room. The experimenters then filled the room with smoke. They found that people were more likely to check on the problem if they were alone than if they were with a group of strangers who continued to fill out their questionnaires (these strangers were actually **confederates** of the experimenter). This experiment made an important contribution to our understanding of human behaviour (see Levine, 2012), but psychologists only acquired this knowledge because the researchers tricked their participants. After all, the alternatives would be starting a *real* fire (which could never be considered for all sorts of reasons) or telling the participants that the fire was *not* real before the research started. The latter simply would not work – a fire does not affect behaviour unless people believe it to be real.

Note, however, that the use of deception is not confined to the laboratory and can be used in field studies where researchers do not want their identity and purpose to be revealed. For example, this was the case when Festinger and his colleagues wanted to infiltrate a cult to see how its members would cope when their prophecy about the world's end failed to come true – a case study we referred to in Chapter 3 (Festinger et al., 1956). Similarly, researchers have examined the circumstances under which a person comes to the aid of a victim by having confederates pose as people in distress (e.g., Darley & Batson, 1973). The ethical dilemma here is clear, and is one we sometimes become aware of when exposed to similar techniques in television programmes that set out to play jokes on members of the general public by placing them in awkward situations.

The way we think about things can have a powerful effect on our behaviour. In some research psychologists use deception to *control* for these effects experimentally. Experimental control of this form occurs in **placebo** studies where participants in one condition think they receive a treatment but in fact receive no treatment. This occurs to control for any effects that might arise from the fact that when the participants think they are receiving a treatment they may get better just because they *expect* to get better. Placebo effects like this are complex and apply in many subtle ways. However, if a control were not put in place it would be impossible to know the extent to which placebo effects contributed to any treatment effects. Moreover, if participants know they are not receiving a proper treatment they might actually go looking for one and their withdrawal from the research could threaten its internal validity (this is the problem of *mortality* that we discussed in Chapter 4).

What are the arguments against deception? Understandably, some people simply feel that it is wrong for researchers to deceive participants whatever the reason. This is a moral issue, but the moral cost must be weighed against the gains to knowledge from the deceptive research. Some issues simply cannot be studied without using deception. The moral burden of deception is one that individual researchers may choose to bear or not to bear, after they have taken account of the reasons for and against the deception. Suffice it to say that most social psychologists see deception as a justifiable technique where there are appropriate safeguards.

The other major argument against deception is that being tricked by the experimenter can be stressful for the participants, not least because it can reveal to people unpleasant things about themselves. The research that illustrates this point best was conducted by Milgram (1963) on obedience. This really kicked off the major debate on ethics in psychology, largely because it was (and still is) among the most provocative and controversial research ever done.

Milgram was interested in the extent to which people were prepared to obey the unreasonable and cruel commands of authority figures. The people who participated in this research were asked to deliver electric shocks to another research participant who performed poorly on a memory task, supposedly as part of a study to investigate the effects of punishment on learning. Consistent with this cover story, the participants were instructed by the experimenter to give increasingly large electric shocks to this person (the 'Learner') every time they made a mistake. In line with the experimenter's instructions, in what as come to be seen as the standard variant of Milgram's paradigm (Reicher, Haslam, & Smith, 2012), most participants continued to administer shocks even after the Learner started to complain and scream – going all the way to a maximum shock of 450 volts (a point labelled 'DANGER: SEVERE SHOCK' – an accurate description given that an alternating current of 100–250 volts is often enough to kill someone). Indeed, most continued doing this even when the person being shocked stopped responding altogether.

It was obvious from participants' responses that when they reflected on what they had done, many participants experienced a great deal of stress. Many of them had questioned the experimenter's instructions, yet they had continued to administer what they thought were potentially lethal shocks. In fact no shocks were administered – the experimenter's cover story was an elaborate deception involving a confederate of the experimenter who only pretended to be shocked. Moreover, rather than wanting to study the effects of punishment on learning, Milgram's real goal was to see how far participants would go in carrying out the

Photo 14.1 Stanley Milgram's 'obedience to authority' studies examined the willingness of participants to administer what appeared to be lethal electric shocks to a 'Learner' when they made mistakes in a memory task. In fact this Learner was Milgram's confederate and the shocks were not real, but the participants did not find this out until they were debriefed. Milgram's study is a standard reference point for ethical debate in psychology – particularly in relation to the use of deception.

experimenter's instructions. Would they be willing to kill a man simply because they were asked to do this by a researcher in a psychology experiment?

As you can imagine, this study has raised many questions about the effect it may have had on participants. Some psychologists argue that such research is harmful for the participants as it causes stress, embarrassment and guilt. They also add that deceptive research like this can have few benefits (Baumrind, 1964, 1985). Extending this point, it has been argued that it was actually Milgram's *assistants* who, by carrying out the deception, displayed the most destructive form of obedience in the research (Harré, 1979; Russell, in press).

However, Milgram actually followed up his participants in order to find out whether they had been harmed (something only a small number of researchers do). Most participants (60%) reported that they had been 'upset' or 'somewhat nervous' at the time, but 84% were 'glad' or 'very glad' to have participated in the study as they had 'learned something of personal importance' and believed that they had made a contribution to a worthy cause – specifically, the progress of science (Haslam, Reicher, Millard, & MacDonald, in press). They arrived at these opinions largely because, after the experiment was over, Milgram provided a detailed **debriefing** that informed participants about the purpose of the experiment and explained to them why the deception was necessary.

It is worth noting, however, that Milgram's participants were healthy adults. Exactly the same study would have been far more objectionable if the participants had been people who were more susceptible to harm (e.g., children, the elderly or the mentally ill). It is also possible that reactivity (in the form of a desire to please the interviewer, as discussed in Chapters 4 and 5) may have led Milgram's participants to downplay the extent of their stress in his post-experimental enquiries. Indeed, Milgram seems to have worked hard to encourage such responses, and, at another level, one might ask – as Haslam and colleagues (in press) do – whether one would really want participants to feel quite so happy about having been prepared to kill an innocent stranger in the name of science. It is also worth pointing out, however, that awkward *political* questions of this form are rarely asked by ethics committees (an observation that touches upon points we will discuss in the next chapter).

The standard way in which such issues are addressed is to ask – in the absence of evidence of harm – whether the risk to the participants was justified given the benefit to human knowledge from the research. In his own defence Milgram pointed out that he had asked psychiatrists to estimate the percentage of people who would obey the experimenter's instructions. Because they assumed that only mentally disturbed people would administer the shocks, their estimate was 1% of the participants, this being the level of serious mental illness in the general population. In fact, none of Milgram's participants were mentally ill, and 65% of his participants were prepared to administer the maximum level of shock. Obviously, if Milgram's research had never been carried out we would never have known that such a high percentage of 'ordinary men' were willing to follow destructive instructions and we would know far less about the processes that underpin such behaviour (Reicher, Haslam, & Miller, in press).

RESEARCH BITE 14.2

Can a prison experiment be ethical?

In 2002 Steve Reicher and Alex Haslam worked with the BBC to reinvestigate issues raised by the Stanford Prison Experiment (SPE) – one of the most ethically controversial psychology studies of all time. The researchers argued that their research was scientifically justified on account of its capacity to contribute to much-needed advance in the theoretical understanding of tyranny. After a nine-month ethical review process that involved implementing multiple safeguards (including setting up an independent on-site ethics panel), the research secured approval and went ahead. Its published findings ultimately presented a range of challenges to conclusions drawn from the SPE.

Reference

Haslam, S. A., Reicher, S. D., & McDermott, M. (in press). Studying harm-doing without doing harm: The case of the BBC Prison Experiment. In R. J. Sternberg & S. E. Fiske (Eds.), *Ethical case studies and commentaries in the behavioral and brain sciences.* New York: Cambridge University Press.

So, although Milgram's research has been heavily criticized on ethical grounds (e.g., Perry, 2012), the study did provide illuminating insights into a particularly important aspect of human behaviour. These insights may, for example, help to explain why otherwise normal people are willing to commit atrocities when told to do so by their superiors. *But was it worth it?* Before you answer this question we should point out that even if this research had not already been conducted (so that the insights it provided still remained to be made), Milgram's work would not be approved by most ethics committees today. What would be the price of *not* having this knowledge?

Whatever your response to these questions, it is apparent that ethics committees are usually very sensitive to the problems caused by doing research, but are much less sensitive to the problems caused by not doing research (Pettit, 1992; Rosenthal, 1994). This is partly because if these committees were to permit harmful research to go ahead, the victims (or their representatives) would hold them responsible. In contrast, the victims of scientific ignorance hardly ever complain.

One other risk of deception is that participants may end up mistrusting all researchers (Baumrind, 1985). That is, after they have found out that the information provided in psychology experiments can be misleading, a person may come to believe that all psychological research involves tricks, even though this is not true (particularly outside social psychology). This is a problem for researchers (in so far as it is an instance of reactivity), but instilling a healthy scepticism into students who will have to read, interpret and perhaps one day conduct research may not be such a bad thing.

Photo 14.2 When conducting research with vulnerable populations, researchers need to be especially mindful of ethical risks. Ethics committees will also be very sensitive to these. In the research being conducted here, this vulnerability is associated with age, but it can arise from an array of other factors such as a person's mental and physical health, or the context in which they are being studied (e.g., during or after a traumatic event).

It is clear from these examples that research can have effects that change people. Features that produce these changes are called **invasive procedures**. Extreme examples might include giving participants drugs (under medical supervision), inserting some psychophysiological recording device into their bodies, or giving people information that they could not otherwise have obtained (e.g., their score on a personality test). Ethical research (e.g., that based on the principles of the *Universal Declaration*) always involves minimizing any long-term effects on participants to those absolutely necessary for the research, and eliminating long-term negative effects.

An interesting question that remains is whether there is actually any evidence of people being harmed by research. To address the issue in the undergraduate population Smith and Richardson (1983) surveyed 464 undergraduates in North America. One-fifth of the participants reported some harm in terms of feeling very nervous, very humiliated, very angry, excessive physical discomfort or that they were very wrongly deceived as a result of participating in research. If we exclude those who felt very nervous without other sources of harm (reasoning that this is less serious than the other types of possible harm) this leaves a total of 15 people, or 3% of the sample, who reported experiencing harm. However, as in the case of Milgram's follow-up interviews, it is possible that these results may have been contaminated by participants' reactivity – leading either to an over- or underestimation of the actual incidence of harm. Very few subsequent studies have detected negative effects of participation in psychological research.

In general, then, it seems that there is little evidence that psychology students are harmed by their participation in normal research in the main areas of psychology – for example, those that involve interaction with other people, working with computer-controlled equipment, or filling in questionnaires. Based on the available evidence, there are only two conclusions we can draw: either researchers have not looked hard enough for the harmful effects of research participation, or the harmful effects are not especially great.

The position taken on this debate depends a great deal upon how fragile research participants (and people in general) are perceived to be (West & Gunn, 1978). Those most concerned about **research risk** tend to see research participants as relatively fragile. Nevertheless, *all* psychologists would accept that the *potential* for harm does exist. This fact needs to be borne in mind at all stages of the research process.

Having considered various points, we are now in a position to summarize some of the key principles that guide ethical research with human participants in psychology. In short, the research should minimize risk to participants, and if there are any negative effects upon participants the researcher has the responsibility to correct those negative effects. Above all, participation should be based on **informed consent**, and participants should be aware of features of the research that could be expected to affect their decision to participate. It is impossible to obtain informed consent when using unobtrusive measurements (Chapter 5), so other techniques should be considered where there is a risk of harm to participants.

The principle that the participant is capable of **discontinuing participation** at any time is also extremely important. If participants feel uncomfortable or for any reason feel that they do not wish to continue taking part, then they must be free to leave at any time. They do not have to give any reason to the researcher.

The other critical feature of all research involving a researcher working with human participants is debriefing. If the research process is to be of any educational benefit for the participants – and it certainly should be – it is only fair that participants are told what the research was about and what it was trying to achieve. This debriefing should occur at the end of the research session, and certainly no later than the end of the testing programme. Above all, it is essential for the dignity of the participants that the researchers explain the nature of any deception used. As Smith and Richardson (1983) found, good debriefing seems to prevent the negative effects of deception. Researchers should try to explain deceptions in a sensitive manner – after all, nobody likes to find out that they have been tricked. They should also explain why the deception was necessary. Poor and insensitive debriefing can often turn relatively minor problems into major problems, while good debriefing can turn potentially major problems into minor ones.

For research conducted with populations that are more vulnerable to research risk (e.g., children, the mentally ill and the elderly), researchers must make extra efforts to ensure that these principles are upheld. For example, informed consent must also be provided by parents or guardians when research involves children.

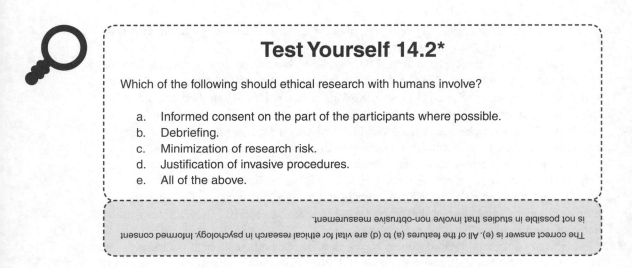

Test Yourself 14.2*

Which of the following should ethical research with humans involve?

a. Informed consent on the part of the participants where possible.
b. Debriefing.
c. Minimization of research risk.
d. Justification of invasive procedures.
e. All of the above.

The correct answer is (e). All of the features (a) to (d) are vital for ethical research in psychology. Informed consent is not possible in studies that involve non-obtrusive measurement.

confederate Someone who works for the experimenter and acts in a certain predetermined way. Normally the confederate pretends to be a genuine research participant, so the use of confederates involves deception.

confidentiality In the research process, confidentiality means ensuring that individual participants cannot be identified. This often means making sure that responses are anonymous.

debriefing Explaining the purpose and procedures of research to participants after its completion. Debriefing should include a sensitive explanation and justification of any deceptions used.

discontinuing participation An ethical principle which guarantees the right of all human participants to cease taking part in research at any time.

informed consent The ethical principle that research participants should be told enough about a piece of research to be able to make a decision about whether to participate in it.

invasive procedures Research procedures which lead to changes in participants.

placebo A device used to control for the effect of participants' expectations about the effects of research participation or the experimental treatment. An example would be giving a control group a sugar tablet rather than the real medical drug given to an experimental group. Neither group would know whether they were receiving the placebo or a real drug (i.e., the participants would be *blind* to the treatment). In other respects the groups would be treated the same.

research risk The possibility of harm to participants, usually in the form of long-term negative effects.

Research with animals

At one time a great deal of research in psychology involved animals. Indeed, in some circles the popular name for psychology was 'rats and stats'. As you have found out, the stats are still there, but there are not as many rats or other animals now. In the three-year period up to April 2013 there were 331,789 journal articles with abstracts on the PsycInfo database and of these 41,874 involved research with animals. In other words, over that period around 13% of the total amount of published research in psychology involved animals. However, animal research raises more than its fair share of debates about ethics.

We must hasten to add that the ethical debate in this area does not arise because psychologists treat animals worse than do other scientists, or other people who work with animals. This is not necessarily because psychologists are more ethical than other scientists, but simply because the nature of psychologists' work means that fewer of them perform procedures that can be distressing to animals (such as surgery). Indeed, a lot of animal research in psychology only involves the *observation* of behaviour. Moreover, most psychologists support the principles of **animal welfare**. Ethical treatment of animals involves things such as housing them in clean cages with adequate food and water, ensuring that the pain and distress they suffer is minimized, and that if it becomes necessary to kill them this is done in a humane and painless way. Ethical treatment of animals is actually in the researchers' interest. This is because if psychologists want to study the normal behaviour of animals it makes no sense to mistreat them (some people would extend this point to argue that it makes no sense to study them in laboratory cages).

Why do psychologists need to study animals? Some psychologists are simply interested in animal behaviour, and these researchers have no choice but to use animal participants. Others study animals because they are interested in questions that studies using human participants cannot address. Imagine that psychologists wanted to know whether a particular part of the brain is essential for controlling the desire to eat. There are only two ways to address this question. The researchers could attempt to find people who have had this section of their brain destroyed in accidents and see whether they still have a desire to eat. The problem is that accidents tend not to destroy isolated regions of the brain. So if it was found that the brain-injured person did not want to eat then this could be due to some other effect of the injury. As in all quasi-experiments, the interpretation of results could be contaminated by these extraneous (uncontrolled) variables.

Given that deliberately destroying parts of humans' brains would render a researcher liable for an extended prison sentence, the only alternative is to take animals with brains that are similar to our own, and conduct invasive research on these animals to see whether the animal still eats. This invasive research might involve the use of electrical probes or the destruction of specific regions of their brain. If psychologists and other scientists did not conduct these studies then important questions (e.g., concerning the biological factors that contribute to dietary disorders) would never be answered. As members of society, all of us have a right to decide whether or not we are prepared to allow animals to be harmed so that these questions can be addressed.

The fact that the work of animal psychologists has come increasingly under attack is correlated with the rise of the **animal rights movement** after the publication of Peter Singer's influential book *Animal Liberation* in 1975 (Herzog, 1995). Many members of this movement believe that animals have the same rights as humans. From this point of view the idea of keeping animals in captivity to observe their behaviour is as offensive as it would be for the researchers to take you prisoner for the same purpose. Obviously, there is a complete conflict of opinions here. The researchers believe that it is essential to study animals in ways necessary to draw the strongest scientific conclusions. Advocates of animal rights believe that the research this entails is unjustifiable. Their argument is not so much that psychologists are not obeying the ethical principles of their science, but more fundamentally that all such research is completely unethical and should be stopped.

This debate will not go away, and will remain acrimonious for the foreseeable future. The clearest conclusion we can draw is that animal research provides a good example of society at large taking an interest in what science does. Although much of the attention is unwanted by the scientists, it has had a positive effect on the welfare of research animals, and virtually all psychologists using animals are now fully committed to the cause of animal welfare (even though most reject the animal rights point of view).

However, the focus on animal research in psychology remains ironic. Much worse treatment of animals can occur in abattoirs, farms, animal refuges, restaurants, commercial research laboratories and people's own homes than in any university psychology laboratory.

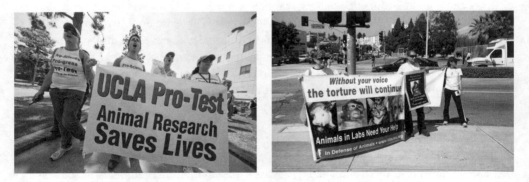

Photo 14.3 Psychological research with animals is a focus for fierce and heated debate. On one side, researchers argue that such research is entirely defensible in light of its benefits for society; on the other, supporters of animal rights contend that it is entirely indefensible on moral grounds.

Animal rights advocates argue that psychologists have a much greater responsibility to act ethically and to reflect community concerns than do other people. However, it seems clear that, regardless of whether research with animals is right or wrong, the attention that university research laboratories receive from the animal rights movement reflects the fact that universities are important and relatively easy targets to influence – not necessarily the fact that university researchers are crueller to animals than most other people (indeed most researchers would contend that they are far kinder). Ultimately, the debate on this issue is as much political as ethical, and it will never be resolved purely by an appeal to ethical principles. This is because ethics are an expression and instrument of society and not everybody in society has the same principles. Instead, like science itself, ethical principles are a source of continuing argument, conflict and struggle.

> **animal rights movement** Groups whose members believe that animals have similar or equal rights to those of human beings.

> **animal welfare** The set of principles that guide humane organizations such as societies for the prevention of cruelty to animals and which promote consideration for the well-being of animals.

Test Yourself 14.3*

Which of the following is true about ethical research using animals?

    a.   It must ensure that discomfort to animals is minimized and harm only occurs where essential.

    b.   Ethics are not a major issue because participants are not deceived.

    c.   Because it is such a controversial topic, the issues it raises are only worth discussing in relation to medical research.

    d.   It is not really relevant to psychology.

    e.   None of the above.

The correct answer is (a). Answer (b) is wrong because deception is only an issue for human participants. Answer (c) is wrong because animal research in psychology and other sciences addresses issues that are just as important as those in medical research, although animal research has declined in popularity, that does not mean that it is not important – 10% of the research published in a big science like psychology is still a lot of research.

Final comment

It is obvious that this chapter has dealt a lot more with opinions than have the previous chapters in this book. Probably some of our own opinions will have become obvious, too, although we have tried our best to frame these in terms of the conflicting sets of arguments that characterize ethical debates both inside and outside psychology.

The fact that conflicts in this area are so pronounced is one reason why research ethics is such an intriguing and integral part of the research process. The science of psychology cannot be separated from society because at all times, whether they like it or not, researchers are a part of society (and quite an important part, too). As such they are guided by values that are *strong* but also *open to challenge*. It should be no surprise, then, if you react more vigorously to the issues raised here than to most of the others discussed in this book.

CHECKLIST
Revisiting the key goals for this chapter

☐ I understand why ethics are a central part of the research process.
☐ I am aware of the core ethical values that should inform psychological research.
☐ I am aware of the key forms of ethical risk associated with psychological research.

Further reading

Over the years, many studies have fuelled debate about ethics in society. However, because Milgram's obedience studies set the agenda for much of this debate, it is worth starting one's reading in this area by examining Baumrind's (1964) critique of this research and Milgram's (1964) own response. Blass's (2004) authoritative and highly readable biography provides fascinating insights into Milgram's work and into his life more generally. It also serves as a window onto the research process more generally, and so is relevant to a number of topics that we have discussed in earlier chapters. Reicher, Haslam, and Miller (in press) also provide a contemporary treatment of these issues in an article that introduces a special issue of the *Journal of Social Issues* published to coincide with the 50th anniversary of the publication of Milgram's initial paper.

Baumrind, D. (1964). Some thoughts on ethics of research: After reading Milgram's 'Behavioral study of obedience'. *American Psychologist, 19*, 421–423.

Blass, T. (2004). *The man who shocked the world: The life and legacy of Stanley Milgram.* New York: Basic Books.

Milgram, S. (1964). Issues in the study of obedience: A reply to Baumrind. *American Psychologist, 19*, 848–852.

Reicher, S. D., Haslam, S. A., & Miller, A. G. (in press). What makes a person a perpetrator? The intellectual, moral and methodological arguments for revisiting Milgram's research on the influence of authority. *Journal of Social Issues.*

Research ethics: A checklist for research evaluation and improvement

Table 14.1

Potential problem	Question to ask	Potential improvement
Breach of confidentiality	Is participants' contribution to research confidential?	Take steps to ensure that as far as possible the identity of individual participants and the results of their participation are kept private. This can often be achieved by referring to participants only by codenames or numbers and/or by keeping records of participants' identities separate from their data. If confidentiality and anonymity are breached this must be explicitly justified and participants need to be informed of this fact before agreeing to participate.
Breach of anonymity	Is participants' contribution to research anonymous?	
Deception	Have participants been deceived about the nature or purpose of research?	Endeavour to tell participants the truth about research and avoid making false or misleading statements or omitting important information. If any deception is deemed necessary, this must be explicitly justified and participants must be sensitively debriefed at the conclusion of the study. If deception or concealment could reasonably be expected to affect the decision to participate (and hence to compromise the principle of informed consent), then participants need to be informed of this fact before agreeing to participate.
Concealment	Has some important information about the research been kept from participants?	
Invasive procedures	Does the research change the participants in any way?	Research should be designed to ensure that, as far as possible, it has no long-term effects on participants and that there are no long-term negative effects. Where there is a risk of this, participants should be informed of this fact and monitored beyond the end of the study to ensure that harm has not occurred and that, if it has, it is corrected.
Research risk	Does the research have any long-term negative effects?	
Inadequate debriefing	At the conclusion of the research have participants been fully informed about the purpose of the research and the nature of, and reasons for, any deception?	At the end of any piece of research participants should be thanked for participating, and the nature and value of the research should be explained to them. Any questions that they have about the research should be answered, and, as far as possible, participants should feel involved and respected in the broad research process (e.g., by being made aware of the scientific benefits associated with the research). This phase of research is particularly important if a study involves invasive procedures, research risk, deception or concealment.

(Continued)

Table 14.1 (Continued)

Potential problem	Question to ask	Potential improvement
Uninformed consent	Have the participants been told enough about the research to make an informed decision about whether to participate in it?	Ensure that participants are given enough information about a piece of research to make a reasonable decision about whether they want to participate in it. If participation involves deception, or other factors that might reasonably be expected to impact on this decision (e.g., in a double-blind trial of a therapeutic technique), participants need to be made aware of this before participating. Where participants are unable to give informed consent (e.g., because they are children or impaired) special safeguards have to be set in place and consent obtained from their legal guardians.
Inability to discontinue participation	Are the participants free to withdraw from the research at any stage?	If participants do not want to continue taking part in a study they must be free to withdraw from it. They should not be placed under pressure to continue and they do not have to give reasons for withdrawing.
Harm to animals	Are animals harmed (psychologically or physically) by taking part in the study?	Animals should not be harmed in the process of conducting research. If they are, or there is a risk of harm, this must be very clearly justified and the scientific benefits of the research must also be very clear. Approval for research with animals is normally granted by a special ethics committee that has a brief to consider broad-ranging welfare issues.
Failure to weigh risks against potential benefit	Have the ethical risks associated with any research been considered in light of potential scientific gains?	Even if it contravenes the ethical guidelines outlined above, research that has clear scientific value should not be rejected out of hand. Instead, the goal of minimizing ethical concern should be weighed against the potential for scientific gain. Different groups will use different scales in this process, but all must strike a workable and moral balance between these elements.
Failure to gain ethical approval	Has the research been approved by a relevant ethical committee or body?	Researchers cannot make decisions about the above issues on their own. Instead, they must present the case for conducting their research to relevant professional bodies (e.g. a university ethics committee). In the process they must justify any procedures that raise any ethical concerns. Only after gaining approval from such a body should the research proceed.

Test Yourself 14.4**

Imagine that you are conducting a psychological experiment that has been approved by your institutional ethics committee and two participants object to answering some questions which they consider to be too personal. As a result, they decide they want to cease participating in the experiment. What are their responsibilities in this case?

a. To complete the experimental session because you would not ask personal questions unless they were really important for science.
b. To explain to you why they wish to leave so that you can conduct debriefing.
c. The participants have no responsibilities, they can leave at any time.
d. To report you to the institutional ethics committee.
e. To discuss your experiment with other students.

Test Yourself 14.5***

Informed consent means that researchers should tell participants about which of the following before they agree to participate in research?

a. The hypotheses.
b. Anything that is likely to affect the participants' decision to participate in the research.
c. Details of any deception.
d. The independent variable.
e. Whether the experiment involves a placebo.

Test Yourself 14.6**

Which of the following statements about Milgram's obedience-to-authority studies is (are) true?

a. They violated the American Psychological Association's standards at the time because they used poor debriefing procedures.
b. They led to important developments in ethical principles in psychological research.
c. They have been criticized for putting participants at risk of harm.
d. Both (b) and (c).
e. They used inadequate follow-up procedures.

The correct answer to 14.4 is (c). Participants are always free to discontinue participation at any time, even if this would be inconvenient for the researcher. If participants feel strongly about an issue then (d) and (e) are options, but they are not *required* to do anything. It is possible, for example, that questions which are deeply personal for one person are not personal for most other people and there is no way the researcher can establish this in advance. Answer (b) is a reasonable thing to do as it may be useful for participants to explain the problems they encountered with the research and to listen to the experimenter's response. However, participants are not required to do this.

(Continued)

(Continued)

The correct answer to 14.5 is (b), but this is mainly because the ethics of deception are complex. However, all ethical guidelines allow deception under some circumstances (so (c) and (e) are wrong), and making participants aware of the *details* of any deception is pointless as this will only ensure that the experiment does not work. There is no reason for the researcher to tell participants about the hypothesis (as (a) suggests) or about the independent variable (as (d) suggests) before the session. Any deception should be explained during debriefing.

The correct answer to 14.6 is (d). Answer (a) is wrong because, although Milgram's studies aroused a great deal of debate at the time, the debriefing was extensive and there were no guidelines on debriefing at the time. This means that (b) is true; (c) is also true (see Baumrind, 1964, 1985). Answer (e) is incorrect because Milgram actually performed very extensive follow-ups of his participants.

Discussion/essay questions

a. Do ethics committees have too little power or too much?
b. Should researchers still be able to use research procedures like those employed by Milgram in the 1960s?
c. To what extent have ethics committees influenced the way in which psychological knowledge has advanced in the last 30 years?
d. Draft some ethical guidelines that you think any research you personally conduct should meet. Justify your decisions.
e. How do you think ethical guidelines for conducting research in psychology will change in the next century? Will this change be for the better?

Conclusion: Managing Uncertainty in Psychological Research

Key goals for this chapter

- Conclude this book by presenting an analysis of psychological research as a process of uncertainty management.
- Clarify the different forms that this uncertainty takes and the key ways in which psychologists manage this.
- Motivate you to use what you have learned through reading this book as a springboard to becoming a very good researcher yourself.

'Where has all this got us?'

We started this book by asking the question 'Why do I have to do this?'. At that point we tried to give you some answers that would motivate you to read on and to try to master the material that we were going to present in the following 14 chapters. If you have stuck to this task (and we hope you have), you should have learned a lot and have a real sense of accomplishment. That being the case, it seems appropriate to conclude by taking stock of the journey and asking where it has brought us.

In this concluding chapter our aim is to summarize some of our ideas about the role that statistics play in the research process and about the relationship between statistics and other aspects of methodology and research design. Central to this summary is the idea that the *challenges* psychologists face when they conduct research relate largely to the question of *how to manage different types of uncertainty in the research process* (Haslam & McGarty, 2001). In many respects this analysis of uncertainty management is one of the most important ideas in

Photo 15.1 Grappling with uncertainty is the business of the research psychologist. This graffito on a wall in Tallinn (the capital of Estonia) asks the question 'Does television imitate life or does life imitate television?'. Finding out sensible ways to tackle such questions (e.g., by looking at the impact of television violence on children; Huesmann, Moise-Titus, Podolski, & Eron, 2003) is a large part of the challenge – but also a large part of the fun – of doing psychological research. What are the big questions that you want to answer?

this book. Although the emphasis in this chapter reflects our personal views, these observations should encourage you to reflect critically on the process of both producing and consuming psychological research.

Managing uncertainty in psychological research

In Chapters 6 to 11 we made an important distinction between two types of statistic: those that describe the properties of particular sets of data, and those that allow us to make inferences about the probable relationship between a set of data and the underlying reality to which the data relate. Each of these types of statistic is associated with a different form of **statistical uncertainty** – **descriptive uncertainty** and **inferential uncertainty**, respectively. It is for the purpose of quantifying statistical uncertainty that most psychological research involves the use of statistics.

As an example, researchers who are interested in the productivity of people in the workplace may want to examine the stress levels of employees who work under artificial light (e.g., factory workers or miners). Part of their investigation might involve administering some psychological tests to 25 workers, where those workers' stress is quantified by assigning them a score between 0 and 100. To summarize the level of stress in this sample the researchers may then compute the group's mean score on this scale. In this and any other psychological research, there will always be a certain amount of descriptive uncertainty arising from the fact that not everyone will produce the same score. Indeed, even if the *same* person completed the test on two consecutive days it is quite likely that they would obtain different scores. The different scores may be due to random error or to other factors (e.g., measurement error or individual differences).

Whether descriptive uncertainty arises from random error or not, it can be quantified by some measure of dispersion – most commonly, the amount of variance (or standard deviation) around a mean. The greater the dispersion in the scores obtained from the research participants, the greater the uncertainty and the less confident the researchers would be in the ability of a measure of central tendency to describe those participants appropriately. If the average stress score for participants in a study was 60 and their scores ranged between 30 and 90, the researchers would be less certain about describing the participants in terms of their average stress level than if the range were between 55 and 65. Descriptive uncertainty would only be completely removed if all participants obtained an identical score.

Descriptive uncertainty is random variation in the sample over which the experimenter has no control and for which no explanation is proposed. Inferential uncertainty, on the other hand, relates to a judgement about whether it is plausible that the results obtained could have been produced by a random process (e.g., drawing random samples from the same population). Inferential uncertainty prevails when any meaningful variation present cannot be distinguished from random variation expected in the population. When inferential uncertainty is low we suspect that something interesting *is* going on. Inferential uncertainty manifests itself in many different forms and the particular form depends largely on the research question that is being addressed. It depends upon three things: (a) the amount of information that we have to indicate that something interesting is going on; (b) random error; and (c) the sample size (or, more particularly, the square root of the sample size).

In the sort of research to which our artificial lighting example relates, researchers would almost definitely want to make a number of inferences and each of these would be associated with some uncertainty. For example, they would probably want to know whether people who work under artificial light differ in their levels of stress from those who work under natural light. Inferential uncertainty could be eliminated by sampling everyone in these two populations and seeing whether they differ. In practice, though, what any half-sensible researchers would do is take a sample of the people from both working conditions. They would then set about quantifying the amount of uncertainty associated with a statement suggesting that the two samples were not drawn from the same population. As with all inferential statistics, this quantification of uncertainty would actually be an estimation. It would be stated as a probability, where a lower probability would signify greater certainty about the inference being made.

In dealing with descriptive and inferential uncertainty, a researcher is often able to quantify the uncertainty accurately, but unable to remove it. Statistics allow researchers to make very precise descriptive and inferential statements, but the elimination of statistical uncertainty is best achieved by methodological changes. Among other things, statistical uncertainty can be minimized by increasing the power of the tests – by increasing the sample size, or by reducing the amount of random variation. Random variation could be reduced by using a within-subjects rather than a between-subjects design or by developing a more reliable measure of the phenomenon under investigation.

If statistical uncertainty *were* completely removed from research, however, it is likely that the psychological issues being addressed by the researcher would be extremely uninteresting. This is because the research would have to involve *complete sampling* of a *completely uniform* population. It is actually hard to think of any research using psychological statistics that would satisfy these requirements and would not be utterly trivial.

The observation that eliminating statistical uncertainty can lead to research that is trivial points to an extremely important tension in psychological research. This arises from the fact that, contrary to the significance fallacy, *statistical significance is not the same as psychological or theoretical significance.* Obtaining a statistically significant result tells us that descriptive and inferential uncertainty are tolerably low. But in the most extreme case statistical significance can amount to a statement of the blindingly obvious (e.g., that all first-year psychology students have one head). As a general rule, psychologists are not (or should not be) interested in truisms – their role is to contribute to and extend knowledge, not just to reproduce it.

Accordingly, an obsession with the reduction of statistical uncertainty can be counter-productive. This is one reason why in recent years the wisdom of a hypothesis-testing approach to statistical inference has come into question (as we noted in Chapter 8). One response to the problem of how to handle statistical uncertainty is to accompany treatments of inferential uncertainty (significance) with treatments of effect size. The aim of including information about effect size is to be sure not only that chance is not a plausible cause of our results, but also that they are of a sufficient size to be interesting or useful (criteria which will vary from area to area and problem to problem).

Statistical uncertainty is only one form of uncertainty faced by researchers, however. A second form, in many ways more serious, relates to confidence that research procedures are directly addressing the question in which researchers are interested and allowing them to answer it. It was this second form of uncertainty that we discussed in the chapters on research methodology in the first half of this book. It can be referred to as **methodological uncertainty**.

As with statistical uncertainty, it is useful to distinguish between two forms of methodological uncertainty. **Internal uncertainty** relates to researchers' confidence in their ability to interpret the results of a study correctly. This term has most in common with the notion of internal validity – the idea that in experimental research the observed effect of a particular manipulation has been correctly interpreted. In Chapter 4 we noted that a large number of features of experimental design can contribute to uncertainty of this form. Our ability to understand why the manipulation of an independent variable brings about change in a dependent variable can be compromised by the effects of maturation, history, reactivity, selection and various other experimental confounds. So, in a study of occupational stress our confidence in interpreting the effects of making one randomly selected group of workers work under non-artificial light would be reduced if participants' behaviour were affected by their knowledge that they were taking part in psychological research (as it was in the Hawthorne studies that we discussed in Chapter 4).

Unlike internal validity, however, the concept of internal uncertainty is not just relevant to experimental and quasi-experimental research. This form of uncertainty is also prevalent in survey research where independent variables are not directly manipulated. In survey research, whenever a relationship between two variables is observed it is inappropriate to draw any conclusions about the effects that one variable has on another. This means that internal uncertainty – pertaining to the interpretation of that relationship – must remain high. Nevertheless, such uncertainty can be reduced in cases where this type of research fails to reveal a relationship between two variables. As we discussed in Chapter 5, this is because a lack of correlation allows the researcher conclusively to *rule out* certain interpretations. For example, if research fails to find a relationship between lighting conditions and stress then internal uncertainty about the psychological interpretation of such a relationship is reduced. In this case, if someone suggests that workers become stressed because they get headaches from poor lighting, we will be reasonably certain they are wrong.

The second type of methodological uncertainty is **external uncertainty**, and this arises when we are not sure that the results we have obtained in our research can be generalized to the population of interest. In many respects this is the most generic form of uncertainty encountered in psychological research, partly because it is closely related to all the other forms of uncertainty that we have already considered. Obviously we do not want to generalize our results unless inferential and internal uncertainty are low. That is, before we can generalize a result we want to be confident that the result is not due to chance, and that it is due to the independent variable rather than some confound. However, it is also the case that we will find it easier to generalize our result when descriptive uncertainty is low (mainly because we will be more confident about what that result is).

In the example of the effect of artificial light on stress, we will have less external uncertainty if we show that the result applies under a wide range of conditions. For example, we will be more confident that we can generalize the results if they are obtained using representative random sampling techniques and a wide range of testing conditions

RESEARCH BITE 15.1
Uncertainty is the only certainty

In one of the most controversial papers in recent years, John Ioannidis (2005) identified a range of reasons why most published scientific findings are false. One of these is that a great deal of science involves reproducing biases and prejudices that prevail within a particular field at a particular point in time. These biases can be built into theory and practice in a great many ways – including the way data are collected, the way they are analysed and the way they are interpreted. We can never know the truth with 100% certainty, he argues, but can get a better grip on this by considering, and trying to integrate, the totality of evidence in a given field rather than obsessing about the statistical significance of small individual studies.

Reference
Ioannidis, J. P. (2005). Why most published research findings are false. *PLoS Medicine*, 2, e124.

and if they have been predicted on the basis of a well-developed theory (e.g., one which asserts that unnatural environments are psychologically damaging). On the other hand, external uncertainty will be high if we use naive empiricism to generalize research findings without recourse to theory or if we draw conclusions on the basis of samples that are not representative of the population of interest on theoretically relevant variables (problems we discussed in Chapter 4).

The concept of methodological uncertainty that we have introduced here does not replace the concept of validity, but rather complements it. Studies themselves can have validity or lack it, but it is researchers and consumers of research who actually express uncertainty about studies. This means that while the validity of a study must be constant over time, methodological uncertainty about that research can change depending on the state of scientific knowledge in a field. For example, this is what happened in the Hawthorne studies as researchers started to question some of the early explanations of the effects of manipulating factory working conditions (e.g., lighting levels). Certain inferences about these findings *always were* invalid – only the researchers' uncertainty changed. However, it was the level of uncertainty about the research, not its validity, that best characterized the state of scientific knowledge at any particular point in time. This reflects the fact that scientific knowledge is contingent on human understanding (and ignorance), not on facts in the abstract.

Because the interpretation of scientific data is a human activity, we often cannot be entirely certain that any particular study is internally valid and we can never be entirely sure that a study is externally valid. However, we can *and do* express varying degrees of certainty about the validity of a piece of research. These statements will often reflect the degree of agreement among researchers about the validity of a particular conclusion. Accordingly, where disputes about methodology occur, these usually involve one group of researchers being confident that conclusions about a study are valid and another group having doubts. Indeed, where *everybody* agrees that the validity of a study is low then it is unlikely that the research would be conducted and it is very unlikely that it would be reported. For experienced researchers, most methodological errors occur when they make what are perceived to be inappropriate claims about the results or implications of studies. This usually means that they have managed uncertainty badly, often by expressing more confidence in their interpretation of the results than appears to be warranted.

You will recall that researchers' ability to quantify statistical uncertainty is high, but it is often difficult to control. The very opposite is true for methodological uncertainty. No procedures have ever been agreed upon for measuring or estimating methodological uncertainty, but a lot is known about how to reduce it. As we noted in earlier chapters, internal uncertainty can be minimized or eliminated by using appropriately controlled experimental designs, while external methodological uncertainty can be reduced through appropriate sampling and the development of psychological theory.

The big question that you may now be asking yourself is, 'If research involves all these forms of uncertainty, how should they be collectively managed?'. In practice, strategic decisions about the management of uncertainty always involve *trade-offs*. Being sure about some things increases uncertainty about others. For example, if we reduce descriptive uncertainty by using a very homogeneous sample of participants in our research, we may increase external uncertainty about the applicability of our findings to a broader population. The relevance–sensitivity trade-off, discussed in Chapter 4, is another example of this point. As descriptive uncertainty is reduced through measurement sensitivity and accuracy, the relevance of research findings to the topic of interest may also be reduced, thereby increasing external uncertainty. Information about all four of the above types of uncertainty is summarized in Table 15.1.

Table 15.1 Forms of uncertainty that are typically addressed in psychological research

		Produced by	**Estimated by**	**Reduced by**
Form of uncertainty				
Statistical	Descriptive	Measurement error	Dispersion	Accurate measurement
		Individual differences		Using homogeneous samples
	Inferential	Chance/error	Probability	Increasing power
Methodological	Internal	Lack of control		Experimental control
	External	Sampling error		Appropriate sampling
		Naive empiricism		Theory development

One very important point to note about the above discussion is that because some of the terminology we have introduced in this chapter is novel (i.e., the terms in bold), you are unlikely to encounter it outside this book. That being the case, you may well ask why we have chosen to burden you with it at this late stage in proceedings. Surely, the last thing you need now is to be weighed down by even more terminology? Mindful of this question, there are three grounds on which we would justify this decision.

Our first justification is simply that we believe this attempted systematization provides a very useful way of summarizing, integrating and understanding the key concepts and procedures that we have been dealing with throughout the book. In short, thinking about doing psychological research as a process of uncertainty management allows us to draw together the many disparate elements of the research process. Managing uncertainty is what the practice of conducting any research is all about – people in different scientific fields simply have to deal with different forms of uncertainty and need to develop procedures and technology that allow them to do this adequately. As we have seen, psychologists have developed a number of statistical and methodological techniques that enable them to manage different forms of uncertainty in different ways. Yet the same is true for physicists, biologists and sociologists. Indeed, a large part of *any* researcher's skill relates precisely to knowledge about what form of management is appropriate for dealing with the particular types of uncertainty he or she confronts.

That being the case, a second justification for this way of thinking about psychological research is that it allows us to restate some core tenets of research practice quite straight-forwardly. That is, it follows from the above analysis that the twin goals of quantitative psychological research are to *minimize methodological uncertainty* and to *quantify statistical uncertainty*. This statement in fact covers most of what we have been concerned with in this book (with the notable exception of qualitative methods, as described in Chapters 12 and 13, where the goals tend to be more diverse). Indeed, we would go so far as to suggest that this is the underlying message in almost all textbooks that attempt to deal with principles of research methodology and statistics. It should be noted, however, that the terms we have developed are not intended to replace the well-established technical jargon that we have used throughout the book. Instead they are simply intended to enable you to develop a more integrated understanding of the place that those terms (and the activities to which they relate) occupy in the research process.

The question you may now ask yourself is whether the management of statistical and methodological uncertainty is all there is to psychological enquiry. Is doing psychological research only a question of engaging in the perpetual struggle with these two, really quite circumscribed, problems? The answer, of course, is 'no'. There are actually many other forms of uncertainty that are relevant to psychological research. Indeed, this provides the third reason for thinking about research practice as we have. Our aim in fencing off these two forms of uncertainty is partly to make it clear that there are other 'bigger picture' forms of uncertainty that are not really addressed in standard prescriptions for doing psychological (or any other) research.

In philosophical terms, the uncertainties we have dealt with can be thought of as *onto-logical* (i.e., they relate to the tangible existence of research findings). However, as we hinted in Chapter 2, there are also other *epistemological* uncertainties that are far less tangible (e.g., whether the research produces genuine or worthwhile knowledge). Among other things, such uncertainties take both a *social* and a *political* form (e.g., whether a given form of knowledge is acceptable in a particular research community, and whether particular groups in society benefit from the research; Ioannidis, 2005). For example, if we think about research into workers' productivity such as that we discussed earlier, we might have uncertainty about whether the research agenda is appropriate and whether the approach taken on an issue ultimately serves particular political interests. In this way the research might be criticized for addressing topics from a position that ultimately serves the narrow economic interests of management rather than the broad interests of the community (e.g., by defining productivity and performance in financial rather than social terms). Although the research area is very different in nature, similar issues pervade enquiry into the biological basis of personality and intelligence as this must always incorporate assumptions about the impact of environmental factors on behaviour. Given that the approach researchers take on *any* psychological issue will always reflect a particular ideological slant (however implicit), it is often appropriate to consider how the answers their research provides are constrained by the questions that are *not* asked.

Along these lines, a number of researchers interested in the social psychology of science have argued that progress in research is often achieved by *creating uncertainty* rather than by reducing it (e.g., Campbell, 1986; McGuire, 1997; Moscovici, 1976; Smithson, 1993). Uncertainty can be created when researchers are forced to confront new uncertainties using new methods (Kuhn, 1962). It can also be created when a researcher goes against the grain by questioning received wisdom and challenging knowledge that has been taken for granted within a particular worldview. This is what happened when Copernicus suggested that the earth went round the sun and when Freud suggested that the unconscious plays a central role in human behaviour. In many ways uncertainty reduction is therefore the business of 'normal science', while uncertainty creation is the stuff of scientific revolution.

We addressed some issues relating to the management of non-tangible forms of uncertainty in Chapter 14 when we discussed research ethics. However, any attempt to deal comprehensively with issues of social and political uncertainty lies well beyond the scope of this book. It is also the case that these other forms of uncertainty are generally discussed much less openly by researchers than the two forms of uncertainty that we have focused on here. Nevertheless, they exert a very profound influence on the research process (see Spears & Smith, 2001). Moreover, every researcher has to deal with these uncertainties one way or another. Sadly, perhaps, this sometimes means ignoring them or simply pretending they do not exist.

Note: Several of the following terms have been introduced in earlier chapters. They are reproduced here to recap key points in the above discussion.

descriptive uncertainty *Statistical uncertainty* arising from variation in observations around any measure of central tendency (or other expected value) and for which the researcher proposes no explanation. It is uncertainty in knowing or predicting individual scores on the basis of a measure of central tendency. This uncertainty is quantified by dispersion measures (e.g., standard deviation, variance, range).

external uncertainty A form of *methodological uncertainty* relating to researchers' ability to generalize their findings appropriately to a relevant population. This uncertainty can be reduced by appropriate sampling and theory development.

inferential uncertainty *Statistical uncertainty* relating to the possibility that an observed result is due to random error or chance. This uncertainty is estimated by a probability value, where a low probability indicates low uncertainty.

internal uncertainty A form of *methodological uncertainty* relating to researchers' ability to interpret correctly the reasons for the relationship between two variables. This uncertainty can be reduced through experimental control.

methodological uncertainty Doubt about the applicability of research findings arising from features of the research procedure. Generally speaking, this uncertainty is difficult to quantify but it can be minimized by appropriate research practice.

statistical uncertainty Doubt about statistics arising from the presence of random error. Generally speaking, such uncertainty is easier to estimate than to reduce.

Final comment

At the start of this book we stated that our objective was to provide a user-friendly introduction to research methodology and statistics. However, before we part company it is probably appropriate to acknowledge that this does not mean that our progress has been all smooth sailing. As the above overview makes clear, we have had to introduce and grapple with a large number of difficult concepts, terms and procedures. In our view none of these is trivial or expendable, and all need to be mastered (or at least addressed) at some stage by anyone who wants to conduct or to understand psychological research.

Despite this, we would go so far as to suggest that the researcher who is always completely on top of all the issues addressed in this book would be the exception rather than the rule. This is not because most researchers are stupid or lazy. The vast majority are neither. Rather it is because the issues themselves are extremely challenging and because things that we understand at one time can become hazy later. That being the case, we would like to think that once you feel confident about handling all the material contained in this book you will be well on the way to becoming an extremely competent researcher yourself.

Photo 15.2 We hope that the preceding chapters have provided you with foundations upon which you can build great research. And, just as importantly, we hope that it has motivated you to try. For, in the end, the success of this book will be measured not by what we have written, but by what you go on to do.

There are very many other complex and difficult issues that you still need to learn about and grapple with, but we have tried to ensure that your efforts to do so will be built upon a solid foundation. While we cannot promise that the new methodological and statistical issues you will encounter will always be easy to understand, we can guarantee that they will be much easier to cope with than would be the case if you had not already done the hard work of tackling the range of issues that have been addressed in the preceding chapters.

As you progress it is likely that you will develop views that diverge from our own and that you may become quite critical of some of the ideas we have presented. That, however, can only be a good thing. Psychological research is never passive and its underlying principles are never just 'given'. For that reason it is every researcher's first responsibility to *think critically*. If this book has helped to make you a more responsible and active participant in the research process, then its most important goal has been achieved.

CHECKLIST
Revisiting the key goals for this chapter

☐ I understand that psychological research is a process of uncertainty management.

☐ I understand the different forms that this uncertainty takes and the key ways in which psychologists manage this

☐ I can use this book as a springboard to becoming a very good researcher myself.

Further reading

Haslam and McGarty's (2001) paper provides a detailed elaboration of the arguments in this chapter, with specific reference to the way that uncertainty has been managed in 100 years of research in social psychology. Of course, having reached the end of this book, we hope that you will now be motivated and equipped to do a great deal more reading in order to find out more about the process of conducting psychological research and about the fruits of that process in particular areas that interest you.

Haslam, S. A., & McGarty, C. (2001). A hundred years of certitude? Social psychology, the experimental method and the management of scientific uncertainty. *British Journal of Social Psychology, 40*, 1–21.

Discussion/essay questions

a. Should the study of statistics and methodology be made optional in psychology courses?

b. Discuss the proposition that the key to successful research is a sound understanding of methodology.

c. Is the general public's limited understanding of research methodology and statistics a cause for concern?

d. What are the main things to be learned from studying psychology?

e. What general skills does a good psychologist need? To what extent are these skills related to an understanding of the research process?

f. Should psychology students be able to choose to study either quantitative or qualitative statistics or should everybody have to have some familiarity with both?

Appendix A

Writing Research Reports in Psychology

Overview

Writing laboratory reports is an essential skill that all psychology students need to master. In the first instance this is because writing reports will be a major component of assessment in any course that you undertake. However, the same skills are involved in writing up any piece of psychological research professionally. Indeed, the guidelines below are based on those laid out in the latest (sixth) edition of the *Publication Manual of the American Psychological Association* (2009) and these (or very similar) guidelines must be followed by all researchers who attempt to publish work in psychology journals.

The overall goal of a laboratory report is to provide the reader with details of the rationale, methodology, results and conclusions of a specific piece of psychological research. The idea is to convey why the research was done, and how what was found contributes to the sum of knowledge in a given area. Psychologists and psychology students spend a considerable amount of time reading formal reports of this form (i.e., in journal articles), and these reports all have a common format to allow readers to access the specific material they are interested in as quickly and easily as possible. First and foremost, then, writing laboratory reports is an exercise in *effective and efficient scientific communication.*

Basic structure

All laboratory reports contain a title, an Abstract, an Introduction, a Method section, a Results section and a Discussion. At the end of the report there is also a references section and sometimes an appendix. In essence, the report tells two stories. The first is a succinct overview of the rationale for the research and its design, together with the key findings and conclusions. This is presented in a short *Abstract* at the start of the report. The next four sections then tell essentially the same story in much more detail.

The *Introduction* introduces (a) the general topic under investigation, (b) the theories that relate to that topic and relevant research that bears upon those theories, and (c) the specific hypotheses examined in the report, with an indication of exactly how these hypotheses are tested. Note that (a) leads to (b) and (b) to (c), in an *ever-narrowing* focus.

Appendix A: Writing Research Reports

The *Method* section provides the reader with specific information about how the study was conducted – who the participants were, what materials or apparatus were used, and what the procedure for running the experiment was. This ensures that readers can be clear about exactly what the researcher did, so that if necessary they would be in a position to replicate that research themselves.

The *Results* section provides information about the data produced by the research, with details of all relevant descriptive and inferential statistics.

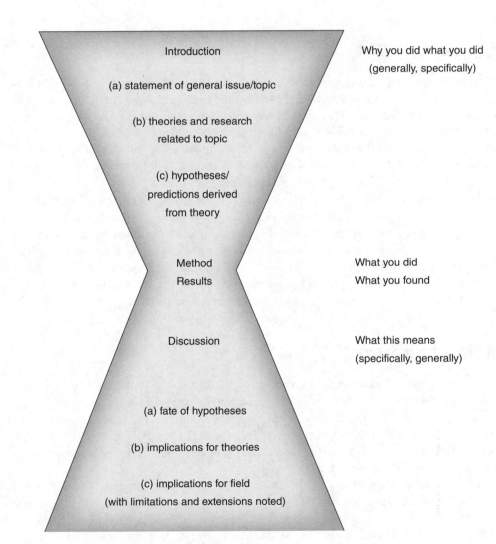

Figure A.1   Structure of a research report

The *Discussion* then discusses (a) the fate of the hypotheses (whether or not they were supported), (b) the implications of this for relevant theories, and (c) the implication of these outcomes for the field as a whole. Limitations of the research are also noted and suggestions are made about important directions for future research. Note that here (a) leads to (b) and (b) leads to (c), in an *ever-broadening* focus.

These four sections represent the body of the report, and together they can be seen to have an hourglass structure, as indicated in Figure A.1. The Introduction starts with broad issues and leads into the tight focus of the research at hand (a focus which is maintained through the Method and Results sections), while the Discussion starts with the issues at hand and leads back to the broad issues raised at the start of the report.

At the conclusion of the report, the *references* section provides information about the source of all the research that has been referred to in the report. An *appendix* then includes any supplementary material too bulky to incorporate in the Method or Results sections and not essential for the report to make sense.

The sections in detail

Title

The title of a report should provide a succinct statement (about 10–12 words) of the core purpose of the research, and for this reason it is usually framed in terms of the key independent and dependent variables and/or a key question that is to be addressed. Additional information that conveys important or distinctive information can be contained in a new clause separated by a colon. However, the title should be as punchy as possible (and definitely no more than two lines long), so avoid unnecessarily long or wordy titles and omit superfluous words. The following are some good and bad examples:

- ✓ The Role of Imagery and Depth of Processing in Memory for Words
- ✓ The Effect of Peer Feedback on Social Behaviour: A Study of Dieting Habits in Adolescents

- ✗ A Study of Students' Memory for Words in the Lab [No IV and irrelevant information]
- ✗ A Survey Asking Why People Diet [No IV]
- ✗ Lab Report 1 [No IV or DV]

Abstract

The Abstract provides a short overview of research. It should be about 120 words long (no more than 960 characters) and is always presented on page 2 of the report. At a minimum it should state what the research involved (e.g., what the IVs and DVs were), who participated in it, and what the key results were. It should also say which theories or predictions were tested and whether these were supported.

The key here is that the Abstract must present the most important information about the report. If research is published the Abstract is usually the only information stored on databases, and so in many instances a reader will make a decision about whether or not to read the entire article based on this information alone.

It is also worth noting that the process of writing the Abstract is good preparation for writing the report as a whole, as it should clarify in your own mind what was important about the research and how the main features of the research fitted together. If you are having problems writing the Abstract, this should warn you that you are not yet ready to write the report or that if you have already written the report your ideas may not be clearly structured.

Writing tip

Writing the Abstract 'cold' can be quite difficult and it is usually much easier to do if you have already written the rest of the report (indeed the standard advice you will be given in most writing guides is 'write the Abstract last'). However, if you start by trying to write the Abstract, you can get a 'feel' for the report as a whole, and also use this task to diagnose problems you are likely to encounter in your report by highlighting sentences that you are having difficulty writing. If these sentences relate to your reasons for doing the study, problems in your Introduction are likely and you may need to do more reading. If the problems relate to describing the mechanics of the study, problems in the Method section are likely, and so on.

Introduction

The Introduction needs to introduce the reader to the scientific problem that is addressed by the reported research. This should be done in a number of steps. The Introduction should start with a broad statement of why the particular topic being addressed is interesting and important. It should then progress to outline theories and other research relevant to that topic and to the research being conducted. It is important that this part of the Introduction focuses on aspects of the existing literature that are relevant to material covered in the remainder of the report, so *be selective* and avoid unnecessary details. Finally, the Introduction should clarify how these broad issues and theories are addressed in the research. This clarification will explain why the research incorporated the particular IVs and DVs that it did (e.g., what theories suggest they are important, which previous research has used them). All this should lead up to the final paragraph of the Introduction that summarizes the aim of the research to be reported and clearly states the hypotheses that are to be tested in the research (or, if not hypotheses, a set of questions that you plan to answer).

The Introduction as a whole should thus tell an internally coherent story about 'why you did what you did'. This story should be accessible to as broad a scientific audience as possible and should make the research that is going to be presented in the report appear to be a balanced and reasonable attempt to deal with an important scientific issue. The point here is to provide a *platform* for the remainder of the report by setting up a framework within which the methodology and findings of the study make sense and can be interpreted.

Two additional points are worth making. First, a very common error in reports is that the link between theory and hypothesis is not fully elaborated in the Introduction. Therefore *make sure that you always explain how an experimental hypothesis (or prediction) is derived from relevant theory.* Second, note that most research does not just address a single issue in isolation. However, the results of any piece of research often shed more light on some issues than on others, and so it is reasonable that the report as a whole focuses on those aspects of research where knowledge is advanced. Bearing this in mind, the Introduction needs to be framed in terms of issues that are going to be important in the remainder of the report, rather than those that might have been important if the research had gone entirely as planned. This point becomes especially relevant as you start to take control of the research process yourself (i.e., as you start to write up projects that you have been responsible for designing and conducting). However, you must still form hypotheses before conducting the research.

Writing tips

Ask yourself 'Why did we do this research?'. Your Introduction needs to provide a sensible answer to this question, so you should not start writing it until you can provide one (at both a general and specific level).

When you have written the Introduction, consider every paragraph in turn. Ask yourself 'How does this paragraph help me to explain why we did this research?'. If the answer is 'it does not', the material may be irrelevant and you should consider reworking or removing the paragraph.

Checklist for Introduction

1 Identify general issue/problem.
2 Outline theories that relate to the problem.
3 Summarize evidence for these theories that is relevant to the present study.
4 Explain how theories will be examined in this study.
5 Summarize the study's aims and hypotheses.

Method

The point of the Method section is to provide enough information for readers to understand clearly what you actually did in the research so that they would be in a position to replicate it themselves if they wished. Here separate subsections usually provide details of the design of the research, the participants, the apparatus or materials involved in conducting the study and the exact procedure. To save space and avoid repetition, these subsections are sometimes combined (e.g., as 'Participants and Design' or 'Materials and Procedure'). If information is important for replication but unwieldy and not essential to understanding how the experiment was conducted, it can be placed in an appendix.

Participants

A short paragraph should indicate who participated in the research and report important demographic features of that research sample (i.e., their age and sex). Other descriptive characteristics of the sample relevant to the research should also be reported. For example, if the research is a study of visual perception it may be important to indicate how many of the participants wore glasses. The method for selecting the participants should also be identified, as well as details of any payment or reward they received in return for participation. The process by which participants were assigned to conditions should also be made clear and information provided about participants who did not complete the study or whose responses were not included in analysis (e.g., because they had participated in the study before).

Design

If the research is experimental, a short design statement is sometimes provided before describing the procedure more thoroughly (this section is optional and not required under APA guidelines). This indicates what the independent variables were, how many levels there were of each (and what the various treatments were) and how they were manipulated (within or between subjects). Key DVs can also be defined. A good design statement might read as follows:

> Mood was manipulated between subjects and participants were randomly assigned to one of three conditions (good mood, neutral mood or bad mood). Responses were obtained on two dependent measures: the Leeds Sadness Scale (LSS) and the Maudsley Mood Inventory (MMI).

Apparatus (or Materials)

This subsection should provide information about important pieces of equipment that were necessary for the study's completion (e.g., a video recorder, computer or electroencephalograph). Details of questionnaires can also be provided. The maxim of relevance is important here: focus on those features of the research that are necessary for replication or which may have had a bearing on the results. For example, the fact that reaction time was measured by hand may be mentioned if you think that measurement error may have been a problem in the research.

Procedure

This subsection provides the reader with a step-by-step account of the participation process. It should describe all relevant events in the research from beginning to end (e.g., where the study took place, how assignment to conditions occurred, the order and timing of dependent measures, the nature of debriefing). However, avoid dwelling on irrelevant details or spending too long describing routine aspects of the research.

Writing tip

Imagine that in 10 years' time someone came to you and said 'I heard about that great study you did and I think it can make a great contribution to psychological science – but I'd like to see it replicated'. You have completely forgotten about the study and all other reports of the research have been lost. However, after rummaging around for a while, you come across the Method section of your report. Ask yourself 'Based on the information in my Method section, would I be able to faithfully reproduce my original research?' If the answer is 'no', think about why this is the case and set about providing the information that would enable you to answer 'yes'.

Results

The Results section summarizes the data obtained in the research and the outcomes of statistical analyses. The section often starts with an overview outlining the basic strategies used to analyse data (e.g., providing information about data aggregation and procedures used to make statistical inferences). It then goes on to report the results of those statistical analyses that relate to the goals of the research outlined in the Introduction, and will be used to draw conclusions in the upcoming Discussion section. The Results section should present the results of statistical analysis and say what those results mean in empirical terms rather than attempting to draw broader practical or theoretical implications from them:

- ✓ Judgements on the 10 trials were averaged for each participant. Mean scores for participants in the two experimental conditions were then compared using a between-subjects t-test. Participants in the fixation condition judged the variable line to be longer than did those in the scanning condition ($Ms = 4.23$, 2.31, respectively), $t(25) = 2.24$, $d = 0.91$, $p = .03$. This result indicates that the Müller–Lyer illusion was stronger for participants in the fixation condition.

- ✓ Participants displayed greater need for achievement in the individual condition than in the group condition ($Ms = 5.43$, 3.21, respectively), $t(24) = 2.24$, $d = 0.91$, $p = .03$.

- ✗ The difference between means was significant, $t(24) = 2.24$, $d = 0.91$, $p < .05$, a result that supports the social relations model but that is inconsistent with the trait model. (Note too that this does not present an exact p-value.)

If the pattern of relevant results is difficult to grasp when described in written text, it may help to place them in *either* a table *or* a figure (i.e., a graph). The table or graph should then be referred to at a relevant point in the text. If you need to provide details of statistical calculations or raw data, these should be provided in an appendix.

Statistical notation in Results sections should generally follow the examples provided in the chapters above. To summarize: M = mean, SD = standard deviation, N = sample size, n = a sub-sample (e.g., the number of participants in one condition).

Writing tips

When you have written the Results section look back at what you wrote in the Introduction and ask yourself 'Does my Results section provide simple and clear information relating to the questions raised in my Introduction?'. This information is absolutely vital (and should represent the core of the Results section), so if it is missing or hidden away, you must take steps to revise the Results section accordingly.

Instructors have differing views about referring to the original hypotheses in the Results section. Many say you should never do this. Others believe that it can be helpful, especially when the results are complex. However, only refer to hypotheses if your instructor considers this appropriate.

Discussion

The Discussion mirrors the Introduction in starting with a summary of the key findings of the research, then broadening to consider how those findings fit with previous research and theory, and their implications for understanding of the research topic as a whole. The overall aim of this section is to provide a satisfactory conclusion to the *research story* that was introduced at the start of the report. As far as possible all loose ends should be tied up, and the reader should be left with a feeling that the research has advanced understanding of the psychological issues it addresses. Note that in order to be useful, research does not need to support all (or any) of the researcher's hypotheses (see Chapter 2).

It is often appropriate to start the Discussion by restating the aim of the experiment and the hypotheses that were under investigation. This helps to refresh the reader's memory and contextualize what follows. The section must then summarize the research findings as they relate to these aims and consider the relationship between the findings and the hypotheses presented at the end of the Introduction. Do the findings support these hypotheses or not?

The Discussion should then continue by clarifying the implications of the results for theories relevant to the topic that is being addressed and for the literature on that topic in general. These considerations should point out any inconsistencies or anomalies between the present and previous findings as well as potential ways of reconciling or making sense of them. It is important here that your observations are guided by the findings at hand, so avoid making unsubstantiated claims or going beyond the available information. It is acceptable to speculate about the broader meaning of your findings, but when these speculations are post hoc (i.e., after the fact) you must make this clear.

Any limitations of the study should also be discussed, as well as methodological changes that might be implemented in future research as a means of surmounting them and taking research forward. The Discussion then typically concludes with a simple summary of the significance of the reported research. If possible, try to end on a positive note that conveys some enthusiasm for the issues at hand. Here and throughout the Discussion you need to indicate to the reader that you have engaged critically and constructively with the research findings. For this reason you should try to avoid banal, clichéd or platitudinous comments that generally suggest a lack of engagement on your part (e.g., 'further research into this important topic will help advance knowledge').

Writing tip

Make a list in point form of the things that you want the reader to have learned from reading your report. These represent the main contribution of the research. Now take a working draft of your Discussion and mark the sections that deal with each point. Ask yourself whether all the points are covered and are given appropriate treatment. If you answer 'yes' to both questions, your Discussion may be close to completion. However, also check the sections that are *not* marked. Ask yourself whether these are all essential to the story that your report tells. If they are not, you probably have some more thinking to do.

Checklist for Discussion

1 Briefly restate the study's aim and summarize the results in relation to hypotheses.
2 Remark on the consistency of the findings with previous literature.
3 Clarify the theoretical implications of the findings.
4 Note methodological or applied implications, including limitations of the study.
5 Make original suggestions for future research.
6 Draw conclusions related to the general issue/problem identified at the outset.

References

This section provides an alphabetical listing of all research material (e.g., articles, books) referred to in the report (for formatting details, see below). Note that this is *not* a bibliography, and so the section should not list material unless it has been explicitly referred to in your report.

Appendices

It may be appropriate (or for assessment purposes you may be required) to include appendices at the end of your report which present bulky and non-essential material that the reader may wish to inspect (e.g., complete questionnaires, details of statistical calculations, raw data). Each appendix should have a descriptive title and must be referred to in the body of the report.

General stylistic issues

A research report is a formal piece of work like an essay or a literature review. For this reason, it needs to be as well written and polished as any other piece of scholarly writing. Sentences should therefore be grammatical and complete, tenses and parts of speech should be used appropriately, and the report as a whole must read well and flow lucidly from one section to another. As well as this, though, the report needs to present information economically and concisely, so you should avoid any temptation to write in a florid or gushing style. Use words carefully and precisely (thinking carefully about the meaning of what you write and whether it is what you intend to say), and avoid colloquial expressions. You should also avoid sexist language. This includes using sex-specific terms (e.g., 'he', 'she', 'his', 'her') when a statement is equally applicable to both men and women. The following examples illustrate some common stylistic errors:

- ✗ The experiment was done in a big lab. [informal/ colloquial]
- ✓ The experiment was conducted in a large laboratory.

- ✗ It is not unreasonable to suppose that this result is indicative of bias on the part of participants. [florid language]
- ✓ This result suggests that participants were biased.

- ✗ The results reject the hypothesis. [imprecise: experimenters reject hypotheses, not results]
- ✓ The results are inconsistent with the hypothesis.

- ✗ Each participants responses were coded by a computer and participant's global scores were recorded on it's hard disk. [incorrect use of apostrophes; note *it's* = *it is*]
- ✓ Each participant's responses were coded by a computer and participants' global scores were recorded on its hard disk.

- ✗ When a participant responded in this way he showed bias. [sexist language, if the participants could be either male or female]
- ✓ When participants responded in this way they showed bias. *Or* This type of response reveals bias.

- ✗ The affect of alcohol is deleterious because it effects people's reaction times. [confusion of effect and affect. Note that *affect* as a noun refers to a feeling or emotion, but as a transitive verb it means to act upon; *effect* as a noun refers to a result or consequence, but as a transitive verb it means to bring about]
- ✓ The effect of alcohol is deleterious because it affects people's reaction times. [here 'effect' is a noun and 'affect' a transitive verb]

Reports are descriptions of studies that have already been conducted, and so they should be written primarily in the past tense. However, at some points in the report it may be appropriate to write in the present tense (e.g., when describing the results of the experiment) or in the future tense (e.g., when discussing issues that subsequent experiments might address). Generally, though, write in the past tense unless there is a good reason not to:

- ✓ The experiment tested the hypothesis that group interaction is stressful. [past tense]
- ✓ These results are consistent with predictions. [present tense]
- ✓ Future research will need to explore this issue further. [future tense]

Many psychologists also prefer reports to be written in the *passive voice* rather than the *active voice*. This is the difference between writing 'The participants were given a standard IQ test to complete' and 'The participants completed a standard IQ test'. The APA actually advocates use of the active voice, so it is a good idea to get guidance from your instructors on this point.

Finally, one extremely important feature of a report (as with a psychology essay) is that it must *reference previous research and ideas appropriately*. As noted above, at various stages in the report (especially in the Introduction and Discussion) you will need to refer to work that has previously been conducted by other researchers. Here you must cite the source of that work appropriately (see later) and acknowledge the source of any of your own ideas that are based on that previous research. This is necessary for a number of reasons, most obviously so that readers can find that source for themselves if they are interested in checking or following up on the observations you make, and so that you do not inappropriately pass off someone else's ideas as your own.

It is important to note here that there is no shame in using and developing other people's ideas (indeed, this is an essential part of scientific progress; see Chapter 2). However, it is wrong to do so dishonestly, either by under-referencing or, in the most extreme cases, by *plagiarizing* (copying the work of others – an academic crime that will be dealt with severely).

Presentational issues

As with the structure and style of the report, a clear set of guidelines covers the way in which the report is presented on the printed page. These guidelines cover a broad range of issues, and it is a good idea to take a look at the *Publication Manual of the American Psychological Association* to see the various areas that are covered. Here, though, we will focus on four important areas: (a) the overall presentation of the report; (b) section headings; (c) figures and tables; (d) numbers in text; and (e) referencing.

Overall presentation

The report as a whole should be typed single-sided on good-quality paper using double spacing and a single, simple and legible font (e.g., 12 point Times). A wide margin (at least 2.5 cm) should be left around the text (providing room for the reader's/marker's comments).

Section headings

These should be placed in all reports as follows (_____ = necessary page break):

Running Head: SHORT HEADER   1

Title   [around 10–12 words]

Author Name

Other information (as required, e.g., a word count)

SHORT HEADER   2

Abstract   [around 120 words]

Text text text text text text text text text text text text text text text text text text

Text text text text text text text text text text text text text text text text

---

SHORT HEADER   3

Title   [Note: Introduction has no heading]

Text text text text text text text text text text text text text text text text text text

text text text text text text text text text text text text text text text text text text

Method

Participants

Text text text text text text text text text text text text text text text text text text

text text text text text text text text text text text text text text text text text text

Design

Text text text text text text text text text text text text text text text text text text

text text text text text text text text text text text text text text text text text text

Materials

Text text text text text text text text text text text text text text text text text text

text text text text text text text text text text text text text text text text text text

Procedure

Text text text text text text text text text text text text text text text text text text

text text text text text text text text text text text text text text text text text text

Results

Text text text text text text text text text text text text text text text text text text

text text text text text text text text text text text text text text text text text text

Figure 1 Figure caption

Table 1

Table Caption

text text text text text text text text text text text text text text text text text text

text text text text text text text text text text text text text text text text text text

text text text text text text text text text text text text text text text text text text

Notes: (if required)

Text text text text text text text text text text text text text text text text text text

Discussion

Text text text text text text text text text text text text text text text text text text
text text text text text text text text text text text text text text text text text text

---

SHORT HEADER   #

References

Text text text text text text text text text text text text text text text text text text
Text text text text text text text text text text text text text text text text text text

---

SHORT HEADER   #

Appendix A

Title

Text text text text text text text text text text text text text text text text text text
text text text text text text text text text text text text text text text text text text

---

SHORT HEADER   #

Appendix B

Title

Text text text text text text text text text text text text text text text text text text
text text text text text text text text text text text text text text text text text text

Tables and figures

These should be numbered consecutively through the report (starting with Table 1 and Figure 1), they should have a simple and clear explanatory title, and they should be positioned as close as possible to the place in the text where they are first referred to. Table titles are positioned at the top of each table, with the first letter of all key words capitalized. Figure captions are presented below each figure, and only the first letter of the first word is capitalized. All features of the tables and figures (e.g., columns, rows, axes) should be appropriately labelled so that the meaning of any given number or data point is unambiguous. Columns in tables should be separated by appropriate spacing rather than vertical lines, although horizontal lines can be used to separate rows where necessary. APA guidelines suggest that labels on the *y*-axis of graphs should be typed vertically (going upward) unless they are very short.

Examples are as follows:

Table 1   *Mean Reaction Time (in Milliseconds) as a Function of Alcohol Use*

Alcohol use	*n*	*M*	*SD*
High	11	173	16.1
Low	23	124	12.4
None	14	120	10.9

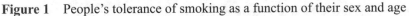

Figure 1   People's tolerance of smoking as a function of their sex and age

Numbers in text

The APA rules for writing numbers in the text of a report are very complex. We recommend that students follow the following relatively simple rule that corresponds to APA style most of the time. Write numbers less than 10 in words and all others in digits. There are two important exceptions: (a) if numbers less than 10 are grouped for comparison with numbers greater than or equal to 10 then write them all as digits (e.g., 'one or two'; '3 vs. 11'; '265 and 102'); (b) use digits for all numbers that represent measurements of units (e.g., for time, age, and positions in a series and sample sizes); and (c) always write numbers in words at the start of a sentence.

Referencing

As noted above, where the work of other researchers is relevant to ideas or findings you refer to in the report, this needs to be referenced appropriately (note that referencing in psychological reports is not done using footnotes). At the relevant point in the text this involves identifying the relevant publication using the researcher's (or researchers') last name(s) and the date of publication. This information is contained in brackets and if multiple authors are referred to these are ordered alphabetically based on the first author's last name. If a paper has more than two authors and the paper is referred to more than once, then when cited for a second time the last names of the second and subsequent authors are truncated to 'et al.'. Examples are as follows:

- ✓ Previous research has shown that people favour members of their own group (Brewer, 1979; Tajfel, Flament, Billig, & Bundy, 1971).
- ✓ The work of Tajfel and colleagues (Tajfel, Flament, Billig, & Bundy, 1971) has shown that people favour members of their own group.

Then later:

- ✓ This point is confirmed by findings from the minimal group studies (Tajfel et al., 1971).
- ✓ This point is confirmed by findings reported by Tajfel et al. (1971).

In psychological reports it is not customary to include extensive direct quotes from other sources. However, when quoting the work of another researcher, the relevant text needs to be surrounded by quotation marks and accompanied by a page reference. Modifications to the text (e.g., to correct errors, regularize grammar or clarify meaning) are indicated by square brackets as in the following example:

In their seminal text, Katz and Kahn (1966, p. 16) note that organizations have classically been defined as 'social device[s] for efficiently accomplishing some stated purpose'.

Whenever a reference to the work of researchers is made in the text, the full reference to that citation is then provided in an alphabetical list of such references provided in the reference section at the end of the report. Here journal articles, book chapters, edited books and authored books are referenced as follows:

Journal article

✓ Bate, P. (1984). The impact of organizational culture on approaches to organizational problem solving. *Organizational Studies*, 5, 43–66.

Authored book

✓ Adorno, T. W., Frenkel-Brunswik, E., Levinson, D. J., & Sanford, R. N. (1950). *The authoritarian personality*. New York: Harper.

Edited book

✓ Cartwright, D., & Zander, A. (Eds.) (1960). *Group dynamics: Research and theory* (2nd ed.). Evanston, IL: Row Peterson.

Book chapter

✓ Brown, R. J. (1978). Divided we fall: Analysis of relations between different sections of a factory workforce. In H. Tajfel (Ed.), *Differentiation between social groups: Studies in the social psychology of intergroup relations* (pp. 395–429). London: Academic Press.

When modelling your own reference list on the above examples, pay careful attention to the order in which each element of the reference is placed, the punctuation, capitalization and italicizing.

Further reading

The *APA Publication Manual* (as it is commonly known) is the standard reference text for writing in psychology. Its guidelines on issues of style and formatting have changed quite considerably over the years and any changes always arouse keen debate (not least because the logic behind these can be very hard to fathom). Nonetheless, it is an authority whose strictures researchers and students cannot afford to ignore.

American Psychological Association (2009). *Publication manual of the American Psychological Association* (6th ed.). Washington, DC: Author.

Sample psychology research report

The following is a sample 1500-word report of an experiment that attempted to replicate a study conducted by Condry and Condry (1976). It is designed to give you an example to refer to when writing your own reports. Be aware that it is tailored to this particular experiment – you will need to make changes to the structure of the argument (as well as to the content) to suit the study you are writing up. Borders indicate separate pages.

A fully formatted version of this report is also available in Online Appendix A. This is annotated to point out a range of important presentational issues that you need to attend to.

PERCEIVED SEX AND EMOTIONAL JUDGEMENT   1

The Role of Children's Perceived Sex in Judgements of Their Emotions

A. Student

University of Yourtown

PERCEIVED SEX AND EMOTIONAL JUDGEMENT   2

Abstract

Many studies have identified sex differences in children's behaviour. However, some of these differences may be the result of stereotypic expectations about the behaviour of girls and boys. The purpose of this study was to determine whether the perceived sex of a child does in fact affect perceptions of its emotional reactions. Undergraduate students ($N = 215$) viewed a videotape of an infant's emotional responses to various stimuli. Half were told the infant was a boy, half that it was a girl. Participants were then asked to rate the emotional reactions of the child. Consistent with the findings of Condry and Condry (1976), the child was generally perceived to be more emotional when it was thought to be a boy. Findings suggest that sex differences revealed by observational studies in which the raters know the sex of the child should be treated with caution.

PERCEIVED SEX AND EMOTIONAL JUDGEMENT   3

The Role of Children's Perceived Sex in Judgements of Their Emotions

Several studies of children have shown that the behavioural and emotional characteristics of young boys differ from those of girls. For example, Fagot (1974) found that boys exhibited a higher degree of motor activity and object manipulation than girls, while girls engaged in more verbal communication. Cramer (1970) observed that 3- to 7-year-old boys were more aggressive and impulsive than girls, who displayed a greater degree of self-control. Jerseld and Holmes (1935, as cited in Condry & Condry, 1976) found that toddler girls expressed a higher degree of fear in response to fear-provoking stimuli than did boys.

Maccoby and Jacklin (1974) have proposed that some of these sex differences may be due to a process of shaping whereby adults only encourage behaviour seen to be appropriate for the child's sex. This explanation assumes that adults have differential expectations regarding the appropriate behaviour for boys and girls. However, it has also been argued that the existence of such differential expectations may also bias observers so that they exaggerate the extent to which boys and girls behave differently (Cooper, 1974).

As with most findings of sex differences, the studies mentioned above used observational methods to rate the behaviour of the child. With this technique, the child's sex is usually known to the observer. Accordingly, it is possible that ratings maybe influenced by the observer's own expectations of sex-appropriate behaviour (Cooper, 1974).

In order to determine whether rated sex differences are influenced by the expectations of the observer, Condry and Condry (1976) asked observers to make judgements of the behaviour

PERCEIVED SEX AND EMOTIONAL JUDGEMENT   4

of a single child. Observers watched a videotape of the child's responses to a number of stimuli and then rated the degree to which they thought each of three different emotions (fear, anger, and pleasure) was present in the child's response. Half the participants were told that they were watching a boy, and half were told that they were watching a girl. When the ratings were aggregated across stimuli and type of emotion, it was found that the child was rated as showing a higher overall level of emotional response if thought to be a boy. Evidence that perceptions of behaviour are influenced by sex stereotypes was also found. When the child was presented with a stimulus that produced a negative, but ambiguous, emotion, the child was rated as more aggressive if perceived to be a boy, but as more fearful if perceived to be a girl.

This experiment attempted to replicate the basic pattern of findings reported by Condry and Condry (1976). Following their results, it was predicted that the perceived sex of the child would influence observers' ratings of its emotional reactions. Specifically, it was hypothesized that a child believed to be a boy would be perceived to be more emotional than one believed to be a girl.

Method

Participants

The participants were 226 undergraduate psychology students attending scheduled laboratory sessions. Of these 139 were women and 87 were men. Data from 11 students (7 women, 4 men) who had read the course manual before the class were not included in subsequent analysis.

PERCEIVED SEX AND EMOTIONAL JUDGEMENT   5

Design

The independent variable was the sex attributed to the child (male or female). This factor was manipulated between-subjects, with participants randomly assigned to groups. The dependent variable was the rated level of emotional reactivity.

Materials and Procedure

Participants were randomly allocated to one of two groups, with each group receiving a different instruction sheet (see Appendix A). Half of the participants were informed that the child was a girl; the other half were told it was a boy. Participants were required to transfer information about the child, including its sex, from their instruction sheet to a rating sheet. This allowed the attributed sex of the child to be manipulated without the experimenter having to state the child's sex publicly.

When they had all done this, participants watched a video depicting a 9-month-old child reacting to five presentations of each of five emotionally arousing stimuli. The stimuli were a toy wombat, a toy rabbit, a toy bear, a jack-in-the-box, and a strange noise. Immediately following the five presentations of each stimulus, participants rated the child's response to that stimulus on three dimensions indicating the amount of pleasure, anger, and fear displayed by the child. Responses were made on 11-point rating scales ranging from 0 (indicating that no emotion was displayed) to 10 (indicating a great deal of emotion).

Results

The data consisted of ratings of the degree of fear, anger, and pleasure shown by the child in response to each stimulus. Ratings were averaged across the presented objects and types of emotion to give a global measure of emotional reaction. Means and standard deviations for these global ratings are presented in Table 1 as a function of the attributed sex of the child.

Table 1   Global Ratings of Emotional Reaction as a Function of Child's Attributed Sex

Attributed sex	n	M	SD
Male	10	64.20	1.31
Female	10	92.43	1.02

From this table it can be seen that ratings of emotion were higher when the child was thought to be a boy, $M = 4.20$, than when it was thought to be a girl, $M = 2.43$. A between-subjects t-test indicated that this difference was significant, $t(213) = 10.92$, $d = 1.50$, $p < .001$. Details of t-test calculations are presented in Appendix B.

Discussion

The aim of this experiment was to see whether ratings of a child's emotionality would be affected by its perceived sex. As hypothesized, the results indicate that a child was rated as more emotional when it was thought to be a boy than when it was thought to be a girl. This pattern replicates Condry and Condry's (1976) findings and supports their conclusion that the perceived sex of a child can influence ratings of its behaviour.

There are two key implications of this finding. First, it serves to question the validity of sex differences reported in rating studies where the observers are aware of a child's sex (e.g., Cramer, 1970; Fagot, 1974). The present results raise the possibility that such findings may reflect observers' expectations, based on sex stereotypes, rather than genuine behavioural differences. Evidence that this stereotypic biasing can occur is also provided by Condry and Condry's (1976) finding that, when presented with a buzzer as a stimulus, their 'boy' was rated as showing anger, while their 'girl' was rated as showing fear. It is possible that similar results would be obtained from more fine-grained analysis of the data collected in the present study (i.e., based on separate analysis of scores on different measures rather than a global measure of emotional reaction) and this should be examined in future studies.

Second, the present findings suggest that biases in the interpretation of a child's behaviour may contribute to subsequent shaping of that behaviour into sex-appropriate forms, along lines suggested by Maccoby and Jacklin (1974). For example, a boy who cries may be treated by his parents as if he is angry, while a girl may be treated as if she is afraid. It is worth noting that Rothbart and Maccoby (1966) actually found that the pattern of such shaping also depended on the sex of the observer: fathers were more permissive with a child they thought was a girl, while mothers were more permissive with a child they thought was a boy. In future research it would therefore be interesting to see whether the pattern of results obtained in the present study varies as a function of the observer's sex.

Conclusion

This study demonstrates that the apparent sex of a child can influence adults' perception of that child's behaviour. This casts doubt on findings of sex differences in studies where the observer

knows the sex of the child and raises the possibility that sex-based biases in the interpretation of behaviour may contribute to shaping of children's behaviour. Clearly this suggests that it might be necessary for future research to replicate important findings of sex differences in studies where the observer remains unaware of the child's sex in order to establish the reliability of those effects and the validity of received interpretations of them.

However, it is worth noting that one important limitation of this study was that the participants were students who on average may have had limited previous experience as observers of children's behaviour. This fact may reduce the study's external validity because similar results might not emerge if participants had greater expertise. For this reason, it would seem prudent to conduct further research to see whether the same biases that emerged in this study also emerge in ratings provided by participants with more direct experience of young children's behaviour. To this end, future studies might attempt to replicate the present study using parents and/or developmental experts as participants.

PERCEIVED SEX AND EMOTIONAL JUDGEMENT   8

References

Condry, J., & Condry, S. (1976). Sex differences: A study of the eye of the beholder. *Child Development, 7,* 812–819.

Cooper, E. S. (1974). Direct observation? *Bulletin of the British Psychological Society, 27,* 3–7.

Cramer, B. (1970). Some sex differences in children between three and seven. *Psychosocial Processes, 6,* 60–76.

Fagot, B. I. (1974). Sex differences in toddlers' behaviour and parental reaction. *Developmental Psychology, 10,* 554–558.

Maccoby, E. M., & Jacklin, C. N. (1974). *The psychology of sex differences.* Stanford, CA: Stanford University Press.

Rothbart, M. K., & Maccoby, E. E. (1966). Parents' differential reactions to sons and daughters. *Journal of Personality and Social Psychology, 4,* 237–243.

PERCEIVED SEX AND EMOTIONAL JUDGEMENT   9

Appendix A

Instruction sheets

[You would place relevant material here. In this instance this would include details of the materials provided to participants]

PERCEIVED SEX AND EMOTIONAL JUDGEMENT   10

Appendix B

SPSS output

[You would place relevant material here. In this instance this could present a copy of IBM SPSS Statistics software (SPSS) output – something that an instructor might require you to include.]

Appendix B

Areas under the Standard Normal Curve

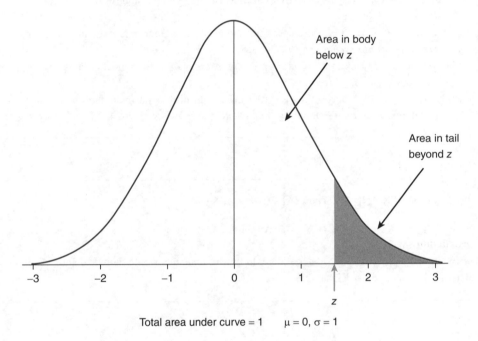

Figure B.1

Table B.1 gives details of the proportion of the area under the standard normal curve lying in the body below and in the tail beyond particular z-scores. The table can be used either to identify probability levels associated with particular z-scores or to identify z-scores associated with particular probabilities.

For example, to find out the probability of events associated with a z-score greater than 1.46, look for 1.46 in the left-hand column of the table labelled 'z' and read off the area that lies in the tail beyond that z-score in the adjacent column. In this case the value is .072. This means that 1.46 cuts off .072 × 100% of the total area. In other words, 7.2% of scores will be greater (and 92.8% will be equal to or less) than 1.46 standard deviations above the mean.

On the other hand, to find out what z-value has to be exceeded to cut off 5% of the area, look for the first value that is equal to, or is less than, .05 in the column labelled 'Area in tail beyond z' and read off the associated z-score. In this case the required value is 1.65. This means that in order to cut off 5% or less of the population, a z-score has to be greater than or equal to 1.65. The value for a two-tailed test would be the value that cuts off .025 (i.e., .05/2) of the population in each tail. The corresponding value of z is 1.96.

Table B.1 Areas under the standard normal curve

z	Area in body below z	Area in tail beyond z	z	Area in body below z	Area in tail beyond z	z	Area in body below z	Area in tail beyond z
0.00	.500	.500	0.38	.648	.352	0.76	.776	.224
0.01	.504	.496	0.39	.652	.348	0.77	.779	.221
0.02	.508	.492	0.40	.655	.345	0.78	.782	.218
0.03	.512	.488	0.41	.659	.341	0.79	.785	.215
0.04	.516	.484	0.42	.663	.337	0.80	.788	.212
0.05	.520	.480	0.43	.666	.334	0.81	.791	.209
0.06	.524	.476	0.44	.670	.330	0.82	.794	.206
0.07	.528	.472	0.45	.674	.326	0.83	.797	.203
0.08	.532	.468	0.46	.677	.323	0.84	.800	.200
0.09	.536	.464	0.47	.681	.319	0.85	.802	.198
0.10	.540	.460	0.48	.684	.316	0.86	.805	.195
0.11	.544	.456	0.49	.688	.312	0.87	.808	.192
0.12	.548	.452	0.50	.691	.309	0.88	.811	.189
0.13	.552	.448	0.51	.695	.305	0.89	.813	.187
0.14	.556	.444	0.52	.698	.302	0.90	.816	.184
0.15	.560	.440	0.53	.702	.298	0.91	.819	.181
0.16	.564	.436	0.54	.705	.295	0.92	.821	.179
0.17	.567	.433	0.55	.709	.291	0.93	.824	.176
0.18	.571	.429	0.56	.712	.288	0.94	.826	.174
0.19	.575	.425	0.57	.716	.284	0.95	.829	.171
0.20	.579	.421	0.58	.719	.281	0.96	.831	.169
0.21	.583	.417	0.59	.722	.278	0.97	.834	.166
0.22	.587	.413	0.60	.726	.274	0.98	.836	.164
0.23	.591	.409	0.61	.729	.271	0.99	.839	.161
0.24	.595	.405	0.62	.732	.268	1.00	.841	.159
0.25	.599	.401	0.63	.736	.264	1.01	.844	.156
0.26	.603	.397	0.64	.739	.261	1.02	.846	.154
0.27	.606	.394	0.65	.742	.258	1.03	.848	.152
0.28	.610	.390	0.66	.745	.255	1.04	.851	.149
0.29	.614	.386	0.67	.749	.251	1.05	.853	.147

(Continued)

Table B.1 (Continued)

z	Area in body below z	Area in tail beyond z	z	Area in body below z	Area in tail beyond z	z	Area in body below z	Area in tail beyond z
0.30	.618	.382	0.68	.752	.248	1.06	.855	.145
0.31	.622	.378	0.69	.755	.245	1.07	.858	.142
0.32	.626	.374	0.70	.758	.242	1.08	.860	.140
0.33	.629	.371	0.71	.761	.239	1.09	.862	.138
0.34	.633	.367	0.72	.764	.236	1.10	.864	.136
0.35	.637	.363	0.73	.767	.233	1.11	.867	.133
0.36	.641	.359	0.74	.770	.230	1.12	.869	.131
0.37	.644	.356	0.75	.773	.227	1.13	.871	.129
1.14	.873	.127	1.64	.949	.051	2.14	.984	.016
1.15	.875	.125	1.65	.951	.049	2.15	.984	.016
1.16	.877	.123	1.66	.952	.048	2.16	.985	.015
1.17	.879	.121	1.67	.953	.047	2.17	.985	.015
1.18	.881	.119	1.68	.954	.046	2.18	.985	.015
1.19	.883	.117	1.69	.954	.046	2.19	.986	.014
1.20	.885	.115	1.70	.955	.045	2.20	.986	.014
1.21	.887	.113	1.71	.956	.044	2.21	.986	.014
1.22	.889	.111	1.72	.957	.043	2.22	.987	.013
1.23	.891	.109	1.73	.958	.042	2.23	.987	.013
1.24	.893	.107	1.74	.959	.041	2.24	.987	.013
1.25	.894	.106	1.75	.960	.040	2.25	.988	.012
1.26	.896	.104	1.76	.961	.039	2.26	.988	.012
1.27	.898	.102	1.77	.962	.038	2.27	.988	.012
1.28	.900	.100	1.78	.962	.038	2.28	.989	.011
1.29	.901	.099	1.79	.963	.037	2.29	.989	.011
1.30	.903	.097	1.80	.964	.036	2.30	.989	.011
1.31	.905	.095	1.81	.965	.035	2.31	.990	.010
1.32	.907	.093	1.82	.966	.034	2.32	.990	.010
1.33	.908	.092	1.83	.966	.034	2.33	.990	.010
1.34	.910	.090	1.84	.967	.033	2.34	.990	.010
1.35	.911	.089	1.85	.968	.032	2.35	.991	.009
1.36	.913	.087	1.86	.969	.031	2.36	.991	.009
1.37	.915	.085	1.87	.969	.031	2.37	.991	.009
1.38	.916	.084	1.88	.970	.030	2.38	.991	.009
1.39	.918	.082	1.89	.971	.029	2.39	.992	.008
1.40	.919	.081	1.90	.971	.029	2.40	.992	.008
1.41	.921	.079	1.91	.972	.028	2.41	.992	.008
1.42	.922	.078	1.92	.973	.027	2.42	.992	.008
1.43	.924	.076	1.93	.973	.027	2.43	.992	.008

Appendix B: Areas under the Standard Normal Curve

z	Area in body below z	Area in tail beyond z	z	Area in body below z	Area in tail beyond z	z	Area in body below z	Area in tail beyond z
1.44	.925	.075	1.94	.974	.026	2.44	.993	.007
1.45	.926	.074	1.95	.974	.026	2.45	.993	.007
1.46	.928	.072	1.96	.975	.025	2.46	.993	.007
1.47	.929	.071	1.97	.976	.024	2.47	.993	.007
1.48	.931	.069	1.98	.976	.024	2.48	.993	.007
1.49	.932	.068	1.99	.977	.023	2.49	.994	.006
1.50	.933	.067	2.00	.977	.023	2.50	.994	.006
1.51	.934	.066	2.01	.978	.022	2.51	.994	.006
1.52	.936	.064	2.02	.978	.022	2.52	.994	.006
1.53	.937	.063	2.03	.979	.021	2.53	.994	.006
1.54	.938	.062	2.04	.979	.021	2.54	.994	.006
1.55	.939	.061	2.05	.980	.020	2.55	.995	.005
1.56	.941	.059	2.06	.980	.020	2.56	.995	.005
1.57	.942	.058	2.07	.981	.019	2.57	.995	.005
1.58	.943	.057	2.08	.981	.019	2.58	.995	.005
1.59	.944	.056	2.09	.982	.018	2.59	.995	.005
1.60	.945	.055	2.10	.982	.018	2.60	.995	.005
1.61	.946	.054	2.11	.983	.017	2.61	.995	.005
1.62	.947	.053	2.12	.983	.017	2.62	.996	.004
1.63	.948	.052	2.13	.983	.017	2.63	.996	.004
2.64	.996	.004	2.76	.997	.003	2.88	.998	.002
2.65	.996	.004	2.77	.997	.003	2.89	.998	.002
2.66	.996	.004	2.78	.997	.003	2.90	.998	.002
2.67	.996	.004	2.79	.997	.003	2.91	.998	.002
2.68	.996	.004	2.80	.997	.003	2.92	.998	.002
2.69	.996	.004	2.81	.998	.002	2.93	.998	.002
2.70	.997	.003	2.82	.998	.002	2.94	.998	.002
2.71	.997	.003	2.83	.998	.002	2.95	.998	.002
2.72	.997	.003	2.84	.998	.002	2.96	.998	.002
2.73	.997	.003	2.85	.998	.002	2.97	.999	.001
2.74	.997	.003	2.86	.998	.002	2.98	.999	.001
2.75	.997	.003	2.87	.998	.002	2.99	.999	.001

Appendix C

Answers to Exercises

Chapter 4. Experimental design

   a.   i. We cannot know whether the treatment only works when participants have a pre-test. The interaction between treatment and testing is also a threat to internal validity.

        ii. History and maturation effects are key threats. In fact this design really only examines the impact of the pre-test.

      iii. This design avoids some external validity problems and is a good choice. Note, though, that sometimes researchers want to examine the effects of treatment on the *same* participants, and this design would not allow them to do this.

      iv. As with (i), pre-testing effects can interact with treatment.

       v. This is actually a very good design as it allows John to look at change in the same participants between the pre-test and post-test – something (iii) did not – but controls for problems associated with (i). However, it uses a lot of participants and experimental resources.

      vi. This design has no treatment, so it can tell John nothing about the effects of the teaching technique.

Chapter 5. Survey design

   a.   i. This is convenience sampling.

        ii. This is not a random sample, but there is a good chance that it could be representative of the population (however, to fully answer this question you would need to have some knowledge about human vision rather than statistics). This is because the colour vision of shoppers is unlikely to differ from that of other members of the population (though note that the sample might well be unrepresentative if the researchers were interested in people's income level or their spending habits).

      iii. Yes, for the reason given above (though note that it would not be appropriate for all psychological research).

   b.   i. There are several problems with this question. Most obviously, the unit of measurement is not specified, so it is unclear whether respondents should provide details of their annual, monthly or hourly income. As it is stated, the question also appears to be very confronting, and respondents may have concerns about revealing private information in this form. A better item would be

What is your annual salary (before tax)? (circle one)

$0–9999 $10,000–19,999 $20,000–29,999 $30,000–39,999 above $40,000

Here responding is not as threatening, and the categories can be constructed in a way that provides the researcher with useful information.

ii. As it is presented here, this question is very vague. It is also likely that, if they took the question literally, almost everyone would answer 'yes', so it is going to provide very little useful information. A better question might be

Do you worry about being able to pay your bills? (circle one)

never   rarely   sometimes   often   always

iii. This question is double-barrelled as it actually contains two questions. Accordingly, if a person answers 'yes', it is unclear which of these they are agreeing with. The question would be better if it was turned into two separate questions:

Are you in a pension plan? (tick one)   yes   no

Are you in a superannuation scheme? (tick one)   yes   no

iv. This question contains an acronym that is likely to confuse respondents. In general, technical language, jargon and acronyms should be avoided unless you are very confident that respondents will be very familiar with these. The question would therefore be improved if it were spelled out as follows:

Do you have an Independent Savings Agreement (ISA)? (tick one)   yes   no

v. This question has a number of problems. First, it is phrased in the negative, which means that if the person disagrees, their response is actually a double negative, and this can be very confusing. Second, the end-points of the scale are not particularly discriminating and so they might not yield the optimal amount of information. Third, like question (ii), the question is rather vague and unspecified. Fourth, it avoids confusion if scales are constructed in such a way that a higher response corresponds to more of the construct than is being measured (in this case, more agreement). In other words, a higher score (e.g., 6) should indicate more agreement than a lower one (e.g., 2). A better item would be

On the scale below indicate your level of agreement with the following statement (circle one number):

I organize my finances well

disagree completely   1   2   3   4   5   6   7   agree completely

vi. This item is badly worded and badly spelled. When preparing a questionnaire it is *very* important to attend to details of content and presentation in order to create a positive impression. If it looks as if you have not put much effort into constructing a questionnaire, why would anyone put any effort into responding? Tidied up, this question might read as follows:

How much do you agree with the following statement (circle one):

I organize my finances well

disagree completely   1   2   3   4   5   6   7   agree completely

Chapter 6. Descriptive statistics

a.   i.

ii.

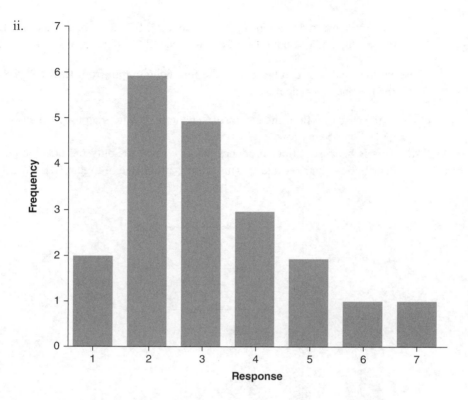

b. i. yes, negatively
    ii. yes, positively
c. i. mean = 4.67, median = 5, mode = 5
    ii. mean = 3.20, median = 3, mode = 2

Statistics

		i	ii
N	Valid	15	20
	Missing	5	0
Mean		4.6667	3.2000
Median		5.0000	3.0000
Mode		5.00	2.00
Std. Deviation		1.71825	1.60918
Variance		2.952	2.589
Skewness		-.668	.818
Std. Error of Skewness		.580	.512
Kurtosis		.119	.248
Std. Error of Kurtosis		1.121	.992
Range		6.00	6.00
Minimum		1.00	1.00
Maximum		7.00	7.00

d. i. range = 6, mean deviation = 1.33, variance = 2.95, standard deviation = 1.72
   ii. range = 6, mean deviation = 1.26, variance = 2.59, standard deviation = 1.61

These various statistics can be seen in the following output from IBM SPSS Statistics software (SPSS) 'Frequencies' analysis:

e. i. In the case of a floor the mean will tend to be greater than the median. The mode will often be very low.
   ii. This is because a floor produces positive skew (as only the positive end of the distribution can have a tail). This point is illustrated in Figure C.1.

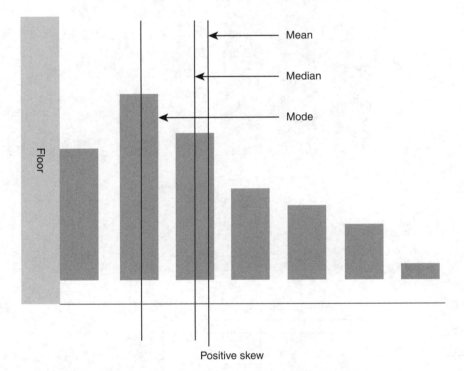

Figure C.1   Effect of a floor on the skewness of a distribution

f. i. The mean number of cars that Americans own should exceed the median because there is a floor at 0 precluding a negative tail to the distribution.
   ii. The mean score on the exam should be lower than the median because there is a ceiling of 100% ruling out a positive tail to the distribution.

g. In his book (which is well worth reading), Gould goes to great lengths to explain why the reduced performance of the best hitters is actually associated with an *increase* in overall batting performance. As Figure C.2 shows, his argument hinges on the fact that despite an overall increase in mean performance, it is still possible for the largest scores to be reduced if variance in hitting performance decreases a great deal as well. Gould's point, and one that we emphasize in this chapter, is that the meaning of single scores (whether they represent a typical score or an extreme one) depends upon the distribution of *all other* scores. In effect, then, *a single score is only given meaning by the distribution from which it is obtained.* Thus, the fact that the best baseball hitters have lower batting averages than they did at the turn of the century *does not* necessarily mean that the standard of baseball batting is declining (contrary to the arguments of a number of media commentators).

Figure C.2 Baseball averages in 1900 and today (Gould, 1997)

Chapter 7. Some principles of statistical inference

   a. 1.08
   b. 14%

    c. 2.12

    d. 1.7%

    e.   i. 18

        ii. If both groups are drawn from the same population we should expect them to appear in the top 20 in the same ratio as they do in the population (though there will be variability around the expected values).

       iii. If you get this one correct, you are doing very well! Go to Table B.1 earlier. The 10th fastest runner in the red team is at the 10th percentile. Look in the body of the table for the z that cuts off 10% (.10). This is 1.28, indicating that the 10th fastest runner has a z-score of 1.28. Multiply 1.28 by 60 seconds and subtract it from 420 seconds to get his or her time (= 343.2 seconds). The 10th fastest runner in the blue team is at the 1.1th percentile. Look in the body of the table for the value of z that cuts of 1.1% (.011). This is 2.30 and indicates that the 10th fastest runner has a z-score of 2.30. Multiply 2.30 by 60 seconds and subtract it from 420 seconds to get his or her time (= 267.6 seconds).

       iv. The law of large numbers tells us the contest is unfair (as does common sense). If the red team were to beat the odds and win the race we would need to conclude that either the red team was incredibly lucky or that the process of dividing the school into two groups (even with random allocation) had changed the performance of the groups – perhaps that the red team was more motivated as a result of being placed in a small team or the blue team was taking it easy.

    f.   i. Adam appears to be the best candidate as he has the highest z-score of 2.33. Bill's z-score is 2.0. Charles' z-score is 2.14.

        ii. 1% (looking at Table B.1, the area in the tail beyond z associated with a z-score of 2.33 is .01).

       iii. If the ability of architecture students in all cities is the same and is always normally distributed with the same variance then we can assume that all three are drawn from the standard normal distribution ($\mu = 0$, $\sigma = 1$). To calculate the proportion of groups with a mean z-score greater than 2.0 (Bill's score) we need to use the sampling distribution of the mean for this distribution. The sampling distribution of the mean for groups of three architects drawn from the three cities will have a mean of 0.0 and will have a standard deviation of 1.0 divided by the square root of 3. The score of 2.0 therefore differs from the population mean of 0.0 by 2×1.73 standard error units. This corresponds to a z-score of 3.46, which (based on information contained in Table B.1) means that less than 1 group in 1000 will have a mean greater than this value.

       iv. The candidates represent an exceptional group of architects.

Chapter 8. Examining differences between means: The *t*-test

a. (Note: Milk $M = 7.00$, $SD = 1.15$; Alcohol $M = 5.70$, $SD = 1.25$.)

   i. Between-subjects

   ii. 2.41

   iii. Yes (with 18 degrees of freedom the critical value of *t* for $\alpha = .05$ is 2.101).

These various statistics can be seen in the following output from SPSS 'Compare Means → Independent Samples T Test' analysis:

Group Statistics

	Condition	N	Mean	Std. Deviation	Std. Error Mean
Drink	Milk	10	7.0000	1.15470	.36515
	Beer	10	5.7000	1.25167	.39581

Independent Samples Test

		Levene's Test for Equality of Variances		t-test for Equality of Means						
									95% Confidence Interval of the Difference	
		F	Sig.	t	df	Sig. (2-tailed)	Mean Difference	Std. Error Difference	Lower	Upper
Drink	Equal variances assumed	.220	.645	2.414	18	.027	1.30000	.53852	.16862	2.43138
	Equal variances not assumed			2.414	17.884	.027	1.30000	.53852	.16809	2.43191

b. (Note: $D = 1.30$, $SD = 1.83$)

   i. Within-subjects

   ii. 2.25

   iii. No (with 9 degrees of freedom the critical value of *t* for $\alpha = .05$ is 2.26).

These various statistics can be seen in the following output from SPSS 'Compare Means → Paired Samples T Test' analysis:

Paired Samples Statistics

		Mean	N	Std. Deviation	Std. Error Mean
Pair 1	Milk	7.0000	10	1.15470	.36515
	Beer	5.7000	10	1.25167	.39581

Paired Samples Correlations

		N	Correlation	Sig.
Pair 1	Milk & Beer	10	-.154	.671

Paired Samples Test

		Paired Differences							
					95% Confidence Interval of the Difference				
		Mean	Std. Deviation	Std. Error Mean	Lower	Upper	t	df	Sig. (2-tailed)
Pair 1	Milk – Beer	1.30000	1.82878	.57831	-.00823	2.60823	2.248	9	.051

c. As illustrated in Chapter 6, the scores from throws of a single die have a *uniform* or flat-rectangular distribution. The distribution obtained from adding the sum of many dice throws is approximately normal. The *t*-test is a normal theory test and works most efficiently when the data analysed are drawn from a normally distributed population. This point underpins the *assumption of normality.*

d. i. Both tests would use a within-subjects *t*-test.
   ii. The alpha level chosen for each test would reflect the level of uncertainty that was acceptable. If we wished to be sure that there were no side-effects we might use a very large alpha level like .25. That is, we would not want to use a therapy unless we were very confident that there would be no side-effects (note that in a real study we would actually look at the proportion of participants who experience side-effects rather than just whether there were side-effects on average!). Before we use the expensive therapy, though, we would want to be very confident that it was effective. We might use a stringent alpha level for this purpose such as .001.
   iii. The fact that participants discussed their responses before making them means that those responses are not independent. This violates the *assumption of independence*, so these data should be treated with caution. Indeed, there may not even be much point in analysing the data because they may be contaminated by the exchange of information.

e. Yes. Using a one-sample *t*-test (with α set at .05) the mean score is significantly greater than 100, $t(9) = 3.03$, $p = .014$.

This can be seen in the following output from SPSS 'Compare Means → One-Sample T Test' analysis:

One-Sample Statistics

	N	Mean	Std. Deviation	Std. Error Mean
Score	10	112.3000	12.82402	4.05531

One-Sample Test

	Test Value = 100					
					95% Confidence Interval of the Difference	
	t	df	Sig. (2-tailed)	Mean Difference	Lower	Upper
Score	3.033	9	.014	12.30000	3.1262	21.4738

Chapter 9. Examining relationships between variables: Correlation

a.

Age and Speed: $r = -.82$; Age and Attention: $r = .34$; Age and Accuracy: $r = .59$.

b. Only the correlation between Age and Speed is significant at the .01 level (with 10 degrees of freedom, the critical value of r for $\alpha = .01$ is .708).

These results can be seen in the following output from SPSS 'Correlate → Bivariate' analysis – indeed, this allows you took look at all these correlations (as well as correlations between the three dependent variables) at the same time:

Correlations

		Age	Speed	Attention	Accuracy
Age	Pearson Correlation	1	-.823**	.345	.587*
	Sig. (2–tailed)		.001	.273	.045
	N	12	12	12	12
Speed	Pearson Correlation	-.823**	1	-.569	-.547
	Sig. (2–tailed)	.001		.054	.066
	N	12	12	12	12
Attention	Pearson Correlation	.345	-.569	1	-.241
	Sig. (2–tailed)	.273	.054		.451
	N	12	12	12	12
Accuracy	Pearson Correlation	.587*	-.547	-.241	1
	Sig. (2–tailed)	.045	.066	.451	
	N	12	12	12	12

**. Correlation is significant at the 0.01 level (2–tailed).
*. Correlation is significant at the 0.05 level (2–tailed).

c. Age and Speed: large effect size; Age and Attention: moderate effect size; Age and Accuracy: large effect size.

d. 68% (i.e., $-.82^2 \times 100$).

e. i. A within-subjects t-test shows that the reading ability scores increase from age 9 to age 12 ($D = -2.7$, $SD = 2.06$, $t(9) = -4.15$, $p < .01$). Using the formula for effect size given on p. 229, $r = .81$. This is a strong effect.

These statistics can be seen in the following output from SPSS 'Compare Means → Paired Samples T Test' analysis:

Paired Samples Statistics

		Mean	N	Std. Deviation	Std. Error Mean
Pair 1	NineYears	11.7000	10	2.00278	.63333
	TwelveYears	14.4000	10	2.83627	.89691

Paired Samples Correlations

		N	Correlation	Sig.
Pair 1	NineYears & TwelveYears	10	.689	.028

Paired Samples Test

		Paired Differences					t	df	Sig. (2–tailed)
		Mean	Std. Deviation	Std. Error Mean	95% Confidence Interval of the Difference				
					Lower	Upper			
Pair 1	NineYears – TwelveYears	-2.70000	2.05751	.65064	-4.17185	-1.22815	-4.150	9	.002

ii. As can also be seen in this output, the correlation between reading ability at age 9 and age 12 is .689 ($p = .028$). This is also a strong effect.

iii. It is possible, and indeed common, for there to be a sizeable difference between the mean score on two variables and for there to be a sizeable correlation between them because repeated measures t-tests and correlation actually answer different questions. In this case it is possible for there to be an increase in reading ability and for ability at the different ages to be related to each other if the change in reading ability is relatively similar for all participants. This is because the correlation between two variables is not affected at all by making a constant change (a transformation) to all of the scores on one or both variables. For example, if we divided *all* of the reading ability scores by 2 we would find that we still obtain the same correlation and t-test score. However, if we only divided the scores at age 12 by 2 we would find that the correlation between reading ability at the different times would remain the same but that the within-subjects t-value would be very different. If you think about it, correlations would be a lot less useful if they did change when we made a constant change to one or the other variable. It would mean, for example, that the correlation between age and intelligence would be different when you measured age in years rather than months. Clearly this would be very confusing and it would make the statistic meaningless.

Chapter 10. Comparing two or more means by analysing variances: ANOVA

a. i.

Tests of Between–Subjects Effects

Dependent Variable: MoralReasoningScore

Source	Type III Sum of Squares	df	Mean Square	F	Sig.	Partial Eta Squared
Corrected Model	5869.400[a]	3	1956.467	22.487	.000	.652
Intercept	121440.400	1	121440.400	1395.778	.000	.975
AgeGroup	5869.400	3	1956.467	22.487	.000	.652
Error	3132.200	36	87.006			
Total	130442.000	40				
Corrected Total	9001.600	39				

a. R Squared = .652 (Adjusted R Squared = .623)

ii. From this ANOVA table it is clear that the F-value for Age Group is associated with a p-value of less than .001 and so there are strong grounds for rejecting the null hypothesis that the level of moral reasoning is the same in all age groups.

Moreover, the pattern of means revealed in the following table of descriptive statistics indicates that, as hypothesized, moral reasoning increases as children get older:

Descriptive Statistics

Dependent Variable: MoralReasoningScore

AgeGroup	Mean	Std. Deviation	N
10–11	37.6000	9.10677	10
12–13	52.8000	11.94245	10
14–15	58.7000	5.96378	10
16–17	71.3000	9.32202	10
Total	55.1000	15.19244	40

As the effect size here is large (i.e., $\eta_p^2 = .652$), this effect also appears to be psychologically, not just statistically, significant.

    b.   i.

Tests of Between–Subjects Effects

Dependent Variable: MoralReasoningScore

Source	Type III Sum of Squares	df	Mean Square	F	Sig.	Partial Eta Squared
Corrected Model	6831.400ᵃ	3	2277.133	37.587	.000	.758
Intercept	138297.600	1	138297.600	2282.766	.000	.984
AgeGroup	4536.900	1	4536.900	74.887	.000	.675
AreaCrimeRate	1537.600	1	1537.600	25.380	.000	.413
AgeGroup * AreaCrimeRate	756.900	1	756.900	12.494	.001	.258
Error	2181.000	36	60.583			
Total	147310.000	40				
Corrected Total	9012.400	39				

a. R Squared = .758 (Adjusted R Squared = .738)

    ii. From this ANOVA table it is clear that the *F*-value for the between-groups age group effect is associated with a *p*-value of less than .001 and so there are strong grounds for rejecting the null hypothesis that the level of moral reasoning is the same in all age groups. The between-groups Crime Rate Area effect is also associated with a *p*-value of less than .001 and so there are strong grounds for rejecting the null hypothesis that the level of moral reasoning is the same in areas of high and low crime. As well as this, the between-groups interaction effect is also associated with a *p*-value of less than .001 and so there are strong grounds for rejecting the null hypothesis that the effects of age and area are simply additive.

This can be seen by plotting the means below in a line graph – where the non-parallel lines provide evidence of an interaction between these two variables:

AgeGroup * AreaCrimeRate

Dependent Variable: MoralReasoningScore

AgeGroup	AreaCrimeRate	Mean	Std. Error	95% Confidence Interval	
				Lower Bound	Upper Bound
10–11	High	37.600	2.461	32.608	42.592
	Low	58.700	2.461	53.708	63.692
12–13	High	67.600	2.461	62.608	72.592
	Low	71.300	2.461	66.308	76.292

Moreover, it can be seen from the values of η_p^2 that the size of all these effects is large, accounting for more that 25% of the variance in the data in each case (i.e., $\eta_p^2 > .25$).

Chapter 11. Analysing other forms of data: chi-square and distribution-free tests

a.   i. The expected frequency of female board members = $Np = 138 \times .4 = 55.2$.

   ii. As $N > 25$, we can use the normal approximation to the binomial distribution to find out how likely it is that a distribution of board members as skewed as this would arise from a random process. Here the base-rate information tells us that p (the probability of an employee being female) = .4 and q (the probability of an employee being male) = .6. Thus

$$z = \frac{x - NP}{\sqrt{Npq}}$$

$$= \frac{44 - (138 \times .4)}{\sqrt{138 \times .4 \times .6}}$$

$$= (44 - 55.2)/\sqrt{33.12}$$

$$= -11.2/5.75$$

$$= -1.95$$

We can see from Table B.1 that this z-score corresponds to a one-tailed probability of .026. The researchers would therefore be entitled to reject the null hypothesis (that the observed deviation from the expected frequency occurred by chance), and to claim support for their alternative hypothesis. Note, too, that the decision to use a one-tailed test could be justified on the grounds that this hypothesis had been specified in advance.

b. i. The expected frequency (f_e) of correct identification = np (where n is the number of participants in each condition (30) and p is the probability of correct identification (.5)). Thus $f_e = 30 \times .5 = 15$.

ii. To answer this question we need to compare the observed frequency ($f_o = 16$) with the expected frequency ($f_e = 15$). Because $N > 25$, we can use the normal approximation of the binomial distribution to find out how likely it is that a number of correct identifications as high as this would arise from a random process. Here p and $q = .5$, so

$$z = \frac{x - NP}{\sqrt{Npq}}$$

$$= \frac{16 - (15)}{\sqrt{30 \times .5 \times .5}}$$

$$= 1/\sqrt{7.5}$$

$$= 0.36$$

From Table B.1 we see that this z-score corresponds to a one-tailed probability of .641. There are thus no grounds for rejecting the null hypothesis that the observed deviation from the expected frequency occurred by chance.

iii. We can answer this question using the chi-square test for goodness of fit, which can be accessed at the www.quantpsy.org/chisq/chisq.htm website. When we enter these data we get the following output from Preacher (2001, April):

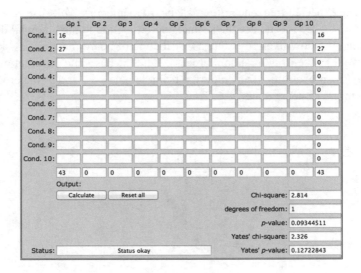

From this we can see that the computed value of χ^2 corresponds to a p-value of .09. With conventional levels of α (i.e., .05) there are therefore no grounds for concluding that learning context (song or poem) had an impact on recognition.

    iv. We can answer this question using the chi-square test of independence. If we put this into the program at www.quantpsy.org/chisq/chisq.htm we get the following output:

	Gp 1	Gp 2	Gp 3	Gp 4	Gp 5	Gp 6	Gp 7	Gp 8	Gp 9	Gp 10	
Cond. 1:	28	16									44
Cond. 2:	29	27									56
Cond. 3:											0
Cond. 4:											0
Cond. 5:											0
Cond. 6:											0
Cond. 7:											0
Cond. 8:											0
Cond. 9:											0
Cond. 10:											0
	57	43	0	0	0	0	0	0	0	0	100

Output:

Calculate   Reset all

Chi-square: 1.412

degrees of freedom: 1

p-value: 0.23472467

Yates' chi-square: 0.97

Status: Status okay

Yates' p-value: 0.32468018

So with a conventional level of α (i.e., .05) there are therefore no grounds for concluding that learning context (song or poem) has more impact on the amnesiacs' memory than on the memory of controls. In other words, the results provide no basis for rejecting the null hypothesis that learning context (song or poem) is unrelated to participant type (control or amnesiac).

    v. Effect size can be measured by a phi coefficient where $\varphi = \chi^2/N = 1.41/100 = 0.14$. This is therefore a small effect (i.e., less than .1).

    vi. If there had been evidence of a relationship between learning context and participant type, the data for controls would suggest that their responses might have been affected by a ceiling effect (see Chapter 9). This is because there was no opportunity for learning material in song form to improve recognition as the participants who learned the material in poem form were already performing the task almost perfectly. This suggests that, in a future study, it might therefore be a good idea to make the task harder. Note, though, that as a result of a relevance–sensitivity trade-off (see Chapter 4), this might in turn mean that the manipulation of learning context has less impact on amnesiacs.

In case you are interested, the description of this study is based on research conducted by Haslam and Cook (2002).

c.   i. Noting that the criticism is worth considering, the researchers could reanalyse their data using a distribution-free test. The obvious candidate here is the Mann–Whitney test (although the researchers should note that this can tell them whether there are differences in the distributions of sample data, not necessarily whether these differences are in central tendency).

ii. When we conduct the Mann–Whitney test in SPSS this generates the following output:

Mann–Whitney Test

Ranks

	Year	N	Mean Rank	Sum of Ranks
Rank	2011	15	19.67	295.00
	2012	15	11.33	170.00
	Total	30		

Test Statistics[a]

	Rank
Mann–Whitney U	50.000
Wilcoxon W	170.000
Z	−2.592
Asymp. Sig. (2–tailed)	.010
Exact Sig. [2*(1–tailed Sig.)]	.009[b]

a. Grouping Variable: Year

b. Not corrected for ties.

This tells us that the average rank (placing) of students in 2011 was 19.67 and in 2012 it was 11.33. This is associated with a Mann–Whitney U-value of 50 and an associated z-value of −2.592 and a probability (p) of .010. It suggests that such a difference in rankings is very unlikely to be the result of chance. Accordingly, we have a sound basis for concluding that performance had improved in 2012. Note that in this case a t-test would have led us to the same conclusion.

Chapter 12. Classical qualitative methods

a. Repertory grid analysis

This exercise is based on a number of studies that have been conducted to inform the travel industry about the experiences of holidaymakers in particular tourist destinations. For example, Pike (2003) used repertory grid analysis to explore the experiences of holidaymakers in New Zealand, while Embacher and Buttle (1989) used the same method to examine what British holidaymakers thought of Austria as a summer holiday destination in comparison with other potential places they might have gone to.

Embacher and Buttle's study provides some indication of how your analysis might be conducted and of the way in which results could be presented. In particular, a modified version of the grid that resulted from their analysis is as follows:

Table C.1

					Constructs	
Austria	Switzerland	Canada	Italy	Spain	similarity (✓)	contrast (✗)
✓	✓	✓	–	✗	genuine	artificial
✓	✓	✓	✗	–	natural countryside	man-made, built up
✗	✗	✗	–	✓	organized tourism	less organized tourism
✗	✗	–	✓	✓	reliable weather	unreliable weather
✗	✗	✗	✓	✓	cheap	expensive

From this analysis the researchers concluded that Austria appealed to British holidaymakers for very similar reasons to Switzerland (in particular, the genuine nature of their tourist experience and the natural countryside), but quite different reasons from Italy and Spain. In this sense, Austria's 'brand' is very similar to that of Switzerland but very different from that of Italy and Spain. Those in the tourism industry might clearly be able to use such information (and the information from your report) to understand who their key competitors are, and where they might want to lure new tourists from. For example, in this instance, it would make more sense for tourism operators to try to target their marketing at people who normally go to Switzerland on holiday than at those who normally go to Spain or Italy.

b. Content analysis

i. The sampling domain is the major national newspapers published on one particular day. Obviously, this domain could be enlarged in various ways (e.g., by including magazines or regional newspapers). Whether or not this would constitute an improvement depends on the questions being asked and the types of conclusions one wishes to draw. For example, including magazines would represent an improvement if one wanted to make arguments related to the range of forms in which people are exposed to written material about mental illness.

  ii. Coding units could take any number of forms and these would depend on the research question you were interested in. Depending on this, they might, for instance, identify references that (a) are favourable or unfavourable, (b) treat mental illness as curable or incurable, or (c) advocate or oppose drug treatment.

  iii. The best way to ensure that your coding is reliable is to use multiple independent coders and then examine the correspondence in their assignment of material to particular categories. This can be done by measures of inter-rater reliability.

  iv. Again, this would depend on the goals of the study, but in principle the data could be subjected to either qualitative analysis (e.g., using grounded theory) or quantitative analysis (e.g., using methods described in Chapter 11).

c. Thematic analysis

A very similar study to this was conducted by Gareth Hall and his colleagues in a study looking at the commitment of Welsh rugby fans to their team. In this, the authors ran seven focus groups with a total of 45 supporters (29 men and 16 women). In the authors' report of their findings they presented the following table that summarizes the four core themes that they identified (Hall et al., 2012, p. 147):

Table C.2

Theme	Characteristics
Affective loyalty	Strong emotional attachments that influenced psychological resistance to change.
Involvement	Ideological behaviours in terms of effort to attend games and join in fan-like behaviour (e.g. jeering opposition and singing). Used to evaluate which fans were atypical fans (fair-weather fans, both in- and out-group) and which were exemplars of the fan base (die-hard fans).
Distinctiveness	The use of apparel to enhance acceptance as a fan of a specific team and also further maximise visual distinction from rival fans; avoid incorrect categorization.
Individualism	Two types of individualism; high levels of team-specific knowledge as a positive attribute and low levels of attendance and willingness to stick with the team through defeats or changes in personal circumstances (moving home) as a negative attribute.

The authors argued that their work could be used to refine previous analysis of sports fans' identification with their team and to develop better measures of this identification. One of the key questions that this research raises – and that the authors argue needs to be addressed in future research – relates to the complex ways in which support for a local team maps onto, and interacts with, support for the national team. As they put it, 'Understanding when and how fans understand and distinguish their commitments between club, national side, and national identity would be a fruitful direction in understanding fandom across all levels of sports' (Hall et al., 2012, p. 150).

Chapter 13. Contextual qualitative methods

a. Grounded theory

This example is based on research conducted by Burgoyne (1997), and so it is instructive to read the report of this research to see how she tackles the problem. Among other things, Burgoyne:

    i. develops a coding system in which the coding categories focused on representations of (a) issues and orientations (whether the article had a patient-centred view or a service-centred view), (b) who should make allocation decisions (e.g., doctors, patients, authorities) and (c) what the decision criteria should be (e.g., cost, care, individual rights, age);

    ii. identifies links between particular orientations (e.g., a patient-centred view) and an emphasis on particular decision criteria (e.g., care, individual rights);

    iii. suggests that particular links (e.g., between being patient-centred and making decisions on the basis of individual rights) were more likely to be made in certain forms of newspaper (tabloid vs. broadsheet);

    iv. concludes that representations of health-care rationing were unrelated to the conceptions developed by economic theorists to describe issues surrounding resource allocation;

    v. argues that the lack of consensus in the representation of health-care rationing contributed to, and was symptomatic of, difficulties in having informed public debate on the topic.

b. Interpretative phenomenological analysis (IPA)

This example corresponds to a very large number of studies that have used IPA to investigate patients' experiences of particular health conditions. As an example, Smith and Osborn (2003, pp. 59–60) present the following interview schedule that they had used to explore the experiences of patients who were undergoing renal dialysis to treat kidney disease, and this gives some indication of how you might construct you interview schedule:

    A. Dialysis

      1. Could you give me a brief history of your kidney problem from when it started to your beginning dialysis?
      2. Could you describe what happens in dialysis, in your own words?
      3. What do you do when you are having dialysis?
      4. How do you feel when you are dialysing?

      prompt: physically, emotionally, mentally.

5. What do you think about?

6. How do you feel about having dialysis?

   prompt: some people/relief from previous illness/a bind.

7. How does dialysis/kidney disease affect your everyday life?

   prompt: work, interests, relationships.

8. If you had to describe what the dialysis machine means to you, what would you say?

   prompt: What words come to mind, what images? Do you have a nickname for it?

B. Identity

9. How would you describe yourself as a person?

   prompt: What sort of person are you? Most important characteristics: happy, moody, nervy.

10. Has having kidney disease and starting dialysis made a difference to how you see yourself?

    prompt: If so, how do you see yourself now as different from before you started dialysis? How would you say you have changed?

11. What about compared to before you had kidney disease?

12. What about the way other people see you?

    prompt: members of your family, friends? changed?

C. Coping

13. What does the term 'illness' mean to you? How do you define it?

14. How much do you think about your own physical health?

15. Do you see yourself as being ill?

    prompt: always, sometimes? Would you say you were an ill person?

16. On a day-to-day basis, how do you deal with having kidney disease (the illness)?

    prompt: Do you have particular strategies for helping you? ways of coping, practical, mental.

17. Do you think about the future much?

c. Discourse analysis

This text is discussed by Hepburn (2003), who also examines the general issue of public displays of memory. In relation to this and other similar data, she notes that the act of remembering is a public one and that it has many purposes. Among other things, her analysis:

i. identifies a number of distinctive features of this text, including (a) the long pauses, (b) the contrast between being able to remember some things but not others, and (c) the differentiation between accepting a statement and not being able to deny it;

ii. notes that Clinton here is trying (a) to appear cooperative, (b) to appear honest and trustworthy, but (c) not to perjure himself (i.e., by telling a lie);

iii. argues that to achieve these various goals, Clinton has to steer a very difficult path between (a) saying that he remembers the phone call (in which case he might have to answer difficult questions about it) and (b) denying memory of it (which might seem uncooperative and implausible). To do this, he needs to give the impression of someone who is *trying* to remember but is not able to – and it can be argued that this is what the various features of the account are designed to do;

iv. argues that this example illustrates the way in which, ultimately, memory and cognition are public acts and that, as such, they are far more nuanced than traditional approaches (e.g., in social and cognitive psychology) might suggest. So, rather than being able to say that a given memory is right or wrong, available or unavailable (as a quantitative analysis might require us to do), we see that natural acts of remembering often require people to avoid these binary choices.

References

Abramson, L. Y., Seligman, M. E. P., & Teasdale, J. D. (1978). Learned helplessness in humans: Critique and reformulation. *Journal of Abnormal Psychology*, *87*, 49–74.

Allport, G. W. (1937). *Personality: A psychological interpretation*. New York: Henry Holt.

American Psychological Association. (2009). *Publication manual of the American Psychological Association* (6th ed.). Washington, DC: Author.

American Psychological Association. (2013). *Directory of national associations of psychology*. Washington, DC: Office of International Affairs.

Aronson, E. (1997). The theory of cognitive dissonance: The evolution and vicissitudes of an idea. In C. McGarty & S. A. Haslam (Eds.), *The message of social psychology: Perspectives on mind in society* (pp. 20–35). Oxford: Blackwell.

Bakker, M., & Wicherts, J. M. (2011). The (mis)reporting of statistical results in psychology journals. *Behavior Research Methods*, *43*, 666–678.

Bandura, A., Ross, D., & Ross, S. (1961). Transmission of aggression through imitation of aggressive models. *Journal of Applied Social Psychology*, *63*, 575–582.

Barber, T. X., & Silver, M. J. (1968). Fact, fiction, and the experimenter bias effect. *Psychological Bulletin*, *70*, 1–29.

Baumeister, R. F., Vohs, K. D., & Funder, D. C. (2007). Psychology as the science of self-reports and finger movements: Whatever happened to actual behavior? *Perspectives on Psychological Science*, *2*, 396–403.

Baumrind, D. (1964). Some thoughts on ethics of research: After reading Milgram's 'Behavioral study of obedience'. *American Psychologist*, *19*, 421–423.

Baumrind, D. (1985). Research using intentional deception: Ethical issues revisited. *American Psychologist*, *40*, 165–174.

Berkun, M. M., Bialek, H. M., Kern, R. P., & Yagi, K. (1962). Experimental studies of psychological stress in man. *Psychological Monographs: General and Applied*, *76*(15), Whole No. 534.

Billig, M. (2011). Writing social psychology: Fictional things and unpopulated texts. *British Journal of Social Psychology*, *50*, 4–20.

Birnbaum, M. H. (2004). Methodological and ethical issues in conducting social psychology research via the Internet. In C. Sansone, C. C. Morf, & A. T. Panter (Eds.), *The SAGE handbook of methods in social psychology* (pp. 359–382). Thousand Oaks, CA: SAGE.

Blass, T. (2004). *The man who shocked the world: The life and legacy of Stanley Milgram*. New York: Basic Books.

Boyatzis, R. E. (1998). *Transforming qualitative information: Thematic analysis and code development*. London: SAGE.

Braun, V., & Clarke, V. (2006). Using thematic analysis in psychology. *Qualitative Research in Psychology*, *3*, 77–101.

Brocki, J. M., & Wearden, A. J. (2006). A critical evaluation of the use of interpretative phenomenological analysis (IPA) in health psychology. *Psychology and Health*, *21*, 87–108.

Burgoyne, C. B. (1997). Distributive justice and rationing in the NHS: Framing effects in press coverage of a controversial decision. *Journal of Community and Applied Social Psychology*, *7*, 119–136.

Campbell, D. T. (1986). Science's social system of validity-enhancing collective belief change and problems of the social sciences. In D. W. Fiske & R. A. Schweder (Eds.), *Metatheory in social science: Pluralisms and subjectivities* (pp. 108–135). Chicago: University of Chicago Press.

Campbell, D. T., & Stanley, J. C. (1963). *Experimental and quasi-experimental designs for research.* Chicago: Rand McNally.

Chalmers, A. F. (1978). *What is this thing called science?* Milton Keynes: Open University Press.

Chew, C., & Eysenbach, G. (2010). Pandemics in the age of Twitter: Content analysis of Tweets during the 2009 H1N1 outbreak. *PLoS One, 5*(11), e14118.

Cho, H., & LaRose, R. (1999). Privacy issues in Internet surveys. *Social Science Computer Review, 17,* 421–434.

Clare, L. (2003). Managing threats to self: Awareness in early stage Alzheimer's disease. *Social Science and Medicine, 57,* 1017–1029.

Cochrane, R., & Duffy, J. (1974). Psychology and the scientific method. *Bulletin of the British Psychological Society, 27,* 117–121.

Cohen, J. (1988). *Statistical power analysis for the behavioral sciences* (2nd ed.). Hillsdale, NJ: Erlbaum.

Cohen, J. (1994). The earth is round ($p < .05$). *American Psychologist, 49,* 997–1003.

Cohen, J. (1995). The earth is round ($p < .05$): Rejoinder. *American Psychologist, 50,* 1103.

Condry, J., & Condry, S. (1976). Sex differences: A study of the eye of the beholder. *Child Development, 7,* 812–819.

Converse, J. M. (2009). *Survey research in the United States: Roots and emergence 1890–1960.* New Brunswick, NJ: Transaction.

Cook, J., Dickinson, H., & Eccles, M. (2009). Response rates in postal surveys of healthcare professionals between 1996 and 2005: An observational study. *BMC Health Services Research, 9,* 160.

Cook, T. D., & Campbell, D. T. (1979). *Quasi-experimentation: Design and analysis issues for field settings.* Chicago: Rand McNally.

Darley, J. M., & Batson, C. D. (1973). From Jerusalem to Jericho: A study of situational and dispositional variables in helping behaviour. *Journal of Personality and Social Psychology, 42,* 497–505.

Dawes, R. M. (1996). The purpose of experiments: Ecological validity versus comparing hypotheses. *Behavioral and Brain Sciences, 19,* 20.

De Groot, A. D. (1965). *Thought and choice in chess.* The Hague: Mouton.

Dey, I. (1993). *Qualitative data analysis.* London: Routledge.

Douglas, K. M., McGarty, C., Bliuc, A. M., & Lala, G. (2005). Understanding cyberhate: Social competition and social creativity in online White Supremacist groups. *Social Science Computer Review, 2,* 68–76.

Ekman, P., Levenson, R. W., & Frieson, W. V. (1983). Autonomic nervous system activity distinguishes among emotions, *Science, 221,* 1208–1210.

Embacher, J., & Buttle, F. (1989). A repertory grid analysis of Austria's image as a summer vacation destination. *Journal of Travel Research, 27,* 3–7.

Eysenck, H. J., & Eysenck, S. B. G. (1985). *Personality and individual differences.* London: Plenum Press.

Fagerland, M. W. (2012). *t*-tests, non-parametric tests, and large studies – a paradox of statistical practice? *BMC Medical Research Methodology, 12,* 78.

Fereday, J., & Muir-Cochrane, E. (2008). Demonstrating rigor using thematic analysis: A hybrid approach of inductive and deductive coding and theme development. *International Journal of Qualitative Methods, 5,* 80–92.

Festinger, L., Riecken, H., & Schachter, S. (1956). *When prophecy fails.* Minneapolis: University of Minnesota Press.

References

Feyerabend, P. K. (1975). *Against method: Outline of an anarchistic theory of knowledge*. New York: New Left Books.

Fiedler, K. (2011). Voodoo correlations are everywhere – not only in neuroscience. *Perspectives on Psychological Science, 6*, 163–171.

Fraser, L., & Lawley, M. (2000). *Questionnaire design and administration*. Brisbane: Wiley.

Fraser, S. (Ed.). (1995). *The bell curve wars: Race, intelligence and the future of America*. New York: Basic Books.

Freud, S. (1933/1964). *New introductory lectures on psychoanalysis* (J. Strachy, trans.). New York: Norton.

Frick, R. W. (1995). A problem with confidence intervals. *American Psychologist, 50*, 1102–1103.

Gauthier, J., & Pettifor, L. (2012). The tale of two universal declarations: Ethics and human rights. In M. M. Leach, M. J. Stevens, G. Lindsay, A. Ferrero, & Y. Korkut (Eds.), *The Oxford Handbook of International Psychological Ethics* (pp. 113–133). Oxford: Oxford University Press.

Gilbert, G. N., & Mulkay, M. J. (1984). *Opening Pandora's box: A sociological analysis of scientists' discourse*. Cambridge: Cambridge University Press.

Goldacre, B. (2008). *Bad science*. London: HarperCollins.

Gould, S. J. (1981). *The mismeasure of man*. New York: Norton.

Gould, S. J. (1997). *Life's grandeur: The spread of excellence from Plato to Darwin*. London: Vintage.

Graham, J. W. (2009). Missing data analysis: Making it work in the real world. *Annual Review of Psychology, 60*, 549–576.

Green, C., & Gilhooly, K. (1996). Protocol analysis: Practical implementation. In J. T. E. Richardson (Ed.), *Handbook of qualitative research methods for psychology and the social sciences* (pp. 55–74). Leicester: BPS Books.

Gribbin, J., & Rees, M. (1990). *The stuff of the universe: Dark matter, mankind and the coincidences of cosmology*. London: Heinemann.

Grice, H. P. (1975). Logic and conversation. In P. Cole & J. Morgan (Eds.), *Syntax and Semantics* (Vol. 3, pp. 41–58). San Diego, CA: Academic Press.

Grice, J. W. (2002). Idiogrid: Software for the management and analysis of repertory grids. *Behavior Research Methods, 34*, 338–341.

Grice, T. (2005). Social identity and communication during organisational change. PhD thesis, University of Queensland.

Hall, G., Shearer, D., Thomson, R., Roderique-Davies, G., Mayer, P., & Hall, R. (2012). Conceptualising commitment: A thematic analysis of fans of Welsh rugby. *Qualitative Research in Sport, Exercise and Health, 4*, 138–153.

Hammond, G. (1996). The objections to null hypothesis testing as a means of analysing psychological data. *Australian Journal of Psychology, 46*, 104–106.

Harré, R. (1979). *Social being: A theory for social psychology*. Oxford: Blackwell.

Haslam, C., & Cook, M. (2002). Striking a chord with amnesic patients: Evidence that song facilitates memory. *Neurocase, 8*, 453–465.

Haslam, C., Haslam, S. A., Knight, C., Gleibs, I., Ysseldyk, R., & McCloskey, L.-G. (2014). We can work it out: Group decision-making builds social identity and enhances the cognitive performance of care home residents. *British Journal of Psychology, 105*, 17–34.

Haslam, S. A. (2004). *Psychology in organizations: The social identity approach* (2nd ed.). London: SAGE.

Haslam, S. A., & McGarty, C. (2001). A hundred years of certitude? Social psychology, the experimental method and the management of scientific uncertainty. *British Journal of Social Psychology, 40*, 1–21.

Haslam, S. A., & McGarty, C. (2004). Experimental design and causality in social psychological research. In C. Sansone, C. C. Morf, & A. T. Panter (Eds.), *Handbook of methods in social psychology* (pp. 237–264). Thousand Oaks, CA: SAGE.

Haslam, S. A., & Reicher, S. D. (2006). Stressing the group: Social identity and the unfolding dynamics of responses to stress. *Journal of Applied Psychology*, *91*, 1037–1052.

Haslam, S. A., Reicher, S. D., & McDermott, M. (in press). Studying harm-doing without doing harm: The case of the BBC Prison Experiment. In R. J. Sternberg & S. E. Fiske (Eds.), *Ethical case studies and commentaries in the behavioral and brain sciences.* New York: Cambridge University Press.

Haslam, S. A., Reicher, S. D., Millard, K., & MacDonald, R. (in press). "Happy to have been of service": Box 44 in the Yale archive as a window into the engaged followership of participants in Milgram's "obedience" experiments. *British Journal of Social Psychology.*

Hathaway, S. R., & McKinley, J. C. (1943). *Manual for the Minnesota Multiphasic Personality Inventory.* New York: Psychological Corporation.

Haule, J. R. (2010). *Divine madness: Archetypes of romantic love.* Carmel, CA: Fisher King Press.

Helliwell, J. F., & Barrington-Leigh, C. (2011). How much is social capital worth? In J. Jetten, C. Haslam, & S. A. Haslam (Eds.), *The social cure: Identity, health, and well-being* (pp. 55–71). London: Psychology Press.

Henrich, J., Heine, S. J., & Norenzayan, A. (2010). Most people are not WEIRD. *Nature*, *466*, 29.

Henwood, K. L., & Pidgeon, N. F. (1992). Qualitative research and psychological theorizing. *British Journal of Psychology*, *83*, 97–111.

Henwood, K. L., & Pidgeon, N. F. (1994). Beyond the qualitative paradigm: A framework for introducing diversity within qualitative psychology. *Journal of Community and Applied Social Psychology*, *4*, 225–238.

Hepburn, A. (2003). *An introduction to critical social psychology.* London: SAGE.

Herrnstein, R. J., & Murray, C. (1994). *The bell curve: Intelligence and class structure in American life.* New York: Free Press.

Herzog, H. A. (1995). Has public interest in animal rights peaked? *American Psychologist, 50*, 945–947.

Holmes, J., & Marra, M. (2002). Humour as a discursive boundary marker in social interaction. In A. Duszak (Ed.), *Us and others: Social identities across languages, discourses and cultures* (pp. 377–400). Amsterdam: John Benjamins.

Howe, M. J. A., Davidson, J. W., & Sloboda, J. A. (1998). Innate talents: Reality or myth? *Behavioural and Brain Sciences*, *21*, 399–342.

Huesmann, L. R., Moise-Titus, J., Podolski, C. L., & Eron, L. D. (2003). Longitudinal relations between children's exposure to TV violence and their aggressive and violent behavior in young adulthood: 1977–1992. *Developmental Psychology*, *39*, 201–221.

Huff, D. (1993). *How to lie with statistics.* New York: Norton.

Hunter, M. A., & May, R. B. (1993). Some myths concerning parametric and nonparametric tests. *Canadian Psychology*, *34*, 384–389.

Ioannidis, J. P. (2005). Why most published research findings are false. *PLoS Medicine*, *2*, e124.

Jankowicz, D. (2005). *The easy guide to repertory grids.* Chichester: Wiley.

Jobson, S. A., Nevill, A., & Atkinson, G. (2009). Choose your primary outcome variables with care. *Journal of Sports Sciences*, *27*, 313–314.

Judd, C. M., McClelland, G. H., & Culhane, S. E. (1995). Data analysis: Continuing issues in the everyday analysis of psychological data. *Annual Review of Psychology*, *46*, 433–465.

Kelly, G. A. (1955). *The psychology of personal constructs* (2 vols.). New York: Norton.

Keppel, G., & Wickens, T. (2003). *Design and analysis: A researcher's handbook* (4th ed.). Upper Saddle River, NJ: Pearson Prentice Hall.

Kerr, N. L. (1998). HARKing: Hypothesizing after the results are known. *Personality and Social Psychology Review*, *2*(3), 196–217.

Kline, P. (1994). *An easy guide to factor analysis.* London: Routledge.

References

Knight, C. (2009). *The psychology of organizational space: Identity, engagement and empowerment.* PhD thesis, University of Exeter.

Krippendorff, K. (2012). *Content analysis: An introduction to its methodology* (3rd ed.). London: SAGE.

Kuhn, T. (1962). *The structure of scientific revolutions.* Chicago: University of Chicago Press.

Kulish, N., & Holtzman, D. (2010). Femininity and the Oedipus complex. In L. G. Fiorini & G. Abelin-Sas Rose (Eds.), *On Freud's "femininity"* (pp. 35–55). London: Karnac Books.

Lassen, N. A., Ingvar, D. H., & Skinhoj, E. (1978). Brain function and blood flow. *Scientific American, 239,* 50–59.

Latane, B., & Darley, J. M. (1970). *The unresponsive bystander: Why doesn't he help?* New York: Appleton Century Crofts.

Ledgerwood, A., & Sherman, J. W. (2012). Short, sweet, and problematic? The rise of the short report in psychological science. *Perspectives on Psychological Science, 7,* 60–66.

Leong, T. L., & Austin, J. T. (1996). *The psychology research handbook: A guide for graduate students and research assistants.* Thousands Oaks, CA: SAGE.

Levine, J. M. (2012). Helping in emergencies: Revisiting Latané and Darley's bystander studies. In J. R. Smith & S. A. Haslam (Eds.), *Social psychology: Revisiting the classic studies* (pp. 192–208). London: SAGE.

Lopez, A. D., Mathers, C. D., Ezzati, M., Jamison, D. T., & Murray, C. J. (2006). Global and regional burden of disease and risk factors, 2001: Systematic analysis of population health data. *The Lancet, 367,* 1747–1757.

Louis, W. R., Mavor, K. I., & Terry, D. J. (2003). Reflections on the statistical analysis of personality and norms in war, peace, and prejudice: Are deviant minorities the problem? *Analyses of Social Issues and Public Policy, 3,* 189–198.

Magee, B. (1974). *Popper.* London: Woburn Press.

Makel, M. C., Plucker, J. A., & Hegarty, B. (2012). Replications in psychology research: How often do they really occur? *Perspectives on Psychological Science, 7,* 537–542.

Manstead, A. S. R., & McCulloch, C. (1991). Sex role stereotyping in British television adverts. *British Journal of Social Psychology, 20,* 171–180.

Maxwell, S. E., & Delaney, H. D. (1990). *Designing experiments and analyzing data: A model comparison perspective.* New York: Harper Collins.

McGarty, C. (1999). *Categorization in social psychology.* London: SAGE.

McGuire, W. J. (1997). Going beyond the banalities of bubbapsychology: A perspectivist social psychology. In C. McGarty & S. A. Haslam (Eds.), *The message of social psychology: Perspectives on mind in society.* Oxford: Blackwell.

McNicol, D. (2004). *A primer of signal detection theory.* Hillsdale, NJ: Erlbaum.

Miles, J., & Shevlin, M. (2001). *Applying regression and correlation: A guide for researchers and students.* London: SAGE.

Milgram, S. (1963). Behavioral study of obedience. *Journal of Abnormal and Social Psychology, 67,* 371–378.

Milgram, S. (1964). Issues in the study of obedience: A reply to Baumrind. *American Psychologist, 19,* 848–852.

Milgram, S. (1974). *Obedience to authority.* New York: Harper & Row.

Milner, B. (1966). Amnesia following operation on the temporal lobes. In C. M. W. Whitty & O. L. Zangwill (Eds.), *Amnesia* (pp. 109–133). London: Butterworth.

Morphew, C. C., & Hartley, M. (2006). Mission statements: A thematic analysis of rhetoric across institutional type. *Journal of Higher Education, 77,* 456–471.

Moscovici, S. (1976). *Social influence and social change.* London: Academic Press.

Orne, M. (1962). On the social psychology of the psychological experiment with particular reference to demand characteristics and their implications. *American Psychologist, 17*, 776–783.

Orne, M. (1969). Demand characteristics and the concept of quasi-controls. In R. Rosenthal and R. Rosnow (Eds.), *Artifacts in behavioral research* (pp. 143–179). New York: Academic Press.

Ozonoff, S. (2011). Editorial: The first cut is the deepest: Why do the reported effects of treatments decline over trials? *Journal of Child Psychology and Psychiatry, 52*, 729–730.

Paulos, J. A. (1990). *Innumeracy: Mathematical illiteracy and its consequences*. New York: Vintage Books.

Perry, G. (2012). *Behind the shock machine: The untold story of the notorious Milgram psychology experiments*. Brunswick, Victoria: Scribe Publications.

Pettit, P. (1992). Instituting a research ethic: Chilling and cautionary tales. *Bioethics, 6*, 89–112.

Piaget, J. (1952). *The origins of intelligence in children* (M. Gabain, trans.). New York: International Universities Press.

Pidgeon, N. F., & Henwood, K. L. (1997). Using grounded theory in psychological research. In N. Hayes (Ed.), *Doing qualitative analysis in psychology* (pp. 245–273). Hove: Psychology Press.

Pike, S. (2003). The use of repertory grid analysis to elicit salient short-break holiday destination attributes in New Zealand. *Journal of Travel Research, 41*, 315–319.

Popper, K. (1968). *The logic of scientific discovery*. London: Hutchinson.

Potter, J. (1996). Discourse analysis and constructionist approaches: Theoretical background. In J. T. E. Richardson (Ed.), *Handbook of qualitative research methods for psychology and the social sciences* (pp. 125–140). Leicester: BPS Books.

Potter, J. (1997). Discourse analysis as a way of analysing naturally occurring talk. In D. Silverman (Ed.), *Qualitative research: Theory, method and practice* (pp. 144–160). London: SAGE.

Potter, J. (2004). Discourse analysis. In M. Hardy & A. Bryman (Eds.), *Handbook of data analysis* (pp. 607–624). London: SAGE.

Potter, J., & Reicher, S. (1987). Discourses of community and conflict: The organization of social categories in accounts of a riot. *British Journal of Social Psychology, 26*, 25–40.

Preacher, K. J. (2001, April). Calculation for the chi-square test: An interactive calculation tool for chi-square tests of goodness of fit and independence [Computer software]. Available from http://quantpsy.org.

Prentice, D. A., & Miller, D. T. (1992). When small effects are impressive. *Psychological Bulletin, 112*, 160–164.

Ray, W. J. (1993). *Methods: Towards a science of behavior and experience* (4th ed.). Pacific Grove, CA: Brooks/Cole.

Rees, T., Salvatore, J., Coffee, P., Haslam, S. A., Sargent, A., & Dobson, T. (2013). Reversing downward performance spirals. *Journal of Experimental Social Psychology, 49*, 400–403.

Reicher, S. (2000). Against methodolatry: Some comments on Elliott, Fischer, and Rennie. *British Journal of Clinical Psychology, 39*, 1–6.

Reicher, S. D. (1984a). Social influence in the crowd: Attitudinal and behavioural effects of deindividuation in conditions of high and low group salience. *British Journal of Social Psychology, 23*, 341–350.

Reicher, S. D. (1984b). The St. Paul's riot: An explanation of the limits of crowd action in terms of a social identity model. *European Journal of Social Psychology, 14*, 1–21.

Reicher, S. D., & Haslam, S. A. (2006). Rethinking the psychology of tyranny: The BBC Prison Experiment. *British Journal of Social Psychology, 45*, 1–40.

Reicher, S. D., Haslam, S. A., & Miller, A. G. (in press). What makes a person a perpetrator? The intellectual, moral and methodological arguments for revisiting Milgram's research on the influence of authority. *Journal of Social Issues*.

References

Reicher, S. D., Haslam, S. A., & Smith, J. R. (2012). Working towards the experimenter: Reconceptualizing obedience within the Milgram paradigm as identification-based followership. *Perspectives on Psychological Science, 7*, 315–324.

Reicher, S. D., & Hopkins, N. (1996). Self-category constructions in political rhetoric: An analysis of Thatcher's and Kinnock's speeches concerning the British miners strike (1984–5). *European Journal of Social Psychology, 26*, 353–372.

Reicher, S. D., & Hopkins, N. (2001). *Self and nation: Categorization, contestation and mobilization.* London: SAGE.

Reicher, S. & Stott, C. (2011). *Mad mobs and Englishmen? Myths and realities of the 2011 Riots.* London: Constable.

Richardson, J. T. E. (Ed.). (1996). *Handbook of qualitative research methods for psychology and the social sciences.* Leicester: BPS Books.

Roethlisberger, F. J., & Dickson, W. J. (1964). *Management and the worker.* Cambridge, MA: Harvard University Press.

Rosenthal, R. (1966). *Experimenter effects in behavioral research.* New York: Appleton Century Crofts.

Rosenthal, R. (1994). Science and ethics in conducting, analyzing, and reporting research. *Psychological Science, 5*, 127–133.

Rosenthal, R., & Fode, K. L. (1963). The effect of experimenter bias on the performance of the albino rat. *Behavioural Science, 8*, 183–189.

Russell, N. (in press). The emergence of Milgram's bureaucratic machine. *Journal of Social Issues.*

Ryan, M. K., & Haslam, S. A. (2004). Introducing the glass cliff. http://news.bbc.co.uk/2/hi/uk_news/magazine/3755031.stm (retrieved February 11, 2013).

Ryan, M. K., & Haslam, S. A. (2007). The Glass Cliff: Exploring the dynamics surrounding the appointment of women to precarious leadership positions. *Academy of Management Review, 32*, 549–572.

Ryan, M. K., Haslam, S. A., & Postmes, T. (2007). Reactions to the glass cliff: Gender differences in explanations for the precariousness of women's leadership positions. *Journal of Organizational Change Management, 20*, 182–197.

Sansone, C., Morf, C. C., & Panter, A. T. (Eds.). (2004). *Handbook of methods in social psychology.* Thousand Oaks, CA: SAGE.

Schuman, H., & Kalton, G. (1985). Survey methods. In G. Lindzey & E. Aronson (Eds.), *The handbook of social psychology* (3rd ed., Vol. 1, pp. 635–697). Reading, MA: Addison-Wesley.

Seligman, M. E. P., & Maier, S. F. (1967). Failure to escape traumatic shock. *Journal of Experimental Psychology, 74*, 1–9.

Shaw, M. L. (2011). The analysis of a repertory grid. *British Journal of Medical Psychology, 53*, 117–126.

Sherif, M. (1956). Experiments in group conflict. *Scientific American, 195*, 54–58.

Siegel, S. (1956). *Nonparametric statistics for the behavioral sciences.* New York: McGraw-Hill.

Silverman, D. (Ed.) (2011). *Qualitative research* (3rd ed.). London: SAGE.

Simmons, J. P., Nelson, L. D., & Simonsohn, U. (2011). False-positive psychology: Undisclosed flexibility in data collection and analysis allows presenting anything as significant. *Psychological Science, 22*, 1359–1366.

Singer, P. (1975). *Animal liberation.* New York: Random House.

Smart, R. (1966). Subject selection bias in psychological research. *Canadian Psychologist, 7*, 115–121.

Smith, J. A., & Osborn, M. (2003). Interpretative phenomenological analysis. In J. A. Smith (Ed.), *Qualitative psychology: A practical guide to research methods* (2nd ed., pp. 51–80). London: SAGE.

Smith, J. R., & Haslam, S. A. (Eds.). (2012). *Social psychology: Revisiting the classic studies.* London: SAGE.

Smith, S. S., & Richardson, D. (1983). Amelioration of deception and harm in psychological research. *Journal of Personality and Social Psychology*, *44*, 1075–1082.

Smithson, M. (1993). Ignorance and science: Dilemmas, perspectives and prospects. *Knowledge: Creation, Diffusion, Utilization*, *15*, 133–156.

Smithson, M. (2000). *Statistics with confidence*. London: SAGE.

Spears, R., & Smith, H. J. (2001). Experiments as politics. *Political Psychology*, *22*, 309–330.

Sternberg, R. J. (1995). *In search of the human mind*. Orlando, FL: Harcourt Brace.

Stewart, V., Stewart, A., & Fonda, N. (1981). *Business applications of repertory grid*. London: McGraw-Hill.

Stott, C., Hutchinson, P., & Drury, J. (2001). "Hooligans" abroad? Inter-group dynamics, social identity and participation in collective "disorder" at the 1998 World Cup finals. *British Journal of Social Psychology*, *40*, 359–384.

Strauss, A., & Corbin, J. (1994). Grounded theory methodology: An overview. In N. K. Denzin & Y. S. Lincoln (Eds.), *Handbook of qualitative research* (pp. 273–285). London: SAGE.

Stroebe, W., Postmes, T., & Spears, R. (2012). Scientific misconduct and the myth of self-correction in science. *Perspectives on Psychological Science*, *7*, 670–688.

Svenson, O. (1981). Are we all less risky and more skilful than our fellow drivers? *Acta Psychologica*, *47*, 143–148.

Svyantek, D. J., & Ekeberg, S. E. (1995). The earth is round (so we can probably get there from here). *American Psychologist*, *50*, 1101.

Tabachnick, B. G., & Fidell, L. S. (2012). *Using multivariate statistics* (6th ed.). New York: Harper Collins.

Tajfel, H. (1970). Experiments in intergroup discrimination. *Scientific American*, *223*, 96–102.

Tassell, N. A., & Lock, A. J. (2012). Cultural considerations for professional psychology ethics: Te tirohanga ahurea hei whakatakato tika, whakapakari te aro ki te tangata: Te ahua ki Aotearoa. *Ethics and Social Welfare*, *6*, 56–73.

Tesch, R. (1990). *Qualitative research: Analysis types and software tools*. New York: Falmer.

Tilley, N. (1993). *Understanding car parks, crime, and CCTV: Evaluation lessons from safer cities*. London: Home Office Police Department.

Tukey, J. W. (1991). The philosophy of multiple comparisons. *Statistical Science*, *6*, 100–116.

Turner, J. C. (1981). Some considerations in generalizing experimental social psychology. In G. M. Stephenson & J. H. Davis (Eds.), *Progress in applied social psychology* (Vol. 1, pp. 3–34). Chichester: Wiley.

Turner, J. C. (1985). Social categorization and the self-concept: A social cognitive theory of group behaviour. In E. J. Lawler (Ed.), *Advances in group processes* (Vol. 2, pp. 77–122). Greenwich, CT: JAI Press.

Tuttle, B. (2010). The true meaning of shopping. *Time*, December 14. http://business.time.com/2010/12/14/the-true-meaning-of-shopping/ (retrieved February 4, 2013).

Tversky, A., & Kahneman, D. (1971). Belief in the law of small numbers. *Psychological Bulletin*, 76, 105–110.

Tversky, A., & Kahneman, D. (1974). Judgement under uncertainty: Heuristics and biases. *Science*, *185*, 1123–1131.

Valentine, E. R. (1982). *Conceptual issues in psychology*. London: Allen & Unwin.

Von Stumm, S., Hell, B., & Chamorro-Premuzic, T. (2011). The hungry mind: Intellectual curiosity is the third pillar of academic performance. *Perspectives on Psychological Science*, *6*, 574–588.

West, S. G., & Gunn, S. P. (1978). Some issues of ethics and social psychology. *American Psychologist*, *33*, 30–38.

References

West, S. G., Newsom, J. T., & Fenaughty, A. M. (1992). Publication trends in the *Journal of Personality and Social Psychology*: Stability and change in topics, methods and theories across two decades. *Personality and Social Psychology Bulletin*, *18*, 473–484.

Wetherell, M. (2008). Subjectivity or psycho-discursive practices? Investigating complex intersectional identities. *Subjectivity*, *22*, 73–81.

Wetzels, R., Matzke, D., Lee, M. D., Rouder, J. N., Iverson, G. J., & Wagenmakers, E. J. (2011). Statistical evidence in experimental psychology: An empirical comparison using 855 *t*-tests. *Perspectives on Psychological Science*, *6*, 291–298.

Wilkinson, L., & The Task Force on Statistical Inference. (1999). Statistical methods in psychology journals. *American Psychologist*, *54*, 594–604.

Woolgar, S. (1988). *Science: The very idea.* London: Tavistock.

Woolgar, S. (1996). Psychology, qualitative methods and the ideas of science. In J. T. E. Richardson (Ed.), *Handbook of qualitative research methods for psychology and the social sciences* (pp. 11–24). Leicester: BPS Books.

World Health Organization. (2012). *Mental Health: Depression.* www.who.int/mental_health/management/depression/definition/en/index.html (retrieved September 22, 2013).

Wright, D. B. (2009). Ten statisticians and their impacts for psychologists. *Perspectives on Psychological Science*, *4*, 587–597.

Yin, R. K. (1994). *Case study research design methods* (2nd ed.). Thousand Oaks, CA: SAGE.

Author Index

Author Index

Subject Index

Note: This index lists all terms for which glossary definitions are provided. Page numbers of these definitions are in **bold**. References to Test-Yourself questions and exercises are in *italics*.

Subject Index